Articles on American Slavery

An eighteen–volume set collecting nearly four hundred of the most important articles on slavery in the United States

Edited with Introductions by
Paul Finkelman

State University of New York,
Binghamton

A Garland Series

Contents of the Series

Vol. 10

Economics, Industrialization, Urbanization, and Slavery

Edited with an Introduction
by Paul Finkelman

Garland Publishing, Inc.
New York & London
1989

Library of Congress Cataloging-in-Publication Data

Economics, industrialization, urbanization, and
slavery/ edited with an introduction
by Paul Finkelman.

p. cm.—(Articles on American slavery; vol. 10)

Includes bibliographical references.

ISBN 0–8240–6790–8(alk. paper)

1. Slavery—Economic aspects—Southern States.
2. Southern States—Economic conditions.
3. Southern States—History—1175–1865.
I. Finkelman, Paul. II. Series.

E441.E26   1989
306.3'62'0975—dc20   89–23537

Printed on acid-free, 250-year-life paper
Manufactured in the United States of America

Design by Julie Threlkeld

General Introduction

Few subjects in American history have been as compelling as slavery. This should not surprise us. Slavery affected millions of Americans, north and south. Afro-Americans, Euro-Americans, and Native Americans were involved in the system. All antebellum Americans were affected, directly or indirectly, by slavery. Slavery especially affected Americans from 1861 until well after Reconstruction. As Lincoln noted in his famous second inaugural address: "The slaves constituted a peculiar and powerful interest. All knew that this interest was somehow the cause of the war."

The goal of this series is to reprint the key articles that have influenced our understanding of slavery. This series includes pioneering articles in the history of slavery, important breakthroughs in research and methodology, and articles that offer major historiographical interpretations. I have attempted to cover all major subtopics of slavery, to offer wide geographic representation and methodological diversity. At the same time, I have resisted the temptation to reprint highly technical articles that will make sense only to specialists in certain fields. For example, I have not included a number of important slavery related articles on economics, law, theology, and literary criticism (to offer just a few examples) because they appeared to be beyond the interest of most generalists.

I have used articles from a wide variety of scholarly journals. I have also used essays and articles in edited volumes, as long as the main focus of those volumes was not slavery, abolition, or black studies. It is my hope that such books are readily available to scholars and students and will show up through card catalogues or on-line catalogue searches. For the same reason I have not reprinted chapters from books about slavery, which are often found in anthologies. With a few exceptions, I have not reprinted articles that later became chapters of books on the same subject. In a few cases I have strayed from this general rule of thumb. I have also generally avoided essay reviews of books, unless the essays go well beyond the common book review or even essay review format. I have also tried to avoid certain famous historiographical controversies that resulted in large numbers of essays being collected and published. With some exceptions, therefore, I have not included the many articles attacking the "Elkins" thesis or Fogel and Engerman's Time on the Cross. Students and scholars interested in these two enormously important scholarly works, and the criticism of them, will find a great deal on both in their card catalogues. Finally, I have also excluded articles from Encyclopedias and dictionaries. These editorial decisions mean that many famous essays and articles will not be found in these volumes. Indeed, a few very important scholars are not represented because all of their work has been in books that are directly on the subject of slavery. Finally, some important articles were left out because we were unable to secure permission from the copyright holders to reprint them in this series.

This project was made easier by the hard work and dedication of Carole Puccino and Leo Balk at Garland Publishing, Inc. A project of this magnitude would not be possible without the help of a number of other scholars, who read lists of proposed articles and discussed the whole problem of slavery with me. I am especially grateful for the help and suggestions of Catherine Clinton, Robert Cottrol, Jill DuPont, Seymour Drescher, Linda Evans, Ronald Formasano, John Hope Franklin, Kermit L. Hall, Robert Hall, Graham Hodges, Michael P. Johnson, Charles Joyner, Alan Kulikoff, Greg Lind, David McBride, Randall Miller, Alfred Moss, James Oakes, Albert J. Raboteau, Judith Schafer, Robert Sikorski, John David Smith, Jean Soderlund, Margaret Washington, William M. Wiecek, Julie Winch, Betty Wood, and Bertram Wyatt-Brown. Two SUNY-Binghamton students, Marci Silverman and Beth Borchers, helped me with much of the bibliographic work on this project. Carol A. Clemente and the inter-library loan staff at SUNY-Binghamton were absolutely wonderful. Without their patience, skills, and resourcefulness, I would have been unable to complete these volumes.

—*Paul Finkelman*

Contents

Introduction

Historians disagree as to whether racism preceded slavery or was a result of slavery. This is the "chicken and egg" question of slavery. Scholars do not disagree, however, on the reason for the origin of slavery: the institution began as an economic institution. Slavery began as a system of labor exploitation in an agrarian setting. From there slavery developed into an institution with social, cultural, and political overtones.

In the antebellum period southern slavery also ceased to be wholly agricultural and rural in nature. While most slaves remained rural agricultural workers, in 1860 the South's twenty largest cities contained nearly 100,000 slaves. In more than half of these cities slaves made up more than twenty-five percent of the urban population.

Urbanization and industrialization were tied together, although not all industrialized slaves lived in cities. The title of one book, *Coal, Iron, and Slaves*,[1] suggests that industrial slaves might be found in rural coal and iron ore mines, but that they were also found working at the urban mills of Richmond's Tredegar Iron Works. In 1860 more than 200,000 slaves worked in the South's coal, iron, and gold mines, as well as on steamships and railroads, and in the shipyards of Baltimore and Norfolk. The major agricultural products of the South also led to industrial work for slaves, who were employed in tobacco factories and warehouses, rope factories, rice and sugar packing operations, and, of course, textile mills.

Despite the widespread use of slaves in industries, it is generally agreed that slave labor retarded southern industrial growth, if for no other reason than that slaves could be more profitably used as agricultural laborers, and southern capital could usually be more profitably invested in slaves and land than in most other businesses. In addition, social status and political influence in the South was directly tied to slaveholding and plantation agriculture. Thus, leaders of the South, and those who would be leaders, rose to power and status and kept both, in part, by owning slaves and land. Although slaves as workers were well suited to industrial uses, legal and social barriers undermined the urbanization and industrialization of slavery.[2] Nevertheless, both urbanization and industrialization play an important part in the economic and social history of slavery.

Even more important is the question of slavery and economic profitability. Put simply, was slavery profitable? For many years scholars thought that antebellum slavery was either declining in profitability or not profitable at all. The decline of cotton prices between 1800 and 1860, along with a three-fold increase in the cost of slaves, led scholars to think that slaveholding was an economic failure. Starting with a seminal essay by Conrad and Mayer,[3] economic historians have published material to show that slavery was, in fact, profitable. The debates now are over how much profit was made, how much of that profit "trickled down" to the slaves, and how long the profitability of slavery might have been maintained.

Much controversy surrounded the publication in 1974 of *Time on the Cross*,[4] which asserted not only that slavery was profitable, but that slaves were well-treated, rarely whipped, and allowed to develop stable families, because poor treatment would have been economically counterproductive. While rejected by most scholars, this book has stimulated an enormous amount of research into the field of slavery and economics.

Slavery has led to a great deal of literature at the convergence of economics and history. Much of this has been reprinted here, or cited in the bibliography at the end of this essay. There is also an extensive technical literature on the economics of slavery. This literature is often of interest to economists, who use slavery, and the available data from the antebellum period, to test theoretical economic models. That literature is not reprinted here.

—Paul Finkelman

Notes

1. Ronald Lewis, *Coal, Iron, and Slaves: Industrial Slavery in Maryland and Virginia, 1715–1865* (Westport Conn.: Greenwood Press, 1979).

2. For one example of the legal problems caused by industrial slavery, see Paul Finkelman, "Slaves as Fellow Servants: Ideology, Law, and Industrialization," *American Journal of Legal History* 31 (1987) 269–305, reprinted in Volume 11 of this series.

3. Alfred H. Conrad and John R. Mayer, "The Economics of Slavery in the Antebellum South," *Journal of Political Economy* 66 (April, 1958) 95–130, reprinted in Volume 1 of this series. Though it deals with the economics of slavery, this key article was deemed more appropriate to the volume on the historiography of slavery.

4. Robert Fogel and Stanley Engerman. *Time on the Cross*, 2 vols. (Boston: Little Brown, 1974).

Further Reading

Aitken, Hugh, ed.   *Did Slavery Pay? Readings in the Economics of Black Slavery in the United States* (Boston: Houghton, Mifflin, 1971).

Anderson, Ralph V., and Robert E. Gallman.   "Slaves as Fixed Capital: Slave Labor and Economic Development," *Journal of American History* 64 (1977) 24–46.

Conrad, Alfred H., John R. Mayer.   "The Economics of Slavery in the and Antebellum South," *Journal of Political Economy* 66 (April, 1958) 95–130, reprinted in Volume 1 of this series.

David, Paul A.	*Reckoning With Slavery* (New York: Oxford University Press, 1976).
Fogel, Robert, and Stanley Engerman.	*Time on the Cross*, 2 Vols. (Boston: Little Brown, 1974).
Genovese, Eugene D.	*Political Economy of the South: Studies in the Economy and Society of the Slave South* (New York: Pantheon, 1961).
Goldin, Claudia A.	*Urban Slavery in the American South, 1820–1860: A Quantitative History* (Chicago: University of Chicago Press, 1976).
Gray, Lewis C.	*History of Agriculture in the Southern United States to 1860*, 2 Vols. (Washington: Carnegie Institution of Washington, 1932).
Green, Rodney D.	"Industrial Transition in the Land of Chattel Slavery: Richmond, Virginia 1820–1860," *International Journal of Urban and Regional Research* 8 (1984) 240–53.
Gutman, Herbert.	*Slavery and the Numbers Game* (Urbana: University of Illinois Press, 1975).
Haskell, Thomas L.	"Were Slaves More Efficient? Some Doubts about *Time on the Cross*," *New York Review of Books* 21 (September 19, 1974) 38–42.
Kulikoff, Alan.	"Black Society and Economics of Slavery," *Maryland Magazine of History* 70, No. 2 (Summer, 1975) 203–10.
Lewis, Ronald.	*Coal, Iron, and Slaves: Industrial Slavery in Maryland and Virginia, 1715–1865* (Westport, Conn.: Greenwood Press, 1979).
Lewis, Ronald.	"The Use and Extent of Slave Labor in the Virginia Iron Industry: The Ante-Bellum Era," *West Virginia History* 39 (1977) 141–56.

Miller, Randall.   *The Cotton Mill Movement in Antebellum Alabama* (New York: Arno Press, 1978).

Moes, John E.   "Absorption of Capital in Slave Labor in the Ante-Bellum South and Economic Growth," *American Journal of Economics and Sociology* 20 (1961) 535–41.

Starobin, Robert.   *Industrial Slavery in the Old South* (New York: Oxford University Press, 1970).

Wade, Richard.   *Slavery in the Cities* (New York: Oxford University Press, 1964).

Wright, Gavin.   "Economics of Slavery," in Randall Miller and John David Smith, *Dictionary of Afro-American Slavery* (Westport: Greenwood Press, 1988) 201–08.

Wright, Gavin.   *The Political Economy of the Cotton South: Households, Markets, and Wealth in the Nineteenth Century* (New York: W.W. Norton, 1978).

Economics,
Industrialization,
Urbanization,
and Slavery

Natives and Immigrants, Free Men and Slaves: Urban Workingmen in the Antebellum American South

IRA BERLIN

and

HERBERT G. GUTMAN

OF NECESSITY, HISTORICAL RESEARCH IS PIECEMEAL. But the growth of historical understanding is not simply an additive process. Instead, new discoveries transform older conceptions and necessitate reconsiderations at the highest interpretive level. A re-evaluation of the place of immigrant workers in antebellum Southern cities suggests how the process works, for it forces a reformulation of ideas about the entire structure of the urban work force and raises questions about the nature of Southern society, urban and rural, and the beliefs of Southerners, native and immigrant, free and slave.

FEW OF THE BULWARKS OF SOUTHERN DISTINCTIVENESS have withstood the battering ram of historiographic iconoclasm better than the overwhelmingly native origins of the Southern people. While scholars of all persuasions have challenged the unique character of the South's economy, its social structure, its politics, and its institutions, the weight of historical evidence has left this mark of Southern difference undisturbed.[1] Even a passing acquaintance with transatlantic migratory patterns

An early version of this paper was prepared in 1975–76 while its authors were fellows at the Shelby Cullom Davis Center for Historical Study at Princeton University. They remain indebted to the center's director, Lawrence Stone, for encouragement and support. Rebecca Scott ably assisted with the initial research and analysis. Judith Rowe and Nita Roberts of the Princeton University Computer Center and Bertha Butler of the Computer Science Center at the University of Maryland guided the statistical aspects of this study. Another version of this paper was thoughtfully criticized at the 1981 Annual Meeting of the Organization of American Historians by Harold Woodman. Research grants from the Ford Foundation and the Rockefeller Foundation facilitated additional research, and we thank Robert Schrank and Joel Colton, respectively, for making this work possible. We also want to acknowledge the thoughtful criticisms offered by W. Elliot Brownlee, George Callcott, Eric Foner, Ronald Hoffman, Michael P. Johnson, Bruce C. Levine, Sidney Mintz, Joseph P. Reidy, and Leslie S. Rowland.

[1] For a recent attempt to deny the distinctive nature of Southern society, see Edward Pessen, "How Different from Each Other Were the Antebellum North and South," *AHR*, 85 (1980): 1119–49; also see the comments that follow in "*AHR Forum*—Antebellum North and South in Comparative Perspective: A Discussion," by Thomas Alexander, Stanley L. Engerman, Forrest McDonald and Grady McWhiney, and Edward Pessen, *ibid.*, 1150–66.

1175

1

affirms that few of the thousands of Europeans who journeyed to the United States in the years before the Civil War settled in the slave states. At mid-century, when fully one Northerner in seven had been born outside the United States, only 5 percent of the Southern free population was foreign born, and a disproportionate number of these resided in the border states. Ten years later, the margin had widened as European migrants surged into the North, while they continued to dribble into the South. On the eve of the Civil War, when fewer than one free Southerner in fifteen had been born outside the United States, immigrants composed nearly a fifth of the population of the free states.[2]

Historians have found this massive imbalance reason enough to ignore immigrants in antebellum Southern society and to argue that slavery repelled foreign settlers. While lavishing attention on the role of foreign-born people in the transformation of pre–Civil War Northern society, scholars have neglected their place in the development of the antebellum South. This is particularly true in accounts of the immigrants' part in the making of the urban working class. Although the portrait of antebellum class formation in the cities of the North has been constructed as a rich ethnic mosaic, in the urban South the process has been etched in black and white.

The conventional treatment of Southern urban workers leaves little room for immigrants—indeed, for white labor generally. Drawing on the antislavery argument, particularly that of political abolitionists, historians have emphasized that the presence of slave labor degraded free white workers. With William Seward, they have maintained that slavery denied the white workingman employment and expelled him "from the community because it cannot enslave and convert him into merchandise." The rules of the free market economy simply did not apply to labor in a slave society. As Charles Nordhoff, another opponent of slavery, observed, it mattered nothing to the slaveholder "how low others can produce the article; he can produce it lower still, so long as it is the best use he can make of his [slaves'] labor, and as long as that labor is worth keeping. A free white mechanic is at the mercy of his neighbor, the capitalist, in a slave state, because, if the capitalist does not like the price, he can go and buy a carpenter and sell him again when the work is done." Conceding that slaves worked at lower rates than free laborers, historians have concurred in the abolitionist argument that, "when the two are brought into competition, white labor is crowded out."[3]

---

[2] U.S. Bureau of the Census, *The Seventh Census of the United States, 1850* (Washington, 1853), xxxvi–xxxviii, and *Population of the United States in 1860* (Washington, 1864), 620–23. If slaves are included in the analysis, the proportion of immigrants in the Southern population shrinks (to about 3 percent in 1850, 5 percent in 1860), and the differences between the proportion of immigrants in the North and that in the South grows. For a survey of recent scholarship about immigrants in the Old South, see Randall M. Miller, "Immigrants in the Old South," *Immigration History Newsletter*, 10 (1978): 8–14. Also see the discussions in Clement Eaton, *The Growth of Southern Civilization* (New York, 1971), 150–76, 221–70; Ella Lonn, *Foreigners in the Confederacy* (Chapel Hill, N.C., 1940), 1–32; Herbert J. Weaver, "Foreigners in the Ante-Bellum Towns in the Lower South," *Journal of Southern History*, 13 (1947): 62–73, and "Foreigners in Antebellum Mississippi," *Journal of Mississippi History*, 16 (1954): 151–63; William L. Barney, *The Secessionist Impulse: Alabama and Mississippi in 1860* (Princeton, 1974), 26–43; and Edward L. Ayers, *Vengeance and Justice: Crime and Punishment in the Nineteenth Century* (New York, 1984), chap. 3.

[3] Nordhoff, *America for Free Working Men* (New York, 1865), 1–39; and David Bertelson, *The Lazy South* (New York, 1967), 201. For an important exception to this conventional wisdom, see Carville Earle and Ronald Hoffman, "The Foundation of the Modern Economy: Agriculture and the Costs of Labor in the United States and England, 1800–60," *AHR*, 85 (1980): 1055–94.

TABLE 1
Selected Southern Urban Populations, 1850–1860

City	Total Population in 1860	Percentage of Increase/Decrease from 1850 to 1860	Percentage of Population in 1860		
			White	Free Black	Slave
RICHMOND	38,000	+38	62	7	31
CHARLESTON	41,000	− 6	58	8	34
MOBILE	30,000	+43	71	3	26
NASHVILLE	17,000	+67	77	4	19
LYNCHBURG	7,000	−18	56	5	39
BATON ROUGE	5,000	+27	68	9	23

NOTE: Percentages here and in all subsequent tables do not always add to 100; owing to rounding; total population rounded to thousands.
SOURCES: U.S. Bureau of the Census, *The Seventh Census of the United States, 1850* (Washington, 1853), and *Population of the United States in 1860* (Washington, 1864).

According to the extant historiography, black freemen and bondsmen did most of the labor in the South, including most of the artisanal work. In his classic study, Charles H. Wesley put the proportion at about 80 percent. Others have suggested the same without Wesley's precision. Historians have maintained that native-born white workingmen fled the slave states when they could. Those who remained in the South protested slave competition but had little success against the potent combination of slaves, who monopolized skilled labor, and masters, who reaped a handsome profit from their slaves' work. Such circumstances could hardly encourage foreign immigration, and those few feckless migrants who alighted in the slave states generally found employment at tasks that masters deemed too dangerous for their valuable slaves.[4] Foreign-born workers have thus appeared marginal, rather than central, to an understanding of the working population of the urban South.

The dominance of the urban work force by black laborers has been challenged implicitly by recent work on urban bondage, which emphasizes the sharp decline of slavery in the cities in the late antebellum years. But scholars have posed the question of urban slavery far too narrowly. They have vigorously debated whether the peculiarities of urban bondage pushed or the nature of plantation demand pulled slaves out of the cities, while ignoring the character of the urban work force and the relations between slaves and free workers. Even the most detailed scholarship has left the immigrant the South's invisible man.[5]

Yet the peculiar pattern of European migration and settlement in the slave states gave immigrants importance far beyond their numbers and projected foreign-born workers into a place in the Southern working class that rivaled the role played by

[4] Wesley, *Negro Labor in the United States* (New York, 1927), chaps. 1–3; Herman Schlüter, *Lincoln, Labor, and Slavery* (New York, 1913); Kenneth M. Stampp, "The Fate of the Southern Antislavery Movement," *Journal of Negro History*, 28 (1943): 10–22; Roger Shugg, *Origins of Class Struggle in Louisiana* (University, La., 1939), 20–110 but esp. 86–92; Robert S. Starobin, *Industrial Slavery in the Old South* (New York, 1970), 146–89 but esp. 153–63; and Frederick Law Olmsted, *Journey in the Seaboard Slave States* (New York, 1856), esp. 193.

[5] Richard C. Wade, *Slavery in the Cities: The South, 1820–1860* (New York, 1964); and Claudia D. Goldin, *Urban Slavery in the American South, 1820–1860: A Quantitative History* (Chicago, 1976).

TABLE 2

Occupational Distribution of Employed Free Adult Men, 1860

City	Number	Percentage of Employed Adult Free Men		
		Non-workers	Skilled Workers	Unskilled Workers
RICHMOND	7,954	38	42	20
CHARLESTON	6,985	45	35	20
MOBILE	7,306	38	30	32
NASHVILLE	4,307	41	35	24
LYNCHBURG	1,273	48	34	18
BATON ROUGE	887	40	47	13

SOURCE: Computed from the U.S. manuscript census schedules, 1860, Records of the Bureau of the Census (Record Group 29), National Archives, Washington [hereafter, U.S. Census MSS., RG 29].

immigrants in the North. Although a comparatively small number of Europeans migrated to the South during the nineteenth century, those who did generally settled in cities. South Carolina, Georgia, and Alabama had few immigrants, but Charleston, Savannah, and Mobile had many. At mid-century, the foreign-born population of these states reached 3 percent only in the case of South Carolina. But more than a fifth of Charleston's residents, more than a quarter of Savannah's, and almost a third of Mobile's had been born outside the United States.[6] Moreover, since men formed a disproportionately large share of the foreign settlers in Southern cities, immigrants composed a still larger share of the urban male work force than they did of the urban population as a whole. As a result, like Mobile (where half of the employed free men had been born outside the United States), many urban places in the Lower South could be appropriately described as immigrant cities.[7]

The same processes that drew immigrant men disproportionately to Southern cities concentrated them in specific places in the social structure of the urban South. As a group, immigrants entered Southern society at the bottom of the free social hierarchy and made up a large part of the lower ranks of urban society. On the eve of the Civil War, native-born white men composed better than two-thirds of the male merchants, political officials, and professionals in Mobile, Charleston, and other Southern cities, while foreign-born men equaled a similar proportion of petty proprietors—grocers, restauranteurs, stable keepers, and the like. Immigrants were

[6] J. D. B. DeBow, *Statistical View of the United States* (Washington, 1854), 399. This disjunction between rural and urban patterns of immigrant settlement also existed in those areas of the South that received the largest numbers of foreign settlers. In 1860, immigrants composed 13 percent of Louisiana's population but foreign-born men and women accounted for almost two-fifths of the inhabitants of New Orleans; U.S. Bureau of the Census, *Population of the United States in 1860*, 615.

[7] The data on nativity of employed free men in Mobile, along with similar information of employed men in Baton Rouge, Charleston, Lynchburg, Nashville, and Richmond have been calculated from a tabulation of all men for whom either an occupation or property (real or personal) is listed in the 1850 and 1860 manuscript censuses, the 1850 and 1860 manuscript slave schedules, and the 1850 and 1860 manuscript industrial schedules, National Archives, Washington, Record Group 29.

TABLE 3
Skill Distribution of Free Working Men, 1860

City	Number of Free Working Men	Percentage Skilled	Percentage Unskilled
RICHMOND	4,929	68	32
CHARLESTON	3,846	63	37
MOBILE	4,552	49	51
NASHVILLE	2,533	60	40
LYNCHBURG	661	66	34
BATON ROUGE	529	79	21

SOURCE: Computed from the U.S. Census MSS., RG 29.

also disproportionately represented among urban workingmen, the largest occupational group in every major Southern city. Immigrants commonly dominated the free male working population and formed a large proportion of the entire male working population, free and slave. For that reason, foreign settlers helped shape social relations in the urban South and had a profound influence on class and racial relations throughout Southern society.

The composition of the urban male work force on the eve of the Civil War suggests the significance of immigrant workers in Southern cities.[8] Four Southern cities and several towns have been studied: Richmond, the South's premier industrial city with a population of some 38,000 in 1860, of which more than 60 percent were whites, about 30 percent were slaves, and less than 10 percent—the remainder—were free Negroes; Charleston, an older Atlantic port with a population slightly larger but of similar composition to that of Richmond; Mobile, an expanding cotton port of some 21,000 whites, 7,500 slaves, and fewer than 1,000 free people of color; and Nashville, a rapidly expanding interior marketing and transporting center, three-fourths of whose residents were white. In addition, two smaller cities have been examined: Lynchburg, a regional Virginia tobacco manufacturing center of 7,000, with proportionally few immigrants, and Baton Rouge, a Louisiana river town of 5,000, with proportionally many immigrants. Except for Charleston and Lynchburg, these cities grew rapidly during the antebellum period. In some respects, their populations increased more rapidly than those of Northern cities.[9] (See Table 1) In these selected cities and throughout the urban South, laboring men were sharply divided by legal status, nativity, and race. Native-born white men monopolized occupations in the upper ranks of Southern society. The vast majority of merchants, bankers, factors, doctors, and lawyers in these cities

[8] This essay focuses on the role of men in the Southern urban working population. We are preparing a companion essay that examines the composition of the female sector of the work force of Southern cities. The presence of large numbers of slave women, almost all of whom worked, had a profound impact on the role of free working women and throws into sharp contrast the lives of all women in Northern and Southern cities. In this essay, unless otherwise stated, work force and working population refer to *male* work force and *male* working population.

[9] Leonard P. Curry, "Urbanization and Urbanism in the Old South: A Comparative View," *Journal of Southern History*, 40 (1974): 43–60.

TABLE 4

Employed and Propertied Adult Free Men by Nativity and Race, 1860

City	Number	Percentage by Nativity and Race				
		Southern-Born White	Northern-Born White	Foreign-Born White	Free Black	Unknown Origin
RICHMOND	8,122	51	7	31	8	3
CHARLESTON	7,256	41	6	42	8	3
MOBILE	7,457	31	16	50	2	1
NASHVILLE	4,415	50	13	31	3	3
LYNCHBURG	1,295	70	3	16	7	4
BATON ROUGE	927	44	11	39	5	1

SOURCE: Computed by the U.S. Census MSS., RG 29.

were white men born in the slave states, frequently in the states in which they resided. Generally, the more successful—as measured by wealth and slaveowner-ship—the greater the likelihood that these men had been born in the South. At the bottom of free society, the free laboring population was a good deal more hetereogenenous. Native-born Southern whites, Northern-born whites, foreign-born whites of various nationalities, and free Negroes (almost all of whom had been born in the South but who divided among themselves by their degree of racial admixture) formed the free working class. The remaining portion of the laboring population, the slaves, was also almost entirely native born and, like the free Negroes, divided by color—black and brown. By its legal status, nativity, and race, each group played carefully defined and usually distinctive roles within the urban work force.[10] Free workers constituted a majority of the adult free men in all cities studies. Except in Mobile, skilled workers predominated among these free wage earners. (See Tables 2, 3, and 4.)

On the eve of the Civil War, immigrants composed a large portion of the free urban work force—sometimes stretching to a clear majority. Generally, the further south the city, the greater the proportion of workers of foreign birth. In Mobile, that classic immigrant city, almost two-thirds of the free workingmen were immigrants. Although the proportion of the foreign-born free workers was smaller in Charleston and Baton Rouge, it still equaled about half of the free work force. Immigrants were not nearly as prominent in the cities of the upper South, especially in land-locked interior cities like Lynchburg. Even in Richmond and Nashville, however, foreign settlers totaled 40 percent of the free workingmen. (See Table 5).

[10] For purposes of this essay, workingmen have been divided into two categories: skilled and unskilled. Among those classified as unskilled are day laborers, boathands, draymen, dock workers, sailors, and tobacco factory workers. The skilled workingmen have been further divided into two subcategories: those working in the building trades (including bricklayers, carpenters, painters, plasterers, plumbers, and stonemasons), and other skilled workers (including bakers, barbers, blacksmiths, bookmakers, brewers, butchers, carriage makers, cabinet makers, clock makers, confectioners, engravers, founders, jewelers, pilots, printers, shoemakers, tailors, tanners, wheelwrights, and watchmakers).

TABLE 5
Adult Free Workingmen by Nativity and Race, 1860

City	Number	Percentage by Nativity and Race			
		Southern-Born White	Northern-Born White	Foreign-Born White	Free Black
RICHMOND	4,929	39	8	39	14
CHARLESTON	3,846	28	6	52	14
MOBILE	4,552	19	14	64	3
NASHVILLE	2,533	42	12	41	5
LYNCHBURG	661	62	4	20	14
BATON ROUGE	529	35	11	47	7

SOURCE: Computed from the U.S. Census MSS., RG 29.

Black freemen and Northern-born whites also played an important part in the laboring population of the urban South. Free Negroes or free people of color—the specific nomenclature depended on the region—made up a small and variable portion of the urban working class in every Southern city. In some places, like Charleston and Richmond, they constituted an important minority of the free workingmen—amounting to more than one in seven. Elsewhere, however, they slipped to numerical insignificance. In Mobile, free men of color totaled only 3 percent of the free workingmen. Northern-born white workers also varied widely in number from place to place, although they played a more important role in the newer cities of the west and the Lower South than in the older ones in the Upper South. They, too, equaled about 4 to 14 percent of the free work force. Taken together, free Negroes and Northern-born whites totaled about a fifth of all free workingmen in Southern cities. (See Table 5.)

Although the proportion varied from city to city, immigrants, free Negroes, and Northern-born whites together constituted nearly three-quarters of the free workingmen in Charleston and about 60 percent of those in Richmond and Nashville. In Mobile, immigrants, Northern-born whites, and free people of color totaled a full 80 percent of the that city's free workingmen. Except in the interior marketing and manufacturing center of Lynchburg, white workers native to the South made up only a minority of the urban South's free working class. Within the context of an overwhelmingly native-born regional population and the predominately native origins of the upper ranks of urban society, native-born Southern white workers were a conspicuous minority in most Southern cities. (See Table 5.)

Whatever the dynamics of slavery in the city, enslaved black laborers remained an indispensable part of the urban work force on the eve of the Civil War. Although their share of the total urban labor force shrank during the late antebellum years, nearly all slaves did manual labor of one kind or another, and they remained a large component of the laboring population everywhere except in the border cities. In Charleston, Richmond, Mobile, and Nashville, adult slaves still

TABLE 6
Workingmen by Status, Nativity, and Race, 1860

City	Number	Slave	Percentage of Workingmen			
			Southern-Born White	Northern-Born White	Foreign-Born White	Free Black
RICHMOND	9,557	48	20	4	20	7
CHARLESTON	7,887	51	14	3	25	7
MOBILE	7,002	35	13	9	41	2
NASHVILLE	3,408	26	31	9	30	4
LYNCHBURG	1,623	60	24	2	8	6
BATON ROUGE	843	37	22	7	29	5

NOTE: For the classification of workingmen, see note 10, above.
SOURCE: Computed from the U.S. Census MSS., RG 29.

constituted between one-half and one-quarter of the workingmen, skilled and unskilled.[11] In Lynchburg, they constituted over 60 percent of the workingmen. The presence of slaves reduced proportionately the weight of various groups of free workingmen in the urban working class and made Southern whites (like everyone else) a still smaller proportion of the whole. Only a minority of Southern urban workers had been born in the South and shared the most prized Southern attributes: whiteness and freedom. Most urban workers were born alien to the dominant characteristics of Southern culture. (See Table 6.)

Slaves, free Negroes, immigrants of various nationalities, Northern-born whites, and Southern-born whites played different roles in the Southern urban work force. By the various combinations of color, status, and nativity, workers toiled at different skill levels, practiced different trades, and labored in different sectors of the economy. (See Table 7.) For free workingmen, these differences can be discerned by disaggregating the census enumerations. The antebellum census, however, provides no occupational designations for slaves—an omission that has fueled erroneous speculation about the kind of work slaves did in Southern cities.[12] So many free men (immigrants and native born) practiced skilled crafts in Southern cities that it is unlikely urban slaves could have been similarly skilled. Had slaves possessed skills in the same proportion as free workers, the ranks of unskilled labor and domestic service would have gone unfilled and Southern cities would have been like no others in the Western world. An analysis of patterns of slave ownership and employment on the assumption that a slave's work was related to his master's— that an adult slave man owned by a blacksmith was likely to be a blacksmith, while an adult slave man owned by a banker was not—and within the context of the known occupational structure of the free working class confirms this inference. It also provides a rough estimate of the level of urban slave skill and a still rougher guide to the character of urban slave occupations.

[11] All slave men between age fifteen and sixty are presumed to have worked and are included in the work force. For a more extended discussion of slave occupations, see pages 1185–87, below.
[12] A recent example is Robert William Fogel and Stanley L. Engerman, *Time on the Cross: The Economics of American Negro Slavery*, 2 vols. (Boston, 1974).

TABLE 7
Free Workingmen, Skilled and Unskilled, by Nativity, and Race, 1860

City	Number	Percentage of Workingmen			
		Southern-Born White	Northern-Born White	Foreign-Born White	Free Black
A: Skilled Free Workingmen					
RICHMOND	3,341	48	10	36	6
CHARLESTON	2,413	38	6	40	16
MOBILE	2,211	25	17	54	3
NASHVILLE	1,522	46	17	33	4 -
LYNCHBURG	434	70	5	18	7
BATON ROUGE	416	36	12	44	8
B: Unskilled Free Workingmen					
RICHMOND	1,588	20	4	46	30
CHARLESTON	1,433	11	5	72	11
MOBILE	2,341	14	12	69	4
NASHVILLE	1,011	35	4	51	9
LYNCHBURG	227	46	2	25	27
BATON ROUGE	113	34	5	57	4

NOTE: For the classification of workingmen, see note 10, above.
SOURCE: Computed from the U.S. Census MSS., RG 29.

An examination of slave ownership in Mobile, Charleston, and Nashville reveals that most artisans (here including those who might classify themselves as manufacturers employing skilled workers—founders as well as blacksmiths, contractors as well as carpenters) did not own slaves, and those who did controlled only a small portion of the city's slave population. Workers were the largest occupational group, but slave ownership by workers (almost always artisans) never exceeded 15 percent of the slave men. (See Table 8.) Moreover, women (usually adolescent girls) composed a disproportionate share of artisan-owned slaves, suggesting that, when a skilled worker purchased a slave, the slave was usually a servant for the owner's household rather than a journeyman for his shop.[13]

With slave prices rising rapidly in the 1850s, slave hiring grew more commonplace throughout the urban South. Many free workers may have been among those who rented rather than purchased slaves. Both masters and slaves found slave hiring profitable. It provided slaveowners—particularly widowed women—a steady

[13] For example, in 1860 only 40 percent of the slaves employed by Richmond's white men (including tobacco manufacturers) were women, but women accounted for 60 percent of the slaves employed by white artisans. A similar pattern can be found in Lynchburg, another city where the distribution of slaves was reported by employer rather than by owner. Elsewhere, the disparity between the white male ownership and the white artisan ownership was smaller, and, in Charleston, artisans proportionately owned more men than the white male population as a whole. See note 16, below.

9

TABLE 8

Ownership or Employment of Adult Slave Men, 1860

City	Total Number of Slaves	Occupation of Owners or Employers							
		Merchants, Planters, Professionals, and Politicians	Manu-facturers	Petty Entre-preneurs	Artisans	Unskilled Laborers	White Women	Free Blacks	Unknown
RICHMOND[a]	4,628	22	58	6	6	1	5	0	3
CHARLESTON[b]	4,042	50	0	4	14	1	22	1	8
MOBILE[b]	2,450	60	5	4	8	1	17	0	5
NASHVILLE[c]	877	38	5	23	11	3	10	0	9
LYNCHBURG[a]	962	31[d]	53	6	4	0	2	0	4

[a] Slaves listed by their employers.
[b] Slaves listed by their owners.
[c] Slaves listed in some wards by their employers, in some wards by their owners.
[d] Includes eighty-four slave men, about 8 percent of the male slaves, employed on the railroad.
SOURCE: Computed from U.S. Census MSS., RG 29.

10

income, and it gave slaves an added measure of control over their own lives. Slave hiring increased despite a variety of complaints from white workers fearful for their jobs and white residents fearful for their lives.[14] But slave hiring did not enlarge artisan employment of slaves in most cities. In Richmond and Lynchburg (where census takers noted slave employment rather than slave ownership), large tobacco manufacturers hired most of the slaves. When viewed from the perspective of employment rather than ownership, artisan control of slaves increased slightly. But throughout the urban South, merchants, professionals, and manufacturers (in factory towns like Richmond and Lynchburg) remained the largest employers of slave labor, and, for the most part, these employers required unskilled, rather than skilled, laborers.[15] (See Table 8.) While some merchants and manufacturers may well have employed slave artisans, some free artisans doubtless worked their slaves in menial roles. In any case, when slave artisans—estimated as all slave men owned by free white artisans—are placed within the context of the artisan class, their share of the skilled work force exceeds 8 percent in Charleston but nowhere else. Even when the estimated number of slave artisans is doubled (that is, every slave man owned by a white artisan plus an equal number owned by others), slaves still composed less than 15 percent of the artisan population in Mobile, Richmond, and Nashville. Thus, as a general rule, urban slaves appear to have toiled in either the most backward sector of the economy as domestic servants and day laborers or in the most advanced sector of the economy as factory hands. (See Table 9.)

Only in Charleston did slaves make up a large portion of the mechanic class. Charleston artisans owned slaves in numbers that proportionately nearly doubled the rate of artisan slave ownership in Mobile, Richmond, or Nashville. Moreover, unlike the pattern of artisan slave ownership in those cities, Charleston artisans held slave men in disproportionate numbers.[16] Those Charleston artisans who did not own slaves also had ample opportunity to hire them, since city-bound planters and white women owned a larger proportion of their city's slave population than in any of the other places investigated. Thus a tradition of slave artisanry reaching back into the eighteenth century—built upon the high level of skill demanded by the rice economy and sustained by a cultural milieu more akin to the West Indies than the mainland—existed in Charleston on the eve of the Civil War.[17] If every slave man owned by a Charleston artisan practiced his master's trade, Charleston's slaves

[14] For discussions of slave hiring, see Wade, *Slavery in the Cities*, 38–54; Starobin, *Industrial Slavery in the Old South*, 128–37, 211–12; Clement Eaton, "Slave-Hiring in the Upper South: A Step toward Freedom," *Mississippi Valley Historical Review*, 46 (1959–60): 663–78; and Richard B. Morris, "The Measure of Bondage in the Slave States," *ibid.*, 41 (1954–55): 219–40.

[15] For the best discussions of Southern tobacco manufacturing prior to the Civil War, see Joseph C. Robert, *The Tobacco Kingdom: Plantation, Market, and Factory in Virginia and North Carolina, 1800–1860* (Durham, N.C., 1938); and John O'Brien, "Black Richmond, 1850–1870" (Ph.D. dissertation, University of Rochester, 1978), chap. 1. Also see Starobin, *Industrial Slavery in the Old South*.

[16] In 1860, 51 percent of the slaves owned by Charleston's white men were women, but only 39 percent of the slaves owned by white artisans were women. See note 13, above.

[17] Artisan ownership of slaves was commonplace in post-Revolutionary Charleston, the largest slave city in the nation. In 1790, more than half of Charleston's artisans owned slaves, and their slaves amounted to nearly a quarter of the city's slave population. The nature of the available evidence makes it impossible to determine how many of the artisans' slaves were men, but the size of their holdings suggests that many used slaves in their shops as well as in their homes. For example, 60 percent of Charleston carpenters owned slaves. Almost three-quarters of these slaves were held in units of six or more, units large enough to extend beyond the domestic

Table 9
Skill Distribution among Free and Slave Workingmen, 1860

Using Minimal Estimate of Skilled Slaves

	Richmond[a]		Charleston[b]		Mobile[c]		Nashville[d]		Lynchburg[e]		Baton Rouge[f]	
	Skilled	Unskilled	Skilled	Unskilled	Skilled	Unskilled	Skilled	Unskilled	Skilled	Unskilled	Skilled	Unskilled
NUMBER	3,619	5,938	2,978	4,909	2,407	4,595	1,612	1,797	473	1,150	451	392
PERCENTAGE												
Southern-born White	45	6	31	3	23	7	43	20	63	9	33	10
Northern-born White	9	1	5	2	16	5	16	2	4	0	11	2
Foreign-born	33	12	32	21	50	36	31	28	16	5	41	16
Free Black	5	8	13	3	3	2	3	5	6	6	7	1
Slave	8	73	19	71	8	49	6	44	10	80	8	71

Using Maximal Estimate of Skilled Slaves

	Richmond[g]		Charleston[h]		Mobile[i]		Nashville[j]		Lynchburg[k]		Baton Rouge[l]	
	Skilled	Unskilled	Skilled	Unskilled	Skilled	Unskilled	Skilled	Unskilled	Skilled	Unskilled	Skilled	Unskilled
NUMBER	3,896	5,661	3,544	4,343	2,603	4,399	1,710	1,698	521	1,102	485	358
PERCENTAGE												
Southern-born White	41	6	26	4	21	8	41	21	58	9	31	11
Northern-born White	8	1	4	2	15	6	15	3	4	0	10	2
Foreign-born	31	13	27	24	46	37	29	30	14	5	38	18
Free Black	5	9	11	4	2	2	3	5	5	6	7	1
Slave	14	71	32	67	15	47	11	40	18	79	14	68

ASSUMPTION: The percentage of slaves who were skilled—that is, if x percent of slaves were skilled, then the skill distribution among workers by status, nativity, and race was as described in the corresponding table— a = 6 percent; b = 8 percent; c = 8 percent; d = 11 percent; e = 5 percent; and f = 11 percent; g = 12 percent; h = 28 percent; i = 16 percent; j = 22 percent; k = 10 percent; and l = 22 percent.

SOURCE: Computed and estimated from the Census MSS., RG 29.

12

would have contributed nearly a fifth of the skilled workingmen in that city. If in addition to those owned by artisans, other slave men also engaged in skilled labor, the proportion of artisanal work performed by slaves would have been higher still. In Mobile, Richmond, and Nashville, all of which developed during the nineteenth century, far fewer slaves practiced skilled trades, and skilled bondsmen composed only a small proportion of the mechanic class. Although urban slaves everywhere enjoyed greater mobility and cultural autonomy than their counterparts in the countryside, only in Charleston—and cities where similar conditions existed—did large numbers of bondsmen practice skilled trades. Elsewhere, few seem to have escaped the dull, demeaning, and backbreaking work that also characterized slave labor in the countryside.

Although slaves were the single largest source of unskilled labor in Southern cities, many free men also worked at unskilled menial jobs. Assuming that all slave men not employed as artisans worked as laborers, slaves supplied slightly better than 70 percent of the unskilled and service workers in Richmond and Charleston, 50 percent in Mobile, and more than 40 percent in Nashville. In short, even where slaves performed most of the unskilled work, free workers still composed a substantial minority of the unskilled laborers. In some slave cities, like Nashville, free workers did most of the unskilled, menial work performed by men. (See Tables 7B and 9.)

Irish immigrants generally dominated the ranks of unskilled urban free men thoughout the urban South. In Charleston, fully 60 percent of the free unskilled laboringmen had been born in Ireland, and, although that proportion slipped substantially in Mobile, Richmond, and Nashville, it remained above 40 percent. In occupational terms, the nativist slander that an Irishman was a "nigger" turned inside out contained a considerable element of truth in such places. Immigrants of other nationalities, along with free Negroes, accounted for most of the remainder of the unskilled free workingmen. (See Tables 7B, 10.)

But, even more than among workingmen generally, native-born whites were conspicuous in their absence from the ranks of the unskilled; and, in the cities of the Lower South in particular, it would have been difficult to find a Southern-born white man shouldering a shovel or lifting a hod. Unskilled Southern-born whites constituted no more than 8 percent of the employed free men in the Southern cities studied. In Charleston, fewer than one Southern white man in fifty—compared to more than half of the Irishmen—did unskilled labor. (See Table 11.) While the structure of the urban laboring class confirmed the degraded status of blacks and identified the Irish with the slave, native-born Southern whites insulated themselves from such imputations.

needs of most households and to contain several slave men. Some Charleston carpenters held so many slaves that their number almost compelled commercial exploitation. A full 25 percent of slaveowning carpenters owned ten or more slaves. These estimates result from linking the 1790 Charleston manuscript federal census and the 1790 Charleston city directory. The directory lists occupations, and the census gives the number of slaves residing in individual households. Any computation of slave ownership (using the federal census before 1850), however, is compromised by the fact that some slaves within a given household may not have been owned by the head of the household; such computations must, therefore, be considered rough estimates. Jacob Milligan, comp., *The Charleston Directory* (Charleston, 1790); U.S. Bureau of the Census, *Heads of Families at the Time of the First Census of the United States, Taken in the Year 1790* (Washington, 1908), 31–34.

13

TABLE 10
Irish and Free Negro Men in the Free Work Force, 1860

City	All Free Workingmen (Percentage)		Unskilled Free Workingmen (Percentage)	
	Irish	Free Negro	Irish	Free Negro
RICHMOND	18	14	46	30
CHARLESTON	29	14	60	11
MOBILE	28	3	43	4
NASHVILLE	23	5	45	9
LYNCHBURG	—	14	23	27
BATON ROUGE	—	7	31	4

SOURCE: Computed from the U.S. Census MSS., RG 29.

As among the unskilled workers, color, status, and nativity sharply divided skilled workers. Except for the Irish, the vast majority of immigrant workingmen practiced artisanal trades, and immigrant artisans composed a disproportionate share of the skilled urban work force. (See Table 7A.) In Richmond, for example, nine out of ten British and German workingmen practiced skilled trades. Although immigrant workers could be found in almost every urban craft, they were especially important in urban service trades like tailoring and shoemaking. In Mobile and Charleston, four of five free shoemakers had been born outside the United States, a proportion only slightly smaller in Richmond and Nashville. Foreign-born workers similarly dominated blacksmithing in Lower South cities and composed a disproportionate share of the blacksmiths even in the urban Upper South.

Free Negro men contributed to the urban artisan class in a special way.[18] First, they were generally confined to one or two trades that whites had denominated "nigger work" and that were usually identified with servile, dirty, or distasteful labor. Although such trades differed from place to place, barbering and butchering typified such occupations. While free Negroes totaled 3 percent of the skilled free workingmen in Mobile and 16 percent of those in Charleston, they equaled, respectively, 20 and 78 percent of the free barbers in those two cities. Second, mulattoes generally composed a disproportionate share of the skilled freemen. This division between mulattoes and blacks was especially evident in the cities of the Lower South. Men of mixed racial origins composed over three-quarters of Charleston's free Negro barbers, one of the most lucrative and prestigious free Negro occupations, but less than one-quarter of the free Negro day laborers. Even in Upper South cities, Negro freemen of mixed racial origins enjoyed a higher skill level than those denominated black.

Southern-born white men also held a distinctive place within the ranks of the urban artisan class. They tended to congregate in a few occupations, most notably in the building trades and in crafts like piloting and printing in which native birth provided them with obvious advantages. Generally, over half the Southern-born

[18] Ira Berlin, *Slaves without Masters: The Free Negro in the Antebellum South* (New York, 1974), 217–49; and Leonard P. Curry, *The Free Black in Urban America: The Shadow of the Dream* (Chicago, 1981), 15–36.

TABLE 11
Unskilled Southern-Born White Workingmen, 1860

City	Number	Percentage of All Employed Free Men	Percentage of All Workingmen (Free and Slave)	Percentage of Free Workingmen
RICHMOND	324	4	3	7
CHARLESTON	158	2	2	4
MOBILE	342	5	5	8
NASHVILLE	360	8	11	14
LYNCHBURG	100	8	6	15
BATON ROUGE	38	4	4	7

SOURCE: Computed from the U.S. Census MSS., RG 29.

white artisans labored as printers and pilots and in the building trades. In some places this proportion reached three-quarters. Even in the building trades, however, Southern whites did not always predominate. While more than half the Southern-born white artisans in Charleston and Mobile worked in the building trades, they equaled no more than 40 percent of building-trade workers. In Charleston, about one in three skilled Southern-born white workingmen labored as carpenters, but the typical free Charleston carpenter was either a free Negro, a Northern white, or an immigrant. (See Table 12.) Outside of these trades, Southern-born whites were grossly underrepresented in the artisanal classes of Southern cities.

A work force with a disproportionately large immigrant artisanal sector and an overwhelmingly black and immigrant unskilled sector did not appear suddenly in Southern cities on the eve of the Civil War. Slave labor had characterized Southern urban life from the beginning of settlement, and the number of European immigrant workers had grown steadily during the middle decades of the nineteenth century. Indeed, in the Lower South, the evolution of an urban work force in which immigrants played a central role appears to have taken place well before mid-century. By 1850, immigrants already numbered almost half of the free workingmen of Charleston and three-fifths of those of Mobile—and an even larger proportion of the unskilled free workers in these cities. In both cities, two of three unskilled free men had been born outside the United States. In the Upper South cities of Richmond and Nashville, however, foreign-born workers still played a minority role in the free labor force at mid-century—although a substantial one. During the decade before the war, immigrant workers entered these Upper South cities in large numbers and increased their share of the working class not only at the expense of slaves—as scholars have emphasized—but also at the expense of native-born white workers.

While historians have focused their attention on the proportional decline of urban slavery, the most significant change in the composition of the urban work force was the increase of immigrant and the decline of native white workers. In Nashville, for example, the number of slave men increased by more than 50 percent between 1850 and 1860, but the number of immigrant workingmen

15

TABLE 12
Free Building-Trade Workingmen by Nativity and Race, 1860

| City | Number | Percentage by Nativity and Race | | | |
		Southern-Born White	Northern-Born White	Foreign-Born White	Free Black
RICHMOND	933	66	7	20	8
CHARLESTON	876	41	5	32	21
MOBILE	804	30	20	45	5
NASHVILLE	687	64	13	22	1
LYNCHBURG	160	84	2	9	5
BATON ROUGE	188	52	13	23	12

SOURCE: Computed by the U.S. Census MSS., RG 29.

increased threefold, with foreign-born artisans doubling and immigrant laborers increasing by some 500 percent. Meanwhile, the number of native-born white workingmen increased by less than 40 percent, lagging behind the allegedly declining slave population. In some artisanal trades, native-born whites suffered an absolute decline. A similar development took place in Richmond. There the slave population grew by about 20 percent as tobacco manufacturers scoured the countryside for hirelings. But the number of immigrant workers more than doubled, while native white workers increased at a pace akin to those in Nashville. In the Lower South ports of Charleston and Mobile, the composition of the work force changed less dramatically during the 1850s, because the central importance of immigrant workers had already been established. But, in the cities of both the Upper and the Lower South, immigrants made especially large gains in the skilled trades, so that their dominance of artisan work increased even faster than their prominence in unskilled labor. Throughout the urban South, foreign-born workers remained the most dynamic element in the working class and increased their dominant position. (See Table 13.)

Skilled free workers, unskilled slaves, immigrants of all sorts playing roles that historians have previously given over to others—this portrait of the composition of the urban work force brings Southern cities much closer to the description of a Charleston boardinghouse rendered by a British merchant in 1860: "Fully one-half the large number of guests in the House seemed as if they had just stepped out of Houndsditch, and remind me of what a friend in Mobile said, that 'I should meet more Jews in Charleston than I could see in Jerusalem.'"[19]

KNOWLEDGE OF THE COMPOSITION of the wage-earning population of the urban South has profound implications for comprehending the development of Southern

[19] W. Corsan, *Two Months in the Confederate States, Including a Visit to New Orleans under the Domination of General Butler* (London, 1863), 9–10.

society. Just as the new understanding of the role of immigrant workers in Southern cities forced a reconsideration of the structure of the entire work force (slave and free), so the new understanding of the South's urban work force necessitates a re-evaluation of the social order of the antebellum South. The reconsideration of urban laboring people raises questions about the development of Southern society, the character of slavery and the evolution of Afro-American culture, and the nature of politics in the urban South and the role of immigrants in

TABLE 13

Increase and Decrease of Urban Workingmen
between 1850 and 1860 by Race, Status, and Nativity

City	*Percentage of Increase or Decrease*				
	Southern-Born Whites	Northern-Born Whites	Foreign-Born Whites	Free Blacks	Slaves
RICHMOND	+37	+97	+166	+42	+27
CHARLESTON	+11	−24	+25	−11	−46
MOBILE	+73	+43	+81	+51	+17
NASHVILLE	+38	+106	+223	+162	+55

SOURCE: Computed by the U.S. Census MSS., RG 29.

the growing sectional controversy. The answers to these questions will ultimately rest on the results of investigations that have hardly begun. Based on this re-evaluation of the composition of the Southern urban working population, some suggestions can be made, if only to indicate the direction that those investigations might take.

First, this analysis of the composition of the urban working population raises questions about the culture of native Southern whites who remained in the countryside, despite opportunity in the city, and of those who migrated to cities but avoided manual work, skilled as well as unskilled. The answers to these questions suggest how the requirements of cotton agriculture and the great prosperity of the late antebellum countryside made yeoman farmers unlikely migrants to the cities. They also suggest the Southern yeomanry's deep attachment to the land and to its own unique culture as well as suggesting the strength of the unspoken entente between planters and yeomen, which guaranteed the security of the yeoman's separate world. It re-emphasizes the importance of understanding the history of rural plain people.[20]

[20] Steven Hahn, *The Roots of Southern Populism: Yeoman Farmers and the Transformation of the Georgia Upcountry, 1850–1890* (New York, 1983); Eugene D. Genovese, "Yeoman Farmers in a Slaveholders' Democracy," *Agricultural History*, 44 (1975): 331–42; and Frank L. Owsley, *Plain Folk of the Old South* (Baton Rouge, La., 1949).

The power of that distinctive way of life often survived the transfer to the city and shaped the lives of country folk in the urban South. As expanding centers of commerce, every Southern city housed a small army of clerks—young, generally unmarried men who boarded together and aspired to counting houses of their own. In overwhelming proportions, these young men had been born in the South, and (given the growth of Southern cities) probably in the countryside. In Charleston, for example, two-thirds of the clerical workers were native to the South and generally to the state of South Carolina, and a similar pattern could be found in other Southern cities.[21] Thus, differences between those who labored in clerical, commercial occupations and manual, industrial ones were compounded by distinctions of nationality throughout the urban South.

Second, understanding the composition of the work force of the urban South raises questions about the changing character of slavery and its development during the nineteenth century. Slaves had played a far different role in the post-Revolutionary urban South than in the mid-nineteenth century. It is not simply that there were proportionately fewer of them in the cities of the pre–Civil War period, a point that has consumed far too much of recent scholarly debate on the subject. More importantly, during the colonial period slaves had actively participated in almost all major artisanal trades; on the eve of the Civil War, except in a few cities with roots deep in the eighteenth century, they did not.[22]

The large number of slave artisans in the post-Revolutionary South helps explain how free Negroes came to enjoy a comparatively high level of skill during the nineteenth century, despite the early presence of politically active white artisans. Most free Negroes obtained their liberty during the period when slaves were still deeply involved in the artisanal economy. They maintained their skills through the antebellum years while slaves were systematically stripped of their crafts. A possible interpretation for the decline of slave skill argues that competition from newly arrived immigrants muscled slaves out of the artisan crafts. Yet, this explanation fails to account for the Negro freemen's ability to maintain their occupational position. In any three-way competition among white, slave, and free black workers, black freemen would probably be the most vulnerable. Yet, free Negroes maintained their occupational position, and the level of free Negro skill appears to have had little connection with the proportion of immigrants in any Southern city. It is possible, then, that the erosion of slave skill began before the great nineteenth-century European migrations and had far more to do with the expansion of the cotton economy than with the entry of foreign-born workers into the South. The opening of new lands to staple production required skilled labor to construct

[21] Clerical workers include accountants, agents, bookkeepers, clerks, and salesmen. Of the 890 clerical workers in Richmond, 83 percent were born in the slave states; of 1,146 in Charleston, 65 percent; of the 1,278 in Mobile, 71 percent; and, of the 554 in Nashville, 60 percent. This information was computed from the U.S. Census MSS., RG 29.

[22] Allan Kulikoff, "Tobacco and Slaves: Population, Economy, and Society in Eighteenth-Century Prince George's County, Maryland" (Ph.D. dissertation, Brandeis University, 1976), 235–39; Gerald W. Mullin, *Flight and Rebellion* (New York, 1972), chaps. 3–4; Philip D. Morgan, "Black Society in the Lowcountry," in Ira Berlin and Ronald Hoffman, eds., *Slavery and Freedom in the Age of the American Revolution* (Charlottesville, Va., 1983); and Louis Morton, *Robert Carter of Nomini Hall: A Virginia Tobacco Planter in the Eighteenth Century* (Williamsburg, Va., 1964). Also see the evidence cited in note 17, above.

quarters for master and slaves and to build and repair barns, carts, presses, and a variety of agricultural machinery. Slave artisans may have been the first to go west, pulled out of the cities in large numbers by the rapid spread of plantation agriculture across the South. In a time of great economic growth, artisan standing provided scant protection from sale. Indeed, it may have encouraged physical removal to distant rural workplaces, a process that reduced the number of slave artisans in cities, transformed urban skills into rural skills, and cut the generational lines by which slaves transferred their crafts. If a Richmond carpenter, who might otherwise pass his skill to his son in Richmond, was sold to Alabama, his son would be left without skill and he would be left without a son to reproduce his skill. The long-term loss of slave skill affected not only urban slaves but rural ones as well. In 1860, according to several estimates, well under 10 percent of rural slave men enjoyed artisanal status.[23]

The loss of skilled standing deeply affected the behavior and values of blacks, both slave and free, during the nineteenth century. In a variety of ways, it may have weakened black resistance to white domination. In almost all early working-class movements, the worldliness and confidence engendered by skill propelled artisans to positions of leadership.[24] Yet, the destruction of slave skill had other, less obvious—and perhaps even more insidious—effects. It appears to have slowed considerably the rate of self-purchase, a practice common among urban slaves elsewhere in the hemisphere. Without skills, even the most industrious slaves had difficulty buying their way out of bondage. Like the sharp decline of manumission at the beginning of the nineteenth century, the inability of slaves to purchase liberty severed the bonds that had existed between slaves and free blacks at the end of the eighteenth century when slaves moved into the free Negro caste in great numbers.[25] Already torn by differences in status, the black community faced still another obstacle to caste unity. Skill differences pushed black freemen and slaves further apart than they would have been if they had shared a common occupational experience.

After emancipation, the distinctive occupational traditions of former free and former slave blacks made those who had enjoyed freedom more important within the larger community yet, paradoxically, hampered their ability to act with authority. Free Negroes provided a disproportionate share of post–Civil War black leadership not only because they had been free but also because they carried the

[23] Roger Ransom and Richard Sutch, "The Impact of the Civil War and Emancipation on Southern Agriculture," *Explorations in Economic History*, 12 (1975): 1–28. In a study based on the mortality schedule of the U.S. Census (1850 and 1860), Michael P. Johnson has calculated the rate of slave skill to be about double the estimate of Ransom and Sutch; Johnson, "Slave Occupations and Marriages," unpublished essay courtesy of the author. For additional evidence on the scarcity of artisanal skills among exslaves during and just after the Civil War, also see Herbert G. Gutman, *The Black Family in Slavery and Freedom, 1750–1925* (New York, 1976), 39–41, 233, 479–83.
[24] The classic study of such leadership is E. P. Thompson's *The Making of the English Working Class* (New York, 1963). For the role of American artisans in developing working-class movements, see Alan Dawley, *Class and Community: The Industrial Revolution in Lynn* (Cambridge, Mass., 1976); and Paul G. Faler, *Mechanics and Manufacturers in the Early Industrial Revolution* (Albany, N.Y., 1981). For a cross-cultural comparison, see Bryan Palmer, "Most Uncommon Common Men: Craft and Culture in Historical Perspective," *Labor/Le Travailleur*, 1 (1976): 5–31.
[25] Berlin, *Slaves without Masters*, 15–50, 138–60.

19

artisanal tradition within the black community. Yet former slaves and former freepeople had not known each other well, particularly in the urban South. Fearful of the fate of slave craftsmen, free Negro artisans may well have hesitated to identify fully with the newly emancipated unskilled masses. That most of them took the risk says something about the dynamics of Reconstruction, but in the end their worst fears were realized.[26] Slaves did not lose skills as a result of emancipation; they had few to lose. Free Negroes suffered badly. An examination of the occupational structure of the black community in Mobile and Richmond in 1880 indicates that generational lines of craft transfer had been smashed within the black community. Although blacks maintained their pre–Civil War skill level through Reconstruction, the internal composition of the black artisan class changed dramatically. Compared to skilled white workers, black artisans—probably descendants of free Negroes—were top heavy with age in the major crafts. The vestiges of traditional black artisanal skills, which had reached a high point in the late eighteenth century and were maintained through the antebellum period by free Negroes, were liquidated in the last decades of the nineteenth century.[27] Artisanship and petty enterprise often went together, so that the decline in artisan skills also stifled small businesses. Booker T. Washington thrived in this constricted setting, but urban blacks migrating to Northern cities in the early decades of the twentieth century carried few skills and little business experience with them.

Finally, the composition of the work force of Southern cities raises questions about the immigrants who constituted so large an element in the free working population of Southern cities. Although a full understanding of their place as workers in Southern society requires close attention in particular cities to the ways immigrants lived, where they resided, what institutions they formed, and how they related to others, some preliminary probing suggests the dimensions of the issue.[28]

In the free states, immigrant workers stood at the center of the most important changes in economy, society, and politics during the late antebellum years. Newly arrived workers, particularly skilled ones, carried artisanal traditions from the Old World to the New, where they fused with the indigenous artisanal traditions of American mechanics and craftsmen. These beliefs, deriving in large measure from

[26] Thomas Holt, *Black over White: Negro Political Leadership in South Carolina during Reconstruction* (Urbana, Ill., 1977); David C. Rankin, "The Origins of Black Leadership in New Orleans during Reconstruction," *Journal of Southern History*, 40 (1974): 417–40; Charles Vincent, *Black Legislators in Louisiana during Reconstruction* (Baton Rouge, La., 1976); Loren Schweninger, *James T. Rapier and Reconstruction* (Chicago, 1978); Howard N. Rabinowitz, ed., *Southern Black Leaders of the Reconstruction Era* (Urbana, Ill., 1982); and especially David C. Rankin, "The Impact of the Civil War on the Free Colored Community of New Orleans," *Perspectives in American History*, 11 (1975): 379–416.

[27] Gutman, *Black Family in Slavery and Freedom*, 433–60, 476–519, 623–44. By 1880, the percentage of all skilled white workers under the age of thirty in Richmond was 46 percent and all skilled black workers under thirty 30 percent, and in Mobile in the same year the percentages, respectively, were 41 percent and 23 percent; the percentage of all white carpenters under the age of thirty in Richmond was 25 percent and of all black carpenters 9 percent; in Mobile the percentages respectively were 27 percent and 13 percent. This information was computed from the U.S. Census MSS., RG 29.

[28] The only book-length study of an antebellum Southern white immigrant and predominantly working-class community is Earl F. Niehaus's *The Irish in New Orleans, 1800–1865* (Baton Rouge, La., 1965). Also see Christopher Silver, "A New Look at Old South Urbanization: The Irish Worker in Charleston, South Carolina, 1840–1860," *South Atlantic Urban Studies*, 3 (1979): 141–72. John F. Nau's examination only begins at mid-century but contains material of interest; Nau, *The German People of New Orleans, 1850–1900* (Liedens, 1958). For a work that concentrates on German political leaders and intellectuals, see Dieter Cunz, *The Maryland Germans: A History* (Princeton, N.J., 1948).

the common character of artisan life and work throughout the Atlantic world, celebrated independence and emphasized a man's right to the fruits of his own labor as central to that independence. Such ideas mixed readily with republican notions about the rights of man and with nationalistic ideas about the rights of American citizens. Together these beliefs drew workers into the ongoing struggle against slavery, as an institution fundamentally opposed to those values that the artisanal experience taught guaranteed freedom. Artisans, some of them nascent manufacturers, played a large role in the rise of political antislavery in the free states, as they not only came to see slavery as a threat to their own liberty but also developed a deep sympathy for the plight of the slave. Such abstract beliefs did not, however, necessarily negate longstanding antipathy toward black people. Indeed, disdain for blacks persisted among Northern white workingmen, reinforced by the historic suspicion of small propertyholders toward the propertyless as well as fear of competition from the emancipated. To accommodate opposition to both slavery and the slave, the abolitionist movement frequently—though not always—advanced with opposition to blacks. Free soilism and Republicanism took both egalitarian and racist forms in the free states.[29]

Immigrant workers who arrived in the South carried ideas and traditions about the meaning of work and its relation to liberty similar to those carried by workers who migrated to the North. (In fact, many arrived first in the free states and then traveled south, and others moved back and forth between Northern and Southern cities.[30]) Deeply rooted beliefs about the connection between labor and liberty and cherished ideas about the connections of both to republicanism took on special meaning in a slave society. Although many quickly adopted Southern racial prejudices and some became slaveholders, immigrant workers generally remained suspicious of chattel bondage. Proportionately, immigrant workers owned or employed fewer slaves than did native-born workers. If some workers, skilled and unskilled, ultimately came to see black bondage as protection for white liberty and insurance for their own elevated position in a split labor market, others believed slavery to be an ever-present threat to their freedom. As in the North, this opposition to slavery took a variety of forms and did not necessarily assure sympathy for the slave. Hatred of slavery and the slave frequently became one.

Still, whatever the precise target, worker complaints about slave competition as a threat to their own liberty grew during the antebellum years. True to the proslavery argument, some of these complaints had no abolitionist import and sought only the removal of slaves from specific trades or from artisan work generally. Such petitions bespoke opposition not to slavery but to slaves. Frequently, they explicitly accepted slavery. Slaveholders generally found it easy to deflect these attacks and direct them to the most vulnerable element of the black population, the black

---

[29] Eric Foner, *Free Soil, Free Labor, Free Men: The Ideology of the Republican Party before the Civil War* (New York, 1970); Leonard L. Richards, *Gentlemen of Property and Standing* (New York, 1970); Dawley, *Class and Community*, chaps. 1–4; John Jentz, "The Antislavery Constituency in Jacksonian New York," *Civil War History*, 27 (1981): 101–02; David Montgomery, "Labor and the Republic in Industrial America," *Le Mouvement Social*, no. 111 (1980): 201–15; and Bruce Carlan Levine, "'In the Spirit of 1848': German-Americans and the Fight over Slavery's Expansion" (Ph.D. dissertation, University of Rochester, 1980).

[30] According to the historian of Charleston's Irish population, most of that city's Irish workers entered the U.S. in the North and then migrated to Charleston, and others, searching for work, migrated seasonally between Northern and Southern cities; Silver, "A New Look at Old South Urbanization," 145–46.

freemen. Attempts to proscribe free Negroes consistently met with greater success than did attempts to limit the use of slave workers. But some free workers, frustrated by the ability of slaveholders to preserve the widest range of opportunities for employing their valuable property, threatened to strike out at slavery. "In placing the negro in competition with white mechanics," noted a Charleston workingman in the city's leading daily, "you drag down the latter to a level with the former. This is well calculated to breed discontent and hatred on the part of the white mechanic, and make him an enemy of our institution."[31]

The everyday realities and necessities of working-class life may have reinforced disdain for racial bondage and increased sympathy for slaves among free workers, particularly immigrants. In the absence of residential segregation, workers of all sorts lived in close proximity. In Richmond, Frederick Law Olmsted found "a very considerable population of foreign origin," many of them "very dirty German Jews . . . thickly set in the narrowest and meanest streets, which seem otherwise inhabited by negroes."[32] Often neighbors practiced a common trade, as did free black carpenter Richard Washington and Irish carpenter George Mahone, who shared a house with their families in Richmond's second ward. Such men probably did not attend the same church, but they may well have shared in the conviviality of back-alley groceries and groggeries scattered throughout every Southern city. There free workers might strike a profitable bargain for some item of slave-stolen merchandise, or a fugitive slave might purchase a set of freedom papers. Much to the disgust of the leaders of Southern society, many white workers did not understand the niceties of Southern race relations or, if they did, did not seem to care. Few workingmen sold slaves liquor, rented them rooms, and aided them in eluding slavery.[33] "Not only free Negroes," complained a Richmond newspaper in 1860, "but low white people can be found who will secret a slave from his master." Other acts of striking generosity punctuated these commonplaces to suggest how closely shared experience might bind workers together. In 1847, the First African Baptist Church of Richmond sent forty dollars overseas to assist victims of the Irish famine, and ten years later that same church donated a small sum to the city's Irish poor.[34]

[31] Berlin, *Slaves without Masters*, 229–33, 349–51; *Charleston Courier*, December 7, 1860, as quoted in Michael P. Johnson, "Wealth and Class in Charleston in 1860," in Walter J. Fraser, Jr., et al., eds., *From the Old South to the New: Essays on the Transitional South* (Westport, Conn., 1981), 74, 80 n.

[32] Olmsted, *Journey in the Seaboard Slave States*, 55; and Curry, *Free Blacks in Urban America*, 49–80.

[33] The manuscript census schedules for the large Southern cities we have examined indicate that small shopkeepers were disproportionately foreign-born. These shopkeepers usually had started as wage earners, and they often became wage earners following business failure. Richard Wade has found much evidence of a traffic in petty theft between urban slaves and white shopkeepers. According to Earl Niehaus, Irish grocers were arrested for receiving sugar and flour stolen by New Orleans slaves. Liquor, apparently, was often traded for stolen goods. Wade, *Slavery in the Cities*; and Niehaus, *Irish in New Orleans*. The alliance between immigrant shopkeepers and black slaves often was simply a matter of convenience for both. But, with freedom, it became increasingly important and, in some places, served as the basis for the alliance between black and white Republicans. See, for example, the alliance between black editor John P. Mitchell, Jr., and Irish grocer James Bahen in Richmond; Michael P. Chesson, "Richmond's Black Councilmen," in Rabinowitz, *Southern Black Leaders of the Reconstruction Era*, 202–06, 216.

[34] *Richmond Daily Dispatch*, December 21, 1860; and Minutes of the First African Baptist Church, March 1847, October 1857, First African Baptist Church, Richmond, Virginia. Frederick Law Olmsted, visiting the Midlothian Coal Mines outside Richmond, recorded an incident that characterizes far more of the interchange between newly arrived immigrants and black slaves than historians have allowed. Olmsted observed, "Not long since, a young English fellow came to the pit, and was put to work with a gang of negroes. One morning, about

Of course, common conditions did not always promote common understanding or mutual respect. Often just the opposite resulted. Shared values and behavior evolved slowly, unevenly, and imperfectly among Southern urban workers during the antebellum years. Conflict among immigrant, native-born, and black workers divided working people, as did internal differences within each group—between British and Irish immigrants, native-born Northern and Southern whites, Catholic and Protestant immigrants, and black freemen and bondsmen. If white workers, immigrant and native, protested black competition and tried to push black craftsmen from their crafts, native-born workers joined the Plug Uglies, Rip Raps, Blood Tubs, and other nativist gangs to oust the immigrants. Slaves sought the protection of their masters and free Negroes their patrons to secure their jobs and protect their persons. The record of this intraclass hostility is full, and the presence of slavery aggravated and enlarged it.[35]

But, if free workers were pulled in all directions, their allegiance to the slave regime was never firm. Men and women who had fled the landlord-dominated societies of Western Europe were hardly predisposed to sympathize with the planter class. Slavery remained the linchpin of the Southern order, and the relationship of free workers to that institution continued to be ambiguous at best. Many were too newly arrived to understand it, and some found good reason to oppose it. Some foreign-born workers had been schooled in antislavery beliefs in Europe, including British artisans who had observed or participated in the abolitionist debates, and many others had learned to wield the phrase "wage slavery" to their advantage. The defenders of slavery, who sometimes argued that all work should be done by slaves and even that all workers should be slaves, alienated free workers by undervaluing their labor and, at times, slandering their persons. A whiggish Richmond newspaper's boast that the major advantage of slave labor was its "exclusion of a populace made up of the dregs of Europe" could not have won the approbation of most free workers in that city.[36]

---

a week afterwards, twenty or thirty men called on him, and told him that they would allow him fifteen minutes to get out of sight, and if they ever saw him in those parts again they would 'give him hell.' They were all armed, and there was nothing for the young fellow to do but to move 'right off.'

'What reason did they give him for it?'

'They did not give him any reason.'

'But what had he done?'

'Why I believe they thought he had been too free with the niggers; he wasn't used to them, you see, and he talked to 'em free like, and they thought he'd make 'em think too much of themselves.'" Olmsted, *Journey in the Seaboard Slave States*, 47–48.

[35] For hints of intraclass conflict, see William D. Overdyke, *The Know-Nothing Party of the South* (Baton Rouge, La., 1950). But the composition of the nativist movement (its leaders and its followers) awaits careful study. The class composition of nativist political "gangs" in places like Baltimore also needs study. Anti-immigrant political violence involved far more than minor electoral brawls. In the Louisville election day riot of August 1855 ("Bloody Monday"), twenty-two persons were killed, three in four of them foreigners. The election riots in New Orleans in both 1854 adn 1856 were nearly as violent. One of them lasted ten days. Afterward, the vote in Irish districts fell by two-thirds. Irish school teachers and policemen lost their jobs. Some Irish persons lost their lives. In 1856, some Irish residents of New Orleans petitioned the Mexican government, seeking land to colonize there. "The initiation of order," said the *New Orleans Delta* of native American violence, "is accompanied by murder." See Niehaus, *Irish in New Orleans*, 84–97. For evidence of clientage connections between free blacks and wealthy whites, see Berlin, *Slaves without Masters*, 316–40; and Michael P. Johnson and James L. Roark, "Charleston's Free Colored Elite and the Secession Crisis," unpublished essay courtesy of the authors.

[36] *Richmond Whig*, n.d., as quoted in Russell B. Nye, *Fettered Freedom* (East Lansing, Mich., 1959), 311; also see *ibid.*, chaps. 7–8. It would be useful to imagine what the immigrant English puddler and Irish drayman in Richmond thought when reading in the *Richmond Examiner* that the nation's first immigrants had fled "religious

The evolving defense of slavery, which left little room for free workers, suggests the deep distrust in which Southern slaveholders held free workers and their belief that free workers were not reliable allies. No doubt Southern leaders were hypersensitive to all opposition and apt to read antislavery sentiment into the most casual dissent. Still, as the sectional conflict escalated, their conviction deepened that a Southern counterpart to the Northern free soil movement was developing among Southern workingmen, a movement hostile not only to blacks but also to capitalized black labor—meaning slavery. In 1849, after touring Mobile, Savannah, and Augusta, a correspondent of John C. Calhoun observed that these cities had become unsound on the slavery issue and blamed the growing number of foreign-born workers. "The issue of Free Labour against Slave Labour," he predicted, "will soon be made in the South." Such concerns multiplied in the 1850s. A Charleston daily declared that alien mechanics were a "curse rather than a blessing to our peculiar institution." And, when Little Rock artisans protested against competition from free black and slave laborers, the *Arkansas True Democrat* warned that such a "movement, carried to its fullest extent, would abolish slavery in the South. If the mechanic can justly complain of the competition of slave labor, those engaged in every other industrial pursuit can complain of the negro on the farm."[37]

The slave masters' fear of subversion rested partly in the habits of artisanal and ethnic cohesion, which often overlapped and reinforced each other in ways that planters, like Northern capitalists, believed to be hostile to their rule. But slaveholders also feared that enfranchised and politically active white workingmen saw their interests as different from those of the planter class. In this context, the politics of the 1850s can be understood as an attempt by planters not only to counter subversion from without but also subversion from within.

Seeing the seeds of Southern free soilism among urban immigrant workers, the most astute planters resisted the movement to exclude black laborers, slave and sometimes even free. "Drive out negro mechanics and all sorts of operatives from our Cities, and who must take their place?" asked Christopher G. Memminger, the future Confederate secretary of the treasury, in 1849. "The same men who make the cry in the Northern Cities against the tyranny of Capital—there as here would drive before them all who interfere with them—and would soon raise the hue and cry against the Negro, and be hot Abolitionists—and every one of those men would have a vote."[38]

The fear of internal subversion laced Southern politics in the decade before the war and created knotty contradictions that not even the most sophisticated Southern politician could comb out. For example, while some planters argued that

---

and political persecution" but its new immigrants migrated "merely as animals in search of a richer and better pasture," lacked "moral, intellectual, or religious wants," and were ("the mass of them") "sensual, groveling, low-minded agrarians." Or when the same newspaper reminded its readers that, "while it is far more obvious that negroes should be slaves than whites, for they are fit only to labor, not to direct, yet the principle of slavery is itself right and does not depend upon differences of complexion." "Slavery black and white," the *Richmond Examiner* affirmed, "is necessary."

[37] Calhoun, as quoted in Shugg, *Origins of Class Struggle in Louisiana*, 144; Charleston *Standard*, June 18, 1853; and Little Rock *Arkansas True Democrat*, September 29, 1858.

[38] Memminger, as quoted in Starobin, *Industrial Slavery in the Old South*, 210.

reopening the African slave trade would secure nonslaveholder loyalty by allowing them to participate directly in slaveownership, others saw the influx of slaves as a means of ridding Southern cities of politically unreliable immigrant workers. Thus, what began as an attempt to unify the white South sharpened internal divisions and left planters and workers further apart than ever. A similar dynamic can be seen operating in the movement to re-enslave free blacks. Radical Southerners believed that re-enslavement provided greater security for the slave regime. Not only would it free the South of another subversive group, but, by selling enslaved free blacks to nonslaveholders, re-enslavement—like the reopening of the slave trade—would also garner nonslaveholder loyalty. Again, opposition came from a variety of quarters, and this time it not only enlarged the gulf between slaveholders and nonslaveholders but also divided the slaveholders among themselves. If some masters maintained that liquidation of the free Negro caste would secure slavery, others believed that the threat of re-enslavement would drive free Negroes out of the South and leave planters even more dependent on white workingmen. In the eyes of these slaveowners, white workers, not free blacks, offered the greatest threat to slavery. Thus, as slaveholders wrestled with the problems of internal division, they enlarged those divisions and also created new fissures in their own ranks. Little wonder the Confederacy came into the world amid contradictory calls for a white man's democracy and open attempts to disenfranchise some whites, particularly immigrant workers.[39]

FROM THE FIRST SHOT AT SUMTER, Southern leaders remained unsure of working-class loyalties. Just after the 1860 election, writing from New Orleans, politician John Slidell observed that in that city "seven-eighths at least of the vote for Douglas were cast by the Irish and Germans, who are at heart abolitionists."[40] While there were few Irish abolitionists among the workers in any Southern city, such doubts about the allegiance of the largely foreign-born work force only intensified with the onset of civil war. Some immigrants found themselves jailed for speaking their minds too freely on the subject of slavery. From New Orleans, the employer of one newly arrived Englishman appealed to the British government to have his employee released from jail; the immigrant worker had been charged with "using language hostile to slaveholding and introducing in the State [Louisiana] books and papers of similar character." Thirty months later, the British consul at Charleston reported to the Home Office that "labouring men"—immigrant workers surely prominent among them—"are frequently discharged from their employment and subjected to contumely for not taking up arms. They are frequently arrested and sent to gaol, as liable to conscription." In 1864, the president of an Alabama railroad conveyed to the Confederate secretary of war his suspicions about the

[39] Ronald Takaki, *A Pro-Slavery Crusade: The Agitation to Reopen the African Slave Trade* (New York 1971); Berlin, *Slaves without Masters*, chap. 11; Michael P. Johnson, *Toward a Patriarchal Republic: The Secession of Georgia* (Baton Rouge, La., 1977), chap. 5; and Fred Siegal, "Artisans and Immigrants in the Politics of Late Antebellum Georgia," *Civil War History*, 18 (1981): 221–30.
[40] Slidell, as quoted in Peyton McCrary, *Abraham Lincoln and Reconstruction: The Louisiana Experiment* (Princeton, 1978), 56. Also see Johnson, *Toward a Patriarchal Republic*, 97.

skilled founders and puddlers at the huge Selma iron works. He observed that "all of these workmen are foreigners from Europe, or natives of the northern states, the majority being foreigners," and then made the common complaint: "These men do not feel identified in any great degree with the South and are not imbued with sentiments and feelings calculated to impress them so strongly in favor of our cause, as to induce them to make any great sacrifice of interest or feeling in its behalf." In spite of the Union noose tightening around the Confederacy, these foreign workers demanded higher wages and abandoned the Selma works even when their demands were met. Perhaps native-born workingmen would have ordered their loyalties in a similar fashion, but the beleaguered railroad executive doubted it.[41]

Dissaffected immigrant workers rallied to the Union flag at the first opportunity and, in places like New Orleans, which early fell to the Union army, provided the basis for a Unionist party. Elsewhere, immigrant workers had to wait until the war's end to demonstrate their political beliefs, but, when given the opportunity, many did so. In 1865, when the Union army occupied Charleston, federal officers promptly recruited two regiments among the loyal natives—one black, one Irish. A Union soldier, parading through Charleston, noted that the crowds who gathered to watch the column move through the city were "chiefly negroes and Irish, and their delight at seeing us was unbounded, the Irish being quite as enthusiastic in the expression of joy as the negroes."[42]

Estimates of the extent of antebellum free soilism, wartime disaffection and disloyalty, and postwar Republicanism among the immigrant workers of the urban South require much more refinement before they can go beyond the complaint of Slidell and others. But, whatever free workers thought about slavery, there can be no doubt that slave masters understood the demands of free workers for the elimination of slave competition as more than a conflict of interest with slaveholding; indeed, ultimately they saw it as a conflict of principles. This understanding held enormous importance in the hothouse of antebellum and reconstruction politics. While the full dimensions of this conflict remain to be explored, its partial outcroppings confirm that immigrant workers in the urban South cannot simply be incorporated into the extant understanding of the nature of Southern society, the evolution of slavery, or the character of antebellum politics. Instead, they demand reconsideration of all.

[41] Daniel Godwin to Newlop Ireland, n.d., enclosed in Ireland to Lord Russell, February 19, 1861. Public Record Office, London, Foreign Office 5/793; Consul Walker to Russell, August 21, 1863, *ibid.*, Foreign Office 5/907; and J. W. Lapsley to J. A. Seddon, February 15, 1864, National Archives, Washington, War Department Collection of Confederate Records, Secretary of War, Letters Received, ser. 5, Record Group 109, L-67 1864. In North Carolina cities, urban workers also played a role in the Unionist "Heroes of America." See William T. Auman and David D. Scarboro, "The Heroes of America in Civil War North Carolina," *North Carolina Historical Review*, 58 (1981): 350–51.

[42] McCrary, *Lincoln and Reconstruction*; General Rufus Saxton to E. M. Stanton, March 1, 1865, S-154 (1865), National Archives, Washington, Records of the Adjutant General's Office, Colored Troops Division, Letters Received, ser. 360, Record Group 94; and *War Letters, 1862–1865, of John Chipman Gray and John Codman Ropes* (Boston, 1927), 459.

Slavery as an Obstacle to Economic Growth in the United States: A Panel Discussion

PANEL MEMBERS: Alfred H. Conrad (City University of New York); Douglas Dowd (Cornell University); Stanley Engerman (University of Rochester); Eli Ginzberg (Columbia University); Charles Kelso (Harvard University); John R. Meyer (Harvard University); Harry N. Scheiber (Dartmouth College); Richard Sutch (Massachusetts Institute of Technology)

ALFRED H. CONRAD (for JOHN R. MEYER and himself): Every economist must be pleased to start some hares; it can become embarrassing, however, when they begin to breed like rabbits. In the ten years since we first tried our slavery model in public, in Professor Gerschenkron's history seminar, more than thirty published arguments addressed to that model have come to our attention. We don't pretend to know whether that represents an increased output over preceding decades. Besides, in our youthful enthusiasm we gave the impression that we were disposing, once and for all, of a piece of intellectual game that was already rather high. In any event, the apparent egocentricity that turned up all those papers and articles may be explained, if not justified, by Ralph Barton Perry's dictum that every reader looks up two references in an index: sex, and his own name.

The recent discussion on the profitability of slavery in the antebellum South can be surveyed along three lines. First, a number of questions of fact, or evidence, have been raised. Second, the capital model that we used has been criticized as irrelevant. And third, the model, as a piece of economic analysis, has been attacked as insufficient to answer the historical questions we put to it.

As for factual or data questions, Fritz Redlich is not a man to

EDITOR'S NOTE: This panel discussion, held under the chairmanship of Professor Moses Abramovitz, was recorded on tape, transcribed, and edited. In its present printed version it represents the editor's interpretation of what each participant intended to say. Many uncertainties in transcription were encountered, however, particularly during the discussion from the floor. An attempt has been made to preserve the atmosphere of oral debate, and statements made should not necessarily be taken as representing the considered judgments of the persons involved. The staff of the Eleutherian Mills Historical Library carried out the initial transcription, and their help is gratefully acknowledged.

28

mince words. He has characterized Part II of our paper, which is where the model works, as simply "fictitious." He means more by this remark than what is implied by saying that *I Promessi Sposi* is a work of fiction and not an historical account of the Counter-Reformation in the Duchy of Milan, or that John Motley could not really know the drunken indiscretions of Egmont or the midnight fears of William of Orange (though Motley may come closer to Mr. Redlich's definition of history than does Fishlow or Fogel, for example). What he *means* is that our Table 9 presents estimated returns on investments in prime field hands under a number of assumptions as to yield per hand, capital outlay, farm-gate cotton price, and slave longevity. Modal values and other measures of central tendency were used where we had distributions of estimated values, but the range over various land fertilities and capital outlays was given in full, so that the sensitivity of our results to different price and interest rates might be tested. The individual values are old-style historical facts; the modal values are statistical estimates, which is a class neither necessarily nor epistemologically equivalent to fiction. We were aware that the census data on longevity were questionable, and we considered whether the estimates were consistent with population trends. Such a comparison is presumably a form of "source criticism." But how does one estimate the rate of return on a piece of capital *without* estimating its life expectancy?

What new information, then, has emerged from the recent literature? Eugene Genovese urges that the medical costs should be at least 50 per cent higher and perhaps double our estimate. He raises the cost of overseers from a range of $5 to $15 per hand, to $22.50. He points to our unfortunate assumption that a stock consisting largely of mules and oxen could be self-reproducing, but he doesn't really reveal how large a proportion of horses and donkeys would be sufficient to maintain the stock—in Mississippi cotton counties, for instance, horses accounted for one-quarter to almost half of the total work animals in 1860, depending upon the size of the farm. He would raise our food and clothing expenses, and he would have us add as costs "several dollars worth of Christmas presents per slave," the "regular and expensive vacations in watering places," and the large sums planters spent on tutors, academies, and finishing schools for their children. However secure or insecure may be the inference that the regular vacations were widespread in the South, the gross analytic error of counting trips to Saratoga as costs should make it unnecessary to pursue the question further.

A more serious factual objection was raised by Edward Saraydar. He argued in a note in the *Southern Economic Journal* that we used data from plantations that *purchased* all provisions as though they represented the costs on self-sufficient plantations. Combining such underestimates of costs with *upward*-biased average yields from specialized plantations, we would obviously have overestimated the rate of profit. Saraydar redid the average yields by returning to the 1850 Census, but at the cost of several downward biases and one arithmetic oversight. Richard Sutch, after raising a disturbing question about the relevance of our model, which we will discuss below, observed, first, that our yields did come from self-supporting plantations, and second, that yields estimated from the 1860 Census data are much closer to the ones we used than to Saraydar's estimates. Mr. Sutch then went on to calculate the rate of appreciation on slaves—an annual increase of 7.56 per cent— from population and slave price increases. To remove speculative effects, he turned more directly to cotton plantations and estimated the internal rate of return exclusive of the rising slave prices, by limiting the appreciation rate only to the 2.15 per cent slave population increase. He found that cotton farming was clearly profitable in the new South and concluded that land prices in the new areas could not rise fast enough to capture the full rent, from which one should predict the press of cotton production (as it actually occurred) into the new western lands.

Robert Evans has contributed to the evidence on slave-hiring practices—and, incidentally, on training and skills—and on the internal slave trade. Most of the interest in his two papers arises from the alternative model that he proposed for estimating rates of return, but his evidence on slave-hire-to-purchase ratios and trading differentials both lend strong support to the conclusion that the slave economy was viable. When he compares the specific slave *trade* returns to skilled wage rates, he finds some compensation in the traders' labor income, presumably to pay for the social disrepute in which the trade was held. But even admitting the difficulties of comparing occupational requirements, the evidence does not indicate that the traders were treated as pariahs.

In criticizing Evans, and later in a review of our book, Thomas Govan raised again (cf. his 1942 work) several factual questions, the most troubling of which relate to the depletion of the fertility of cotton lands. Our discussion of soil exhaustion is a "perverse belief" and a "disregard of reality." From the other side, however, Genovese claimed that we did not take sufficient account of the soil depletion pressed upon the South by the slave-and-cotton economy, and he cites further evidence on fertilizer requirements as well as contemporary discussion. At the worst, we may have been clumsy in identifying the central tendency.

We would argue with Fogel and others that the social savings Genovese computed and the rates of return we calculated could both well be *facts*. But that is not the point. There has been much use of the word "guessing" in the discussion, but very little unearthing of new, direct evidence to refute the estimates we used. Only Sutch and Evans have contributed new evidence and in both cases it buttresses the case for the profitability of slavery.

There has been novelty in the model-building department, however. Let us start by reviewing what we actually did. In order to estimate the profitability of Southern slavery we computed the rate of return on an investment in slaves by the familiar procedure of capitalizing an income stream. In order to include all the relevant income we considered two production functions, one, for the production of cotton, in which the labor of prime field hands was the major input, and a second, in which the natural increase of the marketable slave population was looked upon as the production of capital goods. It should not be necessary to repeat that we did not need to assume, and that we never did assume, the existence of specialized breeding farms, in order to make the computation meaningful. However, to answer some of the denials that have appeared in the literature, let us repeat that we found enough references to "breeding wenches" and "proven breeders" in the secondary and primary source material to suggest, at least, that some ante-bellum Southerners got the idea.

We also did not estimate the returns *as-if* there were breeding farms. Slaves, like other people, reproduced themselves, and their childen were sold as capital instruments. We estimated the returns from that appreciation of the capital stock of the slave South. We made the estimates because it has been argued, repeatedly, that southern slavery had been about to disappear because it was not profitable. We asserted that the values which we derived from the market data led directly to the inference that enough individual men in the South were making a commercial profit that large-scale slavery was not likely to disappear automatically.

A number of alternative models have appeared in the last few years. We have already mentioned Robert Evans' procedure. He computed the net yearly income from the yearly hire received by owners of slaves when they were rented out to work. The advantage of this procedure is the relatively direct, as opposed to residual, nature of the income data. A major danger, of course, is that evidence from slave hires might be biased in the direction of a special class of slave stock. Evans did try to restrict his observations to unskilled labor, but we have been unable to judge his success in this regard. The rates of return on slave capital from his computation are safely above contemporary railroad bond yields and short-term money rates.

Yasukichi Yasuba introduced the problem of *economic* rent—the difference between the price of capital instruments and the net reproduction cost—in an alternative evaluation of the viability of slave system as a whole. For a given region or crop, he argues, the market price is relevant, but for the viability of the system as a whole, only the costs of reproduction of the capital—that is, the costs of rearing slaves—are relevant. He rewrote our basis postulate, therefore, as follows:

. . . If the portion of the price of slaves which represents capitalized rent was increasing, it is a sign of the increased profitability of slavery . . . To say that capitalized rent was positive is the same thing as to say that the rate of return based on the reproduction costs of slaves was above the market rate of interest, provided that non-economic factors did not affect the determination of the price and there was no lag nor anticipation in capitalization . . .

Because the supply of slaves, especially after the prohibition of further imports from Africa, was largely independent of profits, a discrepancy between prices and costs could last longer than would be the case for ordinary capital. This, he argued, is precisely what happened: the demand curve shifted to the right more rapidly than the supply curve could shift, with the result that the economic rent persisted, and indeed increased, over the ante-bellum period. Capitalized rent rose continuously from 1821 to 1855, with a decline between the prosperous late 1830's and the depressed early 1840's. On this basis, as distinguished from our findings on the marginal efficiency of slave capital, valued at market prices, Yasuba concluded that the slave system was viable.

32

This argument was pressed further by Richard Sutch and Douglass North. Much further, since North concluded that we failed to accomplish our objective and simply perpetuated the miserable controversy around profitability and viability. In fact, he says, "there is no possibility that slavery was economically not viable." Given the existence of rent on land and on slaves, short-run unprofitability would result in a readjustment of land rents or slave prices, sufficient to restore equilibrium. Only if the wages of free labor fell to subsistence, they argue, so that slave prices fell to zero, or at least below their cost of reproduction (in which case the rents would fall to zero), could the system become economically nonviable. If this argument simply refers to the fact that with upward sloping supply curves there will apparently always be a margin of private rent, then it must come up against Mrs. Robinson's demonstration that the rising supply curve is a necessary, but not sufficient, condition for the existence of rent in a particular industry. To be more specific, refutation of the arguments of those who said slavery was uneconomic, required proof that slave markets were viable and operative. Those who insist that there was "no possibility of slavery being unprofitable" come very close to assuming away the central question by simply assuming that viable slave markets existed. Furthermore, North is arguing as if slavery were a self-contained system. Actually, the cotton-slave-plantation system was *not* a closed system; it had to bid slave labor away from other uses. One of the results of our study was the demonstration that slave labor was highly mobile. Quasi-rents probably existed in the alternative uses and would have to be part of the plantation bid. Therefore, the presence of some rent or quasi-rent in the price of slaves and of cotton lands is not enough to make viability a foregone conclusion. Something more remains to be proved.

Sutch and North both recognize that if the slaves were less efficient than free labor, slave prices need not have fallen to zero to render the system nonviable. The lower limit would be the subsistence or reproduction cost of slaves; in the face of all the literature on the inefficiency of slave labor, this hardly seems an empty question. Slave rents or quasi-rents should have been continuously threatened by the supply of presumably more efficient free labor. Now, in order to argue that market prices will respond successfully to such erosion, one must visualize that the declining stream of rents is instantaneously reflected in falling slave prices, and that those prices will not hover above the subsistence margin set by the difference in productivity. The stream of rents yielded by slaves from the time they could cover their variable—that is, subsistence or reproduction—costs, to the time when they retired or expired, is the key variable. It is not self-evident that the capitalized sum of that stream must always equal the prices of slaves in a period of declining prices and yields. With any lag in price adjustments, the system might well become nonviable. North's closing point, that if slave prices were pegged by the requirements of conspicuous consumption, land prices must have fallen to an equilibrium solution, seems to ignore the possibility that the land would be in demand for the production of cotton or many other commodities with more efficient free labor. We may have underestimated the returns by using market price rather than the cost of reproduction, but we were certainly not tilting at windmills.

In general, an exclusive reliance upon calculation of quasi-rents to establish the economic viability of slavery *as a system* greatly oversimplifies. And it was definitely not the context in which the historical arguments were conducted. Rather, those who contended that slavery was uneconomic argued that slave markets were pathological and disequilibrated. Stress was placed upon investor irrationality and a divergent pattern in the development of cotton and slave prices. The specific contention was that in the immediate antebellum period a rational investor would not find it profitable to "buy into" the slave system. We demonstrated that this was certainly not obvious and almost certainly was fallacious.

Importance also attaches to differences in the pattern of economic viability of slavery by regions and particular applications, particularly since much political controversy in the pre-Civil War period centered about the issue of whether new lands should be admitted to slave culture. We demonstrated that this emphasis upon growth of slave lands was hardly quixotic. An expanding slave system was much more profitable than a stagnant system, not only for those who occupied the new lands, but for those who remained back on the older lands of the South, engaged in a combination of agriculture and slave breeding. Indeed, looking at the political controversies of the period immediately prior to the war, it is perhaps not too extravagant to claim that the war might have been avoided if southerners had been satisfied to restrict their slave system to lands on which it was already established.

34

In another set of papers the irrelevance of our model has been argued on very different grounds. From a variety of starting points, Douglas Dowd, Eugene Genovese, Harold Woodman, Thomas Govan, and Fritz Redlich all arrived at the conclusion that we could not settle any significant issues with a business model, or a capital model, because slavery was not *simply* a business or a capitalist enterprise. There may be a meaningful distinction to be drawn between the question of the *relevance* of a model of the slave system as a business enterprise, and the *sufficiency* of such a model for the problems of growth and development. Let us look first at the question of relevance.

Why is our economic model argued to be irrelevant by these historians? In Douglas Dowd's words:

... For the southerner to convert himself to beliefs and behavior which would support and comport with slavery required a concentration so intense that all else became secondary—including the process of capital accumulation . . . Who would be inclined to use the term "capitalist" to describe the owners of Southern wealth? Apart from a William Gregg here and there, southern capital was *planter* capital. Planters were of course interested in profits; so were medieval "businessmen" (as jarring a term as "southern capitalists"). But neither group approached the question of capitalist accumulation in the sense in which the northern manufacturers did . . .

In Genovese's terms, the argument runs as follows:

... however brisk the slave trade, considerable sentimental pressure existed to inhibit a purely rational approach to buying and selling slaves. Any notion that slaveholders as a class could or would have abandoned their estates to invest in more remunerative pursuits . . .—in other words, to transform themselves into ordinary capitalists—rests on a vulgar economic determinist outlook, contradicts the actual historical experience, and ignores the essential qualities of slave-based Southern life.

. . .

The question of whether or not the slaveholders earned a return equal to that accruing to Northern capitalists is not an especially significant political or social question.

. . .

Economists have assumed that an affirmative answer would prove slaveholding to have been just another business; as Schumpeter warns us, statistics can never disprove what we have reason to know from simpler and more direct methods.

Now, to be accused of vulgar economic determinism, which must be related to vulgar Marxism, is a serious business, and we would like to say something on that point. First of all, we were not at-

tempting to prove that slaveholding was "just another business"—
that explication has nothing to do with our thesis, and is itself un-
true. We were looking for evidence on profits, because their alleged
absence has been offered as a reason why the American Civil War
was unnecessary. We believe that we did find evidence of competitive profit rates in slavery and concluded, first, that they were an
additional and significant reason, along with any possible Southern
quixoticism and Gothic imagination, to explain the South's willingness to fight; and second that those profits could have provided the
capital for further growth.

Having read our Schumpeter, too, we are prepared to wear the
Marxist shoe, if it fits. But we reserve the right to reject the vulgar
model, on grounds of taste. Let us see if we can outline a Marxist
interpretation of history that will admit the relevance of our capital
model. We shall borrow liberally, but not slavishly, from Maurice
Merleau-Ponty.[1] Discussions of Marxism and historical determinism
have often been conducted as if causality implied that each event
had to have a linear relationship with another event, about which it
could then be determined whether it was "economic" or "ideological," or even *simply* economic or ideological. Marxism, or economic
explanation, is then thought to be vanquished when one can point
to "ideological" causes. But neither materialistic history nor econometric history is more abstract than idealistic history or spiritualistic
history. At the heart of the Marxist interpretation is the idea that
nothing can be isolated in the total context of history, but also that
because of their greater generality economic phenomena make a
greater contribution to historical discourse. Now, to recognize that
the economic phenomena do not explain everything is not the same
as to relegate the production of material conditions to the outbuildings of history. We don't believe that slaves were simply or merely
capital, or that the southern gentleman was simply or merely *homo
faber*, but that does not make a capital model irrelevant or a precise
limitation of the opportunity costs of the enterprise a waste of time,
nor does it render the capitalization of an income stream from slaves
a figment or a fiction. History passes through *homo faber*, and the
production of material conditions, the production and transformation of laws, customs, beliefs, styles of civilization, even the content

[1] Maurice Merleau-Ponty. *Sense and Non-Sense.* Translated by H. L. and P. A.
Dreyfus. (Evanston, Ill.: Northwestern University Press, 1964), chs. viii, ix.

of consciousness—all these are mutually penetrating and fully reciprocal.

Let us quote from the last paragraph of our conclusion, before
going on to consider the *sufficiency* of our model:

> Although profitability cannot be offered as a sufficient guarantee of the con-
> tinuity of southern slavery, the converse argument that slavery must have
> destroyed itself can no longer rest upon allegations of unprofitability or upon
> assumptions about the impossibility of maintaining and allocating a slave
> labor force. To the extent, moreover, that profitability is a necessary condi-
> tion for the continuation of a private business institution in a free-enterprise
> society, slavery was not untenable in the ante-bellum American South.

In this last part, now, we will be less polemical. The arguments of
Genovese, Dowd, and many before them, have linked Southern
slavery directly to Southern stagnation. In Genovese's words:

> Even if it could be established that plantation profit levels did stay high and
> that long-range prospects looked good, it would not follow that capital was
> being accumulated in a manner guaranteeing a politically viable economic
> development.

Frankly, we never had a model sufficient to deal with this question.
About the best we can do on this matter is to define the problem
in terms of some recent work on agrarian reform and Southern development.

There are two essential points that are frequently overlooked
when the discussion settles down to Southern backwardness. To
begin, the ante-bellum Southern economy was not stagnant. North,
Easterlin, Williamson, and Nicholls have all demonstrated that the
prosperity of the plantation economy was real, that income grew as
rapidly in the prewar South as in the rest of the nation, and that
cotton was the most important influence in the ante-bellum growth
of the economy. Apparently, though, retardation did occur in the
rate of Southern economic growth in the period between 1860 and
approximately 1880. As Engerman has pointed out, it was 1890 before the South again achieved the per capita income levels enjoyed
in 1860. In very large measure both the absolute and relative failure
of the South to achieve standards of economic welfare comparable
to the rest of the country can be attributed to the losses or the
growth not achieved in the two decades of the 1860's and the 1870's.
Stanley Engerman and Louis Rose have examined the devastation

and capital losses due to the war and the emancipation, and William Nicholls has discussed with deep insight how in the postwar period agrarian values persisted, then rigidified, and finally corrupted the southern social structure to the point where tradition hardened into a dense barrier against further progress.

Perhaps the most important single illustration of the war's disruptive impact is to be found in the pattern of British cotton imports during the second half of the nineteenth century. Statistics on these are shown in Table 1. Quite noticeably, a sharp rise in world prices for cotton in the early 1860's elicited a rather rapid increase in the supply of cotton from areas outside the American South. In particular, an almost fourfold increase occurred in the average level of East Indian cotton exports to Britain between 1860 and 1865. By contrast, almost fifteen years were required to displace this new cotton from the British market after the war terminated; it was not until the 1880's that the South had regained its absolute and relative prewar position in the British markets once more. Displacement from conventional market outlets would, of course, have retarded southern development during the 1860's and 1870's even without any war-induced physical destruction.

The timing of southern economic retardation also seems important. If most southern underdevelopment is attributable to only two decades of stagnation, difficulty resides with any insistence that it was slavery or some southern slave-induced mentality that lies at the root of southern economic problems. Such an argument is confronted with the difficulty of explaining why these problems should have been particularly pronounced or observable only during two decades. Why was Southern growth not retarded during the height of the slaveholding period or just before the Civil War? Or why did slavery-induced mental attitudes not prove such a hindrance after 1880? By contrast, hypotheses that emphasize war dislocations and destruction are completely consistent with retardation's being restricted to the war period and its immediate aftermath.

Economic considerations or (if you wish) profit-seeking are also quite sufficient to explain the South's concentration upon agricultural development. The South seemed fully capable of developing manufacturing capacity when technological or economic circumstances made such a course attractive, as in the pre-Civil War period and subsequently around the turn of the century. When steam-powered textile mills became possible or more economical than

Table 1
PRICES AND QUANTITIES OF BRITISH COTTON IMPORTS, 1850 TO 1889

Year or Decade	Imports by Origin (in thousands of bales per year)						Average Prices by Types		
	American	Brazilian	Egyptian	Peruvian	East Indian	Total	American	Brazilian	East Indian
1850's	1,638	132	103	9	406	2,288	5 11/16	7 7/16	4 5/8
1860	2,581	103	109	10	563	3,366	6 1/4	8 3/16	5
1861	1,841	100	98	10	987	3,036	8 9/16	9 3/4	6 9/16
1862	72	134	147	20	1,072	1,445	17 1/4	18 7/8	12 7/8
1863	132	138	248	23	1,391	1,932	23 1/4	24 1/4	19 1/4
1864	198	212	319	60	1,798	1,587	27 1/2	28 3/4	21 1/2
1865	462	340	414	131	1,408	2,755	19	19 1/4	14 1/2
1866	1,163	407	200	112	1,867	3,749	15 1/2	17 1/8	12
1867	1,226	437	198	129	1,511	3,501	10 7/8	11 5/8	8 3/4
1868	1,269	637	201	101	1,452	3,660	10 1/2	11 5/8	8 1/2
1869	1,040	514	226	106	1,496	3,382	12 7/8	12 1/2	9 3/4
1870's	1,977	388	277	102	899	3,643	7 7/8	8 3/8	5 3/4
1880's	2,755	246	260	57	631	3,949	5 11/16	6 5/8	4 1/8

Note: Taken from the *Cotton Trade of the United States* as in turn derived from the Senate Report on Cotton Production and Consumption, Fifty-third Congress, third session, Report 986.

529

water-powered mills, the locus of the textile industry slowly but surely shifted from New England to the South, eventually resulting in the substantial post-World War II trauma of New England textile mill towns.

In short, the South was not an isolated, self-contained economy. It is a gross exaggeration to talk about the ante-bellum Southern states as a colonial or tributary economy, locked into dependence upon the North. The terms of trade with England, as well as with New England, were excellent, and the South was well represented in the national government.

Of course, agricultural development, whether a "prerequisite" for industrialization or not, might hold back the initial growth of the industrial sector, especially if agriculture is stuck in a traditional and static position. In that case, agrarian reform is apparently the prerequisite. Alexander Gerschenkron identifies two aspects of this reform:

> . . . it is supposed to increase the productivity of agriculture so that its growing produce will allow shifts of population out of agricultural areas and will support the increasing numbers of men engaged in non-agricultural pursuits. . . . it is supposed to eliminate the traditional restraints on the mobility of the agrarian population and its freedom to exercise a free choice of occupation.

Now, some increase in productivity in the ante-bellum cotton culture can be easily demonstrated, but there is a distinguished chorus to remind us that having once revived the almost moribund institution of slavery as an answer to labor shortage, the South stopped where it was, eagerly abetted in this tendency by its machines—the slaves. Abolition, then, was apparently necessary as the first item on the reform agenda, though the postwar experience must make us question whether it could lead to an essentially different system of cultivation. In the American South it is not obvious that the problem was ever one of moving from a communal to an individualistic system of production.

With regard to eliminating traditional restraints on mobility, obviously the slave population was without free choice of occupation. But, given the market conditions for cotton, and the ease with which market incentives drew production to the fertile western lands, it is not clear exactly what increased mobility might have accomplished for Southern agricultural development in the prewar period.

40

Indeed, let us speculate that the crucial moment for agrarian reorganization and the formation of prerequisites came not in 1860, in the United States, but in the last decade of the eighteenth century. At that point southern agriculture had recovered effectively and rapidly from the Revolutionary War. Then, in 1794, there came the gin and forty-cent cotton. Some kind of structural response was called for, especially in the face of an impending labor shortage. Two alternatives seem plausible: (1) a thoroughgoing agrarian reform to freehold, individualist cultivation, as in the northern cereal lands; or (2) the extension of slavery and the evolution of the slave market to facilitate the movement of productive resources to the West. The actual choice that was made does not seem to have been necessarily eccentric or irrational. Certainly that was not the moment at which agrarianism became stagnant, rigid, and inimical to development in the South. Instead of searching, fruitlessly, for the signs of morbidity which were supposed to lead inexorably to a "genuine" agrarian reform, we can observe that slavery was profitable, indeed viable, and that the moral conflict, instead of appearing to be an avoidable blunder, takes on real meaning. What remains is the devastation of the War years, and the failure of the thoroughgoing reform to take hold. There is still much to be explained, and it may be at this point, where the institutions are less boldly outlined, that the social history is most sorely needed.

DOUGLAS DOWD: Whether in the slavery or the new economic history controversies of the past decade, one moves to a feeling that the participants are often talking past one another, talking to themselves and to what may loosely be thought of as their respective adherents. The new economic historians, it may be said, put one in mind of rather light-hearted evangelists; while those who dissent from their innovations seem, by comparison, stuffy, old-fashioned, fearful of the new truths, perhaps of truth itself.

As is well-known, when controversies take on such characteristics, it is because procedures and conclusions, rather than assumptions and aims, form the stuff of the controversy. Only apparently are the discussions concerned, then, with the same subject matter, for the parameters are different, and they are different because—quite appropriately for both parties—the purposes are different. The slavery controversy provides a useful basis for an exploration of this question, not least because it came as the opening gun of the new economic history, a decade ago, when Messrs. Conrad and Meyer presented their twin papers on methodology and on slavery to the joint EHA-NBER meetings and I served as a critic.

Then, as still today, I puzzled over what Conrad and Meyer were trying to show. If they were attempting to demonstrate that Ulrich B. Phillips (in his *American Negro Slavery, inter alia*) was wrong, there was much more than the profitability of slavery on which to focus, for by the time they wrote Phillips had been quite thoroughly discredited on both narrow and broad questions, perhaps most completely by Kenneth Stampp (in his *Peculiar Institution*). I had thought, by then, that contemporary historians had come to view Phillips and his works more as sociological than as historical materials; documents, almost, revealing how a partisan of the Lost Cause viewed the evolution of that society. And was it not generally accepted by students of the South that writers like Phillips took the position that slavery was unprofitable because to do otherwise would muddy the more fundamental justifications for the system?

There is often something to be said for precise refutations of mistaken notions, to be sure. But what can be said that is positive diminishes to the degree that a general analysis would do. It is of course reasonably obvious that in any functioning social system, slave or otherwise, there will be incomes that are high at the top and decrease as one moves to the bottom of the social scale; and that power will be roughly proportionate to income and wealth. What is less obvious are the costs of a given system—costs in terms of alternatives foregone, as well as the social and human costs of the existent reality.

For the American South, it surely was good business sense that led planters to emphasize cotton cultivation, slaveholding, and slave-breeding; and good business sense was also good economic sense, if the short run and the interests of those in power are taken as guiding criteria. But when we speak of economic development it is not business sense or economic sense for the short run as viewed by those in power that are, or should be, taken as the appropriate referents for judgment; for then we are speaking not only of structural realities and changes in the economy, but also of far-reaching social and political structures and changes.

As I said a decade ago, one cannot evaluate the meaning of slavery as though it were merely one kind of a labor force rather than another, *ceteris paribus*. Slavery normally implies and requires, and especially in the United States implied and required, a slavery-dominated society as much as a society dominating slaves. In turn, this meant that whatever business considerations might support the continuation of the slave-cum-cotton system, these were immeasurably reinforced by the social and political imperatives—ever more on the defensive in the ante-bellum South—of maintaining a slave society. Is this not made more evident when we examine the post-Civil War development of the South?

I should have thought it would be unnecessary to raise these questions once more, except that here we are meeting again on the subject; and, more vividly, we are aware of new work tending to move in the same directions as the earlier work of Conrad and Meyer. I have been away from the United States for a year, having just returned a week ago. Consequently, I have been unable to read Stanley Engerman's latest contributions on the South, slavery, and the Civil War. But may I not assume that Robert Fogel represented Mr. Engerman accurately in his article[2] on the new economic history? There it is said:

> The retarded development of the South during the last third of the nineteenth century and the first half of the twentieth was due not to stagnation during the slave era, but to the devastation caused by the Civil War. As Stanley Engerman points out, if *ante-bellum* growth-rates had continued through the war decade, southern *per capita* income would have been twice the level that actually prevailed in 1870. So disruptive was the war that it took the South some thirty years to regain the *per capita* income of 1860 and another sixty years to reach the same relative position in national *per capita* income that it enjoyed at the close of the *ante-bellum* era. The case for the abolition of slavery thus appears to turn on issues of morality and equity rather than on the inability of a slave system to yield a high rate of economic growth (p. 647).

In a paper delivered to this Association in 1956, in which I attempted to explain the late nineteenth- and early twentieth-century retardation of the southern economy, I did not say, nor do I recall anyone else having said, that southern stagnation was due to "stagnation during the slave era." But I do recall arguing that it was the consequence of slave society, in all its ramifications, that explains that stagnation. To reopen that argument here and now would be impossible, as well as unrewarding, just as it would be impossible to come to grips even partially with all the questions that arise from

---

[2] Robert W. Fogel, "The New Economic History: Its Findings and Methods," *Economic History Review*, XIX (Dec. 1966), 642-56.

the works of Messrs. Conrad, Meyer, Fogel, Engerman, and others now cultivating the new vineyards. But perhaps our brief excursion can provide a basis for fruitful discussions in the meeting today.

Perhaps I am mistaken, but I believe I am correct in seeing the new economic history as an attempt to incorporate the methodology of neoclassical economics and the procedures of econometrics with the materials and the questions of economic history—with the added notion that economic history will thereby be strengthened, made more scientific. In its essence this entails the central use of partial equilibrium analysis. Such an approach may or may not be appropriate for the analysis of questions of narrow focus and very short time periods, where the pound of *ceteris paribus* can serve as a temporary safe haven for "other things." Can it do so when we concern ourselves with changes taking a long period, and that neither begin nor end with economic, let alone quantitative, matters?

It was of utmost significance that slavery in the United States could not be maintained without vitally affecting "all other things," whether that slavery was profitable or not. As Stanley M. Elkins has so capably shown in his *Slavery*,[3] American Negro slavery was the very "worst" the world had known, in its nature and in its consequences, whether it be compared with ancient or contemporaneous slavery (in, for example, Brazil or the Caribbean). What does "worst" signify in this context, and why should it have been so? Slaves have always and everywhere been cruelly treated (and always with exceptions), and black slaves especially. Even so, their treatment, their rights (or total lack of rights), their "family" lives, the depths to which racism sank, the manner in which the present and long-distant future of black slaves (even, as we know, their past) was distorted and doomed—in social, psychological, political, and of course economic terms—in the United States reached the lowest of depths. Why should this be so, in the land of the free and the home of the brave? Was not economic individualism adhered to in the South? It surely was, extending even to trafficking in human beings as commodities. Did not the Enlightenment, did not Christianity, extend into the American South? Most assuredly, but as with economic individualism, certain exotic notions had to be grafted onto otherwise healthy plants. To achieve such exoticism took a mighty effort, an effort that became obsessive, compulsive, and

[3] Stanley M. Elkins, *Slavery* (New York: Grosset and Dunlap, 1963).

sickening not just to those who lived under the system, but also to those who lived from it and with it and for it.

Which brings me to the postwar period, if a bit abruptly, with Mr. Engerman's contributions in mind. Without asking how *ante-bellum* growth rates could have continued indefinitely; without asking, that is, how the South could have maintained its power in the nation while it also maintained slavery (with or without westward expansion); without asking whether or not there was some determining relationship between the Civil War and the socioeconomic system of the South and its power struggle with the North; without asking any of these questions, let us point to some questions that relate growth to development, and war destruction to growth and development.

Keeping in mind the well-recognized distinctions between growth and development, between quantitative and qualitative change (and keeping in mind, too, their connections), let us examine the notion of *"ante-bellum* growth rates continuing through the war decade" and even more, beyond that time. By 1860, the South showed few significant signs of moving away from its dependence on slaves and cotton. The signs that such a concentration might be something less than promising had begun to appear already during the Civil War; but what were then mere whispers turned into a roar in the years after 1870. Were the falling cotton prices (among other prices) in the last quarter of the century a function largely, if at all, of the Civil War? Is there any reasonable basis to assume either (1) that slave-breeding would have maintained the supply of slaves within economically viable magnitudes, or (2) that political realities would have allowed the reopening of the external trade? Has anyone specified how the maintenance of slavery (and the power of those who would so maintain it) in the United States in the late nineteenth century might be made compatible with economic development? Or how its forceful abolition (apart from the Civil War) would have been accomplished? Or its peaceful abolition, by those squarely dependent upon it? Is there any ground for believing that the kinds of structural (economic, political, social) changes that are implied by economic development would have ensued in a South whose economy could no longer "thrive" on the basis of agriculture (for the majority of either its white or its black population)? And, given that the slaves were in fact (legally) emancipated, how does one explain the persistence of all the essential qualities of *ante-*

45

bellum southern society in *post-bellum* southern society, down to
the very recent past? Civil war damage? But is it not difficult to
believe that for eighty years the southern economy was retarded by
war destruction, in the light of what we have seen of so many other
war-damaged economies in our own lives? Can the answers to any
of these questions be turned to the advantage of the relevant conclusions of the new economic history? Or to its procedures? Can we
learn nothing about our own economic development from our studies of the complex interrelationships of development (or its lack)
in the contemporary underdeveloped world?

Furthermore, and in a different vein: What is the point of the
analyses that have occupied these studies? "The case for the abolition of slavery" *of course* "turns on issues of morality and equity
rather than on the inability of a slave system to yield a high rate of
economic growth." To state otherwise would be to say, one pre-
sumes, that an economically viable slave system is to be recommended to . . . whom? The underdeveloped countries? Of course
not, and the sneers of the new economic historians to such a query
are appropriate. But then what is the point? If students of the South
had earlier believed the system was profitable, what then, besides
elegance, was the point of going on? Or did we have to be told, once
more, that the Civil War was terribly destructive? Are we going
back to Ranke, "simply" recording the facts, with technical trimmings? Or are there more vital tasks facing social scientists today;
more vital, more demanding, more promising?

Of course slavery was profitable. And of course imperialism has
been profitable. And of course the status quo in today's underdeveloped countries is profitable. Profitable, in all cases, to investors,
whose definitions of profit do not go beyond the balance sheet and
the income statement, and whose definitions of propriety are quite
identical with their definitions of property. And of course slavery
damaged both whites and blacks in the long run (and most, also, in
the short run). And imperialism damages most citizens of both
metropolis and colony, in the long run; and similarly with underdevelopment. Nor is it difficult to show that the damage that accrues
from such systems is not solely, or mostly, economic; it is social,
psychological, political, cultural. As it is also true that economic
development both requires and brings about social, political, psychological, and cultural changes.

We are concerned in these meetings with obstacles to economic development, a focus that requires us to look at reality. That is a considerable improvement over the earlier inclinations of economists to develop and to use abstract models that, if they had any application at all, were relevant only to highly industrialized, political stable societies, operating within basically capitalist institutions. But improvements do not constitute sufficiencies; and especially they do not if their effect is to fragmentize an area of inquiry that requires broadening, deepening, and an enhanced sense of relevance.

Because in practice the meaning of economic development extends out and down so broadly and deeply, the analysis of development, not to say its implementation, must be as broad and as deep. This is to say that "experts" in economic development must take on the staggering task of attempting to understand the functioning of *societies*, and the manner in which *social* change takes place. One of my criticisms of the new economic history, and not only in its manifestations as regards the South, is that its methods, its thrust, are in exactly the opposite direction from that so desperately needed in the field today. Market relationships (for capital, commodities, labor) are indeed central to the functioning of an economy, as the heart is to the body. But the heart functions in relationship with a nervous system, and a circulatory system, and, among other things, in an environment. If the problem is a heart murmur, perhaps—no more than perhaps—total concentration on the heart itself will do. But those who will understand a cardiac condition, and prescribe for it, require themselves to understand the body in all its essential functions and characteristics. The lack of economic development is a problem in today's world that does not fall within the purview of the man who thinks in terms of heart murmurs. And the South had a cardiac condition in the nineteenth century.

To say that slavery was profitable and yet it inhibited economic development is not to say that slavery but that slave society in the United States in the nineteenth century, during and after its existence, inhibited economic development. But this is to say something else: Both before and after emancipation, social, economic, and political power in the South was held by those who had helped to create, and fought to maintain, slavery; nor was there a lack of interested parties in the North either before or after the War. For the South to develop economically, it was essential—and it is essential —either for a social upheaval within the South to take place, and/or

47

for steady pressures, positive and negative, to be introduced from "outside." Power—its sources and its uses—has to be changed; that is, its possessors have to be changed.

What is true for the South is true for other societies that would develop. To detail such changes, let alone to understand, advocate, and support them, on a country-by-country basis is not only to move out from partial equilibrium analysis, but to move into the swirl and turbulence that characterize the world. And that suggests the stance of the committed and concerned social scientist—distasteful though such an idea is to our profession—more than that of the cheerful and comfortable economist.

ELI GINZBERG: Let me suggest to you how someone who has been working for the last thirty years on human resources in connection with economic development thinks about the argument at hand. I am well placed to do so at the moment because I've just finished a book called *People and Progress in East Asia.* It has nothing to do with slavery. I have, however, remembered my chapter titles, and they may serve as a kind of mirror for the discussion at hand. The first point is, if you're going to have economic development, it must be tied in with the concept of nationhood with the exercise of some kind of governmental power that is effective over a region. The one thing we know about the American slave system is that it finally operated in such a way as to destroy the Union for a time. So some connection must be made between discussions of profitability and the destruction of the Union. Professor Conrad did mention that possibly slavery would have been profitable had it been contained in the original states, but we know that's just what the slave owners would not settle for. Lincoln offered them that as a compromise; they refused to accept it, from which I deduce that maybe they knew their interests best and thought they would die on the vine if they accepted the offer. That was Lincoln's estimate, and that's why he made the offer. I think, therefore, you just cannot deal with such short-run approaches without setting the question into at least the national frame.

The second point I wish to make is that economic development has something to do with the standards of living of the mass of the population. There were large numbers of slaves in the South, and in some states they were in the majority. Now I suppose you can have very rapid development with very substantial inequalities of income. I submit that probably sooner or later fundamental conflict arises here. We may have misled many developing countries by failing to understand the importance of energizing rural life and giving the people who have a contribution to make to increased output some share in a better life. This is just what slavery did not do. I have no doubt, therefore, that in the short run it was profitable for the slave owners to exploit their slaves, but I would argue that, for the long run, this was really not a profitable way to expand the economy at something like an optimum level.

Let's take the question of education in the South. We know that it was forbidden to educate a slave. Not only does this mean that few of them were educated, but that it was a crime to do so. That means that the South inhibited economic development by insisting that it would not make use of the latent potential of a large part of its labor force. One of the most important aspects of the acquisition of skills is that it depends largely on the individual having some incentive to increase his skills, so that he and his family can get some advantage from it. It is my understanding that in a system of slavery this was generally impossible. We know there were a few slaves in the cities who made a deal with their masters but they were exceptional. In the nature of the case there was no incentive for the bulk of the Negro population in the South to improve themselves. In fact, they got into very bad habits of doing as little as possible, except under maximum coercion. Once again, it is perfectly possible to argue that slavery was a profitable system. The question is: how profitable, for whom, and for how long? And on those three counts I would say history is clear. Slavery broke up the Union, it had to be expanded in order to stay profitable, and it was a poor way of using the human resources of the region.

Let's take the question of management or entrepreneurship. We know that thought control became such an essential part of the South that anybody who dissented had to leave the South. I submit again that is a bad way to run the economy. Hitler did it, but not very successfully. If one of the systems of coercion that is needed to operate an economy is the suppression of dissent, that economy is in a bad way. And we know that many able people of the South left the South, if they could possibly get away. The whole tendency of the system was antidevelopmental, except within the narrow context of "getting a few more dollars out of your slaves." That's not sufficient because economic development requires specialization and more specialization. And that's exactly what was impossible with an agricultural system like this. You could use the land for ten years, twenty years, thirty years, forty years, and then you finally had to get new land. Slaves could not be used in a factory system because factory employment and slavery did not mix. There were, of course, a few slaves in the mines and a few out on contract. On the whole, the system of social control was in fundamental conflict with long-term economic development. I think that is the critical point. I would like to remind you that the first legal case on slavery in the history of the United States that I have been able to uncover was in 1629 in Jamestown. The issue had very little to do with economics, but much to do with social control. This was a case of punishing a white man who had slept with a Negro woman. The colonists understood quite well at that point in time that it was only through very rigid social controls that they could maintain the kind of society they wanted to maintain. I remind you finally that the title of my book, *The Troublesome Presence,* comes from a quotation of Abraham Lincoln in his eulogy of Henry Clay. Lincoln said that Henry Clay sought to remove the "troublesome presence" of the *free* Negro from the backs of the slave owners. I submit that if the only way you can have economic development is to ship a labor force back to Africa, you may be in trouble.

RICHARD SUTCH: I thought that we were going to be talking today about capital and capital formation and savings, but I don't think I have heard the words "capital absorption" yet. Nor have I heard any refutations of the sort of capital absorption arguments that used to appear in the literature. The argument would be that because the owners of slaves were investing their capital in slaves, they weren't investing in manufacturing plants. What I propose to do is offer a few ideas about capital formation and savings. I shall argue that there was capital absorption but of a different type than that usually talked about.

The implications of slavery for capital formation depend rather crucially on the model of savings' behavior that we are using. One of the rather widely accepted post-Keynesian models of savings is the life-cycle hypothesis associated with Modigliani and Brumberg. A student at M.I.T., Robert Hall, has written a paper, as yet unpublished, which points out that the Modigliani-Brumberg life-cycle hypothesis implies that there is a burden of slavery. This burden is exactly analogous to the burden of the national debt, which Modigliani has pointed out is implied by any sort of life-cycle hypothesis of savings. The life-cycle hypothesis of savings implies, among other things, that in the long run there is stability in the ratio of wealth to income. Consequently, if there is an increase in, say, the national debt, people will hold this debt and displace from their portfolios tangible capital; on an individual level, they are interested in returns, regardless of whether the returns are on tangible or intangible capital. This argument, I think, is fairly well known. Exactly in the same way, there would be a burden from slavery. Robert Hall has computed an estimate of what this burden would be. Using, I believe, Professor Gallman's income estimates, he concluded that in 1860 the gross national product of the United States would have been 17 per cent higher than it actually was, had not this capital absorption taken place. That is, gross national product would have been 4.9 billion dollars, rather than the 4.2 billion dollars which Gallman estimated. The effect is substantial because slaves accounted for about one quarter of the total wealth in 1860. It does not necessarily follow that the burden was borne exclusively by the South. Presumably, had the plantation owners, in the absence of slavery, sought other forms of investment, they would have invested wherever they thought the return was highest. That might not have been Southern manufacturing. More probably it would have been in the expansion of plantation agriculture. It might also have been in Northern manufacturing or in bonds of the British government. Unless we specify what alternative investments were available, we cannot say that the burden of slavery would have fallen on the South, but we can say that it must have fallen somewhere in the economy.

STANLEY ENGERMAN: I would like to reply briefly to some of the comments made by Professor Dowd. In my judgment the Conrad and Meyer argument about whether slavery was profitable to the planters and the planter class is now agreed upon by most people. The statistical work and the reasoning seem to be largely accepted. The focus of the debate has become the question of Southern growth rates, the importance of the slave system in Southern growth before the Civil War and its lingering effects after the Civil War. One important series, the importance of which is often overlooked, is the series of regional income estimates prepared by Richard

Easterlin. Professor Easterlin, no doubt, has certain reservations about placing considerable weight on these estimates, but the direction in which they lead is quite suggestive.

There are really two questions. One can discuss how rapid were the growth rates that did occur in the period 1840–1860. This, of course, is the question which Professor Easterlin has asked and to which he wants an answer. The second question, the one which is implied by Professor Dowd, is, given the land-labor endowment, and given certain things which we feel about the relationship between slavery and entrepreneurship, how rapidly *could* this Southern economy grow? The really difficult questions are the questions which downplay Southern development and try to argue that development could have been more rapid. This may be true; no one has yet simulated the Southern economy in the absence of slavery; no one has asked what would have happened. One point to note, however, is the much more stringent requirement being imposed upon the South than on the North.

The question of income distribution—whether it was more or less equal in the North than in the South—is still unresolved and very few data are available. If one accepts the suggestion made by Professor Kuznets that with the development of urban areas you get a more skewed distribution than in agricultural areas, it's not clear that the South and the North differed greatly in income distribution. Perhaps more important, the relationship between income distribution and growth is still debatable. It might be argued that the South would have grown more rapidly if there had been no conspicuous consumption; but in the North there was much conspicuous consumption. The building of mansions was not solely a Southern problem; it was certainly occurring in the North. There were art collections in the North and various other forms of what, from the point of view of economic growth, may be called social waste. If you ask of the South: "What is the maximum amount of capital formation which could have occurred in the absence of conspicuous consumption?" and don't ask that question about the North, you will get a rather misleading answer.

The third point is the question of the efficiency of the labor force. Paul Gates, discussing Northern agriculture after the Civil War, has reported farmers' complaints about the hired hands, the gist of which was that the hired hands were lazy, they didn't show up when you wanted them, they couldn't work with machinery, they destroyed the animals, and so on. To raise these questions about the slaves in the South and not apply the same stringent criteria to the North seems to me misleading. We know from the Easterlin data that the South was growing rapidly from 1840 to 1860, and this estimate includes both whites and Negroes in the population base. We also know that, including Negroes, Southern per capita income was higher than in the Western agricultural areas. The picture of the prewar South as a stagnant, poor society is belied by the evidence.

A question has been raised about income distribution and whether the South had such a poor income distribution that growth was inconceivable in the long run. The evidence that we have now on income distribution is insufficient to support that conclusion. The only estimate which I have ever seen on income distribution in the South in the traditional sources is the estimate from *The Cotton Kingdom* prepared by William E. Dodd. It is not clear how the data were prepared, and the implications are so astounding that it is hard to believe that they have any validity. That extreme conclusion doesn't appear to be correct. What we have at the moment (awaiting the results of research now under way) is in effect no information. I may suggest, however, that many statements about income distribution in the South before the Civil War are made in apparent ignorance of the income distribution which existed in the 1920's and the 1930's, and still exists today. Genovese, for example, attempts to show the small size of the market in the South by arguing that Southern income distribution was skewed because the top 6 per cent of the landowners in his sample of Mississippi counties had 33 per cent of the land. A number of adjustments must of course be made, but data on wealth distribution in the 1920's suggest that the top 2 per cent of the families then had about 32 or 33 per cent of national wealth. Questions of income distribution and its effect on economic growth are still open.

The final remark I wish to make about Professor Dowd's comments has to do with another implication of the Easterlin results. Easterlin has no estimate for 1870, but he does have regional relatives for 1880, 1900, and 1920. It appears from these estimates, linked to mine, that from 1870 to 1920 the South was growing as rapidly as the rest of the country, and that the South started to converge on the national average after 1920. The questions would be, first, should we have expected earlier convergence, as is apparently implicit in the argument? And secondly, what occurred in the South to prevent a catching-up? To argue that, starting from 1870, the Southern economy was stagnant is belied again by the Easterlin data. How did growth occur? The South still had close to a world monopoly in cotton, in the sense that it was by far the largest producer; and the demand for cotton was expanding in this period. The South grew from 1870 to 1900 in roughly the same way as it had grown before. It grew because of a rise in the demand for cotton in the world market and the continuing profitability of cotton.

One final point about westward expansion: In most arguments which an economist will accept it is agreed that there was sufficient land in the old boundaries of the South on which to expand, but that land values were such that it was more profitable to expand outward. There is little reason to suggest that once outward expansion was precluded it was impossible to reinvest and redevelop the existing soil.

CHARLES KELSO: I shall confine my comments to two topics: first, an approach to the problem of "obstacles" which we have under consideration in this program; and second, a reexamination of one aspect of the empirical validity of the profitability models. The approach which I propose is based on the distinction between growth and development pointed out by Professor Dowd. We can view growth as a two-dimensional concept, these dimensions being expansion and development. The current experiences of several underdeveloped countries demonstrate that in a sparsely settled, backward area there can indeed be growth without development, merely through the expansion of the existing system. Consequently, it is important to analyze the differential impact of slavery on these two aspects of growth.

For many purposes, the South has been divided into two geographic areas, the old and the new South. The former is composed of the states of earlier settlement, which in the decades preceding the Civil War experienced an outflow of slaves, either through their sale or the migration of their owners. The latter represented the unsettled areas or relatively newly settled regions of the South and Southwest, which were on the receiving end of the slave trade and migrations. These two areas actually faced two distinct problems. In the old South, market-oriented or staple agriculture was relatively well established and there existed little room for expansion.

Thus the only avenue for growth in the old South was through development. On the other hand the new South offered great opportunities for growth through expansion. In addition, slavery in the new South was an important link in the developmental process, in that it brought with it the concept of production for the market, which had been subordinated to self-sufficiency by the nearly subsistence yeomen who had preceded the planters in this area. Thus, we can speak in terms of slavery as an obstacle to development in the old South as compared to slavery as an obstacle to expansion in the new South. It seems doubtful that in 1860 the agricultural system in the new South had been established long enough for slavery to have become an obstacle rather than an agent of development, although this is possible. However, as the opportunity for expansion became more and more remote, the question of blocked or retarded development would have almost inevitably become the dominant consideration.

I would now like to turn to the question of profitability. Unfortunately, much heat has been generated over the appropriate data for use in the profitability models and much too little has been said about their relevance to the real world. I submit that their validity is impaired (although, surprisingly enough, their results are borne out) by expanded analysis.

Ever since Olmsted named his study of the Southern economy *The Cotton Kingdom*, almost all of the studies of slavery, with a few notable exceptions, have emphasized cotton. On the microeconomic level, most of the important questions about cotton planting have been explored, but the same questions for the other four staples of the economy—tobacco, sugar, hemp, and rice—have been neglected, as have the relationships among these five. In 1849, all of the cotton, sugar, and rice grown in the United States was produced in the South, defined as the thirteen states nominally committed to the Confederacy, plus Maryland. In addition, 95 per cent of the country's tobacco and 93 per cent of the hemp were also raised in the South. On the basis of estimates by Professor Gallman, the approximate shares of these products in value-added in staple production were: cotton, 77 per cent; tobacco, 9 per cent; cane sugar, 7 per cent; hemp, 4 per cent; and rice, 3 per cent. The distribution of the nondomestic agricultural slave labor force among these industries was 72.6 per cent, 14 per cent, 6 per cent, 5 per cent, and 2.4 per cent, respectively. The differences between these two distributions reflect both variations among the labor-output ratios and the existence of large numbers of free laborers involved in cotton production. In any event, failure to study the employment of almost three tenths of the agricultural slave labor force is a sizeable omission. Its true significance is revealed only through the geographic distribution of the various crops. Again, using 1849 as a bench mark, we find that the old South, or the slave-selling states of Maryland, Virginia, North Carolina, Tennessee, Kentucky, and Missouri, produced only 10 per cent of the cotton crop, eight tenths of which came from Tennessee alone. On the other hand, the same group of states produced 99 per cent of the tobacco crop and practically all of the hemp as well. Thus, the ratio of total value-added in tobacco production to that of cotton in the old South was on the order of 1.1 to 1, while that of tobacco plus hemp to cotton was 1.7 to 1. At the same time, 95 per cent of the sugar was raised in Louisiana, and 92 per cent of the rice came from a belt along the coast of South Carolina and Georgia. While rice never really rivaled cotton, the ratio of value-added in sugar to that in cotton was 1.1 to 1 in Louisiana.

It is thus apparent that any explanation of profitability based exclusively on cotton is inadequate, especially with respect to the subregional differences emphasized by Professors Conrad and Meyer. In order to complete the test of their hypothesis it was necessary to construct a model for each of the omitted crops. The models used were the familiar Keynesian type found in all the current studies. The $1,210 average per hand investment required in tobacco was comparable to the investment in cotton postulated by Conrad and Meyer for the tobacco-producing region. The average per hand investments in sugar and rice were $1,840 and $2,230, respectively, somewhat higher than the $1,700 investment in cotton "on the best lands of the new Southwest, the Mississippi alluvium, and the better South Carolina and Alabama plantations." The results of these models are quite interesting. Within the relevant range of price variation, the internal rate of return on tobacco planting was found to be from 2 to 6 per cent; on sugar, from 7¼ to 13 per cent; and on rice, from ⸱ to 16 per cent. This supports the results and conclusions already advanced by Conrad and Meyer.

These findings reinforce the hypothesis that slavery was highly profitable in the new South and at least as profitable as alternative investments in the old South if we include the returns from the slave trade. They also imply the allocative efficiency of the capital market, not only in that comparable capital outlays in each area yielded comparable returns, but also by the fact that higher returns were earned on projects which required higher initial outlays and therefore entailed higher risks. Finally, with reference to the framework developed previously, these results support the two simplified conclusions which seem to have been drawn on the basis of earlier studies. First, inasmuch as the profitability of slavery in the old South was comparable with that of industrial-development opportunities, slavery *could* have been an obstacle to growth by channeling capital into planting, a venture more socially respected than industrial enterprise, thereby retarding development. Second, the high profits received on the investment in slaves in the new South provided incentive for expansion and, hence, in this respect, slavery was an aid rather than an obstacle to growth.

HARRY SCHEIBER: In regard to Mr. Engerman's statement that the Conrad and Meyer statistics are now apparently thoroughly accepted on their own terms, regardless of the merits of the framework within which they are presented, I would point out that Eugene Genovese has taken strong exception to the rounding procedures and the impact of rounding procedures on their hypothesis.[4] It would be helpful if, in this panel, Messrs. Conrad and Meyer would reply to Genovese's criticism that the productivity of the slave labor in cotton has not been accurately represented. In the second place, I would point to the irony of using, as Professor Conrad has, alternative investment outlets and their yields. This involves holding all other things equal; but what we are talking about when we refer to interest rates on alternative investment outlets are interest rates in an economy which included a slave South. Finally, in the category of what we really don't know about the South, the question of the South's relative income is still very much an open question. Professor Easterlin's estimates are very tentative, and I would agree with Mr. Engerman that there is considerable work to be done before we can safely argue that the South was sharing fully in growth even in the 1850's and before we can argue that this trend could reasonably have been expected to continue.

[4] The reference is to Eugene D. Genovese. *The Political Economy of Slavery* (New York: Pantheon Books, 1966), pp. 47, 63.

Perhaps all the rest of what I have to say has to do with what we don't know about the pre-Civil War South. In the first place, we don't really know what the productivity per unit of slave labor input was, as compared with the world of what might have been —that is, what the productivity of slave labor might have been in a system other than outright thoroughgoing chattel slavery. There are examples in the American continents of slavery other than chattel slavery with very different kinds of incentives built in, very different opportunities, and very different effects. Furthermore, we don't know as yet, and I am not sure the new economic history can help us with this, what the impact of the plantation system was. I would not use the polite terminology, "system of social control"; let's just call it a plantation system that embraced the caste system. Let us address ourselves to the question of what both the long-term and the short-term economic effects of a caste system of labor and social control were upon the South. We can be reasonably confident that, because of the exploitative potential offered by slave labor and the advantages that it gave to the large planter, he could influence land policy, land acquisition, local tax decisions, and so on. We do know that the large planters in one region after another in the South found it possible to obtain the best land. This is, of course, likely to skew all of our calculations as to the productivity of labor and the profitability of slavery. The question of how this influence was obtained is one that is not going to yield answers without considerations well beyond those posed within the self-admittedly limited framework that Messrs. Conrad and Meyer have provided. We must ask about the impact of the caste system on the productivity of labor in its broadest sense. What was the potential in this labor force? Mr. Ginzberg has spoken eloquently on this point and I need add little more except to say that this was not an adaptable labor force. It is worth remembering Olmsted's statement that the central question to which Southern planters seemed to be addressing themselves was how, without quite destroying the capability of the Negro for any work at all, they could prevent him from learning how to take care of himself. The impact of this kind of labor force on efforts toward diversification, both within agriculture and in the Southern economy as a whole, are problems that are worth pondering.

A word now about comparisons with the West. It seems to me

that it would be fruitful to explore patterns of local and regional stagnation and decline. There are areas of the West which, by the 1850's, were undergoing population decline, areas in which there was soil exhaustion, and so on. But one must differentiate this from what I would call the systemic economic stagnation that was manifest, for example, in South Carolina in the 1850's. One must look at the total economic context, as I think Genovese has done and as Professor Dowd has done so adequately.

Finally, I would emphasize, with almost everyone who has spoken here, the need to consider the national and international context of the profitability of slavery. The question that I raised at the outset on interest rates—alternative investment outlets—is but one example. One must ask questions not merely concerning the long-term impact of the caste system on regional growth but also concerning the short-run and the long-run impact of the slave system on U.S. growth and on the U.S. response to opportunities and constraints in the world market in the pre-Civil War period itself.

JOHN R. MEYER: Professor Dowd has characterized economists as cheerful and comfortable. This is welcome indeed after all these years of being the dismal scientists. But I feel that Professor Dowd, and perhaps Professor Ginzberg by implication, attributed thoughts to us that we never really expressed. What Professor Dowd objected to in particular, if I understood him correctly, was our implication, or perhaps direct statement, that slavery did not inhibit economic development. The fact of the matter is that our original article contained no such remark. Indeed, the article, which was written before Professor Easterlin's figures were available, accepted the then conventional wisdom that the South did develop more slowly than the rest of the country. We wondered why. We speculated that slavery might have had something to do with it, but we found the usual arguments somewhat hard to accept. We considered militarism, posturing, the seignorial tradition, too much consumption, capital absorption, and other things. All these arguments had at least a superficial plausibility. But we could see no reasons for accepting or rejecting any of them and took a neutral view on the question of whether slavery did or did not inhibit Southern economic development. Perhaps I should add that we have certainly never espoused the contrary view that slavery was a great aid to economic development. The evidence (as far as the short-run effects went) and the arguments for this proposition seemed implausible to us.

Since then more evidence has appeared. We have Easterlin's figures; we have Engerman's careful reworking of them; we have the work of Williamson, North, Fogel, and others. So we have at least some reasonable picture of what did happen. There are reasons for reservations about absolute accuracy, but it appears that in the prewar period the South did develop reasonably rapidly, about as quickly as the rest of the country. It had a 10- to 20-year hiatus between 1860 and 1880, and then resumed its rate of growth, but nevertheless even with a high rate of growing it did not catch up with the rest of the country. It began to close the gap only slowly. Now, in the face of this evidence, I shall, perhaps unfairly, characterize Professor Dowd's present argument saying: "I accept the fact that slavery probably was profitable; capitalists had been making profits all around the world, and they were doing it in the South too; calculated from the standpoint of those who owned the system, it certainly was profitable. Furthermore, I am willing to concede that growth in the South in the prewar period was about as rapid as the rest of the country, but they paid a price, between 1860 and 1880, for that slavery. And the reason for this was that it permeated all of their attitudes; it ruined their entrepreneurial spirit, and did all sorts of other harmful things to their state of mind." This may be a caricature, but I think it is not too far from the spirit of Professor Dowd's argument.

Having done that, Professor Dowd also rejected the argument made by Engerman that the reduced rate of growth in the war period and the immediate postwar period in the South had something to do with war destruction. He pointed out that war destruction does not set back economies that much. I suppose the obvious comment for Professor Engerman to make is that in the period after World War II there was something known as the Marshall Plan. As I understand my American economic history, we had the Thaddeus Stevens Plan in the post-Civil War period, a rather different approach to the problem.

If we look at what has happened to regional income distribution over the last one-hundred years, what we observe is generally a convergence. But the slowest growing region in the country has tended to be New England. The Southeast, in contrast, has been one of the more rapidly growing regions over the last hundred years in per capita income levels. The Southeast may not equal the far West or the Southwest, but it has been doing very well indeed and certainly better than New England which has been the real, tardy, reluctant laggard in this income growth race. I would say that what has happened to New England has something to do with steam power displacing the region's unique position in terms of water-power sites for producing textiles and other industrial products. The area has lost certain kinds of technological advantages, but I am led to speculate whether Professor Dowd would not honor us with an analysis of how the abolitionist attitude must have contributed to this startlingly poor performance by New England.

[Professor Irwin Feller of Pennsylvania State University, from the floor, asked a question concerning a possible connection between social structure and the persistence of a one-crop economy.]

ENGERMAN: That point falls under the question which I chose not to answer: the question of what would have happened under a certain alternative set of assumptions. Before the Civil War when the slave system was presumably locked in cotton, the economy was expanding rapidly, and demand for the crop was increasing. If the cotton business was good, the fact that planters stayed in the business is not too surprising for the period before the war. We also know, however, that there were movements into and out of cotton production in the decline of the late 1830's and early 1840's. There was some mobility of slaves. As for what happened after the war, perhaps growth could have been higher under another set of circumstances. But again we find that growth was high, and the fact that the region restricted itself to one crop, then adjusted after 1870 when textile production began, certainly did not lead to a decline in the South *vis-à-vis* the rest of the country.

DOWD: The point made by the questioner is, in part, what I am trying to say. But what I am trying to say is much more than that. It is certainly true that the social system of the South was such as to force energies, emotions, and attitudes to be concentrated on the maintenance of that social system; and this meant also maintaining what the social system did in its economic ramifications. This made it a less flexible system, not just before but also after the Civil War.

May I now respond to some of the remarks made by the various commentators, including Professor Meyer. First, I feel that Professor Ginzberg is really in agreement with me. All the things he talked about were things that I said ought to be talked about. All these matters are in that *ceteris paribus* pound that we use so frequently in economics, which is fine so long as we are talking about very short-run considerations.

This brings me to perhaps my most important point. It has been said over and over again, in answering my argument that the South did not develop, that the South grew at this time, or at that time, at this rate or at that rate. Either I have been misreading the improvement that has taken place in economics in the past fifteen years, where distinctions between growth and development have once again been recognized, or I have misunderstood the speakers' emphasis. What has happened is what I have been trying to say happens so frequently. Words and concepts that the economist should take very seriously are juggled back and forth as though they were synonyms. Growth and development are *not* synonymous terms; they are related terms. The one may or may not imply the other; but they are not the same thing. The fact that the South grew between 1840 and 1860 has no necessary implications about development. Development implies structural change in the economy and a change in the nature of the society.

If one looks at the history of the American South, one finds that it was a very prosperous region relative to the rest of the world in the pre-Civil War period, and that it was at that time reasonably prosperous relative to the rest of the United States. But the social system was deteriorating in terms of its long-run potential. That long-run potential is the sort of thing we refer to when we speak of economic development. My own interest in the South does not have one particular date or one decade or two as its reference. What we are concerned with is the American South, a region which, in the very period in which the American nation was growing *and* developing, grew but did not develop. And when it grew, it grew on the basis of cotton alone, either cotton production or cotton textile production. The maintenance of a lopsided economy—lop-sided industrially as well as agriculturally—is the opposite of development. By all the usual measures of economic development, the South before 1930 in every conceivable respect fitted into the notion of an underdeveloped region. When Professor Conrad says, "the critical decade for the South was really in the last decade of the eighteenth century," I would like to remind him that the most rapid period of industrialization and articulation of the American economy as a whole was in the twenty-five years or so preceding World War I. And this was exactly the period, 1890 to 1920, in which the South underwent its crucial reversion to an emphasis on racism. This is the period in which all those characteristics appeared that today we are trying to fight socially. This happened as a reaction to the possibility that white supremacy might begin to end. The whole business goes back to that point. This was the legacy of a social system which was profitable.

ROBERT FOGEL, University of Chicago: The underlying disagreement stems from the fact that Professor Dowd insists that bad social systems, undesirable social systems, undesirable political systems, and undesirable moral systems cannot be vigorously growing economic systems. Let us consider the argument that slavery eventually had to have a bad effect on the capacity of the Southern economy to produce goods and services for the population; or the related notion that slavery would eventually have retarded the rate of growth, or that slavery would have become unprofitable if it had been confined to the states in which it existed. I have attempted to estimate what would have happened to the profitability of slavery in the absence of a civil war. It turns out that the relative profitability of slavery between 1860 and 1890 would have increased. Whether we like it or not, the demand for American cotton continued to grow down to the early 1920's more rapidly than the South was able to respond and supply. It is quite wrong to say the price of cotton fell. The real price of cotton rose over time. It is clear, then, that cotton over this period faced a booming market. This is not the typical situation of an underdeveloped country. All that remains of Professor Dowd's argument, then, is that when the capacity to grow finally petered out in the 1920's, the South could not convert to some other system. But no evidence is provided for that assertion. In fact we know that the South successfully converted between the mid-1920's and the 1940's, even though both you and I would agree it has held on to many political characteristics we consider undesirable.

CHARLES WILBER, American University: If we define development as involving higher per capita incomes, increased skill levels, increased educational levels, and a greater range of job opportunities, I wonder if the slavery system may not have hindered development. The income level today of that segment of the labor force that is descended from slaves is about half that of those not involved in slavery, and their educational level is considerably lower; by any of these criteria they have hindered Southern development. They are far below the level attained by those whose lives were not subjected to slavery. Could it be that this was an effect of slavery?

MEYER: Let me repeat once again that our paper did not imply or suggest either that slavery was a help or a hindrance to Southern economic growth. That was not really in our purview. The question has been raised, subsequent to our initial paper, whether it retarded Southern growth in the prewar period and what was its legacy on the Southern growth rate in the immediate postwar period. I suspect that Professor Dowd's views on the unfortunate political and social aspects of slavery, its legacy to this country and the South, are much the same as ours. But that is not the issue we are discussing here, so we can put it to one side.

There is a real intellectual issue, however, that divides Professor Dowd and ourselves, on measures or definitions of growth and development. We want some precision in those measures. Professor Dowd suggested per capita educational achievements. I would suggest that that is only a partial measure of development. I would also say that skill levels, value-added estimates, income per capita, and so on, all have a role. He also suggested that income growth necessitates something called "balanced economic growth," suggesting that there had to be a diversity of job opportunities, or skills, or enterprises in order to have development in the strict sense as contrasted with growth. I suggest Professor Dowd should not push this thought too far because a lot depends on geography. The South was a subregion in a larger economy. But this idea can be pushed to absurd extremes. Consider the case of a small farm in Texas or Kansas where oil is discovered and drilling begins, and per capita income rises from oil revenues. I suppose one would have to say this small area and these particular people are not developing. On the other hand, if the wealth created by the oil discovery is available for other purposes and the farmer educates his children better, his educational measure would go up. This balanced-growth argument, in short, raises a host of questions about regional specialization and national specialization, about problems of measurement that depend on the exact geographic area referred to. I would suggest that we still have a long way to go in clarifying the distinction between how we would measure growth and development and how Professor Dowd would.

CHARLES HESSION, Brooklyn College: I would like to ask about a question of fact. There is a postscript in the article on slavery in which the suggestion is advanced that it was not slavery that retarded economic growth in the South, but perhaps the plantation system. The reader is left with the impression that Conrad and Meyer finally take the position that the indirect effect of the plantation system, as so defined, on Southern economic development was adverse. Would the authors comment on that particular passage?

CONRAD: Since we published our paper ten years ago we have had two lines of criticism. One has petered out; the other has flourished. The first one is characterized by a letter from Athens, Georgia, suggesting that we would not dare say these things in Athens, Georgia. The kind of criticism that still flourishes goes as follows: I am less than five days back from Pakistan. Each time I come back somebody says, "What are you doing? Selling slavery to the Pakistani?" I am not selling slavery in Pakistan, but I have learned a good deal there. I have learned that there is a simplistic distinction between growth and development which is just as dangerous to me as a simplistic identification of the two concepts. There is a stage in economic education in which everybody identifies growth and development; there ought to be a stage somewhat later in the game when you learn not to make them diametrically opposite. Development should not mean factories. Development does not mean a simplistic textbook notion of a balanced economy. It does not mean putting tomato-paste factories in countries where they do not have tomatoes, or putting fifteen tractors on a 300-acre plot. It need not mean the usual paraphernalia of industrialization; it may mean a good wheat crop. Hopefully this will make a great deal of difference in growth. It will also make a great deal of difference in development. It may also signify the difference between Pakistan and India at this time. India has taken a lot of nonsense about balanced growth and industrialization and hard goods as the basis of economic development. The same monsoon that brings a good wheat crop in Pakistan may barely reduce hunger in East Punjab. I suspect the difference comes from accepting simplistic distinctions between growth and development.

My second point is about education: We all measure education in terms of the number of years completed in high school or various other such measures and we correlate economic development and productivity with education so measured. One of the things I have learned in the last three years is that education also means going from an eighteen-inch hoe to a long-handled hoe; it means making a bullock instead of taking vicarious satisfaction from the possession of a bull.

I don't quite understand Professor Scheiber's problem with interest rates. If you want to find an opportunity cost, you must find an alternative occupation for the resources or the funds, which does not share the income of the activity which you are examining. With regard to savings rates, may I suggest that the savings rate may have something to do with the opportunity to invest? Then, regarding the question raised by Scheiber and Genovese about our rounding procedures: Yes, we did misplace one turning point by going to two decimal places instead of three and we are admittedly wrong. Concerning the other factual question that Mr. Genovese has raised—the expensive vacations necessary for the South—I am afraid I don't believe that expensive vacations are elements of cost and should have been in our computation. On the question of the mule population we were very wrong. We are both city boys and we forgot that mules don't make mules. On the other hand we have since had pointed out to us that there were enough horses and donkeys to keep the mule population increasing.

A question was raised about our postscript in the book on the plantation system. Let me call attention once again to the paragraph in our article that I have already quoted (see above, page 527). The point that you are making is there very rigorously stated. Having said that the elimination of slavery could not be argued on the basis of its unprofitability, John Meyer and I then, accepting the notion that the South had not grown or developed, proceeded to look for reasons. At the time we wrote that essay, we did not have Easterlin's results in hand and we were still laboring under the assumption that Southern growth had been lagging badly. In order to find the reasons we considered the possibility of the plantation as an industrial structure. This may have been wrong but at least we were facing the question.

What concerns me most is the notion that if you name a number of things that must prove that slavery was bad, then, if it was bad, it cannot have been profitable. It is not necessary that we believe that evil states are unprofitable or inefficient in order to remain moral men. We seem to come back all the time to the idea that, because slavery was evil, it must also have been inefficient. I don't believe that. The sooner we start to make these distinctions, the sooner will we be able to deal with the evil things in this world.

GINZBERG: May I remind Professor Conrad and Professor Meyer that I began by saying that I did not take economics very seriously and I therefore read their piece not once but twice, and I thought it a reasonable piece. I tried to make the simple point that a discussion of profitability, without a discussion of viability, does not seem to be even good elementary economics. I argued that the profitability of Southern slavery has to be reconsidered in the light of the fact that it was the expansionary demands of slaveholders that precipitated the Civil War. You just can't disregard the fact that a civil war occurred because of the inherent dynamic capitalistic drives of these people. If they had been satisfied with a more moderate profit, slavery might have lasted for a hundred years. That was what Lincoln offered them. The United States has in the year 1967 (not 1867) as yet found no way of effectively integrating the Negro population into our economy. And I submit that, despite growth and development, the question may be moot as to whether and how much more development and how much more growth we are going to have unless we do a somewhat better job with "the Southern question." Long-term effects are important in this connection. In 1967, we are still rejecting for military service in the United States over 70 per cent of all Negroes from the Southeastern states. That means they cannot meet eighth-grade standards. I submit that to talk about the "great development" of the South, in the light of that fact, leaves something to be desired.

MEYER: Greater precision is required here. Professor Ginzberg should please note that we were talking about Southern rates of development compared to the rest of the United States. That is what we were contending were quite high. A region may have a very high rate of development from a low base and at the end of five, six, or seven years still have a fairly low absolute level of development.

ENGERMAN: With reference to what Professor Meyer just said, one of the implications is that the South in 1860 was not impoverished relative to the rest of the nation. The white population probably had a per capita income which exceeded that of the North and the West averaged together; even if you include the Negro population, per capita income in the South was reasonably high in comparison to the West. The second point is a reference to Professor Ginzberg's remarks: He is not really asking a question about the economics of slavery. He is asking the question which my father-in-law asks whenever I give him something to read on slavery. His question is: What would have happened if you had not brought the Negroes over? Would America's wealth be higher or lower? The question that is really being asked is not about the profitability of slavery but about the profitability of importing persons as slaves and retaining them after being freed.

PETER TEMIN, Massachusetts Institute of Technology: I would like to reply to Professor Meyer's continual call for precision because I think he is obfuscating an important issue. I don't have Professor Easterlin's figures with me, but as I recall they indicate that the South grew rapidly before the Civil War, roughly at the rate of the country as a whole; that it stagnated from 1860 to 1880; and then, after 1880, it resumed approximately its former rate of growth but at a lower level relative to the rest of the country. That is, after the Civil War it did not return to its previous position relative to the rest of the country, but it grew at approximately the same rate as the rest of the country, at a lower level. The losses suffered during the war were permanent or at least very long-run losses. The question I would like to present is: Why did this happen? One could refer to destruction of Southern capital. But was there that much destruction? The elasticity argument, as presented by Professor Meyer, is certainly a possibility, but it would seem that we need rather more independent evidence on elasticity before resting such a large thesis on that basis. The question is whether this might have something to do with the social system, with the lack of flexibility that was cited as being related to slavery.

E. A. J. JOHNSON, Johns Hopkins University: It seems to me that Mr. Meyer is quite right when he points out that this controversy centers around the definition of development. That very bland term has been bandied around without any attempt to make it very precise. I am not going to offer a simplistic definition because after three or four years in Yugoslavia and a year in Greece and two periods of residence in India, I am not foolish enough to come forward with any simplistic definition. I do think, however, it might have been well if cognizance had been taken of the definition proffered by Svennilson. We are talking about the transformation of the economy. It could be argued, perhaps, that the rate of transformation in the South was lower than that of the North. The concept of transformation consists of four elements. First, there is a tendency toward greater capital intensity. Second, new enterprises develop, with a stimulating effect on industry as well as investment. Third, there occur changes in the direction and composition of foreign trade, primarily in the direction of greater diversification. And fourth, there are changes in the occupations and education of labor. One might proceed in terms of this kind of concept, rather than bland terms such as "growth" and "development."

MEYER: Even very good definitions have problems. For example with reference to occupational diversification and so on, possibly the state of Oregon would be one of the least developed states in this Union because of its heavy emphasis on logging and its closely related lumber and furniture industries. And yet I suspect that if you were to go to Oregon you would not say it was as underdeveloped as some other states of the Union, for example, the South. Or one might take a smaller geographic region. There is a fair diversity of occupations represented in Harlem, for example. By these standards Harlem looks quite developed. Any such definition is a good beginning, but not the end of our problem. Regarding Professor Temin's point, we may note that it took twenty-five years for excess capacity in world cotton production to be absorbed; the South felt for a long time the impact of the disruption of the world cotton market.

DOWD: My concern is not that Conrad and Meyer have shown that slavery was profitable. I agree with them; I agreed with them ten years ago; I agree with them today. But I say that despite that, it required a social system for its persistence which inhibited economic development. The fundamental question is: What do economic historians do? It is at least possible to make distinctions—distinctions between what is important in the sense of social relevance, and what no longer has to be discussed because everyone

69

agrees or because it makes little difference. What difference does it make whether slavery was profitable or not? No difference whatsoever. But it makes a very big difference in the profession of economic history whether we decide that we can understand the prospects for change in one way or in another way. That is all I have ever been concerned with.

The new economic history reminds me very much of the new economics of the past twenty-five years or so. It has an attractive set of techniques easily used by those who have had a certain amount of training in those techniques. It creates great temptations in the way of taking one aspect of an argument and presenting that as the whole problem. It also yields a curriculum for undergraduate and graduate students that is very demanding and that deflects them from other things. Professors must recognize how complex reality is, and make it possible for their students to study the complexity of reality.

MEYER: Professor Conrad and I did not pick this subject because we thought that it was necessarily something that was earthshaking or that a lot of people would be interested in it. It came out of two separate but parallel and almost simultaneous discussions—on my part with Professor Gerschenkron and on his part with Professor Williamson—about the untidy state of economic history and the lack of good economic theory and good economic measurement in economic history. Both Professor Gerschenkron and Professor Williamson confronted us with a challenge: Prove it by doing something more systematic. And we took the subject of slavery. Neither of us said that this is something that all young economic historians, sociologists, or plain historians should become involved with. It has little to do with the question of social relevance. It does, however, have something to do with precision and measurement in economic history.

Disciplining Slave Ironworkers in the Antebellum South: Coercion, Conciliation, and Accommodation

CHARLES B. DEW

WHEN JOHN C. CALHOUN learned in 1845 that his son-in-law, Thomas Clemson, was planning to break up his plantation and rent out his slave force, Calhoun promptly reminded him of the probable human consequences of such a move. The hirer of the slaves would have no incentive to "take good care of them," Calhoun warned. "The object of him who hires, is generally to make the most he can out of them, without regard to their comfort or health," he continued, and Calhoun was so convinced of the evils of slave hiring that he offered to buy the slaves himself if Clemson could not find other decent masters who would purchase them.[1]

Several historians of American slavery who have commented recently on slave hiring, and particularly on the hiring of slaves for industrial purposes, share Calhoun's bleak assessment of this phase of the South's peculiar institution. "The overwork of hired slaves by employers with only a temporary interest in their welfare was as notorious as the harsh practices of overseers," notes Kenneth M. Stampp. "Slaves hired to mine owners or railroad contractors were fortunate if they were not driven to the point where their health was impaired."[2] In the view of Stampp and a number of other scholars, slave hiring and industrial slavery were among the most brutal and exploitive aspects of the American slave system; these historians tend to see hiring out and industrial employment, like slave trading, as

This paper was originally presented at the 1973 meeting of the Organization of American Historians, and I wish to thank Professor Bennett H. Wall of Tulane University for his helpful criticisms on that occasion. I should also like to thank the members of the Corcoran Department of History at the University of Virginia who kindly invited me to spend a year as a visiting teacher at that institution and thus gave me ready access to the manuscript collections at the University of Virginia Library which form the core of this study. Research in other depositories was assisted by a grant from the Research Council of the University of Missouri, Columbia, and by a summer stipend from the National Endowment for the Humanities, and I am deeply grateful for this support.

[1] J. C. Calhoun to T. G. Clemson, Oct. 27, 1845, John C. Calhoun Papers, Clemson University Library, Clemson, S. C.

[2] Kenneth M. Stampp, *The Peculiar Institution: Slavery in the Ante-Bellum South* (New York, 1956), 84.

areas where the business aspects of the institution were most highly developed
and where the humanity of the slaves was most likely to be ignored.[3]

Other recent students of slavery, particularly Clement Eaton and Richard
B. Morris, have suggested a somewhat different picture. "Court records . . .
contain rather frequent references to cruel treatment, overwork, and neglect
of hired slaves," writes Professor Eaton. "Yet considerable evidence . . . indicates that many of the plantation slaves of the Upper South desired to be
hired in the cities and in industries to secure the privileges, social opportunities, rewards, and freedoms which they could not enjoy on the plantation."[4] Both Eaton and Morris see slave hiring and industrial work contributing to the development of improved living conditions for slave laborers
and argue, in Morris's words, that these improvements represented a "trend
toward upgrading slaves into a shadowland of quasi-freedom" in the late
antebellum era.[5] Although there is considerable doubt about some of the
implications of the Eaton-Morris analysis, particularly their suggestion that
this trend toward greater freedom posed a threat to the continued existence
of slavery itself, they would seem to be on the right track. A close examination of one phase of Southern industrial slavery that used large numbers
of hired bondsmen—the manufacture of iron—reveals a complex relationship between master and slave that rested more on a subtle process of
mutual compromise and accommodation than on excessive use of physical
force and coercion. This is not by any means intended to suggest that force
was not used, for it clearly was, or to suggest that the slave iron worker
lived and labored as a free person; he or she was still a slave, and in Southern industrial slavery, as in all slave systems, the master ultimately possessed
far superior weapons if a test of wills threatened to go beyond what the master
considered reasonable bounds. But unless an outright threat to the master's
authority or a direct challenge to the slave system itself occurred, the
Southern iron men examined for this article proved, for a number of reasons,
to be willing to meet their slave hands in a rather vague and nebulous
middle ground where black and white could live with and work alongside
each other and where the slave had considerable influence over his working conditions, his family arrangements, and the course of his everyday
life.

In order to present this thesis in as clear and brief a fashion as possible,
this article concentrates on the operations of William Weaver and several

[3] Robert S. Starobin, *Industrial Slavery in the Old South* (New York, 1970), especially chs. 3
and 4, and his article, "Disciplining Industrial Slaves in the Old South," *Journal of Negro
History*, 53 (1968): 111–28; Samuel Sydney Bradford, "The Ante-Bellum Charcoal Iron Industry
of Virginia" (Ph.D. dissertation, Columbia University, 1958), especially chs. 4 and 5, and his
article, "The Negro Ironworker in Ante Bellum Virginia," *Journal of Southern History*, 25
(1959): 194–206.
[4] Clement Eaton, "Slave-Hiring in the Upper South: A Step toward Freedom," *Mississippi
Valley Historical Review*, 46 (1960): 668–69; Richard B. Morris, "The Measure of Bondage
in the Slave States," *ibid.*, 41 (1954): 231–39.
[5] Morris, "Measure of Bondage," 239.

other ironmasters whose furnaces and forges lay in the Valley of Virginia. More detailed evidence is available on the antebellum Virginia iron industry than for any other Southern state, but research in the surviving records of iron establishments that were located in other areas of the South indicates that Virginia's labor practices were characteristic of the industry throughout the slave states.[6] The emphasis on a specific group of men in a specific area also reflects a conviction that only through close and detailed case studies of the ways in which slavery functioned on a day-to-day basis can we begin to understand what it meant to be a slave in any phase of the American slave system, industrial or agricultural, urban or rural. One of my purposes is to suggest that the material for studies in microcosm of this sort is available and that records generated in the daily functioning of the system can give us some insight into the slave's own reaction to his or her bondage. Perhaps an imaginative use of primary sources of this kind can free historians from an almost exclusive dependence on published fugitive accounts or the Slave Narrative Collection of the Library of Congress in our renewed efforts to get inside the most peculiar of American institutions.[7]

WILLIAM WEAVER was something of a legend in his own lifetime. Although born in Pennsylvania, he spent most of his adult life in the valley region of Virginia where he amassed, for his day, a sizable fortune from his iron, farming, and milling operations. In 1860 Weaver, then seventy-nine years old, estimated to the federal census taker that his real and personal property was worth over $130,000, a figure that was probably reasonably accurate since Weaver owned thousands of acres of land and held sixty-six slaves in 1860—thirty-one adult men, fifteen adult women, and twenty children.[8] Weaver's scientific farming experiments on the steep slopes of the North

6 The employment of slave labor at iron works outside Virginia is discussed in detail in the Louisa Furnace Account Books, which deal with the operations of a Tennessee blast furnace, in the Southern Historical Collection, University of North Carolina, Chapel Hill, N.C.; the Shelby Iron Works Collection, which describes the operations of a major Alabama iron complex, in the University of Alabama Library, University, Ala.; and the Lucy Wortham James Collection, which contains most of the extensive records of the Maramec Iron Works of Missouri, in the Western Historical Manuscripts Collection, University of Missouri, Columbia, Mo. On the use of slave ironworkers in Georgia, see the Augusta *Daily Constitutionalist*, Oct. 29, 1859, and the material relating to the Etowah Iron Works in "Confederate Papers Relating to Citizens or Business Firms," War Department Collection of Confederate Records, Record Group 109, National Archives, Washington, D.C. See also Starobin, *Industrial Slavery*, 100–01; Lester J. Cappon, "Iron-Making—A Forgotten Industry of North Carolina," *North Carolina Historical Review*, 9 (1932): 340–41; and Ernest M. Lander, Jr., "The Iron Industry in Ante-Bellum South Carolina," *Journal of Southern History*, 20 (1954): 350–51. I wish to thank Dr. Robert H. McKenzie of the University of Alabama for kindly providing information on the slave labor practices of the Shelby Iron Works.

7 Two suggestive studies that rely heavily on the Slave Narrative Collection and fugitive accounts have recently appeared. See George P. Rawick, *From Sundown to Sunup: The Making of the Black Community* (Westport, Conn., 1972); and John W. Blassingame, *The Slave Community: Plantation Life in the Ante-Bellum South* (New York, 1972).

8 Manuscript Population and Slave Schedules, Rockbridge County, Virginia, Eighth Census of the United States, 1860, National Archives Microfilm Publications, M653.

River and Buffalo Creek in his home county of Rockbridge gained wide notoriety and earned him a reputation as an innovating and successful farmer.[9] But it was in the iron trade that Weaver concentrated his energies, his financial resources, and the bulk of his slave labor force.

During the 1850s Weaver operated two iron manufacturing installations, both of which employed slave labor extensively and both of which were typical of the slave-manned furnaces and forges that dotted upland areas in Virginia, Tennessee, Kentucky, North and South Carolina, Georgia, Alabama, and Missouri prior to the Civil War. Weaver centered his operations at Buffalo Forge, near Lexington, Virginia, where a picked group of slave operatives worked four fires and two water-powered hammers that annually produced about one hundred tons of bar iron for the Lynchburg and Richmond markets. The pig iron to sustain the operations at Buffalo Forge came from Weaver's Etna Furnace, a charcoal blast furnace located in an adjoining county, which produced some seven hundred tons of pig iron per year. The Etna pig iron not consumed at Weaver's forge was sent by boat down the James River and Kanawah Canal and offered for sale by commission merchants in Lynchburg and Richmond.[10]

Iron manufacturing in the antebellum South was a labor-intensive industry. Since Weaver's Etna Furnace, like practically all Southern blast furnaces, used charcoal for fuel, dozens of workers were needed to chop wood, man charcoal pits, and haul the charcoal frequently long distances to the furnace site. At the ore banks, which might also be several miles from the furnace, miners dug iron ore, while other miners were needed to extract limestone to use as flux in the manufacturing process. When an adequate supply of what furnace men referred to as "stock"—ore, charcoal, and limestone—had been assembled, a process that often required two or three months, the furnace was "blown in" and the production of pig iron begun. Once in operation, workers fed measured amounts of iron ore, charcoal, and limestone into the blast furnace day and night until the blast was completed. Since blasts frequently lasted four to five months, and sometimes longer, and since farming operations were also conducted at most Southern iron works, including Weaver's installations, a constant interchange of slave labor between industrial and agricultural tasks took place at furnaces and forges throughout the South and allowed ironmasters to employ their extensive labor force year round.

At most Southern blast furnaces slave labor played a large role in almost all phases of pig iron production. As founders, colliers, miners, teamsters, wood choppers, and general furnace hands, slaves constituted the bulk of the laboring force. An average charcoal blast furnace required some sixty or

---

[9] "Farming of Mr. William Weaver, of Rockbridge County, Virginia," *Farmers' Register*, 10 (1842): 411–13.

[10] For a description of Weaver's iron properties, see J. P. Lesley, *The Iron Manufacturer's Guide to the Furnaces, Forges, and Rolling Mills of the United States* (New York, 1859), 73, 181.

Fig. 1. William Weaver (1781–1863). From a daguerreotype made in the late 1850s by an unknown photographer. Photograph courtesy the Rockbridge County Historical Society, Lexington, Virginia.

seventy slave workers, in addition to a white manager and a handful of skilled laborers, usually but not always white, who were responsible for supervising various stages of production. Since Weaver owned only thirty-one adult male slaves in 1860 and many of these worked at his forge he, like most Southern iron men, was forced to hire a considerable number of slaves each year—as many as ninety or a hundred hands—in order to sustain both of his iron-making enterprises and his farming operations.[11]

The labor demands at Buffalo Forge were less than those at Weaver's blast furnace. At the forge a force of slave heaters and hammermen turned Weaver's pig iron into "merchant bars," the term used in the nineteenth century to describe refined iron that had been hammered or rolled into

[11] William Weaver to James D. Davidson, Jan. 10, 1855, James D. Davidson Papers, McCormick Collection, State Historical Society of Wisconsin, Madison, Wis.

standard-size bars. A number of slave hands at Buffalo Forge were highly skilled artisans owned by Weaver: Henry Mathews, who was proficient as a blacksmith, rough carpenter, forge hand, and farmworker; Jim Garland and a slave named Tooler who operated Weaver's chafery and refinery forges and there worked the iron prior to its being wrought into bars; two heaters, Henry Towles and Henry Hunt, Jr., the son of one of Weaver's older slaves of the same name who had evidently been brought up in the iron trade at Buffalo Forge; Sam Williams, an exceptionally skilled iron-worker who apparently hammered out finished bars; and Mark, Charles, Garland, and Warder who each had responsibility for a six-mule team and wagon. Weaver's select group of forge hands and teamsters was supplemented by an additional force of slave workers hired by the year to work in less skilled forge operations, in Weaver's flour mill at Buffalo Forge, and as agricultural laborers on Weaver's extensive and scattered farm properties.[12]

The necessity for an accommodation between William Weaver and his slaves, both those he owned and those he hired, lay ultimately in Weaver's dependence on these men for the success of his operations. First of all, to carry on his various manufacturing and farming activities he needed large numbers of slave hands, not all of whom could he afford to purchase. As mentioned previously, he annually sought as many as ninety to a hundred slaves, and the process of hiring so many hands was by no means routine or automatic. A number of difficulties were involved, and these difficulties were compounded in the late antebellum period by the fact that slave labor was becoming increasingly scarce and expensive in Virginia. In the 1820s Weaver normally paid $45 or $50 per year to hire slave hands, with the $50 hire representing Weaver's upper limit for superior workers.[13] By the mid-1850s, however, the price had risen well above those levels, as Weaver's hiring agent reported to him in December 1855:

They [the owners] are asking $135 to $150 for good hands, no one can tell what the price will be, untill new years day. . . . you have no idea of the trouble there is in hiring hands here, at this day, there is all sorts of trickery and management, I don't expect to be able to hire more than thirty or forty hands, we may get fifty; but I can assure you, the prospect is very glomy.[14]

One of Weaver's nephews, James C. Davis of nearby Gibraltar Forge, seeking hands in the same neighborhood, a few days later reported similar difficulties and explained the reason for the troublesome situation. "Hands are hiring a little higher this year than last; the cause of it is the high price of

---

[12] See entries in Buffalo Forge Negro Books, 1850–58 and 1865–72. Weaver-Brady Records, University of Virginia Library, Charlottesville, Va.

[13] James C. Dickinson to Weaver, Jan. 2, 1828, William Weaver Papers, *ibid.* (hereafter these papers will be cited as Weaver Papers, Virginia).

[14] Henry A. McCormick to Weaver, Dec. 29, 1855, *ibid.*

the produce of farms & the consequent demand for their labor in that direction."[15] "There are not so many Iron & no more railroad men in the field," he wrote two days later, "but the farmers make a formidable phalanx of opposition. Some of them are giving $140 & $150 for men, & $70 to $90 for women," he added. "Women are higher than ever known before."[16]

As these letters indicate, the competition among various industrial and agricultural groups for slave labor was stiff in Virginia in the mid-1850s, but this was by no means a novel situation. In the 1820s and 1830s canal-building and gold-mining interests had offered strong hiring competition, and bursts of railroad construction in Virginia in the 1840s and 1850s brought another major employer into the field. Throughout the late antebellum decades agents for the urban tobacco factories and the Richmond area coal mines, cotton mills, and iron works also sought large numbers of slave hands each year.[17]

Given the increased problems involved in hiring an adequate labor force, it was imperative that Weaver and the other ironmasters avoid the reputation that they abused slaves in their employ. If slaves returned home to their owners with stories of hard driving and excessive punishment, an iron man like Weaver could be seriously handicapped in his efforts to hire in subsequent years. That ironmasters were sensitive to any suggestion that they abused slaves and that they sought to avoid excessive physical punishment if at all possible is indicated by an exchange of correspondence in 1849 between the manager of an iron furnace in Rockbridge County and the owner of a hired slave who claimed the manager had mistreated him. First, the letter from the slaveholder to the ironmaster, Francis T. Anderson of Glenwood Furnace:

My boy Edmond that I hired to . . . you got here the eight of this month [November 1849], he says that your overseer is so cruel that he could not stand him. I have hired him out for the three last years and the Gentleman was very much pleased with him. I know he will do his work as well as any negroe unless the person that overlooks him is barbourse I write this to let you know that I have given him a pass and started him back to you, this morning, if you thrash him do not be two rough and I know he will do his work as well as any other negroe at your furnice.[18]

[15] James C. Davis to William W. Davis, Jan. 5, 1856, William W. Davis Papers, University of Virginia Library, Charlottesville, Va.

[16] J. C. Davis to William W. Davis, Jan. 7, 1856, Jordan & Davis Papers, McCormick Collection, State Historical Society of Wisconsin, Madison, Wis.

[17] See John Chew to Weaver, Dec. 5, 1830; and James Coleman to Weaver, Feb. 5, 19, 1856, both in William Weaver Papers, Duke University Library, Durham, N.C. (hereafter these papers will be cited as Weaver Papers, Duke); Tuyman Wayt to Jordan & Irvine, Jan. 6, 1830; and Pallison Boxley to Jordan & Irvine, Jan. 13, 1831, both in Jordan & Irvine Papers, McCormick Collection, State Historical Society of Wisconsin, Madison, Wis.; see also advertisements of companies seeking to hire slave hands in Richmond *Daily Dispatch*, Jan. 5, Dec. 18, 31, 1853; Dec. 22, 1856; Jan. 1, 1857; Jan. 7, Dec. 10, 31, 1858; and Apr. 6, 1859.

[18] John T. Day to Shanks, Anderson & Anderson, Nov. 9, 1849, Anderson Family Papers, University of Virginia Library, Charlottesville, Va.

After receiving this letter, the furnace owner had his manager draft a statement concerning the conduct of this worker and the circumstances surrounding his punishment and subsequent departure from the furnace:

Your letter under date of 9th Nov. is before me and contents noticed, in answer I must inform you that your man Edmund has behaved very badly & told you lies.

I have never struck him one lick on account of his work, the place he lived at last year Mr. Stevens is in the neighbourhood of our Furnace, where he had some 2 or 3 wives and would be there nearly every night in the week and Mr. Stevens complained to me that Edmund kept a continual uproar and fighting with other negroes, and that he could not stand it. I then told Edmund not to go there, and I also told Mr. Stevens if it hapened again to take Edmund and bring him to me which he did and I gave him a good dressing and have not seen him since, which was the early part of the summer. Since that time he has been plundering the neighbourhood & steeling & lying in peoples barns and robing their spring houses &c.

You will please inquire of the negroes which came from the same neighbourhood namely—Ben Swan, Randle Swan, Fister, Burbage, and Beverly Beasly all of them will pr¹ ⁄e the correctness of my statement.[19]

There are a number of significant points in this exchange, but two elements deserve special mention: first, that Edmond, the slave, knew he could get the ear of his master by pleading, in effect, "ironmaster brutality," and although his owner sent him back to the furnace, he did so with the admonition that Edmond not be severely punished; and second, that the owner of the furnace kept a copy of his manager's explanation in his files to protect himself and his enterprise from the charge that slaves were abused at his iron works.

A runaway incident that occurred at Weaver's Etna Furnace in the 1850s led to a similar revealing exchange of correspondence. A hiring agent who had secured several slave wood choppers to work at the furnace had just learned some disturbing information, as he noted in a letter to Weaver dated November 11, 1857:

I received a letter from some one with no name to it saying that Robert had left you and the reason assigned was that your [furnace] manager wished him to work in the Ore Bank and it was so dangerous that all your white hands had quit on that account. if so I am surprised for I had always thought you a different man and had always represented you as being one of the safest men to hire to as regards the treatment in the Vallie and besides I have always hired Robt William & Prince as wood choppers and I have no doubt it was done without your knowledge. if Robt has left please let me hear from you immediately as I dont want the Boy to give either of us any trouble.[20]

Weaver immediately asked his furnace managers for an explanation and received a full account of the difficulty concerning Robert:

[19] T. H. Burns, agent for Shanks & Anderson, to John T. Day, Dec. 18, 1849, *ibid.*
[20] Thomas R. Towles to Weaver, Nov. 11, 1857, Weaver Papers, Duke.

Fig. 2. Glenwood Furnace, Rockbridge County, Virginia, as it appears today. This stack, thirty-eight feet high, was erected in 1849 and is typical of the charcoal blast furnaces built and manned largely by slave labor in Virginia during the late antebellum decades. Photograph courtesy Mr. T. T. Brady, Richmond, Virginia.

On inquiry I find there is something in relation to Bob from which a tale could be manufactured, to wit. On Tuesday a week William [W. Rex] requested Bob to go to the Bank (he picking him out on a/c of being near his wife's) William thinking all [was] right left, but afterwards finding that he did not go up, saw him again on Tuesday last at which time Bob said very imputantly that you had a letter at the forge to the effect that a particular understanding was made that he (Bob) was not to work in the Bank. If that is the case (says William) I dont expect you to work there. He William at the same time requesting him (Bob) to come [to the] Furnace stating to Bob that he would write to you & if it was not in your hands he bob might expect a punishment. That was all that was said & the last & Bob is now away. Of course there is not one word of truth in regard to white hands in [the] Bank & *no danger there either.*[21]

21 Charles K. Gorgas to Weaver, Nov. 17, 1857, *ibid.* William W. Rex, a nephew of Weaver's, was one of the managers at Etna Furnace.

Once again, the ironmaster's inquiry and the manager's detailed explanation of the incident indicate that employers were well aware that they could not afford to ignore charges that they neglected owners' instructions about working conditions or that they dealt too severely with slave laborers.

Although ironmasters apparently tried to avoid excessive reliance on harsh physical punishment, there is ample evidence that the whip was employed at antebellum iron works in Virginia. The point seems to have been not to overuse the lash, to employ it to the extent that the slaves became recalcitrant or demoralized and owners became apprehensive over the health and safety of their hired bondsmen. One letter in particular touches on the entire question of discipline and coercion in such a revealing way that it deserves to be quoted at some length. The letter describes the trials of James C. Davis who was attempting to rehire a specific group of slave workers in eastern Virginia for another year's labor at his Gibraltar Forge near Lexington. His problem was not only to convince the master that they should go back to the forge but also to persuade the slaves, and one slave in particular, to return. He described his difficulties with this group of hands in a detailed letter addressed to his father, William Weaver Davis, at the forge, dated January 5, 1856:

There is some difficulty about Dickinson's hands & I hardly know how to act. When they came from over the mountain they wished to go back: & under the impression that they still wished so I hired them of Dickinson at the Ct House tuesday. Shortly after I hired them he came & told me that Elick did not wish to go, that a railroad man had offered him five dollars cash in his hands to go with him & that tickled his fancy.

But the owner thought that Elick would "get over that & be willing to go with you." If the slave's reluctance to return continued, however, Dickinson said that he would not force him to go but he promised at the same time to send the other hands. "But yesterday I received a letter from him saying that his boys had come to him & avowed they would not go, & if they did go they would run off after they got there," Davis continued. "Now I believe that this is nothing but an empty threat for the purpose of scaring their master & that it only requires decisive measures to bring them straight." If the slaves actually carried out their runaway attempt, "they would be apt to run before they got there [Gibraltar Forge] & not after they crossed the blue Ridge [Mountains], for they know that they dont understand the country well enough to start when so far from home." And if they ran away before they reached the mountains, "they will come down in Dickinson's neighborhood & he will be perfectly willing to take them back & so no harm will result in that case." Davis was reasonably certain the hands would not try to flee after they reached the forge, because in addition to their "not being used to the country," they were not "skilled in the wiles of running away," and thus would be recaptured before they could get very far. "All this is on the hypothesis that Elick goes with them," Davis noted. "If he is cooled down & kept in Jail until I choose to let him off & the others sent on I dont apprehend any difficulty whatever: because he is the ringleader and has persuaded the other's . . . who were willing to go back up to last Monday when I saw them at the Ct House." Davis could not surrender his claim to these men because "the hands through the country are hired," and, in addition, he had gotten the slaves "cheaper than I could get hands again even if I could find any for hire." He then outlined his scheme for dealing with this difficult situation:

I wrote to Mr Dickinson by this morning's mail that I could not let them off, but for him to take them to the Ct House monday morning, put Elick in Jail before the eyes of the others without saying a word as to the meaning of it, then take the others & send them on the [railroad] cars for Staunton with a pass to Gibraltar [Forge]: and after they are gone to take Elick out of Jail & hire him out there at the Ct House by the day, letting on to him that he (Dickinson) will hire him where he wishes to go when he finds a place, which he might do if I found I could make it suit to let him off; if not, I would take him over when I went. I think this plan will work.

In closing this letter the much-troubled ironmaster vented his anger and frustration with a verbal blast at Elick, the "ringleader":

This negro's perversity is but another instance of the assimilation of the negro to the dog. Inorder to make a dog like and follow you, you must whip him occasionally & be sparing of favors, or he will turn at last & bite the hand that feeds him. So with this boy. Of all those five negroes he was the only one that escaped the lash: & frequently received favors that I would have denied the others. Now he not only turns from me but tries to lead them away likewise.[22]

Several things in this letter deserve comment. First, although five of the six slaves involved had been whipped by their employer, they initially expressed a willingness to return to the same man for another year's work. Since hands were scarce at this time, their master could have hired them out elsewhere with no difficulty and clearly would have done so if the men had objected earlier about going back to the forge. Even more significant, it would seem, is the psychological game the hiring agent was forced to play with Elick and the other slaves who looked to him for leadership. The ironmaster wanted and needed these hands, but he could not simply assemble them into a coffle and drive them over the mountains. Because the master did not want to force his slaves to work where they were unwilling to reside, the hirer planned a rather elaborate charade to isolate Elick, get the other men ("who are not skilled in the wiles of running away") on a train, and place them in unfamiliar country where they would probably be unable to find their way back home if Elick failed to follow them or if, after rejoining the group at the forge, he continued to create dis-

[22] James C. Davis to William W. Davis, Jan. 5, 1856, Davis Papers.

satisfaction among the other hands. The entire incident suggests a rather complex give-and-take between master, slave, and employer that rested not on brute force but on a series of adjustments and accommodations in which the slaves did anything but sit passively by while their fate was decided. Four days later Davis reported that the owner had indeed hired the men to another party, and young Davis urged his father to insist that the hands be delivered up to them as originally promised or that a damage suit be brought against the slaves' master; "there being no hands for hire I cannot hire others in [their] place," Davis told his father, and "consequently we cannot prosecute our business."[23]

This incident illustrates another key point: a vital factor in any industrialist's ability to hire slave labor was the willingness of the slave to reside at his work site for the year. Owners of slaves were reluctant to send their bondsmen to locations where the slaves did not want to go, as one master told Weaver in 1828:

Our agreement was, if Brandus was not willing to go to you, I should not force him and on seeing Mr. Brawly, who says the boy is anxious to remain with him therefore I cannot think of compelling him to go any where it is not his wish, as that has always been my rule.[24]

This master expressed his position in exceptionally strong language, but the position itself was by no means exceptional, as a hiring agent in eastern Virginia informed Weaver in 1854 when Weaver asked the agent to secure slaves for his iron works. "I am willing to hire hands for you," the man replied, and added that he would also be hiring for another Rockbridge County ironmaster, "but that will make no in[ter]ferance as persons let their [hands] go pretty much where they please," he assured Weaver.[25]

In addition to any humanitarian considerations, owners worried that a dissatisfied slave might run away, and there was no guarantee that a valuable slave hand would run back to the protection of his master when he left a furnace or forge. As a result owners, like Elick's master in the long letter cited above, frequently respected the wishes of their slaves and refused to hire them to places where they feared the slaves might be dissatisfied, as one slaveowner wrote Weaver in 1830:

I am sorry to inform you that one of the men I hired you (Isaac) has expressed such an unwillingness to return to you, that I feared should I send him over he would run away, and perhaps be of little or no service to you during the year— I therefore thought it best to hire him in Amherst [County] where he is willing to stay, for the same you were to give—I return your bond for him in this letter. I am very sorry this has happened as perhaps it may put you to some in-

[23] James C. Davis to William W. Davis, Jan. 9, 1856, Cyrus H. McCormick Papers, McCormick Collection, State Historical Society of Wisconsin, Madison, Wis.
[24] C. Wiglesworth to Weaver, Dec. 31, 1828, Weaver Papers, Duke
[25] T. R. Towles to Weaver, Nov. 27, 1854, *ibid.*

convenience, but I hope not much. When I hired him I was under the impression he would be willing to serve you,—but I find he is not.

Another slave belonging to this same owner was also reluctant to return to Weaver's employ but agreed to do so under certain circumstances:

Sam has requested me to ask the favor of you, to permit him to stay at the establishment at which you live; he says he greatly perfers it. He also was unwilling to return; but says he would have no objection, provided, he could live at your own establishment. I hope, if it will not put you to much inconvenience, you will grant his request.[26]

The slaves' wishes obviously counted for something, and the industrial employer who was unwilling to meet the basic requests of his laboring men was risking present difficulties with his work force and future problems with his hiring.

EVEN AFTER an ironmaster secured an adequate slave force, he faced other serious problems. Key factors in the success of any manufacturing concern were the efficiency, skill, and productivity of the workers; industrialists employing slave labor on a large scale faced a formidable task in attempting to discipline and, even more important, motivate unfree labor. Weaver, of course, had the power to inflict physical punishment on any recalcitrant or troublesome slave worker, but excessive dependence on force could easily backfire and lead to even greater evils: further demoralization among his slaves, a rash of runaways, an unsavory reputation among slaveowners, slave abuse of draft animals, theft, arson, or acts of industrial sabotage carried out by skilled artisans, any of which could seriously disrupt normal furnace and forge operations. The slaves, in short, were in a position to do considerable physical and financial damage to Weaver's interests, even if they limited their activities to passive forms of resistance like work slowdowns or slipshod performance of their duties. In an effort to deal with the closely related problems of discipline and motivation, Weaver very early in his career as an iron manufacturer (at least as early as the 1820s when surviving records begin) instituted an incentive system to encourage slaves to meet and exceed their tasks. Men who did more than their required amount of work were rewarded with payment, in either cash or goods, for their extra labor, or "overwork" as it was called. In adopting this incentive system Weaver was instituting a technique that had been used in Southern iron works as early as the 1790s and that continued to be used until the end of the Civil War.[27] The object of the overwork system was to make

[26] William Staples to Weaver, Jan. 4, 1830, Weaver Papers, Virginia.
[27] Starobin, *Industrial Slavery*, 101; see also Charles B. Dew, "David Ross and the Oxford Iron Works: A Study of Industrial Slavery in the Early Nineteenth-Century South," scheduled for publication in the *William and Mary Quarterly*, April 1974.

the industrial slave a disciplined and productive worker without having to rely heavily on physical coercion.

Payment of wood choppers for overwork illustrates the way the system operated for almost all slaves at Weaver's installations. The normal task for a wood chopper in the Virginia iron region was 1½ cords per day, working a six-day week—Sunday was a traditional day of rest. Both employer and slave seem to have recognized the 1½ cord requirement as the standard task, and any ironmaster who attempted to increase the customary amount of work would be engaging in a risky enterprise that might well result in extra trouble instead of extra wood. For any wood that a slave chopped over and above his 1½ cord task, he was given credit on the company's books at the rate of 40 cents per cord, the same rate at which white wood choppers were paid. The same general system operated for every job at Weaver's furnace and forge: skilled slave ironworkers could earn overwork payments for producing more than their required quota of iron, ore-bank hands could mine and wash extra ore, colliers could tend the charcoal pits in their time off, shoemakers could make additional shoes, and even unskilled hands could earn credit, at the rate of 50 cents per day, for working at night, on Sundays, and over the traditional Christmas holidays. Other means of earning credit included weaving coal baskets; raising hogs, chickens, and eggs; packing pork; and growing corn on individual plots. Emergency situations also provided the slaves with the opportunity to earn money: if a mine had to be emptied of water, a road needed to be repaired after a storm, or a dam had to be rebuilt after a freshet.[28] Finally, some slaves were credited with a small "allowance," in effect a regular wage for, evidently, assuming responsibility for various phases of the furnace or forge operation. The highest allowance paid by Weaver, $5 a month for twelve months, went to a hired slave named Joshua Crews who worked at Etna Furnace. The exact nature of Crews's duties is unclear, but since another slave was credited for "5 Sundays at Furnace under Joshua" and since Crews's compensation was exceptionally high, $60 for the year, it seems certain that he held an important supervisory post at the furnace, perhaps a job similar to that performed by a black driver on a large plantation.[29] Other slave hands who were paid allowances of lesser amounts whose duties can be determined include Washington Coleman, a collier, who probably received his $8 "coaling allowance" in 1857 for supervising one or more charcoal pits, and Bill Jones, who was paid $1 a month for "ore carts" and was evidently in charge of the mule-drawn ore train at Etna Furnace that brought ore to the furnace site from a bank some ten miles distant.[30]

[28] See entries in Etna Furnace Negro Books, 1854–61 and 1857–60, and Buffalo Forge Negro Book, 1850–58, both in Weaver-Brady Records, Virginia.
[29] See entries for Joshua Crews and Tom Duecen, Etna Furnace Negro Books, 1854–61 and 1857–60.
[30] Etna Furnace Negro Book, 1857–60.

Entries in the Buffalo Forge and Etna Furnace "Negro Books," as these ledgers were called, indicate that most of the slave hands, both skilled and unskilled, used the overwork system to earn their own money. The most significant thing about these entries is the way in which they suggest how a sizable number of blacks took advantage of the system to carve out something of a private and individual life for themselves. Admittedly, in the process of earning overwork compensation the slaves were in one sense doing the ironmaster's bidding; they finished their required tasks before they began working for themselves and thus responded positively to the employer's attempt to motivate them. But on another level the slaves were, it seems fair to say, being their own men. They could do extra work if they wished, or they could take their time off as leisure. Even in the simple act of accepting or rejecting the overwork system, they were achieving, in at least one small phase of their existence, some measure of self-choice. If they did choose to do additional labor, the sums they earned were theirs to control, and they gained an even greater measure of personal initiative. An examination of several individual accounts will perhaps indicate what is being suggested here.

In 1858 one of Weaver's hiring agents secured four hands—Jack, Jim, Bill, and Dabney Willoughby—from a family in eastern Virginia to work for the year. The four men were assigned to Etna Furnace where they labored as wood choppers and miners. During the year the four built up overwork credits on Weaver's books for sums ranging from $10.50 to $13.50. They drew against their credit at the company store for small "luxury" items like coffee and sugar, but in June three of the men decided to use part of their money to buy themselves vacation time at home. Their request for leave was granted, and they left the furnace. While they were away they were debited at the standard overwork rate of 50 cents per day for their time off—ten days for two of the men and two weeks for the third. They returned to Etna at the end of their stay at home and served out the balance of the year. The fourth member of this group, Jim Willoughby, evidently decided not to spend his money in this fashion in order to draw as much cash as possible at the end of the year. In December, just before the four men returned home for Christmas, he drew his remaining credit in cash, which amounted to $10.[31]

Husbanding of cash was characteristic of a number of slave hands; men like Mat Robinson, a miner, earned $5.00 in overwork in one year, spent a carefully allotted 50 cents of it for tobacco, and then drew $4.50 in cash in December; Elec the Collier, as he was listed in the books, earned $13.75 for extra coaling and by raising a hog in 1857 and collected $10.00 in cash at the Christmas break. At the other end of the spectrum was a slave like John Sims, a furnace laborer, who spent his overwork faster than he could

[31] *Ibid.*

Fig. 3. A late nineteenth-century photograph of Buffalo Forge, Virginia, showing many of the buildings in existence during the antebellum period. In the foreground are the grist mill (center), the blacksmith shop (right), and the carpenter shop (extreme left). The harness shop is the square building in the right center, visible between the grist mill and the blacksmith shop. Immediately behind and to the left of the grist mill is the Buffalo Forge store, where slaves drew on their overwork accounts for food, tobacco, cloth, and other merchandise. The flour mill can be seen in the left background, and the mule stable stands between this building and the carpenter shop. The guest cottage and Weaver's home are on the hill overlooking these structures (right background). Photograph courtesy Mr. T. T. Brady, Richmond, Virginia.

earn it on tobacco, coffee, and clothing. Sims ended the year 1858 owing the company store $6.84 but was able to work off his debt the following year by Sunday labor and ore washing, and he made enough additional compensation to continue his purchases of coffee and tobacco on a fairly regular basis.[32]

Sims's case illustrates a second major intent of the overwork system. In addition to motivating the slaves to become efficient and productive workers, it could be used by the employer as a disciplinary tool. Sims had a taste for consumer goods that outran his ability to pay for them, and the furnace manager allowed him to indulge himself to the point where Sims was forced to do extra work in order to pay off his debt. The ledgers also show that slaves who failed to meet their normal task could have the value of their unfinished work deducted from whatever credit they had built up. Two hired slaves, Reubin and Dudley Camack, were, respectively, five and

[32] *Ibid.*

Fig. 4. Black and white colliers atop a charcoal pile in the upper South during the nineteenth century (probably the 1870s). Note the chopped wood stacked and ready for coaling in the left background. Photograph courtesy Mr. William T. Turner, University of Kentucky, Hopkinsville Community College.

seven cords of wood short when a check of wood choppers was made in August 1858. As a result, they were debited for their shortages at the rate of 40 cents per cord, the same amount paid for cutting extra wood. Several other slaves suffered similar deductions for unfinished tasks as miners and wood choppers. In all of these cases, however, the slaves were able to work off their debt and build up additional credit in their favor, usually by turning to some alternative form of labor for which they received payment. The two Camack slaves, for example, removed their debt for unfinished wood chopping by Sunday labor. In fact it may be that these two men purposely came in short on their wood cutting, intending to make up their deficiency by working together on Sundays. This is suggested by the fact that most of the slave choppers met the $1\frac{1}{2}$ cords per day task with relative ease, and, in this particular case, both of the men worked the same number of Sundays, twenty. They drew on their accounts for flour, coffee, sugar, and tobacco during the year and ended their term of service in December with cash coming to them.[33] Wood choppers were not highly skilled workers in the charcoal iron industry, but they still could amass consider-

[33] *Ibid.*

87

able amounts of overwork credit if they chose to do so. To cite one example, over a two year period a black chopper named Daniel Henry working at Glenwood Furnace in Rockbridge County cut 248½ cords over his required task, worked 36 Sundays, and made 36 standard-size charcoal measuring baskets in his spare time. His overwork earnings for the two years totaled $127.66, which he drew mainly in coffee and other store purchases during the year, but he had enough credit remaining at the end of each year to make fairly substantial Christmas purchases—$22.58 in 1847 and $13.50 in 1848.[34]

The slaves who were generally in the best position to take advantage of the overwork system, however, were the more skilled artisans. Weaver's own forge hands regularly earned relatively large sums by heating, working, and finishing extra tonnages of iron at Buffalo Forge. Sam Williams, Henry Towles, Jim Garland, Henry Mathews, Tooler, and Henry Hunt, Jr., all slave ironworkers owned by Weaver, were paid from $3 to $5 per ton for their overwork, and all of these men used their exceptional position to good advantage. Henry Towles, for example, who was a heater at the forge, was credited with $31.80 in overwork in 1852, $36.16 in 1853, $55.28 in 1855, and $93.53 in 1856. In 1858, when his account was transferred to a new ledger, he carried a balance of $102.53 in his favor to the new book. Towles drew most of his overwork in cash, but another of Weaver's forge hands, Henry Hunt, Jr., used the credit he earned primarily to buy quality clothing, like three $6 coats and a $4 pair of pants in 1850 and "1 fine suit (coat & pants)" valued at $18 in 1854.[35] The individualism of each slave shows through clearly in these and other accounts: John White, who chopped 43¼ extra cords of wood in 1856, Allen Jackson, who devoted his off hours in 1856 to raising chickens and a hog, and Landis Cartmill, a skilled basket weaver who earned $17.32 in 1857 by making fifty-two charcoal baskets for Etna Furnace.[36]

The case of Sam Williams demonstrates the degree to which a skilled industrial slave could use his training and ability to live a life that probably deserves to be called quasi-free, or something like it. Williams worked molten iron into finished merchant bars at Buffalo Forge and received the highest overwork rate paid to any of Weaver's forge hands, $5 per ton. He, like a number of Weaver's skilled slaves, also had individual plots of land at the forge that were laid off and planted in the spring by the regular force of agricultural workers. These farm hands, including the white overseer, a white agricultural laborer, and several slaves, planted the plots along with Weaver's own fields as part of the spring corn planting.[37] Williams and the

[34] Glenwood Furnace Negro Book, 1847–49, Anderson Ledgers, University of Virginia Library, Charlottesville, Va.

[35] Buffalo Forge Negro Book, 1850–58.

[36] Etna Furnace Negro Book, 1857–60.

[37] Entries for Apr. 23, 27, 1861, Daniel C. E. Brady, Home Journal, 1860–65, McCormick Collection, State Historical Society of Wisconsin, Madison, Wis.

other forge hands then worked their own lots during the summer, and when they brought in their crops they could either sell them to Weaver or consume them themselves. By working extra tonnages of iron, growing corn, and raising hogs, Williams earned enough cash during the 1850s to supplement his own and his wife's diet with regular purchases of sugar and coffee, buy "3 yds. cotton cloth for Nancy," his wife, to cite one 1855 entry, and, most surprising of all, open a savings account at a Lexington bank.[38] Williams, who was forty years of age in 1860, played an important part in establishing the high reputation that Weaver's "W" brand bar iron enjoyed among Virginia blacksmiths and commission merchants, and Williams obviously used his skills to improve materially the quality of the life he and his wife were able to lead under slavery.[39]

One of the most significant ways in which the overwork system allowed male slaves to achieve some measure of personal dignity and pride was the opportunity it gave men like Sam Williams to provide cash or small luxuries for their wives. Tooler, a skilled slave artisan who had been raised at Buffalo Forge, drew $5 in cash to send to his wife in 1850, and other entries in his account show that he used part of his overwork credit in 1852 to make three trips to Lynchburg, perhaps to see his wife. Other examples of men using their overwork credit to acquire items for their wives include Bill Jones, the ore cart supervisor at Etna Furnace, "1 pair Brogans for his wife," $2, and for a slave identified as "Daniel Dumb Boy," several entries for "cash to Louisa."[40]

Additional evidence of slave marriages appears elsewhere in the records of Weaver's enterprises. A number of slaves, both hired and owned by Weaver, who had wives in the vicinity regularly left Buffalo Forge after the work day ended on Saturday to visit their wives and returned in time for work on Monday morning.[41] Slave men whose wives lived longer distances away sometimes tried to deal with this separation in their own way.

---

[38] Buffalo Forge Negro Book, 1850–58; John A. Rex to J. D. Davidson, Feb. 25, 1855, Davidson Papers. The text of the letter from Rex, another one of Weaver's nephews, to Davidson, a Lexington lawyer, reads as follows: "I wish to ask you one question whether Sam Williams can draw his money from the Savings Bank or if he cannot. As Sam and Henry Nash has got a bet for his watch against the said Nash['s] watch. It is my opinion that he can draw his money if he gives the Directors of the Bank 10 days notice. After he receives the money he wishes to show it to Henry Nash, and then he will return the said money back to the Bank again. As I was witness to the said bargain." Davidson noted on the rear of this letter that he had directed Rex "to confer with Wm Weaver" about the matter. Henry Nash was a free black cooper who lived in the vicinity of Buffalo Forge. Manuscript Population Schedules, Rockbridge County, Virginia, Eighth Census of the United States, 1860.

[39] Williams's age is given in a "Descriptive List of Negroes at Buffalo Forge, Rockbridge Co., Va.," 1865, Weaver Papers, Duke; he is described as five feet ten inches tall and his color is listed as "yellow." On the quality of Weaver's iron, see William D. Couch to Weaver, Feb. 9, 1859; McCorkle & Co. to Weaver, Feb. 22, 1859; and Thomas G. Godwin to Weaver, Mar. 2, 1859, all *ibid.*

[40] Buffalo Forge Negro Book, 1850–58, and Etna Furnace Negro Book, 1857–60; Jordan Davis & Co. to Weaver, Oct. 11, 31, 1851, Weaver Papers, Duke.

[41] See entries in Brady, Home Journal.

Booker, a slave chopper at Etna in 1854, was noted in the furnace time-book as having "lost two weeks going to see his wife." Perhaps he had permission to make this trip, however, since his overwork account shows that he was docked only 50 cents, one day's pay, on April 28, 1854, as a "day lost going to see wife."[42] Even more revealing is a letter from Weaver's manager at Etna Furnace describing his difficulties with two hands in 1862:

You ask about Griffen. I consider him a triffling hand.—He laid up here very often & for long periods—but it was only when we worked him about the Furnace[;] he laid up so often that we had finaly to take him away. Par objected to changing so often. tell him that you will put him in the wood chopping when he gets well. & I will guarentee he will soon be out—that is his object now in laying up. I found that he laid up very seldom when he could get a chance to run to his wife.[43]

The incidence of slave resistance at Weaver's installations is difficult to judge, but if this letter is indicative, the problems of slave motivation and efficiency were not by any means completely solved by the overwork system. In order for the system to work, Weaver's slave hands had to exceed their required tasks voluntarily, and if the slave were a skilled artisan, Weaver and his managers were apparently willing to tolerate a certain amount of neglect of duty in order to avoid difficulty with key black personnel. This point can be illustrated by the work records of several of the Buffalo Forge slaves contained in a daily journal kept by Weaver's nephew-in-law and second in command, Daniel C. E. Brady, from October 1860 to June 1865. Tooler, one of Weaver's heaters, is frequently described by Brady as "loafing," but there is no indication that Tooler was disciplined, physically or otherwise, for his performance; when he was running out iron or drawing bars he regularly earned substantial overtime credit that was not docked for his slipshod work on other occasions. Edgar, a miller who worked at Weaver's flour mill, is another slave who is listed as "loafing" on numerous occasions, again with no record of punishment. Most of the Buffalo Forge slave hands, however, are regularly listed at their jobs with no indication that Weaver or Brady were dissatisfied with their performance. Sam Williams is typical of this larger group; "Sam at work" is the most consistent entry in Brady's journal, perhaps because Williams was putting something away for himself at that bank in Lexington.[44]

Unskilled slave workers had much less leverage with Weaver and his managers, of course, but they did have the power to accept or reject the master's incentives and they had rights set by tradition if not by law—like a reasonable daily task, Christmas holidays, and Sundays off—that they would go considerable lengths to defend. The slaves' insistence on their

[42] Etna Furnace Time Book, and Etna Furnace Negro Book, 1854-61, Weaver-Brady Records, Virginia.
[43] W. W. Rex to Brady, Mar. 22, 1862, Weaver Papers, Virginia.
[44] Entries in Brady, Home Journal.

annual Christmas vacation is demonstrated in a report Weaver's furnace managers made in November 1830 explaining why they would not be able to keep the furnace in blast during the entire month of December:

We had thought [of] blowing through the Christmas holy days and going on as long as possible, but as our white hands are few and the most part of the blacks will be going home and the few remaining not willing to be closely confined we have concluded to stop up for a short time during Christmas.[45]

Similarly, a potentially explosive altercation at Etna Furnace in 1854 showed the risks one of Weaver's own slaves was willing to take in order to maintain Sunday as a day he alone controlled.

Anthony was told saterday evening to start to [Buffalo] forge this morning [Sunday]—I waited till about 10 oclock and finding that he had not started I asked him the reason[.] he said it was Sunday and that he was not going till tomorrow—with some other impudence to me I collared him and he resisted & struck me—I struck him on the head with a rock. you please will see about the matter.

The irate manager closed his letter with a significant postscript: "He said that this was Sunday and his day and that he was not going [to] take it up in going to your place."[46] Unfortunately there is no information in surviving records that reveals whether Weaver inflicted further punishment on his bondsman, but the incident shows clearly the determination of one slave to preserve his day of rest and probably speaks for a view that was universally held among Southern slaves, industrial and otherwise.

The most serious labor difficulties at Weaver's installations were caused by slaves running away, but this evidently did not become a major problem until late in the Civil War. Between 1829 and 1861 at least thirteen slaves ran off from Weaver's employ, with the bulk of these flights (ten of the thirteen) occurring during several years in the late 1820s and early 1830s when a manager at one of Weaver's iron works evidently caused a considerable amount of dissatisfaction among the slave force. All but one of these runaways were hired slaves who returned to the counties in eastern Virginia from which they had been secured and there either hid out in the vicinity of their homes until recaptured or, in several instances, came in to their owners with accounts of mistreatment by overseers, sickness, or bad food.[47] But the runaway problem did not seriously endanger Weaver's furnace and forge operations at any time during the antebellum period, and

---

45 Jordan Davis & Co. to Weaver, Nov. 24, 1830, Weaver Papers, Duke.
46 John K. Watkins to Weaver, July 30, 1854, *ibid.*
47 William Watson for Joel W. Brown, Jailor, to Post Master, Lexington, Va., Apr. 19, 1829; W. E. Dickinson to Abraham Davis, Apr. 19, 1829; James C. Dickinson to Weaver, May 10, 1829; James Rose to Weaver, Mar. 8, 1830; Elizabeth Mathews to Weaver, Mar. 29, 1830; Lewis Rawlings to Weaver, Aug. 22, 1832; Charles Perrow to Weaver, Sept. 17, Oct. 26, 1833; and John A. Turpim to Weaver, Aug. 28, 1854, all in Weaver Papers, Duke; Henry A. McCormick to Weaver, Dec. 29, 1855, Weaver Papers, Virginia; see also entries under "Lawson," Etna Furnace Negro Book, 1857–60.

this was true of the first three years of the war as well.[48] In June 1864, however, a large scale cavalry raid by Union forces commanded by General
David Hunter swept through the valley iron district and provided several
of the Buffalo Forge slaves with an opportunity to gain their freedom.
"I regret to inform you that your boy Beverly went off with the enemy
upon that raid through this country on 12 June," Daniel Brady informed
the owner of a hired slave. "I lost three of my own men at the same time,"
he continued, and "I was fortunate in escaping myself & sustaining no loss
of other property."[49] In all, five Buffalo Forge slaves made it to freedom
with Hunter's troopers; and included in the three escaped slaves who had
belonged to Weaver was Warder, a skilled teamster who had hauled pig
iron and supplies between Etna Furnace and the forge for a number of
years. More of the Buffalo Forge hands undoubtedly would have fled had
they not been moved to an isolated farm on the day the federals occupied
Lexington.[50] The forge property itself escaped destruction, and Union
troops did not reappear in the vicinity for the remainder of the war.

When a reasonably good chance for successful escape presented itself,
black ironworkers, like the vast majority of slaves throughout the South,
wasted little time in striking for freedom. In the absence of such an opportunity, however, Weaver's black artisans and laborers appear to have
learned how to live with, and cope with, industrial slave conditions. Perhaps the most impressive evidence underscoring this point came in the
transition from slavery to freedom at the close of the Civil War. Three
brief entries in journals kept at Buffalo Forge by Daniel Brady describe
events of monumental significance for the black men, women, and children
working and living there:

Friday May 26, 1865 Declared free by order of the military authorities.
Saturday May 27, 1865 All hands quit work as they considered themselves free.
I made a speech to them, & read the order No 2 of Genl Gregg. J G Updike,
Alex Hamilton, Jno D Ewing, W W Rex & Thos Edwards present.
Monday May 29, 1865 Commenced work on free labor.[51]

Brady, who assumed ownership and primary direction of all of Weaver's
properties when Weaver died in March 1863, did not write down what he
said in his address, but subsequent events make clear that he told the newly
freed blacks that he intended to keep Buffalo Forge in operation and continue farming on the Weaver lands. Those workers who wished to keep their
jobs could do so, and they would be paid on a piecework or wage basis depending on the specific position they held. The general orders that Brady
read to the assembled workers had been issued by General J. Irvin Gregg, the

[48] Two slaves tried to escape in 1863 but were apprehended in Lynchburg. Brady to James
D. Davidson, Dec. 9, 1863, Davidson Papers.
[49] Brady to James Stewart, July 7, 1864, Weaver Papers, Virginia.
[50] Entries for June 11, 12, 14, 1864, Brady, Home Journal.
[51] Buffalo Forge Journal, 1859-66, Weaver-Brady Records, Virginia; Brady, Home Journal.

federal commander of the military subdistrict of Lynchburg, on May 18, 1865, and they were published in the Lynchburg press five days later. Gregg's orders contained both a declaration of the former slaves' rights and a statement of their responsibilities:

The operation of existing laws is to make them *free*, but not to give them any claim whatever upon, or rights in connection with the property of former owners. They are at liberty to make any contract or agreement concerning themselves that a white man may, and equally bound to abide by it.

The former masters had "the right to refuse them anything that he might deny to a perfect stranger," the orders continued, "and is no more bound to feed, clothe, or protect them than if he had never been their master." The freedmen might "remain with him if he and they both desire it, and agree on the terms, in which case each party is equally bound by the contract." The orders concluded by admonishing blacks "that they must work for their support now, the same as before they were free; in some instances, perhaps, even harder" and informed them that "destitute" rations would not be issued to able-bodied laborers unless they could show they had tried but were unable to obtain work. A final paragraph read:

All colored persons living in the country, are informed that it is much better for them to remain there than to come to the already over-stocked city, and that they will not be permitted to come here for work or subsistence, unless they cannot obtain them where they are.[52]

With Brady offering continued employment and with the military authorities in Lynchburg telling the freedmen in rather blunt language to keep their present jobs, some forty-three men and women, almost the entire black work force at Buffalo Forge when emancipation occurred, accepted labor contracts. Work resumed "on free labor," as Brady described it in his journal on May 29, 1865, three days after the slaves learned officially that they were free.[53]

The length of time the freedmen remained at Buffalo Forge offers the only real evidence as to their motives for staying on. For some, the military's position seems to have been a deciding factor. Two men who had been hired at the beginning of 1865 left within a matter of days after signing their contracts and two of Weaver's former slaves quit in mid-July. Six men who had been hired from the same household—George, Bob, John, William, Alfred, and Stephen Glasgow—all signed three-month contracts to chop wood, served out the terms of their agreement, and then departed. Perhaps Gregg's General Orders No. 2 had some influence on them and on the remainder of those who did not work beyond 1865; eleven of the

[52] Lynchburg *Daily Virginian*, May 23, 1865.
[53] Buffalo Forge Negro Book, 1865–72.

forty-three who signed initial contracts had left by August 30 and seven more departed by the end of the year. For the twenty-one who can be identified as working into 1866 and beyond, however, the decision to remain seems to have been a choice they themselves made. Included in this number were almost all of the skilled artisans who had drawn and hammered Weaver's iron during the antebellum and Civil War years.[54]

For those freedmen who began working at Buffalo Forge on the morning of May 29, 1865, conversion to a wage basis presented few problems since all the laboring force was familiar with the overwork system. Now the men would be paid for all the work they did, and they would assume the responsibility of providing for themselves and their families. Sam Williams, Henry Towles, Henry Mathews, Henry Hunt, Jr., and Tooler all signed contracts to work for three months at $4 per ton for all the iron they produced, while they furnished their food and other supplies out of their wages. Sam Williams's wife, Nancy, went to work as a dairymaid at $4 a month. Williams and his wife were still working at Buffalo Forge in 1872, as were Towles, Mathews, and Hunt, when their accounts were transferred to a new ledger, and they can no longer be traced in surviving records; Tooler's accounts were closed in December 1868. Most of the remaining freedmen at Buffalo Forge who had once belonged to Weaver also accepted initial contracts of three months' duration for work as forge hands, wood choppers, shoemakers, carpenters, teamsters, and farmworkers. As mentioned above, employment was also offered to those men who had been hired at the beginning of 1865 for a year's labor. A number of these men had been employed by Weaver and Brady on a regular basis for a considerable length of time, some since the 1850s, and they formed the bulk of the freedmen who signed on as wood cutters, at the rate of 66 2/3 cents per cord. Generally those men who had been hired as slaves stayed for shorter periods of time than the more skilled workers who had previously been owned by Weaver. But a sizable number of the former hired slave hands served out their three-month contracts, others remained until the end of the year, and several worked for two or three years.[55]

LOOKING BACK over the entire black labor experience at Weaver's iron works, the smooth and rapid conversion to a free labor situation in 1865 seems particularly significant. Both skilled and unskilled workers in appreciable numbers made the transition to a wage basis at the jobs they had held as slaves, a pattern that was repeated by slave artisans and laborers at other

[54] *Ibid.* In the case of four of the forty-three who signed contracts, it is impossible to determine from their accounts how long they remained.
[55] *Ibid.*

iron works not only in Virginia but elsewhere in the South.[56] Even though local military officers might not like it, those workers who did not wish to remain at Buffalo Forge could leave; some did so at once, some left after several weeks or at the expiration of their initial contracts, and some stayed for years. Those who remained for more extended periods did so not because of military compulsion or because slavery had infantilized them or rendered them incapable of making a decision without white guidance; they stayed, it seems clear, simply because they saw an opportunity to use the skills they had acquired under slavery to earn a living for themselves and, for those with wives and children, for their families. Equally important, it seems fair to say that they had not been so mistreated as industrial slaves that they could not continue to work in the same job at the same place after emancipation. This is not meant to suggest that slavery under Weaver, Brady, and their various managers was an institution that lay lightly on the shoulders of the black laborers who worked Weaver's furnace, forge, and fields. Weaver's slaves were sometimes whipped,[57] black (and white) iron-workers occasionally suffered from the poor quality or inadequate food and clothing available at the blast furnace site,[58] and Weaver was not above selling several slaves into Louisiana in the late 1850s when he thought their conduct warranted it.[59] Perhaps most important of all, the black men and women who manned Weaver's operations had to cope psychologically with the prospect that the rest of their lives would in all likelihood be spent in bondage. But at the same time, day in and day out, the central tendency at Weaver's installations was for slavery to function more through mutual accommodation than outright repression. Because Weaver had to go into a tight hiring market year after year and because the success of his various enterprises was, in many ways, controlled by the slaves he employed, measures like compensation for overwork grew into features of

[56] Records documenting the transition of a large number of black workers from slave to free labor almost identical to that which occurred at Buffalo Forge can be found in the Graham Ledgers and Papers, dealing with the operations of David Graham's iron works in Wythe County in southwestern Virginia, in the University of Virginia Library, Charlottesville, Va.; see especially Ledgers "L" 1857–59, "M" 1859–64, "N" 1864–68, and "E" 1868–71. For the post-war use of a substantial force of former slave workers by the most important Richmond iron manufacturer, see Charles B. Dew, *Ironmaker to the Confederacy: Joseph R. Anderson and the Tredegar Iron Works* (New Haven, 1966), 313–14; for a similar transition of black labor labor from slavery to freedom at a major Alabama iron works in 1865, see Robert H. McKenzie, "The Shelby Iron Company: A Note on Slave Personality after the Civil War," *Journal of Negro History*, 58 (1973): 341–48.

[57] At least two instances of hired slaves being whipped can be documented; see Jordan Davis & Co. to Weaver, May 26, 1830; and William W. Rex to Brady, Oct. 26, 1860, both in Weaver Papers, Duke.

[58] See Jordan Davis & Co. to Weaver, Mar. 25, Aug. 11, 1830; Jordan Davis & Co. to Abraham W. Davis, Aug. 24, 1830; Charles K. Gorgas to Brady, Mar. 11, Apr. 2, 1860; William W. Rex to Brady, May 29, June 29, Sept. 6, 21, 26, Oct. 13, 1860; and Rex to Weaver, Aug. 7, 1860, all *ibid.*; Gorgas to Weaver, Mar. 29, Apr. 6, 1859; and Rex to Brady, Mar. 15, 1861, Weaver Papers, Virginia.

[59] J. E. Carson to Weaver, Mar. 12, May 30, June 27, 1859; William W. Rex to Weaver, Aug. 15, 1860; and G. W. Johnson to Weaver, Oct. 29, 1860, all in Weaver Papers, Duke.

primary importance in the functioning of his slave system. And because of things like the overwork system, black and white managed to find a way to live together at Weaver's iron works without maltreatment and excessive use of physical force permanently poisoning relations between the two groups. In this instance, industrial slavery did not totally degrade and brutalize the black workers; in fact it seems in some ways to have done something quite different, to have provided these men with an environment in which they could develop some sense of personal dignity and individual initiative in spite of the psychological and physical confines of their bondage. Or at least so it appears. If this analysis is correct, then we clearly need to take a closer look at the industrial phase of the South's peculiar institution. Such an examination may tell us a good deal about the nature of slavery in the American South.

Sam Williams, Forgeman:
The Life of an Industrial Slave in the Old South

CHARLES B. DEW

WILLIAM WEAVER was the leading ironmaster in Rockbridge County, and perhaps in the entire Valley, when he died at his home at Buffalo Forge, Virginia, in March 1863. During his eighty-three years he had built up a legendary fortune which, at the time of his death, included his iron-making facilities and rich farmlands centered at Buffalo Forge, over 20,000 additional acres of land scattered across three Virginia counties, and a force of seventy slaves—twenty-six men, fourteen women, and thirty children—that made him the largest slave owner in the county.[1] The inventory of his estate provided a detailed listing of his personal property—his "goods and chattels," in the language of the law—and along with entries for items like feather beds, rocking chairs, farm implements, and draft animals was a careful enumeration and appraisal of his slave holdings.[2] The lengthy list evaluating Weaver's slaves included the following brief notations:

One male slave	Sam Williams	$2,800.00
One male slave	Sam Williams Senior	0 000.00
One female slave	Sally	500.00
One female slave	Nancy	1,500.00
One female slave	Lydia	2,000.00
One female slave	Caroline and two children	2,500.00
Two female slaves	Mary Caroline and Julia	600.00

These entries constituted one of the rare instances when the name of Sam Williams and the names of his father (Sam Williams,

Senior), his mother (Sally), his wife (Nancy), two of their children (Lydia and Caroline), and two of their grandchildren (Mary Caroline and Julia) appeared on a legal document. And it is symbolic of the status of slaves as property that two of Sam and Nancy Williams's grandchildren—Caroline's "two children" in the appraisal—were not even identified by name on this occasion. The public record, in short, is sparse indeed on the life of Sam Williams and his family.

As might be expected, Sam Williams did not leave letters, diaries, journals, or other manuscript materials behind, either— the kind of documentary evidence that Weaver and his family left in abundance. Like most slaves in the American South, Sam Williams never learned to read or write; the closest thing we have to a document written by him is an "X" he made over his name on a work contract he entered into in 1867.[3] No member of the Williams family, as far as we know, ever talked to an interviewer from the Federal Writers' Project or from Fisk or Southern University when their invaluable oral histories of slavery were being compiled in the nineteen-twenties and thirties.[4] Yet it is possible to discover a great deal about Sam Williams and his family, and I would offer that they are, on many grounds, eminently worth knowing. They deserve our attention not only because they were people caught up in the American system of human bondage and thus illustrate something of the nature of the antebellum South's most significant institution. They also warrant our best efforts at understanding because, if we look carefully, we can catch at least a glimpse of them as men and women who lived out human lives despite the confines and cruelties of their enslavement. Their love and affection, their joys and sorrows, their times of trial and moments of triumph come through to us —imperfectly, to be sure, but visibly nonetheless, in spite of their inability to speak to us through traditional historical sources. This essay will attempt, in some small measure, to speak for them.

William Weaver became an ironmaster, a slave owner, and a Virginian almost by accident. He was born in 1781 on a farm near Philadelphia, and he spent most of his first forty or so years in and around that city, where he developed a series of successful business enterprises. As a merchant, miller, and textile manufacturer, Weaver began accumulating enough surplus capital to look elsewhere for profitable investments, and the War of 1812 seemed to create some excellent prospects in the Valley of Virginia.[5] The brisk wartime demand for iron prompted him to form a partnership in 1814 with Thomas Mayburry, another Philadelphia merchant, who had several years' experience in the Pennsylvania and Maryland iron business. The firm of Mayburry & Weaver purchased two iron properties in the Valley in the summer of 1814: Union Forge (which Weaver later renamed Buffalo Forge), located on Buffalo Creek some nine miles south of Lexington in Rockbridge County, Virginia; and Etna and Retreat furnaces, two charcoal blast furnaces approximately eighteen miles southwest of Union Forge in neighboring Botetourt County.[6] Retreat Furnace was abandoned rather quickly, but the firm launched extensive rebuilding projects at Etna Furnace and Union Forge and soon had both properties in full operation.[7]

Weaver did not move to Virginia immediately, however. Mayburry came down to manage the ironworks and supervise renovations at both installations, but Weaver remained in Philadelphia to raise needed capital and look after his business interests there. Over the next few years, Weaver sank close to $40,000 into the Virginia iron-making venture.[8] Among the more valuable acquisitions made with this money during the early years of Mayburry and Weaver's partnership was a growing force of slaves at both Etna Furnace and Union Forge.

The first slaves acquired by the firm were purchased in the fall of 1815. The seller was John S. Wilson, one of the Virginia ironmasters from whom Weaver and Mayburry had bought their furnaces and forge the previous year. Wilson had a number of slaves he wished to dispose of, and Mayburry wanted and needed these hands, but the two men could not agree on a price. Wilson apparently grew tired of dickering with Mayburry and decided he might be better off talking directly to the man who controlled the firm's finances.

In late October 1815, he journeyed north to Philadelphia, and there he and Weaver completed the deal. Weaver paid $3,200 for eleven slaves, divided into two very distinct groups. The first parcel consisted of an ironworker named Tooler, his wife, Rebecca, and her four children, all boys: Bill, seventeen, Robert, seven, Tooler, four, and Joe, two. The father and the oldest son, Bill, promised an immediate return to the firm since their services would be available without delay. It would be several years before Robert, Tooler (Jr.), and Joe could enter the work force, but since they were all boys, there was a strong likelihood that they might also be productive furnace or forge hands at some future point.

The second group of slaves Weaver bought from Wilson, however, contained no males at all. This parcel was made up of a slave woman named Mary and her four daughters: Sally, thirteen, Amey, ten, Louisa, six, and Georgianna, two.[9] In this instance, Weaver appears to have been looking toward the future labor needs of his ironworks in a far different way from the way he did with the acquisition of Tooler and his family. By securing the ownership of Mary and her daughters, Weaver was, in effect, seeking to ensure that his slave force could be built up, at least to some extent, by natural increase. Mary clearly seems to have been, in Weaver's eyes, a "breeding woman," to use a phrase Weaver himself employed on another occasion to describe a similar situation.[10] The sale papers contain no mention of Mary's husband, and there is no indication in the surviving records that he was ever acquired by Weaver or Mayburry. He may have lived near Etna Furnace or Union Forge, so the sale of his wife and daughters to Weaver might not have separated the family. Since Mary had several more children after Wilson sold her, there is a strong possibility that her husband lived close by, but there is no way to be sure. One thing is certain, however. In obtaining Mary and her daughters, Weaver made an investment that was to pay rich dividends. In the years that lay ahead, this slave family would play a monumental role in shaping the fortunes of Weaver's iron-making venture in Virginia, a role that was in many ways as significant as that of Weaver himself.

Mary and her children settled at Etna Furnace. There, probably in 1817 when she was fifteen years old, Sally—Mary's oldest daughter—married a man named Sam Williams, who was one of the skilled slave ironworkers Weaver and Mayburry were constantly seeking to add to their labor force. Sam and Sally Williams had their first child, a girl, in 1817, and they named her Mary, undoubtedly for her grandmother. Three years later, Sally gave birth to another child, a boy this time, and she and her husband named their new baby after his father, Sam Williams.[11]

Very little is known about Sam Williams, Sr., because most of the records dealing with Weaver's early iron-making activities in Virginia have not survived. According to a slave register compiled at Buffalo Forge during the Civil War, Sally's husband was born in 1795, but that date was probably a rough approximation.[12] The appraisal of him at the time of Weaver's death in 1863— "no value"—suggests that he was physically or mentally incapacitated and unable to perform useful work at age sixty-eight or so, an assumption reinforced by the fact that other slave men of similar age had values of $200 to $300 beside their names on the 1863 estate inventory. Other fragmentary evidence indicates the cause of his disability. In 1832 when one of Weaver's managers was in desperate need of a skilled worker to fill in temporarily for a sick hand, he spoke to Sam about taking a turn at the forge. Sam refused; "he objects [because of] . . . his eyes (which is in fact a very great objection might in all probability loose [sic] them if continued in the forge)," the manager told Weaver.[13] Ironworkers, both black and white, were in constant danger of eye injuries from sparks and flying bits of red-hot metal, and Sam Williams, Sr., seems to have suffered such an injury, or perhaps a series of them. Clearly his eyes were badly damaged while he was still a relatively young man; he would have been in his middle or late thirties in 1832 and, if sound, still in his most productive years as a slave—a "prime hand," in the language of the trade. He may well have been blind by 1863, when the county appraisers examined, itemized, and evaluated "the goods and chattels of William Weaver deceased" and entered a string of zeroes after the name Sam Williams Senior.

Toward the end of 1823, when Sam and Sally Williams's boy, Sam, was three years old, Weaver took up residence at Union Forge. Weaver's presence in Virginia was the result of the floundering financial condition of his iron-making enterprise there. Despite the substantial amount of capital that he had poured into the blast furnace and forge operations since 1814—almost $40,000 —Mayburry & Weaver had still not returned a profit on their investment (which seems to have consisted largely of Thomas Mayburry's rather limited managerial skills and William Weaver's money). With that much money at stake, Weaver felt that he had no choice but to move to the Valley and try to pull things together.[14] Not long after his arrival at the forge, he renamed the property after the creek that supplied water power to the works.

101

The name Union Forge had not brought much luck to the two Yankees who made up the firm of Mayburry & Weaver; perhaps Buffalo Forge would do better.

A year's experience of working firsthand with Mayburry apparently convinced Weaver of something he had suspected for some time—that his partner was incompetent. As a result Weaver moved early in 1825 to dissolve their partnership and divide the assets of the firm.[15] Prominent among these assets were the "Wilson negroes," the name that both Mayburry and Weaver regularly used to describe the first slaves bought by the partnership in 1815. Their argument over the ownership of the "Wilson negroes"—Tooler and his wife and children, and Mary and her children (including Sally Williams) and grandchildren (including Sam Williams, Jr.)—soon brought to light an interesting fact, one that revealed a great deal about Weaver and his business practices. When Weaver purchased these slaves from John Wilson in 1815, he took title to them in his own name, not in the name of the firm of Mayburry & Weaver. He had done this, he assured Wilson at the time, only because he feared that Mayburry "might have some religious scruples" about owning slaves.[16] Mayburry did not discover Weaver's delicate concern for the health of his soul until Weaver moved to dissolve their association in 1824, nine years after these slaves had been purchased, and demanded that Mayburry surrender the entire Wilson slave force. Mayburry, who was living at Etna Furnace, where a number of these slaves worked, refused to do so, on the quite reasonable grounds that Weaver had duped him in the original transaction. Their clash over these slaves was one of a series of heated disputes between the two men that led to Weaver's filing suit against Mayburry and throwing the entire matter into the tortuously slow machinery of the Virginia chancery courts.[17] It was eleven years before the two former partners finally reached a compromise (in the form of an out-of-court settlement) that brought a measure of satisfaction to both men. Their settlement, made in the summer of 1836, also brought with it the seeds of bitter anguish for many of the slaves involved.

In their article of agreement signed on August 3, 1836, Weaver and Mayburry agreed to a division of the "Wilson negroes." On January 1, 1837, Mayburry was to turn over to Weaver the bulk of these slaves still in his possession. Since Weaver already had

Tooler and his wife and children at Buffalo Forge, that family remained intact under Weaver's ownership. Mary's family was not so fortunate, however. Mayburry still had Mary and her children and grandchildren at Etna Furnace, and his share of the human assets of the firm was to include Mary and three of her younger children: two boys, John, born in 1816, and Hamilton, born in 1823, and her youngest child, a daughter, Ellen. Two of Mary's older daughters, Sally Williams and Louisa, along with their children, were to pass into Weaver's possession on New Year's Day, 1837.[18]

The division took place as scheduled at the beginning of 1837. Mayburry surrendered Sally and Louisa and their children to Weaver at Buffalo Forge; he retained, as their agreement stipulated, Mary and John, Hamilton, and Ellen. When Mayburry left the vicinity shortly thereafter to take up a new iron-making venture in northern Rockbridge County, he took Mary and her three young children with him.[19] As a result, Mary's family was broken in order to provide Mayburry and Weaver with a fair division of the property belonging to their former partnership. Mary—young Sam Williams's grandmother—had been stripped of a substantial portion of her family, but subsequent events were to show that she and the children who went with her were not forgotten by those who were left at Buffalo Forge early in 1837.

Sam Williams would turn seventeen sometime during that year, and this birthday would occur at a new home under a new master. But he could take some comfort from the knowledge that his immediate family would be there with him. Sam Williams, Sr., had been under Weaver's control for a number of years prior to 1837, as the 1832 letter regarding his deteriorating eyesight indicates, and his mother, Sally, had, of course, come to Weaver in the division, along with young Sam's brothers and sisters. The family had grown substantially during the last few years and now included at least four children: Sam; his older sister, Mary; a younger sister, Elizabeth, born in 1825; and a younger brother, Washington, born in 1827.[20] The birthplace of Sally Williams's sons was indicated clearly in the Buffalo Forge records as they entered Weaver's labor force; their names were recorded as "Sam Etna" and "Washington Etna."[21] The reason for this seems clear. It simply was easier to write "Sam Etna" than "Sam Williams, Jr." whenever an entry had to be made under his name, and it identified him clearly as one of the "Wilson negroes" born and raised at Etna Furnace. And if you were going to refer to one brother that way, why not do it for both of them? From the master's point of view, it made perfectly good sense. Sam Williams took quite a different view of the matter, however. He knew who he was, and he did not like being called "Sam Etna." It would take him a long time, but eventually he would get his name back.

To be precise, it took sixteen years. On a page in the Buffalo Forge ledgers covering his work for the year 1853, his name appears two ways: as "Samuel Etna" and as "Sam Williams."[22] The most logical explanation for the change is that Sam himself wanted it made. By the 1850s he was important enough to Weaver's operations to get his way, particularly since his request must have struck Weaver as a fairly minor matter. One suspects that Sam viewed the subject in quite a different light. From this point on, as far as the records were concerned, he was "Sam Williams" at Buffalo Forge; his father was "Sam Williams Senior."[23]

Since the early Etna Furnace records have not survived, there is no way to trace young Sam Williams's life prior to his arrival at Buffalo Forge in 1837. If his youth was spent like that of most slave boys who grew up at iron-making facilities in the South, he probably had no regular duties until he reached age eight or so, when he would have been expected to assume some light chores, such as helping to look after the younger slave children during the day. By age twelve or fourteen, he would have entered the regular work force, perhaps as a furnace boy doing odd jobs or as a leaf raker at the charcoal pits.[24] The elder Sam Williams's failing eyesight probably prevented him from training his teenage son in his ironworking skills, a method of transmitting knowledge and expertise that occurred frequently at Virginia furnaces and forges in the nineteenth century.[25] He may have been untrained when he arrived at Buffalo Forge as a sixteen-year-old youth on New Year's Day, 1837, but William Weaver could clearly see that Sam Williams's boy had the potential for forge work.

His assets were several. First of all, he came from a family that produced good mechanics. Intelligent Southern iron men looking for slave recruits for critical furnace and forge jobs paid close attention to things like heredity, and Weaver was certainly no fool when it came to the iron business. He seemed to feel about black ironworkers the same way he felt about white ironmasters. You had to have "the proper head for it," Weaver told his nephew-in-law, Daniel C. E. Brady, when he was trying to persuade Brady and his wife to move to Buffalo Forge during the 1850s. "Training alone will not [do] as nature must do something, in order to make a good Iron Master."[26] Nature seemed to have done a great deal for Sam Williams. He had the necessary size and strength; he stood five feet ten inches tall when he achieved his full stature, which made him one of the tallest slave hands at Buffalo Forge. And his color suggested to white Southerners of that place and time that he was likely to possess intelligence and good judgment as well. A physical description of him drawn up during the Civil War listed his color as "yellow."[27] He had, at some point in his ancestry, a strong admixture of white blood.

Where this miscegenation occurred in the Williams family remains a mystery. Since he took the elder Sam Williams's name as his own, one assumes that both his father and mother were slaves, and that Mary, his grandmother, was also enslaved, as the property settlement signed with Mayburry in 1836 made clear. It could well be that his maternal or paternal grandfather was white, but there is no way to know. Whatever the case, Weaver obviously knew he had a likely candidate for his forge gang when Sam "Etna" came into his possession in 1837.

After a year in which the only work recorded for him at Buffalo Forge consisted of field labor with the farmhands, Sam entered the forge in 1838 at the age of eighteen.[28] Weaver undoubtedly had Sam go down to the forge and watch the black refiners and hammermen at their jobs before deciding whether he wanted to train as a forgeman. This was Weaver's usual practice with potential recruits for his ironworking crew, and there is no reason to suspect that he did things differently this time.[29] It was far better to have a willing apprentice than a surly, rebellious underhand who would turn out poor-quality work, try to escape, or perhaps sabotage the forge machinery. As Sam walked in to the stone forge building that stood alongside Buffalo Creek, he would have seen an impressive, even awesome, sight: charcoal fires burning at white heat; slave refiners and their helpers working bars of pig iron in those fires until the iron turned into a ball of glowing, pasty metal, then slinging this semimolten mass of iron onto their anvils, where they pounded and shaped it under the rhythmic

105

blows of their huge, water-powered hammers. Through successive reheatings and poundings, Weaver's refiners removed enough of the impurities in the pig iron to work it into something called an "anchony." Turning out high-quality anchonies was the most important single job in the forge, and that was what Weaver wanted Sam Williams to do.[30]

Weaver himself described an anchony in a court deposition he gave in 1840. It was a piece of malleable iron about six inches square weighing between 80 and 150 pounds, "with a blade of iron about the length of my cane," Weaver noted (his cane measured thirty-two inches); "one end of the blade has what is called the *tail end,* which contains iron enough generally to make a shovel mould, and out of which shovel moulds are generally made," he added.[31] Producing this rather strange-looking item was no easy task. The key point in the refining process was exactly when the pig iron heating in the refinery fire had reached just the right temperature and consistency for pounding and shaping on the anvil block. Bringing the pig iron "to nature," as this was called, was the most difficult forge skill to learn, and it could be acquired only by many months of apprenticeship to a master refiner.[32] If Sam Williams decided that he wanted to follow in his father's footsteps and became a refiner, he would have to start as an underhand at the fires of men like Phill Easton, John Baxter, or the Hunt brothers—Harry and Billy—all of whom were skilled slave refinery hands at Buffalo Forge in the late 1830s.[33]

Pounding out anchonies was the most critical part of the forge operation, but it was only the first half of the manufacturing process. The final stage came when a second group of operatives, the hammermen, reheated the anchonies and worked them at another forge called a chaffery. The hammermen produced iron bars of various standardized shapes, sizes, and lengths—"merchant bars," in the language of the iron trade—which would be shipped to market and sold. Merchant bars kept the wheels of agriculture turning. Blacksmiths hammered these bars into the things needed on (or off) the farm that had to be made out of iron: horse and mule shoes, wagon tires, nails, tools, agricultural implements, and the like.[34] The slave hammermen at Buffalo Forge at the time of Sam Williams's arrival—Tooler (the son of the ironworker of the same name and one of the original "Wilson negroes"), his brother

Bob (another "Wilson negro"), and Garland Thompson—were, like the refiners, prize hands worth a substantial premium on the open market.[35]

Weaver was well aware of their value to him. Without his forge, and the slaves who ran it, William Weaver would have been just another valley farmer—a prosperous one, to be sure, but a farmer nonetheless. There would have been nothing wrong with that, of course; most of his Rockbridge County neighbors were farmers, and agriculture was certainly an honorable occupation in the Old South. But Buffalo Forge and his skilled crew of slave hands made him much more—they made him an ironmaster, a person of premier importance in the local economy and someone to be reckoned with, politically and socially, in the Valley. "Some of my Friends in Phila. wondered why I did not reside amongst them," he confided to a friend in Lexington in 1848. "I replied— At home I was but a small person—but that I was somebody—The people knew me—and in crowded Phila. I would be nobody."[36] Weaver was much more than "a small person" in Rockbridge County, and he knew very well where the source of his prestige lay. It lay in that stone forge building that stood beside Buffalo Creek—in the massive hammers and charcoal fires and in the black men who worked them so skillfully.

To retain his status, and the wealth that went with it, Weaver had to train and hold good slave artisans and replace those hands who were growing too old (like Billy Hunt) or were too infirm (like Sam Williams, Sr.) to work. One suspects that when young Sam Williams decided he wanted to be a forgeman, William Weaver could not have been happier.

The advantage of doing forge work would not have been unknown to Sam Williams, either. In making himself indispensable to Weaver's iron-making operations, he would be gaining a significant amount of influence over his own fate. There was no sure guarantee against punishment or sale; like all Southern masters, Weaver could do pretty much what he wished in the way of punishment, and if he should fall deeply into debt or die suddenly, his slave force could be dispersed either by sale or the division of his estate. Barring that sort of catastrophe, however, Sam would be in a much stronger bargaining position as a skilled forge hand than in any other occupation at Buffalo Forge. If he trained as a refiner and showed an aptitude for the work, he would have talents his owner would need and even be willing to pay him for.

Compensation for extra work was almost a universal feature of the labor system at slave-manned furnaces and forges in the Old South, and Buffalo Forge was no exception. Slaves had a daily or weekly task to accomplish, but they were paid for anything they turned out over and above that amount—"overwork," it was called.[37] The task for refiners at Weaver's forge and everywhere else in the Valley was a ton and a half of anchonies per week (the quota required of hammermen was a "journey" of 560 pounds of bar iron per day).[38] These amounts had been the customary tasks for years, and old traditions like this were hard to change. Slaves as well as masters knew what the tasks were, and any attempt by ironmasters to increase work quotas or to abolish compensation for overwork entirely would have been a very risky venture. It did not take much, for instance, to break a hammer "helve"—the huge wooden beams that supported the 500- to 600-pound cast-iron hammerheads in the forge. And every time a helve broke, the forge had to shut down for at least a day or two for repairs. Sabotage of this sort would be relatively simple to accomplish, and who could say whether it was deliberate? Helves did, after all, wear out and break in the normal course of forge operations. It was this sort of unspoken threat that gave slave forgemen considerable protection against an increase in their tasks and helped them preserve their right to earn compensation for themselves.

Payment for overwork came in several forms, and the option as to how this pay would be taken lay with the slave. The slaves at Buffalo Forge could take it in cash; they could take it in credit at Weaver's store and draw against it for items they wished to buy; they could use their overwork to secure time off from their regular duties; and finally, if Weaver permitted, they could attempt to purchase their own freedom.[39] This last option was almost never granted. In 1830, Weaver allowed an elderly slave forge hand whom he had purchased in the Lynchburg area to buy himself and return to his former home.[40] But this appears to be the only time Weaver made such a concession to any member of his slave force. Even without the opportunity to try to attain freedom, however, the overwork system had obvious advantages for the slave, as Sam Williams's life at Buffalo Forge would illustrate in rich and elaborate detail.

Sam's first year in the forge, 1838, was a year of apprenticeship. He served as an underhand to both John Baxter and Harry Hunt, and under their guidance he sought to master the refiner's art: learning to put up and maintain the special refinery fire, heating the pig iron and bringing it "to nature," and then pounding the red-hot metal under the huge hammer into those oddly shaped anchonies.[41] He undoubtedly cost Weaver some money that year in wasted pig iron and excessive use of expensive charcoal, but the only way to learn was by doing.

Sam had expert teachers. Harry Hunt, for instance, was fifty years old in 1838 and had been a refiner for well over twenty-five years. He, like many other slave ironworkers, had been born to the trade. In his case, this meant birth, youth, and young adulthood at the Oxford Iron Works in Campbell County, Virginia, not far from Lynchburg. His father had been a limestone miner at Oxford Furnace, and Harry and his brother Billy had been trained in the forge at Oxford. There they had refined for David Ross, one of the most famous Virginia ironmasters of the Revolutionary and post-Revolutionary eras. Ross's death in 1817 and the subsequent sale of his estate sent a number of his best ironworkers across the Blue Ridge Mountains and into the Valley, where the Virginia iron industry was moving during the early years of the nineteenth century and where ironmasters like William Weaver were eagerly seeking skilled furnace and forge workers.[42]

Harry Hunt knew his job, and Sam learned quickly. Before his first year was out, he had sufficiently mastered the techniques of refining to earn a modest amount of overwork: "½ ton over iron 2.00."[43] It was not a great deal of money, especially when compared to what some of the other skilled forgemen were able to put away for themselves. But it was a start toward something better, toward a life in which his skills could help make things a little more comfortable and perhaps a bit more predictable and secure. By 1840, he had added reason to be concerned about a more comfortable present and a more certain future.

Sometime during the year 1840, Sam Williams married. His wife was a slave woman named Nancy Jefferson, who was also owned by William Weaver. She was twenty-three years old that

year, three years older than Sam, but the difference in age meant
little.[44] Sam had finished his forge training by then and was now
one of Weaver's master refiners.[45] His future was probably as
secure as any slave's could ever be, and he was ready to assume
the responsibilities of a husband and, soon, a father. Their marriage was not a legal one, of course. Slave marriages had no
standing in Virginia law, or in that of any other Southern state.
But time would clearly show that Sam Williams and Nancy
Jefferson viewed themselves as man and wife. The date of their
marriage was not recorded in the journals and papers kept at
Buffalo Forge, but they knew the year was 1840 and they never
forgot it.

The birth of their first child did appear in the Buffalo Forge
records, however, and for good reason. The birth of a new baby
in the slave quarters meant an addition to the master's wealth
and potential work force. So, when Elizabeth Williams came into
the world later that year, note was taken of the event.[46] Elizabeth,
or Betty, as she was more frequently called, was undoubtedly
named after Sam's younger sister, Elizabeth, who is mentioned in
early legal documents dealing with the dispute over the "Wilson
negroes."[47] This sister was not one of those children taken by
Mayburry in the 1837 division, but there is no record that she
came to Weaver, either. She may well have died before her name-
sake was born to Sam and Nancy Williams in 1840. If she was
living in that year, she would have been fifteen. The practice of
naming children after older, and particularly lost, relatives would
recur frequently in the Williams family in the years that lay
ahead. Much of the family's history would be mirrored in those
names.

Sam Williams's marriage and the birth of his daughter gave
him added incentive to exploit the possibilities opened up by the
overwork system. He had earned some relatively small amounts
of money prior to 1840: a total of $3.00 in 1837, the same in 1838,
and just over $4.50 in 1839.[48] He would not be content with
earnings of this size in 1840, however. Early in the year, he began
devoting a considerable amount of his spare time to "tar burning,"
as it was called. He would collect the heart of fallen pine trees
from the woods around Buffalo Forge, stack it closely on a low,
hard-packed mound of earth with gutters running out from the
center, cover the resinous pine with dirt, and light it. As the wood

110

smoldered, the gum would flow out as tar through the trenches cut in the earth.[49] Sam would collect this "tair," as it was spelled in the Buffalo Forge books, and sell it to his master. Weaver was willing to pay twenty-five cents a gallon for it—pitch and tar were always needed around installations dependent on water power—and Sam's long hours in the woods produced no less than fifty-nine gallons of tar before the year was out.[50]

He also did something else in the year he was married that he had not done during his three previous years at Buffalo Forge— he worked through the Christmas holidays. The break beginning on Christmas Day and ending with a return to work on New Year's Day was a traditional period of rest for Weaver's slave hands, as it was for most slaves throughout the South. The forge would close down for Christmas, but there were plenty of other things to do—stock to feed and water, roads and walks to shovel if it snowed, ice to cut from the forge pond and haul to the ice house if a cold snap hit. Sam worked five days out of the seven-day Christmas break in 1840 and earned $2.50 for his labor (fifty cents a day was the usual pay for anyone, white or black, who did common labor, so Sam was not paid "slave wages" for his holiday work). By his tar burning, forge overwork, and Christmas labor in 1840, he earned $22.42, well over four times what he had made for himself in any previous year at Buffalo Forge.[51]

There is no way of knowing why Sam worked so hard in 1840, but it seems safe to assume that his efforts were spurred by a desire to be able to do more for his wife and his new baby. This view is reinforced by the record of his purchases during the year: sugar and molasses (treats all three of them could enjoy), coffee for himself and Nancy, and crocks for her to use for household storage. Unfortunately, several of the larger expenditures he made in 1840 were not spelled out in the books, like his store "order" of $4.00 on March 7 and a similarly vague general entry on September 5 for $9.16.[52] These sizable store purchases probably included items for Nancy and Betty, but we cannot be sure.

Sam and Nancy Williams's family grew steadily over the next several years. In 1842, a second daughter, Caroline, was born, and she was followed by two more girls, Ann, born in 1843, and Lydia, born the next year.[53] Sam's overwork increased along with the size of his family. He continued his tar burning in 1841, but on a reduced scale. He concentrated more and more on his work at the refinery forge in his effort to earn extra income for himself and his wife and daughters. This made sense. As his skills improved, so did his chance to earn overwork pay by hammering out extra pounds of anchonies. It was now easier for him to make his task of a ton and a half of refined iron per week, and anything he turned out above that amount meant money in his pocket or credit at the Buffalo Forge store. He was paid $8.82 for pounding out over two tons of extra iron in 1841, while his tar production dropped off to thirty-six and a half gallons (which still earned him $9.12). Once again, his purchases at Weaver's store suggest that he was using his overwork compensation to buy things his family could use—items like sugar, calico, ticking, drill, jeans cloth, and trimmings. And a week before Christmas in 1841, he spent $1.25 for a silk handkerchief.[54]

Sam's growing prowess as a refiner and his continued support of his family are apparent in his overwork accounts during the next few years. No records have survived for 1842 and 1843, but he made a total of $31.00 in overwork pay in 1844, most of which he earned at his forge. As a master refiner, he was paid for his overwork at the same rate a white artisan would have been paid for the same job—$8.00 per ton, with three-fifths of that going to Sam as the refiner and two-fifths going to his underhand. Sam's five tons of "over iron" in 1844 translated into a credit of $24.00 on Weaver's books. The debit side of the ledger is incomplete for 1844, but fortunately some of his purchases were listed, particularly his holiday buying at the end of the year. One item he bought early in 1844 is especially interesting: "10 yds. best silk" on February 20. This certainly was a present for Nancy, and since their daughter Lydia was born sometime during that year, this gift of silk may have been to celebrate that occasion. As Christmas approached, he made several additional purchases. On December 21, he bought four pounds of sugar for his mother, Sally, undoubtedly to give to her for Christmas (the cost was seventy-seven cents). Three days later, on Christmas eve, he took $1.00 in cash from his account, spent $2.00 for eight yards of calico, and drew against his store credit for no less than $20.00 for a "Blue Coat Fine." Whether this last item was for himself or Nancy is not clear, but even after spending that sum (for what must have been a very fine coat), he still had a balance to his credit of $5.21. That amount was carried over on the books to the next year, which was always done when one of Weaver's slaves had not spent his full earnings by the end of the year. And Sam almost invariably carried at least a small balance in his favor into the new year.[55]

During the next several years, Sam's overwork earnings continued to mount. By the early 1850s, he was regularly making over $50.00 per annum, and in 1855 and 1856, the last two years for which his complete accounts are available, his compensation reached even greater levels. In 1855, his overwork amounted to $92.23, and the next year, for the first time, it exceeded $100.00— $103.00, to be exact, $100.00 of which he made by refining twenty tons of "Over Iron."[56]

There is no need to make a detailed list of his purchases during this ten- to twelve-year period, but some of the things he did with his money suggest a good deal about this man and his attitudes and priorities. He supplemented Weaver's standard rations of pork and cornmeal with regular purchases of flour, sugar, coffee, and molasses, and he frequently bought cloth for Nancy to sew into garments for the family. His overwork kept him, and perhaps Nancy as well, supplied with tobacco. And his gifts to various members of his family continued. His mother received fifty pounds of flour from him in February 1845, and he gave his father a pound of coffee in April 1846—to cite two instances where the items were specifically identified in the records as going to his parents. Nancy, as might be expected, received a number of presents: a pair of buckskin gloves at Chritsmas in 1848; a shawl in May 1849; nine yards of silk in October 1851. One of his special purchases for his children was eight and three-fourths yards of cloth for a bedspread for Ann when she was ten years old.[57]

The most fascinating items of all that he acquired during these years were the articles of furniture he bought for the cabin that he, Nancy, and the girls shared. His major Christmas gift to the family in 1845 consisted of a table (at $3.00) and a bedstead (which cost $9.00), both of which he purchased at the Buffalo Forge store on Christmas eve of that year. He added significantly to the cabin's furnishings six years later when he apparently attended an estate sale held in the neighborhood. In April 1851, he made two acquisitions "at Blackford's Sale": a set of chairs, for which he paid $7.25, and, probably his most revealing purchase of the entire antebellum era, "1 looking glass," priced at $1.75.[58]

113

There are many reasons why any family would want to own a mirror—perfectly natural reasons, such as curiosity about one's appearance or a touch of vanity, perhaps. Sam and Nancy Williams had growing daughters, too. Betty was eleven, Caroline was nine, Anne was eight, and Lydia was seven, in 1851. But a *slave's* buying a mirror suggests something more. It would seem to indicate a strong sense of pride in one's self and one's family that transcended their status as slaves. Why else would Sam spend that kind of money on such a purchase? One dollar and seventy-five cents represented the sweat and sore muscles that went into several hundred pounds of overwork iron. One almost suspects that that looking glass, packed carefully in a wagon and hauled home from "Blackford's Sale," stood as a symbol of Sam and Nancy Williams's feelings about themselves and their children. And there were other signs of pride as well.

In 1849, Sam began making fairly frequently cash withdrawals against his overwork account. Some of this money he undoubtedly used to buy items at rural stores that dotted the nearby country-side, places like Saunder's Store, which stood just across Buffalo Creek from the forge. But he was not spending all of it in this way. The individual withdrawals were small at first, a dollar or two, generally, but they soon added up: $24.00 taken out in cash in 1849 (as opposed to $6.75 in 1848, $5.00 in 1847, and $1.50 in 1846); $23.25 in 1850; a jump to $41.16 in 1851, followed by a one-year fall-off to $16.00 in 1852; and then a sharp increase to almost identical sums of $51.00 in 1853, $57.00 in 1854, $56.87½ in 1855, and $57.81 in 1856. In 1857, the last year in which the withdrawals can be traced in full, he took out $25.50 in cash.[59] Part of the money that he pocketed during these years ended up in a rather remarkable place, as indicated by a letter written by Weaver's young forge clerk in 1855. On February 25 of that year, John A. Rex, a twenty-three-year-old nephew of Weaver's who had come down from Pennsylvania to help out at Buffalo Forge, described an incident that had recently occurred there. "I wish to ask you one question," he wrote James D. Davidson, a prominent lawyer in Lexington who served as Weaver's attorney: "whether Sam Williams can draw his money from the Savings Bank or if he cannot." Sam, it seems, had made a bet with a man named Henry Nash, a free black cooper who lived near Buffalo Forge and who made the barrels for Weaver's flour. Nash refused to believe that Sam had a savings account in the bank in Lexington, and Sam had bet his watch (another impressive acquisition for a slave) against Nash's watch that he did. "It is my opinion that he can draw his money if he gives the Directors of the Bank 10 days notice," Rex continued. "After he receives the money he wishes to show it to Henry Nash, and then he will return the said money back to the Bank again." Rex closed the letter by assuring Davidson that he "was witness to the said bargain."[60]

J. D. Davidson was an experienced attorney, but it is doubtful that he had ever before had to give an opinion as to how a slave should handle his savings account. The only thing he knew to do was advise young Rex "to confer with Wm. Weaver" on the business.[61] Perhaps the master could decide how a man who was himself legally property should deal with his own property, in this case a sizable account in a major Lexington financial institution.

There are several extraordinary things about this incident, not the least of which is the episode of the white forge clerk's holding the bet for a slave and a free Negro and serving as a witness to their wager. But everyday life in the Old South was filled with anomalies of this sort, so perhaps this part of the story was not so remarkable after all. Sam Williams's possession of a savings account was remarkable by any standard, however, and, given the value of the dollar in the 1850s, his account was a large one. We know the size of his savings because just over a year after Rex wrote Davidson about the bet, the lawyer withdrew Sam's money from the bank. It may have been that the bank directors felt uneasy about holding, and paying interest on, a slave's money, particularly after the wager brought up the subject. Or maybe Weaver decided it would be better to handle these funds in some other way. Whatever the reason, on April 22, 1856, Davidson rode out to Buffalo Forge carrying Sam Williams's savings of $91.31. He also brought with him $61.96 belonging to Sam's wife.[62]

Nancy Williams, it turned out, had a savings account, too, and in her own name. Since she was in charge of dairy operations at Buffalo Forge and did a good deal of housework at Weaver's residence, she clearly had had opportunities to earn overwork pay in her own right. The house account books have not survived, so there is no way to discover exactly what she did to make money for herself or to trace the precise amounts of her compensation. But since her savings account was fully two-thirds the size of her husband's, her earnings must have been substantial. Between them, Sam and Nancy had over $150.00 in cash.

What were they saving for? No evidence exists to show that Weaver had given them the right to buy their own freedom or that of their children, so self-purchase apparently was not the reason. The fact that they were saving anything at all suggests that they felt their material standard of living was adequate to the family's needs; if it had not been, they probably would have spent much more than they did on various food items and cloth. The most logical explanation for their extraordinary, and substantial, bank accounts would seem to be that they both had extra overwork funds and that they had simply put their money in a safe place where it would earn interest for them. This conclusion is reinforced by the subsequent history of their accounts at Buffalo Forge.

William Weaver, in effect, replaced the savings bank as the holder of the Williamses' money and as the payer of interest on their accounts. Special entries were made under their separate names in a private ledger kept at the forge, and both Sam and Nancy placed their full savings with Weaver on April 22, 1856, the day Davidson brought their funds out from Lexington. Neither Sam nor Nancy made any withdrawals during the next twelve months, so exactly one year after their initial deposits, Weaver credited both accounts with interest on the full amounts. Sam's $91.31 earned him $10.96, and Nancy's $61.96 made $7.44 for her. The interest rate in both instances was 12 percent.[63]

In the years just ahead, Sam and Nancy would follow quite different courses in handling their savings. In the spring and fall of 1858, Nancy made fairly systematic cash withdrawals of $4.00 to $5.00, and in 1859 she used the remainder of her money for substantial purchases at Buffalo Forge and at two neighboring country stores. On October 27, 1859, she closed out her account by spending $4.82 at Saunder's Store. Sam, on the other hand, kept exactly $100.00 on deposit throughout these years and into the 1860s. He withdrew the interest each year, in either cash or goods, but kept the $100.00 principal fully intact. Weaver regularly credited him with interest on his $100.00, figured after 1860 at 6 percent, and Sam just as regularly drew off his $6.00 a year (for some reason, two interest payments were made in 1862, so Sam took out $12.00 that year). His account was not finally closed out until after the Civil War.[64]

The picture that emerges from this story of two slaves with savings accounts is by no means a simple one. On the surface, one might be tempted to argue that their behavior indicated a placid acceptance of their status and condition. Since they had to complete their required tasks before they could start earning money for themselves, they obviously were turning out a considerable amount of work for William Weaver—working like slaves, so to speak, and taking the bait the master offered to do a good deal more than they had to do. Yet they clearly were doing a great deal for themselves as well, and for their children. They were improving the material conditions under which all of them could live, and they were protecting themselves against the fearful threat that hung over them all—the breakup of the family through sale. Weaver would be very reluctant indeed to part with workers like this man and woman, who meant so much to the smooth running, and the success, of his iron-making and farming activities. Nor would he want to run the risks that would certainly occur if he tried to sell Sam and Nancy Williams's daughters off Buffalo Forge. Through their overwork, both Sam and Nancy could help to shield and provide for each other and for their children. The psychological importance of this to them—the added access it afforded Sam to the traditional responsibilities of a husband and father, and Nancy to the role of wife and mother—cannot be overemphasized. Their feelings and emotions can be shared by anyone who has ever tried to make a good and decent life with another person and has helped to bring children into a fragile and uncertain world.

The nature of Sam's attitude toward his work does not have to be left totally to the imagination, however. Thanks to the arrival at Buffalo Forge of a new manager in 1857 and his meticulous record keeping, we can follow Sam at his forge and in the fields for months on end. The insights to be gained from a close look at his daily activities during the late 1850s and early 1860s are revealing.

By the mid-1850s, Weaver was no longer capable of supervising the complex industrial and agricultural operations at Buffalo Forge by himself. He was in his seventies, his health was uncertain, and just moving around the property was becoming more and more difficult for him.[65] As a result, he began a campaign to persuade his favorite niece and her husband to move down from Philadelphia and take over the management of day-to-day affairs at the house, the forge, and the farms. Weaver had brought a number of young relatives down from Pennsylvania over the years, but none had worked out to his full satisfaction. He had no one in his immediate family to take over for him; he had not married until 1830 when he was forty-nine, and his wife, a Philadelphia widow named Elizabeth Newkirk Woodson, was only four years younger than he was. She had died in 1850, and they had had no children.[66] So he set his mind on persuading his niece Emma Matilda Brady and her husband, a young Philadelphia banker named Daniel C. E. Brady, to move to Buffalo Forge and assume direction of things there.[67] "I am old, all but 75," Weaver wrote to Daniel Brady in 1855, and he was worried about what would happen after his death. "The great object with me is, that my servants shall remain where they are, and have humane masters," he went on. "This point is the only difficulty on my mind in relation to my Estate. Giving them their freedom, I am satisfied, would not benefit them as much as having good masters, and remain where they are. You I presume understand my intentions, —and if you get here I hope they will be carried out. The means will be given you to do so," Weaver promised, an unmistakable hint that Emma and Daniel Brady would inherit his considerable estate if they and their three children moved permanently to Virginia.[68]

Late in 1857, the Bradys closed up their affairs in Pennsylvania and moved to Buffalo Forge. There were only two children with them when they came: Anne Gertrude, who was nine, and Charles Patrick, who was seven. Their younger son, William Weaver Brady, had died in the spring of 1856, when he was only two and a half years old. They gave their next baby the same name, but he died the same day he was born, in August 1857. Perhaps the loss of these two boys, as well as business reverses Daniel Brady had recently suffered in Philadelphia, had something to do with their decision to start a new life for themselves in the Valley of Virginia.[69]

The arrival of the Bradys was an event of major significance in the lives of the slaves at Buffalo Forge. It must have relieved

118

much of the anxiety that would have been growing in the quarters as Weaver's age advanced and his health deteriorated. Now there was a clear prospect that the Buffalo Forge slave community would remain intact after Weaver's passing, that families would not be broken and friends separated by a division of the master's estate. Weaver obviously had not consulted with his slaves about what arrangements they would prefer after his death. One suspects very strongly that if he had, he would not have continued to believe that they would rather have "humane masters" to succeed him than to have their freedom. But aside from manumission, there was probably nothing more important to these black men and women than the strong probability that they could all "remain where they are," as Weaver put it, after he was gone. The Bradys' coming (and the fact that they already had a son, seven-year-old Pat, who might also inherit the place one day) would have been the cause for some quiet rejoicing in the slave cabins that dotted the landscape around Buffalo Forge.

A historian seeking to reconstruct the lives of these slaves also has reason to celebrate the arrival of the Bradys. Daniel Brady was a remarkably careful and devoted keeper of records. Soon after his arrival, he began a regular daily journal in which he wrote down the work routine for each day—what the weather was like, which slaves were doing what jobs, how much work they did, who was sick, who was pretending to be sick. If some notable event occurred at or around Buffalo Forge, if a freshet interrupted forge operations or washed out roads and fences, if a snowstorm hit and prevented work, that information also went into his journal. The result is a running description of slave activities at Buffalo Forge that fills three neatly written volumes and covers a span of over seven years, from March 1858 to June 1865.[70] These years, perhaps the most critical in the entire history of the slave South, are the ones in which we can follow the life of Sam Williams in the greatest and most elaborate detail.

When Sam was putting in a routine day at his refinery forge, Brady simply noted "Sam at work" in his journal. And Sam was "at work" most of the time. He and his underhand, a slave named Henry Towles, were the steadiest pair in the forge, but they also had their own ideas about when they had worked long enough and hard enough to deserve a break. The summer of 1860 was such a time. Sam and Henry Towles manned their forge through some very warm days at the beginning of July, but by the middle of the month they had obviously had enough. Henry said he was too ill to work on Wednesday, July 18, and Brady apparently believed him. "Henry Towles sick," he recorded in his journal. Jim Garland, a slave who served as a swing hand between the field gang and the forge, was brought in to relieve Henry, and he and Sam put in a full day together. The next day, the temperature reached 100 degrees at one o'clock in the afternoon, and the heat in the forge must have been stifling. Henry did not show up for work that day, either. "Henry Towles sick i.e. loafing" was Brady's assessment. Sam and Jim Garland continued to work, so the forge had its supply of anchonies that day, but Sam was working under very trying conditions, and no one knew it better than he did. He and Jim finished out the week, however, with "Henry Towles loafing" both Friday and Saturday.[71]

On Monday, July 23, it was Sam's turn, and he may not even have made a pretense of being sick. Henry returned to work that day; he could handle Sam's job, with Jim Garland's help. Sam was now "loafing," according to Brady, and he stayed out "loafing" the entire week. Brady realized he had pushed his hands about as far as he could in the oppressive heat, and he probably was not surprised on Saturday when his two chaffery forgemen, Tooler and Harry Hunt, Jr., also took matters into their own hands. "Tooler & Harry drew a few pounds and then broke down to loaf," he wrote. He decided about the middle of the day that there was no sense fighting it any longer: "All hands had a ½ [day] holiday."[72] From Brady's vantage point, Saturday, July 28, had been a difficult day. The slaves undoubtedly took just the opposite view.

Sam's vacation was not over yet, though. He did not go back to work for three more weeks. From Monday, July 30, to Saturday, August 18, Brady noted with regularity that Sam was "loafing" each day.[73] Even the appearance on August 7 of J. E. Carson, a Rockbridge County slave trader, did not drive Sam back to his post. If Sam were going to be intimidated into returning to work, the slave dealer's visit to Buffalo Forge should have done it. Carson was no idle threat. In the spring of 1859, he had carried one of Weaver's slaves, a man named Lawson, to New Orleans and sold him, and Carson had purchased a slave woman and her children from Weaver several months later. Lawson had tried to run away; the woman had apparently disrupted the quarters by her licentious behavior.[74] Weaver, as was his custom, simply got rid of unruly slaves. But Sam's extended period of "loafing" was not enough to convince Weaver that he should part with his most valuable forgeman. Carson did buy a slave from Weaver on August 7. When he left after dinner on that day, he took away a runaway field hand, Bill Greenlee, in handcuffs.[75] Sam did not return to his forge until Monday, August 20. He had been off the job four full weeks.[76]

Sam returned to work as if nothing had happened. Jim Garland went back into the fields, and Sam and Henry Towles took up where they had left off a month or so earlier. As far as we know, neither Weaver nor Brady attempted to do anything to coerce him back to work earlier. If they did, Brady made no mention of it in his journal. Carson's trip out to the forge was not staged for Sam's benefit. The slave trader had captured Bill Greenlee, the runaway, and was bringing him back to Buffalo Forge in shackles to haggle with Weaver over his price. Sam's vacation, if that word fits the occasion, seems to have been something he felt was due him. He had worked hard that year up to his four weeks of "loafing." His overwork accounts unfortunately do not go beyond 1858, but Weaver's cash books show a number of payments to him between late 1859 and the summer of 1860:[77]

December 24, 1859	To Sam	$10.00
February 11, 1860	"	5.00
March 25, 1860	"	10.00
May 10, 1860	"	1.00
July 10, 1860	"	5.00

It had taken a lot of extra pounds of iron to make this kind of money. And a month after he returned to work, he began receiving cash payments from Weaver again, a strong indication that he was working overtime after he rejoined Henry Towles at the refinery forge:[78]

September 24, 1860	To Sam	$2.50
November 13, 1860	"	1.00
December 1, 1860	"	5.00

Perhaps most significant of all, his savings account, which Weaver was holding, was not touched during or after his month-long absence from his job.

What this fascinating incident suggests is that Sam was fully aware of the power he possessed and the quite distinct limits of that power. He knew that his skills were critically important to his master and that this gave him a considerable amount of leverage in his dealings with Weaver and Brady. In his view, he deserved some time off, and he chose the hot, muggy dog days of July and August 1860 to take it. It was probably no accident that he did not leave his forge until Henry Towles returned. This kept the situation from assuming potentially dangerous and threatening dimensions. Since they were off one at a time, Jim Garland could come in to spell each one of them temporarily, and forge operations could continue. Iron making would not grind to a complete and costly stop because Henry was feigning illness and Sam was "loafing" back at his cabin. Thus Weaver and Brady would not be backed into a corner where they would be forced to crack down on their two refinery hands. Sam knew just how far he could go with his resistance, and he was careful to keep the situation under control.

At the same time, he had enough pride in himself to insist, through his actions, that there was a line beyond which he would not allow himself to be pushed. Months of steady labor, followed by forge work in temperatures reaching 100 degrees, was one step over that line. He took off for a month, and there were certainly risks attendant on that. But they would probably be manageable risks, and that was the way things turned out. By tolerating his absence, Weaver and Brady tacitly recognized that Sam had the power to force reasonable, limited, and temporary changes in his work regimen; they also silently acknowledged that, in a certain sense, he was justified in what he was doing. None of this fits the classic definition of what Southern slavery was supposed to be: total dominance by the white master and total subservience by the black slave. But social institutions have a way of getting fuzzy around the edges, especially when they are as complex as the institution of human bondage.

Sam Williams won this confrontation, probably because of who he was and because his challenge to the system was guarded and oblique and had a limited objective—rest from work. Bill Green-lee's case was quite a different matter. He was twenty-eight years old and a "prime field hand," but he was, from the perspective of Weaver's labor needs, still only a field hand.[79] Even more important, his defiance of the slave regime was open and direct and had an objective that no slaveholder could tolerate—freedom. Not surprisingly, Weaver brought the full force of the system swiftly and brutally down on him. The example of the unsuccessful runaway's being taken off in chains was immediately before the eyes of Sam Williams and every other slave at Buffalo Forge, and that was undoubtedly the way Weaver wanted it. Even Sam's status as a master refiner probably would not have protected him if he had carried his resistance as far as Bill Greenlee did his.

Bill's attempt to escape and Sam's much more limited protest raise one of the ultimate questions about American slavery. What, in fact, was the better part of valor for a slave? Should one fight, confront, resist openly, run away, do everything one could to bring the system down? Or should one maneuver as best one could within the system, stay with one's family and try to help and comfort them, and attempt to carve out the best possible life, despite the physical and psychological confines of enslavement? These were questions each slave had to decide; they were not easily answered then and they are not easily answered now. But most, like Sam Williams, chose the latter course. To have done otherwise would have placed almost everything he loved in jeopardy. And Sam—husband of Nancy, father of Betty, Caroline, Ann, and Lydia, and son of Sally and Sam Williams, Sr.—had a great deal to lose.

The exact date when Sam and Nancy Williams's oldest daughter married was not entered in the Buffalo Forge records, but it was probably sometime in 1857. Betty was seventeen then, and she and a man named A. Coleman, who apparently belonged to a neighboring slaveholder, became husband and wife.[80] On February 18, 1858, she gave birth to her first child, a boy, and they named him Alfred Elliott Coleman.[81] The baby may well have been named for his father, but since we know only the initial of his father's first name, we cannot be sure. Sam and Nancy were grandparents now, and Sam had just that much more reason to try to shelter his family from the worst aspects of the slave regime.

Perhaps nothing was more indicative of the precariousness of
their existence than the events of December 1859. Daniel Brady
was away on a cattle drive to Richmond during the first part of
the month, but one of the clerks took note of the events that were
pressing in on the black men and women there. On Friday,
December 2, 1859, "John Brown of Ossawatiamie [*sic*] Noteriety
to [be] hung at Charlestown Va. to day, for Insurrection," he wrote
in Brady's journal.[82] The day was unusually warm and sultry for
December, a sign that something worse was on the way. The rains
came the next day, Saturday, and enveloped Buffalo Forge in a
cold, biting drizzle that continued from early morning until well
into the night. It was not the best day for a wedding, but it was
the day Caroline Williams and Andrew Reid, a slave teamster who
lived nearby, had chosen to be married. Caroline, like her older
sister Betty, was seventeen at the time of her marriage, and, again
like her sister, had taken for her husband a man who was not one
of Weaver's slaves. Another slave girl at Buffalo Forge, fifteen-
year-old Amy Banks, was getting married at the same time; her
husband-to-be, James Carter, belonged to Charles H. Locher, who
operated the cement works at Balcony Falls on the James River,
a few miles south of Weaver's place.[83] A double wedding, with
both grooms coming from off the property, meant a large gathering
of slaves; and the timing—the day after John Brown was hanged
—was undoubtedly the reason why a distinctly unwelcome group
of uninvited guests turned up at Buffalo Forge that day. On
Saturday, December 3, the Rockbridge County slave patrol came
calling.[84]

Something akin to panic had swept over much of the South in
the wake of John Brown's October raid on Harper's Ferry, and
the Valley of Virginia was no exception. The only way to prevent
slave rebellions, whites argued, was through an overwhelming show
of force and the immediate suppression of the slightest hint of
insurrectionary activity.[85] It was not work for the squeamish. We
do not know what, if anything, Weaver's slaves said about John
Brown, but one of them apparently said or did something the
patrol did not like. The hated "paddyrollers," as the blacks called
them, left Buffalo Forge after the wedding party broke up on
Saturday, but they were back the next day.

Overnight the temperature plunged and the first snow of the
season fell at Buffalo Forge. Sunday dawned bright and clear, one

of those magnificent early-winter days in the Valley when the air is crisp and fresh and the cloudless sky forms a stunning contrast to the snow-covered Blue Ridge. The tranquility of this December day was soon shattered by the clatter of horses' hooves, as the slave patrol rode up the hill to Weaver's house. Perhaps a snide remark had been directed their way the day before, the day of the wedding, and had festered in the patrollers' minds during the night. Maybe it was nothing more than rumors of some loose talk among the slaves at the forge. It did not take much to set off the paddyrollers in the overheated atmosphere brought on by John Brown's raid. Whatever the reason may have been, their return visit resulted in an ugly incident that struck close to Sam Williams. The patrol singled out Henry Towles, Sam's helper at the refinery forge, for punishment; the twenty-three-year old forge hand was taken out, stripped, and whipped.[86] Towles, whose wife, Ann, and three young children lived with him at Buffalo Forge, did not return to work until December 15.[87] It had taken him ten days to recover from the beating administered by the Rockbridge County patrol.

Two weeks later, as the Valley lay under a new two-inch blanket of snow, a much happier event occurred at Buffalo Forge. At eight o'clock in the morning on December 29, Betty Coleman gave birth to her second child, and this time it was a girl. Both mother and daughter were fine.[88] Sam and Nancy Williams now had a granddaughter as well as a grandson at Buffalo Forge.

It had been a month of stark contradictions. The love and hope expressed in the marriage of two young people, followed by the pain and despair brought on by the brutal whipping of one of their own people, had been followed by the joy surrounding the birth of a healthy child. Those events spoke eloquently of the pleasure and anguish that mingled together in the lives of these black men and women, at Buffalo Forge and throughout the South.

Much of the history of American slavery could also be said to reside in the name of Betty Coleman's new baby. She and her husband called their newborn child Mary Caroline.[89] Her middle name was almost certainly given her in honor of her Aunt Caroline, who had celebrated her marriage just two weeks earlier. What better way could there be for Betty to show love and respect for her sister and, in the process of naming her new child, to

125

demonstrate the transcendent importance of the family to them all? The baby's first name, Mary, went back much farther in the history of the family, back to little Mary's great-great-grandmother. That Mary, mother of Sally Williams, grandmother of Sam Williams, was the woman taken by Thomas Mayburry when he and Weaver divided the "Wilson negroes" over two decades before. Memories of her, it seems fair to say, were still alive in the minds of her descendants at Buffalo Forge, a family that in 1859 spanned four generations there.

John Brown's raid was a prelude to the war that would free them all, although many of them would not be there when emancipation came in 1865. William Weaver was also not there. His final illness set in on a bleak day in mid-March 1863, just over a week after he had celebrated his eighty-third birthday. He died on March 25, 1863, and, true to his word, he left most of his considerable fortune to Daniel and Emma Brady.[90] "As I have kept the great bulk of my estate together partly to provide for the comfort of my servants I desire that they should be treated with kindness and humanity," he had written in his will.[91] The Bradys, from all we can tell, honored his wishes. Only one of his former slaves was put on the block after Weaver was gone. Bill Comiskey, a woodchopper, came in from the coalings with syphilis late in October 1863; a month later he was sold.[92] It was death, not the auctioneer's hammer, that took so many from Buffalo Forge before the day of freedom arrived.

The years of the Civil War were a time of mounting expectations among slaves everywhere in the South, and we can be reasonably sure that such was the case at Buffalo Forge. The Rockbridge Grays, a company in Stonewall Jackson's legendary brigade, had been recruited from the area right around the forge and had drawn off most of the young white men from that section of the county.[93] Even the most isolated slave could see the significance of that fact. And then the refugee families had come streaming past Weaver's place, sometimes spending the night in the big house, while their slaves took their rest in the quarters—and undoubtedly passed on the latest news to the black men and women there.[94] In Sam and Nancy Williams's case, however, the joy and hope inspired by the prospect of freedom must have been tempered by the grief and sorrow they had to live with during these years.

By the fall of 1862, their family had grown significantly. Their daughter Caroline had given birth to her first child, Mary Martha Reid (yet another Mary in the Williams family tree) in October 1860, and Betty Coleman had had her third baby, Julia, in November 1861. Less than a year later, in September 1862, Caroline had delivered another healthy child, a boy, William John Reid (one of Mary's children taken by Mayburry in 1837 had been named John).[95] But that September was also the month when death had begun stalking the Williams family at Buffalo Forge.

Caroline's boy, William John Reid, was born on September 5, 1862. Nine days later, Betty Coleman's four-year-old son, Alfred Elliott, complained of a sore throat. When Daniel Brady examined the boy, he saw unmistakable signs of impending disaster at Buffalo Forge. Alfred Elliott Coleman had diphtheria. Since immunization and effective treatment were not available, it was bound to spread quickly, and no one, black or white, would be safe from its ravages. In rapid succession, Betty, Caroline, and Lydia, three of Sam and Nancy Williams's four daughters, came down with the disease.[96]

When death came to Betty Coleman, it must have been a relief from terrible torment. The first signs of her diphtheria appeared on September 19, and it was clear from the large yellow streaks extending deep into her throat that she had a severe case, much worse than her son's. When a membrane formed at the top of her throat, Brady cauterized it, and she vomited up large, leathery pieces of tissue. She died late in the afternoon on Wednesday, September 24.[97] She was twenty-two years old and the mother of three small children, one of whom, Alfred Elliott, was fighting his own struggle against diphtheria. Her father and his forge helper, Henry Towles, dug her grave in the slave cemetery at Buffalo Forge the next morning, and that afternoon, under a clear, cool autumn sky, she was buried. Brady gave all hands the afternoon off so that they could be present at her funeral. Sam was not asked to return to his forge until the following Monday.[98]

For over two months, diphtheria lingered at Buffalo Forge, and before it ran its course, fifteen of Weaver's slaves contracted the disease. Alfred Coleman, Caroline Reid, and Lydia Williams gradually recovered, although the caustic and turpentine with which their throats were treated must have caused them enormous pain. Daniel Brady was also stricken. He was confined to his

bedroom for several weeks, but his case did not turn out to be one
of the fatal ones. Three more slaves at Buffalo Forge did die of
diphtheria following Betty's fatal attack, however, and before
October had ended, her son was also dead. Alfred Elliott Coleman,
perhaps weakened by his bout with diphtheria, died on October
31, 1862. Brady listed the cause of his death as an infestation of
worms.[99] In the space of six weeks, Sam and Nancy Williams had
lost their firstborn child and their oldest grandchild.

More grief was in the offing. Sam Williams was at his forge on
May 5, 1864, when news came that his mother was dead. Brady
noted that she died of "paralysis," probably a stroke. Sam and a
number of the older slaves were released from their duties on the
morning following her death, and later that day, Friday, May 6,
a beautiful spring day in the Valley, she was buried in the slave
cemetery at Buffalo Forge.[100] The cemetery, which stood in a
grove of locust trees on a hill behind the mansion, commanded a
magnificent view of the Valley—the pale haze of the Blue Ridge,
the dense green forests of oak, hickory, walnut, and cedar, the
rich fields of wheat, oats, and corn, the waters of Buffalo Creek
freshened by the spring thaw. There her wooden coffin was lowered into the earth, and a plain, uncarved shaft of limestone was
set up to mark her grave.[101] She had been among family and
friends in the last days of her life, and they were doubtless there
for her funeral: Sam Williams, Sr., in frail health but still alive;
her son Sam; her daughter-in-law Nancy; her grandchildren and
great-grandchildren; and her friends of many years' standing. Not
the least of the comforts that came to the enslaved was represented
by that gathering of black men, women, and children on a hilltop
overlooking Buffalo Forge in the spring of 1864—the solace and
strength that came from family and community in times of trial
and sadness.

Sam and Nancy Williams's time of troubles was still not over.
Tragedy seemed to haunt them in late 1864 and early 1865 as the
end of the war and the moment of freedom drew closer and closer.
In the fall of 1864, their twenty-year-old daughter Lydia, who was
unmarried, contracted typhoid fever. On October 7, 1864, as her
condition worsened, her older sister, Caroline Reid, gave birth to
her third child, a girl. The baby was named Lydia Maydelene
Reid in honor of Caroline's stricken sister. Two days later, on
Sunday, October 9, Lydia Williams died. Sam's forge was idle on

Monday as he spent the day with his family. On Tuesday morning, the black families of Buffalo Forge once again climbed the dirt road behind the big house to the locust grove on the hill. There Sam and Nancy laid their youngest child to rest.[102]

It was not finished even then. By early 1865 it was clear that a third Williams daughter was gravely ill. Caroline Williams Reid had "consumption," or tuberculosis, and there was no cure. She died on Thursday, January 12, 1865; she was twenty-three years old and the mother of three small children. Sam remained at home that day, and he would have been sorely needed by Nancy, by his one remaining daughter, Ann, and by his grandchildren. Betty Coleman had left two young children behind when she died in 1862, and now there were Caroline's three: Mary Martha, three years of age, William John, two, and Lydia Maydelene, who was only three months old.[103] If ever there was a time when a man and woman, slave or free, black or white, needed to be with each other and with their own, this was surely such a time. Sam and Nancy Williams were there, together.

They were also there when freedom came to Buffalo Forge in the spring of 1865. Brady's matter-of-fact entries for three days in late May tell the story:[104]

Friday May 26, 1865	Declared free by order of military authorities.
Saturday May 27, 1865	All hands quit work as they considered themselves free.
Monday May 29, 1865	Commenced work on free labor.

Sam and Nancy Williams were among those who signed three-month contracts on May 29, Sam as master refiner at the forge and Nancy as head dairymaid.[105] Sam continued refining until 1867, when outside competition finally forced Brady to abandon iron making at Buffalo Forge.[106] Sam shifted to farming on Brady's land in that year and, not surprisingly, became the most successful sharecropper, black or white, on the place.[107] And when he and Nancy finally moved off the property in 1874, they went only a short distance away—to an adjoining farm, owned by one of Brady's neighbors, where many of Sam's friends lived and where he found employment as an agricultural laborer.[108]

129

Space does not permit a full discussion here of Sam and Nancy Williams's life in freedom, but a few points that shed light on their experience in slavery deserve at least a brief mention. Their marriage and their family, so critically important to their survival in former times, was no less vital to them now. We can catch a glimpse of this at two poignant moments. One occurred in 1866 when they entered the office of the Freedmen's Bureau in Lexington. They had come to register their marriage, to legalize that slave union which had taken place twenty-six years before. "Samuel Williams and Nancy Jefferson as man and wife since 1840," the clerk recorded. Sam correctly listed his age at forty-six, Nancy as forty-nine; their only surviving child, their daughter Ann, was twenty-four.[109]

Fourteen years later, in 1880, there is another revealing moment, this one at the time when the census taker was making his rounds in southern Rockbridge County. He reported that Samuel Williams, farmhand, age sixty-one, and Nancy Williams, housewife, age sixty-three, lived in the same household in the Natural Bridge section of the county. Checks placed in the appropriate boxes indicated that neither could read or write. There was a third member of the family, however. Living with them, the census taker noted, was Lydia Maydelene Reid, their granddaughter. The baby who had been only three months old when her mother had died in 1865 was now a girl of fifteen.[110]

How long Sam and Nancy Williams lived on after 1880 is unclear. Lydia married in January 1882 and left the household to begin raising a family of her own. Her husband was a young man named Charles Newman, and their first child, a girl, was born in November 1882; they named her Mary Ann Newman.[111] We do not know exactly when Sam and Nancy died—it was sometime before 1900—but we can be reasonably sure where they are buried.[112] Shortly after the Civil War, the black men and women at Buffalo Forge organized their own church. For a nominal sum, Daniel Brady sold the church trustees a small tract of land just a mile south of the forge; among the trustees of the Buffalo Forge Colored Baptist Church (soon renamed the Mount Lydia Church) was one Samuel Williams.[113] The freedmen erected a wooden church and schoolhouse and laid out a cemetery on this land in 1871.[114] The church building has long since disappeared, and today the cemetery site is covered with trees and a heavy growth of underbrush. But if one looks closely enough back among the trees and under the dense carpet of honeysuckle, one can discern small, uncarved, triangular-shaped pieces of limestone. Almost certainly, one of these simple limestone markers stands over the grave of Sam Williams. It is equally certain that a similar stone on the grave nearest his marks the final resting place of Nancy, his wife. The points of all these stones face in the same direction—toward the sky.

NOTES

1. Weaver's property was located in Rockbridge, Botetourt, and Amherst counties. On the quantity of land held by Weaver, see his property-tax receipts in James D. Davidson Papers, McCormick Collection, State Historical Society of Wisconsin, Madison (hereafter cited as Davidson Papers, McCormick Collection); articles of agreement between William Wilson and Thomas Mayburry and William Weaver, July 30, 1814, Jordan and Irvine Papers, ibid. (hereafter cited as Jordan and Irvine Papers, McCormick Collection); entries for William Weaver in Manuscript Census of Agriculture, 1860, Virginia (microfilm copy, Virginia State Library, Richmond). Weaver's slave holdings at the time of his death are given in "An appraisement of the goods and chattels of William Weaver, deceased," June 1, 1863, William Weaver Papers, University of Virginia Library, Charlottesville, Va. (hereafter cited as Weaver Papers, Virginia).

2. "An appraisement," June 1, 1863, Weaver Papers, Virginia.

3. "Article of agreement . . . between Danl. C. E. Brady . . . and Sam Williams (Freedman)," January 1, 1867, Weaver-Brady Papers in the possession of T. T. Brady, Richmond, Va. (hereafter cited as Weaver-Brady Papers, T. T. Brady). I would like to thank Mr. Brady for kindly granting me access to these papers and for his generous assistance on numerous occasions when I needed help on points relating to Buffalo Forge and the Weaver and Brady families.

4. See Charles L. Perdue, Jr., et al, eds., *Weevils in the Wheat: Interviews with Virginia Ex-Slaves* (Charlottesville, 1976), and George P. Rawick, ed., *The American Slave: A Composite Autobiography*, 41 vols. (Westport, Conn., 1972, 1977, 1979).

5. "Weaver Family: Memo and Historical Notes," Weaver-Brady Family Record Book, Weaver-Brady Papers, T. T. Brady.

6. Articles of agreement between William Wilson and Thomas Mayburry & William Weaver, July 30, 1814, Jordan and Irvine Papers, McCormick Collection.

7. Mayburry to Weaver, September 15, October 18, 1815, February 4, 1816, in Case Papers, Weaver v. Mayburry, Superior Court of Chancery Records, Augusta County Court House, Staunton, Va. (hereafter cited as Case Papers, Weaver v. Mayburry).

8. Statement of Thomas Mayburry, October 1, 1821, ibid.

9. John S. Wilson to Weaver, October 24, 1815, ibid. All ages given on the bill of sale were approximations.

10. See deposition of James C. Dickinson, August 15, 1836, in Case Papers, Weaver v. Jordan, Davis & Co., Superior Court of Chancery Records, Rockbridge County Court House, Lexington, Va. (hereafter cited as Case Papers, Weaver v. Jordan, Davis & Co.).

11. Bond of Mayburry for the forthcoming of slaves, December 20, 1828, Case Papers, Weaver v. Mayburry; "An appraisement," June 1, 1863, Weaver Papers, Virginia.

12. "Names, births & c: of Negroes," Weaver-Brady Papers, T. T. Brady.

13. W. W. Davis to Weaver, July 7, 1832, William Weaver Papers, Duke University Library, Durham, N.C. (hereafter cited as Weaver Papers, Duke).

14. Mayburry to Weaver, October 18, November 10, December 19, 1817, March 29, July 16, 1818, September 22, 1819, August 19, 1821, June 15, November 14, 1822, Case Papers, Weaver v. Mayburry; deposition of William Weaver, December 10, 1840, Case Papers, Alexander v. Irvine's Administrator, Superior Court of Chancery Records, Rockbridge County Court House (hereafter cited as Case Papers, Alexander v. Irvine's Administrator).

15. "Articles of agreement . . . between Thomas Mayburry and William Weaver," February 9, 1825, Weaver Papers, Duke.

16. John S. Wilson to Mayburry, March 1, 1825, Case Papers, Weaver v. Mayburry.

17. See deposition of Thomas Mayburry, April 22, 1839, Case Papers, Weaver v. Jordan, Davis & Co.

18. "Article of agreement . . . between Thos. Mayburry & Wm. Weaver," August 3, 1836, Weaver Papers, Duke.

19. Ibid.; deposition of Thomas Mayburry, April 20, 1839, Case Papers, Weaver v. Jordan, Davis & Co.

20. Bond of Thomas Mayburry for the forthcoming of slaves, December 20, 1828, Case Papers, Weaver v. Mayburry; "Names, births & c: of Negroes," Weaver-Brady Papers, T. T. Brady; Buffalo Forge Negro Books, 1830–40, 1839–41, 1844–50, 1850–58, Weaver-Brady Records, University of Virginia Library, Charlottesville (hereafter cited as Weaver-Brady Records, Virginia).

21. Buffalo Forge Negro Books, 1830–40, 1839–41, 1844–50, 1850–58, Weaver-Brady Records, Virginia.

22. Ibid., 1850–58.

23. "An appraisement," June 1, 1863, Weaver Papers, Virginia.

24. See Charles B. Dew, "David Ross and the Oxford Iron Works: A Study of Industrial Slavery in the Early Nineteenth-Century South," *William and Mary Quarterly*, 3rd ser., 31 (1974), 197–98.

25. Ibid., pp. 197, 210–11; "List of Slaves at the Oxford Iron Works in Families and Their Employment, Taken 15 January 1811," William Bolling Papers, Duke University Library, Durham, N.C. (hereafter cited as Bolling Papers, Duke).

26. Weaver to Brady, March 4, 1856, Weaver Papers, Duke.

27. "Descriptive List of Negroes hired . . .," Confederate States Nitre and Mining Service, 1865," Weaver-Brady Papers, T. T. Brady.

28. Buffalo Forge Negro Book, 1830–40, Weaver-Brady Records, Virginia.

29. Weaver to James D. Davidson, November 4, 1849, Davidson Papers, McCormick Collection.

30. See Arthur Cecil Bining, *Pennsylvania Iron Manufacture in the Eighteenth Century*, 2nd ed. (Harrisburg, Pa., 1973), pp. 72–73.

31. Deposition of William Weaver, December 10, 1840, Case Papers, Alexander v. Irvine's Administrator; Weaver's cane is in the possession of Mr. D. E. Brady, Jr., Buffalo Forge, Va.

32. Samuel Sydney Bradford, "The Ante-Bellum Charcoal Iron Industry of Virginia" (Ph.D. diss., Columbia University, 1958), p. 134; Bining, *Pennsylvania Iron Manufacture*, pp. 72–73.

33. Buffalo Forge Negro Books, 1830–40, 1839–41, Weaver-Brady Records, Virginia.

34. Bining, *Pennsylvania Iron Manufacture*, pp. 73–74.

35. Buffalo Forge Iron Book, 1831–62, Weaver-Brady Records, Virginia; Moses McCue to Weaver, July 3, 1829; Weaver Papers, Duke; deposition of William Weaver, December 10, 1840, Case Papers, Alexander v. Irvine's Administrator.

36. Weaver to Davidson, June 12, 1848, Jordan and Irvine Papers, McCormick Collection.

37. See Buffalo Forge Negro Books, 1830–40, 1839–41, 1844–50, 1850–58, Weaver-Brady Records, Virginia. The best general discussions of the overwork system are Robert S. Starobin, *Industrial Slavery in the Old South* (New York, 1970), pp. 99–103, and Ronald L. Lewis, *Coal, Iron, and Slaves: Industrial Slavery in Maryland and Virginia, 1715–1865* (Westport, Conn., 1979), pp. 119–27.

38. Depositions of John Doyle, February 5, 1840, Anthony W. Templin, January 24, 1839, John Jordan, July 22, 1836, and Henry A. Lane, February 5, 1840, Case Papers, Weaver v. Jordan, Davis & Co.

39. Buffalo Forge Negro Books, 1830–40, 1839–41, 1844–50, 1850–58, and Etna Furnace Negro Book, 1854–61, Weaver-Brady Records, Virginia.

40. Wm. C. McAllister to Weaver, February 22, 1830, Weaver Papers, Duke.

41. See entries for Sam Etna, John Baxter, and Harry Hunt in Buffalo Forge Negro Book, 1839–41, Weaver-Brady Records, Virginia.

42. See "List of Slaves at the Oxford Iron Works . . . 1811," Bolling Papers, Duke; Dew, "David Ross and the Oxford Iron Works," pp. 189–94, 222–24.

43. Buffalo Forge Negro Book, 1839–41, Weaver-Brady Records, Virginia.

44. Marriage Register for Rockbridge County, Sub-district "A," 6th District, Virginia, Records of the Bureau of Refugees, Freedmen, and Abandoned Lands, Record Group 105, National Archives, Washington, D.C. (hereafter cited as Marriage Register for Rockbridge County, Freedmen's Bureau Records, RG 105, NA).

45. As indicated by his entries in Buffalo Forge Negro Book, 1839–41, Weaver-Brady Records, Virginia.

46. "Names, births & c: of Negroes," Weaver-Brady Papers, T. T. Brady.

47. Bond of Thomas Mayburry for the forthcoming of slaves, December 20, 1828, Case Papers, Weaver v. Mayburry.

48. Buffalo Forge Negro Book, 1830–40, Weaver-Brady Records, Virginia.

49. For a description of this process, see W. McKee Evans, *Ballots and Fence Rails: Reconstruction on the Lower Cape Fear* (Chapel Hill, 1967), pp. 195–96.

50. Buffalo Forge Negro Book, 1839–41, Weaver-Brady Records, Virginia.

51. Ibid.

52. Ibid.

53. Marriage Register for Rockbridge County, Freedmen's Bureau Records, RG 105, NA; "Names, births & c: of Negroes," Weaver-Brady Papers, T. T. Brady.

54. Buffalo Forge Negro Book, 1839–41, Weaver-Brady Records, Virginia.

55. Ibid., 1844–50.

56. Ibid., 1850–58.

57. Ibid.

58. Ibid., 1844–50, 1850–58.

59. Ibid.

60. John A. Rex to Davidson, February 25, 1855, Davidson Papers, McCormick Collection.

61. Notation on reverse, ibid.

62. D. C. E. Brady Private Ledger, Weaver-Brady Papers in the possession of Mr. D. E. Brady, Jr., Buffalo Forge, Va. (hereafter cited as Weaver-Brady Papers, D. E. Brady, Jr.). I would like to thank Mr. Brady for kindly granting me access to these papers and for his generous assistance when I need help on points relating to Buffalo Forge and the Weaver and Brady families.

Without his aid and that of his brother, Mr. T. T. Brady, the research for this essay could not have been completed. I am deeply grateful for all they have done.

63. Ibid.

64. One can follow their accounts by tracing the entries under their names in: Buffalo Forge Ledger, 1851–59, Weaver-Brady Papers, T. T. Brady; Buffalo Forge Ledger, 1859–78, Weaver-Brady Papers, D. E. Brady, Jr.; Buffalo Forge Journal, 1859–66, Weaver-Brady Records, Virginia; and Buffalo Forge Journal, 1866–78, Weaver-Brady Papers, D. E. Brady, Jr.

65. Weaver to Brady, August 27, 1855, March 4, 1856, Weaver Papers, Duke.

66. Weaver family history compiled by D. E. Brady, Sr., October 28, 1951, Weaver-Brady Papers, D. E. Brady, Jr.; "Weaver Family," Weaver-Brady Family Record Book, Weaver-Brady Papers, T. T. Brady.

67. Weaver to Brady, August 27, 1855, March 4, 1856, and to Emma M. Brady, March 21, 1856, Weaver Papers, Duke.

68. Weaver to Brady, August 27, 1855, ibid.

69. "Brady Family" and "Gorgas Family," Weaver-Brady Family Record Book, and [D. C. E. Brady] to Davidson, July 27, 1867, Weaver-Brady Papers, T. T. Brady.

70. Daniel C. E. Brady, Home Journal, 1858–60, Weaver-Brady Records, Virginia; Daniel C. E. Brady, Home Journal, 1860–65, McCormick Collection (hereafter cited as Brady, Home Journal, Virginia; Brady, Home Journal, McCormick Collection).

71. Ibid., Virginia.

72. Ibid.

73. Ibid.

74. Ibid.; J. E. Carson to Weaver, March 12, May 30, June 27, 1859, Weaver Papers, Duke; Weaver to Carson, July 2, 1859, Buffalo Forge Letterbook, 1858–65, Weaver-Brady Records, Virginia; entries for June 9, July 30, 1859, Buffalo Forge Cash Book, 1849–62, ibid.

75. W. W. Rex to Weaver, August 15, 1860, Weaver Papers, Duke; entry for August 7, 1860, Buffalo Forge Cash Book, 1849–62, Weaver-Brady Records, Virginia; Brady, Home Journal, Virginia.

76. Brady, Home Journal, Virginia.

77. Buffalo Forge Cash Book, 1849–62, ibid.

78. Ibid.

79. "Names, births & c: of Negroes," Weaver-Brady Papers, T. T. Brady.

80. Ibid. Betty's husband's name was given at the time one of their children married in 1876; see marriage registration of Mary C. Coleman and Steward Chandler, July 27, 1876, Register of Marriages, Book 1A, 1865–89, Rockbridge County Court House, Lexington, Va. (hereafter cited as Rockbridge County Marriage Register, 1865–89).

81. "Names, births & c: of Negroes," Weaver-Brady Papers, T. T. Brady.

82. Brady, Home Journal, Virginia.

83. Ibid.; Ch. H. Locher to Weaver, December 3, 1859, Weaver-Brady Papers, T. T. Brady; "Names, births & c: of Negroes," ibid.; Marriage Register for Rockbridge County, Freedmen's Bureau Records, RG 105, NA. Caroline's husband's name was given at the time one of their children married in 1882; see marriage registration of Lydia Reid and Charles Newman, January 4, 1882, Rockbridge County Marriage Register, 1865–89.

84. Brady, Home Journal, Virginia.

85. Clement Eaton, *The Freedom-of-Thought Struggle in the Old South* (New York, 1964), pp. 102–3; Eaton's chapter "The Fear of Servile Insurrection" provides an excellent discussion of overall white attitudes. See also Charles B. Dew, "Black Ironworkers and the Slave Insurrection Panic of 1856," *Journal of Southern History*, 41 (1975), 327–33.

86. Brady, Home Journal, Virginia.

87. Ibid.; "Names, births & c: of Negroes," Weaver-Brady Papers, T. T. Brady.

88. Ibid.

89. "Names, births & c: of Negroes," Weaver-Brady Papers, T. T. Brady.

90. Brady, Home Journal, Virginia; Last Will and Testament of William Weaver, January 8, 1863, William Weaver Papers, Washington and Lee University Library, Lexington, Va. (hereafter cited as Weaver Papers, W & L).

91. Last Will and Testament, January 8, 1863, Weaver Papers, W & L.

92. Entry for October 24, 1863, Brady, Home Journal, McCormick Collection; "Names, births & c: of Negroes," Weaver-Brady Papers, T. T. Brady.

93. Oren F. Morton, *A History of Rockbridge County, Virginia* (Staunton, Va., 1920), pp. 126, 425–27; entry for April 20, 1861, Brady, Home Journal, McCormick collection.

94. Entries for March 7, April 28, 1862, Brady, Home Journal, McCormick Collection.

95. "Names, births & c: of Negroes," Weaver-Brady Papers, T. T. Brady.

96. Brady, Home Journal, McCormick Collection; see entries under "Diptheria & Sore Throat 1862," rear flyleaf, vol. 1, ibid.

97. Ibid.

98. Brady, Home Journal, McCormick Collection.

99. "Names, births & c: of Negroes," Weaver-Brady Papers, T. T. Brady; "Diptheria & Sore Throat 1862," Brady, Home Journal, McCormick Collection.

100. Brady, Home Journal, McCormick Collection.

101. Ibid. Mr. D. E. Brady, Jr., pointed out to me the site of this cemetery; a number of the gravestones are still there.

136

102. "Names, births & c: of Negroes," Weaver-Brady Papers, T. T. Brady; Brady, Home Journal, McCormick Collection.

103. Ibid.

104. Buffalo Forge Journal, 1859–66, Weaver-Brady Records, Virginia; Brady, Home Journal, McCormick Collection.

105. See entries under "Sam Williams" and "Nancy Williams," Buffalo Forge Negro Book, 1865–73, Weaver-Brady Records, Virginia.

106. Ibid., "Sam Williams"; "Account Sales Iron made by Rocke & Murrell," Lynchburg, Va., 1865, 1866, Weaver Papers, Duke.

107. "Article of agreement . . . between Danl. C. E. Brady . . . & Sam Williams (Freedman)," January 1, 1867, Weaver-Brady Papers, T. T. Brady; entries for Sam Williams and other sharecroppers in D. C. E. Brady, Home Journal, 1865–76, ibid. (hereafter cited as Brady, Home Journal, T. T. Brady).

108. The last entries for Sam Williams are dated 1874 in Brady, Home Journal, T. T. Brady; Manuscript Population Schedules, Rockbridge County, Va., Tenth Census of the United States, 1880, National Archives Microfilm Publications, T9.

109. Marriage Register for Rockbridge County, Freedmen's Bureau Records, RG 105, NA.

110. Manuscript Population Schedules, Rockbridge County, Va., Tenth Census of the United States, 1880.

111. See marriage registration of Lydia Reid and Charles Newman, January 4, 1882, Rockbridge County Marriage Register, 1865–89; birth registration of Mary Ann Newman, Birth Register No. 2, 1878–1896, Rockbridge County Court House, Lexington, Va.

112. A search of the index and population schedules for the 1900 Census failed to turn up the names of either Sam or Nancy Williams; Card Index (Soundex) to the 1900 Population Schedules, Virginia, National Archives Microfilm Publications, T1076; Manuscript Population Schedules, Rockbridge County, Va., Twelfth Census of the United States, 1900, National Archives Microfilm Publications, T623.

113. Deed between D. C. E. Brady, et al., and Samuel Williams, et al., October 9, 1871, Deed Book MM, Rockbridge County Court House, Lexington, Va.

114. "Col. Baptist Church of Buffalo Forge, Va.," account with D. C. E. Brady, 1871, Weaver-Brady Papers, T. T. Brady.

A STAPLE INTERPRETATION OF SLAVERY AND FREE LABOR*

CARVILLE V. EARLE

THE economic interpretation of labor systems offers a powerful explanation of the geography of slavery and free labor in antebellum Anglo-America.[1] Although the past decade has produced a crippling assault on this thesis, I shall contend that recent critics misapplied the economic model, erroneously concluded that slavery was the most efficient agrarian labor system in North America, and incorrectly inferred that the North rejected slavery for ideological-moral reasons rather than economic ones. When these critics assumed the comparability of slave-free-labor efficiencies during a yearly time span, they unwittingly placed wage labor in an untenable position. Wage labor was competitive for part of a year but never on an annual basis. Farmers who needed labor for a few days, weeks, or months found the use of hired labor decidedly cheaper and more efficient economically than slaves. The decisive factor in the farmer's choice of either slave or free labor came down to the annual labor requirements of his staple crop: crops such as wheat, which required only a few weeks of attention, lent themselves to wage labor; whereas crops such as tobacco or cotton, which demanded sustained attention during a long growing season, lent themselves to slave labor. The introduction of these appropriate free-labor costs into a labor-efficiency model reveals that the geography of antebellum slavery and free labor conforms rather well to economic theory. Farmers and planters used the economically rational labor supply; and more specifically, northern farmers rejected slavery because it was less efficient than free labor, not because slavery was morally or ideologically repugnant.

The causal link between staple crops and labor supply is revealed most clearly where regions shift from one staple to another. Of special interest are those regions that changed from "few-day" staples to "multiple-day" staples, or vice versa, with the attendant adjustments in labor supply. Accordingly, this paper examines two regions of staple change: the tobacco-to-wheat transition on the eastern shore of Maryland during the eighteenth century, and the wheat-to-corn transistion in the antebellum Lower Midwest. In Maryland, tobacco produced by slaves prevailed until the 1720's; but as wheat took hold, hired labor proved more efficient and gradually replaced slaves. Privately manumitted slaves swelled both the free black population and the general wage-labor force. Matters were reversed in the emerging corn belt of southern

---

* Earlier versions of this paper were presented at the Eastern Historical Geography Association meeting held at the University of Delaware in the fall of 1976 and to the History Seminar held at the University of Maryland Baltimore County. I am indebted to the participants in these sessions and to Franklin Mendels and Allan Bogue for their comments and suggestions.

[1] Until now, the economic interpretation of slavery and free labor has been sustained on argument more than on substantive evidence of labor efficiency. The best statement connecting plantation crops and slavery appears in Lewis C. Gray: History of Agriculture in the Southern United States to 1860 (2 vols.; Peter Smith, Gloucester, Mass., 1958), Vol. 1, pp. 462–480. Also, see Robert Baldwin: Patterns of Development in Newly Settled Regions, *Manchester School of Econ. and Soc. Studies*, Vol. 24, 1956, pp. 161–179; and Douglass C. North: Agriculture in Regional Economic Growth, *Journ. Farm Econ. Proc.*, Vol. 41, 1959, pp. 943–951. A cogent review of the issues is in Stanley L. Engerman: Some Considerations Relating to Property Rights in Man, *Journ. Econ. Hist.*, Vol. 33, 1973, pp. 43–65.

● DR. EARLE, an associate professor of geography at the University of Maryland Baltimore County, is a Fellow of the Charles Warren Center for Studies in American History, Harvard University, Cambridge, Massachusetts 02138, for the 1977/1978 academic year.

and central Ohio, Indiana, and Illinois. Wheat was the initial staple, produced by wage labor and by family farm members. But owing to the expansion of corn in the 1840's and 1850's, to the demanding cultivation requirements of corn as compared with wheat, and to rising wage rates, hired labor was steadily pushed into economic competition with slaves. The corn-hog region gave increasingly vocal support to proslavery politics, parties, and legislation and helped force through severely restrict- ive state laws that curtailed the civil rights of free blacks and led them toward servitude if not enslavement. Slavery was headed for the North in the wake of a corn economy; the only way to halt the laws of economics and preserve northern free labor was to destroy the peculiar institution in a civil war.

The economic interpretation of labor systems is controversial, and the wise course is to proceed cautiously. I begin by briefly reviewing the economic model of labor choice and the critics of an economic interpretation before I turn to the refined staple model and to the two regions of study.

LABOR: SLAVE OR FREE

Interpretations of slavery and free labor, whether economic or noneconomic, begin at the same place: the calculation of relative labor efficiencies. The rational capitalist farmer, faced with a choice of slavery or free labor, chooses in accordance with Evsey Domar's model of labor profitability.[2] The farmer compares outputs and costs of slaves and freemen and uses the labor supply that offers the greatest return. Stated more generally, the farmer prefers free labor when $P_f - P_s > W_f - W_s$, where P_f is the net average productivity of free labor, P_s is the net average productivity of slave labor, W_f is the cost of free labor, and W_s is the subsistence and discounted costs of slave labor. The model is simplified when slave and free-labor outputs are shown as equivalent or nearly so, in which case labor choice becomes a matter of least cost, and free labor is used when $W_s > W_f$. Domar, though he did not test his model with data from the United States, speculated that such a test would probably show slavery as the most efficient labor supply for the entire nation; and, therefore, northern rejection of slavery must be interpreted on noneconomic gounds. Yet Domar was ambivalent. As an economist, he knew that if his hunch proved correct, it would seriously undermine economic rationality as a behavioral model.

I know of two tests of Domar's model, albeit crude ones. Each sustains his hunch about the economic superiority of slavery. In 1967, Arthur Zilversmit presented a double-barreled argument on northern labor before 1800.[3] First, he concluded that slave and free-labor outputs were similar, thus casting doubt on the assumption that the incentive of freedom resulted in greater productivity than slavery. Recently and independently John Hicks reached the same conclusion on theoretical grounds.[4] Having set productivities equal, Zilversmit turned to the cost side, compared slave prices with white servant prices and annual free wage rates, and concluded plausibly

[2] Evsey Domar: The Causes of Slavery or Serfdom: A Hypothesis. *Journ. Econ. Hist.*, Vol. 30, 1970, pp. 18–32. Economic historians have acknowledged Domar's contribution, but they have given too much attention to the land-labor ratio as a determinant of wage rates while disregarding empirical tests of the labor efficiency model. Wage labor can be used in societies with high land-labor ratios, as will be pointed out below.

[3] Arthur Zilversmit: The First Emancipation: The Abolition of Slavery in the North (Univ. of Chicago Press, Chicago, 1967), pp. 33–53. Also, Leon F. Litwak: North of Slavery: The Negro in the Free States, 1790–1860 (Univ. of Chicago Press, Chicago and London, 1961), pp. 3–29.

[4] John Hicks: A Theory of Economic History (Clarendon Press, Oxford, 1969), pp. 122–140.

that slaves, when the costs were discounted over their useful lives, were much less expensive than either wage labor or servant labor. Although more refined economic calculations might increase Zilversmit's slave costs, his conclusions that slavery was the most efficient labor system and that its abolition in the North was rooted in ideology, morality, and ethics remain unshaken.

Domar and Zilversmit weakened the economic interpretation of labor, but the most damaging blow was delivered long ago, in 1795. In that year, William Strickland tried to prove that slavery was a poor economic choice in Virginia, but his evidence showed just the opposite: slaves cost less than free labor not only in Virginia but in all of the United States as well.[5]

Strickland's method was straightforward. The Englishman believed the Virginia planters' lament that slaves entailed excessive costs and low returns. He set out to verify these complaints by attacking the cost side of Domar's equation, confident that slaves would cost much more than free labor. Using records of construction costs of the James River Canal, Strickland calculated slave costs at £18 a year, which consisted of annual hire rates for adult male slaves of £9 plus maintenance costs of £9. He then computed daily slave cost at 1s. 2d. and compared this figure with Chesapeake free-labor day rates. Much to Strickland's disappointment, slaves cost the planters less than free whites, who hired out at 1s. 6d. a day. In fact, the cost advantage to slavery was much greater than Strickland's estimates because of his biased accounting. Specifically, slave maintenance costs of £9 are very high, and a more realistic estimate on the order of £3 to £6 a year drives down daily slave costs to 9s. 4d. or 11s. 7d., respectively. These figures make the costs of slaves lower than the costs of either free Negroes or free whites. Slavery won on the cost side in Virginia and also in the northern states, where free labor received 1s. to 2s. per day, according to Strickland's own estimates.

Strickland persisted in pressing his thesis of the economic inferiority of slavery. Having lost on the cost side, he launched a vicious attack on slave output—Domar's productivity. Slaves were depicted as inert, recalcitrant, slovenly, and prone to willful destruction and pilfering. Given these traits, Strickland concurred with "the received opinion of the country, that slave-labour is much dearer than any other; and that the price paid for the *time* of a slave, by no means shows the amount of value of his labour; it certainly is much higher than it appears to be; though not knowing the quantity of labour performed by slaves in general in a given time, in a sufficient number of instances, I have not data whereon to calculate the exact value."[6] This tactic will not do.

Low slave productivity cannot be inferred from Strickland's exaggerated stereotype of black behavior. Slaves may have been at times lazy, slovenly, and subversive in the fields, but the evidence we have from colonial America suggests that white freemen behaved in similar ways;[7] and furthermore, measures of physical productivity thus far assembled show no appreciable differences in output between white and black, or slave and free. For instance, Chesapeake tobacco growers between 1660 and

---

[5] William Strickland: Journal of a Tour in the United States of America, 1794–1795, With a Facsimile Edition of William Strickland's "Observations on the Agriculture of the United States of America" (edited by J. E. Strickland; New-York Hist. Soc., New York, 1971), pp. 31–36.

[6] *Ibid.*, pp. 33–34.

[7] See, for example, David Bertelson: The Lazy South (Oxford Univ. Press, New York, 1967); and Edmund S. Morgan: American Slavery American Freedom: The Ordeal of Colonial Virginia (W. W. Norton & Company, Inc., New York, 1975).

1770 consistently produced between 1,500 and 2,200 pounds per year per laborer, and slaveholding planters produced more tobacco than those planters without slaves.[8] Nor is there any compelling reason for believing that free labor produced more corn or wheat than slaves, per unit of labor input.[9] In short, Strickland's invective against the productivity of slaves must be dismissed. The rest of his argument supports the Domar-Zilversmit thesis that northern farmers who hired free labor chose an inefficient labor force.

The economic interpretation of American slavery and free labor, long sustained by tradition and faith, is in shambles as a result of these recent studies. The suggestion that northern farmers used an inefficient labor supply is subtly shifting the attention of economic history and historical geography from South to North and from economic to noneconomic explanations of northern free labor. The issue is not why the South used slaves but why the North did not use them.[10] In the remainder of this essay I address the borderland between North and South, where both slaves and free labor were accessible. Careful consideration of this borderland reveals flaws in the revisionist inefficiency thesis, while refining and clarifying the staple economic basis of labor choice.

A Staple Economic Interpretation of Labor Systems

Domar's labor efficiency model will explain the geography of labor, provided that labor inputs of freemen and slaves are compared fairly. Returning to that model, let us assume that slave and free-labor outputs are equivalent—a point suggested by the evidence cited above. Entrepreneurs select the labor supply by comparing costs and choosing the least expensive, such that they use slaves when $W_s < W_f$ and free labor when $W_f < W_s$. All this is easy enough; the tough problem is assessing the comparable costs. Heretofore, slave-labor and free-labor costs have been assessed as though each group were employed for a whole year. Such a procedure, while appropriate for slaves as permanent fixtures, has the effect of vastly inflating the costs of hired labor, customarily employed by the day or for several weeks or months but rarely by the year. During these short terms hired labor was competitive with slaves, as long as the number of days of hired labor times the daily wage rate was less than the cost of a slave.

It is precisely at this point that staples play a decisive role by regulating the amount of required labor days. During the growing season, staples vary remarkably in their daily demands for labor. The time-honored distinction between plantation crops and small grains reflects these differences in labor requirements. Plantation crops, such as tobacco, cotton, and wet rice, are so called because they are planted separately and command individual attention by labor during the growing season,

---

[8] Carville V. Earle: The Evolution of a Tidewater Settlement System: All Hallow's Parish, Maryland, 1650-1783, *Univ. of Chicago, Dept. of Geography, Research Paper No. 170,* Chicago, 1975, pp. 24-27.

[9] "I have a hard time believing that slaves could not be used in the mixed farming of the North; much food was produced on southern farms as well, most of the slave owners had very few slaves, and many slaves were skilled in crafts" (Domar, *op. cit.* [see footnote 2 above], p. 30).

[10] Domar urged this refocusing in 1970, but so far the "new" economic historians have disregarded the problem of slave-free labor efficiencies under the same crops and have instead directed their attention to the efficiencies of farms and plantations. These are not the same, as is forcefully pointed out in Paul A. David and Peter Temin: Slavery: The Progressive Institution? *in* Reckoning with Slavery (by Paul A. David, Herbert G. Gutman, Richard Sutch, Peter Temin, and Gavin Wright; Oxford Univ. Press, New York, 1976), pp. 165-230, reference on pp. 202-203.

especially during cultivation.[11] Their frequent and even demands for labor invariably drove up wage labor costs beyond slave costs. By contrast, broadcast grains such as wheat demand labor in concentrated applications. Wheat labor worked sunup to sunset during fall planting and midsummer harvest, but no labor was required between these periods.[12] The economically rational antebellum wheat farmer almost always employed wage labor because the few days of labor required times the daily wage rate usually fell below the cost of slaves.

The plantation–small grain dichotomy, though traditional, confuses the main issue: how many days of attention the staples require during the crop season. Theoretically, the number of days of attention ranges from one to three hundred and sixty-five, and the appropriate dichotomy is thus between few-day and multiple-day crops. For instance, dairy farming, though never regarded as a plantation crop, demands labor during the entire year and is as much a multiple-day staple as plantation cotton or tobacco. Might this fact not explain the otherwise anomalous use of slaves in the dairying zone of colonial Narragansett, Rhode Island?[13] To cite another example, corn requires labor days intermediate between the extremes of wheat and cotton or dairying. The extensive labor demands of corn during the three-to-four month period of plowing and tillage made it adaptable to slaves or freemen, depending on wage rates and slave costs.[14] Using the "required-days" approach suggested here, we may achieve a more realistic assessment of wage costs that faced the farmer who chose between slaves and freemen.

A caveat is in order. Staple labor days are not to be confused with labor intensity. For example, two crops that use equivalent acreage and require identical labor inputs of 300 man-hours may have different allocations of labor during the growing season. One crop may be tended in just thirty days, for ten hours a day, while the other requires seventy-five days at four hours a day. Under prevailing wage rates and slave costs in pre-1860 Anglo-America, the former favored freemen, the latter slaves.[15]

At this point, Domar's model can be refined for free labor by restricting comparison to similar staples. Farmers will choose free labor when $W_r D_l < W_s$, where W_r is the wage rate of free labor and D_l represents the labor days required by the staple.

[11] Gray, *op. cit.* [see footnote 1 above], Vol. 1, pp. 462–480; and Baldwin, *op. cit.* [see footnote 1 above], pp. 161–179.

[12] "Our winter crops of wheat, rley, & c. also the oats flax & buckwheat are so disposed of as to require no further care [until harvest] after the seeds are put into the ground" (R. O. Bausman and J. A. Munroe, edits.: James Tilton's Notes on the Agriculture of Delaware in 1788, *Agric. Hist.*, Vol. 20, 1946, pp. 176–187, reference on p. 181). See also Peter Kalm: Travels into North America (The Imprint Society, Barre, Mass., 1972), p. 77; and John H. Klippart: The Wheat Plant: Its Origin, Culture, Growth, Development, Composition, Varieties, Diseases, etc., etc. Together with a Few Remarks on Indian Corn, Its Culture, etc. (Moore, Wilstach, Keys, Cincinnati, Ohio, 1860), pp. 475–478.

[13] Percy Wells Bidwell and John I. Falconer: History of Agriculture in the Northern United States, 1620–1860 (Peter Smith, New York, 1941), pp. 106 and 109–110.

[14] Bausman and Munroe, *op. cit.* [see footnote 12 above], p. 181; Robert Russell: North America, Its Agriculture and Climate; Containing Observations on the Agriculture and Climate of Canada, the United States, and the Island of Cuba (A. and C. Black, Edinburgh, 1857), pp. 81–82; and Allan G. Bogue: From Prairie to Cornbelt: Farming on the Illinois and Iowa Prairies in the Nineteenth Century (Quadrangle Books, Chicago, 1968), pp. 132–133.

[15] Economists have generally regarded labor inputs in terms of intensity (man-hours or man-days); hence systematic data on the more critical labor input of "required days" are lacking. These data are available, however, in sensitive accounts by agricultural historians. See Bogue, *op. cit.* [see footnote 14 above], pp. 132–133; Gray, *op. cit.* [see footnote 1 above], Vol. 1, pp. 462–480; and Paul W. Gates: The Farmer's Age: Agriculture, 1815–1860 (Harper & Row Publishers, New York, Evanston, and London, 1960).

Staples and Labor in the Colonial Chesapeake

Staple change and labor adjustments in the eighteenth-century Chesapeake lend empirical support to this theoretical discussion. Wheat supplemented and then replaced tobacco as the staple of Maryland's upper eastern shore during the period between 1720 and the Revolution. Although the details of regional economic change demand much more elaboration, the outline of changes in staples and labor is fairly clear.[16] The clayey soils of that region produced a poorer quality tobacco which was less valuable than western shore crops. As grain prices rose after 1720, reflecting demands from southern Europe and the West Indies, slave-owning tobacco planters on the upper eastern shore rationally shifted to grains, especially wheat. This new few-day staple also entailed adjustments in the labor supply. Some slaves were hired out for short terms; others functioned as sharecroppers; and still others were emancipated by their owners. Manumission was abetted, of course, by Quaker abolitionists and revolutionary egalitarianism, but the rock-bottom cause was economic. Wheat was produced more efficiently with freemen than with slaves.[17]

An example may clarify the economic pressures on the average planter during the middle of the eighteenth century. On the typical tobacco plantation one laborer produced 1,000 pounds of tobacco on about three acres. Total labor input was about 185 man-hours, or 23 man-days. More decisive from the standpoint of labor was the number of days of labor attendance required by tobacco, which amounted to as many as 75 days spread over the January-to-November cropping season. The planter who hired free labor at a wage rate of 3s. a day paid out £11 5s.[18] Using slaves effected a considerable savings. A prime male slave field hand cost £5 10s. a year, calculated by using an average slave price of £50 discounted over a useful life of twenty years, or £2 10s. a year, plus annual maintenance costs of £3.[19] Tobacco planters chose slaves for the simple reason that they cost less than half of what free labor cost.

---

[16] This discussion of economic change on the eastern shore derives from many sources, too numerous to be listed here. See especially Carville Earle and Ronald Hoffman: Staple Crops and Urban Development in the Eighteenth-Century South, *Perspectives in Amer. Hist.*, Vol. 10, 1976, pp. 7–78; and Paul G. E. Clemens: From Tobacco to Grain: Economic Development on Maryland's Eastern Shore, 1660–1750 (unpublished Ph.D. dissertation, Dept. of History, Univ. of Wisconsin, Madison, 1974).

[17] On manumission and free blacks on the eastern shore, see the impressive study by Ira Berlin: Slaves without Masters: The Free Negro in the Antebellum South (Vintage Books, New York, 1974), pp. 15–78. Also, Kenneth L. Carroll: Religious Influences on the Manumission of Slaves in Caroline, Dorchester, and Talbot Counties, *Maryland Hist. Mag.*, Vol. 56, 1961, pp. 176–197; and *idem*, Maryland Quakers and Slavery, *ibid.*, Vol. 45, 1950, pp. 215–225. These studies emphasize religion and revolutionary ideology as the chief causes of manumission and the growth of the free black community; yet these interpretations fail to explain the strength of slavery sentiment among tobacco-producing Quakers on Maryland's western shore and the manumission activity that began before the Revolution. In 1790, the proportion of free Negroes to all Negroes was highest in the upper bay counties of Maryland ("Return of the Whole Number of Persons within the Several Districts of the United States, According to 'An Act Providing for the Enumeration of the Inhabitants of the United States,' Passed March the First, One Thousand Seven Hundred and Ninety-One" [Childs and Swaine, Philadelphia, 1791], p. 47). On slave hire and hire rates, see Strickland, *op. cit.* [see footnote 5 above], pp. 31–36; and "Letters of Father Joseph Morley, S.J., and Some Extracts from his Diary (1757–1786)," *Records Amer. Catholic Hist. Soc.*, Vol. 17, 1906, pp. 180–210 and 289–311, especially p. 300.

[18] These estimates, their sources, and a preliminary, if crude, statement of the argument made here appear in Earle and Hoffman, *op. cit.* [see footnote 16 above], pp. 36–39 and 68–78.

[19] Slave prices appear in Clemens, *op. cit.* [see footnote 16 above], p. 171; "Historical Statistics of the United States, Colonial Times to 1970" (2 parts; Bur. of the Census, Washington, D.C., 1975), Part 2, p. 1174; Allan Kulikoff: Tobacco and Slaves: Population, Economy and Society in Eighteenth-Century Prince George's County Maryland (unpublished Ph.D. dissertation, Dept. of History, Brandeis Univ., Waltham, Mass., 1976), pp. 485–488; and Harry J. Carman, edit.: American Husbandry (Kennikat Press, Port Washington, New York, 1964), p. 164. Twenty years as the useful life for adult male slaves for discounting

Conversely, assume that wheat became more profitable and that the planter turned to farming. His slave prepared and sowed ten acres in August and September, and harvested 100 bushels from this land the following July. The labor input of about 25 man-days for wheat resembled that for tobacco; but wheat required a mere 25 days in attendance, one-third the attendance requirement of tobacco. Slave costs in wheat remained the same as in tobacco, £5 10s., but hired labor costs, at 25 days times 3s. per day, fell to £3 15s. For the wheat farmer, wage labor was decidedly cheaper than slaves, by £1 15s.[20]

These cost savings resulted in substantial productivity gains for free labor in wheat. A farmer who invested his savings of £1 15s. in additional day labor gained 12 labor days in wheat production. Put differently, the farmer expanded wheat output from 100 bushels to nearly 150 bushels—a gain of 50 percent over slave output. This superior productivity of free labor in wheat resulted, therefore, from cost savings to free labor and from the divisibility of its labor inputs, such that labor could be hired in small daily increments. On the other hand, this productivity had little or nothing to do with the output incentives mythically attached to the condition of freedom.[21]

The unique harvest regimen of wheat gave a divisible labor supply another advantage. The maturation of wheat allowed only about ten days in July for harvest. As the grain passed quickly through the dough or harvest stage, the seeds became dead ripe, shattered, and fell to the ground as reaped. Reaping at the maximum rate of an acre a day, a slave was hard-pressed to finish ten acres of wheat. Wage labor assured that the harvest would be completed on time. Instead of hiring one laborer for ten days, the farmer might hire two men for five days, thus minimizing the loss of grain by overripening and shattering.[22]

Slaves and wheat made an unhappy marriage on Maryland's eastern shore. Slaves were more expensive and less productive than wage labor, and pressures for adjustments from slaves to hired labor were inevitable. After 1750, slave owners pursued several alternatives: slaves were hired by the day or week during the harvest bottleneck; sharecropping schemes were suggested to reduce slave costs while keeping available a harvest labor force; and private manumission of slaves increased. Although these adjustments toward free labor are the most important changes, the range of solutions was limited only by the ingenuity of individual planters as they sought to wed staples and labor supply.[23]

The changeover from slaves to free labor on the eastern shore was excruciatingly slow; yet we have no reason to expect instantaneous labor adjustment to the economic model. In the first place, although slaves had become decidedly inefficient, they nonetheless involved a heavy sunk cost not easily recouped. More decisively, whole-

---

purposes is suggested in Carman [see above], p. 164; and Clemens, *op. cit.* [see footnote 16 above], pp. 47–53. However, calculating slave life expectancy is an intractable problem. Among Prince George's County whites in the eighteenth century, expectation of life at age 20 was 27 additional years (Kulikoff [see above], pp. 38–41). Maintenance costs are from Carman [see above], p. 164.

[20] Earle and Hoffman, *op. cit.* [see footnote 16 above], pp. 68–78.

[21] The belief that freedom was a production incentive and resulted in productivity gains over slavery probably rests on free labor's superior output in broadcast grain production—a superiority we have attributed to the few required days of labor and the divisibility of free labor. The incentive of freedom disappeared in tobacco production, where a slave doubled the output of freemen for a given cost.

[22] Klippart, *op. cit.* [see footnote 12 above], pp. 475–478; and Leo Rogin: The Introduction of Farm Machinery in Its Relation to the Productivity of Labor in the Agriculture of the United States During the Nineteenth Century (Univ. of California Press, Berkeley, 1931), p. 78.

[23] Berlin, *op. cit.* [see footnote 17 above], pp. 15–78; Carroll, Religious Influences [see footnote 17 above], pp. 176–197; Letters of Father Joseph Morley [see footnote 17 above], p. 300; and Strickland, *op. cit.* [see footnote 5 above], pp. 31–36.

sale labor change involved the risk that sudden changes in relative labor costs or in the technology of staple production could turn against free labor. For instance, slaves could have produced wheat at less cost than free labor if the wheat harvest was extended by rescheduling planting, if free wage rates rose, or if slave costs fell. Crop scheduling appealed to George Washington, and no doubt eastern shore farmers tried it. By planting fall wheat at staggered intervals or by sowing several varieties, the fields might mature at different times and spread the harvest over more than ten days. Washington then saw how slaves could be used to advantage: "if Wheat of different kinds are sowed so as to prevent the Harvest coming on at once, it is my opinion that hirelings [wage labor] of all kinds may be dispensed with."[24] Using our previous calculations, free labor probably handled fourteen to fifteen acres and slaves ten acres; accordingly, expanding the wheat harvest beyond fifteen days, at one acre harvested a day, would have resulted in a clear-cut advantage for slave labor. Fortunately for northern free labor, Washington's cropping scheme was never successfully implemented, as John H. Klippart observed nearly a century later,[25] and almost two centuries passed before Warren Thornthwaite worked out the intricacies of crop calendars.

A second condition that favored slave-produced wheat was higher wage rates. In 1769, when Washington toyed with crop scheduling, wheat was in great demand, prices were high, and a bumper crop drove wages up. Day wages rose from a norm of 3s. to 5s. a day for skilled harvesters.[26] At that rate, ten acres of wheat production cost £6 5s., compared with £5 10s. for a slave. Understandably, slave owners were reluctant to free their slaves until they were assured of a steady, abundant, and low-cost supply of free labor. The year 1769 was atypical, however. Although similar wage peaks hit sporadically through 1860, wage costs generally remained relatively lower than slave costs. When the situation occasionally reversed, farmers supplemented the supply of free labor with marginal lower-cost laborers such as convicts or free Negroes.[27]

Thirdly, wheat farmers would have used slaves if slave costs had fallen; indeed, theory implies such an adjustment and the mechanisms responsible. Assuming a single region in which wheat is produced, the demand curve for slaves shifts downward as slave inefficiencies in wheat production are perceived. While slave prices, and hence discounted costs, are falling, slave masters simultaneously may reduce maintenance costs by cutting expenditures for food, health care, clothing, and shelter.[28] In practice, however, such cost adjustments by markets and masters seem to have been blunted because of external markets for slaves. Prices for Chesapeake slaves rose rather than fell, suggesting that lower slave demand on the eastern shore was compensated by augmented demand from the expanding tobacco economy of the western shore. The existence of this neighboring slave market thus was decisive in

[24] George Washington: The Diaries of George Washington, 1748–1799 (edited by J. C. Fitzpatrick; 4 vols.; Houghton Mifflin Company, Boston and New York, 1925), Vol. 1, p. 338, cited in Gray, op. cit. [see footnote 1 above], Vol. 1, p. 550.

[25] Klippart, op. cit. [see footnote 12 above], pp. 475–478.

[26] Gaspar John Saladino: The Maryland and Virginia Wheat Trade from Its Beginnings to the American Revolution (unpublished M.A. thesis, Dept. of History, Univ. of Wisconsin, Madison, 1960), p. 45; Bidwell and Falconer, op. cit. [see footnote 13 above], pp. 117–118; and Historical Statistics, [see footnote 19 above], Part 2, p. 1196.

[27] In the antebellum Midwest, free Negroes were used principally during bumper harvests (David E. Schob: Hired Hands and Plowboys: Farm Labor in the Midwest, 1815–1860 (Univ. of Illinois Press, Urbana, Chicago, and London, 1975), pp. 83–87.

[28] This argument appears in Richard Sutch: The Profitability of Ante Bellum Slavery—Revisited, South. Econ. Journ., Vol. 31, 1965, pp. 365–377, reference on pp. 365–366.

propping up eastern shore slave prices and costs, despite slave inefficiencies in wheat. Put pithily, freedom on the eastern shore depended on the existence of slavery in a nearby region. The market failed to make slaves competitive with free labor, but masters had another avenue by lowering maintenance costs. Whether they proceeded ruthlessly by reducing medical care, housing, and clothing of slaves or by affording quasi-freedom via sharecropping and eventual manumission remains an issue of overriding importance.[29]

Slavery lost out in the wheat-producing eastern shore precisely because none of these three conditions—harvest extension through crop scheduling, rising wage rates, or declining slave costs—seems to have been met. For these reasons, a few-day crop such as wheat fostered the development of a labor force that was free, flexible, and divisible in its inputs.

STAPLES AND LABOR IN THE ANTEBELLUM MIDWEST

Slavery decayed, albeit slowly, on Maryland's eastern shore with the change from tobacco to wheat. But what of the reverse situation, where few-day wheat gave way to a multiple-day crop? The test case here comes from the antebellum Midwest and deals with the transition from wheat to a corn-hog complex that took place just before the Civil War. This staple change posed a momentous threat to northern wage labor in particular and to society in general. I begin at a more mundane level by comparing the costs of slave labor and free labor under wheat and its successor, Indian corn. Having demonstrated slave efficiency in corn production, I turn to proslavery attitudes and legislation in the Midwest.

Antebellum labor costs provide the basic economic information. Slave costs are from Alfred H. Conrad and John R. Meyer's estimate of $51 as the annual cost of a slave between 1830 and 1850. They arrive at this figure by first discounting the price of a twenty-year-old male slave ($900 to $950) over a useful life of thirty years, or $30, and adding yearly maintenance costs of $21 for a total of $51.[30] Farm-labor wages come from Stanley Lebergott's wage series for the various states under consideration.[31] Comparison of slave and wage costs from these sources show that wage labor hired by the year was expensive and could not compete with slaves. For example, in 1830 the average monthly wage in the United States of $8.85 totaled $95.20 for twelve months—almost double the cost of a slave.[32] These figures cast serious

---

[29] On slave prices, see Clemens, *op. cit.* [see footnote 16 above], p. 171; Historical Statistics, [see footnote 19 above], Part 2, p. 1174; and Kulikoff, *op. cit.* [see footnote 19 above], pp. 485–488. These prices are not entirely satisfactory, for we need a series specifically for the eastern shore after 1750. However, rather high slave prices are suggested in Letters of Father Joseph Morley [see footnote 17 above], p. 300. Slave clothing allowances, as an indicator of maintenance costs, seem to have remained the same from the 1720's to the Revolution, but the evidence is fragmentary (Clemens, *op. cit.* [see footnote 16 above], pp. 47–53 and 175.

[30] Alfred H. Conrad and John R. Meyer: The Economics of Slavery in the Ante-bellum South, *in* The Reinterpretation of American Economic History (edited by Robert W. Fogel and Stanley L. Engerman; Harper & Row, Publishers, New York, Evanston, and elsewhere, 1971), pp. 342–361, especially pp. 345–347. The farmer who was considering the adoption of slavery would probably have purchased a prime male field slave rather than an infant or child slave; hence the appropriate costs are given by slave market prices rather than the considerably lower costs of slave reproduction and rearing. For the latter costs, see Yasukichi Yasuba: The Profitability and Viability of Plantation Slavery in the United States, *Econ. Studies Quart.*, Vol. 12, 1961, pp. 60–67.

[31] Stanley Lebergott: Manpower in Economic Growth: The American Record since 1800 (McGraw-Hill Book Company, New York, Chicago, and elsewhere, 1964).

[32] Monthly wages are with board included (*ibid.*, p. 539).

doubt on Clarence H. Danhof's belief that freemen were commonly hired for eight to ten months during the cropping season; eight months of labor in 1830 cost more than $70, still far in excess of slave costs.[33] Long labor contracts of this sort were used selectively, notably during the first years of farm making and sod busting; but otherwise the eight-to-ten-month laborer cost too much. Other students of farm labor lean toward shorter-term hire, ranging from a daily basis to several months at a time; and their impressions and evidence conform remarkably well with the hypothesis of labor costs presented here.[34] Given the prevailing wage rates in midwestern states in 1850, three to five months was the theoretical maximum for wage-labor hire; beyond that time, slaves became cheaper than freemen. Parenthetically, we may note that free labor had improved its economic position vis-à-vis slaves between 1750 and 1850. In the earlier year, the annual cost of a slave equaled about 36 days of wage labor as compared with 65 days of hired labor in 1850 Ohio.

Wheat was the initial staple of the Midwest, and its labor requirements fell easily within the economic range of free labor. The link between day labor and wheat should be clear from the earlier discussion of the Maryland case, and repetition for the Midwest is unnecessary. However, subtle changes in nineteenth-century wheat production gave day labor even greater advantages. The harvest-labor bottleneck of ten days to two weeks persisted into the nineteenth century, but labor demands became even more intense because farmers increased output per acre from the colonial norm of ten bushels to twenty to thirty bushels or more. Accordingly, labor time spent in harvesting and gathering the wheat, despite some efficiencies introduced by the cradle and the flail, increased from 60 percent of total labor time to about 83 percent in the prereaper nineteenth century. Harvesting and getting in an acre of wheat, according to Leo Rogin, required about five days.[35] That meant that a slave could harvest just two to three acres of wheat, while divisible day labor, hired at the 1850 Ohio wage rate for the time equivalent of a slave's cost and allocating five-sixths of the hired labor to harvest, handled ten or eleven acres of wheat. In other words, a slave harvested and gathered two to three acres for $51.00, or a cost of $17.00 to $25.50 per acre. Day laborers, paid $51.00, harvested and gathered ten to eleven acres, at a cost of $4.64 to $5.10 per acre. Furthermore, day laborers cost less than monthly labor. The hire of two laborers for three months each cost $66.00 at the 1850 Ohio rate; and they harvested and gathered four to six acres, at a cost of $11.00 to $16.50 per acre.[36]

As long as wheat persisted as the midwestern staple, day labor was economically superior to both slaves and monthly hired hands. Nor did this superiority of the day

---

[33] Clarence H. Danhof: Change in Agriculture: The Northern United States, 1820–1870 (Harvard Univ. Press, Cambridge, Mass., 1969), pp. 73–78. This criticism should not impugn the remainder of this excellent and essential book.

[34] Bogue, op. cit. [see footnote 14 above], pp. 182–187; Merle Curti: The Making of an American Community: A Case Study of Democracy in a Frontier County (Stanford Univ. Press, Stanford, Calif., 1959), pp. 145–149; Paul W. Gates: Frontier Estate Builders and Farm Laborers, in The Frontier in Perspective (edited by Walker D. Wyman and Clifton B. Kroeber; Univ. of Wisconsin Press, Madison, 1957), pp. 143–164; and Schob, op. cit. [see footnote 27 above], pp. 69, 103–104, and 258.

[35] Rogin, op. cit. [see footnote 22 above], pp. 229–243; and Gates, Farmer's Age [see footnote 15 above], pp. 156–169. See also Paul A. David: The Mechanization of Reaping in the Ante-bellum Midwest, in Industrialization in Two Systems: Essays in Honor of Alexander Gerschenkron by a Group of His Students (edited by Henry Rosovsky; John Wiley & Sons, Inc., New York, London, and Sydney, 1966), pp. 3–39.

[36] The discussion, of course, concerns prereaper harvest technology. I have used the 1850 Ohio daily hire rate, without board, of $0.78 and the monthly hire rate, with board, of $11.00 (Lebergott, op. cit. [see footnote 31 above], p. 539; and Schob, op. cit. [see footnote 27 above], p. 259). Somewhat higher daily rates of $1.27 for 1849–1853 have been recorded in Illinois, particularly for harvest cradlers (David, op. cit. [see footnote 35 above] pp. 35–37).

hand diminish with increased scale of operation—a point demonstrated later in the century in the bonanza wheat farms of the Red River Valley, where day laborers at the critical seasons vastly outnumbered laborers hired by the month or season.[37]

The midwestern staple economy altered between 1800 and 1860, and pressures to adjust the labor supply became evident a decade or two before the Civil War. The wheat staple suffered from disease and humidity, particularly in the south central tier of Ohio, Indiana, and Illinois; and as wheat became less attractive, the southern demand for hogs and pork encouraged a corn-hog staple economy. Wheat was supplemented and then displaced by these new regional staples.[38] From the standpoint of labor requirements, corn lay intermediate between wheat's few days and the multiple labor days of tobacco and cotton. More precisely, a laborer in corn tended about twenty-five acres and invested perhaps 850 man-hours, compared with wheat's ten acres and 600 man-hours.[39] From plowing through the third cultivation the individually planted and tended corn plant demanded exceptional attention. The corn farmers of Illinois, for example, planted in April or early May and cultivated three times before July 4, when the crop was "laid by." Afterward, labor needs were light until harvest. Although corn harvesting was backbreaking and sweaty work, corn did not create a harvest labor bottleneck as did wheat. The crop was ready for harvest in September, but there was no urgency because the ears could stand in the fields throughout the winter and into early spring. As a result, corn was usually harvested by family members or neighbors during idle moments, rather than by expensive wage labor. Thus for corn it was the plowing and tillage in spring and early summer that established the period of peak labor demand.[40]

Corn farmers sought labor for the three to four months from April or May through July. Day labor was prohibitively expensive, and corn farmers engaged labor on short-term contracts of ten weeks to four months.[41] But this shift upward in labor costs pushed freemen into competition with slaves (it makes no difference that state legislatures and referenda had outlawed slavery in the Midwest in the first quarter of the century). For instance, an Illinois farmer who hired a four-month laborer with board in 1850 spent $12.55 a month and $50.20 for four months, whereas a slave would have cost the farmer $51.00. Wage rates had risen by 1860, when the four-month laborer cost $54.88.[42] These wage rates, I might add, are conservative figures; David

---

[37] Fred A. Shannon: The Farmer's Last Frontier: Agriculture, 1860-1897 (Harper & Row, Publishers, New York, Evanston, and London, 1968), pp. 154-161.

[38] Midwestern economic change is thoroughly discussed in J. E. Spencer and Ronald J. Horvath: How Does an Agricultural Region Originate? Annals Assn. of Amer. Geogrs., Vol. 53, 1963, pp. 74-92. See also Bogue, op. cit. [see footnote 14 above], pp. 156-172; and John G. Clark: The Grain Trade in the Old Northwest (Univ. of Illinois Press, Urbana and London, 1966), pp. 147-171 and 197-211. Regional boundaries were hazy. The Lower Midwest continued to produce wheat after corn and hogs were the main staples. But toward the Great Lakes, wheat remained dominant and the corn-hog complex penetrated more slowly. See the maps of corn and wheat production in Charles O. Paullin: Atlas of the Historical Geography of the United States (edited by John K. Wright; Carnegie Inst. of Washington and the Amer. Geogr. Soc. of New York, Washington, D.C. and New York, 1932), Plate 143.

[39] Shannon, op. cit. [see footnote 37 above], p. 143.

[40] Russell, op. cit. [see footnote 14 above], pp. 81-82; and Bogue, op. cit. [see footnote 14 above], pp. 132-133.

[41] "The general practice in Central Illinois is to hire about the 1st of April for the 'crop (corn) season,' or until after harvest, which includes wheat, oats, hay, & c." (The Merchants' Magazine and Commercial Rev., Vol. 41, 1859, p. 760.) The small grain harvest was in July, so the author meant that labor was hired from April to the end of July, or for four months. Also, see Russell, op. cit. [see footnote 14 above], pp. 81-82.

[42] Lebergott, op. cit. [see footnote 31 above], p. 539. The labor problem was most severe between 1854 and 1857, when wage rates peaked. David shows that Illinois common laborers received $1.25 a day compared with $0.85 in 1849-1853—an increase of 35 percent. Adjusting our monthly rates according to this

E. Schob has indicated that the four-month rate may have been $13.00 to $18.00 a month rather than $12.55.[43] By the mid-1850's, slave labor probably was less costly than free labor in the production of corn, a multiple-day staple crop.[44] To make matters worse, slaves had long since mastered the techniques of corn production, and they employed these in Kentucky, just across the river from freedom.

The political implications of this analysis are far-reaching. As slavery became more efficient than free labor, we should and do find an acceleration of proslavery advocacy and legislation emanating from the central and lower midwestern corn region during the 1840's and 1850's. Slavery was headed north. The threat was no more nor less than the imminent dissolution of northern society based on free labor. Slavery took on a new urgency, and its enemies, so disarrayed before 1850, molded a unified opposition, focused on the northern margins of the corn belt. Their choice was simple: allow slavery to survive anywhere in the United States and corn farmers eventually would adopt the institution; destroy slavery completely and thus remove this labor supply as a competitor for freemen. The efficiency of slaves in corn culture helps put a new perspective on otherwise confused political behavior in the antebellum Midwest, to which we now turn.

The midwestern states in the first quarter of the nineteenth century prohibited the institution of slavery by referenda. This made economic sense because slavery was already a dead letter for the majority of farmers who produced a wheat staple and used more efficient free labor.[45] But these referenda posed an ominous threat: if laws and referenda could prohibit slavery, they could also introduce the peculiar institution when it became profitable. That day was not far off, as economic change swept over the Lower Midwest and as corn-hog farming supplemented or displaced wheat during the 1830's and 1840's. Slave costs still exceeded those of free labor, but the gap was narrowing. Accordingly, the corn region gave little support to the enemies of slavery; they found more fertile ground for their abolitionist societies, antislavery newspapers, and third-party efforts in the northern wheat counties. The sectional rift was apparent in the elections of 1844, 1848, and 1852, when the northern counties cast increasingly larger votes for antislavery third parties, while the nascent corn-belt counties voted overwhelmingly for the regular parties, particularly the Democrats.[46]

---

percentage increase, we find that monthly wages would have risen from $12.55 in 1850 to $16.94 in 1854–1857, making a total wage bill of $67.75. Slave costs fell below this (David, *op. cit.* [see footnote 35 above], p. 36).

[43] Schob, *op. cit.* [see footnote 27 above], p. 104.

[44] Slave costs rose during the 1850's but at a less rapid rate than free-labor costs. Slave prices moved up to $1,306 between 1856 and 1860. Discounting this price over thirty years and adding $21.00 for maintenance put slave costs at about $64.50—or $3.00 less than the four-month hire rate for free labor, as calculated in footnote 42. For slave prices, see Yasuba, *op. cit.* [see footnote 30 above], pp. 60–67. During the 1850's, midwestern real wages generally exceeded all other regions except the east south central states, thus compounding the pressure on free labor in this region (Philip P. Coelho and James F. Shepherd: Regional Differences in Real Wages: The United States, 1851–1880, *Explorations in Econ. Hist.*, Vol. 13, 1976, pp. 203–230).

[45] Eugene H. Berwanger: The Frontier Against Slavery: Western Anti-Negro Prejudice and the Slavery Extension Controversy (Univ. of Illinois Press, Urbana, Chicago, and London, 1967), pp. 7–29; Theodore Calvin Pease: The Story of Illinois (A. C. McClurg & Co., Chicago, 1925), pp. 96–113; and Jacob P. Dunn: Indiana: A Redemption from Slavery (Houghton, Mifflin and Company, Boston and New York, 1888).

[46] Theodore Clarke Smith: The Liberty and Free Soil Parties in the Northwest (Russell & Russell, New York, 1967), pp. 325–331; Paullin, *op. cit.* [see footnote 38 above], Plates 105, 114, and 115; and Arthur Charles Cole: The Era of the Civil War, 1848–1870 (Illinois Centennial Commission, Springfield, 1919), pp. 101–201.

Northern support for third parties intensified when they added a new and powerful argument against slavery—an argument that becomes more reasonable when it is placed in the context of the increasing efficiency of slavery in the Lower Midwest. Salmon Chase and the Free-Soil party adopted all of the standard attacks on the immorality of slavery and on its exclusion from the territories, and they went even farther. Northern society, they proclaimed, faced the grave danger of an inexorably expanding slave power or slavocracy. Slavery threatened free labor, which was the underpinning for northern civilization. Chase's argument has been treated unkindly by political historians. Should we accept their verdict that he and his supporters were paranoid, grossly distorting the dangers of slave encroachment in the North, or crassly political, manipulating issues and voters through the use of exaggerated rhetoric and playing on the racial fears of midwesterners?[47] Quite the opposite, if the economic analysis presented here is correct. Chase was on sound ground; if he was guilty of anything, it was of detecting the threat of slavery to the North before more ordinary men and of misplacing blame on a conspiracy of expansionist-minded southern slaveowners instead of on a conspiracy of economics favoring the corn staple and pushing up wage rates in the late 1840's and 1850's.[48]

Chase's argument did not win the day immediately. His fear that slavery would expand into the old Northwest was not shared by his natural allies in northern Illinois, Indiana, and Ohio. They faced a more pressing problem—control of an expanding free Negro population. Their anti-Negro attitudes, racism by another name, led them into an uneasy coalition with proslavery advocates in the corn belt. This coalition in the late 1840's and early 1850's voted repeatedly against free Negroes, excluding fugitive slaves and free Negroes from these states and circumscribing the civil and political rights of those who were already there. African colonization for midwestern free Negroes also held broad appeal.[49]

The cement of racism began to crack in the mid-1850's. Upstaters who detested Negroes and wanted to get rid of them perceived that downstaters wanted to strip free Negroes of their rights in order to enslave them or else facilitate the introduction of slavery. The subtle schemes of proslavers were laid bare in an 1855 committee report of the Indiana legislature: African colonization, it claimed, originated "in the basest motives and most mercenary considerations. It is one of the offspring of slavery . . .

---

[47] See the perceptive examination of Chase in Eric Foner: Free Soil, Free Labor, Free Men: The Ideology of the Republican Party before the Civil War (Oxford Univ. Press, London, Oxford, and New York, 1970), pp. 73–102. Chase and other antislavery advocates are cast as irresponsible fanatics in Avery Craven: An Historian and the Civil War (Univ. of Chicago Press, Chicago and London, 1964). Benson has suggested that Chase and men of his persuasion were guilty of overblown campaign rhetoric and reckless demagogy which got out of hand in the late 1850's. I disagree. See Lee Benson: Toward the Scientific Study of History: Selected Essays of Lee Benson (J. B. Lippincott Company, Philadelphia, New York, and Toronto, 1972), pp. 225–340, especially pp. 297–303.

[48] Foner's thesis that northern fears of an aggressive, expanding slave power played a decisive role in the coming of the war is pursued by Larry Gara: Slavery and the Slave Power: A Critical Distinction, in Beyond the Civil War Synthesis: Political Essays of the Civil War Era (edited by Robert P. Swierenga; Contributions in American History No. 44; Greenwood Press, Westport, Conn., and London, 1975), pp. 295–308. A leading advocate of corn culture, the midwestern Yankee Solon Robinson, produced a lengthy apologetic for slavery in DeBow's Review in 1849. The timing of his conversion, coming as it did when corn culture was expanding into the Lower Midwest and labor rates were rising, seems more than coincidental (Solon Robinson: Negro Slavery at the South, in Solon Robinson: Pioneer and Agriculturalist [edited by Herbert Anthony Kellar; 2 vols.; Indiana Hist. Bur., Indianapolis, 1936], Vol. 2, pp. 253–307).

[49] Berwanger, op. cit. [see footnote 45 above], pp. 30–59. For a slightly different view of midwestern racism, see John M. Rozett: Racism and Republican Emergence in Illinois, 1848–1860: A Re-evaluation of Republican Negrophobia, Civil War Hist., Vol. 22, 1970, pp. 101–115.

intended to remove the free blacks from the country in order to increase the value and security . . . of slaves."[60] Even more drastic action had been taken by proslavers in Illinois. The legislature of 1853 put through a law that compelled free Negroes new to the state to pay a fine of $50 plus court costs; Negroes unable to pay this exorbitant sum were hired out for six months to the highest bidder. Indiana carried a similar law on the books, and efforts to strengthen its provisions were narrowly defeated in 1851.[61] That these laws favored black servitude, and potentially permanent bondage, did not escape the opponents of slavery. A delegate to Indiana's constitutional convention of 1850 clearly understood the implications of the attack on the free Negro.

> If I am not mistaken the favorite proposition, and it has been already avowed and advocated here, is, that all persons in whose blood negro descent shall be detected, shall be arrested and sold for six months to the highest bidder and the proceeds applied to the operations of the Colonization Society! And what a spectacle will Indiana in that attitude present to the civilized world? We reprobate slavery and the slave trade, denounce the one as inhuman and the other as piracy punishable with death. And yet what is it proposed to do? Nothing less than to erect shambles at every county seat, enjoin it upon officers to sell, not slaves, but those who are confessedly free, into slavery, differing only from the Southern States, as to its duration.[62]

Identical concern surfaced in Illinois, where the law of 1853 permitting court-appointed sale of free Negroes was regarded by some as a harbinger of slavery.[63]

Proslavery efforts became more blatant as pressures for a more efficient slave labor supply emanated from the corn belt. Dumas Van Deren succinctly summarized the corn farmers' interests in 1854. He and other Illinoians were

> prepared to pronounce openly our full and candid preference in favor of slave labor in agricultural business. . . . We have discovered that the novelty of free labor is a mere humbug. . . . We have been endeavoring to learn the sentiments of our people upon this subject, and have been astonished to see with what unanimity they express themselves in favor of the introduction of slave labor. I have conversed with many of our best farmers who were raised in the eastern States, and they will give their hearty co-operation in effecting this object.[64]

By about mid-decade, the northern counties comprehended that the immediate threat was slavery and not the free Negro. Chase was vindicated and his fear of the slave power carried justifiable weight in the emerging Republican party.

The prospect of slavery in the Lower Midwest made the Civil War inevitable and irrepressible; more important, this threat made the issue of the annihilation of slavery a matter of some urgency.[65] For every cent that free wages increased, for every farmer

---

[60] Quoted in Emma Lou Thornbrough: The Negro in Indiana: A Study of a Minority (Indiana Hist. Bur., Indianapolis, 1957), p. 86.

[61] N. Dwight Harris: The History of Negro Servitude in Illinois and of the Slavery Agitation in that State, 1719–1864 (A. C. McClurg & Co., Chicago, 1904), pp. 188 and 235–236; Cole, Era of the Civil War [see footnote 46 above], pp. 224–229; and Thornbrough, *op. cit.* [see footnote 50 above], pp. 58–59.

[62] "Report of the Debates and Proceedings of the Convention for the Revision of the Constitution of the State of Indiana, 1850" (2 vols.; A. H. Brown, Indianapolis, 1850), Vol. 1, pp. 457–458.

[63] Harris, *op. cit.* [see footnote 51 above], pp. 237–238; and Gustave Koerner: Memoirs of Gustave Koerner, 1809–1896 (edited by Thomas J. McCormack; 2 vols.; Torch Press, Cedar Rapids, Iowa, 1902), Vol. 2, pp. 29–32.

[64] Cited in Arthur Charles Cole: Lincoln's "House Divided" Speech: Did It Reflect a Doctrine of Class Struggle? (Univ. of Chicago Press, Chicago, 1923), pp. 32–33.

[65] A recent quantitative study of the causes of the Civil War concludes that "northern preferences to eliminate slavery were more than twenty times as strong as those to preserve the Union" (Gerald

who adopted corn as his staple, the potential for slavery became ever stronger. Yankee morality would not hold the line against slavery because, according to one southern critic, their morality was only superficial: "once persuaded to consider this question [of slave labor] . . . it is not apprehended that moral qualms will hinder their action. It requires the least rudimental knowledge of Yankee nature, and no argument at all to show, that where a real interest, and a question of abstract morality conflict in a Yankee's mind, abstract morality will sustain a grievous overthrow." [56] This jaundiced southerner understood well the moral fragility of the North, but he seriously misunderstood that the real interest of the Lower Midwest departed sharply from its northern margins. In the latter areas slavery remained an alien and inefficient labor system that contributed nothing to society except the problem of the free Negro. These northern counties became bastions of free labor, free soil, and antislavery in the late 1850's. [57] Excluding slavery from the territories or confining it to the South did not go far enough. They had to destroy it forever so it would not tempt the "real interest" of corn-growing midwesterners. Such was the unequivocal course of action laid out by Abraham Lincoln on June 16, 1858:

> In my opinion, it [slavery agitation] *will* not cease, until a *crisis* shall have been reached, and passed. A house divided against itself cannot stand. I believe this government cannot endure, permanently *half* slave and *half* free. I do not expect the Union to be dissolved—I do not expect the house to *fall*—but I do expect it will cease to be divided. It will become *all* one thing or *all* the other. Either the opponents of slavery, will arrest the further spread of it, and place it where the public mind shall rest in the belief that it is in course of ultimate extinction; or its *advocates* will push it forward, till it shall become alike lawful in *all* the States, old as well as *new*—*North* as well as *South.* [58]

Corn culture, rising wages, and incipient slavery in the Lower Midwest had brought the nation to its greatest impasse.

I have tried to show that moral fiber cannot explain the geography of slavery and free labor and that, conversely, the economics of staple crops and labor costs can. Before 1860, slavery was not good or bad, it was merely efficient or inefficient—and labor decisions were made accordingly. We can no more extol the principles of slave emancipators on Maryland's eastern shore nor the Republicans of the northern Midwest who brought the issue of slavery to war than we can denigrate as unprincipled the proslavery advocates in the midwestern corn belt. They all subscribed to and acted on the same set of economic principles. The thesis that moral superiority motivated antislavery northerners must be shown for what it is: a comfortable liberal myth which obviates examination of the basic amorality of the antebellum American economic system.

Gunderson: The Origin of the American Civil War, *Journ. Econ. Hist.*, Vol. 34, 1974, pp. 915-950). This finding is consonant with the argument presented here: if the North had allowed the South to secede peacefully or had they compromised on the issue of slavery in order to preserve the Union, slavery would have persisted and would shortly have expanded into the Lower Midwest. The extermination of slavery, either peacefully or forcefully, was the only course open to the Upper Midwest and the Republican party.
[56] This essay carries the ominous title, "African Slavery Adapted to the North and North-west," *DeBow's Review*, Vol. 25, 1858, pp. 378-395.
[57] Cole, Era of the Civil War [see footnote 46 above]. pp. 101-201.
[58] Abraham Lincoln: The Collected Works of Abraham Lincoln, 1848-1858 (edited by Roy P. Basler; 8 vols.; Rutgers Univ. Press, New Brunswick, N.J., 1953). Vol. 2, pp. 461-462.

The Effects of Slavery Upon the Southern Economy: A Review of the Recent Debate

Stanley L. Engerman*

The economic effects of slavery have long been a subject of great interest.[1] Hotly debated in the antebellum period, the question has been discussed extensively by historians ever since. Over the years there emerged among historians a general consensus which held that slavery not only prevented the economic development of the South, but that by 1860 it had become unprofitable to the slaveholders. Consequently the slave system was economically decadent before the onset of the Civil War. The chief architects of this interpretation were Ulrich B. Phillips and Charles W. Ramsdell. Although challenged by several writers in the 1930's and 1940's, the Phillips-Ramsdell position continued to be dominant until the late 1950's. However, during the past decade a series of attacks on the views of Phillips, Ramsdell, and their main supporters has substantially modified the old consensus.

In this critical review of the long debate on the economics of slavery I shall discuss both the basic arguments of the Phillips-Ramsdell view and the recent attacks on it. It will be important to distinguish three related but different issues often confused in the debate. These are:

1. The profitability of slavery to the individual slave-owner.
2. The viability of slavery as an economic system.[2]
3. The effects of the slave system on the economic development of the South.

The answers to these questions do not necessarily fall into a simple pattern; a positive answer to any one does not imply the answer to the others. Much disagreement in the literature can be traced to the failure to recognize the differences among these questions.

*The author is indebted to Robert Fogel, Robert Gallman, Sherwin Rosen, and Edward Zabel for comments and suggestions. Parts of this article will appear in a modified form in the introduction to Section VII of Robert W. Fogel and Stanley L. Engerman (editors), *The Reinterpretation of American Economic History*.

EEH/Second Series, Vol. 4, No. 2. Graduate Program in Economic History, University of Wisconsin, 1967.

I. THE PHILLIPS-RAMSDELL POSITION

Historical work on the slavery question has been dominated by the writings of Ulrich B. Phillips.[3] Phillips discussed almost all the economic aspects of slavery and much of the subsequent debate has been within the framework which he set forth. Phillips' study led him to conclude that slavery was economically unprofitable to the planter, was undoubtedly moribund on the eve of the Civil War, and that it was the crucial factor in the presumed retarded development of the southern economy. Phillips granted that his conclusions were not always true, since slavery had been established and initially expanded "because the white people were seeking their own welfare and comfort." However, he argued, "in the long run [private gain and public safety] were attained at the expense of private and public wealth and of progress."[4]

Central to this position was his view that the Negro slave was an innately ignorant savage and an inefficient worker who could handle only simple tasks and who required constant control. To use such crude labor the plantation system, which provided the necessary supervision, was essential. Therefore, the slave system and the plantation system became identical in the South.

In an early article, Phillips presented his basic arguments for the conclusion that slavery had become unprofitable and moribund by the time of the Civil War.[5] His major piece of evidence was a comparison of the ratio between the price per pound of cotton and the price of male field hands. Observing a ten- to twelve-fold increase in the ratio of slave prices to cotton prices between 1800 and 1860, he stated (without supporting evidence) that such an increase was much too great to be explained by increased slave productivity. He went on to point out that the cost of using slave labor included: "expense of food, clothing and shelter"; interest on the capital invested in the slave; economic insurance against death, illness or escape; the "wear and tear" of years; and taxation on the capitalized value of the slave. While no conclusions were drawn concerning the sum of these costs, in context they seem clearly designed to buttress the argument of unprofitability. Phillips noted that account should have been taken of the market value of off-spring, but he claimed this was offset by the cost of supporting the aged. The existence of high and rising slave prices he attributed to overspeculation—"an irresistible tendency to overvalue and overcapitalize slave labor."

Phillips stated that another important factor in bidding up the price of slaves was economies of scale in cotton production. This, he contended, would explain in part the high and rising slave prices since a price in excess of the value of each particular slave would be paid. It also explained why larger plantations expanded relative to smaller holdings, and how these larger plantations could have shown profits while losses were widespread. For this reason, according to Phillips, all funds that the planter could earn or borrow went to purchase slaves, "not into modern implements or land improvements."[6]

The existence of a demand for slaves for purposes of prestige and conspicuous consumption was also mentioned as a cause of high slave prices. Implicit is the statement that only part of the slave's price was based upon the value of production, the remainder representing a form of consumption expenditure by the owners of slaves.[7] If this were true, slavery could be viable even if it were an unprofitable investment as measured by the return from business operations alone. The large extent of the prestige demand, however, was considered an important element in explaining the low rate of capital formation and economic growth in the southern economy.

Phillips argued that the slave system further retarded southern economic development because "the capitalization of labor and the export of earnings in exchange for more workmen, always of a low degree of efficiency," deprived the southern economy of capital which presumably could have been used for other (industrial) purposes, and made the South a chronic debtor to northern merchants and bankers.[8] Phillips' argument about labor capitalization and export of earnings is rather confusing. He realized that after the closing of the external slave trade in 1808 the export drain went to the Upper South rather than outside the southern states. However, he claimed, "there it did little but demoralize industry and postpone to a later generation the agricultural revival"—but the mechanism explaining this outcome was never clearly stated.[9] The capitalization of the labor force presumably reduced labor elasticity and versatility: "it tended to fix labor rigidly in one line of employment."[10] This was significant in the South's one-crop economy, particularly since the profitability of cotton production exhibited considerable cyclical variation. However, Phlilips was not clearly on the side of those blaming the South's ills on agricultural specialization. At one point he argued that slavery "deprived the South of the natural advantage which the cotton monopoly should have given it."[11]

Given all the adverse effects, why maintain the system? Because it was essential to keep the "savage instincts from breaking forth"—in other words, for race control and protection.[12] Maintaining slavery and letting slaves produce agricultural commodities was, in Phillips' opinion, less expensive than sending slaves back to Africa or supporting the police and army which would have been required if the slaves were freed.

The Phillips position was modified and extended in an influential article by Charles W. Ramsdell, which claimed that while profitable before 1860, slavery had become unprofitable and moribund by that year.[13] Ramsdell held that economic factors would have made slavery unprofitable to the planting class and that slavery would have ended in the late nineteenth century without the Civil War. In his view, the decline of slavery was likely because the planters had reached the end of the land upon which cotton could be grown profitably. Ramsdell suggested that by 1860 the western limits of slavery had been reached in Texas, and no room existed for expansion northward. Geographic containment would have caused a rise in the labor/land ratio and, as a consequence, slave prices would have fallen until it became too expensive for the owners to maintain their slaves. The end result would have been manumission.

The Ramsdell position—frequently called the natural limits hypothesis—is theoretically plausible, but Ramsdell argued as if there were little room for downward adjustment of slave prices before freedom of the slaves would become an attractive alternative to owners. He also exaggerated the potential pressure on slave prices by ruling out the possibilities that soil in the older areas might be refurbished or that slaves might be profitably employed in other agricultural or non-agricultural pursuits. Nevertheless the natural limits hypothesis has attracted a large number of adherents.

The Phillips position received new support during the 1930's when several southern historians turned to the records and diaries of individual plantations.[14] Focusing on the profitability of slavery to the planter, they uncovered evidence which appeared to indicate a low rate of return in most of the cases reviewed. Although the accounting techniques used were open to question, and it was never established whether those plantations whose records were used were representative, these studies were used to buttress the Phillips position.

The most recent support for the Phillips conclusion has come from writers who have revived antebellum arguments concerning the effects of slavery upon the course of southern economic development. While generally accepting the profitability of slavery to the planter, they argue that the socio-economic system associated with slavery nevertheless retarded the growth of the overall southern economy. Perhaps the most prominent exponent of this position is Eugene Genovese, who stressed the effects of the slave system upon the size of the internal market in the South.[15] Genovese posited that the skewed income distribution which slavery created made for low demand for domestically manufactured goods within the South; wealthy planters preferred to import goods, slaves had no purchasing power, and low income whites had little market impact. This situation contrasted with that of the North and Midwest where a large "middle-class" market was held to have led to the internal development of industry and a more diversified economy. Genovese argued that this restriction of the internal market deprived the South of economies of scale upon which to create an efficient industrial base. The result was a rural, agricultural southern economy dependent upon outsiders for modern industrial goods. An additional effect of the skewed income distribution was that it caused, or at least permitted, conspicuous consumption and lavish living on the part of the rich planters. Consequently savings and capital formation were reduced.

Douglass North has recently put forward the suggestion that the most important effect of slavery upon capital formation was to be found in the small amount of investment in human capital in the South.[16] Unlike Phillips, who had earlier made a similar point, North considered the South wasteful of the potential of both white and Negro workers. Phillips had argued that slavery prevented the development of a skilled labor force by discouraging the non-planter whites, but he dismissed the possibility of improving the skills or intelligence of the Negro.

II. The Revisions

The attack on the arguments of Phillips, Ramsdell, and their followers began in the thirties when Lewis Gray and Robert Russel presented strong arguments for the profitability and viability of slavery, although both did consider the South stagnant relative to the rest of the nation.[17] Gray's work was particularly important since it clearly set forth most of the general considerations to be found in the recent discussions of profitability and viability. However, Gray did conclude that slavery indeed retarded the growth of the southern economy. In the early forties Thomas P. Govan pointed to serious mistakes in several of the studies based on plantation records. He contended that correction of these mistakes led to the conclusion that slavery was profitable.[18] Kenneth Stampp, in his thorough study of slavery (published in 1956), reached the same conclusion as did Govan, and he went on to dismiss most of the arguments which had been used to connect slavery and the backwardness of the southern economy.[19] However, it apparently was not until after the appearance of the widely discussed essay on "The Economics of Slavery in the Antebellum South," by Alfred H. Conrad and John R. Meyer that the old interpretation lost its clearly dominant position.[20]

1. Profitability to the Planter

As noted above, Phillips' contention that slavery was unprofitable to the planters found support in several studies of plantation records. Recent attacks on these studies have come from two directions. First, the records were found to be incomplete and to contain a crucial conceptual error. Second, economists have applied the traditional tools of economic analysis to test for the profitability of slavery in a manner which removed the reliance upon the fortunes of those particular plantations whose complete records survived. The results of this analysis contradicted the Phillips hypothesis.

It was never clear how much reliance should be placed upon conclusions drawn from the analysis of those few plantations whose records survived. Not all plantations kept records and even fewer were preserved. Special factors could have affected each plantation, but no adjustment can be made without prior knowledge of the biases. It is therefore not certain that the existing sample of plantations is representative. There were long and short cycles in prices and output, regional variation was pronounced, and there were apparently differences based upon size of plantation. Conrad and Meyer did use these records, but they used only certain of the data they contained as sample observations in determining estimates of particular variables. They did not generalize from the profit position of a small number of plantations.

Moreover, the use of plantation records by Phillips and his followers contained several errors, the importance of which were first stressed by Govan, and later reiterated by Stampp. A conceptual error in accounting technique led to an erroneous conclusion. Phillips included interest on the capital invested in slaves and land as costs in his discussion of the expenses of plantation owners. The later accounting studies similarly included the imputed interest on invested capital as a cost to be deducted from revenues in calculating net profits. This net profit figure was then divided by the capital value of the plantation to measure the average rate of return on capital. Since the rate of return computed in this manner was below the rate of return on alternative investments, slavery was considered unprofitable.

Govan and Stampp both pointed out that this was an illegitimate calculation, since it resulted in double-counting the cost of capital. Net profits are computed by deducting all expenses (including depreciation) from gross revenues. A positive residual includes the imputed return on the capital of the owner, as well as the wages of management and "pure profits." When imputations for capital cost and the wages of management are deducted any positive sum remaining would be "pure profits." The existence of such "pure profits" would indicate that the investment was profitable. There is no need to then compare this with the alternative rate of return, since deducting the imputed capital cost allows for this. The same test could be made by deducting from net profits the imputed wages of management, computing the rate of return upon this investment, and then comparing it with the rate of return upon alternative assets. If the rate of return on the investment exceeds that upon alternative assets, the investment is considered to be profitable. Both methods described provide the same answer; what is shown to be profitable by one computation is profitable under the other. (Accounting and economic approaches differ in the way costs are measured—the accounting calculations using historical costs and the economic current opportunity costs.) [21]

An important omission from plantation income was the capital gain derived from the reproduction of the slave labor force. As long as slave children could be sold or used on the plantation, this was an additional source of income. A capital gain was also to be derived from the increased value of existing slaves. The slaves held in the 1850's were usually purchased in earlier years at below their current market value. Other errors were the exclusion of slave household services and slave land clearing and maintenance services, and the treatment of the personal expenditures of planters as costs rather than as a use of profits. Govan and Stampp argued that correcting the omissions and errors of earlier historians showed that their samples clearly demonstrated high rates of return to slave ownership in the antebellum period.

The path-breaking essay by Conrad and Meyer was more general in scope, based on an economist's as opposed to an accountant's approach to the problem. Rather than confining their attention to measuring the rates of return of particular plantations, they asked whether, on the average, a planter who purchased slaves and land at an "average" price for the period (1830-1860) could have expected to make as high a rate of return as if he had invested in some alternative asset. While not arguing that every plantation made money, their important conclusion was that, on the average, profits were to be made from slave ownership.

In their analysis, Conrad and Meyer separated the slave economy into two sectors, and estimated the profitability of slave ownership in each. Male slaves were regarded as capital goods used in the production of marketable output of agricultural staples. Female slaves, however, not only were used to produce staples but also were the source of additional slaves. Thus the female slave could be considered a capital good who produced the capital goods used to produce final output.

By regarding both male and female slaves as capital goods, Conrad and Meyer were able to test for the profitability of slavery by computing the rate of return on the total investment in slaves, including the land and other assets which the slave used. The basic computation involved solving to find that rate of return which equated the cost of obtaining slaves with the net stream of earnings derived from using the slaves. Separate rates of return were computed for male and female slaves.

These calculations involved the estimation of four variables. First, the period over which the stream of earnings was obtained was estimated by using an average life expectancy drawn from mortality tables. Second, the total cost of the investment in the slave and the complementary assets was derived from information on slave prices collected by Phillips, with various sources providing the basic information for other assets. Third, the rates of return from bonds and commercial paper were used to compare with the rate of return on slaves. The fourth variable, the annual value of earnings from the slave's productive activities was computed differently for males and females. For the male, gross earnings were measured by multiplying the estimated quantity of cotton produced per slave by the farm price per pound of cotton. Net earnings were obtained by subtracting the costs of maintaining and supervising the slave from gross earnings. For the female, net earnings depended not only on the value of the cotton she produced but also on the market value of offspring. The computation involved estimates of the expected number of offspring, a deduction for nursery and other costs of raising the offspring to the age at which they were sold (assumed to be 18), and a deduction for maintenance and supervision costs. In effect, all the costs of raising slave children to productive age were charged against the female slaves, and all proceeds from sales were attributed to her.

Conrad and Meyer estimated the rate of return from slave ownership for different types of land using various selling prices of cotton. For the majority of plantations they estimated the return on male slaves to range between 4½ per cent and 8 per cent. On poor soils, such as upland pine or the worked-out lands of the east, the rate of return varied from 2.2 per cent to 5.4 per cent. On the best lands of the South the returns varied from 10 per cent to 13 per cent. These rates of return meant that males yielded a rate of return equal to or in excess of the return on alternative assets on all but the poorest lands.

For female slaves a rate of return was computed for land of average quality only. If the females had only five marketable offspring, the estimated lower limit, the rate of return was 7.1 per cent. If there were ten offspring, the estimated upper limit, the rate of return was 8.1 per cent. Conrad and Meyer then argued that slaveholders in the older regions of the South, where males were yielding a low rate in cotton production, were able to achieve a profitable rate of return by selling the offspring of their female slaves to the newer areas where profitable cotton production was possible. They demonstrated the existence of this type of slave reallocation by pointing out differences in the age structure of slaves in the newer and older states, as well as by citing testimony of contemporaries.[22]

The computations of Conrad and Meyer have been attacked as showing too high a rate of return from investment in slaves. While their estimates of each of the four variables—slave life expectancy, capital costs, the rate of return on alternative assets, and the income obtained from slaves—have been criticized, the revision which most sharply challenges their conclusion is Edward Saraydar's downward adjustment of the productivity of prime male fields hands in cotton production.[23]

Saraydar was interested in testing a more restricted hypothesis about slave profitability than were Conrad and Meyer. He was concerned only with the profitability of owning male prime field hands; thus ignoring the gains from slave offspring which Conrad and Meyer accounted for in computing the rate of return upon females. This means that Saraydar understated the profitability of slave ownership to the individual plantation owner (as well as to the southern economy) as long as female slaves were a profitable investment. The specific formulation of the test for the profitability of male slaves used by Saraydar was the same as that of Conrad and Meyer. He computed the rate of return from the use of males in cotton production using averages of the period 1830-1860. His one major change was to provide an alternative measure of physical productivity in cotton operations. Rather than an average of estimates presented in various "contemporary journals," Saraydar used a sample of counties taken from the 1849 census to estimate slave yields in various parts of the South. The particular year chosen, 1849, was justified as being one of average crop size for the 1830-1860 period. Saraydar selected counties in which little was produced besides cotton, and then adjusted the total slave population to obtain an estimate of the average number of field hands. Dividing total cotton output in these counties by the estimated number of field hands gave cotton productivity per field hand. This resulted in a lowering of the all-south average yield per field hand from Conrad and Meyer's 3.75 bales to 3.2, and the yield on alluvial soil from 7.0 bales to 3.6.[24] Using these lowered yields, Saraydar computed sharply lower rates of return on male slaves. On average land the computed rate of return was below that upon alternative assets, and only on the best alluvial land were field hands a profitable investment to the planter. Even there the rates of return were distinctly lower than the rates computed by Conrad and Meyer .

Both Saraydar's form of the test for the profitability of slavery and his specific productivity estimates were challenged in turn by Richard Sutch. Sutch incorporated into one production function the computations which Conrad and Meyer did separately for males and females, thus providing for a single overall test of slave profitability. In effect, Sutch's formulation considered the plantation owner to purchase a slave whose price was determined by applying to Phillips' data the age-sex composition of the slave population and allowed the owner to benefit from the growth of the slave labor force. Unlike Conrad and Meyer, however, the benefits of the increased labor were not attributed to the female alone. This formulation meant that the purchase of a slave provided a permanent stream of income to the owners as long as average slave productivity exceeded average costs of rearing and maintenance. By applying this production function to Saraydar's figures, Sutch estimated rates of return on slave ownership roughly similar to those of Conrad and Meyer.

Sutch, however, also attacked Saraydar's estimates of income from slaves by preparing specific tests of profitability for the years 1849 and 1859. His main correction of Saraydar's 1849 figures was the use of the higher cotton price of that year, while for 1859 both the higher cotton price and increased physical productivity were used. However, these corrections provide too favorable an estimate of slave profitability for the thirty-year period studied. Although the 1849 crop was below that of the preceding two years, it was rather high for the decade of the 1840's, and Sutch's argument that the marked price rise that year is indicative of a small crop is weak. The 1849 price was unusually high—only one year of the seventeen from 1839 to 1855 had a higher cotton price. The 1859 crop, on the other hand, was abnormally large. It was almost half-again as large as that of the average of the 1850's, and was not exceeded until 1879. Thus, while they indicate that Saraydar's adjustments may not be relevant for those specific years, Sutch's corrections of price and ÿield seem excessive when applied to the years between 1830 and the outbreak of the Civil War.

There are several questions concerning the profitability of slaves in cotton production which require further analysis. First, the argument that profits should be measured using data from a large span of years to compute averages does create some problems and gives an element of arbitrariness to the calculations. Since prices and output of cotton varied considerably during the thirty years presumably averaged, and slave prices did move sharply, the measurement of profitability is sensitive to the particular numbers chosen. The use of averages also ignores the possibility of an upward trend in slave productivity above that attributable to the movement to newer soils. Computations for specific years may provide a better indication of profitability than does the thirty-year average, though sensitive to the particular years studied. Saraydar and Sutch, of course, may both be correct. Slavery may have been unprofitable in the earlier part of the interval studied, but profitable in the 1850's.

Second, the use of an average price of slaves for the entire South overlooks the fact that the market adjustment between the Upper South and the Lower South did not lead to price uniformity. Evans' data suggest an average price spread of about 25 per cent in the years from 1830 to 1860, with no marked trend in the size of the differential over time.[25] The use of Lower South slave costs in all regions results in an understatement of the rate of return in the older regions, though the computations for the better soils are not affected.

Third, better estimates of slave productivity are necessary. To obtain these more detailed work on census manuscripts and plantation records is necessary. Questions as to the degree of self-sufficiency on plantations, the possible production of other marketed crops on what are primarily cotton producing plantations, the other functions of an income-yielding nature performed by slaves, and the quantity of cotton produced by whites both on and off plantations require further study, some of which is currently being undertaken.[26]

What Saraydar has done is to throw into some doubt the profitability of owning male slaves. This does not mean that slavery would be unprofitable to planters, as long as females were owned and produced marketable offspring. Saraydar's result, in fact, suggests that female slaves were underpriced, given the market value of slaves. If he were correct we would expect the price of male field hands to fall below that of females, since it is the offspring who are the source of profits. It is the maintenance of the higher price on male slaves which raises questions about the meaning of Saraydar's (and Conrad and Meyer's) separate production functions for male and female slaves, as well as the accuracy of Saraydar's yield estimates.

Moreover, a study by Robert Evans using a different set of data and testing the same hypothesis as did Saraydar, reached the same conclusion as Conrad and Meyer. Evans estimated the rate of return on male slaves only, excluding the value of offspring. He used data on the prices paid to hire slaves as estimates of the income to be derived from using slaves. If the slaves hired were equal in productivity to the slaves used elsewhere, the hiring rate should provide an estimate of the income produced per slave. Evans' treatment of the problem of slave mortality also differed from Conrad and Meyer's. Evans adjusted slave incomes for the proportion of deaths each year rather than using an average expected life span. Rates of return were computed for five-year periods between 1830 and 1860. They ranged from 9.5 per cent to 14.3 per cent in the Upper South, and between 10.3 per cent and 18.5 per cent in the Lower South. Evans further tested the sensitivity of his results to possible errors in the data, and concluded that it was improbable that his conclusion was in error. The maximum cumulation of probable errors would not be sufficient to reduce the rate of return from ownership of male slaves below the return from alternative assets.

We should be clear as to exactly what has been measured in these studies. If Conrad and Meyer and Evans are correct, a planter who purchased either a male or female slave at the market price could have made a rate of return equal to or better than that upon alternative investments. This would mean that prestige demand does not have to be used in explaining the price of slaves. It means further that regardless of how inefficient slave labor was relative to white labor, the planters who employed slaves were profiting from their use. The market price could be justified on the basis of the productivity of the male slave in market activities, and labor productivity plus the value of the slave offspring in the case of the female. By arguing that most planters made profits, these studies made a presumption of viability. The finding of profitability also means that any retardation the South experienced could not be attributed to sub-marginal investments made by slaveowners.

2. Viability to the Economy

Yasuba, Evans, and Sutch have each pointed out that the conclusion that slavery was profitable to the planter did not prove the viability of the slave system. It is possible that a profitable rate of return be made on the market price of existing slaves although the system was moribund. If the value of slaves (as reflected in the market price) was below the rearing cost, there would be an adjustment over time, resulting in a decline in the number of slaves until the institution disappeared. If the demand for slaves fell, but the market price for a reduced number of slaves was equal to the rearing cost, the slave industry would decline without disappearing. However, not only was the market price of slaves in excess of rearing costs in the years before the Civil War, but as Yasuba has demonstrated, this surplus—or capitalized rent—was growing in the late 1840's and 1850's.[27]

Capitalized rent would exist in the price of slaves as long as the market price exceeded the cost of producing slaves—the cost of raising them to the age at which they became productive or were sold. This surplus was not eliminated because once the importation of slaves from Africa was forbidden, the increase in supply set by either biological or institutional constraints was not sufficient to reduce the market price of slaves to their rearing cost. The surplus of market price over cost of production is the measure of the potential fall in slave values which could have occurred without making slavery unprofitable to the southern economy.[28] A falling price of slaves due to a decline in demand would mean that it was possible for the same rates of return to be made on the market price of slaves before and after the decline in demand.[29] However, this price decline, resulting in a capital loss to those who owned the slaves, need not imply that slavery as an institution was not viable, as long as the lowered price still exceeded the costs of producing slaves.

Thus studies which indicate slave purchasers made a rate of return roughly equal to that upon alternative assets would not be surprising. Rather, since supply was inelastic at any moment of time, the price of slaves was set by the demand for them. It therefore would mean that the price of slaves was set at a figure which yielded the market rate of return to the purchaser.

The level of the price of slaves could be based upon elements of both prestige demand and demand for use in production. As long as the total price southerners were willing to pay for slaves exceeded rearing costs, the institution was viable. However, Conrad and Meyer and Evans argued that the market price could be justified on the basis of slave productivity alone. This means that slavery's viability was not attributable to an element (prestige demand) which caused apparent business losses and lowered southern capital formation. (If prestige demand were high it would not necessarily mean that, properly defined, business losses occurred, or that capital formation was reduced. Rather, the profitability test should be based upon the business value of slaves—deducting the imputed consumption element—and the capital formation comparison would need to bring in the expenditures upon goods for conspicuous consumption in the North, which also reduced the investible surplus.)

Yasuba separately estimated the rent element in the price of male slaves and of female slaves. Since the form of the calculation attributes the value of the offspring to the female slave, the rent on the female is based not only upon her productivity in growing cotton, but also upon the future value of her marketable offspring. Thus, the demand for female slaves would be based upon expectations covering not only her life-span but also that of her offspring. If there was an anticipation of an early end to slavery, for economic or other reasons, the demand for female slaves would decline. That Yasuba finds the rent rising before 1860 implies that the southern planters did not expect slavery to decline, let alone be abolished, until at least several decades elapsed. Whatever merit there is in the natural limits hypothesis, its presumed effects were not anticipated in the South before the Civil War. Indeed the magnitude of the rent calculated by Yasuba makes it clear that a substantial decline in slave values would have had to occur for the institution to be threatened.[30]

Richard Sutch independently arrived at the same result concerning slavery's viability as did Yasuba, although he stated his argument differently. Sutch's analysis was based upon a comparison of the costs of using free labor with the costs of using slave labor to the economy (the annual "maintenance cost" plus the amortization of rearing costs). The value of the marginal productivity of the slave to the southern economy exceeded the costs of using the slave, thus creating an economic surplus. The free laborer was paid the value of the marginal product, so that no such surplus existed. If we assume that slave and free labor are equally productive, and that the cost of using slaves was at a subsistence level, then slavery would be viable as long as the free wage rate exceeded subsistence. (If the productivity of the two types of labor differed, the condition for viability is that the ratio of the cost of using slave labor to the wages paid free labor be less than the ratio of their marginal value products.) This would be equivalent to Yasuba's result if slavery were profitable to the planter, since the present value of the surpluses from the use of slave labor would then be equal to the capitalized rent in the price of the slave.[31]

The discussion of the viability of the slave economy points out that the rate of return to the southern economy from its investment in slave labor exceeded the rates of return earned by planters. This was because the latter studies measured the rate of return based upon the market price of the slave, while, as Yasuba notes, for the economy it would be based upon rearing costs. The difference between rearing costs and the market price resulted in capital gains for slaveholders—the question of who received the capital gains depending upon the foresight with which slave values were predicted once the importation of slaves was prohibited.

3. A Stagnant Economy?

The strongest argument against slavery on economic grounds has been the image of a poor and stagnant southern economy in the antebellum period. Some historians have argued that slavery was both profitable and viable, but have introduced other factors to contend that the long-run effect of the slave system was to retard southern economic development. As described in Section I, major emphasis has been upon the presumed effects of the slave system upon income distribution (and thus the size of the internal market) and the rate of capital formation. Stagnation has also been attributed to southern specialization in the production of agricultural staples, particularly cotton, for export. A long debate has taken place as to whether slavery caused specialization, or whether specialization in cotton promoted slavery. In either case, analogy has been made with the supposed weak position of agricultural export producers in the world today. The argument is that a shift away from agricultural specialization would have led to a more rapid rate of economic growth in the South.

Many discussions of the antebellum southern economy start with the presumption of a low income, slow growing region. Thomas Govan had used the wealth estimates of the 1850 and 1860 censuses to question the concept of a stagnant southern economy, but it is only with the recent estimates of regional income by Richard Easterlin that this point can be examined in more detail. By applying Easterlin's estimates of the income shares by region to Robert Gallman's estimates of national income for 1840 and 1860 we can calculate the level of income by region for the two decades preceding the Civil War, and compute regional growth rates. The regional income estimates can be placed on a per capita basis by dividing by regional population.[32]

Easterlin's estimates of regional income include slaves as part of the population and their "incomes" (maintenance costs) in the income total for each region. On this basis the level of southern per capita income in 1860 was 80 per cent of the national average (Table 1). While less than 60 per cent of the per capita income in the Northeastern states, it was higher than the per capita income in the North Central states. Comparing rates of growth of per capita income between 1840 and 1860, the southern economy does not appear stagnant. The southern rate of growth, 1.6 per cent, exceeded that of the rest of the nation, 1.3 per cent.[83]

The pattern of income change within the southern economy is of interest. The per capita income within each component section grew at a rate below the national average. Nevertheless, it is clear that growth did occur within the period in each of the sections. The shift of southern population into the richer West South Central states, particularly Texas, explained the high southern growth rate. However, since it says nothing about the imminence of any possible decline in that area nor anything about declines in the older parts of the South, this population redistribution cannot be used to support the natural limits thesis. As Sutch has argued, the greater profitability of slavery in the New South immediately prior to the Civil War meant that land (and slave) prices had not reached equilibrium. The low level of land rent is indicative of a relative abundance of cheap lands.[84] Similarly the higher levels of land values in the Old South do not suggest that this area had lost economic potential.

The comparisons in the previous paragraphs included slaves in the population and their "incomes" in the income totals. For those imbued with twentieth-century mores this seems the obvious thing to do, but we should remember that to southern planters slaves were intermediate goods, used in the production process, not individuals for whom society was producing final output. From the viewpoint of these planters, the comparisons of per capita income should be based upon the income of the free population only, deducting the "maintenance cost" as the expense of using slave labor.[85] This redefinition of "Southern society" raises both the level and rate of growth of southern per capita income relative to that of the rest of the nation. With the exclusion of slaves from "society" the level of southern per capita income in 1860 exceeds the national average. Southern per capita income was two-thirds again as large as the per capita income of the North Central states, and the gap between the South and the Northeast is reduced by over 50 per cent. Treating slaves as intermediate goods also has an effect upon rates of growth. The southern growth rate becomes 1.8 per cent, in contrast with the rest of the nation's 1.3 per cent.

Given these findings, how do we account for the widespread im-

TABLE 1

PER CAPITA INCOME BY REGION, 1840 AND 1860
(IN 1860 PRICES)

	Slaves as Consumers		Slaves as Intermediate Goods[1]	
	1840	1860	1840	1860
National Average	$ 96	$128	$109	$144
North:	109	141	110	142
Northeast	129	181	130	183
North Central	65	89	66	90
South:	74	103	105	150
South Atlantic	66	84	96	124
East South Central	69	89	92	124
West South Central	151	184	238	274

[1]"Maintenance cost" equal to $20.

Source: See text and footnotes 32 and 35.

pression of southern backwardness? Three factors seem most important. First, the fact that the South had only 33 per cent of the nation's popultaion in 1860 (24 per cent of the free population) means that comparisons based upon total output (perhaps useful in discussing war potential) provide a less favorable comparison for the South than do the per capita measures.[36] Second, the commercial dependence upon the North for financial and transport services, as well as for manufactured goods, upset the southerners, who seemed unwilling to acknowledge fully their comparative advantage in the production of cotton and other staples. Third, if growth is equated with urbanization and industrialization, the South does compare unfavorably with the rest of the nation. Comparisons with the agricultural states of the North Central region, however, are less unfavorable to the South. The percentage of population in urban areas in 1860 was 36 per cent in the Northeast, 14 per cent in the North Central states, and 7 per cent in the South. Of the total national employment in manufacturing in that year, 72 per cent was in the Northeast, 14 per cent in the North Central states, and 10 per cent in the South. (The population shares were 36 per cent, 29 per cent, and 33 per cent, respectively).[37]

The last two of the indicators have been widely used as proxy measures for southern economic development, in the absence of a more complete set of income estimates. Thus their usefulness as proxies has been superseded by Easterlin's measures, which directly give us the information we want. While it is true the South lacked industry and was not urbanized relative to the rest of the nation, this clearly did not mean that the South was a poor or a stagnant area.

Other of the arguments which have been used to suggest southern backwardness can also be misleading. The particular nature of cotton as a crop may explain the low level of farm mechanization in the South, since cotton was profitably farmed without mechanical equipment. It is of interest that no important cotton harvesting equipment was adopted until the middle of the twentieth century. Profitability of new lands can explain the frequent mention of presumably exhausted soil in the older areas of the South. Given a choice between investing in older soils (fertilizing) and in new soils (clearing), at the relative prices existing before the Civil War, movement to new soil was apparently economically rational. It is not clear, moreover, that this behavior would not have changed had the relative prices for these types of investment in land shifed.

Emphasis by Phillips on the effects of slavery upon capital formation has made this a standard argument for southern retardation. The slave system has been considered to be the cause of low southern investment in physical capital, since investment in slaves presumably absorbed capital which would have had other uses in the economy.[38] However, once the external slave trade was forbidden, there was no capital drainage out of the South—funds were merely being transferred from one region to another within the southern economy. Therefore, it is necessary to determine what the seller of the slave did with his funds.[39] It is, in fact, possible that slave ownership increased the ability of southerners to borrow from the North (as well as the planter's ability to borrow within the South) by providing a marketable asset which could be used for collateral on loans, and thus permitted increased capital formation.

Other explanations of low southern capital formation can also be questioned. That a skewed income distribution and the social climate attributable to slavery resulted in conspicuous consumption and waste of money on the part of the plantation owners has often been argued.[40] At present, however, no reliable income distribution statistics exist for the antebellum South which can be compared with other regions and years. For a rough indication of the inequality of the income of the free population in 1860, I have estimated the share of income going to the top approximately 1 per cent of free southern families in 1860. The basic assumption is that all the top income earners were plantation owners. By using data on the size distribution of plantations by number of slaves owned, it was estimated that the share of free southern income going to the top 1 per cent of the free population was about the same as the income share of the top 1 per cent of the population in 1929.[41] While crude, it does suggest the need for more detailed examination of southern income distribution.

The essential point of the conspicuous consumption argument is not that planters purchased more land and slaves—this could represent a productive use of capital—but that they lived too lavishly. This is usually supported by fragmentary mentions of wasteful expenditures by planters. Unfortunately, we again lack sufficient data to determine if the spending propensities were higher in the South than in the North, as well as if the South had more and/or richer upper income families. We do know, however, that the large consumption expenditures do not imply low savings. In the somewhat atypical year of 1928, the per capita consumption of the top 1 per cent of income earners in the United States population was about $5200, while that of the remaining 99 per cent was under $600. Certainly this is a pronounced difference, and given normal human reactions this could (and did) lead to discussions of wasteful expenditures by the rich. Yet in this year the top 1 per cent had a savings-income ratio of 43.3 per cent, and accounted for over 100 per cent of estimated personal savings.[42] This suggests the possibility that the effects of large consumption expenditures on southern capital formation may be overstated. That conspicuous consumption which did exist was probably carried on mainly by planters who were wealthy by the standards of the times. Their conspicuous consumption possibly absorbed only part of their incomes, and their savings rates could have exceeded the national average. Indeed, given what we now know about the relationship between income and savings, it is quite possible that savings in the South were higher than they would have been with a less skewed income distribution.

Another way in which slavery was presumed to have retarded southern capital formation was by necessitating debt payments to be made to the North. Payments on loans led to a drain of funds from the South, as did southern purchases of services from the North. However, the existence of such flows are part of the costs to be paid for profitable borrowing and specialization. Certainly the existence of capital imports for the South need not result in any reduction in income or capital formation. If the capital imports permitted a higher level of investment in the South it could have raised, rather than lowered, the rate of growth of the economy.

It has been argued that the income estimates do not provide the relevant comparisons—that the South should have industrialized for long-term growth irrespective of its prewar condition. This implies that a deliberate effort should have been made to shift resources from agriculture to manufacturing. This policy has been advocated on two grounds. The first is that the southern entrepreneurs were backward, and therefore were unwilling or unable to take advantage of modern developments. It appears, however, that the South did not ignore all modern developments. The South had 31 per cent of the nation's railroad mileage, with per capita mileage only slightly below the national average.[48] This network was financed predominantly by indigenous capital, a fact which is of interest for the capital formation hypothesis discussed above. While the track to area ratio was lower in the South than elsewhere, the southern economy was favored by a transportation network based upon navigable streams and rivers. Thus the absence of an entrepreneurial spirit within the confines of the slave system is not clearly established.

The second reason for advocating a shift to manufactures is the proposition that growth based upon an agricultural export commodity was doomed to ultimate failure. The more rapid the shift away from cotton, the better the longer-term prospects for the southern economy. Implicit in this is the statement that southern whites would not have responded to changing profit opportunities. This statement is usually justified by the argument that industrialization was prevented because it would have meant the end of slavery. While the hypothesis that with the existence of shifts in profitability the South would not have shifted into industry is widely debated, it should be repeated that cotton production was apparently profitable in most of the antebellum period, that geographic mobility in response to income differentials existed, and that, at least within agriculture, there were responses to changing profitability.

In concluding this section, we can raise further questions about two of the arguments previously given for slavery's deleterious effect upon southern economic development. The first, arguing for retarded development of the internal market, needs more justification. The question is not slave purchasing power but the amount of demand which existed for products the slaves consumed. Southern discussions of the clothing and shoes for slaves which were imported from the North suggest the existence of a substantial market for consumer goods on plantations. That the planters paid for these goods rather than the slaves does not diminish the effect on demand. It can be argued that the products ordered by planters were more standardized and amenable to mass production techniques than would have been the situation if the slaves were themselves the source of demand.

Given the small optimal size of manufacturing plants in 1860, it seems probable that the southern market could have been large enough to support internal industry, if the South's comparative advantage had been manufacturing. Estimates presented by Genovese of cash expenditures per person in the South suggest that the region could have supported over 50 cotton textile plants and more than 200 boot and shoe establishments of Massachusetts size. While an admittedly crude calculation, it is more probable that the estimates are too low rather too high.[44] For a more complete answer the important questions are those of plantation self-sufficiency and the nature of the products purchased by southerners. To settle this, detailed records of the magnitude and composition of southern purchases from other regions and from abroad are needed.[45]

The second argument, the relative deficiency of education in the South, is clearly supported by the relevant data. The education of slaves was forbidden by law, while that of the whites was certainly below that in the rest of the nation.[46] However, given the world demand for cotton and the rate of growth of income in the antebellum South, it may be that whatever costs it did impose were negligible relative to the effects in the late nineteenth and twentieth centuries. Here again, more research is needed in order to establish the size of the penalty paid by the South for its educational backwardness before the Civil War.

III. CONCLUSION

The recent works of historians and economists have resulted in revisions of the conclusions about the economics of slavery which derive from the pioneer works of U. B. Phillips. Indications are that on the eve of the Civil War slavery was profitable to the planters, viable, and consistent with a growing economy.

There are many aspects of the overall impact of slavery which have not been discussed. The effects on political decision-making, the psychology of the white population, and the propensity to innovate, for example, must be answered before a full determination of the social and economic effects of the slave system can be made.[47]

Perhaps the basic economic question would be the comparison of southern developments under free and slave labor. It is possible that growth might have been more rapid and the returns to investment higher had the slave system never been introduced. Yet we do know that up to the Civil War the South had a relatively high level of per capita income, that because of the surplus above subsistence costs the planters as a class made a return on their investments in slaves greater than that on alternative investments possible at that time, and that even if slave labor had been less efficient than free, its use probably did not cause losses to the owners. While the broader and more difficult questions are still unanswered, the recent revisions have improved the analytical and factual framework in which they can be pursued.

The University of Rochester

NOTES

1. For another critical review of the debate, from a different perspective, see Harold D. Woodman, "The Profitability of Slavery: A Historical Perennial," *Journal of Southern History*, 29:303-325 (August, 1963).

2. Viability is defined as the ability of an industry to continue existing. In economic terms an industry would be considered viable if a market rate of return could be made on the replacement cost of capital used. In the case of slavery the test for viability is the equating of the present value of the future stream of income from slaves with the costs of rearing them. If the present value, computed on the basis of the market rate of interest, was less than the present value of rearing costs, slavery would have been economically unviable—there would have been no incentive for anyone to raise slaves.

3. The most pertinent of these are: "The Economic Cost of Slave-holding in the Cotton Belt," *Political Science Quarterly*, 20:257-275 (June, 1905); and *American Negro Slavery* (New York, 1918).

4. Phillips, "Economic Cost," p. 259.

5. *Ibid., passim.*

6. *Ibid.*, p. 272. The question of economies of scale in cotton production is one of the key questions concerning the plantation which remain to be answered. The primary evidence for increasing returns to scale is the increased plantation size and concentration of holdings in larger plantations before 1860. See Lewis Cecil Gray, *History of Agriculture in the Southern United States to 1860* (2 vols., Washington, 1933), 478-480, 530. William Parker apparently doubts the existence of economies in production attributable to the costs of management and equipment, or at least he doubts that they alone can explain the observed size distribution of plantations. William N. Parker, "The Slave Plantation in American Agriculture," First International Conference of Economic History, *Contributions and Communications* (Paris, 1960), 321-331.

7. Rising slave prices in this period could be attributed to either increased consumption of prestige by slaveowners or to increased value of slave production in business operations (with the consumption expenditure remaining constant), or to some combination of the two. The observation that the price of slaves fluctuated with the price of cotton does not itself suggest that southerners were behaving to maximize profits from business operations alone. Such variations are

consistent with the hypothesis that the expenditure for prestige remained constant.

8. Phillips, "Economic Cost," p. 275.

9. *Ibid.*, p. 273.

10. *Idem.* Phillips later argued that the slave system had the advantage of providing for mobility of the labor force (*Slavery*, p. 395). The distinction intended was apparently that between occupational mobility and geographic mobility.

11. *Ibid.*, p. 275.

12. *Ibid.*, p. 259.

13. Chas. W. Ramsdell, "The Natural Limits of Slavery Expansion," *Mississippi Valley Historical Review*, 16:151-171 (September, 1929).

14. See, in particular:

> Ralph Betts Flanders, *Plantation Slavery in Georgia* (Chapel Hill, 1933).
>
> Charles Sacket Sydnor, *Slavery in Mississippi* (New York, 1933).
>
> Charles S. Davis, *The Cotton Kingdom in Alabama* (Montgomery, 1939).

15. Eugene D. Genovese, "The Significance of the Slave Plantation for Southern Economic Development," *Journal of Southern History*, 28:422-437 (November, 1962). Reprinted in his *The Political Economy of Slavery: Studies in the Economy and Society of the Slave South* (New York, 1965), 157-179.

16. Douglass C. North, *The Economic Growth of the United States, 1790-1860* (Englewood Cliffs, 1961), 133-134. See also his *Growth and Welfare in the American Past: A New Economic History* (Englewood Cliffs, 1966), 90-97.

17. Robert R. Russel, "The General Effects of Slavery upon Southern Economic Progress," *Journal of Southern History*, 4:34-54 (February, 1938), and *Gray, op. cit.*, 462-480, 940-942.

18. Thomas P. Govan, "Was Plantation Slavery Profitable?" *Journal of Southern History*, 8:513-535 (November, 1942).

19. Kenneth M. Stampp, *The Peculiar Institution: Slavery in the Ante-Bellum South* (New York, 1956), 383-418.

20. Alfred H. Conrad and John R. Meyer, "The Economics of Slavery in the Ante Bellum South," *Journal of Political Economy*, 66:95-130 (April, 1958). Reprinted in their *The Economics of Slavery and Other Studies in Econometric History* (Chicago, 1964), 43-92.

21. For a criticism of the accounting calculations, based as they are upon historical cost, see Yasukichi Yasuba, "The Profitability and Viability of Plantation Slavery in the United States," *The Economic Studies Quarterly*, 12:60-67 (September, 1961).

22. They also directly answered Phillips' charge that slaves were overpriced by pointing to a sharp rise in productivity in this period, justifying the rise in slave prices in terms of cotton prices. (See *op. cit.*, pp. 116 and 117, particularly Table 17). However, the increase in productivity they show may be too large. First, their estimates ignore the secular and cyclical variations in the proportion of slave labor used in cotton production. Second, a published estimate of man-hours per bale of cotton shows a fall from 601 in 1800 to 439 in 1840 and 304 in 1880. Department of Agriculture, *Progress of Farm Mechanization* (Miscellaneous Publication No. 630, Washington, 1947), p. 3. This study, however, shows no change in yield per acre between 1800 and 1840, which is surprising given

the move to presumably more fertile soils.

23. Edward Saraydar, "A Note on the Profitability of Ante Bellum Slavery," *Southern Economic Journal*, 30:325-332 (April, 1964).

24. Saraydar also claimed that Conrad and Meyer must have overstated alluvial yields since the average yield per acre for the nation didn't reach their implied level until after World War II. Richard Sutch pointed out that alluvial yields in 1879 exceeded those implied by Conrad and Meyer. Richard Sutch, "The Profitability of Ante Bellum Slavery—Revisited," *Southern Economic Journal*, 31:365-377 (April, 1965), with "Reply" by Saraydar, 377-383.

25. Robert Evans, Jr., "The Economics of American Negro Slavery," in National Bureau of Economic Research, *Aspects of Labor Economics* (Princeton, 1962), 185-243. The Phillips estimates do show an increased differential in favor of the Lower South after 1856.

26. Robert Gallman and William Parker have been studying the manuscript census for southern states in 1860. In a related study, James T. Foust and Dale Swan have been examining the effects upon measured productivity of owners of small plantations (six or fewer slaves) working in the field alongside their slaves.

27. Yasuba's calculations are based on the estimates of Conrad and Meyer. Even if, as discussed above, the latter overstate cotton yields per slave the existence of rent and the trend remain.

28. As Sutch pointed out, flexibility also existed in the price of land.

29. This point is overlooked by Govan in his discussion of the Evans paper. He rejected as implausible Evans' finding that the profits of slave purchasers not only did not fall, but actually rose in the early 1840's. Thomas P. Govan, "Comments" in National Bureau of Economic Research, *Aspects of Labor Economics* (Princeton, 1962), 243-246. Yasuba found the capitalized rent in this period lower than in preceding and succeeding intervals, which meant that the market price of slaves fell more than their rearing costs. Thus it was possible for those who purchased slaves in this period to have made high rates of return, since they obtained slaves at a lower price. Apparently investors as a group were overly pessimistic.

30. John Moes has suggested another possible economic end to slavery. If the productivity of the freed Negro was sufficiently in excess of his productivity while enslaved he would have been able to compensate his owner for granting freedom. John E. Moes, "Comments," in National Bureau of Economic Research, *Aspects of Labor Economics* (Princeton, 1962), 247-256.

31. If slavery were unprofitable this would mean that rent as measured by Yasuba, based upon the excess of market price at age 18 above rearing costs, would exceed that implied by Sutch, which is based upon the excess of productivity above rearing and maintenance costs.

32. Richard A. Easterlin, "Regional Income Trends, 1840-1950," in Seymour Harris, ed., *American Economic History* (New York, 1961), 525-547; Robert E. Gallman, "Gross National Product in the United States, 1834-1909," in Conference on Research in Income and Wealth, Volume Thirty, *Output, Employment, and Productivity in the United States After 1800* (New York, 1966), 3-76; Department of Commerce, *Historical Statistics of the United States: Colonial Times to 1957* (Washington, 1961), Series A123-180, p. 13. There were a number of revisions applied to Easterlin's data in obtaining the estimates of Table 1. The major revision was the estimation of income for Texas in 1840, so that Texas

could be brought into the southern region in both years. To downward bias the growth rate Texas per capita income in 1840 was assumed equal to the 1860 level. The 1840 population was interpolated between the 1836 and 1846 estimates presented in Lewis W. Newton and Herbert P. Gambrell, *A Social and Political History of Texas* (Dallas, 1932), p. 280. Thus the regional breakdown in Table 1 differs from Easterlin's in including Texas in the South, but accords with his placement of Delaware and Maryland in the Northeast. The Mountain and Pacific states were excluded from the national and regional totals in both years.

Easterlin's estimates are the most detailed available for this period, but, of course, may not be perfectly accurate for the conclusions made. Genovese, for example, has stressed the inferior quality of livestock in the South. (See "Livestock in the Slave Economy of the Old South—A Revised View," *Agricultural History*, 36:143-149 (July, 1962). Reprinted in his *The Political Economy of Slavery*, 106-123.) The importance of such biases awaits further study. However, two points should be made. First, it is improbable that such corrections could reverse the finding that growth did occur in the slave economy. Second, while it is possible that such corrections would reduce the level of southern income in 1860, it need not effect the relative growth rate if the same relative quality existed in 1840 and 1860.

33. As I have indicated elsewhere, southern backwardness appears to be mainly attributable to the effects of the Civil War and its aftermath. If per capita income in the South had grown as rapidly between 1860 and 1870 as it had between 1840 and 1860, the 1870 level would have been about twice the observed level. Stanley L. Engerman, "The Economic Impact of the Civil War," *Explorations in Entrepreneurial History*, Second Series, 3:176-199 (Spring, 1966).

34. Sutch, *op. cit.*, p. 377.

35. The "maintenance cost" per slave used in these calculations was $20 (see Gray, *op. cit.*, p. 544). It should be noted that while a higher maintenance cost would reduce the relative per capita income of free southerners in 1860, it would raise the rate of growth of their income between 1840 and 1860. E.g., if a $30 figure were used the southern per capita income would have been $144, compared to the North's $142, but the growth rate would have risen to 1.9 per cent, with that of the North remaining the same as in the previous calculation. For similar comparisons see Easterlin, *op. cit.*, p. 527, and Robert William Fogel, "The Reunification of Economic History with Economic Theory," *American Economic Review*, 55:92-98 (May, 1965).

36. Hinton Helper's classic attack was restricted to measures of total output, overlooking population differences. Hinton Rowan Helper, *The Impending Crisis of the South: How to Meet It* (New York, 1963). His comparison was based upon a more complicated model, since it is also intended to explain the net outflow of population from the South. Southern total income grew at 4.1 per cent from 1840 to 1860 as contrasted with the rest of the nation's rate of 4.7 per cent. The northeastern growth rate, however, was only 4.0 per cent (With slaves treated as intermediate goods, the southern growth rate becomes 4.2 per cent, still below the rest of the nation's rate of 4.7 per cent.)

37. Bureau of the Census, Sixteenth, *Population* (Washington, 1942), Vol. I, p. 20. Census, Eighth, *Manufactures of the United States in 1860* (Washington, 1865), p. 729.

38. Moes has pointed out a theoretically plausible way in which such a decline

in investment could have occurred. If in a non-slave society expenditures on rearing children are considered consumption to the parents while in a slave society such expenditures are considered part of capital formation, slave societies which have the same savings-income ratio as non-slave societies would devote less to non-human capital. However, if the ratio of savings to income was higher the more unequally income was distributed, the slave society might devote more to all types of capital formation than the non-slave. John E. Moes, "The Absorption of Capital in Slave Labor in the Ante Bellum South and Economic Growth," *American Journal of Economics and Sociology*, 20:535-541 (October, 1961).

39. It is not clear in which direction within the South net capital flowed. If a slave was sold from an older region to a new region, there would be a net flow of funds to the older area in exchange for human capital. If the planter moved with his slaves there would be a net inflow of human and other capital into the new region, with no corresponding outflow. See William L. Miller, "A Note on the Importance of the Interstate Slave Trade of the Ante Bellum South," *Journal of Political Economy*, 73:181-187 (April, 1965).

40. The distribution of income in the South is still debated. For an argument that inequality was not as great as often implied, see Frank Lawrence Owsley, *Plain Folk of the Old South* (Baton Rouge, 1949). For a rebuttal to this position see Fabian Linden, "Economic Democracy in the Slave South: An Appraisal of Some Recent Views," *Journal of Negro History*, 31:140-189 (April, 1946).

41. The key assumptions were that only plantation owners fell in the top 1 per cent of income earners, and that dividing estimated plantation income by five (the average family size) does not change the rankings. Thus what is actually measured is the share of income going to families owning large plantations. The size distribution of plantations is in Census, Eighth, *Agriculture of the United States in 1860* (Washington, 1864), p. 247 and errata sheet. Each slave was considered to represent capital (including land, etc.) of $2500. Capital was then decapitalized at 6 per cent, roughly the market rate of interest. If slavery were unprofitable, the capital estimate would be decapitalized at a lower rate, and the income amount and share would be correspondingly lower. Total free southern income was taken from the detail underlying Table 1. The top 0.8 per cent of free population, representing plantations with over 50 slaves, received 15 per cent of income, while the top 1.2 per cent (plantations with over 40 slaves) received 18.5 per cent. In 1929 the top 1 per cent of the population received 17.2 per cent of income (economic variant). See Simon Kuznets, *Shares of Upper Income Groups in Income and Saving* (National Bureau of Economic Research Occasional Paper 35, New York, 1950), p. 67. For a study of the wealth distribution in 1860, based on census manuscripts, see Robert E. Gallman, "The Social Distribution of Wealth in the United States," unpublished paper presented to the International Economic History Conference, August, 1965.

42. See Robert J. Lampman, *The Share of Top Wealth-Holders in National Wealth, 1922-56* (Princeton, 1962), p. 236. This is the boldest comparison, but more typical years of the 1920's can be used to demonstrate the same point. In 1925, e.g., the ratio of consumption per capita of the upper 1 per cent to that of the rest of the population was 9:1; yet the upper income groups had a savings-income ratio of 42.9 per cent, and acounted for 51 per cent of personal savings.

43. See George Rogers Taylor, *The Transportation Revolution, 1815-1860* (New York, 1951), p. 79. Similarly, Allen Fenichel shows that in 1838 (the only

ante bellum year for which data exist) the South had 38.2 per cent of the nation's total capacity of steam power in manufacturing. Allen H. Fenichel, "Growth and Diffusion of Power in Manufacturing, 1838-1919," in Conference on Research in Income and Wealth, Volume Thirty, *Output, Employment, and Productivity in the United States After 1800* (New York, 1966), 443-478.

44. Genovese estimates 1860 cash expenditure in Mississippi at about $25 per person (Genovese, *Political Economy*, p. 169). If we assume this amount to hold throughout the southern states, this amounts to about one-fourth of southern per capita income in that year. Making the extreme assumption that outside of the South all income went into cash expenditures, while the southern share was only one-fourth, and that expenditures on boots and shoes and cotton textiles were proportional to all cash expenditures, we can use the value of output of those sectors to estimate total southern cash expenditures on the specific goods. Total value of output and average output per Massachusetts plant are from Census, Eighth, *Manufactures*, pp. xxi and lxxiii. In 1860 there were 217 cotton textile plants and 1,354 boot and shoe establishments in Massachusetts.

45. For an attempt to measure this trade see Albert Fishlow, *American Railroads and the Transformation of the Antebellum Economy* (Cambridge, 1965), 269-288, as well as the articles by Fishlow and Fogel in Ralph L. Andreano, ed., *New Views on American Economic Development* (Cambridge, 1965), 187-224.

46. See Albert Fishlow, "The Common School Revival: Fact or Fancy?," in Henry Rosovsky, ed., *Industrialization In Two Systems: Essays in Honor of Alexander Gerschenkron* (New York, 1966), 40-67.

47. For a study of some of these effects see Stanley M. Elkins, *Slavery: A Problem in American Institutional and Intellectual Life* (Chicago, 1959).

EXPLORATIONS IN ECONOMIC HISTORY 18, 304–308 (1981)

The Slavery Debate: A Note from the Sidelines

STEFANO FENOALTEA*

Duke University

The groves of academe, as the inhabitants know, are a malarial jungle infested by snakes, snipers, and booby traps; only rarely does scientific argument ascend from guerrilla operations to global conflict in the classic style. Our own discipline is much blessed: the ongoing Great War between the Central Empires of Fogel and Engerman and the Allied Powers of near everybody else is a model of the kind, long-lasting, wide-ranging, and splendidly expensive in men and materiel.[1] But in the heat and din of battle, the problems of tactics are all-absorbing, and strategic considerations easily lost sight of. How easy it is to win the battle but lose the war, or win the war but lose the peace! Might not the notes of a neutral observer from another theater help even the combatants to reflect upon their war aims?

In a sense, the slavery issue is as old as the "new" economic history, which is just now coming of age.[2] The early questions of slavery's profitability and viability have been set aside: viability despite high slave prices was established by the observation that the latter were demand prices rather than supply prices;[3] private profitability is taken for granted, since there is little evidence to the contrary (and equally little evidence for it, given that neither expected earnings nor ex ante discount rates can be observed);[4] and social profitability is too complex a question to be usefully approached by cliometric modeling.[5] The issues central to

---

* I wish to thank Hugh Aitken, Martin Bronfenbrenner, Stephen DeCanio, Robert Gallman, Richard Hydell, John Meyer, and Gavin Wright for their comments, without attributing to them the views expressed here.

[1] See especially Fogel and Engerman (1974), David *et al.* (1976), Fogel and Engerman (1977), David and Temin (1979), Haskell (1979), Schaefer and Schmitz (1979), Wright (1979), and Fogel and Engerman (1980).

[2] Conrad and Meyer (1958).

[3] Yasuba (1961).

[4] The basic issue here is whether slave-owners were profit maximizers. The standard test has been to see whether slave prices were justified by slave earnings and interest rates; if not, that would be evidence that planters accepted a substandard rate of return, or

304

Time on the Cross, and to the subsequent debate, are relatively new ones: the "efficiency of slavery" on the one hand, and the nature of the slave-management system on the other. What is striking is the peculiar *combination* of positions adopted on these issues by the participants in the debate, which suggests that each group is busily undermining its own argument.

The first (but not the main) message of *Time on the Cross* is that slave agriculture was more efficient than free agriculture. Now "efficiency" is not a neutral word: efficiency is good, inefficiency is bad, and a more efficient system better than a less efficient one. What Fogel and Engerman actually did, of course, was to measure the ratio of output to a weighted sum of inputs in slave and free agriculture, and compare these ratios.[6] The prudent interpretation of differences in such ratios is that they are due to poor measurement, and especially to incomplete measurement of the relevant inputs: the students of aggregate technical change, who pioneered such measures (in an intertemporal, rather than intersectoral, context), concluded that the difference in measured productivity was best called "the measure of our ignorance."[7] A cautious scholar obtaining Fogel and Engerman's result might thus have concluded that the inputs into the slave sector's production function had been less completely specified than those into the non-slave sector's: in essence, that we know less about slave agriculture than about free agriculture. Not a dramatic conclusion, perhaps, but eye-catching enough to the *cognoscenti*.

It is plausible to assume that the critical mismeasurement is in the labor input, since it is relatively difficult to measure, and in any case more heavily weighted than the other inputs combined. If the measured productivity differential survives the refinement of the labor measure from a crude number-of-people figure to a less indirect number-of-man hours figure (as it appears to do), in turn, it is plausible to attribute the residual to the (still unmeasured) difference in the intensity of each labor hour.[8] Simply put, the evidence suggests that slaves worked harder than

---

(equivalently) valued slaves as consumption goods as well as productive assets. The empirical block to such a test, as noted, is that the relevant earnings and interest rates are the expected future ones, and not the currently observed ones. There is yet a deeper problem: if planters did not maximize profits out of humanitarian feelings about how hard their slaves *should* be worked, the slaves' current earnings would not be maximized; but those earnings could still be normally capitalized into slave prices. The slaves' price–earnings ratio may thus be entirely beside the point.

[5] The cliometricians who have paid sophisticated attention to this point—summarized, if one will, in the distinction between economic growth and economic development—do not appear to dispose of analytical tools superior to those of ordinary historians. See especially Wright (1978); also, for example, Genovese (1965).

[6] Fogel and Engerman (1974), vol. 2, p. 131 ff.

[7] Abramowitz (1956), p. 11; Domar (1962), p. 599. For a radically nihilistic view, see McClelland (1978), p. 375.

[8] Fogel and Engerman (1980), pp. 686, 688.

free men. This result may have been novel to those—if there ever were any—who genuinely believed the racist hokum about shiftless niggers and all that; at least to an Italian, who would say "lavorare come un negro" where English-speakers say "work like a dog," it is almost spectacularly platitudinous. Moreover, the picture that emerges from the attribution of the measurement error to the labor input is one that substantially confirms the traditional view that Southern agriculture used human effort where Northern agriculture used capital and improvements; and it is precisely this "backwardness," this failure to substitute capital for labor, that the nontechnical observer seems to identify with inefficiency. In short, it would appear, efficiency in its narrow textbook sense is neither here nor there; what Fogel and Engerman call the relative efficiency of Southern agriculture is simply what was previously called its relative *inefficiency*, and the apparent novelty of *Time on the Cross* on this particular issue reduces essentially to a play on words.[9]

The truly novel argument made by *Time on the Cross* is that the superior "efficiency" of slavery—the superior intensity of slave labor, if, at the limit, it is only that—was attributable not to the threat (and use) of the lash but to humane treatment, moral suasion, and promises of rewards. The most important message of the work, certainly the basis for its public notoriety, is that slavery was relatively benign: slave-breeding, harsh material conditions, interference with family life, whippings, exploitation, debauchings are either insignificant or outright "myths." Whatever the ultimate reasons for this interpretation—perhaps the desire to bring even slavery into that Elysian neoclassical world in which people interact only to their mutual benefit, perhaps the dangerous presumption that it is the destiny of cliometrics to correct the blunders of traditional historians, perhaps even the siren-song of the spectacular—two things seem clear. The first is that it is not warranted by the evidence: it convinced no one beyond a few early, impressionable reviewers, and the close criticism of David, Gutman, Sutch, and Temin has effectively disposed of it.[10] The second is that it is, from Fogel and Engerman's own point of view, a remarkably unpromising, not to say self-defeating, basis on which to explain the superior "efficiency" of slave agriculture. The slave-owner has no advantage over the employer of free men in his ability to offer, and elicit effort by means of, ordinary rewards; but only

[9] As I have argued elsewhere (Fenoaltea, 1973), the controversy surrounding Fogel's earlier assessment of the importance of American railways turns on a similar sleight of hand (in this case, the substitution of "necessity" for "sufficiency"). What is most curious, in all this, is the prevailing willingness supinely to accept the argument on the misleading terms that underlie the proposed (counterintuitive, and false) reinterpretation of history.

[10] David et al. (1976). While noncliometricians also contributed to the debate, the fundamental criticism of *Time on the Cross* came, as it perhaps had to come, from within the guild.

slaves can be driven with the whip.[11] If slaves were more productive than free labor, is it not presumably because they were threatened rather than cajoled, because slavery was terrible rather than benign?

Here, then, is the central *curiosum* of the slavery debate. The best evidence that slavery was harsh and terror-driven is the superior "efficiency" of slavery; the best evidence that slavery was mild and benevolent would be that slaves worked no harder than free men. *Time on the Cross* argues that slavery was benign, and advances the productivity argument that undermines that view; *Reckoning with Slavery* argues that slavery was harsh, and attacks the productivity argument that supports that view. Might it not behoove both groups to pause and reconsider their scientific objectives?[12] My own suggestion (as the reader has inferred from my use of indicatives and conditionals) is that David *et al.* should make their stand on the nature of the slave-system, where their case that it was indeed inhuman and inhumane seems unassailable, and embrace the Fogel–Engerman argument that slaves were "more efficient" (worked harder) than free labor. The latter result seems relatively robust, for all their arguments to the contrary;[13] and, to repeat, it is a powerful weapon in their own hands if only they choose to adopt it. With equal consistency, Fogel and Engerman could embrace the criticisms of their relative efficiency findings, and make their stand on the benign nature of slavery—or, with I think far greater empirical justification, vice versa. If they were to maintain their findings on relative productivity, where their cliometric contribution seems greatest (and, please, abandon the biased and misleading term "efficiency"), and recant the interpretation of slavery advanced in *Time on the Cross* (or at least consent not to repeat it, without admission of guilt),[14] all could agree

[11] The inability of the plantations to survive Emancipation on a wage-labor basis indicates that their productivity depended on the merciless driving of the slave gangs, rather than on conventional economies of scale; see also Fogel and Engerman (1980), pp. 677–679, 682, 686. By the same token, the "rewards" for which slaves labored were typically relief from lash-driven field work and the like; for a broader discussion of such incentive systems, and the limits to their profitability, see Fenoaltea (1980).

[12] Scientific objectives are not the only ones, of course, and others may be at the root of the animus that mars *Reckoning with Slavery*. The eagerness to find fault with everything in *Time on the Cross* not only reproduces, as in a mirror, the inconsistencies of that work; it also leads to a basically negative critique, insensitive to the need to offer a coherent picture to replace the one under attack. Wright's contribution to the volume is here the laudable exception; and other authors may have made their positive contribution elsewhere, e.g., Ransom and Sutch (1977).

[13] Fogel and Engerman (1980).

[14] There is some evidence that they may be leaning in this direction: note the focus of Fogel and Engerman (1977, 1980), and the growing stress on the gang and hard work as the source of the slaves' superior productivity (also Haskell, 1979). On the other hand, Fogel and Engerman still seem determined to convince us that their measures establish the superior *efficiency* of slavery, and actually claim a consensus on this point (1980, p. 672).

that slaves were harshly driven, and (therefore) worked *come negri*. A classic conflict would come to an equally classic end: a return to the *status quo ante bellum*. A good time was had by all, and a Thucydides, or an Aristophanes, could write it up for posterity.

REFERENCES

Abramowitz, M. (1956), "Resource and Output Trends in the United States Since 1870." *American Economic Review* 46, 5–23.

Conrad, A. H., and Meyer, J. R. (1958), "The Economics of Slavery in the Ante Bellum South." *Journal of Political Economy* 66, 95–130.

David, P. A., Gutman, H. G., Sutch, R., Temin, P., and Wright, G. (1976), *Reckoning with Slavery*. New York: Oxford Univ. Press.

David, P. A., and Temin, P. (1979), "Explaining the Relative Efficiency of Slave Agriculture in the Ante-Bellum South: Comment." *American Economic Review* 69, 213–218.

Domar, E. D. (1962), "On Total Productivity and All That." *Journal of Political Economy* 70, 597–608.

Fenoaltea, S. (1973), "The Discipline and They: Notes on Counterfactual Methodology and the 'New' Economic History," *Journal of European Economic History* 2, 729–746.

Fenoaltea, S. (1980), "Slavery and Supervision in Comparative Perspective: A Model." Presented at the Cliometrics Conference, Chicago.

Fogel, R. W., and Engerman, S. L. (1974), *Time on the Cross*. Boston: Little, Brown.

Fogel, R. W., and Engerman, S. L. (1977), "Explaining the Relative Efficiency of Slave Agriculture in the Ante-Bellum South." *American Economic Review* 67, 275–296.

Fogel, R. W., and Engerman, S. L. (1980), "Explaining the Relative Efficiency of Slave Agriculture in the Ante-Bellum South: Reply." *American Economic Review* 70, 672–690.

Genovese, E. D. (1965), *The Political Economy of Slavery: Studies in the Economy and Society of the Slave South*. New York: Pantheon.

Haskell, T. L. (1979), "Explaining the Relative Efficiency of Slave Agriculture in the Ante-Bellum South: A Reply to Fogel and Engerman." *American Economic Review* 69, 206–207.

McClelland, P. D. (1978), "Cliometrics versus Institutional History." In P. Uselding (Ed.), *Research in Economic History*. Greenwich, Conn.: Jai Press. Vol. 3.

Ransom, R. L., and Sutch, R. (1977), *One Kind of Freedom: The Economic Consequences of Emancipation*. New York: Cambridge Univ. Press.

Schaefer, D. F., and Schmitz, M. D. (1979), "The Relative Efficiency of Slave Agriculture: A Comment." *American Economic Review* 69, 208–212.

Wright, G. (1978), *The Political Economy of the Cotton South*. New York: Norton.

Wright, G. (1979), "The Efficiency of Slavery: Another Interpretation." *American Economic Review* 69, 219–226.

Yasuba, Y. (1961), "The Profitability and Viability of Plantation Slavery in the United States." *The Economic Studies Quarterly* 12, 60–67.

THE LOW PRODUCTIVITY OF
SOUTHERN SLAVE LABOR:
CAUSES AND EFFECTS

Eugene D. Genovese

THE ECONOMIC BACKWARDNESS that condemned the slaveholding South to defeat in 1861-1865 had at its root the low productivity of labor. This factor expressed itself in several ways. Perhaps most significant was the carelessness and wastefulness of slaves. Bondage forced the Negro to give his labor grudgingly and badly, and his poor work habits retarded those social and economic advances that could have raised the general level of productivity. Less direct, as we shall presently see, were limitations imposed on the free work force, on technological development, and on the division of labor.

Although the debate on slave productivity is an old one, few arguments have appeared during the last hundred years to supplement those of contemporaries like John Elliott Cairnes and Edmund Ruffin. Cairnes made the much-assailed assertion that the slave was so defective in versatility that his labor could be exploited profitably only if he were taught one task and kept at it. If we allow for some exaggeration, Cairnes's thesis is sound. Most competent observers agreed that slaves worked badly, without interest or effort. Edmund Ruffin (although sometimes arguing otherwise) pointed out that whereas at one time cheap, fertile farmland required little skill, soil exhaustion had finally created conditions demanding the intelligent participation of the labor force.[1] Ruffin neither developed his idea nor drew the appropriate conclusions. The systematic education and training of the slaves would have been politically dangerous. Furthermore, the use of skilled workers would have made a smaller labor force desirable. This, in turn, re-

MR. GENOVESE, *the author of a number of recent articles on Southern slavery, is assistant professor of history at Rutgers.*

[1] Cairnes, *The Slave Power* (London, 1863), p. 46; Ruffin, *The Political Economy of Slavery* (Washington, 1857), p. 4; *Farmers' Register*, III (1863), 748-749. The best introduction to the literature is still Ulrich B. Phillips, *American Negro Slavery* (New York, 1918), chap. xviii.

quired extensive markets for surplus slaves and therefore could not be realized in the South as a whole. Other Southerners simply dropped the whole matter with the observation that the difference in productivity between free and slave labor only illustrated how well the Negroes were treated.[2]

Ample evidence indicates that slaves worked well below their capabilities. In several instances in Mississippi, when cotton picking was carefully supervised in local experiments, slaves picked two or three times their normal output. The records of the Barrow plantation in Louisiana reveal that inefficiency and negligence were the cause of two-thirds of the punishments inflicted on slaves, and other contemporary sources are full of corroborative data.[3]

However much the slaves may have worked below their capacity, the limitations placed on that capacity were probably even more important in undermining productivity. In particular, the diet to which slaves were subjected must be judged immensely damaging, despite assurances from contemporaries and later historians that the slave was well-fed.

The slave usually got enough to eat, but the starchy, high-energy diet of corn meal, pork, and molasses produced specific hungers, dangerous deficiencies, and that unidentified form of malnutrition to which the medical historian, Richard H. Shryock, draws attention.[4] Occasional additions of sweet potatoes or beans could do little to supplement the narrow diet. Planters did try to provide vegetables and fruits, but not much land could be spared from the staples, and output was minimal.[5] Protein hunger alone—cereals in general and corn in particular cannot provide adequate protein—greatly reduces the ability of an organism to resist infectious diseases. Even increased consumption of vegetables probably would not have corrected the deficiency, for as a rule the indispensable amino acids are found only in such foods as lean meat, milk, and eggs. The abundant pork provided was, however,

[2] See the *Southern Quarterly Review*, XIX (1851), 221. Ruffin also sometimes argued this way.

[3] Charles Sackett Sydnor, *Slavery in Mississippi* (New York, 1933), p. 16; E. A. Davis (ed.), *Plantation Life in the Florida Parishes of Louisiana: The Diary of B. H. Barrow* (New York, 1943), pp. 86 ff.

[4] "Medical Practice in the Old South," *South Atlantic Quarterly*, XXIX (1930), 160-161. See also Felice Swados, "Negro Health on Ante-Bellum Plantations," *Bulletin of the History of Medicine*, X (1941), 460-461; Eugene D. Genovese, "The Medical and Insurance Costs of Slaveholding in the Cotton Belt," *Journal of Negro History*, XLV (1960), 141-155.

[5] "Probably at no time before the Civil War were fruits and vegetables grown in Mississippi in quantities sufficient to provide the population with a balanced diet," writes John Hebron Moore, *Agriculture in Ante-Bellum Mississippi* (New York, 1958), p. 61. At that, slaves undoubtedly received a disproportionately small share of the output.

largely fat. Since the slave economy did not and could not provide sufficient livestock, no solution was at hand.[6]

In the 1890's a dietary study of Negro field laborers in Alabama revealed a total bacon intake of more than five pounds per week, or considerably more than the three-and-one-half pounds that probably prevailed in antebellum days. Yet, the total protein found in the Negroes' diet was only 60 per cent of that deemed adequate.[7] Recent studies show that individuals with a high caloric but low protein intake will deviate from standard height-weight ratios by a disproportionate increase in weight.[8] The slave's diet contained deficiencies other than protein; vitamins and minerals were also in short supply. Vitamin deficiencies produce xerothalmia, beriberi, pellagra, and scurvy and create what one authority terms "states of vague indisposition [and] obscure and ill-defined disturbances."[9]

There is no secret to why slaves appeared healthy: their diet was well-suited to guarantee the appearance of good health and to provide the fuel to keep them going in the fields, but it was not sufficient to insure either sound bodies or the stamina necessary for sustained, really productive labor. We need not doubt the testimony of William Dosite Postell, who presented evidence of reasonably good medical attention for slaves and of adequate supply of food bulk. Rather, it is the finer questions of dietary balance that concern us. At that, Postell has provided some astonishing statistics that reinforce the present argument: 7 per cent of a sample of more than 8,500 slaves from Georgia, Mississippi, Alabama, and Louisiana above the age of fifteen were either physically impaired or chronically ill.[10]

The limited diet was by no means primarily a result of ignorance or viciousness on the part of masters, for many knew better and would like to have done better. The problem was largely economic. Feeding costs formed a burdensome part of plantation expenses. Credit and market systems precluded the assignment of much land to crops other than cotton and corn. When so assigned it was generally the poorest land available, and the quality of foodstuffs consequently suffered.

[6] Eugene D. Genovese, "Livestock in the Slave Economy of the Old South—A Revised View," *Agricultural History*, XXXVI (1962), 143-149.

[7] W. O. Atwater and Charles D. Woods, *Dietary Studies with Reference to the Negro in Alabama in 1895 and 1896* (Washington, 1897). Adequate animal proteins plus corn probably would have sufficed to prevent nutritional deficiencies. See C. A. Elvehjem, "Corn in Human Nutrition," *Proceedings of the Fourth Annual Meeting of the Research Institute* (Washington, 1955), p. 83.

[8] See J. Masek, "Hunger and Disease," in Josué de Castro (ed.), *Hunger and Food* (London, 1958).

[9] Josué de Castro, *The Geography of Hunger* (Boston, 1952), p. 48.

[10] *The Health of Slaves on Southern Plantations* (Baton Rouge, 1951), especially pp. 159 ff.

For example, experiments have shown that the proportion of iron in lettuce may vary from one to fifty milligrams per hundred, according to soil conditions.

The slave's low productivity resulted directly from inadequate care, incentives, and training,[11] and from other well-known factors such as the overseer system. But just how low was it? Can the productivity of slave labor, which nonstatistical evidence indicates to have been low, be measured? An examination of the most recent, and most impressive, attempt to assess it suggests that it cannot. Alfred H. Conrad and John R. Meyer have arranged the following data to demonstrate the movement of "crop value per hand per dollar of slave price" during the antebellum period: size of the cotton crop, average price, value of crop, number of slaves aged ten to fifty-four, crop value per slave, and price of prime field hands.[12] Unfortunately, this method, like the much cruder one used by Algie M. Simons in 1911 and repeated by Lewis C. Gray, does not remove the principal difficulties.

First, the contribution of white farmers who owned no slaves or who worked in the fields beside the few Negroes they did own, cannot be separated from that of the slaves. The output of slaveless farmers might be obtained by arduous digging in the manuscript census returns for 1850 and 1860, but the output of farmers working beside their slaves does not appear to lend itself to anything better than baseless guessing. There is also no reason to believe that slaves raised the same proportion of the cotton crop in any two years, and we have little knowledge of the factors determining fluctuations.

Second, we cannot assume that the same proportion of the slave force worked in the cotton fields in any two years. In periods of expected low prices slaveholders tried to deflect part of their force to food crops. We cannot measure the undoubted fluctuations in the man-hours applied to cotton. The Conrad-Meyer results, in particular, waver; they show a substantial increase in productivity before the Civil War, but the tendency to assign slaves to other crops in periods of falling prices builds an upward bias into their calculations for the prosperous 1850's. It might be possible to circumvent this problem by calculating for the total output instead of for cotton, but to do so would create

[11] The thesis presented by U. B. Phillips, Avery O. Craven, Lewis C. Gray, and others that the slave worked badly not because he was a slave but because he was a Negro cannot survive critical examination. For a critique, and a summary of evidence showing that Negroes brought to the U.S. were drawn from agricultural economies which demanded hard, disciplined labor, see Eugene D. Genovese, "The Negro Laborer in Africa and the Slave South," *Phylon*, XXI (1960), 343-350. See also Mamadou Dia, *Réflexions sur l'économie de l'Afrique noire* (rev. ed.; Paris, 1960), p. 23.

[12] "The Economics of Slavery in the Ante-Bellum South," *Journal of Political Economy*, LXVI (1958), 95-130, especially Table 17.

even greater difficulties, such as how to value food grown for plantation use.[13]

Not all bad effects of slavery on the productivity of the society were so direct. Critics of slaveholding have generally assumed that it created a contempt for manual labor, although others have countered with the assertion that the Southern yeomen was held in high esteem. True, the praises of the working farmer had to be sung in a society in which he had the vote, but an undercurrent of contempt was always there. Samuel Cartwright, an outspoken and socially minded Southern physician, referred scornfully to those whites "who make negroes of themselves" in the cotton and sugar fields.[14] Indeed, to work hard was "to work like a nigger." If labor was not lightly held, why were there so many assurances from public figures that no one need be ashamed of it?[15]

There were doubtless enough incentives and enough expressions of esteem to allow white farmers to work with some sense of pride; the full impact of the negative attitude toward labor fell on the landless. The brunt of the scorn was borne by those who had to work for others, much as a slave did. The proletarian, rural or urban, was free and white and therefore superior to one who was a slave and black, but the difference was minimized when he worked alongside a Negro for another man. So demoralized was white labor that planters often preferred to hire slaves because they were better workers.[16] How much was to be expected of white labor in a society that, in the words of one worried editor, considered manual labor "menial and revolting"?[17]

The attitude toward labor was thus composed of two strains: an undercurrent of contempt for work in general and the more prevalent and probably more damaging contempt for labor performed for an-

[13] Other questions are also raised by their price data; cotton statistics were not kept with the degree of accuracy required for really sophisticated analysis, for example. In any event, the authors have not demonstrated a significant increase in productivity at all. They show no increase for the depressed 1840's, but 20 per cent for the 1850's. These results emerge from a certain carelessness in rounding off figures. Crop value per hand per dollar of slave price is indexed at .05 for 1840; .05 for 1850; and .06 for 1860. But if we carry out the arithmetic two more decimal places we get .0494 (1840), .0538 (1850), and .0562 (1860)—i.e., a 9 per cent increase for the depressed 1840's and only 4 per cent for the 1850's. These results are implausible and, in any case, contradict their own conclusions.

[14] J. D. B. De Bow, *The Industrial Resoucres of the Southern and Western States* (New Orleans, 1852-53), III, 62.

[15] "Let no one be ashamed of labor," insisted William W. Holden of North Carolina; "let no man be ashamed of a hard hand or a sunburnt face." *Address Delivered Before the Duplin County Agricultural Society* (Raleigh, 1857), p. 7.

[16] Cornelius O. Cathey, *Agricultural Developments in North Carolina, 1783-1860* (Chapel Hill, 1958), pp. 54-55.

[17] *Southern Cultivator*, V (1847), 141.

other.[18] These notions undermined the productivity of those free workers who might have made important periodic contributions, and thus seriously lowered the level of productivity in the economy.

Few now doubt that social structure has been an important factor in the history of science and technology or that capitalism has introduced the greatest advances in these fields. For American agricultural technology, the craftsman, the skilled worker, and the small producer—all anxious to conserve labor time and cut costs—may well have provided the most significant technological thrust. Specifically, the great advances of the modern era arose from a free-labor economy that gave actual producers the incentives to improve methods and techniques.[19] In nineteenth-century America, writes one authority, "the farmers . . . directed and inspired the efforts of inventors, engineers, and manufacturers to solve their problems and supply their needs . . . [and] the early implements were in many cases invented or designed by the farmers themselves."[20]

If workers are to contribute much to technology, the economy must permit and encourage an increasing division of labor, for skilled persons assigned to few tasks can best devise better methods and implements. Once an initial accumulation of capital takes place, the division of labor, if not impeded, will result in further accumulation and further division. Such extensive division of labor cannot develop in slave economies. The heavy capitalization of labor, the high propensity to consume, and the weakness of the home market seriously impede the accumulation of capital. Technological progress and division of labor result in work for fewer hands, but slavery requires all hands to be occupied at all times. Capitalism has solved this problem by a tremendous economic expansion along varied lines (qualitative development), but slavery's obstacles to industrialization prevent this type of solution.

In part, the slave South offset its weakness by drawing upon the technology of more progressive areas. During the first half of the nineteenth century the North copied from Europe on a grand scale, but the South was limited even in the extent to which it could copy and was especially restricted in possibilities for improving techniques once they had been acquired. The regions in which transference of technical

[18] This latter attitude may be an automatic ingredient of a slave society. Karl Polanyi suggests that Aristotle, reflecting the Greek view, held work for others degrading. Polanyi et al. (eds.), *Trade and Market in the Early Empires* (Glencoe, Ill., 1957), p. 77.

[19] Edgar Zilsel, "The Sociological Roots of Science," *American Journal of Sociology*, XLVII (1942), 557 ff.

[20] Fowler McCormick, *Technological Progress in American Farming* (Washington, 1940), p. 9.

skills has always been most effective have been those with an abundance of trained craftsmen as well as of natural resources.[21] In the North a shortage of unskilled labor and a preoccupation with labor-saving machinery stimulated the absorption of advanced techniques and the creation of new ones. In the South the importation of slaves remedied the labor shortage and simultaneously weakened nonslave productive units. The availability of a "routinized, poorly educated, and politically ineffectual rural labor force" of whites as well as Negroes rendered, and to some extent still renders, interest in labor-saving machinery pointless.[22]

Negro slavery retarded technological progress in many ways: it prevented the growth of industrialism and urbanization; it retarded the division of labor, which might have spurred the creation of new techniques; it barred the labor force from that intelligent participation in production which has made possible the steady improvement of implements and machines; and it encouraged ways of thought antithetical to the spirit of modern science. These impediments undoubtedly damaged Southern agriculture, for improved equipment was largely responsible for the dramatic increases in crop yields per acre in the North during the nineteenth century.[23] The steady deterioration of American soil under conditions imposed by commercial exploitation, we now know, has been offset primarily by gains accruing from increased investments in technological improvements. Recent studies show that from 1910 to 1950 output per man-hour doubled only because of the rapid improvements in implements, machinery, and fertilizer.[24]

The farmers of the South were especially hurt by technological backwardness, for the only way in which they might have compensated for the planters' advantage of large-scale production would have been to attain a much higher technological level. The social pressure to invest in slaves and the high cost of machinery in a region that had to import much of its equipment made such an adjustment difficult.

Large-scale production gave the planter an advantage over his weaker competitors within the South, but the plantation was by no means more efficient than the family farm operating in the capitalist economy of the free states. Large-scale production, to be most efficient under modern conditions, must provide a substitute for the incentives possessed by the individual farmer. The experience of Soviet agriculture,

[21] Léon H. Dupriez (ed.), *Economic Progress* (Louvain, 1955), pp. 149-169.
[22] James H. Street, *The New Revolution in the Cotton Economy* (Chapel Hill, 1957), p. 34.
[23] Leo Rogin, *The Introduction of Farm Machinery . . . in the United States During the Nineteenth Century* (Berkeley, 1931), chap. i.
[24] Cited by Ronald L. Mighell, *American Agriculture: Its Structure and Place in the Economy* (New York, 1955), pp. 7-8.

with its politically induced collectivization, has again demonstrated that the prerequisite for efficient large-scale commodity production is a level of industrial technology such as is only now being attained even in the most advanced countries.[25]

Let us turn now to a detailed consideration of the plantation division of labor. Although few scholars assert that the Southern slave plantations were self-sufficient units, most assume a fair degree of division of labor in their work forces. The employment of skilled artisans is usually treated as a minor matter not worth serious attention. An examination of plantation manuscripts, and data in the manuscript census returns, however, shows that considerable sums were paid for the services of artisans and laborers, and that home manufactures were not well developed.

According to one study, the Confederacy was unable to repeat the achievements of the colonies during the Revolutionary War, when family industry supplied the war effort and the home front. Although household manufacturing survived longer in the slave states than in other parts of the country, slave labor proved so inefficient in making cloth, for example, that planters preferred not to bother. In those areas of the South in which slavery predominated, household manufactures decreased rapidly after 1840, and the system never took hold in the newer slave states of Florida, Louisiana, and Texas.[26] Whereas in the North its disappearance was occasioned by the development of much more advanced factory processes, in the South it was part of a general decline in skill and a lowering of technique.

An examination of manuscript census data for selected counties in 1860 bears out these generalizations. It also shows that the large plantations, although they usually produced greater totals than the small farms, did very poorly in the production of home manufactures. In Mississippi's cotton counties the big planters (thirty-one or more slaves) averaged only $76 worth of home manufactures during the year, whereas other groups of farmers and planters showed much less. In the Georgia cotton counties the small planters (twenty-one to thirty

[25] Paul A. Baran, *The Political Economy of Growth* (New York, 1957), pp. 267 ff., 278-283, insists that collectivization was justified because the only alternative to it in a country lacking enough urban purchasing power to support high food prices would dry up rural sources of capital accumulation by heavier peasant consumption. He adds that the U.S.S.R. had to force the pace of industrialization for political and military reasons and that grain deliveries to cities had to be guaranteed. These arguments, however valid, do not contradict the observation that collectivization removed a good part of the peasants' incentives without providing them with implements and machines. See W. Arthur Lewis, *The Theory of Economic Growth* (Homewood, Ill., 1955), pp. 134 ff., for a summary of experiences with large-scale farming.
[26] Rolla M. Tryon, *Household Manufactures in the United States, 1640-1860* (Chicago, 1917), pp. 5, 184 ff., 295-298, 371.

slaves) led other groups with $127, and the big planters produced only half as much. Fifty-eight per cent of the big planters in the Mississippi counties examined recorded no home manufactures at all, and most agriculturalists in the Georgia counties produced none. In Virginia the same results appeared; in tobacco counties the big planters led other groups with $56 worth of home manufactures, and in the tidewater and northern wheat counties the big planters led with only $35.[27]

The Richmond *Dispatch* estimated in the 1850's that the South spent $5,000,000 annually for Northern shoes and boots.[28] Although the figure cannot be verified, there is no doubt that Southerners bought most of their shoes in the North. One of the bigger planters, Judge Cameron of North Carolina, owner of five plantations and 267 slaves in 1834, had to purchase more than half the shoes needed for his Negroes despite his large establishment and a conscientious attempt to supply his own needs.[29] Most planters apparently did not even try to produce shoes or clothing. When a planter with about thirty slaves in Scotland Neck, North Carolina, made arrangements to have clothing produced on his estate, he hired an outsider to do it.[30] Yet, until 1830 shoes were produced in the United States by tools and methods not essentially different from those used by medieval serfs,[31] and not much equipment would have been needed to continue those methods on the plantations. Even simple methods of production were not employed on the plantations because the low level of productivity made them too costly relative to available Northern shoes. At the same time, the latter were more expensive than they ought to have been, for transportation costs were high, and planters had little choice but to buy in the established New England shoe centers.

Plantation account books reveal surprisingly high expenditures for a variety of tasks requiring skilled and unskilled labor.[32] A Mississippi planter with 130 slaves paid an artisan $320 for labor and supplies for a forty-one-day job in 1849. Other accounts show that Governor Hammond spent $452 to have a road built in 1850; another planter spent

[27] For the sampling and computing methods employed here see Eugene D. Genovese, "The Limits of Agrarian Reform in the Slave South" (Ph.D. diss., Columbia University, 1959), appendices.
[28] De Bow, *Industrial Resources*, II, 130.
[29] Cameron Papers, CXIII, University of North Carolina.
[30] Simmons Jones Baker Account Book, misc. notes, University of North Carolina.
[31] Blanche Evans Hazard, *The Organization of the Boot and Shoe Industry in Massachusetts Before 1875* (Cambridge, 1921), p. 3.
[32] The use of white labor for ditching is frequently cited, but the size of expenditures is not generally appreciated. One planter paid $170 in 1852, another $250 in 1859. Such sums were not trifles, especially for small planters. See Moses St. John R. Liddell Papers, 1852, Louisiana State University; entry of Feb. 8, 1859, Leonidas Pendleton Spyker Diary, *ibid.*

$108 for repair of a carriage and $900 for repair of a sloop in 1853, as well as $175 for repair of a bridge in 1857; a third spent $2,950 for the hire of artisans in 1856 on a plantation with more than 175 slaves.[33]

The largest expenses were for blacksmiths' services. A Panola, Mississippi planter listed expenditures for the following in 1853: sharpening of plows, mending of shovels, and construction of plows, ox-chains, hooks, and other items. In 1847 a Greensboro, Alabama, planter, whose books indicate that he was businesslike and efficient, spent about $140 for blacksmiths' services on his large plantation of seventy-five slaves.[34] One South Carolina planter with forty-five slaves had an annual blacksmith's account of about $35, and expenditures by other planters were often higher.[35]

Even simple tasks like the erection of door frames sometimes required the services of hired carpenters, as was the case with a Jefferson County, Mississippi, planter in 1851.[36] If buildings, chimneys, or slave cabins had to be built, planters generally hired free laborers or slave artisans.[37] Skilled slaves had unusual privileges and incentives, but there was not much for them to do on a single plantation. Rather than allow a Negro to spend all his time acquiring a skill for which there was only a limited need, a planter would hire a bondman for short periods. Even this type of slave specialization was frowned upon by many planters, who considered the incentives and privileges subversive of general plantation discipline.

It may have paid to keep all available slaves in the cotton fields during periods of high prices, but during low prices the reverse was probably true. At those times the factors forcing a one-crop agriculture and the low productivity of nonfield labor wrought devastating results. The South's trouble was not that it had few shoe and clothing factories, or that it lacked a diversified agriculture, or that it lacked enough

[33] Haller Nutt Papers, 1849, Duke University; James H. Hammond Account Book, 1850, Library of Congress; Stephen D. Doar Account Books, 1853, 1857, ibid.; Charles Bruce Plantation Accounts, 1856, ibid.

[34] Everard Green Baker Papers, I, University of North Carolina; Iverson L. Graves Papers, XV, ibid.; Henry Watson Papers, 1847, Duke University. Graves spent twenty dollars to sharpen and repair tools during four months of 1853.

[35] De Bow, Industrial Resources, I, 161. One planter with fifty slaves spent about $75 in eight months. Killona Plantation Journals, I, 60 ff., Dept. of Archives and History, Jackson, Miss. See also William McKinley Book, p. 17, University of North Carolina; Robert Withers Books, I, 46, ibid.; James Sheppard Papers, Apr. 9, 1849, ibid.

[36] Entry of Jan. 4, 1851, Duncan G. McCall Plantation Journal and Diary, Duke University. The plantation possessed seventy-five slaves.

[37] Entry of Jan. 6, 1851, ibid.; entry of Jan. 15, 1857, Spyker Diary. Spyker, with more than one hundred slaves, spent over $200 for the services of a mason. A letter to Mrs. Howell Cobb (1846) indicates that Negro cabins were generally built by hired labor at up to $250 per cabin. Ulrich B. Phillips, Plantation and Frontier Documents: 1649-1863 (Cleveland, 1909), II, 38.

other industrial enterprises. The trouble was that it suffered from a lack of all three at the same time. The slight division of labor on the plantations and the slight social division of labor in the region forced the planters into dependence on the Northern market. The result was to raise the cost of cotton production during periods of low as well as high cotton prices. Even during the extraordinary years of the Civil War, when Southerners struggled manfully to feed and clothe themselves, the attempt to produce home manufactures met with only indifferent results.[38] These observations merely restate the problem of division of labor in the slave South: the low level of productivity, caused by the inefficiency of the slaves and the general backwardness of society, forced increasing specialization in staple crop production under virtual colonial conditions.

The broad problem of improved farm equipment deserves further amplification. "There is nothing in the progress of agriculture," the United States Agricultural Society reported in 1853, "more encouraging than the rapid increase and extension of labor-saving machinery."[39] As already suggested, the South did not profit much from these technological advances, nor did it contribute much.[40]

The most obvious obstacle to the employment of better equipment was the slave himself.[41] In 1843 a Southern editor sharply rebuked planters and overseers for complaining that Negroes could not handle tools. Such a complaint was, he said, merely a confession of poor management, for with proper supervision slaves would provide proper care.[42] The editor was unfair. Careful supervision of unwilling laborers would have entailed either more overseers than most planters could afford or a slave force too small to provide the advantages of large-scale operation. The harsh treatment that slaves gave equipment shocked travelers and contemporaries, and neglect of tools was among the most common reasons given for inflicting punishment on Negroes.[43]

[38] Mary Elizabeth Massey, *Ersatz in the Confederacy* (Columbia, S.C., 1952), chap. i and *passim*.

[39] *Journal of the United States Agricultural Society*, I (1853), 132.

[40] Cathey, commenting on the agitation for improved implements in North Carolina in the 1850's, says that, surprisingly, none of those demanded were produced on a large scale within the state and no local inventor profited much from his efforts. *Agricultural Developments*, p. 68. In view of the small market, however, the result is no surprise—unless undue attention is paid to the statements of agricultural reformers or to the illusory valuations that sometimes appeared in census returns.

[41] The familiar generalization that slaves so mistreated equipment that planters were reluctant to purchase good implements has received new support from Moore's study, *Agriculture in Ante-Bellum Mississippi*, p. 41.

[42] *Southern Planter* (Richmond), III (1843), 205-206.

[43] See "Instructions to Overseer," James H. Hammond Plantation Book, 1832-39, Library of Congress.

In 1855 a South Carolina planter wrote in exasperation that

The wear and tear of plantation tools is harassing to every planter who does not have a good mechanic at his nod and beck every day in the year. Our plows are broken, our hoes are lost, our harnesses need repairing, and large demands are made on the blacksmith, the carpenter, the tanner, and the harnassmaker [sic].[44]

The implements used on the plantations, therefore, were generally much too heavy for efficient use. The "nigger hoe," often used in relatively advanced Virginia, was far heavier than the "Yankee hoe," which slaves easily broke. Those used in the Southwest were almost three times the weight of those manufactured in the North for Northern use.[45] Curiously, in many cases equipment was too light for adequate results. Whereas most planters bought extra heavy implements in the hope that they would withstand rough handling, others resigned themselves to breakage and bought the cheapest possible.[46]

We do not know the proportion of Southern implements made by local blacksmiths, but the difference in quality between them and Northern goods was probably not so great as one might think. Local blacksmiths made wretched goods, but those made in the North especially for the Southern market were well below national standards. J. D. Legare, editor of the *Southern Cabinet*, visited Northern implement factories and was "struck" by the inferior grade of goods sent south. The materials and workmanship were much worse than those put into goods for the Northern market. The reason for the double standard, as Legare admitted, was that planters demanded inexpensive items.[47] Information on implements produced in the North for the Southern market is scarce. John Hebron Moore quite plausibly suggests that a few unscrupulous Northern manufacturers gave the rest a bad reputation by misrepresentations and other unethical practices.[48] Misrepresentations aside, frequent complains suggest that the implements were often inferior to those designated for the North. M. W. Philips demonstrated that Northern plows lasted three times as long as local Mississippi products,[49] but the question at issue is not the quality of Northern equipment but the quality that Southerners could and would buy.

[44] *Farmer and Planter*, VI (1855), 43.

[45] C. G. Parsons, *Inside View of Slavery* (Boston, 1855), p. 94; Harold F. Williamson (ed.), *The Growth of the American Economy* (2nd ed.; New York, 1951), p. 120.

[46] On the coastal plain of the Southeast during the twentieth century the persisting lack of capital has caused continued reliance on harrows and plows that are too light for most purposes.

[47] *Southern Cabinet*, I (1840), 531-536.

[48] Moore, *Agriculture in Ante-Bellum Mississippi*, p. 168.

[49] *Ibid.*, p. 166.

In 1857 an agricultural journal carried a special report by a former editor who had visited the South Carolina state fair and had inspected plows made by Southern manufacturers. He described the instruments as poor, of indifferent quality and crude construction, adding that most Southern producers had advanced only to the point at which James Small of Berwickshire had left the plow in 1740.[50]

Good plows in 1857 sold for fifteen or twenty dollars, although perhaps some of those selling at five or ten dollars were adequate. An eighty-acre Iowa farm in one estimation, had at least $375 worth of implements in addition to good plows and small tools.[51] Cultivators and harrows cost from five to twenty dollars; a grist mill from fifteen to thirty dollars; a treadmill horsepower from eighty-five to 150 dollars; a seed drill sixty dollars; a reaper-mower 135 dollars; and so forth. Planters, M. W. Philips noted, usually refused to buy anything except the cheapest of essential items. "We of the South have a jaundiced eye," he wrote. "Everything we view looks like gold—costly."[52]

Plows such as those generally in use in Arkansas were valued at five dollars, and perhaps of greater significance, an average cotton-producing unit of one hundred acres was said to have only fifteen dollars' worth of equipment other than plows.[53] A Mississippi planter valued his thirty "indifferent" plows at seventy-five dollars; even if he had made a liberal allowance for depreciation, he was clearly using the poorest kind of equipment.[54] As an indication of the quality of the work done by local blacksmiths, one planter spent a total of five dollars for ten turning plows in 1853.[55] Gray claims that most Southern plows were worth only three to five dollars. There is little reason to question either this estimate or his opinion that they probably did not last more than a year or so.[56]

Most planters in Mississippi, wrote Philips, thought they could use one kind of plow for every possible purpose.[57] The weakness was doubly serious, for the one kind was usually poor. The most popular plow in the Lower South—at least well into the 1840's—was the shovel plow, which merely stirred the surface of the soil to a depth of two or three inches.[58] Made of wrought iron, it was "a crude and inefficient instru-

---

[50] *Farmer and Planter*, VIII (1857), 245.
[51] Williamson, *Growth of the American Economy*, p. 132 and n. 22.
[52] *Farmer and Planter*, II (1851), 19.
[53] *De Bow's Review*, XII (1852), 72.
[54] Valuation figures for 1847, Sheppard Papers.
[55] Expenditures for Feb.-May, 1855, Graves Papers, XV.
[56] Lewis C. Gray, *History of Agriculture in the Southern United States to 1860* (Washington, 1933), II, 796.
[57] *American Cotton Planter*, II (1854), 244.
[58] *Southern Cabinet*, I (1840), 199; Williamson, *Growth of the American Economy*, p. 118.

ment which, as commonly employed, underwent no essential improvement throughout its long career."[59] It was light enough for a girl to carry and exemplified the "too light" type of implement used on the plantations.

In the 1850's the shovel plow slowly gave way in the South to a variety of light mouldboard plows, which at least were of some help in killing and controlling weeds. Good mouldboard plows should have offered other advantages, such as aid in burying manure, but those in the South were not nearly so efficient as those employed in the free states.[60] In 1830, Connecticut manufacturers began to produce large numbers of Cary plows exclusively for the Southern market. These light wooden plows with wrought-iron shares were considered of good quality. Unfortunately, they required careful handling, for they broke easily, and they could not penetrate more than three or four inches below the surface. During the early 1820's Northern farmers had been shifting to cast-iron plows that could cover 50 per cent more acreage with 50 per cent less animal- and man-power.[61] When cast-iron plows did enter the South, they could not be used to the same advantage as in the North, for they needed the services of expert blacksmiths when, as frequently happened, they broke.[62]

Twenty years after the introduction of the cultivator in 1820 Northern farmers considered it standard equipment, especially in the cornfields, but cultivators, despite their tremendous value, were so light that few planters would trust them to their slaves. Since little wheat was grown below Virginia the absence of reapers was not especially important, but the backwardness of cotton equipment was. A "cotton planter" (a modified grain drill) and one man could do as much work as two mules and four men,[63] but it was rarely used. Similarly, corn planters, espe-

[59] Rogin, *Introduction of Farm Machinery*, p. 54.

[60] On the advantages of the mouldboard plow for weeding and burying manure see E. John Russell, *Soil Conditions and Plant Growth* (8th ed.; London, 1950), pp. 578 ff. These plows were in general use in New England as early as 1840. M. H. Chevalier, "Les charrues anciennes de l'Amérique et de l'Oceanie," Socjété des Ingenieurs Civils de France, *Memoires et compte rendu des travaux*, LXXIII (1920), 71. In recent years some agronomists have challenged the usefulness of deep plowing, arguing that it does more harm than good. The literature is vast, but the issue unresolved. A firm conclusion about the methods used by antebellum planters must therefore wait. It is significant, however, that the planters' failure to plow deeply was not due to any special knowledge or experience, but rather to their lack of proper equipment.

[61] Rogin, *Introduction of Farm Machinery*, pp. 8-9, 30-31. The Cary plow was also called the Dagon, the Degen, the Connecticut, and various other names.

[62] Craven maintains that in Maryland and Virginia farmers and planters used excellent equipment after 1840. See his *Soil Exhaustion as a Factor in the Agricultural History of Virginia and Maryland, 1606-1860* (Urbana, 1926), p. 152. This equipment was excellent however, only in comparison to that used further south.

[63] Williamson, *Growth of the American Economy*, p. 126; *American Cotton*

cially the one invented by George Brown in 1853, might have saved a good deal of labor time, but these were costly, needed careful handling, and would have rendered part of the slave force superfluous. Since slaveholding was a matter of prestige and status, and since slaves were an economic necessity during the picking season, planters were not interested.[64]

The cotton picker presents special, complicated, technical, and economic problems. So long as a mechanical picker was not available a large labor force would have been needed for the harvest, but in 1850 Samuel S. Rembert and Jedediah Prescott of Memphis did patent a mule-drawn cotton picker that was "a simple prototype of the modern spindle picker."[65] Virtually no progress was made on the original design until forty years later, and then almost as long a span intervened before further advances were made. The reasons for these gaps were in part technical and in part the economic pressures arising from slavery and share-cropping. Although one can never be sure about such things, the evidence accumulated by historians of science and technology strongly suggests that the social and economic impediments to technological change are generally more powerful than the specifically technical ones. The introduction of a cotton picker would have entailed the full mechanization of farming processes, and such a development would have had to be accompanied by a radically different social order. Surely, it is not accidental that the mechanical picker has in recent decades taken hold in the Southwest, where share-cropping has been weak, and has moved east slowly as changes in the social organization of the countryside have proceeded. Even without a mechanical picker the plantations might have used good implements and a smaller labor force during most of the year and temporary help during the harvest. In California in 1951, for example, 50 per cent of the occasional workers needed in the cotton fields was obtained from within the county and 90 per cent from within the state. Temporary employees were obtained from among rural and town housewives, youths, and seasonal workers anxious to supplement their incomes.[66] There is no reason to believe that this

---

Planter, XII (1858), 115. Grain drills sold for about $100 in the South, according to the *Farmer and Planter*, II (1851), 161. See also *De Bow's Review*, VI (1848), 133.

[64] George F. Lemmer says that tobacco and hemp growers in Missouri failed to keep pace with grain growers in the use of improved implements and machinery because tobacco and hemp machinery did not improve much. See his "Farm Machinery in Ante-Bellum Missouri," *Missouri Historical Review*, XL (1946), 469, 479. We need to know why labor-saving machinery for those crops was not developed. The answer—or at least part of it—may be traced to the use of slave labor in the tobacco and hemp regions; free labor predominated in the grain regions.

[65] Street, *New Revolution*, p. 92.   [66] *Ibid.*, p. 197.

alternative would not have been open to the South in the 1850's if slavery had been eliminated.

A few examples, which could be multiplied many times, illustrate the weakness of plantation technology. A plantation in Stewart County, Georgia, with a fixed capital investment of $42,660 had only $300 invested in implements and machinery. The Tooke plantation, also in Georgia, had a total investment in implements and machinery of $195, of which a gin accounted for $110. Plantations had plows, perhaps a few harrows and coulters, possibly a cultivator, and in a few cases a straw-cutter or corn and cob crusher. Whenever possible, a farmer or planter acquired a gin, and all had small tools for various purposes.[67]

The figures reported in the census tabulations of farm implements and machinery are of limited value and must be used carefully. We have little information on shifting price levels, and the valuations reported to the census takers were not standardized. The same type of plow worth five dollars in 1850 may have been recorded at ten dollars in 1860, and in view of the general rise in prices something of the kind probably occurred.[68]

Even if we put aside these objections and examine the investments in selected counties in 1860, the appalling state of plantation technology is evident. The following table presents the data from the manuscript census returns for 1860. Of the 1,969 farmers and planters represented, only 160 (or 8 per cent) had more than $500 invested in implements and machinery. If we assume that a cotton gin cost between $100 and $125, the figures for the cotton counties suggest that all except the planters (those holding twenty slaves or more) either did without a gin or had very little else. Note that an increase in the slave force did not entail significant expansion of technique. In the cotton counties, as the size of the slaveholdings increased, the investments in implements and machines increased also, but in small amounts. Only units of twenty slaves or more showed tolerably respectable amounts, and even these were poor when one considers the size of the estates.[69]

[67] David Hillhouse Memorandum Book, p. 25, Alexander Robert Lawton Papers, University of North Carolina. For the Tooke Plantation see Ralph B. Flanders, "Two Plantations and a County in Ante-Bellum Georgia," *Georgia Historical Quarterly*, XII (1928), 4. See also Cameron Papers, CXIII; Hairston Plantation Book, 1857, University of North Carolina; 1849 inventory in Killock Plantation Books, VII, *ibid.*; Newstead Plantation Diary, 1861, *ibid.*; Andrew Flinn Plantation Book, 1840, University of South Carolina; Plantation and Account Book, 1851, pp. 1, 83, Eli J. Capell and Family Papers, Louisiana State University; Joseph M. Jaynes Plantation Account Books, p. 15, Duke University.

[68] Commodity prices rose from 23 to 35 per cent from 1849 to 1857, and then slumped somewhat following the crisis. In 1859 prices were from 10 to 16 per cent higher than they had been in 1849. See Snyder-Tucker and Warren-Pearson indices in Bureau of the Census (comp.), *Historical Statistics of the United States, 1789-1945* (Washington, 1949), pp. 232-233.

[69] "The averages of southern states were high not only because sugar-refining

MEDIAN VALUE OF FARM IMPLEMENTS AND MACHINERY
IN SELECTED COUNTIES, 1860[a]

Sample Counties	Number of Slaves on Farms and Plantations[b]							
	0	1-4	5-9	10-20	21-30	31-60	61-100	100+
Virginia Tobacco Counties (Amelia, Buckingham)	$40	$ 50	$ 50	$100	$150	$320	$ 925	
Virginia Tidewater (Gloucester, Charles City)	30	35	70	150	200	500	725	
Virginia Northern Wheat Counties (Fauquier, Prince William)	60	100	150	300	425	1200	1350	
Georgia Upland (Walker, Gordon)	10	75	100	215	450	300		
Georgia Cotton (Dougherty, Thomas)	25	75	135	200	350	400	500	
Mississippi Cotton (De Soto, Marshall)	50	100	150	300	500	700	1000	1200

a Calculated from the manuscript census returns for 1860; see note 27.
b The number of persons in each group was as follows:

Virginia Tobacco:	67	45	45	52	23	20	6
Virginia Tidewater:	41	26	31	24	12	9	
Virginia Northern Wheat:	175	59	62	62	19	7	
Georgia Upland:	364	37	27	17	4	3	
Georgia Cotton:	43	19	18	21	13	22	
Mississippi Cotton:	204	83	89	92	47	45	5

Gray has suggested that the poor quality of Southern implements was only partly due to slave inefficiency. Other contributing factors were the lack of local market places for equipment, the ignorance of the small farmers and overseers, prejudice against and even aversion to

and cotton-ginning machinery were expensive but, more important, because the larger plantations were almost congeries of farms. The value of farm machinery per acre of improved land is a better index. For representative southern states, the figures are Virginia $0.82; North Carolina, $0.90; Alabama $1.16; Mississippi $1.74; and Louisiana $6.80. For representative northern states the figures are Massachusetts $1.80; Ohio $1.38; New York $2.03; and Pennsylvania $2.14." Paul W. Gates, *The Farmer's Age, 1815-1860* (New York, 1960), p. 291.
70 Gray, *History of Agriculture*, II, 794.

innovations, and a shortage of capital in the interior.[70] Each of these contributing factors was in itself inevitable in a slave society. The weakness of the market, which has been discussed elsewhere,[71] led to a lack of markets. The social structure of the countryside hardly left room for anything but ignorance and cultural backwardness. The social and economic pressures to invest in slaves and the high propensity to consume rendered adequate capital accumulation impossible. The psychological factor—hostility to innovation—transcended customary agrarian conservatism and was related to the patriarchal social structure.

The attempts of reformers to improve methods of cultivation, diversify production, raise more and better livestock, and so forth, were undermined at the outset by a labor force without versatility and the possibility of increasing its productivity substantially. Other factors would have to be examined in order to understand fully why the movement for agricultural reform had to be content with inadequate accomplishments, but consideration of the direct effects of slave labor alone tells us why little could be done.

[71] See Eugene D. Genovese, "The Significance of the Slave Plantation for Southern Economic Development," *Journal of Southern History*, XXVIII (1962), 422-437.

The Significance of the Slave Plantation
for Southern Economic Development

By EUGENE D. GENOVESE

Historians are no longer sure that plantation slavery was responsible for the economic woes of the Old South. The revisionist doubts rest on two propositions of dubious relevance. The first is that slave labor could have been applied successfully to pursuits other than the raising of plantation staples; the second is that slave agriculture was possibly as profitable as were alternative industries and can not be held responsible for the unwillingness of Southerners to use their profits more wisely.[1] The first confuses slave labor and its direct effects with the slave system and its total effects; it is the latter that is at issue, and the versatility of slave labor is a secondary consideration. The second rests on the assumption that the master-slave relationship was purely economic and not essentially different from an employer-worker relationship. Yet, when confronted with the issue direct, who could deny that slavery gave rise to a distinct politics, ideology, and pattern of social behavior and that these had immense economic consequences?

We need not examine at the moment the precise relationship between slavery and the plantation. Certainly, plantation economies presuppose considerable compulsion, if only of the *de facto* type now prevalent in Latin America. The historical fact of an ante bellum plantation-based slave economy is our immediate concern, although, undoubtedly, post bellum developments preserved some of the retardative effects of ante bellum slavery.

Those retardative effects were too many even to be summarized here. A low level of capital accumulation, the planters' high propensity to consume luxuries, the shortage of liquid capital aggravated by the steady drain of funds out of the region, the low productivity of slave labor, the need to concentrate on a few staples, the anti-industrial, antiurban ideology of the dominant planters,

[1] See, for example, the well known writings of R. R. Russel, including his "The General Effects of Slavery upon Southern Economic Progress," *Journal of Southern History*, IV (February 1938), 34-54, or the more recent statement of Alfred H. Conrad and John R. Meyer, "The Economics of Slavery in the Ante-Bellum South," *Journal of Political Economy*, LXVI (April 1958), 95-130.

the reduction of Southern banking, industry, and commerce to the position of auxiliaries of the plantation economy—all these are familiar and yet need restudy in the light of the important work being done on the economics of underdeveloped countries. For the present let us focus on another factor, which in itself provides an adequate explanation of the slave South's inability to industrialize: the retardation of the home market for both industrial and agricultural commodities.

Thirty years ago Elizabeth W. Gilboy complained that economic historians studying the process of industrialization were too much concerned with supply and insufficiently concerned with demand.[2] Her complaint was justified despite brilliant work on the problem of markets by a few outstanding men from Karl Marx to R. H. Tawney and Paul Mantoux. Since then, demand has received much more attention, although possibly not so much as it deserves. Important essays by Maurice Dobb, Simon Kuznets, H. J. Habakkuk, and Gunnar Myrdal, among others, have helped to correct the imbalance,[3] as has new research on European industrialization and the economics of underdeveloped countries. If there is one lesson to be learned from the experience of both developed and underdeveloped countries it is that industrialization is unthinkable without an agrarian revolution which shatters the old regime of the countryside. While the peasantry is tied to the land, burdened with debt, and limited to minimal purchasing power, the labor recruitment and market pre-conditions for extensive manufacturing are missing. "Land reform"—*i.e.* an agrarian revolution—is the essential first step in the creation of an urban working class, the reorganization of agriculture to feed growing cities, and the development of a home market.

There are several ways in which agricultural reorganization can provide markets for manufactures; for our immediate purposes we may consider two. First, when the laborers are separated from the land, as they were during the English enclosures, they necessarily increase the demand for clothing and other essentials for-

[2] Elizabeth W. Gilboy, "Demand As a Factor in the Industrial Revolution" in *Facts and Factors in Economic History; Articles by the Former Students of Edwin F. Gay* (Cambridge, Mass., 1932), 620-39.

[3] Maurice Dobb, *Studies in the Development of Capitalism* (New York, 1947), 6 ff, 87 ff, 98 ff, 290-96; Simon Kuznets, "Toward a Theory of Economic Growth" in Robert Lekachman (ed.), *National Policy for Economic Welfare at Home and Abroad* (New York, 1955), 12-77; H. J. Habakkuk, "The Historical Experience on the Basic Conditions of Economic Progress" in L. H. Dupriez (ed.), *Economic Progress* (Louvain, Belgium, 1955), 149-69; Gunnar Myrdal, *Rich Lands and Poor* (New York, 1957), *passim*, 23-38 especially.

merly produced at home. Paradoxically, this expansion of the market is compatible with a marked reduction in the laborers' standard of living. Second, the farmers left on the countryside to produce for growing urban markets provide an increased demand for textiles, agricultural equipment, and so forth.

The rapid extension of the rural market was the way of the North, but the slave plantations dominated the South until such time as reorganization was imposed from without by a predatory foe interested primarily in a new system of rural exploitation. An adequate home market could not arise in the ante bellum South and has only evolved slowly and painfully during the last century.

In 1860 about seventy-five per cent of the Southern cotton crop was exported; during no ante bellum year did the grain exports of the United States exceed five per cent of the grain crop. No doubt, cotton profits were an important element in the financing of America's economic growth. The question is, were the profits syphoned off to build up the Northern economy? We know that the credit mechanisms alone, to a considerable extent, did just that. The South's dependence on the export trade, in contradistinction to the North's primary reliance on its home market, indicates not merely a social division of labor but the economic exploitation of the exporting South.

Robert G. Albion, in his excellent examination of the colonial bondage of the South to the North, concludes that the South's lack of direct trade with Europe constituted an irrational arrangement secured by the impudence of New York's aggressive entrepreneurs. We can agree that, had the South imported from abroad as much as the North and West, there could have been no sensible reason to route through New York either the South's cotton or its share of European goods; but Albion's assumption of a rough equality of imports, an assumption shared by contemporaries like George McDuffie and T. P. Kettell, can not be substantiated. The slave South's total market for manufactured goods was small relative to that of the free states; and even though the South depended upon Europe as well as the North for manufactured goods, its imports from Europe were smaller in value than imports into the North and West and smaller in bulk than the staples it exported. If the ships carrying cotton had sailed from Southern ports direct to Europe and back, they would have had to return in ballast,[4] New York's domination of the South's export trade was, therefore, not accidental. Furthermore, if the

[4] See Robert Greenhalgh Albion, *The Rise of New York Port, 1815-1860* (New

South's share in American imports had been as Albion suggests, and if the coastal trade had been as large as he implies, the greater part of the goods sent from New Orleans to the plantation areas would have originated in Europe and been reshipped through New York rather than being—as is known—of Western origin.[5]

Albion's acceptance of the assumption of nearly equal imports is the more surprising in view of the evidence of restricted Southern demand. The Southern cotton, iron, paper, wool, and railroad industries—to mention a few—struggled with indifferent results against a low level of Southern patronage. Antislavery leaders like Henry Ruffner and Cassius M. Clay made slavery's effects on the home market a cardinal point in their indictment. Thoughtful proslavery Southerners also commented frequently on the market problem. The opinion of the editor of the *Southern Agriculturalist* in 1828 that the South lacked sufficient customers to sustain a high level of manufacturing was echoed throughout the ante bellum period. The speech of Col. Andrew P. Calhoun to the Pendleton, South Carolina, Farmers' Society in 1855, for example, was strikingly similar in tone and content. On the other side, someone like Beverley Tucker would occasionally argue that Northerners would never risk a war "which, while it lasted, would shut them out from the best market in the world."[6] It is difficult

York, 1939) and Albion, *Square-Riggers on Schedule; the New York Sailing Packets to England, France, and the Cotton Ports* (Princeton, 1938). For similar arguments presented by contemporaries, see James E. B. De Bow (ed.), *The Industrial Resources, etc., of the Southern and Western States* . . . (3 vols., New Orleans, 1852-1853), 125, 365; and *De Bow's Review*, IV (1847), 208-25, 339, 351. For a perceptive Northern reply, see the anonymous pamphlet, *The Effects of Secession upon the Commercial Relations Between the North and South and upon Each Section* (New York, 1861), 15. For the weakness of the Southern import trade, see George Rogers Taylor, *The Transportation Revolution, 1815-1860* (New York, 1951), 198; Philip S. Foner, *Business & Slavery; the New York Merchants & the Irrepressible Conflict* (Chapel Hill, 1941), 6-7; and Samuel Eliot Morison, *The Maritime History of Massachusetts, 1783-1860* (Boston, 1921), 298-99. Many of the lines carrying cotton from Northern ports were deeply involved in bringing immigrants to the United States, which was one of the reasons why their ships did not have to return from Europe in ballast. John G. B. Hutchins, *The American Maritime Industries and Public Policy, 1789-1914; an Economic History* (Cambridge, Mass., 1941), 262-63.

5 Emory R. Johnson and others, *History of the Domestic and Foreign Commerce of the United States* (2 vols., Washington, 1915), I, 242; R. B. Way, "The Commerce of the Lower Mississippi in the Period 1830-1860," Mississippi Valley Historical Association, *Proceedings*, X (1918-1919), 62; Louis Bernard Schmidt, "The Internal Grain Trade of the United States, 1850-1860," *Iowa Journal of History and Politics*, XVIII (January 1920), 110-11.

6 *Southern Agriculturalist* (Charleston), I (September 1828), 404; *Farmer and Planter*, VI (December 1855), 270-71; *Southern Quarterly Review*, XVIII (September 1850), 218.

to imagine that many, even those who adopted such arguments for political purposes, took seriously a proposition so palpably false.

Alfred Glaze Smith, Jr., and Douglass C. North have traced the low level of Southern demand, in part, to plantation self-sufficiency. This view is not borne out by the data in the manuscript census returns from the cotton belt, which reveal only trivial amounts of home manufactures on even the largest plantations and which bear out the judgments of Rolla M. Tryon and Mary Elizabeth Massey on the weakness of Southern household industry.[7] In De Soto and Marshall counties, Mississippi, the big planters (those with thirty-one or more slaves) averaged only seventy-six dollars worth of home manufactures in 1860, and farmers and small planters averaged much less. In Dougherty and Thomas counties, Georgia, the small planters (those with from twenty-one to thirty slaves) led other groups of slaveholders with one hundred and twenty-seven dollars, and the big planters produced only about half as much. Most of the planters in both clusters of counties recorded no home manufactures at all.[8] Sample

[7] Alfred G. Smith, *Economic Readjustment of an Old Cotton State: South Carolina, 1820-1860* (Columbia, S. C., 1958), 134; Douglass C. North, *The Economic Growth of the United States, 1790-1860* (Englewood Cliffs, N. J., 1961), 132-33; Rolla M. Tryon, *Household Manufacturers in the United States, 1640-1860; a Study in Industrial History* (Chicago, 1917); Mary Elizabeth Massey, *Ersatz in the Confederacy* (Columbia, 1952), 80, 98.

[8] From the five Mississippi and the five Georgia cotton belt countries regarded as typical by Lewis C. Gray in his *History of Agriculture in the Southern United States to 1860* (2 vols., Washington, 1933), I, 334-35, II, 918-21, I have analyzed for each state the two that come closest to the mode in the only variable for which there is clear evidence, the size of slaveholdings. A review of the economic and natural conditions of the South reveals nothing to suggest that the four counties so chosen are not roughly typical of the cotton belt. I have used the four counties primarily for an investigation of purchasing power—to gain clues to the general structure of the market—and the insignificant expenditures recorded indicate that even with due allowance for the possibility of a wide, say 50%, deviation in other counties and for incorrect reporting in the census returns, the results could not conceivably be substantially different.

As a random sample, I selected the first ten names on each page of U. S. Census, 1860, Georgia, Schedule 4, Productions of Agriculture, Dougherty and Thomas counties (Library, Duke University, Durham, North Carolina) and U. S. Census, 1860, Mississippi, Schedule 4, De Soto and Marshall counties (Mississippi State Archives, Jackson). From the U. S. Census, 1860, Georgia, Schedule 2, Slave Inhabitants, Dougherty and Thomas counties, and U. S. Census, 1860, Mississippi, Schedule 2, De Soto and Marshall counties (National Archives, Washington), I determined the number of slaves held by each agriculturist in my sample. Where Schedule 4 gave the amount of produce but not its monetary value, I used a specially prepared price schedule in order to translate the amounts into dollar values. See Eugene D. Genovese, *The Limits of Agrarian Reform in the Slave South* (unpublished Ph.D. thesis, Columbia University, 1959), appendixes.

studies from Virginia's tobacco area, wheat area, and tidewater reveal the same situation. Plantation manuscripts show surprisingly frequent, and often quite large, expenditures for artisans' services and suggest that plantations were much less self-sufficient and exhibited much less division of labor than is generally appreciated.[9] The root of the insufficient demand must be sought in the poverty of the rural majority composed of slaves, subsistence farmers, and poor whites.

In nineteenth-century America as a whole both capital and labor were in short supply. Industrial development was spurred by farmers who provided a large market for goods and tools, and manufacturing arose on the foundation of this immense rural demand. Eastern manufacturers gradually awoke to their dependence on this rural market and by 1854 were supporting homestead legislation not only to gain support for higher tariffs and for purposes of speculation but to expand the market for their goods. Farmers in New England saw their futures linked with industrial development, and their hostility toward commercial middlemen was not usually transferred to the manufacturers.[10] The same was true in the West. As the shrewd Achille Murat noted in the 1830's, the manufacturing interest of the West "is not constituted by the manufactories which exist, but those which they look forward to in prospective." [11] An agrarianism uncompromisingly hostile to industry and urbanization—to what was called "manufacturing as a system"—existed only in the South and can not be separated from the ideological leadership of the

[9] These expenditures were for blacksmiths' services, road building, cabin building, and even for such trivial tasks as the erection of door frames. The accounts often run into hundreds of dollars. See, for example, Moses St. John R. Liddell and Family Papers (Library, Louisiana State University, Baton Rouge), Haller Nutt Papers (Library, Duke University, Durham, N. C.), Everard Green Baker Papers (Southern Historical Collection, University of North Carolina, Chapel Hill), I, 139; Killona Plantation Journals (Mississippi State Department of Archives and History, Jackson), I, 60 ff.

[10] Roy M. Robbins, *Our Landed Heritage; the Public Domain, 1776-1936* (New York, 1950), 177; Joseph Brennan, *Social Conditions in Industrial Rhode Island, 1820-1860* (Washington, 1940), 18; Samuel Rezneck, "The Rise and Early Development of Industrial Consciousness in the United States, 1760-1830," *Journal of Economic and Business History*, IV (1932), 784-811; Isaac Lippincott, *A History of Manufactures in the Ohio Valley to the Year 1860* . . . (New York, 1914), 63-65; Grace Pierpont Fuller, *An Introduction to the History of Connecticut As a Manufacturing State* (Northampton, Mass., 1915), 45; James Neal Primm, *Economic Policy in a Development of a Western State, Missouri* (Cambridge, Mass., 1954), 56-59; Frank W. Taussig, *The Tariff History of the United States* (7th ed., New York, 1923), 68-108; and Bray Hammond, *Banks and Politics in America, from the Revolution to the Civil War* (Princeton, 1957).

[11] Achille Murat, *America and the Americans* (New York, 1849), 19.

slaveholding planters. Even there, those seriously interested in economic progress saw the link between agricultural reform and industrialization and tried to work out proposals for increased manufactures that would be palatable to their fellow slave-holders.[12]

The West was able to import capital because Eastern manufacturers and European creditors were confident of her growth and prosperity. Outside credits at that time had to be accumulated by the importation of commodities and the maintenance of an unfavorable trade balance. The immense internal market guaranteed the West an import surplus until 1850. Its insatiable demand for manufactured articles contributed to the unfavorable trade balance of the United States, but on the whole this was not a serious problem for the country because American importers were strong enough to obtain long-term credits on relatively easy terms; and, during the 1850's, profits from shipping and other invisible gains largely restored the balance.[13] Thus, on the one hand, the national economy was sufficiently strong to overcome the worst effects of a trade deficit, and, on the other hand, the agrarian West was able to obtain the credits required for industrial development. The South did not benefit from this arrangement. It provided an exportable surplus, which, although of great help to the national economy in offsetting the large quantity of imports, was exploited by Northern capital. The invisible gains that were so important to national growth were made partly at the expense of the South.

The population statistics for 1860 offer a clue to the structure of the market. If we exclude Maryland, in which slavery was declining, and Delaware, which was a slave state in name only, the median population per square mile in the slave states was 18, and Kentucky was high with 31. In comparison, Massachusetts had a population of 158 per square mile; Rhode Island, 138; Connecticut, 98; New York, 84; New Jersey, 81; and so forth. In the West, Ohio had 59; Indiana, 40; and Illinois, 31.

These figures do not tell the important part of the story. A country that is sparsely settled, in absolute terms, may have a

[12] For examples, see the remarks of M. W. Philips and John J. Williams, *Mississippi Planter and Mechanic*, II (May 1858), 157-58; of Thomas J. Lemay, *Arator*, I (November 1855), 237; and of Andrew Johnson, *Congressional Globe*, XXIII, 312.

[13] See Simon S. Kuznets, *Economic Change; Selected Essays in Business Cycles, National Income, and Economic Growth* (New York, 1953), 307 ff; and Charles F. Dunbar, *Economic Essays* (New York, 1904), 268.

high population density, in economic terms, if its system of transportation and commodity production are well developed and integrated. For example, the Northern states in 1860 had a much higher population density—from an economic point of view—than the thickly populated countries of Asia. When we consider the superiority of Northern transportation and economic integration, relative to those of the South, we must conclude that the difference in the magnitude of the market greatly exceeded that suggested by the population figures.

Historians have long appreciated—at least since the pioneer researches of U. B. Phillips—that the Southern transportation system tied the staple-producing areas to the ports and that this was the best possible arrangement for the planters. The planters controlled the state legislatures in an era in which state participation was decisive in railroad construction and generally refused to assume the tax burden necessary to open the back country and thereby encourage and strengthen politically suspect farmers. Without a fully developed railroad network tying the South into an economic unit, the absorption of nonstaple producers into the market economy, except in a peripheral way, was impossible. Poor transportation was, for example, one important factor in the retardation of the Southern cotton textile industry.[14]

With good reason alert Southerners spoke of the connection among railroads, markets, diversified agriculture, and manufacturing. James Robb pointedly described improved transportation and greater industry as necessary ingredients in the process of unifying the South. Oscar M. Lieber noted that without an adequate transportation system South Carolina farmers were prevented from entering the market as corn producers. John Bell warmly supported federal land grants to railroads to strengthen the bonds of commodity production.[15] Within the South these men could, at best, expect to be received with an impatient silence. Where their message was sometimes listened to attentively was in the upper South, as for example in what came to be

[14] See Milton S. Heath, *Constructive Liberalism; the Role of the State in Economic Development in Georgia to 1860* (Cambridge, Mass., 1954), 290-91, and Seth Hammond, "Location Theory and the Cotton Industry," *Journal of Economic History*, II (1942), Supp., 101-17. The opposition of entrenched landowning classes to the extension of transportation has been general in colonial, underdeveloped countries. See George Wythe, *Industry in Latin America* (New York, 1945), 4.

[15] De Bow (ed.), *Industrial Resources*, II, 154; Oscar M. Lieber, *Report on the Survey of South Carolina . . . 1857* (Columbia, 1858), 106; *Congressional Globe*, XXI, pt. 1, 867-68.

West Virginia; the subsequent construction of road and railroad links to existing markets generally bound parts of the upper South to the free states and helped remove them from the slave-holders' domain.

In the slave South the home market consisted primarily of the plantations, which bought foodstuffs from the West and manufactured goods from the East. The planters needed increased Southern manufacturing but only for certain purposes. They needed cheap slave clothing, cotton gins and a few crude agricultural implements, rope for cotton bagging, and so forth. This narrow market could not compare with the tremendous Western demand for industrial commodities of all kinds, especially for agricultural implements and machinery on the more capital-intensive Western farms. The Northeast had the capital and skilled labor for fairly large-scale production and had established its control over existing markets in the North and West. Southern manufacturers could not hope to compete with Northern outside the South, and the same conditions that brought about Northern control of the Northern market made possible Northern penetration of the Southern market despite the costs of transportation.

The South was caught in a contradiction similar to that facing many underdeveloped countries today. On the one hand, it provided a market for outside industry. On the other hand, that very market was too small to sustain industry on a scale large enough to compete with outsiders who could draw upon wider markets. Only one fifth of the manufacturing establishments of the United States were in the South, and their average capitalization was well below that of the manufacturing establishments of the free states. Consider the situation in two industries of special importance to the South—cotton textiles and agricultural implements. New England had almost three times as many cotton factories as the entire South in 1860, and yet the average capitalization was almost twice as great. The concentration in this industry had proceeded so far by 1850 that of the more than 1,000 cotton factories in the United States only forty-one had one half the total capital investment. As for the agricultural implement and machinery industry, New York, Pennsylvania, Ohio, and Illinois each had a greater total capital investment than did the entire South, and in three of these the average capitalization was between two and two and a half times as great as the average in the South.[16] This Northern advantage led Edmund Ruffin and T. L.

[16] U. S. Census Office, *Manufactures of the United States in 1860* . . . (Wash-

Clingman, among others, to look forward to a Southern confederacy protected by high tariffs against Northern goods.[17]

In view of the nature of the plantation market it is not surprising that data on the cotton textile industry almost invariably reveal that Southern producers concentrated upon the production of the cheapest and coarsest kind of cloth to be used in the making of slave clothing.[18] Even so, local industrialists had to compete for this market with Northerners who sometimes shipped direct and sometimes established Southern branches and who had facilities for the collection and processing of second-hand clothing.[19] Just as New England supplied much of the South's "Negro cloth," so it supplied much of the boots and shoes. Firms like Batchellor Brothers of Brookfield produced cheap shoes especially for the Southern market and as early as 1837 opened a branch at Mobile to consolidate its Southern market.[20]

Producers of better cotton goods had little hope of making a living in the South. Occasionally, a William Gregg could penetrate Northern markets successfully, but Southern demand for such goods was too small to have much effect on the industry generally. Northern firms like the Pepperell Manufacturing Company or A. A. Lawrence Company did little business in the South. On the other hand a rising demand for textiles in the agrarian

---

ington, 1865), xxi, ccxvii, lxxiii, 729-30; Evelyn H. Knowlton, *Pepperell's Progress; History of a Cotton Textile Company, 1844-1945* (Cambridge, Mass., 1948), 32. The average capitalization of manufacturing establishments was in 1850 more than 25% higher in the free states and territories than in the slave states, and the gap widened in the 1850's when the increase in average capital investment was 68% in the free states and territories and only 51% in the slave states. The lower South (North Carolina, South Carolina, Georgia, Florida, Alabama, Mississippi, Louisiana, and Texas) fell even further behind. The average capitalization here, 38% less than in the free states in 1850, was 47% less by 1860. Furthermore, the rate of increase in the number of establishments during this decade was appreciably greater in the North than in the South.

[17] Edmund Ruffin, Incidents of My Life, 19-20, in Edmund Ruffin Papers (Southern Historical Collection, University of North Carolina); T. L. Clingman's speech to the House of Representatives, January 22, 1850, in *Selections from the Speeches and Writings of Hon. Thomas L. Clingman of North Carolina* ... (Raleigh, N. C., 1877), 233-54, especially 250.

[18] See Patent Office, *Annual Report, 1857, Agriculture, Senate Exec. Docs.*, 35 Cong., 1 Sess., No. 30, pt. 4 (Serial 928), 308-309, 318; and Richard H. Shryock, "The Early Industrial Revolution in the Empire State," *Georgia Historical Quarterly*, XI (June 1927), 128.

[19] Jesse Eliphalet Pope, *The Clothing Industry in New York* (Columbia, Mo., 1905), 6-7.

[20] Blanche Evans Hazard, *The Organization of the Boot and Shoe Industry in Massachusetts Before 1875* (Cambridge, Mass., 1921), 57-58.

West had greatly influenced the New England cotton industry since 1814.[21]

The Southern iron industry, hampered as it was by the restricted railroad development in the slave states, also had a poor time of it. American iron producers generally were handicapped because much of the country's railroad iron was being imported. The small scale of operations and resultant cost schedule, which hurt the industry nationally, hit the Southern manufacturers especially hard. Dependent upon a weak local market, Southern iron manufacturers had great difficulty holding their own even during the prosperous 1850's.

No wonder the Augusta, Georgia, Commercial Convention added to its demand that Southerners buy Southern goods the qualification, unless you can get Northern cheaper. And no wonder the proposal was ridiculed as amounting to "Never kiss the maid if you can kiss the mistress, unless you like the maid better." [22]

We can not measure precisely the extent of the Southern market nor even make a reliable, general, quantitative comparison between the Southern and Western rural markets, but we can glean from various sources some notion of the immense difference. For example, Phelps, Dodge & Co., a prominent cotton shipping firm that also distributed metals, tools, machinery, clothing, and an assortment of other items, reported at the beginning of the Civil War that only five per cent of its sales were to the South and that those were primarily to the noncotton states. We do not know the extent of the firm's participation in the cotton export trade, but it was considerable. Phelps, Dodge & Co. was in an excellent position to exchange industrial goods for cotton, but the Southern demand for imported goods could not compare in bulk or value with the supply of cotton. In the West, on the other hand, farmers and townsmen provided a growing and lucrative market, and the firm had more customers in Ohio than in any state except New York.[23]

An examination of the 1860 manuscript census returns and other primary sources pertaining to two representative cotton counties in Mississippi and to two in Georgia permits us to

[21] Knowlton, *Pepperell's Progress*, 83-84; Caroline F. Ware, *The Early New England Cotton Manufacture; a Study in Industrial Beginnings* (Boston, 1931), 48, 55.

[22] Herbert Wender, *Southern Commercial Conventions, 1837-1859* (Baltimore, 1930), 25.

[23] Richard Lowitt, *A Merchant Prince of the Nineteenth Century, William E. Dodge* (New York, 1954), 31 ff, 37.

judge roughly the extent of the market in the cotton belt by
estimating the expenditures made by planters and farmers in
these counties. (See above, note 8.) The estimates are the most
generous possible and exaggerate the extent of the Southern rural
market in relation to the Western in two ways: There were far
more rural poor with little or no purchasing power in the cotton
belt than in the West, and the concentration of landholdings in
the South resulted in fewer landowners than could be found in a
Western area of comparable size. Thus, even if the estimate of
the expenditures made by these Southern planters and farmers
had been larger than the expenditures of a similar group of individual proprietors in the West—which was by no means true—the
total purchased in each county would still have been far less than
in a comparable Western area. Furthermore, as food was a major
item in the expenditures of the Southerners, the market for industrial commodities was much smaller than might appear.

The concentration of landholding and slaveholding in the
Mississippi counties meant that six per cent of the landowners
commanded one third of the gross income and probably a much
higher percentage of the net. That is, the majority of landowners
were faced with a disproportionately small portion of the total
income accruing to the cotton economy as a whole.

Only the largest planters—ten per cent of the landowners—
spent more than $1,000 a year for food and supplies, and they
rarely spent more. These expenditures include the total purchases
for the slaves. The slaveholding farms and plantations in Mississippi annually spent about thirty or thirty-five dollars per person
for food and supplies; nonslaveholders spent about twenty-five
dollars per person. In Georgia slaveholding farms and plantations
spent about twenty-five dollars per person, and nonslaveholders
were just about self sufficient.[24] In contrast, Philip Foner reports
that contemporary newspapers and other sources indicate that
the small farmers who made up the great majority of the rural
population of the West accumulated store bills of from one
hundred to six hundred dollars.[25] Even if we allow for considerable
exaggeration and assume that the accounts were generally closer
to the lower estimate, these figures, which are exclusive of cash
purchases, mail orders, payments to drummers, and so forth, are

[24] In Mississippi a sample of 584 units with 7,289 slaves and an estimated 2,480
whites spent about $316,500; in Georgia a sample of 100 units with 2,354 slaves
and an estimated 710 whites spent about $73,300.
[25] Foner, *Business & Slavery*, 143.

at least a clue to the impressive purchasing power of the Western countryside.

However imprecise the estimates for the South may be, they indicate the lack of purchasing power among the rural population of the cotton belt and demonstrate how greatly the situation there differed from that in the West. With such a home market the slave economy could not sustain more than the lowest level of commodity production apart from that of a few staples. The success of William Gregg as a textile manufacturer in South Carolina and the data produced by Professor John Hebron Moore showing that a cotton textile industry could and did exist in ante bellum Mississippi would seem to contradict this conclusion; but Gregg, who was aware of the modest proportions of the home market, warned Southerners against trying to produce for local needs and suggested that they focus on the wholesale market. His own company at Graniteville, South Carolina, produced fine cotton goods that sold much better in New York than in the South. Gregg's success in the Northern market could not easily be duplicated by others, and when he discussed the Southern market, he felt compelled, as did Benjamin L. C. Wailes and other astute observers, to advocate production of cheap cotton goods for the plantations.[26] Moore's conclusion that his data prove the adaptability of manufacturing to the lower South requires for substantiation more than evidence of particular successes, no matter how impressive;[27] it requires evidence that Southern producers were strong enough to drive out Northern competition and, more important, that the market was large enough to sustain more than a few firms.

The plantation system did have its small compensations for industry. The planters' taste for luxuries, for example, proved a boon to the Petersburg iron industry, which supplied plantations with cast-iron fences, lawn ornaments, balconies, fancy gates, and other decorative articles.[28] A silk industry emerged briefly

[26] William Gregg, *Essays on Domestic Industry; or An Inquiry into the Expediency of Establishing Cotton Manufactures in South-Carolina* (Graniteville, S. C., 1941), 4; Benjamin L. C. Wailes, *Address Delivered in the College Chapel Before the Agricultural, Horticultural and Botanical Society, of Jefferson College* (Natchez, Miss., 1841), 22-23; *De Bow's Review*, XXIX (October 1860), 496-97; Broadus Mitchell, *William Gregg, Factory Master of the Old South* (Chapel Hill, N. C., 1928), 106.

[27] John Hebron Moore, "Mississippi's Ante-Bellum Textile Industry," *Journal of Mississippi History*, XVI (April 1954), 81.

[28] Edward A. Wyatt, IV, "Rise of Industry in Ante-Bellum Petersburg," *William and Mary College Quarterly*, s. 3, XVII (January 1937), 32.

but was destroyed by climatic conditions as well as by a shortage of capital.[29] The hemp industry, which supplied rope for cotton baling, depended heavily on the plantation market.

Some Southern industrialists, especially those in the border states, did good business in the North. Louisville tobacco and hemp manufacturers sold much of their output in Ohio. Botts and Burfoot of Richmond, Virginia, reported the sale of $1,000-worth of straw cutters in the North during a six-month period. The more successful Southern iron producers were those of the upper South, who were able to sell outside the slave states. Smith and Perkins of Alexandria, Virginia, began production of locomotives and railroad cars in the 1850's and obtained a good many orders from the North; but the company failed because shipping costs made consolidation of its Northern market difficult and because only a few orders were forthcoming from the South. Similarly, the paper industry in South Carolina did well until the 1850's, when Northern orders dropped and no Southern orders appeared.[30] The political dangers of these links with the free states were widely appreciated. The Virginia Commercial Convention, for example, reported that West Virginia was being cut off from the South in this way.[31] During the Civil War, William Henry Holcombe, a thoughtful doctor from Natchez, listed in his diary various reasons for the adherence of the border states to the Union and placed close commercial ties high on the list.[32] One suspects that there was more than hindsight here, for politically sophisticated Southerners were alert to the danger well before 1861. But what could they have done about it?

The inability of the slave South to generate an adequate rural market inhibited industrialization and urbanization, which in

[29] Southerners were very much interested in silk cultivation and manufacture and saw fine market possibilities. See Charles G. Parsons, *Inside View of Slavery; or a Tour Among the Planters* (Boston, 1855), 71 ff; C. O. Cathey, "Sidney Weller: Ante-Bellum Promoter of Agricultural Reform," *North Carolina Historical Review*, XXI (January 1954), 6; Spaulding Trafton, "Silk Culture in Henderson County, Kentucky," *Filson Club History Quarterly*, IV (October 1930), 184-89.

[30] Lippincott, *Manufactures in the Ohio Valley*, 64; *Southern Planter*, III (April 1843), advertisement on back cover; Lester J. Cappon, "Trend of the Southern Iron Industry Under the Plantation System," *Journal of Economic and Business History*, II (February 1930), 361, 371, 376; Carrol H. Quenzel, "The Manufacture of Locomotives and Cars in Alexandria in the 1850's," *Virginia Magazine of History and Biography*, LXII (April 1954), 182 ff; Ernest M. Lander, Jr., "Paper Manufacturing in South Carolina Before the Civil War," *North Carolina Historical Review*, XXIX (April 1952), 225 ff.

[31] De Bow (ed.), *Industrial Resources*, III, 465.

[32] William Henry Holcombe Diary (Southern Manuscript Collection, University of North Carolina), entry for September 6, 1855, but obviously written in 1861.

turn limited the market for agricultural produce and undermined attempts at diversification. With the exception of New Orleans and Baltimore, the slave states had no large cities, and few reached the size of 15,000. The urban population of the South could not compare with that of the Northeast, as is generally appreciated; but, more to the point, it could not compare with that of the agrarian West either. The urban population of the lower South in 1860 was only seven per cent of the total population, and in the western part of the lower South, embracing most of the cotton belt, there was a relative decline during the preceding twenty years. In New England, the percentage was thirty-seven; in the Middle Atlantic states, including Ohio, thirty-five; and perhaps most significantly, in Indiana, Illinois, Michigan, and Wisconsin, fourteen.[33]

The urban market in the South was even less developed than these figures suggest. If we except New Orleans, which was a special case, three cities of the lower South had a population of 15,000 or more: Mobile, Charleston, and Savannah, with a combined population of 92,000. Of this number, thirty-seven per cent were slaves and free Negroes, who may be assumed to have represented only minimal purchasing power. In the 1850's American families certainly did not spend less than forty per cent of their incomes on food, and the importance of a large urban market for foodstuffs may be judged accordingly.[34]

Eugene W. Hilgard, state geologist of Mississippi, explained his state's failure to develop a cattle industry largely by the absence of a local market. Similarly, Oscar M. Lieber, state geologist of South Carolina, warned farmers in a state that was never comfortably self-sufficient in corn not to produce more corn than they could consume, for there was no place to market the surplus. Charles Yancey of Buckingham County, Virginia, wrote that planters and farmers would not grow oats because the only possibility of disposing of them lay in person to person barter.[35]

[33] Urban area defined as incorporated places of 2,500 or more. See U. S. Bureau of the Census, *Urban Population in the U. S. from the First Census (1790) to the Fifteenth Census (1930)* . . . (Washington, 1939).

[34] This estimate is from Edgar W. Martin, *The Standard of Living in 1860* (Chicago, 1942), 11-12, and may greatly underestimate the situation in urban households. According to Richard O. Cummings, laborers in Massachusetts probably spent about three fourths of their weekly wages on food in 1860. R. O. Cummings, *The American and His Food; a History of Food Habits in the United States* (Chicago, 1941), 266.

[35] Eugene W. Hilgard, *Report on the Geology and Agriculture of the State of Mississippi* (Jackson, 1860), 250-51; Lieber, *Report*, 106. See also Patent Office,

The weakness of the market for agricultural produce had many detrimental consequences for the South, of which we may mention only two. First, those sections of the border states which found markets in the Northern cities were increasingly drawn into the political-economic orbit of the free states at the very moment when the slave states required maximum solidarity to preserve their system. Second, the weakness of the market doomed the hopes of agricultural reformers and transformed their cry for diversification into a cry for a backward step toward natural economy.

When that great antislavery Kentuckian, Cassius M. Clay, finally receives from historians the honor and attention that he deserves, he will surely be recognized as one of the most penetrating commentators on the economics of slavery. Consider his remarks on the problem of markets, with which we are presently concerned:

Lawyers, merchants, mechanics, laborers, who are your consumers; Robert Wickliffe's two hundred slaves? How many clients do you find, how many goods do you sell, how many hats, coats, saddles, and trunks do you make for these two hundred slaves? Does Mr. Wickliffe lay out as much for himself and his two hundred slaves as two hundred freemen do? . . . All our towns dwindle, and our farmers lose, in consequence, all home markets. Every farmer bought out by the slave system send off the consumers of the manufacturers of the town: when the consumers are gone, the mechanic must go also . . . . A home market cannot exist in a slave state.[36]

Plantation slavery, then, so limited the purchasing power of the South that it could not sustain much industry. That industry which could be raised usually lacked a home market of sufficient scope to permit large-scale operation; the resultant cost of production was often too high for success in competition with Northern firms drawing on much wider markets. Without sufficient industry to support urbanization, a general and extensive diversification of agriculture was unthinkable. Whatever other factors need to be considered in a complete analysis, the low level of demand in this plantation-based slave society was sufficient to retard the economic development of the South.

Annual Report, 1849, Agriculture, Senate Exec. Docs., 31 Cong., 1 Sess., No. 15, pt. 2 (Serial 556), 137.

[36] Horace Greeley (ed.), *The Writings of Cassius Marcellus Clay* . . . (New York, 1848), 179, 227. For a recent biography, see David L. Smiley, *Lion of White Hall: The Life of Cassius M. Clay* (Madison, Wis., 1962).

The Economics of Emancipation

THIS paper illuminates one particular aspect of the theme of this session, property rights in man. It will deal with various emancipation plans: those actually enacted in various slave societies; those discussed by legislators who debated slave and anti-slave proposals; and those which, being purely fictional, have become part of counterfactual history.

The form which emancipation of slaves took in different slavocracies to some extent reflected their view of property rights in man. In many societies slaves were recognized as property, and, therefore, the freeing of bondsmen without full compensation to their owners was considered illegal. For others, slavery was immoral, and payment to manumit slaves was considered a de facto recognition of the institution of slavery. Some forms of compensated emancipation can also be viewed as early precedents for the doctrine of eminent domain.

In addition one can construe the form which emancipation took in different societies as a reflection of the relative strengths of the slave and non-slave holding classes. This interpretation makes property rights an endogenous variable. Empirical evidence suggests that the smaller the percentage of slave owners relative to the electorate, the less the degree of compensation. In fact, many gradual abolition schemes can be viewed as attempts to lessen the strength of the slave holding class so that noncompensated, immediate abolition could be instituted.

Almost every slave society in the Western hemisphere terminated

I have benefited from presenting versions of this paper at a summer conference on "The Application of General Equilibrium Models to Topics in Economic History" sponsored by the Mathematical Social Science Board of the NSF, the University of Wisconsin Economic History Workshop, and the Queen's University faculty seminar. I would like to thank the following members of these seminar groups and other helpful persons: Stanley Engerman, Ronald Fielding, Isaac Fox, Alan Green, Frank Lewis, Donald McCloskey, Thomas Skidmore and R. Craig West for their comments on this manuscript. Without demeaning the contributions of the others, I would like to single out Frank Lewis and Stanley Engerman for their many insights. The Graduate School of the University of Wisconsin supported this research financially, and NSF Grants GS-27282 and GS-3262 enabled the collection of slave price data used in this paper.

slavery with some form of legislative emancipation. The schemes varied in many respects. Some were gradual and others immediate in nature. That is, under certain plans slaves were emancipated at once, although others were gradual because they either provided for the creation of apprenticeships or stipulated that the children of slaves were to be freed after a specified period of service. Many schemes provided for full monetary compensation to the owners of slaves; some had partial compensation; and still others entailed outright expropriation. For many slavocracies emancipation was the direct result of abolitionist sentiment, although in some cases it was the culmination of years of slave unrest. This paper will briefly review the emancipation schemes enacted in the Western hemisphere prior to the adoption of the Thirteenth Amendment in the United States as background for a discussion of the American slave South. The schemes which will be discussed represent alternatives available to the Union prior to the outbreak of the Civil War. This review will not determine why the various schemes differed, but will instead provide the foundation for the hypothetical schemes to be proposed for the Union in 1860.

A BRIEF REVIEW OF EMANCIPATION SCHEMES

The American North led emancipation in the Western hemisphere with Vermont's proclamation of abolition in 1777.[1] Massachusetts (including Maine) followed close behind and, unknowingly, wrote emancipation into its state constitution. This constitution, as well as the Declaration of Independence, was interpreted by the Massachusetts courts as freeing that state's slaves. Although the slave trade in Massachusetts was declared illegal in 1788, the confusion surrounding court decisions enabled many Massachusetts owners to sell their slaves in the South, thereby avoiding capital loss due to abolition.[2]

Those northern states with the largest numbers of slaves, Pennsylvania, New York and New Jersey, all adopted gradual abolition

[1] See Arthur Zilversmit, *The First Emancipation: The Abolition of Slavery in the North* (Chicago: The University of Chicago Press, 1967) for an excellent discussion of the anti-slavery movement in the North and the slave legislation, proposed and enacted, which it furthered.

[2] See George H. Moore, *Notes on the History of Slavery in Massachusetts* (New York: Negro Universities Press, 1968; originally published, D. Appleton and Co., 1866) for an excellent summary of the events culminating in the emancipation of Massachusetts' slaves.

with Pennsylvania leading the group in 1780. The Pennsylvania law stipulated that all children of slaves would be freed at age twenty-eight. The Supreme Court later interpreted this law as implying that slavery would last only one more generation in Pennsylvania. That is, the children of these emancipated slave children would automatically be freed even if both their parents were slaves at the time of birth.[3]

The New York law provided that all Negro children born after 1799 were free after serving their mother's masters for twenty-eight years if male and twenty-five if female. New Jersey had similar provisions and declared that males would be freed after twenty-five and females after twenty-one years of service if born after 1804. This difference in age for the freeing of male and female slaves in the New York and New Jersey legislation can be rationalized in two ways. First, it could represent the desires of the legislators to free slave children at the age at which they would begin their own families. This implies that females married at an earlier average age than did males.

Another way of viewing this choice of age is in terms of minimizing the number of abandoned children. If the objective of the legislators was to free slave children at the earliest possible age under the constraint that there be few orphaned slave babies, they would choose an age such that the birth price of these children would be, on average, zero.[4] Using data for another region I find that the years outlined by the New York and New Jersey acts conform well to this theory. It can be shown that the emancipation years stipulated in the New York act imply prices at birth of between $1.00 and $3.00

[3] The Supreme Court in Miller v. Dwilling (1826) declared that, "no child can be held to servitude till the age of twenty-eight . . . but one whose mother was . . . a slave at the time of its birth . . . [implies that] the legislature of Pennsylvania though it abolished slavery for life, established . . . a servitude . . . which may continue . . . to the end of the world." The Supreme Court, therefore, decided that "the child of one bound to serve to the age of twenty-eight, was not bound . . . for the same period; but was absolutely free." See Helen T. Catterall, editor, *Judicial Cases Concerning American Slavery and the Negro* (Washington, D.C.: Carnegie Institution of Washington, 1936), IV, Cases from the Courts of New England, the Middle States, and the District of Columbia, p. 282.

[4] If the price at birth were less than zero, the owner should choose to abandon the child, as the maintenance costs during the early period of development are greater than the stream of benefits from the later working stage. A positive price would insure a low rate of abandonment, but would also involve a later age for freedom. Therefore, a zero price would accomplish both a minimal number of orphans and an early age at which freedom would be guaranteed. This interpretation of the New York and New Jersey laws was suggested to me by Stanley Engerman.

for male and female infants, instead of the previously prevailing rate of about $25 per newborn.[5] Because female slaves were more productive in their teens than their male counterparts[6] the earlier emancipation age for females is consistent with this rationalization of the gradual abolition schemes.

Both hypotheses outlined above arrive at the same conclusion concerning the approximate ages for emancipating male and female slaves. Some direct evidence supports the latter view. The New York legislature was greatly concerned about the social problem of orphaned slave children. The 1799 act provided for the public care of these abandoned youths stating that masters would be reimbursed up to $3.50 per month for the support of children who otherwise would be abandoned. In some sense, this provision made gradual abolition more palatable to the slaveowners by enabling, in disguised form, some compensation.

The costs to the slaveowners[7] of the gradual abolition programs outlined above were small, compared to those of immediate emancipation. The loss to slaveowners is the reduction in the price of female slaves due to the owner's not having property rights to the full income stream from the production of children. If the birth price of children becomes zero by the choice of the age at which freedom is granted, the entire rents from the breeding capabilities of females also become zero. The breeding portion of a female slave's price varied with her age. It was between one half and one quarter the price of a slave girl under ten years of age, and between two tenths and one tenth the price of a grown female between twenty and thirty years old.[8]

---

[5] The calculations were performed using Maryland slave price data for the same period. The prices at age 25 and 28 were discounted back to year 0 (birth) and these were subtracted from the prices at birth. The resulting figure is the price at birth of a slave whose services are guaranteed for 25 years (for a female) or 28 years (for a male). A ten percent discount rate is used because this appears to have been the internal rate of return on slave owning.

[6] See Robert W. Fogel and Stanley L. Engerman, "The Market Evaluation of Human Capital: The Case of Slavery," unpublished paper presented to the Annual Cliometrics Conference, Madison, Wisconsin, April, 1972 for a discussion of the differences in slave male and female age-net hire rate profiles. They find that female children begin to earn a positive yearly net hire at age 7½, whereas male children produce positive net earnings at age 8½. Females continue to be more productive than males until they are nineteen years of age. After that point, male slaves produce substantially more net income than do females.

[7] If the schemes were compensated, this would refer to the costs to the taxpayers.

[8] The division of female price between the value of the child-bearing capacity and the value of field productive capacity has been computed by R. Fogel and S. Enger-

Gradual abolition had many beneficial aspects. The costs to slave-owners were low, and it appeared to foster a slow and easy transition for society. But gradual abolition had many drawbacks. It was effective in achieving the abolitionists' goal only if it was not anticipated and if the slave trade between the North and South was closed. If the bill was anticipated, owners could sell their bondsmen to slave areas before an embargo on trade could be declared. In New York, for example, data suggest that the 1799 abolition plan was anticipated by some slaveowners, but that many more took advantage of the loopholes in the gradual abolition law to sell their slaves in the South. It is entirely possible that only 12,000 New York State slaves were freed by abolition legislation, whereas 24,000 were sold to slave states farther South.[9]

In addition to the smuggling problem, which was particularly prominent in the North, gradual abolition in any area would encourage more intensive use of slaves during their productive period. In the New York, New Jersey and Pennsylvania cases, gradual abolition involved the emancipation of slave children after a period of service. These children were probably worked harder than if their owners had property rights to their lifetime earnings streams. In 1817 a bill was passed in New York providing for the freedom of all slaves born before 1799 as of 1827. This must surely have encouraged masters to work their slaves more intensively during the ten years of remaining service. Announced or anticipated gradual abolition of this type certainly would be against the interests of abolitionists, and, of course, of the slaves.

It is perhaps due to smuggling and the "working of slaves to

---

man and is contained in Fogel and Engerman, "The Market Evaluation of Human Capital," Charts V and VI.

[9] The Federal Census reveals that in 1790 there were 21,324 slaves in New York State, and 20,343 in 1800. This indicates a drop of about 5,000 slaves, if a 20 percent rate of net increase is allowed for during the ten year period. This decline in the slave population was partially due to slaveowner anticipation of the 1799 act. The decline in the slave population during the period 1800 to 1820 is even more dramatic. The gradual abolition bill was not actually effective in freeing slaves during this period, although it may have engendered the manumission of certain slaves due to mounting social pressure. The 1800 slave population in New York was 20,343, but the 1820 figure is 10,088. Using again a 20 percent net rate of increase yields 19,205 slaves who were either manumitted, abandoned children, or smuggled South to slave states. One student of New York slave history believes that independent evidence substantiates the latter hypothesis. He cites as evidence that the gains to be made in smuggling an able-bodied slave South were £40 "after commissions, insurance costs and shipping charges were paid." Edgar J. McManus, *A History of Negro Slavery in New York* (New York: Syracuse University Press, 1966), p. 170. Certainly after 1817, when the immediate abolition of slaves was guaranteed in ten years, the gains to be made by circumventing the anti-slave-trade laws were great.

death" that gradual abolition was almost always followed closely behind by immediate emancipation.[10] As suggested in the Introduction to this paper, gradual abolition may also have been used as a way of diluting the slave-owning class so that full emancipation could be enacted with less resistance. New York passed its total emancipation bill in 1817, although the act freed slaves ten years hence. Pennsylvania abolitionists tried to pass a similar piece of legislation, but failed, and slavery was terminated more gradually in that state. New Jersey, in 1846, ended slavery by changing the status of all slaves to that of apprentice.

Emancipation in the British West Indies was sparked by British abolitionists, although slave revolts in Jamaica contributed to the freeing of West Indian bondsmen. The 1820's marked the beginning of a full-scale anti-slavery campaign in Parliament, and legislation in 1824 was passed prohibiting the transportation of slaves from one British colony to another. In 1834, after much debate, the British government put into effect an emancipation plan which provided that field hands would be completely free in six years and non-field hands in four. During the interim they were to work as apprentices to their former masters for forty-five hours a week. They were to be given their customary allowances, and any money they earned in overtime could be used to purchase their remaining years of service.[11] Twenty million pounds was allocated by the Parliament from the public funds of the United Kingdom as an indemnity grant to the slaveowners.[12]

The abolition of slavery in Venezuela was a by-product of the wars for independence of that nation. After independence, in 1821, the Cúcuta Slave Law was passed which provided for the free birth of all slave children, although these minors had to serve their mothers' masters for eighteen years. In 1830 this age was increased to twenty-one, and later the government further extended servitude to age twenty-five. Specific taxes were collected by the government

[10] This would, of course, increase the costs to slave owners of gradual emancipation. The increased cost would be the discounted value of all remaining productive services from male and female (not including breeding rights as these have been subtracted out before) slaves.

[11] The detail of these provisions, as well as the personnel which the British sent to secure them legally for the slaves, indicate that Parliament knew that gradual abolition could involve the working of slaves more intensively. This law was obviously designed to accomplish the abolitionists' goals without the hardship which the Northern gradual abolition laws may have entailed.

[12] This sum was probably not sufficient fully to compensate the owners, and represented about one-twentieth of British total national product in the 1830's.

for the manumission of a number of slaves every year, and this together with gradual abolition served to decrease the slave population in Venezuela. In 1854, after depression, discontent, and revolution, an abolition law was passed providing for the freedom of all slaves and full compensation to their owners.[13]

The emancipation schemes outlined above were all effected prior to the American Civil War and all represented possible avenues of solution to the slave problem in the American South. Of Western hemisphere countries only Cuba and Brazil freed their slaves after the passage of the Thirteenth Amendment. In both, gradual emancipation was instituted and was followed about twenty years later by complete abolition. Therefore, in both countries, slaveowners had the opportunity of working their chattel harder during their remaining years of servitude.

All the emancipation schemes described above involved balancing abolitionist and slave-owning interests. Even in most of the American North, where slaveowners were clearly in a minority, emancipation did not involve the complete confiscation of property. In fact, full abolition bills were passed in all these areas only after years of trying gradual abolition. A slow eroding of the slave-owning forces may have made complete freedom easier to push through the legislature. If, then, the American Civil War was caused in part by slavery, why didn't the Union choose one of the options suggested by the above comparative analysis?

The next section will outline the options that were available to the Union prior to 1861 and will analyze the costs associated with each. These options will be viewed in light of the previous comparative discussion and in terms of the debate on emancipation during the Thirty-seventh (Civil War) Congress.

THE OPTIONS AVAILABLE TO THE UNION IN 1860

Many of the options discussed below may not have been politically feasible in the years preceding the Civil War. In addition, some will doubt that these schemes were alternatives to battle.

---

[13] It is difficult to state whether or not there was full compensation, since payment was based on a schedule of prices set by law. See John V. Lombardi, *The Decline and Abolition of Negro Slavery in Venezuela: 1820-1854* (Westport, Connecticut: Greenwood Publishing Company, 1971), Appendix 1, "Tables Pertaining to Slaves and Manumisos," for information concerning the number of slaves emancipated from 1830 to 1854 and the compensation awards to slave owners through the 1854 Abolition Law. Emancipation in Venezuela is interesting because the slave population was very small and the slavé owning class was rather minor compared to the free population, but compensation was awarded to slaveowners.

These issues are difficult to resolve. Nevertheless, a measurement of the effects of various abolition plans and a comparison of them with the realized costs of the Civil War can still provide useful information. In particular, such an exercise might add credence to the hypothesis that the costs of the war were not correctly anticipated and that for this reason emancipation was rejected by both sides in favor of what appeared to be a better alternative. This research might also serve to reject or substantiate a completely different thesis, that the North was rational in fighting the Civil War because its net benefits from winning were positive.[14]

The first option which will be considered is that of immediate emancipation with full compensation. Full compensation is required for this and the other schemes because it reflects the view of property rights held by the majority of the populace in 1860. Other than certain radical Republicans, few members of the Thirty-seventh Congress believed in the expropriation of slave property; most were in agreement that slaveowners must be fully compensated for their losses.[15] Lincoln, for one, felt quite strongly about the issue of compensation, and doubted the constitutionality of the Emancipation Proclamation because it did not provide compensation. Under this hypothetical emancipation scheme, the Federal government would issue to the states, and then the states to the slaveowners, bonds whose principal was equal to the value of the slaves.[16] Therefore the initial cost of such a program would be the capital value of all the slaves in the United States in 1860.[17] I have estimated the

[14] See, for example, Louis M. Hacker, *The Triumph of American Capitalism* (New York: Columbia University Press, 1947), for a complete discussion of this notion. This paper, though, does not attempt to assess the North's gains from victory in terms of redistributing income from the South to the North. Therefore, this work alone cannot lead to a rejection or acceptance of the "Beard-Hacker" thesis.

[15] Some might challenge this statement with the fact that most of the emancipation schemes discussed and enacted during the Thirty-seventh Congress provided for less than full compensation. For example, the District of Columbia bill appropriated $1 million for compensation to masters or an average of about $300 per slave. The Border State bill also allotted $300 for each slave freed. Although this was slightly less than one-half the price of slaves during 1860 for these areas, it must be remembered that these acts were wartime measures. District of Columbia slaveowners readily sold their slaves at these "low" prices, probably because they feared expropriation if the South won. In addition, many of the bills passed and debated provided for gradual abolition of slaves. Therefore, although the monetary compensation was less than the total value of the slave, the owner had a longer period of service than if emancipation was immediate.

[16] Since slavery was a state issue, the states would have to purchase the rights to the slaves with the Federal bonds.

[17] Since the slave region can be identified with a specific economic and regional group, there may be reasons for a political settlement to result in a compensation transfer greater than the sum of slave prices. This will be considered at a later point.

capital value of all slaves in 1860 to have been 2.7 billion 1860 dollars. This number was calculated using age-specific slave price data recently collected from southern probate records and slave bills of sale.[18]

The financing of so great a venture as the purchase of $2.7 billion worth of capital, when the gross national product was only $4.2 billion, would have required borrowing. In the emancipation schemes which were actually outlined by Congress during the years 1861 to 1863, thirty-year bonds, yielding from five to six percent were to be offered states fulfilling various criteria.[19] Similarly, in this exercise I shall assume that the government buys slaves from their owners with bonds that pay six percent[20] and are refunded, an equal amount each year, over a period of thirty years. If I assume that all persons, except ex-slaves, pay taxes to finance these bonds, refunding the bonds at a constant rate over the thirty-year period implies a per capita tax of $7.25 in 1860. This represents about five percent of per capita income for that year, with this percentage

---

In addition, all slaves are freed at once; therefore one does not have to consider the effects on price of an increasingly smaller stock of slaves. The Federal Government does not have to pay slave owners the area under the demand curve for slaves, but merely their price as slaves in 1860. This becomes clearer if one considers slaves as free men to be equivalent to slaves as slaves. As slaves are freed they become free laborers; therefore the supply function for slaves moves to the left but that for free laborers moves equally in the opposite direction. Thus, the price of workers does not change as slaves are freed.

[18] This capital value is about one billion 1860 dollars less than that computed by Louis A. Rose. See Louis A. Rose, "Capital Losses of Southern Slaveholders Due to Emancipation," *Western Economic Journal*, III (Fall 1964), 39-51. The prices for slaves used in the Rose estimate were partially based on those collected by U.B. Phillips. The lower price series which I have used resulted from a sample collected by R. Fogel and S. Engerman from the identical collection of New Orleans bills of sale which Phillips used. The Fogel and Engerman prices are about 20 percent lower for a "prime field hand" (a slave between the ages of 18 and 30) than those given by Phillips. Phillips' sample is biased upward for an unknown reason. Fogel and Engerman's detailed comments on this problem can be found in a forthcoming article.

[19] For example, the House version of Lincoln's border state bill provided that " 'whenever the President of the United States shall be satisfied that any one of the states of Delaware, Maryland, Virginia, Kentucky, Tennessee or Missouri shall have emancipated [their] slaves . . .' he should cause to be delivered to such state 5 percent, 30 year bonds in an amount equal to $300 for each slave freed." Leonard P. Curry, *Blueprint for Modern America* (Nashville: Vanderbilt University Press, 1968), pp. 47-48. In addition, the House's Select Committee on Gradual Emancipation reported a bill in January 1863 which also authorized the President to issue 30 year, 5 percent bonds to Missouri when that state adopted immediate abolition. *Ibid.*, p. 53. Other bills provided for 6 percent, thirty year bonds. I have chosen the 6 percent figure to bias my costs upward slightly.

[20] One may wonder why the interest rate on the bonds is six percent although the internal rate of return on slaves was somewhat higher. The bonds are far less risky assets than the slaves, and if persons are risk averse a smaller rate of interest would be necessary to induce them to hold bonds instead of slaves in their portfolios.

declining during the thirty-year period because of the growth in both per capita income and population. If southerners are to be compensated for their tax burden too, the per capita cost would be $9.66 in 1860, with southerners receiving a transfer. Certainly, the slaves themselves may have been willing to contribute to their own freedom. If they too are assumed to pay taxes the per capita cost is $6.30, and is $8.40 if southerners are compensated for the tax.[21]

These bonds would be given to the slaveowners in return for the freedom of their slaves, each bond having a principal value equal to that of a slave. The transfer of income in the first part of this analysis is essentially from all whites to the slaves. The net wealth position of the slaveholders remains exactly the same; they should be indifferent between holding slaves or bonds. The slaves are the only gainers in this analysis in that they are essentially given money to purchase their freedom. The entire real wealth position of the United States is assumed not to change.[22]

Had the reference point been 1850 instead of 1860, the debt produced by immediate and fully compensated emancipation would have been smaller. This is due both to the smaller number of slaves in 1850 and to the rapid rise in slave prices from 1850 to 1860.[23] The capitalized value of slaves in 1850 was 1.3 billion 1850 dollars.

[21] These calculations were computed as follows. At six percent, $2.7 billion could be refunded at a constant rate by the taxation of $195,480,000 per year for thirty years. In 1860 there were 26,923,000 whites in the United States; therefore, the per capita tax in 1860 would have been $7.25. Per capita income in 1860 was $141; therefore the tax represented about 5 percent of per capita income. The southern population (that is, the Confederate population) was about 20 percent of the entire nation; therefore the per capita tax would be $9.66 if a refund was to be given the southerners to compensate them not only for their slaves but also for their tax burden. Taxation in this example is assumed to have an equal effect on all. If revenue were raised by a tariff, this might not be the case, and one region could bear a greater percentage of the burden.

[22] The possible exceptions to this statement will be raised in a later section of this paper. Robert Hall in "The Burden of Slavery," unpublished manuscript, Massachusetts Institute of Technology, discusses the possibility of changes in the interest rate due to the existence of slavery, in the same way that the creation of debt can result in a real burden. (See Richard Sutch, "Discussion of Slavery and Economic Growth," JOURNAL OF ECONOMIC HISTORY, XXVII (December 1967), 540-41, for a summary of the Hall paper.) But the perfection of a market for human capital, like the creation of a mortgage market, does not change anything real except the lowering of transactions costs of borrowing or lending. This paper does not consider the issue of transactions cost changes but does implicitly reject the hypothesis in the Hall manuscript. For a discussion of the real differences between a slave and nonslave economy, see Stanley L. Engerman, "Some Considerations Relating to Property Rights in Man," this JOURNAL.

[23] Slave prices, deflated by the Warren and Pearson wholesale price index, rose approximately 5 percent on an average annual basis from 1850 to 1860.

The same scheme as outlined above would have involved a per capita payment of $4.80 in 1850, and less per year thereafter. Per capita income in 1850 (in 1850 prices) was $110; therefore the first payment would have been four percent of per capita income. This, too, would decline during the thirty-year refunding period.

Another emancipation scheme, suggested by the brief review of abolition plans above, was that of gradual abolition with eventual immediate emancipation. This would lower the costs of compensation considerably. The gradual abolition scheme I have considered would free slave children at an age such that their birth price would be zero. This would reduce the probability that the slave children would be abandoned. Using a ten percent discount rate, male children would have been freed at age twenty-five in the Lower South and twenty-six in the Upper South. Female slave children would be completely emancipated at an earlier age on average, at twenty-five in the Lower South but at twenty-two in the Upper South. Since it is assumed that all children are freed so that their birth price is zero, then the entire rent on female slaves due to their breeding capacity is zero. Only the returns to field or household work now comprise a female slave's price. The entire capital loss from this portion of gradual abolition would have been $210 million in 1860.

Gradual abolition was almost always followed by full emancipation. The legislation proposed during the Thirty-seventh Congress recognized that complete and immediate emancipation was to be a difficult social transition. Therefore, most of the bills dealing with abolition provided for complete freedom after a period of time. One proposed measure which would have freed the Border State slaves allowed for a twenty-year transition period. That for Missouri specified complete freedom within thirteen years. If a gradual abolition bill was passed specifying total emancipation after a given period of time, the costs of fully compensating slaveowners would have increased. For instance, if all slaves were to be freed by 1890 there would have been approximately 5.3 million bondsmen emancipated at that date[24] at an 1860 value of about $340 million.[25] To this sum

[24] This computation involves several assumptions. The slave population is assumed to grow at a decadal rate of 22 percent. Survivor information (that is, the percent of any cohort which will survive to the next decade) from the period 1850 to 1860 was used to get the hypothetical number of slaves in each cohort which would have been in the population in 1890. The first effects of gradual emancipation are felt in 1885 when a cohort of twenty-five year-olds is emancipated. By 1890 there are no

would have to be added the 1860 capitalized value of the loss in breeding rights of the females; therefore, the total losses from this form of gradual abolition would have been $550 million in 1860.

One problem with the hypothetical compensated emancipation schemes developed above is that many northerners and southerners believed that the colonization of ex-slaves was a necessary part of abolition plans. Lincoln in particular "doubted that whites and free Negroes could live together in peace, and this led him to advocate colonization."[26] Colonization never became an issue in the Latin American and Caribbean emancipation debates because pre-abolition race relations in these areas made freedom more acceptable than in the United States. One writer has stated that in Cuba, for example, "there was no fear of emancipation . . . for the Cubans had long since accepted both racial miscegenation and an open-class system of social stratification."[27]

If compensated emancipation in the United States were followed by complete colonization of the ex-slaves, the costs of re-settlement would have to be added to the amount of debt created for compensation purposes. In the legislation proposed and passed during the Thirty-seventh Congress, about one-tenth of the total amount allotted to compensation and colonization was to be spent on the latter.[28] This would imply in the above case of immediate and fully

slaves between the ages of twenty and twenty-five. I also assume that childbearing is deferred by these female slaves, so that no children are born into slavery after 1885. An equivalent assumption would be to invoke the Supreme Court's decision in Miller v. Dwilling (1826), which stated that the children of emancipated slave children were free at birth. If this held, and if those children were cared for by their mothers' masters, the costs of gradual abolition would be slightly higher than calculated here.

[25] I assume here that by 1890 the percentage of slaves in the Old and New (or Upper and Lower) South is the same. In addition, the peak prices for male and female slaves in 1860 are increased at an average annual rate of 1.3 percent to 1890. Therefore, the male peak price for an average of the Upper and Lower South would have been $1772 in 1890. That for the females would have been $1275; this does not include the birth rights to the children, since those have been subtracted off by the previous exercise. For a justification of the average annual rate of increase in slave prices from 1860 to 1890 see Robert W. Fogel and Stanley L. Engerman, "The Economics of Slavery," in their *The Reinterpretation of American Economic History* (New York: Harper and Row, 1971), p. 331.

[26] John Hope Franklin, *The Emancipation Proclamation* (New York: Doubleday and Co., 1963), p. 21.

[27] Herbert S. Klein, *Slavery in the Americas: A Comparative Study of Virginia and Cuba* (Chicago: The University of Chicago Press, 1967), p. 258.

[28] The emancipation bill for the District of Columbia appropriated $100,000 for the colonization of about 3,000 slaves. The border state proposal allotted $20 million for this deportation, and that for Missouri "pledged federal support for voluntary colonization." See L. Curry, *Blueprint.*

compensated abolition an average of $78 to be allocated for the colonization of each slave. This can be compared with actual values spent by the Colonization Society. During the period 1816 to 1860 this organization colonized 10,498 free blacks at a cost of $1,806,705, or about $172 per person.[29] The Colonization Society probably spent more per slave than would have been allotted by Congress, and $100 per slave appears reasonable in view of the costs involved and the willingness of the electorate to allocate funds. This would add $384 million to the costs of compensated emancipation, if colonization were a necessary step in the passage of an abolition bill.

Southerners, too, viewed colonization as a necessary adjunct to emancipation. The colonization issue arose during debates in the Virginia Legislature from 1831 to 1832. In summarizing the consensus, Thomas R. Dew stated that "all seemed to be perfectly agreed in the necessity of removal in case of emancipation."[30] In view of this southern opinion, it is interesting to derive the effects of colonization on total factor returns in the South, to see if some factors could have gained from removal of the ex-slaves. It can be shown[31] that under the assumption of a Cobb-Douglas production

[29] Phillip Staudenraus, *The African Colonization Movement, 1816-1865* (New York: Columbia University Press, 1961), p. 15.

[30] Thomas R. Dew, "Review of the Debate in the Virginia Legislature of 1831 and 1832," in Eric L. McKitrick, *Slavery Defended: The Views of the Old South* (New Jersey: Prentice Hall, 1963), p. 21.

[31] The supply function for southern agricultural products can be characterized as Cobb-Douglas and of the form: $Q_a = AK^{(1-\alpha)} [L_w + L_b]^\alpha$, where L_w is free and L_b is slave labor. If the wage rates for these two labor groups are the same, the total factor returns to either w or b can be expressed quite simply. For example, the total return to w is: $\lambda_w = \left[\dfrac{L_w}{L_w + L_b} \right] \cdot \alpha \cdot P_a \cdot Q_a$, where P_a is the price of agricultural goods deflated by the price of all other goods in the economy. The total return to capital can be expressed similarly as: $\lambda_k = (1 - \alpha)P_a \cdot Q_a \cdot L_w$ in this analysis is identified with free laborers and K with slaveowners. To see the effects of compensated emancipation and colonization on λ_w and λ_k, designate two time periods, 0 and 1, the latter corresponding to the colonization case. That is, in time period 1 the only labor is L_w. If the demand function for agricultural products takes the simple form: $Q_a = D_a P_a^{-\eta}$, the gains or losses from colonization can be easily derived. The ratio of the return to free labor in the two time periods is: $\dfrac{\lambda_{w1}}{\lambda_{w0}} = \left[\dfrac{L_w + L_b}{L_w} \right]^{[1-\alpha(1-1/\eta)]}$. Since $0 < \alpha < 1$ and $\eta > 0$, this ratio is always > 1. The corresponding ratio for the capitalists is: $\dfrac{\lambda_{k1}}{\lambda_{k0}} = \left[\dfrac{L_w}{L_w + L_b} \right]^{[\alpha(1-1/\eta)]}$, which is $\gtrless 1$ as $\eta \lessgtr 1$. Therefore, capitalists gain if the demand for agricultural products is

function for agricultural goods in the South, capitalists would have lost from the compensated emancipation and colonization of slaves if the elasticity of demand for agricultural goods were greater than one. They would have gained if it were less than one. Free laborers will always gain. Of course, other models can produce very different results. In addition, to the extent that southerners consumed cotton textiles and staple crops, they would lose from price increases. Northerners would also lose from these increases in price.

The colonization schemes which were discussed during the Thirty-seventh Congress and the 1831-1832 Virginia State Legislature involved groups of slaves much smaller in number than the four million which I am considering here. Certainly the speedy removal of these four million ex-slaves would have been virtually impossible. Nevertheless, the abundance of debate on colonization renders this issue at least a necessary consideration in a discussion of hypothetical emancipation schemes.

THE EX POST COSTS OF THE CIVIL WAR

But to what can the costs of these emancipation schemes be compared? To determine whether the legislators in 1860 were rational it would be necessary to ascertain what the anticipated costs and gains of the Civil War were to the North and the South. This, though, is not possible. Instead, I will outline what the ex post costs of the Civil War were.[32] Although this does not shed much light on the anticipated costs, it allows one to ask whether an emancipation scheme would have been acceptable had the true costs of the war been known.

Direct estimates of the costs of the Civil War involve only scraps of evidence. It is known that the Union and the Confederacy borrowed about three billion 1860 dollars to finance the war and that about 600,000 soldiers died in battle or from battle wounds.[33] But we do not have reliable direct estimates of all losses, such as

---

inelastic. In addition, capitalists are compensated fully for their slaves; therefore they are not losing the annual net hire rate of their now freed bondsmen.

[32] Much of this section is taken from Frank D. Lewis and Claudia D. Goldin, "The Economic Costs of the Civil War," forthcoming manuscript, Queen's University and the University of Wisconsin.

[33] See Chester W. Wright, "The More Enduring Consequences of America's Wars," JOURNAL OF ECONOMIC HISTORY, III, Supplement (December 1943) for a discussion of war deaths, and Charles A. and Mary R. Beard, *The Rise of American Civilization* (New York: Macmillan Co., 1933), II, "The Industrial Era," p. 107, for an estimate of the Northern debt created during the Civil War. The burden of the war expenditures was less than the amount given because much of the money was spent on items such as food and clothing which would have been purchased by civilians in the absence of the war.

capital destruction and political instability. Therefore, I suggest that these costs be measured indirectly.

The costs which will be measured are those to persons alive in 1860,[34] because they determined the course of events culminating in the war. I assume that the costs of the war to the population alive in 1860 can best be viewed as the discounted value of the difference in consumption which would have been achieved without the war and that which was actually observed. The technique for computing these costs involves the construction of a hypothetical consumption stream for the period following 1860, that is, a consumption stream in the absence of the war. The difference between this consumption stream and that which was actually observed, discounted to 1860, is construed to be the cost of the War Between the States. Therefore, the cost is given by:

$$C = \sum_{j=1860}^{n} \left[\frac{C_j' - C_j}{(1+i)^{j-1860}} \right],$$

where C_j' is the hypothetical consumption in year j and C_j is the actual consumption in that year. The discount rate, i, is taken to be .07. The calculation described below takes n as 1909, for after that date the costs, C, are trivially incremented. Given certain assumptions concerning the hypothetical consumption stream, C is calculated to be about 10 billion 1860 dollars.

The hypothetical consumption stream for the period 1860 to 1869 was constructed by assuming that per capita real income would have grown at the average 1839 to 1859 rate had the Civil War not occurred. It also assumes that the hypothetical path grows at a rate such that per capita income in the real and hypothetical worlds are equal by 1885. After that year the per capita growth for both streams is taken to have been the same. One million people are assumed to have died directly from the war.[35] That is, there are one million more persons in the hypothetical than in the actual world in 1869, and these persons die at rates according to data for 1900. Immigration is subtracted from the population increase, because the costs of the war are only to those living in 1860.

---

[34] The persons alive in 1860 are assumed to value the consumption stream of their children and their grandchildren, and to discount it at the rate at which they would their own. The loss of consumption to immigrants who enter after 1860 is not counted in the calculation described below.

[35] Although this is probably an upwardly biased estimate of Civil War-related deaths, the analysis does not take into consideration some of the losses due to war wounds not resulting in death.

To compare the costs of emancipation to the costs of the Civil War it is necessary to assume that the hypothetical world of emancipation without the Civil War would not have involved political instability. One might certainly argue that if the states underwent some form of fully compensated, voluntary emancipation, rather than an imposed settlement after battle, the process of change would have been much smoother. This will be my assumption in this analysis.

The costs of the Civil War, measured by various means, were much above the costs of any one of the compensated emancipation plans. Of course, the nature of the costs of the two alternatives is different. The war involved "dead-weight" losses and a redistribution of income from slave-owning persons to slaves, whereas the emancipation schemes are only income redistribution plans. But to the free persons who could vote in 1860 these costs are both weighed equally in their decisions. The southerners decide on their strategy by assessing the probability of winning the war times the expected net costs or benefits of the war. If they weigh this against a fully compensated emancipation scheme,[36] they should choose battle only if the expected net gains of the war are positive. The northerners also make the same calculation, but they weigh the expected net gains from the war against the costs of financing the compensation scheme.

From a casual glance at the data presented it seems obvious that an incorrect choice was made. Was this a function of a stalemated political process? That is, are there reasons to believe that the emancipation schemes were not feasible as political solutions? Are the costs of the alternatives being measured incorrectly? Certainly, one cannot leave out the fact that the costs of the Civil War were very imperfectly anticipated, and that the expected gains from winning appeared large. In addition, there is still the possibility that the war would have been fought even had one of the emancipation schemes been adopted.

WHY EMANCIPATION SCHEMES WERE NOT PROPOSED AND ENACTED BEFORE 1861

The previous analysis took the sum of all slave rents to equal the amount necessary fully to compensate all slaveholders. If the method of purchasing back the slaves were non-political, that is, if each

---

[36] I assume here that the bonds are financed in such a way that southerners are compensated for their tax burden as well as for their slave property.

slave were bought back individually, then this assessment is correct. But because the slave-owning region would have to decide on the amount necessary for compensation, there are many reasons to believe that the figures given above are underestimates.[37] More correct figures can be obtained if one takes into account the rents accruing to other productive factors in the South due to the existence of slavery.

If slaves were emancipated, with or without colonization taking place, factors which were specific to the slave economy would lose. For instance, if the scale of farms would have to be reduced with large living quarters broken down, additional transition costs would have to be paid. White overseers and other specific factors would lose by the abolition schemes, and these factors would also have to be compensated for emancipation to be amenable to the South as a whole. There is no evidence bearing on the magnitude of these losses, although they probably were trivial in comparison with the capital value of slaves.

Another, even more nebulous, set of losses concerns the positive externalities which the slave system conferred on persons in the South. With emancipation, these positive external benefits would be removed. If the abolition scheme were voted on by the entire slave-owning region, these losses would have to be compensated. One possible external benefit was the satisfaction southerners received from the institution of slavery as a racist device. In addition, the slave system might have represented a "way of life" to southerners as a group. Although each master valued his slave at the market price, which reflected only the productive (and breeding) capabilities of the slave, the slave system as a whole may have been worth more than the sum of these prices.

Even though Lincoln and many influential northerners and southerners wanted colonization, it is possible that southerners as a whole did not. In that case there may have been additional costs to factors in the South had the ex-slaves moved North. Because the relative magnitude of free labor in the South prior to 1861 was small, it is possible that wages did not equalize between the northern and

[37] This argument will not involve bargaining problems. That is, if all costs were known, the South could "hold out" for a much larger sum. In addition, factors such as economies of scale and conspicuous consumption have already been included in the above figures. That is, if slaves afforded economies of scale in staple crop production, whereas free labor did not, then the price of slaves would reflect this advantage. The same argument applies to the possible existence of conspicuous consumption in slave owning.

southern regions. Since slaves could not migrate, factor prices did not have to equalize. Therefore, emancipation would induce a massive migration to the North, with losses of inframarginal products to certain productive factors remaining in the South. This can only be counted as a loss if the southerners did not want the removal of the Negroes. On the other hand, had the southerners elected colonization as part of an emancipation scheme, the Federal Government would not have to pay for the inframarginal losses.

It is possible, therefore, that the capitalized value of slaves was less than the required amount of compensation. Specific factors in the South may have lost; positive external benefits would have been curtailed; and the decline in inframarginal products would have to be compensated. Although it is impossible to assess these amounts, it seems reasonable to assume that they were not double or triple the value of slaves in 1860. Therefore, the required compensation costs still appear to be smaller than the realized costs of the Civil War.

In all probability, the major reason that the war was fought instead of there being a political settlement was that its costs were incorrectly anticipated. The North was obviously surprised by the tenacity of the South, and the South had counted on more support from Great Britain. It appears that neither side thought the war would last more than one or two years. As the war dragged on, Lincoln expressed the opinion that the costs of the war were dreadfully and surprisingly high and that slavery could be "bought out" at a cheaper price. In a letter to J. A. McDougall of California in 1862 Lincoln stated that "[l]ess than one half-day's cost of this war would pay for all the slaves in Delaware at $400 per head . . . [and] less than 87 days cost of the war would pay for all in Delaware, Maryland, District of Columbia, Kentucky and Missouri."[38]

The "Beard-Hacker" thesis also can serve to explain the apparent northern apathy toward a political resolution of the problem.[39] The settlement imposed on the South after the war may have redistrib-

---

[38] John Hope Franklin, *The Emancipation Proclamation*, p. 22.

[39] Louis Hacker's statement of this proposition can be found in the following passage: "The American Civil War turned out to be a revolution indeed. But its striking achievement was the triumph of industrial capitalism. The industrial capitalists, through their political spokesmen, the Republicans, had succeeded in capturing the state and using it as an instrument to strengthen their economic position. It was no accident, therefore, that while the war was waged on the field and through Negro emancipation, in Congress' halls the victory was made secure by the passage of tariff, banking, public-land, railroad, and contract-labor legislation." L. Hacker, *The Triumph of American Capitalism*, p. 373.

uted income to northerners. This implies that persons in the North
need not have weighed the costs of the war against the costs of
compensated emancipation. Instead, they should have compared
the net costs or gains of the war with the costs of compensated
emancipation.

A final reason for the lack of legislative discussion of abolition
prior to 1861 is that slavery may not have been a major cause of
the Civil War. The war may have been fought with or without the
institution of slavery. As a corollary, the Civil War and emancipation may not have been exclusive events. Even had a fully compensated emancipation scheme been passed prior to the firing on
Fort Sumter, the political balance of power would have remained
delicate. The Civil War might still have been fought, and both the
costs of redistribution from non-slave owning to slave and the
costs of the war would have been incurred.

CONCLUDING REMARKS

Although the Union was able to view in historical perspective
emancipation schemes of all types, none were seriously considered
before 1861. After that date abolition plans were discussed only as
part of the Union's war effort. It appears from a summary of the
data in this paper, given in Table 1, that the Union erred. It did
not look to other slavocracies for advice in solving its slave problem, for the realized costs of the Civil War were far greater than
those of various emancipation schemes. Of course, the Union's winning the war may have given the northern states a greater market
basket of goods than just the abolition of slavery. It is possible that
it more carefully weighed the costs and benefits of the war than
has been apparent from this analysis.

The South lost doubly from fighting the Civil War. It not only
paid large amounts for the machinery of war and incurred the
destruction of lives and property, but, in addition, its slaveowners
had their property expropriated after the battles were over. However, the gains to the South of winning the war have not been
assessed, and the expected losses of its entering into battle may
have been small.

Because the paper by Stanley Engerman[40] has discussed the inter-

[40] See S. Engerman, "Some Considerations Relating to Property Rights in Man,"
this JOURNAL.

esting features of slave and non-slave economies, my paper has not focussed on the effects of emancipation on human capital formation, economic efficiency, the labor-leisure choice and other subjects. Instead, I have looked at various schemes of emancipation which were adopted by certain slavocracies. These and the discussions during the Thirty-seventh Congress have suggested various counterfactuals concerning the antebellum United States. My only conclusion is that I have been surprised that so few persons considered emancipation in any form prior to the war. I have suggested various possible reasons, but have no concrete answers.

CLAUDIA DALE GOLDIN, *University of Wisconsin*

TABLE 1
THE COSTS OF FULLY COMPENSATED IMMEDIATE AND GRADUAL ABOLITION IN 1860 AND THE EX POST COSTS OF THE CIVIL WAR

A. *The Costs of Fully Compensated Abolition in 1860*[a]

(1) Capital Value of 1860 stock of slaves	$2.7 billion
(2) Breeding rights of female slaves in 1860	$210 million
(3) Capital value of 1890 stock of slaves in 1860 after gradual abolition[b]	$340 million
(4) Colonization costs in 1860[c]	$384 million

	Per Capita Cost[d]		
	All Free Persons Pay	Only Northerners Pay	Slaves Plus Free Persons Pay
Immediate Abolition (1)	$7.25(5%)	$9.66(7%)	$6.30(4%)
Immediate Abolition (1)+(4)	8.00(6%)	10.70(8%)	6.90(5%)
Gradual Abolition (2)+(3)[e]	1.50(1%)	2.00(1.5%)	1.30(1%)

B. *The Ex Post Costs of the Civil War*

Direct Outlays	$ 3 billion
Deaths to soldiers	635,000
Ex Post Cost defined as the difference in two consumption streams	$10 billion

[a] All costs are expressed in 1860 prices, in 1860.

[b] Gradual abolition is defined as the freeing of all children of slaves after a period of 25 years of service. This is followed by total abolition as of 1890; therefore, the costs of the remaining stock of slaves must be added to the decline in the capitalized value of the females.

[c] Colonization costs for 3.84 million slaves at $100 per slave.

[d] The bonds used to finance these schemes are refunded such that an equal amount of principal and interest is paid each year. The numbers in parentheses are the percent of 1860 per capita income represented by the tax transfer in 1860. The percentage would decline during the thirty-year refunding period.

[e] The costs of gradual abolition involve both the losses of breeding rights to females (2) and the loss of the capital stock of males and females (not including breeding rights) as of 1890, discounted back to 1860 (3).

Source: See text.

7

Urbanization and Slavery: The Issue of Compatibility*

CLAUDIA DALE GOLDIN

I   THE PROBLEM

THE American plantation slave population grew steadily from its inception until its forced demise with the close of the Civil War. But its urban counterpart reached a peak in its growth sometime between 1830 and 1850 and declined during its last decade. Some cities showed a weakening in their slave populations earlier, and a few declined throughout the forty-year period, 1820 to 1860. Many historians and students of the ante-bellum period have tried to discover the cause for this decline and, in general, their answers have been quite similar. It seemed obvious to them that slavery could flourish only in the production of agricultural staples and that it was incompatible with city and industrial life. Some stressed the fact that profitability from slaves was closely connected to the plantation system, but most agreed that slavery did not gain substantial inroads into urban and industrial life because of some inherent incompatibility.

One of the earliest to state the proposition that slavery could not survive in an urban environment was John Elliott Cairnes, whose book *The Slave Power* attempted to influence British foreign policy during the Civil War. Cairnes believed that slavery was an economic system "unsuited to the functions of commerce; for the soul of commerce is the spirit of enterprise . . . found wanting in communities where slavery exists." Slavery was excluded from manufacturing industry and urban areas because it "could only be carried on at a constant risk of insurrection . . . effectually [preventing] . . . such societies from ever attaining any considerable growth." Thus, Cairnes concluded, "excluded by these causes from the field of manufactures and commerce, slavery finds its natural career in agriculture."[1]

° The author thanks her doctoral committee, Robert W. Fogel, H. Gregg Lewis, and Donald McCloskey, all of the University of Chicago, for assistance in completing "The Economics of Urban Slavery" (unpublished Ph.D. dissertation, University of Chicago, 1972) of which this paper is but a part. *Urban Slavery*, forthcoming, will be an expanded version of this dissertation.

[1] John Elliott Cairnes, *The Slave Power* (Torchbook Edition, 1969; originally published London: London, Parker, Son and Bourn, 1862, p. 71.

231

Some writers, with more than slightly racist overtones, believed that slaves could not be trained and that this fact accounted for the inability of the cities to support an ever-growing slave population. Especially prominent among these writers was Ulrich B. Phillips, whose opinion of the Negro led him to believe that slavery "failed to gain strength in the North because there was no work which [N]egro slaves could perform with notable profit to their masters. . . . [But] in certain parts of the South the system flourished because the work required was simple, the returns were large and the short-comings of [N]egro slave labor were partially offset by the ease with which it could be organized."[2] Another historian to hold similar views on this matter was Lewis Cecil Gray, who questioned "the tendency for the slave to displace free labor where conditions were favorable to producing and marketing the staples." He concluded that a major cause of this tendency was that "the rewards and punishments of the plantation system were more powerful stimuli . . . [to] the primitive Negro . . . than the rewards of industry."[3]

The contention that slavery would never be profitable in urban areas was implicit in Charles W. Ramsdell's natural-limit thesis. Slavery was "a cumbersome and expensive system [which] . . . could show profits only as long as it could find plenty of rich lands to cultivate."[4] Therefore, it could survive only in the production of agricultural staples, and as land became more scarce slavery would eventually decline.

More recently, the issue of urban slavery has been raised by Richard C. Wade in his *Slavery in the Cities*.[5] His general thesis, that slavery declined in the cities because it was incompatible with urban life, goes back to earlier theories, especially Cairnes's. The urban slave, according to Wade, had far more freedom than his rural brother because of various institutional changes in the nature of slavery when it came in contact with an urban area.

The trouble with urban slavery, to Wade, was not that slaves were not trainable, as had been assumed by earlier students of the period. Instead, crucial problems arose because, in fact, they were trained

[2] Ulrich B. Phillips, "The Economic Cost of Slaveholding in the Cotton Belt," *Political Science Quarterly*, xx (June, 1905), pp. 257-275.

[3] Lewis Cecil Gray, *History of Agriculture in the Southern United States to 1860* (Washington: Carnegie Institute of Washington, 1933), p. 470.

[4] Charles W. Ramsdell, "The Natural Limits of Slavery Expansion," *Mississippi Valley Historical Review*, 26, No. 2 (September, 1929), pp. 151-171.

[5] Richard C. Wade, *Slavery in the Cities, The South 1820-1860* (New York: Oxford University Press, 1964).

232

and educated to be profitable investments in their urban and industrial settings. Many slaves were apprenticed to learn a trade; others acquired some form of literacy through the Church or through work necessitated by their jobs. Slaves lived apart from their masters in large numbers in the Southern cities, and although this arrangement proved to be acceptable to the individual owners, it created social problems for the urban centers as a whole. In addition, many slaves were given permission from their masters to hire out their own time, an arrangement under which the slave periodically paid his owner a specified sum of money and managed to find jobs himself. In general, the urban environment gave the slave more freedom and more education, and these contributed to the institution's decline. According to Wade, with the white masters no longer having control over their bondsmen and the white citizenry constantly fearing insurrections, city slaves were sold to the plantations. Thus, the root of the decline of slavery in the cities was the inherent incompatibility between slavery and urban life.

Most of the above explanations of why slavery did not flourish in urban areas conclude that it was not profitable in cities and in industry. Many reasons have been given. Some rely on a discredited belief that the Negro was naturally inferior, and some are based on the assumption that the slave could more easily create problems in the cities than on plantations. But, in general, the belief was that slaves were pushed out of the cities—in other words, that the demand for slaves was declining in these areas. However, if this were true one would expect a decline in city slave prices, possibly an absolute one, but at least a decline relative to plantation prices. Much of the city slave labor force had skills specific to urban areas, but the selling price to plantations of these slaves would be equal to that paid for any other prime field hand. If the city demand were declining, city slave prices should then fall absolutely from their previous levels. In addition, transfer costs, within limits, would put a wedge between the price of a slave in a growing area and one in a declining city area. The puzzling feature about an explanation which relies on a declining demand for city slaves is that urban slave wages continued to rise during the period 1820-1860 and "more than matched the general increase."[6]

---

[6] *Ibid.*, p. 244. Wade also states that "hiring rates continued to rise throughout the last ante-bellum decades," which is exactly when many of the cities' slave populations showed the greatest weakening in numbers. Data collected from archival probate records support this statement of Wade's and

233

An explanation which hinges on a generally declining demand for city slaves fails to come to grips with the fact that the rates of change for the slave population in the various cities fluctuated in magnitude and even in sign over the four decades. While some urban areas had large decreases, others had large increases in their slave populations. The declining-demand theory does not enable us to predict these differences. In fact, the most heavily industrial city, Richmond, showed increases in its slave population throughout the forty-year period 1820 to 1860. Wade's analysis of urban slavery would lead us to predict just the opposite. Richmond should have lost slaves as time wore on, since it contained an unusually high proportion of skilled slave labor. This concentration should have created more severe problems for Richmond than for other cities.

Moreover, the exodus of slaves from cities was greater among the unskilled than the skilled. As 1860 approached, the cities were left with a more highly skilled male slave labor force than they had in earlier periods. Unskilled male slaves were sold to the plantations, but the skilled remained in the cities. This, again, is inconsistent with a "push" theory for the decline in urban slaves. That is, if demand for all types of urban slaves were declining we would not expect any change in the skill-composition of those remaining. Furthermore, if Wade's thesis is correct, if urban masters sold their bondsmen because they no longer felt that they had control over them, we again would not expect a change in the male skill-mix of the type indicated. Presumably the educated and skilled slaves were more hostile to slavery, and hence constituted a greater threat than the uneducated slaves.

Not only were the cities left with a more highly skilled male slave population, but they had more females and fewer children by the eve of the Civil War than previously. Thus, if the cities pushed their slaves out, they did so with much discrimination. While we might be inclined to rationalize the greater exodus of unskilled males and children on the grounds that they constituted a more acute threat to safety than did skilled males and women, no evidence to support such a view has yet been marshalled.

These facts may lead us to doubt the thesis that slaves were pushed from the cities by a declining demand for them in urban areas. The balance of this paper explores the alternative hypothesis that slaves

---

show that the rate of change in wages for slaves in Richmond, Fredericksburg, and Lynchburg averaged 6.8% per year for 1850-1860. Those for more rural areas were about 4-5% annually. See C. Goldin, "The Economics of Urban Slavery" (unpublished Ph.D. dissertation, Chicago, 1972).

234

were pulled from the cities. I will argue that the urban demand for slaves was probably increasing over time, accounting for the evidence we have on city slave prices and wages. In general rural demand was also increasing, perhaps at an accelerating rate. Nevertheless, there is evidence to suggest that many city demand functions were increasing at a rate even greater than was that of the overall supply of slaves. It may seem contradictory to argue that the urban slave population was declining even though the demand for urban slaves increased more rapidly than the aggregate slave population. The contradiction is only apparent. It can be resolved by considering the difference between the elasticity of demand in rural and in urban areas. Differences in these elasticities may also explain changes in the rate of change in the quantity of urban slaves. The alternative hypothesis is consistent with the facts observed previously, that unskilled male slaves were sold to the plantations during periods when the price of slaves was very high, and that male slaves with skills more specific to the cities, and females, were retained there.

II THE DATA

TABLE 7-1 presents data on the slave and free populations for the ten major Southern cities and the rate of change in population for these cities for four decades, 1820 to 1860. In most of these cities the slave population increased from 1820 to approximately 1850 and then declined during the last decade. This slave population peak occurred earlier for these cities as a whole because New Orleans dominates the aggregate figures. But when we observe the percentage changes in the slave population for the four decades the picture becomes clearer. Every city, with the exception of Mobile and New Orleans, shows a cyclical pattern in the percentage rate of change of slaves over the four decades. The percentage increase in slaves for the ten-year periods 1820 to 1830 and 1840 to 1850 is greater (or equivalently the decrease, as in the case of Baltimore, is smaller) than for the other two decennial periods. In addition, the swings of these cycles are very large. Many cities experienced large increases in slaves during the first and third decades and decreases during the other two decades. Other cities—for example, Richmond—experienced increases in their slave populations throughout this forty-year period, but, despite this, the increases were cyclical in rate of change. Therefore, it seems clear that a theory which attempts to explain why slavery did not take root in the cities must be consistent with these large cycles in slave population change.

235

TABLE 7-1   PART A: SLAVE AND FREE[a] POPULATIONS FOR 10 CITIES,
1820-1860

Cities	1820 Slave	1820 Free	1830 Slave	1830 Free	1840 Slave	1840 Free	1850 Slave	1850 Free	1860 Slave	1860 Free
Baltimore, Md.	4357	58381	4120	76500	3199	99114	2946	166108	2218	210100
Charleston, S.C.	12652	12128	15354	14935	14673	14588	19532	23453	13909	26613
Louisville, Ky.	1031	2979	2406	7935	3430	17780	5432	37762	4903	63130
Mobile, Ala.[b]	836	1836	1175	2019	3869	8803	6803	13712	7587	21671
New Orleans, La.	7355	19821	9397	20340	23448	78745	17011	99364	13385	155290
Norfolk, Va.	3261	5217	3756	6058	3709	7211	4295	10031	3284	11336
Richmond, Va.	4387	7680	6345	9715	7509	12644	9927	17643	11699	26211
St. Louis, Mo.[c]	1810	8210	2796	11419	1531	14938	2656	⁻5204	1542	159231
Savannah, Ga.[d]	3075	4448	4000	n.a.[e]	4694	6520	6231	9081	7712	14580
Washington, D.C.	1945	11302	2330	16496	1713	21651	2113	37888	1774	59348

[a] Free white and free black
[b] 1820 Mobile returns are for Mobile County
[c] 1820 and 1830 St. Louis returns are for St. Louis County
[d] No Census population data were given for Savannah for 1830. The 1830 slave figure is an approximation based on the manuscript census figures.
[e] n.a. = not available.
SOURCE: United States Census Office, 4th, 5th, 6th, 7th and 8th Censuses.

PART B: DECENNIAL RATES OF CHANGE, SLAVE AND FREE POPULATIONS
FOR 10 CITIES FOR 4 DECADES

Cities	1820-1830 Slave	1820-1830 Free	1830-1840 Slave	1830-1840 Free	1840-1850 Slave	1840-1850 Free	1850-1860 Slave	1850-1860 Free
Baltimore, Md.	−5 %	31 %	−22 %	30 %	−8 %	68 %	−25 %	26 %
Charleston, S.C.	21	23	−4	−2	33	61	−29	13
Louisville, Ky.	133	166	43	124	58	112	−10	67
Mobile, Ala.	41	10	229	336	76	56	12	58
New Orleans, La.	28	3	150	287	−27	26	−21	56
Norfolk, Va.	15	16	−1	19	16	39	−24	13
Richmond, Va.	45	26	18	30	32	40	18	49
St. Louis, Mo.	54	39	−15	31	73	403	−42	112
Savannah, Ga.	30	n.a.	17	n.a.	33	39	24	61
Washington, D.C.	20	46	−26	31	23	75	−16	57

The ten cities in Table 7-1 were chosen because they were the largest Southern cities whose population statistics could be collected for the period 1820 to 1860. Statistics for the period 1850 to 1860 for twelve other cities having total populations which exceeded 5000 in 1860 can be found in Table 7-2.

These data are useful because they show that there is a small bias in using only the original ten cities' slave populations for the last decade; that is, the percentage decrease in the total urban slave population is lessened by the addition of these cities (see Table 7-2). Data for these and other Southern cities are practially nonexistent for the earlier time period, 1820 to 1840. But, since cities other than the original ten were very small prior to 1850, and were questionably

236

urban in nature, no extensive bias is expected from using the data in Table 7-1.

Tables 7-1 and 7-2 would be more pertinent if they reported the labor force, or at least slaves who were of working age. The five censuses, 1820 to 1860, give age breakdowns for slaves, but the age limits they report are not comparable among all decades. That is, the censuses of 1830 and 1840 had different age breakdowns than

TABLE 7-2   SLAVE POPULATIONS FOR
12 ADDITIONAL CITIES, 1850-1860

Cities	1850	1860
Augusta, Ga.	4718	3663
Alexandria, Va.	1061	1386
Fredericksburg, Va.	1174	1291
Lynchburg, Va.	3424	2694
Memphis, Tenn.	2360	3684
Montgomery, Ala.	2119	4400
Nashville, Tenn.	2028	3226
Natchez, Miss.	3031	2138
Newbern, N.C.	1927	2383
Portsmouth, Va.	1751	934
Petersburg, Va.	4729	5680
Wilmington, N.C.	3031	3777

AGGREGATE URBAN SLAVE POPULATION,
1850-1860, FOR TEN ORIGINAL
CITIES AND TWENTY CITIES

	1850	1860
10 Original Cities	76,900	68,000
22 Cities	108,275	104,228

DECENNIAL RATE OF CHANGE, URBAN
SLAVE POPULATION 1850-1860

	1850-1860
10 Original Cities	−9%
22 Cities	−3%

SOURCE: United States Census Office, 7th Census, 1850 (Washington, 1853). United States Census Office, 8th Census, 1860 (Washington, 1864).

237

TABLE 7-3 AVERAGE ANNUAL RATES OF CHANGE OF SLAVE POPULATIONS
AND LABOR FORCES FOR TEN CITIES, THREE REGIONS,
AND THE UNITED STATES

	Total Population				Labor Force[d]			
	1820-30	30-40	40-50	50-60	1820-30	30-40	40-50	50-60
Baltimore	−.006	−.025	−.008	−.028	+.004	−.023	−.006	−.031
Charleston	+.019	−.005	+.029	−.034	+.018	.000	+.036	−.035
Louisville	+.085	+.035	+.046	−.010	+.098	+.031	+.054	−.018
Mobile	+.034	+.119	+.056	+.011	+.037	+.122	+.062	−.001
New Orleans	+.025	+.091	−.032	−.024	+.015	+.097	−.028	−.028
Norfolk	+.014	−.001	+.015	−.027	+.014	.000	+.016	−.017
Richmond	+.037	+.017	+.028	+.016	+.044	+.025	+.031	+.020
St. Louis	+.043	−.060	+.055	−.054	+.045	−.052	+.055	−.060
Savannah	+.026	+.016	+.028	+.021	+.028	+.017	+.033	+.016
Washington, D.C.	+.018	−.031	+.021	−.017	+.026	−.028	+.021	−.029
Total U.S.	+.027	+.021	+.025	+.021	+.025	+.023	+.029	+.021
[a]New South	+.026	+.095	−.014	−.013	+.017	+.100	−.009	−.019
[b]Old South	+.030	−.003	+.027	−.009	+.024	+.009	+.032	−.008
[c]Border States	+.024	−.017	+.029	−.023	+.032	−.014	+.032	−.030

[a] Mobile, New Orleans
[b] Richmond, Savannah, Charleston, Norfolk
[c] Louisville, Baltimore, Washington, D.C., St. Louis
[d] Defined as that portion of the population between the ages of 10 and 55.

those for 1850 and 1860, and those for 1820 are rather poor. Computation of the labor force figures required these to be reworked. Table 7-3 presents such a reformulation of the data and gives the average annual rate of change[7] for slave populations and slave labor forces for the cities studied. These data will be used in section III to compute the rate of change in the demand for urban versus rural slaves. In this way we can discover why urban slavery appears to have declined during the period immediately preceding the Civil War.

Table 7-4 shows the aggregate slave figures for the United States, and the decennial rates of increase for the four decades. The rate of increase for slaves is again not constant but has small cycles, with greater rates of increase for the first and third than for the second and fourth decades. These cycles have been attributed to the cycles in the importation of mature Negroes prior to the embargo placed on slave importations.[8] That is, the two larger rates of increase are

[7] Average annual rates computed using the formula: $X_{(t+10)} = X_t e^{r(10)}$.

[8] See Alfred H. Conrad and John R. Meyer, "The Economics of Slavery in the Ante-Bellum South," reprinted in Conrad and Meyer, *The Economics of Slavery and Other Studies in Econometric History* (Chicago: Aldine Press, 1964), p. 69. Price data for male and female slaves during the period 1796 to 1810 support this hypothesis. In addition, chlorea epidemics in the 1830s and 1850s served to diminish the slave population for those periods.

238

then a result of the two generations following that of these adult slaves. The other two decades are the periods in the intergenerational cycle. Therefore, the aggregate slave population had cycles of population change that were not as violent as those of the cities. It can be shown that a difference in demand elasticities is a sufficient explanation for these large differences in population change.

TABLE 7-4   TOTAL SLAVE
POPULATION FOR THE UNITED
STATES, 1820-1860
(to nearest thousand)

1820	1,538,000
1830	2,009,000
1840	2,487,000
1850	3,205,000
1860	3,954,000

DECENNIAL RATE OF INCREASE
FOR TOTAL SLAVE POPULATION,
1820-1860

1820-1830	30.6%
1830-1840	23.8
1840-1850	28.8
1850-1860	23.4

SOURCE: United States Census Office, 4th, 5th, 6th, 7th and 8th Censuses.

Section III will test the hypothesis that the demand for urban slave labor, rather than declining during the period 1820 to 1860, was increasing. Critical to the empirical work in that section is a set of urban slave prices. The only slave price data available to previous researchers were those compiled by U. B. Phillips.[9] Phillips used prices for prime male field hands, and these prices in average annual rate-of-change form for four trading areas are given in Table 7-5. They are also presented in deflated form, with the Warren and Pearson

[9] These data are appraised prices and are about 20% lower than actual selling prices. Because they include prices for all slaves appraised they are not absolutely comparable to Phillips' data which are only for prime field hands. A more comprehensive discussion of these price data can be found in C. Goldin, "The Economics of Urban Slavery" (unpublished Ph.D. dissertation, Chicago, 1972) and R. W. Fogel and S. L. Engerman, *Time on the Cross: The Economics of American Negro Slavery* (Boston: Little, Brown and Co., 1974.)

239

GOLDIN

TABLE 7-5   PRICE DATA FOR SLAVES IN AVERAGE ANNUAL RATE OF CHANGE FORM

(1) Four Trading Areas, Phillips and Virginia Cities[a]

	Richmond	Charleston	Mid-Georgia	New Orleans	Virginia Cities
1820-1830	−.050	−.047	−.031	−.032	−.015
1830-1840	+.057	+.044	+.025	+.022	+.044
1840-1850	−.007	+.003	+.011	+.010	+.003
1850-1860	+.054	+.043	+.059	+.049	+.053

[a] Richmond, Fredericksburg, and Lynchburg.
SOURCES: U. B. Phillips, *American Negro Slavery* (Baton Rouge: Louisiana State University, 1966). Virginia city prices were collected from probate records, slave sales and inventories, Genealogical Society, Salt Lake City.

(2) Phillips and Virginia City Prices Deflated by the Warren and Pearson Wholesale Price Index for All Commodities

	Richmond	Charleston	Mid-Georgia	New Orleans	Virginia Cities
1820-1830	−.035	−.032	−.016	−.017	.000
1830-1840	+.053	+.040	+.021	+.018	+.040
1840-1850	+.002	+.012	+.020	+.019	+.012
1850-1860	+.043	+.032	+.048	+.038	+.042

SOURCE: Warren and Pearson Wholesale Price Index, *Historical Statistics of the U.S. Colonial Times to 1957* (Washington: GPO, 1960), p. 115.

wholesale commodity index as the deflator. It is clear that in those decades for which the rate of change of the aggregate slave population was the lowest, the price increase was the greatest. Price data have recently been collected from probate records and other archival sources. Prices for one group of Virginia cities are currently available and are also presented in rate-of-change form in Table 7-5. The rate of change in prices for urban slaves is very similar to that for rural slaves in the same region.

Since the price data for almost all the regions[10] show cyclical changes and the population data for the aggregate United States and the cities show similar oscillations, a hypothesis can be advanced to explain the relative decline of urban slavery. If the demand for urban slaves were more elastic than the demand for rural slaves,[11]

[10] The New Orleans price data do not show the same cyclical pattern that the other data show. In addition, the New South cities, Mobile and New Orleans, also show a pattern of change different from that of the other Southern cities. This is because the period 1830 to 1840 was one of rapid growth for these areas. That is, the 1830 price for the New South was much higher than that for other areas.
[11] This appears to have been the case since substitutes for slave labor in the cities were more readily available and appear to have been closer substitutes

240

then the shifts in the supply function which caused the cyclical changes in price could easily have resulted in the cities' undergoing violent population swings. The larger the difference in these demand elasticities, the more pronounced would be the population cycles in the cities than those for the aggregate.

Furthermore, the demand for urban slaves need not have been declining during any of the decades studied for the equilibrium population or labor force to have been diminishing. The larger the difference in the elasticity of demand between urban and rural slave labor, the greater would be the cycles in the cities versus those for the aggregate. In addition, the larger the elasticity of demand for urban slave labor the greater the shift term in the demand function could have been during a period of rising prices and falling urban slave quantities. That is, the decline of urban slavery during the 1850s could have been the result of urban slave owners' cashing in on their capital gains. The cities may have lost slaves even though their demand functions were moving to the right at a rate faster than that for the aggregate.

The 1850s can be viewed as merely part of an over-all forty-year picture. The two decades 1820 to 1830 and 1840 to 1850 were periods of gains in urban slavery or periods during which cities lost very few slaves. But 1830 to 1840 and 1850 to 1860 were decades during which slavery declined or increased very slowly in the cities. The changes which occurred during these periods need not require diverse explanations. The slave-price data and intuitive reasoning about elasticity differences suggest the more integrative hypothesis put forth above. The entire era in this context was marked by the great flexibility of the urban slave institution. Periods of overall rising prices led to the selling of slaves from the cities (or the hiring out of these slaves), and periods of falling prices led to the reverse situation. The last decade of urban slavery may have represented not the decline of the institution but its very ability to survive in a changing economy. Had emancipation not occurred and had the prices of slaves declined, urban slave quantities might have again increased.

III The Demand for Urban Slaves

I HAVE suggested above that the demand for urban slaves need not have declined during the period 1820 to 1860 even though the equilibrium quantities of urban slaves changed radically. In this sec-

---

than those for agricultural slave labor. In addition, the price elasticity of demand for those goods which used urban slave labor in production was probably greater than the price elasticity of demand for agricultural commodities.

241

tion I will demonstrate that, with a very simple economic model, reasonable elasticity values yield surprisingly strong annual growth rates for urban slave demand.

I will assume that each city or region has a demand schedule for slaves which takes the form:

$$Q_i = D_i P_i^{-e_i}, \tag{1}$$

where Q_i is the quantity of slaves in city or region i, P_i is the price for slaves, D_i is the shift term, and e_i is the (constant) price elasticity of demand. It was this price elasticity of demand which I postulated to be larger for urban than for rural slaves, thus accounting for the strange population and labor force cycles experienced in the cities. In this section I will assign various values to e_i to test the hypothesis which Wade and others stressed that D_i, or the shift term, declined over time. To accomplish this, equation (1) must first be expressed in rate-of-change form. Differentiating totally the logarithmic transform of (1) yields:

$$\overset{*}{Q_i} = \overset{*}{D_i} - e_i \overset{*}{P_i}, \tag{2}$$

where an asterisk ($^\circ$) over any variable indicates the rate of change in that variable.

Solving for $\overset{*}{D_i}$ gives:

$$\overset{*}{D_i} = \overset{*}{Q_i} + e_i \overset{*}{P_i}, \tag{3}$$

which will aid in determining $\overset{*}{D_i}$ for various values of e_i.

Let us assume for the moment that the statistical work to follow demonstrates that $\overset{*}{D_i}$ was positive. This would mean that the demand for urban slaves was increasing. What, though, does this imply about the underlying economic and social forces in these cities? A positive $\overset{*}{D_i}$ need not indicate that all citizens felt secure in the cities and that urban slave owners were not taxed in many ways. That is, we cannot infer that the costs of using slaves in the cities did not rise relative to those of the rural areas as 1860 approached. But we can state unequivocally that these costs were outweighed by other forces such as increases in real income or rising wage rates for alternative labor sources.

The issue of increased taxation on slaves is very interesting and deserves further comment. Many have viewed taxes, jail fees, and badge costs as methods of discouraging urban owners and hirers of

242

slaves from using this form of labor in the cities. That is, many see these fees as internalizing the apparent externalities which slaves imposed on the community. Whether these fees did increase over time has not yet been completely resolved,[12] but the relative value of the fines was small in comparison with yearly slave-hire rates. More importantly, a positive $\overset{*}{D}_i$ shows that even if fines increased they were dwarfed by demand increases stemming from other factors.

To determine whether the demand for urban slaves did increase during the forty-year period 1820 to 1860 on a decadal basis, I have used equation (3) to construct Table 7-6. For each city or group of cities we have data on $\overset{*}{Q}_i$ (in Table 7-3) and $\overset{*}{P}_i$ (in Table 7-5), but not on e_i. Therefore, I have selected three values for e_i (.5, 1, 1.5) to see how sensitive the $\overset{*}{D}_i$ results are to the choice of this parameter. Additional research I have done indicates that these bounds are correct.[13]

The results for the cities are quite impressive. For almost all decades, for almost all cities or urban aggregates, the demand for slaves increased—that is, $\overset{*}{D}_i$ was positive. The only cities for which demand may have declined during the controversial decade 1850 to 1860 are Baltimore, Charleston, New Orleans, and St. Louis. Elasticity values greater than .5 reverse this result for Baltimore and New Orleans, and values greater than 1 yield positive $\overset{*}{D}_i$ for all cities.

One very interesting result is that the decade which appears the weakest in terms of the size of $\overset{*}{D}_i$ is not 1850 to 1860 but 1820 to 1830. This finding is not at all obvious from viewing slave-quantity data alone. In fact, the conclusion that urban slavery was "an institution which had been an integral part of urban life in Dixie in 1820" but which "was languishing everywhere in 1860"[14] is typical. My model, though, suggests that the cities should have been gaining even more slaves during 1820 to 1830 to have shown the demand strength they did during 1850 to 1860, when prices rose tremendously. Although many cities lost slaves during 1850-1860, demand strength in that

[12] More recent work I have done shows that these fees probably did not increase from 1850 to 1860. See C. Goldin, *Urban Slavery: 1820 to 1860,* forthcoming.

[13] I have run regressions on a more complete model, and my estimates of e_i range between .10 and 2.8, with the majority of the cities having an elasticity around 1. These estimates are biased downward because there are no data on the wage rate for free whites and blacks. See Goldin, "The Economics of Urban Slavery" (unpublished Ph.D. dissertation, Chicago, 1972).

[14] R. C. Wade, *op. cit.*, p. 243.

243

TABLE 7-6 AVERAGE ANNUAL RATES OF GROWTH IN THE DEMAND[a] FOR URBAN SLAVE LABOR FORCE FOR THREE VALUES OF e FOR 10 CITIES AND 3 AGGREGATES AND THE U.S.

Decades	Old South[b,e]			New South[d,f]			Border States[d,e]			United States Aggregate[h]		
	$e = .5$	$e = 1$	$e = 1.5$	.5	1	1.5	.5	1	1.5	.25	.5	1
1850–1860	+.013	+.034	+.055	.000	+.019	+.038	−.009	+.012	+.033	+.032	+.043	+.064
1840–1850	+.038	+.044	+.050	.000	+.010	+.017	+.038	+.044	+.050	+.030	+.030	+.031
1830–1840	+.029	+.049	+.069	+.109	+.118	+.127	+.006	+.026	+.046	+.037	+.050	+.076
1820–1830	+.024	+.024	+.024	+.009	.000	−.008	+.032	+.032	+.032	+.014	+.007	−.010

Decades	Baltimore[e]			Charleston[g]			Louisville[e]			Mobile[f]		
	.5	1	1.5	.5	1	1.5	.5	1	1.5	.5	1	1.5
1850–1860	−.010	+.009	+.032	−.019	−.003	+.013	+.003	+.024	+.045	+.018	+.037	+.056
1840–1850	.000	+.006	+.012	+.042	+.048	+.054	+.060	+.066	+.072	+.071	+.080	+.089
1830–1840	−.003	+.017	+.037	+.020	+.040	+.060	+.051	+.071	+.091	+.131	+.140	+.142
1820–1830	+.004	+.004	+.004	+.002	−.014	−.030	+.098	+.098	+.098	+.029	+.020	+.019

Decades	New Orleans[f]			Norfolk[e]			Richmond[e]		
	.5	1	1.5	.5	1	1.5	.5	1	1.5
1850–1860	−.009	+.010	+.029	+.004	+.025	+.046	+.041	+.062	+.083
1840–1850	−.019	−.009	.000	+.022	+.028	+.034	+.037	+.043	+.049
1830–1840	+.106	+.115	+.124	+.020	+.040	+.060	+.045	+.065	+.085
1820–1830	+.007	−.002	−.010	+.014	+.014	+.014	+.044	+.044	+.044

Decades	St. Louis[c]			Savannah[a]			Washington[c]		
	.5	1	1.5	.5	1	1.5	.5	1	1.5
1850-1860	−.039	−.018	+.003	+.032	+.048	+.064	−.008	+.013	+.034
1840-1850	+.061	+.067	+.073	+.039	+.045	+.051	+.027	+.033	+.039
1830-1840	−.032	−.012	+.008	+.037	+.057	+.077	−.008	+.012	+.032
1820-1830	+.045	+.045	+.045	+.012	−.004	−.020	+.026	+.026	+.026

[a] $\overset{*}{D} = \overset{*}{Q} + e\overset{*}{P}$, where $\overset{*}{Q}$ = average annual rate of slave labor force; see Table 7-3.

[b] Richmond, Savannah, Charleston.

[c] Mobile, New Orleans.

[d] Louisville, St. Louis, Washington, D.C., Baltimore.

[e] $\overset{*}{P}$ = Virginia city price average annual rates of change, deflated by Warren and Pearson Wholesale Commodity Index, see Table 7-5.

[f] $\overset{*}{P}$ = Phillips' New Orleans price average annual rate of change, deflated by the Warren and Pearson Index, see Table 7-5.

[g] $\overset{*}{P}$ = Phillips' Charleston price average annual rate of change, deflated by the Warren and Pearson Index, see Table 7-5.

[h] $\overset{*}{P}$ = Phillips' Richmond price average annual rate of change, deflated by the Warren and Pearson Index, see Table 7-5.

257

decade was considerable. The decline of urban slavery did not show any inherent weakness in the institution as many have previously believed. On the contrary, it had developed into a very flexible labor source which responded to economic changes in the entire society.

In many cases the increases in the demand for urban slaves more than matched the increases in the supply of slaves. This implies that the cities were contributing to the increase in the price of slaves or, alternatively, were slowing down any price increases during certain decades.

The shift term for the aggregate demand curve has also been estimated. Consistent with prior reasoning, the e_i values for this exercise are somewhat lower than those for the cities. The computed $\overset{*}{D}_i$ can be compared to those for the cities to see how they fared with respect to rural demand.[15] In general, using low e_i values for the aggregate and large e_i values for the cities yields larger $\overset{*}{D}_i$ for the latter than the former.

IV Concluding Remarks

Students of American history have long questioned whether or not slavery would have survived into the twentieth century in the absence of the Civil War. A great majority of them would reply that, as the South urbanized, slavery would have disappeared because slavery and urbanization are incompatible. This paper demonstrates that, at least for the period 1820 to 1860, urban slavery was a vigorous institution and that slavery was flexible enough to be compatible with urban sprawl.

This paper suggests an economic model which rationalizes the ups and downs of city slave populations. It integrates the apparently weak decade of the fifties into a whole picture, resting its explanation on elasticity differences coupled with general price movements for slaves. It then tests the hypothesis put forth by many that the demand for urban slaves declined toward 1860. This appears to be erroneous. In fact, the cities showed strength in almost all decades. Slaves appear not to have been pushed out of the cities by some inner force, such as the citizens' fear of insurrections. Instead, urban slavery responded to economic changes and slaves were pulled out of cities in the 1850s. Urban slavery appears to have been a vigorous and flexible institution as late as 1860.

[15] Actually, the aggregate shift term is estimated, but this can be shown to be equal to $\lambda \overset{*}{D}_r + (1 - \lambda)\overset{*}{D}_c$, where $\lambda = [Qr/Qr + Qc]$ and r = rural and c = city. If λ is large, $\overset{*}{D}_r$ is a close approximation to the aggregate shift term.

246

Slaves for Hire: The Allocation of Black Labor in Elizabeth City County, Virginia, 1782 to 1810

Sarah S. Hughes

FOR six years near the end of the eighteenth century Fanny Baines hired Jacob, an adult slave, to help her operate the 40-acre farm that she rented in Elizabeth City County, Virginia. In most of these years she paid at least twice as much for Jacob's services as she did for the land. She grew no tobacco, but the corn and beef raised on the farm were evidently profitable enough to allow her to continue to pay cash rent for both land and labor.[1]

The experience of Fanny Baines and Jacob was not unusual, for such hiring was integral to the labor system and the institution of slavery in the county between 1782 and 1810. Few of the county's slaves escaped being hired out. Before their childhood ended, most blacks spent at least a year working as hired servants outside their home household, and such uprootings continued periodically throughout their lives. This practice made slave labor available to nearly all of the free whites. Even tenants and owners of farms as small as 25 acres or less could employ slaves. Residents of the village of Hampton also hired domestic servants from among the women and children on the county's larger farms, while the local shipyards, artisans, and merchants rented the labor of more expensive skilled adult male slaves. Although large farms were a principal source of such labor, nearly anyone who owned one or two slaves might occasionally hire them out.[2]

Rather than being an incidental or peripheral aspect of the slave labor market, such arrangements were the key to the survival of slavery in the county. Hiring was a means of adjusting a labor system initiated when tobacco was the profitable staple crop to the needs of the smaller grain-

Ms. Hughes, of Hampton, Virginia, is working on a study of the population and economy of the lower Chesapeake Bay between 1750 and 1860 in collaboration with Brady A. Hughes of Hampton Institute.
[1] Settlement of the estate of Francis Pool, Elizabeth City County Deeds and Wills, Book 12, 381-382, Courthouse, Hampton, Virginia. Unless otherwise stated, all records in the following notes are from Elizabeth City County.
[2] Sarah S. Hughes, "Elizabeth City County, Virginia, 1782-1810: The Economic and Social Structure of a Tidewater County in the Early National Years" (Ph.D. diss., College of William and Mary, 1975), passim.

260

livestock farms of the late eighteenth century. The hire of slaves introduced flexibility in allocating workers in a diversified rural economy with low profit margins. It also allied the large class of poor white farmers with the wealthy against the enslaved blacks, who composed the majority of the people of the county. The result was a form of slavery different from that associated with plantation agriculture. These differences were not simply economic, for their impact was felt by whites and blacks alike and affected relationships between the two groups.

Historians have long known that slaves throughout the South were often temporarily transferred from owners to other employers by hiring. In the eighteenth century the customs controlling the practices were already well established. The usual period of hire was fifty weeks, beginning in early January and ending shortly before Christmas. At the outset of each new year owners who had a surplus of slave labor met prospective hirers at the courthouses to negotiate privately or to participate in public auctions. The hirer paid a cash rent and assumed the costs of feeding, clothing, and housing the slaves, as well as medical expenses and slave taxes. By the beginning of the nineteenth century the courts had defined the responsibilities of lessor and lessee in instances of death, injury, or escape of a hired slave.[3] Despite our general knowledge of the subject, however, there has been little systematic investigation of the incidence and importance of slave hiring in any large region of the South at any period. Most studies have concentrated on the use of hired slaves in cities and industries just before the Civil War. Little is known about the hiring of slaves in the eighteenth century or about their employment in agriculture.[4]

---

[3] On the essential point that the person who hired a slave paid the personal property tax for the year, see the entry of Miles King, executor of Francis and Mary Mallory, "paid taxes of the negroes that could not be hired out in 1789, 1790, and 1791" (Deeds and Wills, Book 34, 102); and Kenneth M. Stampp, *The Peculiar Institution: Slavery in the Ante-Bellum South* (New York, 1956), 68 and 414. The Virginia courts ruled on many of the conflicts that arose between owners and hirers of slaves. An important 1806 decision declared that "where one hires a slave for a year, that if the slave be sick or run away, the tenant must pay the hire; but if the slave die without any fault in the tenant, the owner and not the tenant, should lose the hire," because such death was an act of God. George v. Elliott, 2 Hen. and M. 5, in Helen Tunnicliff Catterall, ed., *Judicial Cases concerning American Slavery and the Negro*, I (Washington, D.C., 1926), 113.

[4] See Richard C. Wade, *Slavery in the Cities: The South, 1820-1860* (New York, 1964), chap. 2; Frederic Bancroft, *Slave-Trading in the Old South* (Baltimore, 1931), chap. 7; Robert Evans, Jr., "The Economics of American Negro Slavery, 1830-1860," in Universities-National Bureau Committee for Economic Research, *Aspects of Labor Economics* (Princeton, N.J., 1962); Clement Eaton, "Slave-Hiring in the Upper South: A Step toward Freedom," *Mississippi Valley Historical Review*, XLVI (1960), 663-670; Richard B. Morris, "The Measure of Bondage in the Slave States,"

During the period under consideration Elizabeth City County, now incorporated as the city of Hampton, was a small rural district on the lower western shore of Chesapeake Bay. At the end of the Revolution it had 2,450 inhabitants, of whom 1,298 were slaves; in 1810, of the county's 3,600 people, 1,734 were slaves. The number of free blacks was very small: eighteen in 1790 and eighty-five in 1810. Three-fourths of the population lived on farms, the remainder in the village of Hampton. The county's location at the tip of a peninsula, jutting into Chesapeake Bay and bounded on the south by the James River, gave its farmers access to the West Indies trade, to ships provisioning for sea voyages, and to the markets of the growing city of Norfolk across the roadstead. This advantageous position seems to have been the principal factor in the commerical success of farms of remarkably small size. Sixty-two percent of the farms of Elizabeth City County were under 101 acres, 33 percent were 101-500 acres, and only 6 percent contained more than 500 acres. It is especially striking that 21 percent were smaller than 26 acres, and 42 percent were under 51. Despite the distribution of land into small parcels, the county was no model of a Jeffersonian society of independent yeomen. Tenancy was widespread; by 1810 about one-third of the land was held by absentee owners and one-half was farmed by tenants. The presence of adult sons and daughters in farm households indicates a surplus of free labor—yet one-half of the population was held in slavery.[5]

All farms of one hundred or more acres were worked by slaves. Ninety-two percent of the farmers owning from 51 to 100 acres used slave labor, as did 76 percent of those owning 50 acres or less. Over one-half (54 percent) of the farms using no slaves were 25 acres or less. By the time of the Revolution tobacco was no longer a crop of commercial importance in Elizabeth City County. Cattle and corn had become the principal products on farms of all sizes. The county had nearly four times as many cattle per hundred persons (including slaves) as did ten counties of southeastern Pennsylvania where livestock was fattened for the Philadelphia market. Cattle were more numerous than swine on most farms. Barreled beef and pork, along with corn, were sold to the ship provisioners of Hampton Roads or exported to the West Indies. Secondary products such as lamb, butter, poultry, cider, oats, wheat, and tobacco were marketed in Norfolk.[6]

The hiring of slaves had become well-established in the county before the Revolution. By the 1780s it was pervasive, and its continuance to 1810 is

ibid., XLI (1954), 219-240; Robert S. Starobin, *Industrial Slavery in the Old South* (New York, 1970); and Ulrich Bonnell Phillips, *American Negro Slavery: A Survey of the Supply, Employment and Control of Negro Labor as Determined by the Plantation Régime* (New York, 1918), chap. 20.

[5] Hughes, "Elizabeth City County," chaps. 2, 6, 7.
[6] *Ibid.*, chaps. 2, 3, 8.

indicated by several sorts of records. Although no contracts specifying terms of hire have been found, the common practice of renting slaves is well documented in personal property tax lists, probate records, and papers relating to the sale or mortgage of personal property or the manumission of slaves. For the beginning of the period, the personal property tax records of 1784, 1785, and 1786 list the given names of slaves after the name of each taxpayer.[7] These lists of slaves show extreme discontinuity within households; one rarely finds exactly the same group of slaves in a household in all three years, indicating that the majority of slaves so listed were not actually owned by the taxpayer. Although some changes can be attributed to births, deaths, or transfers by inheritance, purchase, or sale of slaves, the evidence demonstrates that these were not primary factors.[8] Rather, the discontinuities in household composition are largely explained by the hiring of slaves. Since it was customary for the person who hired a slave in January to pay the annual personal property tax, the hirer's name can be expected to appear on the tax list that was compiled in the late spring of each year; the slaves listed after a taxpayer's name may have been either owned or hired by that person. Thus, the tax records prove a guide not to the ownership of slaves, but to the use of slave labor.

The present study employs a sample of 25 percent of those who paid personal property taxes on slaves in order to estimate the extent of slave hiring. The fifty-seven people in the sample represent a random selection of owners of farms of 1-25, 26-50, 51-100, 101-200, 201-500, and over 500 acres in approximate proportion to the number of each in the county's population, as well as of tenants, residents of Hampton, farmers with major sources of nonfarm income, and free blacks.[9] Probate records, bills of sale, manu-

[7] In these years slaves of all ages are listed; after 1787 only those older than 11 years were taxed. Although the total number of adult slaves (16 years or older) of each taxpayer is shown, the names are usually arranged in random order, so that adults cannot be distinguished from children. Personal Property Tax Records, Elizabeth City County, Virginia State Library, Richmond.

[8] Careless or fraudulent tax returns are a negligible factor because errors in the tithable lists were corrected each year by the county grand jury and court.

[9] See Hughes, "Elizabeth City County," Table II, chap. 6. Tenants and Hampton residents were probably underrepresented by the decision to use 10 names from each group; the total number of each of these two groups in 1784 is not known; free blacks (1), owners of over 500 acres (4), and farmers with major sources of nonfarm income (4) are overrepresented because of their importance as slaveholders. The latter group included a merchant, an owner of a shipyard, the holder of the Norfolk ferry concession, and a ship captain, each of whom owned over 200 acres of farm land as well. Selection of only seven women almost certainly underestimates their importance as owners of slaves, judging from the evidence in wills and inventories, but supports other evidence that women slaveowners, except those who were actually operating farms, normally hired out slaves. Only those who had slave labor in their households for at least two of the three years were chosen for the sample.

TABLE I

ANNUAL HIRE OF SLAVES IN ELIZABETH CITY COUNTY, 1784, 1785, AND 1786, AMONG FIFTY-SEVEN TAXPAYERS

Type of Taxpayer	Not Involved in Slave Hire		Hired or Hired Out Slaves		
	Taxed on Same Slaves, 1784–1786	Possible Natural Increase or Decrease	Definitely Hired Slaves	Definitely Hired Out slaves	Either Hired and/or Hired Out Slaves
Tenants	1		7		2
Owners of:					
1–25 acres	2		1		1
26–50 acres			4		1
51–100 acres			5		3
101–200 acres	1	2			4
201–500 acres				1	3
over 500 acres				2	2
Farm and nonfarm income:					
Hampton residents			6	1	4
Free black			1		3
Total	No. 4	No. 2	No. 24	No. 4	No. 23
	% 7.0	% 3.5	% 42.1	% 7.0	% 40.3
Subtotal	No. 6		No. 51		
	% 10.5		% 89.4		

Source: Personal Property Tax Records. Elizabeth City County, 1784, 1785, 1786, Virginia State Library, Richmond.

missions, mortgages, and land tax lists provide additional data about the slaves of thirty-five of the fifty-seven taxpayers. Table I summarizes the analysis of the sample.

Nearly 90 percent of the taxpayers in the sample were involved, either as lessor or lessee, in the hire of slaves. Only 236, or 39 percent, of the 600 slaves in the sample lived in the same household for three consecutive years. The sample demonstrates the prevalence of hiring but it cannot be used for a precise measure of the percentage of slaves hired out each year because some residents known to have hired or hired out slaves are excluded by the nature of the records. For example, the names of those who hired out all their slaves and who were not liable for taxes on other personal property do not appear on the tax lists. Similarly anyone who retained the same slave in his household between 1784 and 1786 was considered in this analysis of the tax lists to have owned, rather than hired, the slave, although estate settlements show that it was not unusual for a person to hire the same slave for several years. These considerations suggest that the actual proportion of people who engaged in slave hiring must have been larger than the sample indicates. In contrast, in tracing the movement of slaves from household to household on the tax lists there is usually no way to identify which slaves were sold or purchased, or were born or died. In the following discussion of individual cases in the sample, the possibilities other than hiring are considered.

Though historians believe that hiring was widespread in Virginia in the late antebellum period, their highest guesses suggest that only about 3 percent of the state's slaves were hired out each year. The proportion hired out in Elizabeth City County in the mid-1780s must have been far greater.[10] Historical studies to date do not furnish comparable data by which to judge whether hiring on the scale observed in the county in the 1780s was normal, or reflected a regional pattern, or represented an atypical phase in the adjustment of the numbers of bonded workers to changing economic conditions. There is some evidence of extensive hiring elsewhere in Virginia near the end of the eighteenth century. The largest slaveowner in the state, Robert Carter, hired out over two-thirds of his 509 slaves in 1791. After the Revolution, Carter retained personal management of only two of his eighteen farms. He rented out the others, usually in units of about 100 acres, complete with slaves, livestock, and equipment; an individual rent was charged for each slave. He also hired out some slaves separately, and he occasionally hired slaves with special skills.[11] Other owners sometimes advertised as many

[10] Frederic Bancroft estimated over 15,000 Virginia slaves were hired out annually in the 1850s (*Slave-Trading in the Old South*, 404-405). Stampp accepted Bancroft's figure (*Peculiar Institution*, 67-68). In 1850 there were 472,528 slaves in Virginia.

[11] Louis Morton, *Robert Carter of Nomini Hall: A Virginia Tobacco Planter of the Eighteenth Century* (Williamsburg, 1945), 76-77, 106-107, and Appendix Tables 4 and 9.

as thirty slaves for hire, and newspaper accounts of runaways indicate that some escaped slaves had been hired.[12] Gerald W. Mullin notes an increased demand by Virginia businesses for hired slaves at the time of the Revolution. This demand, he suggests, could be met because the "supply was increased, as many tidewater planters switched to general farming and wheat growing, and hired out slaves they could not profitably employ."[13]

Unfortunately, although the tax lists demonstrate that births, deaths, and sales cannot account for the magnitude of annual turnover, it is not possible in twenty-three cases (40 percent of the sample) to determine who was hiring slaves and who was hiring them out. For example, Henry Jenkins, who owned a 200-acre farm, paid taxes on the following slaves:

1784	1785	1786
Sam[1]		
Nan	Nan	Nan
Sall		
Sarah	Sarah	Sarah
Judy	Judea	
Sam[2]	Sam	Sam
Moll	Moll	Moll
		Joe
		Kate
		India

If it is assumed that there were no births, deaths, or sales[14] in the three years, then (1) did Jenkins own only four slaves (Nan, Sarah, Sam[2], and Moll), and hire Sam[1], Sall, and Judy in 1784, Judea only in 1785, and India, Kate, and Joe in 1786, or (2) did he own all ten slaves, and hire out India, Kate, and Joe in 1784 and 1785, Sam[1] and Sall also in 1785, and Sam[1], Sall, and Judy in 1786, or (3) did he own no slaves and hire between five and seven each year?

---

[12] Robert McColley, *Slavery and Jeffersonian Virginia* (Urbana, Ill., 1964), 79; *Norfolk Weekly Journal*, 1797-1798; *American Gazette, and Norfolk and Portsmouth Weekly Advertiser* (Norfolk), 1795-1796; Thad W. Tate, *The Negro in Eighteenth-Century Williamsburg* (Williamsburg, Va., 1965), 103; Phillips, *American Negro Slavery*, 406.

[13] *Flight and Rebellion: Slave Resistance in Eighteenth-Century Virginia* (New York, 1972), 87. Mullin's brief discussion of hiring, focused on slaves employed in industries and urban occupations, does not consider the market for hired slaves among farmers.

[14] If Henry Jenkins's two adult slaves in 1785 were both women, they might have borne three children in 1786 if one had twins. But, the probable incidence of multiple births could not explain all of the similar cases found in the records.

Another example is that of Sam Bright, one of the few slaves in the sample whose given name and surname are both recorded. In 1784 Bright's taxes were paid by Thomas Wootten, but in 1785 by Richard Barron. Lacking other records, there is no way to determine whether Wootten, Barron, or someone else actually owned Sam Bright and who was earning the profits from his hire.

Fortunately, for over 49 percent of the sample it is possible to determine whether a taxpayer was a lessor or lessee of slaves, either from the evidence of the tax lists alone or from supplemetary sources that establish the ownership of the slaves who appear on a tax list. In fewer cases the age and sex of hired slaves can also be determined.

It is remarkable that in a sample in which forty-five of the fifty-seven taxpayers had fewer than ten slaves (in 1784), only four paid taxes on exactly the same slaves in all three years. One of these was a tenant who paid for two children. Two owned farms of 15 and 17 acres; one of these used the labor of two adults and two children, while the other had one adult and one child. The fourth owned 125 acres, on which he employed four adults and two children. The wills and inventories of two of the four, Baldwin Shepard Morris (the tenant) and Joseph Nichols (the possessor of the 125-acre farm), prove that they did own their slaves.[15]

Equally remarkable, only two other taxpayers had holdings of slaves in which all the changes might be reasonably attributed to natural causes. Both William Gooch and John Cary owned medium-size farms. Gooch had fewer slaves than usual for one who owned 110 acres. In 1784 he was taxed for two adults—Abby and Hanna—and two children—Harry and Murtilla—one of whom was evidently fifteen years old. By 1785 one child, Murtilla, had apparently died; in 1786 another, Tom, was born. Tom, too, probably died in childhood, for Gooch's will of 1792 names Abby, Hannah, and Harry, but mentions neither Tom nor other children. His pessimistic phrasing about the distribution of the increase of his slaves, "if there should be any increase," points to the hazards of counting on capital gains from births, although Gooch may have sold children born to Abby and Hannah before he died.[16] John Cary, who owned 175 acres, had more slaves than was usual on a farm of that size. Though he had slightly over half again as much land as Gooch, he held over five times as many slaves. Cary paid taxes in 1784 for twenty-one slaves—nine adults and twelve children—eighteen of whom remained on his list each year. Two slaves apparently died in 1785, and one in 1786, but one child was also born in each of those years.

[15] Inventory of Baldwin S. Morris, Deeds and Wills, Book 12, 556-557. Will of Joseph Nichols, ibid., 544-545; inventory and estate sale, ibid., Book 33, 135.
[16] Will of Mar. 18, 1792, recorded Oct. 25, 1792, ibid., Book 34.

Who hired slaves? Several distinct groups of hirers can be identified, each tending to employ slaves of certain ages, sex, or skills. Tenants and owners of small farms, hiring relatively few slaves, were the largest group who definitely leased slave labor; they number seventeen, or 30 percent, of the taxpayers's sample. Seven were tenants, and ten owned farms ranging from 8 to 100 acres. The proportion of children hired was significantly high among this group. Since these seldom were children hired out with their mothers, they were probably boys and girls of ten to fifteen years, who frequently worked on one farm one year and on another the next. Six Hampton residents (11 percent of the sample) employed mainly women and children to do domestic work. A third category of hirers included wealthier persons who could afford to employ adult male slaves and who often hired out some of their female and child slaves. These Hampton artisans, merchants, shipbuilders, and ship-owners, together with owners of large farms, created a market for the hire of adult male slaves, probably often skilled or semi-skilled, whose labor commanded premium rates. No names of slaves hiring their own time appear in the tax lists for 1782-1810; presumably, a free person paid the taxes of such slaves. The existence of self-hire among slaves is occasionally shown by deeds of manumission, probate records, and grand jury presentments, but such slaves composed only a small proportion of all slaves hired in the county.

Fifteen taxpayers (21 percent of the sample), who owned no slaves, hired black workers; they paid taxes on different individuals in each of the three years. Six were tenants who could usually afford only one adult, or one adult and one child. Three owned small farms (8, 37½, and 100 acres) and normally hired one adult and one child, or two adults, each year. The remaining six were Hampton residents who employed from one to three slaves.

Another group, composed primarily of small farm owners, either owned or hired for a longer term the one or two slaves whose names appear after theirs in each of the three years, but also hired others. This is the most likely explanation, for example, of those instances where a male slave appears consistently among changing companions. Typical of these taxpayers was William Sandy, a tenant, whose adult slave Cutty is listed each year together with a different hired child. Also in this group was John Rosano, a free black, who held his wife Rachel as a slave in 1784 and 1785, and also paid taxes on another adult male, Harry, in 1784 and on a child, Jack, in 1785, but who had no taxable slaves in 1786. Seven farmers who owned and hired slaves had farms of 26 to 100 acres. William Hatton (58 acres) paid in 1784 for Nanny and two nameless children; in 1785 for the children Judith and Ballard; in 1786 for an adult woman, Lucy, and for two children, Ned and Ballard. After Hatton's death, thirteen years later, Ballard was hired out by the estate, an indication that he was or had become the property of Hatton.[17] Similarly, Thomas Payne (35 acres) owned Jack, one of two adult males on whom he paid taxes each year; in 1791 Jack was part of his security for a small debt, and in his will in 1801 he provided for Jack's eventual manumission.[18]

The employers of groups of adult men are much more difficult to trace because the wealthy citizens who could afford their labor also usually owned relatively large numbers of slaves, some of whom were hired out in the same years in which prime or skilled male laborers were hired. A similar pattern is common to a number of these tax lists: a basic group of women and children appears each year (or in two of the three years), along with two to five adult men listed in only one of the years. While it is usually impossible to tell for any given year whether these men were hired or hired out, such a pattern is indicative of a specialized market for adult male slaves. For instance, a farmer who owned a slave woman and her young children might have hired one or two men each year. In addition to their value in heavy farm work, these men were needed in the maritime economy of the county as sailors and as workers for the shipyards and docks of Hampton.

The small-scale maritime industries of Hampton created a fluctuating job market for hired labor, both free and slave. George Hope was typical of the employers who needed men with particular skills. Hope, who operated the largest shipyard in Hampton in this period and owned more than 500 acres (divided into several farms), hired both free and slave adult males each year. In 1784 he hired six free males and five adult male slaves; in 1785, five free males and two adult male slaves; and in 1786, four free males and no slaves. In the following twelve years the number of adult slaves on whom Hope paid taxes continued to fluctuate as his business increased or decreased. In 1792, for instance, he paid taxes on twelve adult slaves, in 1794 on twenty-four, and in 1798 on thirteen. At the same time, he hired out several women and children each year; their names appear, disappear, and reappear in the listings of Hope's taxes.

The people who hired out slaves had backgrounds nearly as diverse as those who were hirers. Three broad groupings of the former can be identified. The twenty-six households (in a total of 231) in 1784 with sixteen to fifty slaves resident (42 percent of all county slaves) had the largest surplus of labor for hire. Those with smaller holdings also leased out slaves from time to time. The third group comprised an unknown number of slave masters, especially women and orphans, who leased all their slaves to others each year,

[17] Estate sale and settlement, William Hatton, *ibid.*, Book 33, 203-204.
[18] Deed of trust, Aug. 20, 1791, Thomas Payne to Charles Bayley, *ibid.*, Book 34; will of Thomas Payne, *ibid.*, Book 12, 94.

had no other taxable personal property, and therefore make no appearance in the tax lists.

John Rogers, a Hampton merchant, was probably typical of many owners of a few slaves who hired out one or two occasionally or regularly. In 1784 he paid taxes for three adult slaves, Lucy, Nanny, and Robin, and two children, Thomas and Sampson. He also owned another child, Lidia, about eight years old, who must have been hired out in 1784. The following year he was taxed for Lidia but not for Nanny and Robin. Since Robin's name reappears on Rogers's 1786 list, he had almost certainly been hired out in 1785, while Nanny may have been hired out for two years, died, or been sold.[19]

Westwood Armistead and Mary Mallory owned and hired out more slaves each year than did John Rogers. They were typical of the small number of planters whose large holdings of slaves were the most important source of adult black workers for hire. Armistead's estate inventory of 1786 shows him to have owned 999 acres of farm land and fourteen slaves. Comparison of names on the inventory with those on the tax lists reveals that he had hired out four adult men in 1784 and 1785, and retained on his farm five adult women and their children.[20]

Mary Mallory's ownership of over forty slaves placed her among the largest slaveholders of the county. Exceptionally complete records for the estate of her husband, Colonel Francis Mallory, who died in 1781, and of her own after her death in 1788 make it possible to determine which men, women, and children were used in her household and which were hired out in each of the three years (Table II). Mary Mallory kept about two-thirds of her slaves to farm 250 acres and to maintain her extravagant mode of life. She hired out about one-half of the men and one-third of the women and the children, either older children hired out separately or younger ones employed with their mothers. The same four men, three women, and three small children were hired out in each of the three years; four men, five women, and seventeen children (including six infants) were never hired out; and

[19] Lucy, the wife of Caesar Tarrant, was manumitted by Rogers in 1793, but their children, Sampson and Lidia, were not freed. When Rogers sold Lidia in 1801, he said she was 25 years old. He had inherited Lucy and her children from his wife's father, the elder Robert Brough, who died in 1770. See instrument of emancipation, Jan. 21, 1793, Lucy and Nancy Tarrant, will of Caesar Tarrant, Feb. 19, 1797, in which he calls Lidia, Sampson, and Nancy (born in 1791) his children. *Ibid.*, Book 34; and bill of sale, John Rogers to Robert Brough, Sept. 1, 1801, *ibid.*, Book 12, 102. Note that without these additional documents it would have been reasonable to assume that Lidia was born in 1785.

[20] Inventory of July 17, 1786, *ibid.*, Book 34. This inventory was taken about two months after the 1786 tax lists were compiled. During the three years, two children were born to Armistead's slaves and one died. His inventory shows little farm equipment for so large an acreage, so he probably used his slaves primarily for domestic work and may have leased his land to tenants.

TABLE II

NUMBER OF MALLORY SLAVES, BY SEX AND AGE, HIRED OUT AND RETAINED
FOR USE ON THE MALLORY FARM, 1784 TO 1786[a]

Number of Slaves	1784	1785	1786
Adult Men			
Hired Out	5	6	6
Retained	6	5	7
Total	11	11	13
Adult Women			
Hired Out	4	3	6
Retained	7	8	8
Total	11	11	14
Children			
Hired Out	4	7	6
Retained	15	16	13
Total	19	23	19
All Slaves			
Hired Out	13	16	18
Retained	28	29	28
Total	41	45	46

Note: [a] None of the Mallory slaves died or were sold between 1784 and 1786. Either seven or eight babies were born in these years.

Source: Personal Property Tax Recs.; Inventory, Dec. 31, 1788, and Partial Settlement of the Estate of Francis and Mary Mallory, Elizabeth City County Deeds and Wills, Book 34, 102–106, 116, 431–438.

three men, three women, and five children were hired out in some years but not in others. A large proportion of the most valuable adult slaves were hired out, while children made up about one-half of the number retained.[21]

Other important sources of slaves for hire are not recorded in the tax lists. These were slaves owned by estates in process of settlement (a period that might extend anywhere from one to twenty years, or even longer), by absentees, by orphans, and by women, all of whom depended on the income from their hired slave labor. Documentary evidence for such cases exists in only a few instances, and the traces of each group remaining in the records are undoubtedly a poor measure of their importance. Women and orphans were probably the most significant "invisible" owners, although absentee ownership may have become more important after the large-scale out-migration of county residents just before 1800.

[21] Inventory, Dec. 31, 1788, and partial settlement of the estates of Francis and Mary Mallory, *ibid.*, Book 34, 102-106, 116, 431-438.

Slaves who could be hired out were the most secure and profitable property a person could leave for the maintenance of dependent heirs at a time when land rent was low, stocks and bonds a speculation, and life insurance little used. Estate planning among the wealthy recognized this fact in wills that specified that slaves were to be hired out annually by the executors for the benefit of heirs.[22] Bequests sometimes included the hire of slaves. Robert Sandefur Russell gave his housekeeper, Mary Saunders, "two years hire of Jem and Ben after their being hired out to pay my debts."[23] Among those who owned few slaves the division of hire could be complicated. Judy Saunders's will said that her "Negro man Will should be hired out by my executor for seven years, the first three years hire I give to my son Robert Saunders towards boarding, clothing, and schooling him, the fourth years hire to my daughter Mary Saunders, the fifth years hire to my daughter Ann Saunders, the sixth years hire to my grand-daughter Mary Saunders, and the seventh years hire to be equally divided between my other two grandchildren, James Saunders Wilson and Ann Wilson."[24] Slaves could also be hired out at the discretion of the estate administrator. Though it was rare for the court to receive a detailed list of the names of such slaves and the amount of annual hire, it is probable that a number of the unitemized credits in estate accounts resulted from the hire of slaves.[25]

The names of a number of women and orphans who definitely owned slaves are also missing from the tax lists. In many cases it cannot be proved

[22] A good example of this type of will is that of Robert Armistead, which names 11 of his 36 inventoried slaves who were to be hired out annually for the support of his mother and daughter. The 10 men and women to be hired out were nearly one-half of his 22 able-bodied adult slaves. Armistead expected his widow to support herself with her dower share of the land and personal property. His will also specified that residual cash be "placed in the Treasury of Virginia," an investment that was rare among county residents. Will of Nov. 12, 1792, and inventory of Feb. 19, 1793, *ibid.*, Book 34.

[23] He also lent Mary Saunders for life the bulk of his other property, including two adult women and two child slaves. The women either died soon afterwards or were also hired out, for Mary Saunders paid no tithable tax on adult slaves until 1809, and then on only one person, although she paid tax on the land lent her by Russell every year from 1801 to 1810. Will of Nov. 5, 1798, recorded July 26, 1799, *ibid.*; Personal Property and Land Tax Records, Elizabeth City County, 1801 and 1810, Va. St. Lib.

[24] Will of July 2, 1794, recorded July 23, 1795, Deeds and Wills, Book 34.

[25] For instance, Robert Smelt's will specifically directed his executors to sell his slaves, but they were hired out for three years before they were sold. Will of May 3, 1795, and settlement of Jan. 23, 1800, *ibid.*, 518-519. Only 16 estate accounts itemized the hire of slaves. In every case in which it is known that all slaves of an estate were hired out, the name of the deceased owner disappeared from the personal property tax lists, but, if the slaves of a deceased owner were not *all* hired out, the person's name remained on the tax list with a notation of "deceased" or "estate" after it.

that these omissions do not result from the death or sale of the slave, or from the removal of the owner from the county, or, in the case of a woman, from her marriage to a man who assumed responsibility for her taxes. The best evidence for the existence of these invisible owners comes from bills of sale or deeds of emancipation that relate the history of a slave's ownership, and these records do yield instances of hiring out.

Sarah Brough, who was born in Hampton before 1770 and died there, unmarried, in 1806, never paid personal property taxes. Yet in 1792 she acquired a thirty-year-old man, Jack Hampton, from the division of her father's estate, and he must have been hired out between that date and 1804, when he was manumitted.[26] Her sister, Amelia Brough, who was a retail merchant in Hampton, owned a number of adult slaves, both inherited and purchased, but her name appears only on the personal property tax lists for 1804, when she paid for one adult slave, and 1810, when she paid for one child. Since some of the slaves she owned during these years are listed in her will of 1821, she must have been hiring out her adult slaves in most years, while possibly retaining the services of the children.[27]

That single or widowed women commonly hired out adult slaves is implied by the fact that although they inherited slaves more often than land, fewer women paid taxes on slaves than on land. This disparity could also have resulted from the fact that slaves were easily moved across county lines within Virginia.[28] These considerations raise the difficult questions of absentee ownership and migration of slaves with their owners. Sarah and Mary Armistead, unmarried daughters of William Armistead, lived in the county until after their father's death in 1799, then moved to Norfolk for several years, but returned to the county by 1809. They owned slaves deeded to them by their father in 1793, others inherited under his will, and still others

[26] Will of Robert Brough, Mar. 1, 1770, original will 160, Courthouse, Hampton, Va.; will of Sarah Brough, Apr. 6, 1808, original will 408; deed of manumission, Sarah Brough to Jack Hampton, Jan. 1, 1804, *ibid.*, Book 12, 285; Personal Property Tax Recs., 1782-1804. There is no evidence that Sarah Brough migrated from the county at any time.

[27] Amelia Brough was one of the few women whose continued residence in the county can be proven, since she paid the $15 retail merchant's tax each year from 1800 to 1810. Personal Property Tax Recs., 1782-1810; bill of sale, Deeds and Wills, Book 12, 356; original will 514. In 1810 she had three slaves living in her household, two of whom were under 12 years old. Other similar cases are discussed in Hughes, "Elizabeth City County," chap. 4.

[28] The numbers of women paying personal property and land taxes are compared in Hughes, "Elizabeth City County," appendix 2. A woman who was lent slaves for life could not, under the Virginia law of dower, take the slaves outside the state. If she tried to do so, she forfeited her rights to all property in the estate. William W. Hening, ed., *The Statutes at Large; Being a Collection of All the Laws of Virginia* . . . (Richmond, 1809-1823), V, 444-448, XII, 145.

purchased after his death. Although they paid no taxes on their slaves until their return to the county, some of the slaves were left there and hired out while the sisters were living in Norfolk. And after returning to the county, the sisters continued to hire out slaves either in Elizabeth City County or in Norfolk, as evidenced by their paying taxes on far fewer slaves than they owned.[29] Mary Young, of Hampton, had six slaves working in adjacent York County in 1810.[30] The only other evidence of the hiring out of slaves to persons in other counties is that three of the twenty-three people who hired slaves owned by estates in probate between 1787 and 1803 were not county residents. There is no way to estimate the extent of inter-county hiring, whether of slaves owned by county residents and sent to work elsewhere or of those left in the county after their owners migrated. The most reasonable assumption is, however, that the well-established practice of slave hire was not limited by county lines, especially when the free population moved easily and frequently across them.

During the period under study Elizabeth City County's population and economy changed significantly. Especially remarkable is the high rate of geographic mobility between 1782 and 1810, when more than half of the free population left every ten years. These emigrants were partially replaced by newcomers from adjacent counties, who made up about one-fourth of the county's free population by 1810. During the decade 1795-1804 the slave population declined sharply, though in the following six years, 1805-1810, its growth once more paralleled that of the free population. These years of intense movement altered the demographic composition of the county. In 1786, 57 percent were slaves and 43 percent were free. By 1810, 50 percent were slaves and 50 percent were free.[31] The departure of free residents was

[29] By 1800 the Armistead sisters owned 22-25 slaves, and in 1802 they bought three men from their brother for $545. William Armistead's deeds of gift of Oct. 3, 1793, and will of Aug. 23, 1799, Deeds and Wills, Book 34; bill of sale, Jan. 12, 1802, *ibid.*, Book 12. In 1809 they paid taxes on five adults and one child aged 12-16, and in 1810, on five adults and two children aged 12-16. In the latter year they owned 81 acres of land, and 12 slaves lived in their census household. Personal Property and Land Tax Recs., 1794-1810. Although they paid no taxes on slaves they owned for 14 years between 1794 and 1809, the records of their father's estate indicate that some of their slaves were hired to work on the family land in 1800, for Sarah Armistead was paid £18 and Mary Armistead £24 for "hire of Negroes." Settlement of estate of William Armistead, Sr., Deeds and Wills, Book 33, 87-88.

[30] The York County manuscript census returns differ from those of surrounding counties in noting 11 absentees whose slaves remained in York County. U.S. Bureau of the Census, Population Schedules of the Third Census of the United States, 1810 (M-14720), Microcopy No. 252, Roll 71. Mary Young paid the tax on one black adult in Elizabeth City County in 1794, but she paid no taxes on slaves in the county in later years. Personal Property Tax Recs., 1782-1810.

[31] Hughes, "Elizabeth City County," chap. 3. Slaves were 58% of the population in 1800, and though their percentage in the population declined steadily afterwards, they remainded a majority until 1810.

partly responsible for a sharp increase in the amount of absentee-owned land; investments by nonresident merchants and planters also contributed to that increase. By 1810, 33 percent of the farms and 36 percent of the total county acreage were owned by absentees.[32] About one-third of the free farm workers, by 1810, were tenants, mainly farming land owned by nonresidents. These tenants, like farm owners, relied on slave labor, although they were more likely to employ only children than were farm owners. Thirty-one percent of the tenants, but only 17 percent of the landowners, had slave children (under sixteen years) on their farms, but used no adult slave labor. While no recorded farm lease includes in its terms the hire of slaves, since their hire was usually a separate transaction, there is every reason to believe that tenants commonly hired the larger part of their slave work force.[33] If the hiring patterns of the 1780s still prevailed in 1810, many owners of small farms also hired slaves. Whether these slaves came from the holdings of an absentee owner or from a county resident, most probably still belonged to the wealthiest families.[34] Two vulnerable slave groups, children and the aged, were notable among the workers on very small farms. Three-fourths (74 percent) of the slaves working on farms of those who owned fewer than 26 acres in 1810 were children under twelve years or adults exempt from taxes by reason of advanced age.[35] That the labor of black children was so prevalent in an agricultural economy where profit margins were small and where, by 1810, 42 percent of all farms were under 51 acres is testimony to the adaptability of slavery. The base of support for the institution among whites was wider than has been supposed: tenants or owners of 7 to 20 acres could afford to own or hire a slave, even if only a child.

What did it cost to hire a slave? The rates of annual hire for men, women, and children were sharply differentiated. Generalizations about average cost are hazardous, for the sums varied greatly according to age, sex, and skill, and from year to year even for the same slave.[36] The itemized

[32] *Ibid.*, chap. 6.

[33] *Ibid.*, chaps. 4, 7.

[34] Because the names of slaves were no longer recorded on the tax lists after 1786, it is impossible to ascertain patterns of slave hire throughout the county after that date. The principal evidence of slave hiring practices for the later years comes from probate records. The manuscript population schedules for the 1790 and 1800 federal censuses were destroyed; the 1810 census indicates the distribution of slaves among free households, but by itself reveals nothing about the extent of slave hiring.

[35] Derived from comparison of the 1810 manuscript population schedule with the personal property tax list. About one-fifth of households with slaves employed only children, but these children (including those 12-15 years) were most often used as domestic workers in Hampton households. These households were 53% of all households employing only children, and their 70 slaves were 68% of the children so employed.

[36] Historians have quoted a wide range of rates of hire for Virginia slaves in the period. Lewis Cecil Gray cites various sources in the 1790s that indicate that slaves could be hired for £8 to £16 per year (*History of Agriculture in the Southern United States to 1860* [Washington, D.C., 1933], I, 468-469, II, 667). Jackson Turner Main

accounts of slave hire in estate settlements for 1787–1803 show that the highest amount paid for the annual hire of any slave was the £16 10s. 10d. ($54.95) which Miles King paid in 1796 for Tom, an adult male.[37] The average payment for the yearly hire of an adult male slave was far less between 1789 and 1799. In 1789 it was £6 13s. ($22.15), but then gradually rose to £13 6s. ($44.28) in 1796, and then fell by 1799 to £9 15s. ($32.47). The mean annual rate of hire of men during the period was £9 7s. 2d. ($31.14). The highest rate in these years rose steadily from £10 ($33.30) in 1789 to the £16 10s. 10d. ($54.95) paid in 1796, then declined to £12 ($39.96) in 1799. In 1789 a man's labor could be obtained for as little as £3 10s. ($11.66), but by 1791 the lowest observed rate had doubled (£7 or $23.31). The mean hire increased at a slower rate; the 1789 figure did not double until 1796.[38]

The rising costs of hiring adult male slaves show some correlation to the pattern of prices of corn, one of the county's main cash crops. The average price of a barrel of corn in 1789 was $2.08; by 1795 it had increased by 38 percent to $2.88.[39] The early 1790s were also a period when shipbuilding in Hampton was thriving, so that demand for labor in that industry, as well as on local farms, contributed to the increase in the rates of hire for male slaves.

In 1789 the average cost of hiring an adult male slave was about one-fourth the wage of free seamen at Hampton. The hirer who paid the average cash rate of $22.15 (£6 13s.) in 1789 also had to house, feed, and clothe the slave. The lowest-paid sailors in the Virginia navy that year received $80 annually plus board, room, and clothing, and some common sailors drew as much as $135 per year in cash wages.[40] Sailors probably were better paid than white farm workers, but no comparable data on wages of other unskilled free laborers in the area have been found. According to George Washington, in 1791 in Virginia the annual cost of a white farm laborer was £10 to £15 and

says that before the Revolution slaves were usually hired for £10 per year and in the 1780s, "as a rule," for £12 per year (*The Social Structure of Revolutionary America* [Princeton, N.J., 1965], 72, 125n). McColley cites exceptionally high rates of hire, ranging from £15 to £30 per year, but gives no specific dates, sections of the state, or sources (*Slavery and Jeffersonian Virginia*, 78).

[37] In 1797, when all local Virginia taxes were first assessed in dollars instead of in pounds, the official conversion rate was $3.33 = £1. Although most personal transactions continued to be in pounds, shillings, and pence, dollar equivalents have been calculated from the official conversion rate to facilitate comparison of rates of slave hire with those of the early 19th century.

[38] Hughes, "Elizabeth City County," Table VII, chap. 4.

[39] *Ibid.*, Table VI, chap. 8. Although corn prices peaked in 1795, the expectation of a continuing price increase probably influenced rates of slave hire negotiated in January 1796.

[40] Seamen of the state boats *Patriot* and *Liberty* were paid these wages if they worked for 12 months in 1788-1789. Auditors Papers 224, Accession No. 13147, Va. St. Lib.

board, while a slave could be hired for £8 to £12 and board, or 20 percent less.[41]

The lowest individual hire of any slave named in the probate records for 1787 to 1803 was the food and clothing exchanged in 1790 for the year's labor of Nancy, a woman owned by the Mallory estate, who two years later earned £4 ($13.32) in addition to her keep.[42] The average payment for the annual hire of adult women shows a slightly different trend from that of male hiring rates. Rather than steadily rising in the early 1790s, the women's rate fluctuated around £3 10s. ($11.66) until 1792, then rose to a peak of £5 5s. ($17.48) in 1795. Between 1796 and 1801, it hovered near £4 10s. ($14.99). The mean annual rate of hire of women between 1789 and 1801 was £4 0s. 2d. ($13.35). While the average rate for men doubled in seven years, that of women increased by only about one-third, but fell less sharply after 1796 than did male rates. The differential between male and female mean rates widened as hiring costs rose. In 1789 mean hire of male slaves was slightly less than twice that of women, but by 1796 the male rate was nearly three times greater than that of females. The yearly variation in the top rates was less for women than for men. Until 1795 none of the women was hired for more than £6 ($19.98); afterwards, with one exception, the highest observed annual hire was £7 10s. ($24.98). The range of rates paid in any one year for women's hire varied more widely than that for men, and there was no consistent increase in the minimum hire of women.[43]

An adult woman accompanied by a small child or children commanded far less than a woman alone. For instance, in 1791, when the average woman could be hired for £3 14s. ($12.32), the mean hire of women with children was £2 ($6.66), the most frequent rate of hire for such women in all years between 1789 and 1801. Children aged about ten to fifteen years could be hired very cheaply. Employers of boys paid as little as ten shillings ($1.67) for one year's labor.[44]

Comparable wage rates for free women and children cannot, of course, be found because large numbers of them were not employed for wages at all. Another way of measuring the relative cost of female and child slaves is to compare their rates of hire to the price farmers received for their corn. Hiring a slave woman in 1789 cost about as much as a farmer received that year for twenty bushels of corn, or the produce of one acre. A boy's hire at ten shillings was equivalent to the price of only 2.8 bushels, or less than one barrel.[45]

---

[41] Cited in Gray, *History of Agriculture*, I, 468.

[42] The variation in Nancy's hire seems attributable to market factors, rather than personal ones, since she was never listed as sick or pregnant in the estate accounts.

[43] Hughes, "Elizabeth City County," Table VII, chap. 4.

[44] *Ibid.* Note that Lidia Tarrant was hired out at age eight.

[45] The woman's hire of £3 12s. = $11.99; the price of corn was 59 cents per

TABLE III

COMPARISON OF MAXIMUM ANNUAL HIRE AND APPRAISED VALUE OF SLAVES IN ELIZABETH CITY COUNTY, 1787 TO 1803

Name of Slave	Age/Sex	Maximum Annual Hire — Virginia Pounds			Appraised Value — Virginia Pounds		Hire as Percentage of Appraisal[a]
		£	os.	od.	£	os.	
Abraham	Adult/M	6	0	0	20	0	30.0
Manuel	Adult/M	9	10	0	40	0	23.7
Moses	Adult/M	12	0	0	59	2	20.3
Colley	Adult/M	15	0	6	75	0	20.0
Johnny (Davis)	Adult/M	12	0	0	60	0	20.0
Ned	Adult/M	9	5	0	50	0	18.5
Mun	Adult/M	11	0	0	60	0	18.3
Sam	Adult/M	8	1	6	45	0	17.9
Will	Adult/M	9	7	0	55	0	17.0
Joe	Adult/M	15	0	0	90	0	16.7
Peter	Adult/M	11	0	0	72	0	15.3
Chelsea	Child/M	3	11	0	25	0	14.2
Johnny	Adult/M	7	16	0	60	0	13.0
James	Child/M	2	0	0	27	10	7.3
Tom	Child/M		12	0	54	4	1.1
Cate	Adult/F	6	0	0	35	0	17.1
Fanny	Adult/F	3	0	0	23	0	13.0
Silphia	Adult/F	4	13	6	40	0	11.6
Sue	Adult/F	3	0	0	27	12	10.9
Rachel	Adult/F	4	15	6	50	0	9.5
Nancy	Adult/F	4	0	0	50	0	8.0
Hannah	Adult/F	2	10	0	50	0	5.0
Peggy and children	Adult/F + ch.	1	4	0	48	0	2.5
Lucy and children	Adult/F + ch.	1	0	0	65	0	1.5

Note: [a] No more than four years elapsed between the dates of appraisal and maximum hire.

Source: Settlements of estates in Deeds and Wills, Books 34, 33, and 12.

278

Table III compares the maximum hire of twenty-four slaves to their appraised value. Clearly, there were important differences between the immediate (hiring) and long-term (appraisal) values of slaves. Abraham, who died in 1791, was described as old and was valued at only £20 in the 1788 inventory of the Mallory estate, yet in the following year someone paid £6 to hire him, and even in 1790, when he was chronically ill, he earned £4 10s., more than was paid for any of the estate's adult women that year. The opposite relationship between rental and appraised values existed for women who had young children and whose need to care for their progeny sharply reduced their hire value but did not affect the amount of the appraisal.[46] Young boys were also appraised in terms of their eventual, rather than immediate, earning capacity.

Only one man had a maximum rate of hire of less than 15 percent of his appraised value, and the average percentage among the twelve men was 19. In periods such as 1792-1796, when high rates of hire prevailed, the investment in an adult male slave could have been recovered within six years. These data from Elizabeth City County confirm the statements of Thomas Jefferson and others that for such slaves the ratio of hire to capital value was 1 to 5.[47] Only one of the women, Cate (a grandmother), had a ratio of annual earnings to capitalization comparable to that of the men. Maximum annual earnings as a percent of appraised value among the nine women ranged from 1.5 to 17, but when one excludes the two women hired out with their children at nominal rates, five of the remaining six had maximum rates of hire of 8 to 13 percent of their value. At these rates it would have taken about ten years to amortize by hiring the investment in an adult female slave who bore no children. It should be noted, however, that women were more difficult to hire out than men. For instance, among the thirty-five slaves whom the Mallory estate attempted to hire out between 1789 and 1792, there were each year three to five women who were ill or pregnant, who needed to care for infant slaves, or for whom jobs could not be found, but only one man, in one year, who was not hired out.[48] A number of the other slave women (especially if accompanied by children) could be placed only if a nominal rent

---

bushel, so 20.3 bushels would have paid for her hire. Production of corn per acre varied between 15 and 25 bushels. *Ibid.*, chap. 8.

[46] For instance, Peggy and her children were hired for £1 4s. in 1792; in prior years she was worth twice as much (£2 10s.) alone.

[47] Cited in Gray, *History of Agriculture*, I, 473; see also McColley, *Slavery and Jeffersonian Virginia*, 78. But note that this was true only when maximum rates of hire prevailed and when the price of slaves was exceptionally low.

[48] See Hughes, "Elizabeth City County," Table X, chap. 4. Pregnant women were also hired out; for instance, Peggy was hired out in the three years, 1789, 1791, and 1792, in which she bore children, as were Lucy and Silphia, although Sarah, Judea, and Rachel were not hired out when pregnant.

TABLE IV

DEPENDENT SLAVES IN THE MALLORY ESTATE: COMPARISON OF NUMBERS HIRED OUT AND NUMBERS SUPPORTED BY THE ESTATE, BY AGE AND SEX, 1789 TO 1792

	1789			1790			1791			1792		
	Adult Men	*Adult Women*	*Children*	*Adult Men*	*Adult Women*	*Children*	*Adult Men*	*Adult Women*	*Children*	*Adult Men*	*Adult Women*	*Children*
Hired Out	8	7	2	7ᵃ	7	3	6	8	6	6	8	5
Not Hired Out												
Reason unknown	1	3	11		2	7		3	6		2	7
Sick		1			1	3		1				
Pregnant		1			2						1	
Died			1	1			1		1		1	
Sold				1								
Baby			3			6			8			11
Total Dependents	1	5	14		5	16		4	14		3	18

Source: ᵃ Sam, hired out part of the year before his death, not included among 7 men hired out. Settlement, guardian accounts, and division of slaves in the estate of Francis and Mary Mallory, Deeds and Wills, Book 34, 102-106, 116, 431-438.

280

were paid. Only one of the men listed in the probate records, "Old Dick," was hired out without payment of substantial cash rent.

One conclusion to be drawn from these data is that women's capacity to bear children was included in their capitalization. Another is that to quote average rates of hire based solely on payments for adult male slaves, as has usually been done, without indicating how much less was paid for the labor of women and children, seriously overestimates the income most slave owners might have received from slave hire.[49] Despite these reservations, if the small number of cases for which we have comparable rates of hire and appraised values are representative, hiring out slaves was a profitable venture in Elizabeth City County at the end of the eighteenth century. Hiring out an adult male yielded a high rate of return. Although the yearly earnings of women slaves were lower, they were more than respectable (even without the bonus of profits eventually to be realized from their children) when compared to Virginia's maximum interest rate of five percent or to United States bonds, which paid three to eight percent interest.[50]

Even when an estate, such as that of the Mallorys, had a large number of dependent slaves to support, and their expenses are deducted from the net earnings of the slaves hired out, the practice was profitable. In the four years following Mary Mallory's death in 1788, the 250 acres of farm land were rented to a tenant, her three minor orphans were lodged in the homes of a married sister and aunt, and most of the able-bodied slaves were hired out. The number of slaves who could be hired out for the support of the Mallory orphans after 1789 was reduced by sale of four to pay accumulated debts of the estate and by a partial division of personal property which gave an older daughter ten slaves. Table IV compares the numbers of men, women, and children who were hired out or retained by the estate between 1789 and 1792.

[49] Among the historians cited, only two, Frederic Bancroft and U. B. Phillips, consider comparative male and female rates of hire. Phillips writes, "Women usually brought about half the wages of men, though they were sometimes let merely for the keep of themselves and their children" (*American Negro Slavery*, 409). He gives no specific rates of hire for women. Bancroft quotes rates both for men and women in the 1850s and notes that women with small children were worth "only one-half, or less, the average price for hire" (*Slave-Trading in the Old South*, 156–161). The only systematic comparison, made by the U.S. government for 1860, shows that Virginia males slaves engaged in agricultural work cost $105 a year, while the rate for women was $46, or 44% of the male rate. *Report of the Commissioner of Agriculture*, H.R. Ex. Doc. 91, 40th Cong., 1st sess., 1867, 416.

[50] The 1788 usury law limited interest to 5% annually. Hening, ed., *Statutes at Large*, XII, 337-338. Federal bonds of the 1790s (including older issues refunded) paid 3, 6, and 8%, but no county residents owned the 8% bonds, though these were popular among Richmond, Petersburg, and Norfolk investors. Records of the Bureau of Public Debt, U.S. Treasury Department, Record Group 53, Vols. 1087, 1137-1140, 1143-1148, 1150, and 1178, National Archives.

Because there were so many small children and infants to care for, the estate was forced to support and pay taxes on eighteen to twenty-one slaves each year.[51] The cash expenditures for the Mallory slaves who could not be hired out averaged £18 2s. 11 1/2d. annually, or a total of £72 11s. 11d. from March 1789 to September 1792.[52] The slaves who were hired out earned £303 10s. 6d. in the four years. When the expenditures for the dependent slaves were deducted, there remained £230 18s. 7d. or about £58 per year, plus the income from rent of the land, for the support of the Mallory orphans. The average annual gross earnings of the slaves hired out as a percentage of the estimated capital value of all Mallory slaves was 7 percent. The average net earnings of all slaves in the estate each year was 5.5 percent of estimated capital value.[53]

Flexibility was the key to the viability of slavery in Elizabeth City County, and the hire of slaves was essential to that flexibility. The pervasive and complex system of hiring offset the inherent rigidity of slavery in several ways. For the owner of slaves, hiring permitted a more efficient allocation of workers of various ages, sexes, and skills. Mature male workers could be shifted from job to job in response to market conditions, skilled men brought premium earnings to their owners as shipyard workers and seamen. In addition, hiring helped cut the costs of maintaining slaves, even if only room, board, and clothing could be obtained for the services of a pregnant woman, or a nominal fee for a child's work. By these means the underemployment of slaves was minimized, and profits even from the labor of children were maximized. Hiring also provided the slaveowner with a form of insurance to protect widows or orphans. And it was in itself very profitable.

Hiring so broadened access to slave labor that it was used even by a large

[51] Among the dependent slaves were 11 babies born between 1789 and 1792. Three women, Old Hannah, Sarah, and Judea, who were never hired out, were evidently responsible for raising the children of hired-out women.

[52] The estate accounts itemize money spent for clothes, blankets, hoes, medicine, doctors, taxes, and some corn. However, not enough food was purchased to have fed all the dependent slaves, even at a starvation level. Nor do the accounts indicate where these slaves lived. Since the relatives who boarded the Mallory orphans charged the estate for their food, it is unlikely that they absorbed the food expenses of their slaves. Probably the dependent slaves continued to live on the Mallory farm and were either provided food by the tenant farmer as part of the contract to lease the land, or were allowed to grow their own food.

[53] The estimates of capital values are based on the 1788 appraisal of all slaves allocated to Mary Mallory and her three minor children. Although no adjustments have been made for increasing or decreasing values by age of the slaves in the years 1788-1792, the appraised cost of the slaves who died or were sold has been deducted from and the value of infants (£10) born the previous year was added to the total capital.

part of the propertyless tenant class. Those who hired slaves benefitted in several ways. Labor was obtained at minimal expense—without the capital investment or risk of loss from death or injury that owning a slave incurred, and at substantially less cost than the wages of a free worker. Counterbalancing this enormous advantage was always the possibility of being outbid or unable to hire slaves when crop prices were highest and peak production was needed. Though in an abstract sense the job opportunities and access to land of young white people, tenants, and small farmers might have been greater had there been no slaves in Virginia, this was not the practical context in which slavery was viewed. Slaves were seen as potential employees, rather than as potential competitors. They were prevented by their legal status from competing for the small number of places in the county as owners of farm land, as tenants, or as farm managers. Only male slaves who were skilled workers in the maritime trades attained even limited privileges in this system.

It must be assumed that slavery in Elizabeth City County was profitable to the whites who, whether rich or poor, deliberately spent income to hire slaves or retained ownership in order to hire them out. In 1810 the percentages of county households that used slave labor were 82.5 among farm owners, 65 among farm tenants, and 81 in the village of Hampton.[54] Although many blacks born in the county were forced to follow their owners' migration or were sold outside the area, the institution of slavery remained secure until the Civil War. Slaves were never less than 41 percent of the total population before 1860.

How did hiring affect relationships between masters and slaves? One may reasonably speculate that the practice minimized patriarchal control over the lives of black people and encouraged them to take responsibility for their own welfare. Yet greater autonomy had social costs for black people: harsh exploitation of adults and children, separations from family and friends, low standards of living, and infrequent manumissions.

Hiring was foremost among the factors that weakened ties between slaves and masters. The discontinuity of work experience was extreme among slaves of taxpayers surveyed between 1784 and 1786, for only 39 percent of those slaves lived and worked in the same household for three successive years. By 1810 the practice of hiring out children separately from their families had become so widespread that about one of eight slave children that year began early in their working lives to adapt to different masters without the buffer of their parents. Two-thirds of the slaves lived in groups of eight to fifty on farms of over 100 acres, and in any year less than 10 percent of all slaves were living alone or with only one other slave in a free household, but because hiring was so common, the life experience of many slaves must have

[54] Hughes, "Elizabeth City County," chaps. 7, 10.

encompassed both situations. Blacks thus knew the cultural and personal autonomy of group life and also had the familiarity with the dominant culture and class that came from the close associations of individual service.[55]

With a substantial number of slaves moving about among the farms, the shipyards, and the homes of Hampton each year, there were ample opportunities for slaves to learn that working conditions varied, that free people were paid wages for the same work, that there were many other slaves in the county. News of the successful revolution in Haiti in 1793 spread quickly among the slaves, and the fear of county leaders that their slaves were conspiring with counterparts in Norfolk and on the Eastern Shore implies much about their freedom of movement. The problem of controlling and disciplining slaves who must have gained a sense of independence under such conditions was intensified by the fact that during most of these years slaves composed more than one-half of the county's population.[56] Most threatening were the few slaves left behind to hire out their own time by owners who migrated from the county. Grand jury charges against absentee owners for letting their slaves "go at large" were an ineffectual means of control.[57] Evidently more effective were the increased slave patrols, which by the end of the period constituted a major expense of local government. Undoubtedly, the economic dependence of both landowning and tenant farmers on slave labor was crucial to maintaining the dominance of the white minority, for the situation left little possibility for an alliance of the poor free people and slaves that would have been requisite to a successful revolt. But fear of slave rebellion was constant, and the slave patrol a consequential duty and expense.

The system had other disadvantages for the slaves. As the patriarchal authority of a master was diminished when slaves were hired out, so also was

[55] See John W. Blassingame, *The Slave Community: Plantation Life in the Antebellum South* (New York, 1972), chap. 7, and Mullin, *Flight and Rebellion*, chaps. 1-3, for discussion of the different personality types that emerged among slaves who always lived with 20 or more slaves and those who worked more intimately in white households.

[56] The breakdown of control over slaves in cities, as conditions similar to those in the county led to blacks' increasing self-confidence, independence, and resentment of slavery, is a major theme of Wade's *Slavery in the Cities*. Also see Mullin's conclusions in *Flight and Rebellion*, 162-163, about the threat posed by acculturated 18th-century Virginia slaves (those who had the broadest knowledge of white society, who had most fully assimilated its language and manners, and who were employed in skilled occupations).

[57] These grand jury charges, though not very frequent, are scattered throughout the court orders of the period. See, for instance, the charge against Mrs. Selden, of Princess Anne County, in 1786, in Court Orders, 1784-1786, 305, and those against Miles King and Wilson Miles Cary in 1809, *ibid.*, 1808-1816, 96. The order books for only six scattered years of the period 1782-1810 have survived, so it is impossible to tell whether the number of slaves left at large increased as out-migration rose.

the sense of responsibility that may have accompanied it. If hiring made slavery a more profitable institution for owners, it did so by making blacks work harder. It also seems likely that the low profit margins of the major county crops and the widespread distribution of slaves among owners of varying degrees of wealth led to more systematic and earlier exploitation of children, both those hired out and those retained on their home farms. The owner who calculated which men, women, and children were more profitably hired out was more capitalist than patriarch.

Few material goods were furnished to slaves in return for their labor. There is no evidence of separate slave quarters in either Hampton or the countryside. Black families with a kitchen, a storehouse, or a shed in which to live were fortunate; the only furnishings they could expect to receive were a mattress covering and a blanket. Scant clothing was provided. For instance, shoes were never bought for any slave of the Mallory estate, and blankets were issued only at four-year intervals. In this wealthy house the average cash expenditure for clothing, pallets, and blankets per slave each year was well under one pound. No record exists of a hired slave being provided with a full set of clothes in any year by owner or hirer. More usual are such ledger entries as "to one shirt and stockings for negro I hired, six shillings, 9 1/2 pence." When the richest farmers and merchants spent so little on their slaves it is unlikely that poorer people provided more. Sixty percent of the free farm families lived in poverty in crowded quarters that seldom had more furnishings than the houses of their early seventeenth-century predecessors.[58] Periodic removal from farms of wealthy people to those of poorer families, whose standard of living was harsh in itself and who had less to cast off or share with people even more oppressed, must have been a hardship for some slaves. Such conditions must have been especially hard for children already lonely and vulnerable because of their separation from family and friends.

County slaves may, by their own efforts, have made shoes, woven material for clothing, and supplemented their diet from gardens, fishing, and hunting small game. They had little control over gaining freedom. Manumission was rare: only thirty-four slaves were freed between 1782 and 1810. Despite the opportunities for slaves to work closely with free families and to know them well under the intimate conditions that prevailed in the smaller households, emancipation seldom resulted. Nor did hiring provide the means for more than a handful of county slaves to acquire freedom by self purchase.[59]

That hiring seldom eventuated in manumission points to differences between the rural hire of slaves in Elizabeth City County and the better-known urban hire of southern cities. Most of the hired slaves in the county

[58] Hughes, "Elizabeth City County," chap. 5.
[59] Ibid., chap. 4.

285

were farm laborers. Few had the opportunities of artisans to purchase their freedom. There was no flow of new slaves into the area that might have benefitted native acculturated blacks. The closing of the external slave trade cut off the supply of Africans in the late eighteenth century, and the relatively stagnant agricultural economy of the county did not pull slaves into its orbit as did growing cities or new cotton plantations. The county's small number of free blacks provided no base for formation of black-controlled institutions, such as the churches of Williamsburg, Norfolk, or Charles City County.

There is little cause to believe that the pattern of slavery in Elizabeth City County was unique, for many counties, especially in eastern Virginia, North Carolina, and Maryland, had similar crops, similar numbers of small farmers and tenants, and similar ratios of slave to free population—all suggesting a resemblance that deserves further study.[60] The regional variant of slavery found in this county may help explain how the institution could continue in some diversified farming economies, as well as the economic self-interest of poor farmers and tenants in aligning themselves with the slaveholding class. Economic and demographic changes in the eighteenth century modified, but did not destroy, slavery in Elizabeth City County. The ambiguous impact of those modifications on the lives of black workers shows that simple models of master-slave relationships cannot adequately explain the Afro-American experience.

[60] Jackson Turner Main first noted that the coastal counties of Chesapeake Bay were a distinct section different in many respects from the tidewater region ("The Distribution of Property in Post-Revolutionary Virginia," *MVHR*, XLI [1954], 241-258). See Harry Roy Merrens, *Colonial North Carolina in the Eighteenth Century: A Study in Historical Geography* (Chapel Hill, N.C., 1964), for characteristics Elizabeth City County had in common with parts of northeastern North Carolina. Also see Edward W. Phifer, "Slavery in Microcosm: Burke County, North Carolina," *Journal of Southern History*, XXVIII (May 1962), 137-160.

"THE DARKEST ABODE OF MAN"

Black Miners in the First Southern Coal Field, 1780-1865

by RONALD L. LEWIS*

ON June 20, 1796, the French nobleman Duc de La Rochefoucauld left Richmond, Virginia, for Monticello to visit Thomas Jefferson. On the way, he stopped to examine several coal mines at Dover, and while the traveler remained unimpressed by their management, he was struck by the fact that "Messrs. Graham and Havans employ about five hundred negroes in this mine, and the business of the farm." [1] Although La Rochefoucauld may have exaggerated the case, he nevertheless touched on the most striking characteristic of southern coal mining. From the very beginning mines in the South depended upon the sinew and sweat of black bondsmen.

Located about thirteen miles west of Richmond, the eastern Virginia coal field provided the first commercial source of domestic coal in the United States. While other states, such as Pennsylvania, had more extensive supplies, Virginia possessed the only coal easily accessible to coastal vessels through the port of Richmond. Consequently, even before the American Revolution, Virginia supplied Philadelphia, New York, and Boston with bituminous coal for home and industry. Not until the 1840s and 1850s, when Pennsylvania was tied together by a network of railroads, did coal from that state become available in the East Coast markets and force Virginia to relinquish its dominance over the trade. Between the American Revolution and the mid-nineteenth century, however, Virginia remained the major supplier of domestic coal on the Atlantic Coast. [2]

Among the earliest mines along the James River were the Black Heath Pits in Chesterfield County near the town of Manchester. [3] Opened in 1788, and operated for the next three decades by Henry (Harry) Heth (1760?-

*Dr. Lewis is an assistant professor of Black American Studies at the University of Delaware, Newark, Delaware. His research for this article was supported by a grant from the University of Delaware Research Fund.

[1] Duc de La Rochefoucauld-Liancourt, *Travels Through the United States of North America, the Country of the Iroquois, and Upper Canada, in the Years 1795, 1796, and 1797* (London, 1799), III, 122-125.

[2] Victor S. Clark, *History of Manufactures in the United States* (New York, 1929), I, 331-332, 520; Samuel Harries Daddow and Benjamin Bannan, *Coal, Iron, and Oil: or, the Practical American Miner* (Philadelphia, 1866), p. 108; Frederick Moore Binder, *Coal Age Empire: Pennsylvania Coal and Its Utilization to 1860* (Harrisburg, Pennsylvania, 1974), pp. 34-35.

[3] "An Account of the Coal Mines in the Vicinity of Richmond, Virginia, Communicated to the Editor in a Letter from Mr. John Grammar Jun.," *American Journal of Science*, I (1819), 126-127. Manchester has since been incorporated into the city of Richmond.

1821), a Revolutionary army officer and enterprising businessman, Black Heath became synonymous with high-quality coal.[4] Although he owned as many as 114 hands in 1812, the number varied substantially between 1800 and 1820, but averaged about 56 per year.[5] Heth hired a large number of slave pit-men as well. Thus, in March 1810, he advertised for "30 or 40 able bodied Negro Men, for whom a liberal price will be given."[6] Bondsmen also constituted the vast majority of the 170 full- and part-time workmen employed at Heth's coal yards during the summer of 1813.[7]

Not only did Heth employ a large number of slaves as miners, he also worked them in every occupation associated with the business, including the most highly skilled. When the collier leased his Stonehenge coal property in 1819, for example, he agreed to furnish the company with "fifty Negroe Men, a Smith & Striker, with Obey the Cork Maker, with Billy Griffen & Gilbert to attend the Engines."[8] Heth had been ill for several years by 1819 and apparently contemplated giving up the business, when he drew up a "List of Negroes which the proprietor will sell all together." Heth enumerated 52 men and women, among whom he included Phill Cox, "a tolerable cooper," as well as a blacksmith, a striker, a carpenter, a bricklayer, and ten laborers.[9] At the time of his death in 1821, Harry Heth owned 41 slaves which had been hired to the company and upon which the remaining partners paid to the estate hiring fees which totaled $11,855.[10] In his memoirs the Confederate general, Henry Heth, grandson of the mine promoter, recalled his childhood at Blackheath, the family estate. Among the general's earliest recollections were the family coal mines and the childhood curiosity which led him to descend into the pits even though his father John Heth had forbidden it. According to the general's *Memoirs*, with the money he had saved for several weeks, along with some cake from his mother's storeroom, young Heth "bribed a foreman of the mine, an old 'darkey,'" to guide him through the underground chambers.[11] Whether

---

[4] Ida J. Lee, "The Heth Family," *Virginia Magazine of History and Biography*, XLII (1934), 277. Henry Heth used the name "Harry" both officially and unofficially. Some idea of his pioneering leadership in coal mining may be inferred from his proposal to establish an institute to train American youths in the technical aspects of mining ("Coal Mines Seminary," in Harry Heth's hand, October 10, 1819, Heth Family Papers, University of Virginia, hereafter cited as Heth Papers, U. Va.).

[5] Personal Property Tax Books for Chesterfield County, 1800-1821, Virginia State Library, Richmond, Virginia, hereafter cited as VSL.

[6] Richmond *Enquirer,* March 2, 1810.

[7] William Pennock to Harry Heth, July 10, 1813, Heth Papers, U. Va.

[8] Agreement, Harry Heth with James and John Bavid, December 8, 1818, *ibid.*

[9] "List of Negroes which the proprietor will sell all together," n.d., 1819, *ibid.*

[10] "Accounts & Receipts," 1821, *ibid.*

[11] James L. Morrison, Jr., editor, *The Memoirs of Henry Heth* (Westport, Connecticut, 1974), p. 11.

slave or free, this black foreman must have possessed considerable experience in coal mining to acquire the knowledge mandatory for underground supervision. Moreover, his presence in such a sensitive position further underscored the commitment of the Heth family specifically, and Virginia coal operators generally, to black labor.

Organized in 1822 by John Heth and Robert Beverley Randolph, the Black Heath Company of colliers sank several shafts varying from 150 to 700 feet. After an explosion which killed 45 blacks and two white overseers in 1836, the company was reorganized into the Maidenhead Pits.[12] The mine never recovered the losses sustained from the explosion, however, and in 1840 sold all of its stock to a group of English capitalists organized into the Chesterfield Coal and Iron Mining Company.[13] Unlike most coal mines in the region, the Chesterfield Company deliberately employed 130 free blacks rather than slaves. It remains unclear why the company followed this policy, whether out of moral compulsion, or the real possibility that owners refused to hire their slaves to the company fearing a loss of their property in another explosion.

By the late 1830s and early 1840s, numerous coal companies operated in the eastern Virginia field. One of the largest of them was the famous Midlothian Mining Company, chartered in 1835.[14] By 1843 the Midlothian mines employed in all their operations "some 150 negroes,"[15] most of whom were slaves.[16] Midlothian did hire some free blacks in addition to slaves. An 1846 advertisement for slave workers notified owners that "The Company have in their employment several free coloured men," but assured squeamish owners that the free blacks were well disciplined.[17]

During the 1850s the Midlothian Company continued to rely on hired slave labor. The 1850 census recorded 123 male bondsmen at the mines, only seven of whom the company owned.[18] By 1860, however, the Midlothian had increased its labor force to 200 workers, at least 100 of whom

[12] Richmond *Enquirer*, March 23, 1839.
[13] Howard N. Eavenson, *The First Century and a Quarter of American Coal Industry* (Pittsburgh, 1942), p. 107; Oswald J. Heinrich, "The Midlothian, Virginia, Colliery in 1876," American Institute of Mining Engineers, *Transactions*, IV (May 1875-February 1876), 309.
[14] A. S. Wooldridge, "Geological and Statistical Notice of the Coal Mines in the Vicinity of Richmond, Va.," *American Journal of Science and Arts*, XLII (October 1842), 6, 8.
[15] Henry Howe, *Historical Collections of Virginia; Containing a Collection of the Most Interesting Facts, Traditions, Biographical Sketches, Anecdotes, etc., Relating to its History and Antiquities* (Charleston, S. C., 1845), p. 232.
[16] Richmond *Whig and Public Advertiser*, July 15, 1846.
[17] *Ibid.*, January 2, 1846.
[18] Manuscript Industrial and Slave Schedules, Chesterfield County, Virginia, Seventh Census of the United States, 1850, National Archives Microfilm Publications.

belonged to the company.[19] Following the Civil War, the company continued to employ blacks, for in 1871 the superintending engineer observed that "most of our labor here is colored labor, although we have a few good white miners amongst us. The men have faced great danger and undergone much hardship bravely."[20]

Ranked among the earliest mines in the eastern Virginia field, from their inception Dover Pits depended on slave miners. While journeying to Monticello, La Rochefoucauld stopped at Dover Pits in 1796 and noted that "about five hundred negroes" worked at the pits and the attached farm.[21] Little else is known about the Dover Pits during the ensuing decades, but apparently they continued to utilize bonded labor in every capacity. Edmund Ruffin, editor of the *Farmers' Register*, visited Dover in 1837 and remarked that

Graham's mining operations had been superintended and directed entirely by a confidential slave of his own, (whom he afterwards emancipated, and then paid $200 a year wages,) and the laborers were also slaves: and they, only, knew anything of the condition of the coal.[22]

During the 1850s, Christopher Quarles Tompkins, a United States and then Confederate colonel and experienced coal operator, began to organize a number of mines, including the original works, into what became known as the Dover Coal Mining Company.[23] Like most mine operators in the district, Tompkins employed numerous slaves in his coal pits. A Richmond newspaper reported an 1855 excursion by "a number of ladies and gentlemen" who descended into the mine "1030 feet deep." The sojourn through these workings fascinated the visitors, one of whom aptly characterized the subterranean maze as "the darkest abode of man." The spectators found that Tompkins employed slaves in these pits as well, forty of whom were

---

[19] *Ibid.*, Eighth Census of the United States, 1860.

[20] Oswald J. Heinrich, "The Midlothian Colliery, Virginia," A.I.M.E., *Transactions*, I (May 1871–February 1873), 356.

[21] La Rochefoucauld, *Travels Through the United States*, III, 123. Traditionally, Dover had been regarded as the oldest commercial coal mine in the South (Kathleen Bruce, *Virginia Iron Manufacture in the Slave Era* [New York, 1960, originally 1930], p. 88). This does not appear to be accurate for the *New York Mercury*, July 22, 1765, carried an advertisement by Garrard Ellyson for the sale of coal from his "bank of COAL in Chesterfield county" (*VMHB*, LXVI [1958], 203).

[22] Edmund Ruffin, "Visit to Graham's Coal Pits," *Farmers' Register*, V (1837), 315.

[23] *Ibid.*; William M. E. Rachal, editor, "The Occupation of Richmond, April 1865: The Memorandum of Events of Colonel Christopher Q. Tompkins, *VMHB*, LXXIII (1965), 189; Ellen Wilkins Tompkins, editor, "The Colonel's Lady: Some Letters of Ellen Wilkins Tompkins, July-December 1861," *ibid.*, LXIX (1961), 387.

hard at work as the party toured the chambers.[24]

In 1863-1864, the Dover, and the Tuckahoe Pits, which now fell under Tompkins's supervision,[25] employed about 150 blacks, of whom a large majority were hired. Of these hands, Dover utilized 103 and Tuckahoe 38, while nine hands labored on the farm connected with the mines. Table I identifies their occupations and hiring prices.

TABLE I

NUMBER AND OCCUPATIONS OF SLAVES AT DOVER AND TUCKAHOE PITS, 1863-1864

Occupation	Number	Approximate Hiring Price Each
Teamster	3	$ 345 per year
Trainer †	5	300
Fireman	3	250
Coal Digger	8	700
Carpenter	3	625
Laborer	28	325
Top Hands	24	325
Miner	10	350
Bricklayer	1	500
Engineer	7	350
Wood Chopper	1	300*
Boy	4	150
Blacksmith	2	1,000*
Slater	3	125
Farmer	6	275
Miller	5	150
Bottom Hand	2	350
Totals	115	$40,485

Source: "Commonplace Book of Christopher Quarles Tompkins, 1863-1867," Tompkins Family Papers, VHS. Compiled and arranged by the author.

*No price was given for the hire of the blacksmiths or the wood chopper. The figures given are conservative estimates.

†A "trainer" pulled a basket-like vehicle with iron runners, called a "corve," filled with coal from the working face section to the main drift where it was hauled to the bottom of the shaft and then to the surface. He was probably being trained by the miner, or the workman who actually dug coal. This was a skilled and sensitive occupation which required highly specialized knowledge and experience.

[24] Lease of John James Flournoy, May 28, 1847, Tompkins Family Papers, VHS, represented the first notice of his use of slave miners; Richmond *Daily Dispatch*, January 11, 1855.

[25] Charles B. Dew, *Ironmaker to the Confederacy: Joseph R. Anderson and the Tredegar Iron Works* (New Haven, 1966), pp. 34, 99, 149-150; "Corporate Holdings, 1866," and Tredegar Journals, December 1826, in the Tredegar Company Records, VSL; Bruce, *Virginia Iron Manufacture*, p. 88; Rachal, "The Occupation of Richmond," *VMHB*, LXXIII, 189-193; the Commonplace Book of Christopher Quarles Tompkins, 1863-1867, hereafter cited as Tompkins Commonplace Book, VHS.

Of the 150 black hands working at the Dover and Tuckahoe Pits in 1863-1864, free blacks comprised 24 of the total. Their occupations and rate of pay, where it was possible to determine, are recapitulated in Table II. Between 1864 and 1865, whites constituted only 21 of the total number of

TABLE II

FREE BLACK OCCUPATIONS AT DOVER AND TUCKAHOE PITS
1863-1864

Occupation	Number	Rate of Pay
Trainer	4	—
Laborer	1	—
Driver	1	—
Engineer	3	$3.00 per day
Sinker	1	$3.00 per day + Bd.
Miner	5	$3-4.00 per day + Bd.
Bottom Hands	2	"By the day on Trial"
Top Hands	3	$2-3.00 per day
Blacksmith	1	—
Bricklayer	1	$500 per year
Unspecified	2	—
Total	24	

Source: "Commonplace Book of Christopher Quarles Tompkins, 1863-1867," Tompkins Family Papers, Virginia Historical Society.

workmen at Dover and Tuckahoe. Since only two of them were "boss men," and a force that large, working in two-shift relays, probably required six or eight supervisors, it is highly likely that blacks filled some of those positions as well.[26]

The figures presented in Tables I and II provide some valuable clues to prevailing labor patterns at slave-operated coal mines, and represent perhaps the only actual analysis of exactly what jobs slaves, free blacks, and whites held at these pits, and the percentage of the total constituted by each. If the Dover and Tuckahoe Pits provide a reasonably accurate picture of employment patterns in the field, as they probably do, whites comprised only about 12 percent, free blacks about 14 percent, and slaves about 67 percent of the total labor force at these early Virginia mines. The status of about 7 percent of the workmen remains unverifiable. The above tables also reflect the long tradition of reliance on slave labor without restriction by race from

[26] "List of White Persons at Dover Pits—1864," and "List of White Hands at Trent's Pits—1865," in Tompkins Commonplace Book, VHS.

occupation or place of work. Thus, bondsmen toiled not only in the dangerous underground operations, they also worked on the surface where it was
relatively safe, and practiced the skilled trades as well as unskilled. These
patterns prevailed throughout the industry until, by 1861, the 22 leading
Virginia coal companies employed 1,847 slave miners.[27] Most Virginia mine
operators would have agreed in principle with one Alabama miner who
observed in 1859 that "Every day's experience confirms my opinion that it
is next to impossible to prosecute my mining interest successfully with free
labor. . . . No reliance whatever can be placed upon it. . . . I must have a
negro force or give up my business." [28]

Eastern Virginia coal pits justified the old refrain about mines being
"dark as a dungeon and damp as the dew, where the dangers are double and
the pleasures are few." In fact, miners conducted a perennial courtship with
danger and accidents plagued masters and slaves alike, although in obviously
different ways. Rock falls represented one of the most persistent threats to
life and limb. In 1812 Heth's foreman informed the operator that several of
the hands had been hurt. Toby had recovered since the visit of Dr. Turpin
and should be able to work soon. Shadrack and Chester, however, were
"hurt with a piece of coal that fell from the roof" and were laid up for a
somewhat longer period of time.[29] Others were not so fortunate. For example, Ned was "Nearly Killed" and had been incapacitated since his accident.[30] And another slave's owner dunned Heth for compensation "for the
. . . man who was killed by accident in your coal pits." [31]

Flooding provided another constant irritant to miners, and contributed to
making their work, according to one contemporary, a "gloomy avocation." [32]
More than an unpleasant working condition, however, flooding represented
a source of grave danger. One Friday afternoon in 1856, for example, Midlothian miners found the water rising rapidly in the "deep shaft," which
acted as a sump. Upon investigation, an overseer found that the water had
risen about forty feet above the bottom of the shaft. He and the general
supervisors attempted to reach the men trapped below by descending the
"rise shaft," by which the coal was brought to the surface, but found that

---

[27] Clement Eaton, *The Growth of Southern Civilization, 1790-1860* (New York, 1961),
p. 231.
[28] W. P. Browne to A. Saltmarsh, September 24, 1859, Browne Papers, Alabama Archives, cited
in Robert S. Starobin, *Industrial Slavery in the Old South* (New York, 1970), p. 23.
[29] N. Sanders to Harry Heth, September 16, 1812, Heth Papers, U. Va.
[30] Robert Brooke to Harry Heth, February 22, 1810, *ibid.*
[31] W. B. Pillsborough to Harry Heth, February 6, 1819, *ibid.*
[32] John Holland, *The History and Description of Fossil Fuel, the Collieries, and the Coal
Trade of Great Britain* (London, 1841), p. 247.

the water had cut all communications in the passage which connected the two shafts. The next morning the relief party rescued two unconscious whites, but the remainder did not share such good fortune; the list of dead included one white man, three company slaves, and four hired bondsmen.[33]

The frequency of devastating fires in the eastern Virginia coal field earned these pits a "well-founded bad reputation." The heat generated from the constant downward pressure, along with the presence of gas, and the loose coal and slate which littered the floors, rendered spontaneous combustion an ever present possibility.[34] As early as 1788 fire forced the closing of some sections of Black Heath Pits. Although sealed off, that initial fire continued to smolder for at least thirty years.[35] Thereafter, fire periodically ravaged Black Heath Pits. Heth's partner, Beverley Randolph, wrote on the morning of August 24, 1810, that "the day before yesterday they [the hands] were driven out by the smoke, which was very abundant all day," and the smoke had turned one of the shafts into a huge chimney.[36] The following day, Randolph informed his partner that conditions had worsened:

This morning I went again into the pit after receiving your letter to see if anything could possibly be done and took three or four of the hands with me, but had not been down five minutes before the hands began to stagger & fall from the effects of the Sulphur, which is intolerably strong. It was with great difficulty that we could get Jim Warren out, and I was very doubtful for some considerable time whether he would recover.[37]

Most frightening of all mine disasters is the explosion, but it also engenders a certain fascination because of its unpredictability and awesome destructive power. Normally caused by improper ventilation, methane gas explosions rocked the eastern Virginia coal field with alarming regularity. The first recorded explosion shook Black Heath Pits in 1817, although it remains unknown how many men died in that mishap.[38] Throughout its existence, the Black Heath Pits periodically suffered explosions. In 1839 a combustion of methane gas resulted in the death of "forty-five negroes and

---

[33] Richmond *Daily Dispatch*, December 15, 16, 1856.

[34] Heinrich, "The Midlothian Colliery, Virginia," A.I.M.E., *Transactions*, I, 346-349, 356, 360, 364.

[35] "An Account of the Coal Mines in the Vicinity of Richmond," *Americal Journal of Science*, I, 126-128; David Street to Harry Heth, August 10, 1810, Heth Papers, U. Va.

[36] Beverley Randolph to Harry Heth, August 24, 1810, Heth Papers, U. Va. Randolph was Heth's son-in-law as well as business partner.

[37] *Ibid.*, August 25, 1810.

[38] "An Account of the Coal Mines in the Vicinity of Richmond," *American Journal of Science*, I, 129.

two white overseers."[39] According to one interested contemporary:

Some years since, when ventilation was less understood than at present, an explosion took place . . . of the most fearful character. Of the fifty-four men in the mine, only two, who happened to be in some crevices near the mouth of the shaft, escaped with life. Nearly all the internal works of the mine were blown to atoms. Such was the force of the explosion, that a basket then descending, containing three men, was blown nearly one hundred feet into the air. Two fell out, and were crushed to death, and the third remained in, and with the basket was thrown some seventy or eighty feet from the shaft, breaking both his legs and arms.[40]

Even though the "most approved methods of ventilating the mines had been introduced" in the interim, another explosion occurred in 1844 at the same pits which resulted from "the leaking out of gas from some deserted works which had been ineffectually dammed off from the new galleries."[41] That explosion claimed the life of eleven men.[42] Still another explosion killed three slaves in 1855.[43] The Midlothian Company, perhaps the most professionally operated mine in the field, had its share of similar disasters. In 1842 the Maidenhead Pits suffered a tremendous concussion. A. S. Wooldridge, company president, described the disaster as follows:

A terrific explosion occurred . . . by which thirty-four persons were instantly killed, and a number of others so badly burned that little or no hopes are entertained of their recovery. . . . Some of the dead men, the flesh charred on their bones, held their shovels in their hands. . . . and Samuel Hunt, a small boy, who had been deprived of reason for the time, by the concussion, was calling loudly to the mule he had been driving to go along. Those who were not dead . . . begged earnestly not to be left, and then prayed loudly for a few drops of cold water to quench their burning thirsts.[44]

Another serious explosion killed about 55 of the slave force at Midlothian in 1855, and before the pits were closed in the 1870s, several additional eruptions took the lives of an unspecified number of black miners.[45]

Because of the dangerous working conditions in antebellum coal pits,

[39] Charles Lyell, "On the Structure and Probable Age of the Coal-Field of the James River," *Quarterly Journal of the Geographical Society of London,* III (1847), 270; Richmond *Enquirer,* March 23, 1839.
[40] Howe, *Historical Collections of Virginia,* pp. 231-232.
[41] Lyell, "On the Structure of the Coal-Field of the James River," *Quarterly Journal of the Geographical Society,* III, 270.
[42] Richmond *Times and Compiler,* November 21, 1844.
[43] Richmond *Whig and Public Advertiser,* November 28, 30, 1855.
[44] Wooldridge, "Notice of the Coal Mines in the Vicinity of Richmond," *American Journal of Science and Arts,* XLII, 2; see also *Mining Magazine,* IV (1855), 316-317.
[45] Heinrich, "The Midlothian, Virginia, Colliery in 1876," A.I.M.E., *Transactions,* IV, 310; Oswald J. Heinrich, "An Account of an Explosion of Fire-Damp at the Midlothian Colliery, Chesterfield County, Virginia," A.I.M.E., *Transactions,* V (May 1856-February 1877), 148-161.

owners frequently were reluctant to hire their slaves for mine labor. This hesitance was reflected in the colliers' continuous advertising campaign in local newspapers to portray the various mines as reasonably safe places in which to work.[46] When slaves were hired, owners and employers alike tried to minimize possible losses of their human property by securing life insurance on the slave miners. As early as 1815, one owner wrote to Harry Heth that he had been "informed that you [Heth] are now anxious to hire hands to work in your coal pits and that you will insure them against accidents which might happen."[47] By the late 1850s, however, insurance companies had become wary of underwriting the lives of slaves who worked in coal pits with a known history of accidents, which further complicated the recruitment of an adequate labor force. In 1858 the manager of Black Heath Pits, where several slaves had recently drowned, observed that "from the impending danger they supposed to exist, slave-owners could not be induced to engage their hands without first effecting an insurance upon them." Yet, because "accidents from similar causes have of late occurred" in which "life had been sacrificed," the insurance companies had become "greatly intimidated" and reluctant to take "risks on hands similarly circumstanced as those who have suffered on previous occasion."[48]

Insurance companies and the owners of hired hands did not represent the only vested interests who resisted the dangers of the mines. Slaves themselves frequently took the initiative on their own behalf. An agent for Harry Heth wrote to the operator in 1813 that slaves refused to work in the pits and had to be forced to obey orders to do so. Both Anderson and Robin had "been twice in danger of losing his life."[49] Another agent informed Heth a few years later that it would be impossible for him to hire any black miners. An owner had promised him six hands, but changed his mind and now "positively objects to their working in the coal pits . . . & the negroes themselves also positively object to going to the pits."[50] Numerous other cases could be cited as well.

A wide variety of responses characterized slave reactions to forced labor in coal mines. Like so many other bondsmen throughout the South, slave miners shirked work, abused the draft animals, stole food, and there are

[46] Richmond *Whig and Public Advertiser*, January 2, 1846; Richmond *Daily Dispatch*, January 11, 29, 1858, December 31, 1859, and January 10, 1860.
[47] B. Dandridge to Harry Heth, April 1, 1815, Heth Papers, U. Va.
[48] Richmond *Daily Dispatch*, January 29, 1858. See also Todd L. Savitt, "Slave Life Insurance in Virginia and North Carolina," *Journal of Southern History*, XLIII (1977), 586n.
[49] Richard Brooke to Harry Heth, January 6, 1813, Heth Papers, U. Va.
[50] Robert Gaines to Harry Heth, December 20, 1815, *ibid.*

a few cases of possible sabotage. Probably the most frequent direct action taken by pit slaves, however, consisted of running away. Thus in 1800, Sam ran off from Black Heath Pits, and from that incident forward, the Heth manuscripts are littered with references to escapees.[51]

Harry Heth also owned a saltworks along the Kanawha River in western Virginia. Since salt furnaces required large quantities of coal, and because few slaves resided in the transmontane region, the collier occasionally sent some of his Black Heath slaves across the mountains to work in the western mines. One of Heth's overseers, David Street, attempted to march a coffle of these pit hands to western Virginia in 1819.[52] As the coffle progressed into the dense forests of the Blue Ridge Mountains, however, several bondsmen escaped. The incident produced a particularly revelatory series of correspondence from the driver to Harry Heth which reflected the determination of some slave miners to gain their freedom. Just before the escape, Street had informed his employer that none "of my men will have it in their power to give me the slip," for he maintained "a strict watch over them and three of them I chained."[53]

The driver's confidence proved to be misplaced, however, for six days later Street wrote that he had run into some "very bad luck. The three negroes Billey and the 2 Johns that I had chained together—Escaped the night of the 13 Instant." The three hands pretended to acquiesce to their fate and Street had intended to remove the leg irons the next day. When the coffle bedded down for the night at a farm along the road, the slaves took affairs into their own hands, for at about 2:00 A.M. "old Shadrick" came to the house and informed Street that the three had escaped.[54] After two days of tracking the fugitives over a distance of sixty miles, Street informed his employer that the three were still traveling together when they were accidentally discovered, and one of the escapees had been captured.

John not being so Expert as the other two they took him. Billey finding that they had took John came back to rescue John with a club and if it had not been that a man hearing the alarm running that way with a gun, Billey would have certainly released John. They are now in the Mountains. . . . I am now waiting for their

[51] See the letters to Harry Heth from Jesse Cole, August 4, 1800; William Kimbrough, June 3, 1801, and June 12, 1801; David Paterson, March 2, 1803; John E. Browne, June 28, 1819; R. Tankersley, August 28, 1819, all in the Heth Papers, U. Va.
[52] Numerous letters during 1815 refer to Heth's venture into mining and manufacture of salt in western Virginia. See for example, Harry Heth to Beverley Randolph, January 24, 1815, and J. Barhu to Harry Heth, February 15, 1915, Heth Papers, U. Va.
[53] David Street to Harry Heth, April 9, 1819, Heth Papers, U. Va.
[54] *Ibid.*, April 16, 1819.

return [in order] to fetch me the nurse. . . . John informs me that Billey's intention was to Kill me if he had it in his power.[55]

Street believed that the runaways intended to cross the James River above Richmond and "make their ways" to Fredericksburg and Gloucester where they had friends who would hide them.[56] What happened to the slaves remains a mystery for all trace of them disappeared from the Heth correspondence. In an ironic turn of events, however, Street also disappeared, and a several-month search apparently failed to locate the driver. The evidence suggests that he probably sold the remainder of the slaves to his brother, who was engaged in the slave trade, pocketed the money, and like so many other scoundrels, vanished into the frontier.[57]

The problem of runaway pit hands was not confined to Black Heath, for contemporary newspapers throughout the antebellum era indicate that running away represented a constant source of aggravation for Virginia mine operators generally.[58] When the Civil War came, many slave miners took advantage of the chaos to grasp for freedom. As the end drew near the trickle of fugitives turned into a flood. According to the operator of Dover Pits, Christopher Quarles Tompkins, when the Union forces occupied the Confederate capital in April 1865, "All the negroes" went "quick for Richmond" and desertion became the "order of the day." In a remarkably dispassionate diary of the events which surrounded the occupation, Tompkins observed that

Of the 108 slaves hired at these pits only four or five left Monday evening, but the next evening there was 30 or 40, the provisions were not entirely issued & some held back to get their weekly allowance of meat &c. The negroes were slow to realize the fact that they were free. Many disclaimed any disposition to be so, particularly Alfred, Phil &c. &c. But by Tuesday evening the fever was so high that every soul who had legs to walk was running to Richmond.[59]

Although most of the free black miners stayed on the job, desertion among the slaves became so complete that Tompkins finally "concluded to stop the pits."[60]

Employment patterns in these early coal mines reflected the general commitment to black labor in southern industry throughout the slave era.

[55] *Ibid.*, April 19, 1819.
[56] *Ibid.*
[57] C. L. Stevenson to Harry Heth, November 5, 1819, Heth Papers, U. Va.
[58] Richmond *Daily Courier*, September 21, 1836; Richmond *Enquirer*, May 23, June 6, 1837, and June 17, 1845; Richmond *Daily Dispatch*, May 5, 1858.
[59] Rachal, "The Occupation of Richmond," *VMHB*, LXXIII, 192-193.
[60] *Ibid.*

Hazardous working conditions occasionally rendered it difficult to hire an adequate number of slave miners. Nevertheless, blacks formed the backbone of the labor force. Moreover, bondsmen toiled at every task associated with coal mining, from the least to the most skilled occupations. By the end of the Civil War, the eastern Virginia coal field had become moribund. The economics of mining dictated that capital be channeled into the development of the seemingly limitless reserves of the Appalachian states. Blacks continued to represent a vital source of labor in the expanding southern coal industry, however. In doing so, they followed a tradition with roots extending back to America's first commercial coal field in eighteenth-century Virginia.

By Randall M. Miller
ASSOCIATE PROFESSOR OF HISTORY
ST. JOSEPH'S UNIVERSITY

The Fabric of Control: Slavery in Antebellum Southern Textile Mills*

¶ *The factory system in one of its earliest forms—the textile mill—made limited strides in the American South during the closing decades of the slave era. While bondsmen were put to work in mills almost from the beginning, the problem of adapting an agricultural work force to the factory system was one that had to be solved simultaneously with the development of the factory system itself. Since then, historians have wondered whether the use of slaves in early industry was an intensification of the human aspects of bondage or whether it represented a marginal improvement in their physical and spiritual welfare. Professor Miller offers no answer to these questions, nor to those of how widespread or how successful was the use of slaves as factory operatives. He demonstrates, however, that apart from the fact that bondsmen took to factory work more readily than poor whites, the problems to be solved by managers, before a successful degree of efficiency could be achieved, were common to all new industrial systems; clearly, the development of an intelligent disciplinary system, enlightened motivation, and good working conditions were as important in using slaves as in using free labor.*

In 1827, an advocate of southern industrialism extolled the virtue of slave labor in textile mills. He argued that slaves were more efficient and less costly to maintain than white laborers and that their market value increased as they acquired industrial and mechanical skills. Moreover, he added, the industrial employment of very young and very old slaves, who were of marginal use in the fields, made productive an otherwise "idle" population. In closing his argument, he brushed aside the dollars and cents of the subject to observe that drafting them for industrial work "would be a real mercy to the slaves—for the labour in a cotton factory is infinitely more easy than in a cotton field." [1]

Few people, then or now, have wholly shared such convictions about industrial slavery in the Old South—and with good reason.

Business History Review, Vol. LV, No. 4 (Winter, 1981). Copyright © The President and Fellows of Harvard College.
* Research for this article was assisted by grants from the Penrose Fund of the American Philosophical Society and the Saint Joseph's University Board on Faculty Research. This article also benefited from the advice and encouragement of Milton Cantor, Charles Dew, Stanley Engerman, Ronald Lewis, Melton McLaurin, John Mulder, Tom Terrill, and Gavin Wright.
[1] *The American Farmer*, IX (October 12, 1827), 235.

The relative efficiency and the costs of slave and free labor in textile mills changed over time and according to place. Different people learned, and adapted to, the manufacturing process at different rates, irrespective of color. The availability of either form of labor derived from the size and character of the local labor pool, the regional price for slaves, the migratory patterns of whites, and the willingness of blacks or whites to enter the mills at prevailing wage rates, or even to work for wages, all of which were factors beyond the control of manufacturers. The roseate view of some early Lowell "girls" notwithstanding, work in American textile mills in general was dull, draining, and dangerous during the nineteenth century; in fact, conditions worsened steadily in the antebellum period as the machines speeded up. Whatever the rigors of toil in the field, they were scarcely improved in the factory.[2]

Still, slaves hired out to, or owned by, textile mills earned good returns for many masters and manufacturers throughout the antebellum period. Bondsmen competed effectively, and in skills and costs they compared favorably with white laborers even in the 1850s when the price of slaves rose sharply. Bondsmen also mastered the machinery and adjusted well enough to work rhythms to allow them a measure of control over their own lives in and out of the factories. In putting blacks to such work, owners and mill operators did not separate the economic advantages of using slaves in mills from the necessity of making factory work acceptable to them. Although the work never became "infinitely more easy" than agricultural labor, it did prove adaptable to some of the needs and aspirations of the slaves.

Like industrial slavery generally, the system in southern textile mills was not monolithic. It evolved slowly and haltingly from the first experiment in a small spinning mill in the 1790s to the

[2] The standard accounts of industrial slavery in the Old South include: Robert S. Starobin, *Industrial Slavery in the Old South* (New York, 1970), for the best overall, if sometimes over-stated, treatment of the subject; Ronald L. Lewis and James E. Newton, eds., *The Other Slaves: Mechanics, Artisans and Craftsmen* (Boston, 1978), which reprints articles and book chapters dealing with slavery in the salt industry (by John E. Stealey), in the tobacco factories (by Joseph C. Robert), and in the hemp industry (by James F. Hopkins), among other subjects. On the coal and iron industries, see Ronald L. Lewis, *Coal, Iron, and Slaves: Industrial Slavery in Maryland and Virginia, 1715–1865* (Westport, Conn., 1979); Samuel Sydney Bradford, "The Negro Ironworker in Ante-Bellum Virginia," *Journal of Southern History*, 25 (May 1959), 194–206; Charles B. Dew, "David Ross and the Oxford Iron Works: A Study of Industrial Slavery in the Early Nineteenth-Century South," *William and Mary Quarterly*, 3rd series, 31 (April 1974), 189–224; Dew, "Disciplining Slave Ironworkers in the Antebellum South: Coercion, Conciliation, and Accommodation," *American Historical Review*, 79 (April 1974), 393–418. On the textile industry, see Ernest M. Lander, Jr., "Slave Labor in South Carolina Cotton Mills," *Journal of Negro History*, 38 (April 1953), 161–173; Norris W. Preyer, "The Historian, the Slave, and the Ante-Bellum Textile Industry," *Journal of Negro History*, 46 (April 1961), 67–82. On the economics of slavery and the textile industry compare Tom E. Terrill, "Eager Hands: Labor for Southern Textiles, 1850–1860," *Journal of Economic History*, 36 (March 1976), 84–99, who argues for the "availability" and utility of free white labor; and Gavin Wright, "Cheap Labor and Southern Textiles before 1880," *Journal of Economic History*, 39 (September 1979), 655–680, who argues that the South did not have "cheap" labor, slave or free, before 1875. The literature on this subject is enormous and growing.

regular recruitment of gangs of bondsmen in the 1850s. It varied according to the size and location of the industrial unit, and the product it turned out; and it varied according to the personalities of the men and women involved—masters and slaves—and the peculiar blendings of white and black, slave and free, young and old in particular industrial settings.

In the early textile mills the plantation, not the factory, fixed the habits of work and discipline. Many of the early southern mills, having been founded and managed by planters, were small, with a few hundred spindles, at most, and a handful of looms, if any, and required no more than ten to twenty workers, who were often slave women and children from the mill owners' plantations. Such factories incorporated the home manufacturing practices of the plantations, where women and children regularly performed the chores of spinning, reeling, and weaving. Many years later former slave Henry Cheatam recalled how "De li'l niggers at night went to de big house to spin an' weave. I'se spun a many roll an' carded a many bat of cotton." Ex-slave Mandy McCullough Cosby gave a fuller description of home manufacturing: "My mother was a loomer. She didn't do nothin' but weave. We all had reg'lar stints of spinnin' to do, when we come from the fiel'." And they spun "ever' night until ten o'clock," she added, because there were spinning wheels in every cabin. For such slaves, the erection of small mills on the plantation provided no profound changes in work patterns. In many ways, these women and children simply exchanged the big house for the mill house as they continued their duties of spinning and weaving.[3]

The typical planter who had turned mill owner ran his factory as an extension of the plantation. He shuttled the slaves back and forth from farm to mill as agricultural needs and the local demand for yarn and cloth warranted. Invariably, however, the needs of planting superseded those of manufacturing—the planter withdrew slaves from his mill during planting and picking time. Work in the mill lasted from dawn to dusk, as on the plantation, but the pace was largely attuned to the skills of the individual worker. The slaves lived among the farm hands, and the rules of the big house and the quarters governed their social behavior.

By the 1840s southerners had begun to concentrate larger amounts of capital and labor in textile manufacturing. As the

[3] On early mills, see, for example, Ernest M. Lander, Jr., *Textile Industry in Antebellum South Carolina* (Baton Rouge, 1969), 3–49; Randall M. Miller, *The Cotton Mill Movement in Antebellum Alabama* (New York, 1978), 9–24; and Allen H. Stokes, Jr., "Black and White Labor and the Development of the Southern Textile Industry, 1800–1920" (Ph.D. dissertation, University of South Carolina, 1977), 13–47. On slaves' spinning and weaving: Henry Cheatam interview, W.P.A. Slave Narrative Collection, Alabama Narratives (Library of Congress); Mandy McCullough Cosby interview, ibid.

number of spindles in a typical mill increased to 1000 or more, weaving became a regular feature of the larger factories. Some plants employed from thirty to forty hands, but several had as many as one hundred and the use of both slaves and free white labor became more extensive than in the early planter-run spinning mills. With this change owners also attempted to introduce greater system in production and labor management. Movement between plantation and factory slowed as manufacturers sought a permanent industrial labor force. Although planters continued to control factory development in the South, and even to run many mills, the day-to-day operations of the textile factories increasingly passed into the hands of intermediaries. Outsiders in the form of northern-born mill supervisors and skilled workers entered the southern mills to train the southern hands and to inculcate "proper" habits and values of work. These developments reflected a trend, not a pattern. Most textile mills remained in the hands of men who were planters first, and the rules of the plantations continued to play an important role in shaping factory discipline and life.[4]

Slaves who worked in southern textile mills never attained the autonomy that marked their counterparts in the southern iron and coal industries. In textile manufacturing slaves were less skilled because the group consisted mainly of women and children who lacked the influence of the skilled, adult male iron workers and coal miners. But blacks in textile mills were not defenseless. They could destroy valuable machinery, burn factories, or run away. They could slow production and commit careless mistakes that disrupted operations. As they became more proficient in spinning and weaving, they also became more valuable, and the success of a large capital investment in textile manufacturing could hinge on the slaves' good performance, indeed on their willingness to perform at all. The masters recognized their dependence on the bondsmen by offering incentives and rewards— free time, overpayment, and internal mobility—to spur them on. Failing that, the masters inflicted punishment, but their growing dependence on slaves militated against excessive, sustained brutality, for the blacks would have none of it. As on plantations and in other southern industries, masters and slaves in the textile

<hr />

[4] On later developments in the textile industry, see Lander, *Textile Industry in Antebellum South Carolina*, 50–98; Miller, *Cotton Mill Movement in Alabama*, 25–239; Stokes, "Black and White Labor," 48–132. See also Richard W. Griffin, "North Carolina, the Origin and Rise of the Cotton Textile Industry, 1830–1880" (Ph.D. dissertation, Ohio State University, 1954); Griffin and Diflee W. Standard, "The Cotton Textile Industry in Ante-bellum North Carolina, Part II: An Era of Boom and Consolidation, 1830–1860," *North Carolina Historical Review*, 34 (1957), 131–164; and Griffin and Harold S. Wilson, "The Ante-bellum Textile Industry of Georgia" (unpublished manuscript).

industry evolved complex, sometimes contradictory, relationships based on mutual respect and dependence.[5]

A Preference For Slave Labor

Managers of textile mills agreed that slaves worked well. Henry A. Donaldson, who left Rhode Island to join Joel Battle in building a cotton plant on the Tar River in North Carolina, employed bondsmen there and later at another mill near Fayetteville. He thought that these people were "equal to whites in aptness to learn and skill to execute." He also reported that all but one of his northern-born superintendents "preferred black help." Slaves were more malleable and more accountable than whites, there was "no turning out for wages, and no time lost in visiting musters and other public exhibitions," and slaves could be attached "permanently to the establishment by purchase." A Georgia commentator maintained that blacks were more profitable than whites because they were "more docile, more constant, and cheaper than free men," and their living habits were "more uniform." In Virginia in 1831 the managers of several cotton mills expressed similar views, and their opinion did not change over the course of that decade. An overseer at a Tennessee mill boasted that slaves there did "their work in every respect as well as could be expected by whites." Even William Gregg, the apostle of employing free white labor in cotton mills, conceded that slaves were suited for factory work. Unlike whites, he said, they required no extra services such as religious instruction and education, they lacked mobility, and they learned to handle the machinery as readily as free labor.[6]

Large factories such as the one at Saluda, South Carolina, also reported proficiency and progress in using slaves. By 1849 this mill had engaged almost one hundred bondsmen, many hired on a yearly basis. They were such good workers that when the stockholders of the company voted to replace them with free white labor because of rising hiring rates, the northern-born superintendent objected. He confessed that he had come to Saluda with

[5] On the coal and iron industries, see Lewis, *Coal, Iron, and Slaves*, 81–146; and Dew, "Disciplining Slave Ironworkers in the Antebellum South," *passim*. Lewis's and Dew's interpretations have strongly influenced my work.

[6] Donaldson quoted in Charles Fisher, "A Report on the Establishment of Cotton and Woolen Manufactures and on the Growing of Wool," Legislative Papers, 1828 (North Carolina Department of Archives and History); *Macon Telegraph*, November 6, 1827; *Niles' Register*, 40 (1831), 282; James Montgomery, *A Practical Detail of the Cotton Manufacture of the United States* (Glasgow, Scotland, 1840), 192; *Southern Quarterly Review*, 8 (1845), 146; William Gregg, *Essays on Domestic Industry* [1845] reprinted in D.A. Tompkins, *Cotton Mill, Commerical Features* (Charlotte, N.C., 1899), 215. See also Augusta *Georgia Courier*, April 12, 1828; *New York Herald Tribune*, March 8, 1860.

many reservations about using slaves in a cotton mill, but one year at Saluda observing their "activity and promptness" dispelled his doubts about their "capacity or availability" in "becoming efficient operatives." In comparing the raw, undisciplined New England workers with bondsmen fresh from the fields, he favored the blacks. They were "early trained to habits of industry and patient endurance." More important, by restricting their intellectual scope to a few industrial processes, "their imitative faculties become cultivated to a very high degree, their muscles become trained and obedient to the will, so that whatever they see done they are very quick in learning to do, without entering into any philosophical inquiry as to the Method of doing it." In the carding and spinning rooms the slaves performed their duties "promptly"—indeed, as well as any hands the superintendent had "ever seen." The head weaver, a woman from Lowell, concurred. She praised their quickness and dexterity but especially their care of the machines. They also seemed to take a proprietary interest in their work. Such reports convinced the stockholders to abandon their plan to hire white labor, and in fact, the company added several slaves to the work force; without any prior experience in a cotton mill, they developed rapidly into "efficient operatives." [7]

The use of slave labor, however, was no guarantee of steady performance and pecuniary success, for blacks required management and training, as did whites. In analyzing the failure of a cotton and woolen mill at Natchez in 1844, historian John Hebron Moore placed the blame on "the shortage of skilled white operatives that necessitated the employment of [unskilled] slave labor." The overseer at the Tallassee factory in Alabama attributed the low productivity of his cotton mill to the inexperience of his young bondsmen, many of whom were "raw from the plantation." Yet he expected them to pay off "after they become practiced." William Lenoir of Tennessee discovered that young slaves learned carding, drawing, and weaving easily enough but needed "considerable practice" at spinning. Despite these problems, most who experimented with slave labor in textile mills believed the bondsmen worth the time and expense required to transform them into good factory hands.[8]

[7] Columbia (S.C.) Daily Telegraph, May 23, 1849; DeBow's Review, 9 (1850), 432–433. Poor management of the factory, however, led to economic reverses. The company sold its slaves in 1853 to cover the mill's debts.

[8] John Hebron Moore, "Mississippi's Ante-Bellum Textile Industry," Journal of Mississippi History, 16 (1954), 83; J. Hastings to James E. Calhoun, May 5, 1845, James Edward Calhoun (Colhoun) Papers (South Caroliniana Library, University of South Carolina); William B. Lenoir to Selina Lenoir, July 13, 1833, Lenoir Family Papers (Southern Historical Collection, University of North Carolina at Chapel Hill).

However much they might have wanted to employ slaves, by the 1850s textile manufacturers found it difficult to purchase or hire them. As cotton prices rose during the decade, men, women, and children became more valuable as agricultural laborers, and many planters who had employed them in factories now put them to work in the fields. Joel Battle, who had used bondsmen in his cotton mill for thirty years, complained in 1851 that they were unavailable for hire at any price because local planters wanted them for field work. He reluctantly accepted white labor in their stead. Many planters who had operated small mills simply quit manufacturing to concentrate their workers in the more remunerative activity of cotton growing. By 1860 only one mill in South Carolina used slaves, and in North Carolina white labor had displaced them completely.[9]

For much of the antebellum era, mill owners relied on local southern labor. Where a high white population density existed, factories had a potentially cheap and abundant supply of operatives, but there were few such places. A few mill owners imported workers either from Europe or from the North, but such practices necessitated offering wages above local levels. This practice was expensive, and factory owners did not generally recover the costs through dramatic increases in factory production; and moreover, not enough immigrant and northern workers came to the South to enlarge the labor pool significantly. This of course increased the attractiveness of slaves, but even though they were a source of portable labor, to purchase slaves for a factory meant that the owner had to buy them in the regional slave market. And that could also be expensive. The only local supplies of "cheap" labor were slaves that the planter-turned-manufacturer could supply from his own plantation. Unable to outbid planters during flush times, owners of large mills in particular switched to free labor, but the shift was not complete or immediate, producing a varied pattern of labor. Some mills were all slave, some were all white, and some were mixed. That the high cost of slave labor in the 1850s did not sweep bondsmen from textile mills, however, suggests their importance and usefulness in cotton manufacturing.[10]

Not all bondsmen who worked in mills were rushed to the fields during the 1850s. Skilled workers remained longer than

<hr/>

[9] Holland Thompson, *From Cotton Field to Cotton Mill* (New York, 1906), 251; Lander, *Textile Industry*, 91; Griffin and Standard, "Cotton Textile Industry in Ante-Bellum North Carolina, Part II," 140–141; Griffin and Wilson, "Ante-Bellum Textile Industry in Georgia," chapter 2.

[10] On importing foreign and northern workers, see, for example, Vicksburg *Sentinel*, November 11, 1844; Huntsville *Southern Advocate*, December 3, 1851; Lander, *Textile Industry*, 91–92.

the unskilled, for it was time-consuming and expensive to train spinners, reelers, weavers, and machinists. Factory owners were thus willing to pay a premium to keep their skilled operatives. Owners of trained slaves also made more money by hiring them out than in drafting them for field work. This tendency to retain skilled workers and give up the unskilled suggests that the movement of slaves out of cotton mills in the 1850s was a response to a greater, almost irresistible, demand for unskilled labor in agriculture, and in no way indicts slavery in the mills for poor performance. Economic demography dictated the recruitment policies of the mill owners. White workers were increasingly available; black ones were not.[11]

But the most available labor was not necessarily the best labor. Factory owners recruited among the poorer whites, and while low wages induced few landholders to enter the mills, money did attract families down on their luck or, more often, women and children looking to supplement family incomes. These people envisioned their factory work as temporary employment, at best. Factory owners also subjected white workers to a battery of reform measures to inculcate steady habits of sobriety, celerity, industry, and frugality, and they preached an evangelical Protestantism that scored idleness as sin and work as good. But all the expenses for Sabbath schools, religious tracts, and stationed preachers as well as all the strictures on strong drink, strong language, and strong play did not make southern whites work to the clock-time rhythms of the factories or internalize "Yankee" values. At an Augusta, Georgia mill, for example, Frederick Law Olmsted learned that the "mean-looking," worthless workers at the factory wasted much of the day "loafing about." In North Carolina, operatives left work to attend militia musters, public exhibitions, and other amusements. Everywhere in the South, white factory hands arrived late, left early, or failed to show up at all. They drank, they swore, they stole, and they drifted away. They were, on the whole, an unreliable work force who clung to the preindustrial work habits and values of rural and village culture.[12]

[11] The discussion of the "availability" and "cheapness" of white and slave labor follows Wright, "Cheap Labor and Southern Textiles." On the tendency to retain skilled workers, see Claudia Goldin, *Urban Slavery in the American South, 1820–1860: A Quantitative History* (Chicago, 1976), 60, who discovered a similar pattern in southern cities generally. The observations on slave hiring and skilled slaves are based on the records of the Tuscaloosa & Northport Manufacturing Company in the Robert Jemison, Jr. Papers (University of Alabama), the McGehee Papers pertaining to the Woodville Cotton Factory (Louisiana State University), the Roswell mill papers in the Barrington King Papers (University of Georgia), among other collections.

[12] On the efforts to inculcate New England values see Randall M. Miller, "Daniel Pratt's Industrial Urbanism: The Cotton Mill Town in Antebellum Alabama," *Alabama Historical Quarterly*, 34 (1972), 5–35; Lander, *Textile Industry*, 60–61, 93–98. Frederick Law Olmsted, *A Journey in the Back Country* (London,

These attitudes and behavior angered and frustrated the southern mill owners who employed them. Shadrach Mims, the agent for Daniel Pratt's mill in Alabama, linked the economic troubles of his factory to the native white workers, drawn from the piney woods, who remained dissipated in morals and health despite Pratt's rigorous program of moral uplift. At one mill in Augusta, Georgia, absenteeism was so common and so high that it undermined the plant's survival. The workers refused to submit to factory discipline. Every day the manager went out to "drum in recruits," who reluctantly came to work. At Graniteville, South Carolina, William Gregg's showcase of the industrial South, turnover was dangerously high, and white workers tirelessly violated the rules on temperance, promptness, and industry. The main factor that kept Gregg from shifting to slave labor was his knowledge that so many whites in the area needed a chance to work.[13]

Many mill owners persisted in using white labor because they had little choice. As a class, mill owners wanted to demonstrate the utility and safety of textile manufacturing to other southerners in order to obtain vital economic and political support for their operations. One of their principal arguments was that textile mills would provide gainful employment for large numbers of poor whites. These people would then remain satisfied with southern institutions because the southern factory, working up the products of slavery, would pass on to them some of the profits of slavery. It was a tortured argument, but a necessary one.

In the late antebellum period, however, growing criticism about unfair competition with slaves developed among southern whites, and although this was largely an urban phenomenon identified with tradesmen, it spilled over into industry. In an atmosphere of heightened racial consciousness during the 1850s, white workers found it unbearable to toil alongside blacks. Where the racially integrated work forces in textile mills had occasioned much favorable comment in the 1830s, now such mixing led to blasts against black encroachment in the work place. Racial mixing at one Georgia textile mill set off one verbal explosion:

1860), 357; Olmsted, *A Journey in the Seaboard Slave States* (New York, 1856), 356, 547–548; Fisher, "Report on the Establishment of Cotton and Woolen Manufactures"; *Camden* (S.C.) *Journal*, November 10, 1827. On white operatives in general, see Richard W. Griffin, "Poor White Laborers in Southern Cotton Factories, 1789–1865," *South Carolina Historical Magazine*, 51 (1960), 26–40, who differs from my interpretation. On the tenacity of preindustrial values among workers newly recruited to industry, see Herbert Gutman, "Work, Culture, and Society in Industrializing America, 1815–1919," *American Historical Review*, 78 (1973), 531–588. Gutman ignores the South in his discussion, but his judgments apply in many instances.
    [13] Shadrach Mims, "History of Prattville," in Susan F.H. Tarrant, *Hon. Daniel Pratt: A Biography with Eulogies on His Life and Character* (Richmond, Va., 1904), 21, 24–25; M.F. Foster, "Southern Cotton Manufacturing," *Transactions* of the New England Manufacturers' Association, Number 68 (190), 164–167; Terrill, "Eager Hands," 95–98.

"*Negroes*, slaves, and White men, and *White Women*, co-operating in a cotton factory! What an association! Disgusting!" Rather than oppose community feeling, mill owners at Columbus, Georgia, closed their factories to slave labor in hope of attracting whites who otherwise would not work in the cotton mills. Likewise, the management of the Augusta Manufacturing Company refused to employ blacks in deference to white sensibilities. The firm justified such an exclusion by asserting that black workers gave off an unpleasant odor and were not mechanically proficient.[14]

The shift toward white labor did not happen everywhere in the South, but occurred mainly in the eastern seaboard states that had a surplus of white workers. In the Old Southwest slavery became more, not less, important in textile manufacturing even in the course of the 1850s because of the shortage of hands. Alabama took the lead. At the Dog River Factory outside Mobile, the owner initially drew upon the local population to supply help for the mill. He offered good wages and comfortable housing as incentives, but he could not keep a satisfactory number of workers at this plant. He imported French weavers and enticed families away from other mills, but still, the work force dwindled. Finally, in the 1850s he filled the openings with his own slaves. Likewise, at Prattville, Daniel Pratt mixed bondsmen into his work force owing to the unpredictability of native white laborers who moved on after a few months on the job, being so wedded to the preindustrial values of work. In 1841 David Scott purchased a slave family for his cotton mill near Tuscaloosa, and as he saw their value and his prestige rise he bought others. By 1857 slaves were "much employed" at his mill, and at least thirty blacks toiled alongside whites with no apparent racial hostility between them. Through natural increase and inflation the value of the original slave family grew to $10,000 by 1858, and most of the original group remained "very useful" workers at the mill, where they had labored for seventeen years.[15]

The same preference for slaves surfaced in other "new" cotton states. Edward McGehee suffered losses using immigrants and native white workers at his Woodville mill in Mississippi. Exasperated by their shoddy performance, he replaced them with bondsmen in 1852. When the Arcadia Manufacturing Company

[14] On the arguments of manufacturers for white labor, see, for example, Miller, *Cotton Mill Movement*, 33–43, 93, 189–191. On black-white tensions, see Ralph B. Flanders, *Plantation Slavery in Georgia* (Chapel Hill, 1933), 205; Sir Charles Lyell, *A Second Visit to the United States* (2 vols., London, 1849), II, 34; Thompson, *From Cotton Field to Cotton Mill*, 251; Terrill, "Eager Hands," 87.

[15] Miller, *Cotton Mill Movement*, 75–76, 209–212; *DeBow's Review*, 25 (1858), 717; Tuscaloosa *Independent Monitor*, September 24, 1857.

near Pensacola, Florida, began operations, the owners purchased slave workers from mills in Virginia because the firm wanted "to avoid the possible inconvenience of white operatives becoming dissatisfied and leaving their work." [16]

By purchasing slaves rather than hiring whites, factory owners hoped to avoid high turnover, save money, and gain stability in their operations. They also hoped they would not have to increase wages higher than their competitors in order to recruit labor, and they hoped they would not have to train workers continuously— expensive in itself—as did factories dependent on unskilled white labor. And they hoped that the mills would absorb a good part of the high cost of slave labor by using women, children, and old people. The mechanism of slavery allowed masters to achieve a high rate of labor participation in the textile industry. Moreover, there were degrees of competence in the category "unskilled." The "marginal, immature, destitute, and illiterate" whites likely to respond to the low wage offers of southern textile firms were very expensive to train to do even the simplest tasks, and they were poor prospects for adjusting to the rigors and rhythms of factory life. It took time to develop the dexterity and speed necessary to tend cotton manufacturing machinery properly and well. [17]

The antebellum South never enjoyed "cheap labor" in its textile mills. The poor quality of white workers and the rising costs of bondsmen contributed to the slow, erratic rate of economic growth in the southern textile industry. Whatever the long-range economic implications of using free or slave labor, southern mill owners had to find workers to turn the spindles and the looms. They mined the best resources at hand, and this sometimes meant slave labor if it was available.

A Policy of Accommodation

Employers and masters adopted a policy of accommodation with their slaves, for it was less disruptive and more productive than using brute force and intimidation. Few owners expected bondsmen to accept their lot without resistance, and indeed, the various incentives and restrictions established revealed this apprehension. But owners did not need total submission, for broken slaves were dull and careless workers. Because valuable textile

[16] McGehee Papers, vol. I, 46, 74–75; *Pensacola Gazette*, September 13, 1845; Starobin, *Industrial Slavery*, 120. This pattern contrasts with Goldin's arguments about the elasticity and worth of immigrant and native white labor in southern cities: Goldin, *Urban Slavery in the American South, passim*.
[17] Wright, "Cheap Labor and Southern Textiles," 658.

machinery made the plants vulnerable to sabotage and "carelessness," masters sought alert, agile, and cooperative individuals, and if they never quite got those kinds of slaves, they made enough concessions to keep the machines running.

The use of incentives—overpayments, holidays, upward mobility—made sense only in the context of possible compulsion. Persuasion and accommodation, incentives and rewards, avoided clashes and promoted worker "efficiency." That was sound economic and social policy, but the shadow of coercion hung over and shaped the contours of accommodation. The threat of physical punishment allowed mill owners to employ less stringent measures to get the slaves to work, and as long as accommodative policies worked, coercion was not necessary.

While the evidence reveals no pattern of excessive or sustained brutality in the textile mills, whippings and other forms of corporal punishment did occur, perhaps with frightening frequency, although the spotty records of southern textile manufacturers are silent on the daily administration of discipline. Given the unblinking commitment to the lash among southerners, and its frequent application by northern manufacturers as well, it is doubtful that southern factory managers shrank from whipping the recalcitrant or careless. But the dictates of factory production discouraged reflexive and excessive thrashing, especially of women and children. A hysterical or injured worker performed poorly at his or her machine. Since textile machinery was set up to run in a line, confusion in one section of operation affected production all along the line. Furthermore, extraordinary or wrongful physical correction might outrage the workers and lead to slowdowns, sabotage, or worse. Because of the tight familial network among slaves, the suffering of any one naturally aroused the sympathy, and perhaps the anger, of the others. The victim might also run away, thereby disrupting factory operations. Although some managers may have left the correction of minor infractions of work rules to slave leaders, more likely they relied on verbal chastisement, demotion to the fields or to dirty work, and forfeiture of overwork payments and other rewards as the principal means of disciplining black operatives, and resorted to the whip after they had exhausted these other means of correction.

Besides the threat of corporal punishment, work in a cotton mill subjected slaves to many dangers. Fires broke out often, particularly in the pickery. Dust and noise were constant hazards, so much so that visitors to southern textile mills often remarked about the "dusty, unwholesome atmosphere." Even the best-run factories posed dangers to health. Shadrach Mims, who ran Daniel Pratt's cotton factory for many years, "completely wrecked" his health working long hours in the choking cotton dust. Few slaves fared better. Diseases also found a haven in the dirty, crowded southern mills. Tuberculosis, pneumonia, and measles were common afflictions. During an epidemic at the Roswell cotton mill in Georgia in 1847–1848, mumps and measles left the factory in "great distress" with over half the work force stricken and three slaves dead.[18]

From such evidence, the historian Robert Starobin concluded that working conditions in southern industry were generally worse than conditions on southern plantations. Of course, factory labor entailed great risks because of the crude machinery, the almost complete absence of safety precautions, and the debilitating effects of cotton dust. But slaves working at cotton gins and presses, sugar refineries, rice mills, and just doing chores on the farms faced almost as many dangers as textile workers. And, contrary to Starobin's insistence, the work day in southern mills was not "longer and harder" than that on the plantations.[19]

In general slaves worked six days a week with time off on Saturday afternoon and all of Sunday. The typical day went from sunrise to sunset, just as on the plantations, although there were exceptions. Occasionally, factory managers pressed slaves into service after dark and on Sundays to meet a rush of orders. At the Battle mill in North Carolina some slaves were "constantly going" because of brisk business. At the Fries woolen mill in Salem, North Carolina, the children worked "a half night each" and were "rather worsted from loss of sleep" during a spurt of business prosperity. Only when orders slackened did the pace of work relax. After spasms of hard driving, Fries compensated his slaves with time off to hunt, skate, and even see a circus passing through Salem. At the other extreme, according to a government report, a Mississippi cotton factory using slave labor introduced the eight-hour day as standard. Nobody else emulated this example.[20]

Life in the mills was not easy. The machinery required constant

[18] Shadrach Mims, "History of Autauga County," (ca. 1886) in *Alabama Historical Quarterly*, 8 (1946), 251; Frederika Bremer quoted in Starobin, *Industrial Slavery*, 49; James Silk Buckingham, *The Slave States of America* (2 vols., London, 1842), II, 113; Barrington King Letterbook, June–August, 1847 and February–April, 1848, King Papers; Adelaide L. Fries et al., eds., *Records of the Moravians in North Carolina* (10 vols., Raleigh, 1922–1966), VIII, 4067; Harvey T. Cook, *The Life and Legacy of David Rogerson Williams* (New York, 1916), 142.

[19] Starobin, *Industrial Slavery*, 35–74.

[20] D. Battle to R.H. Battle, September 19, 1844, Battle Papers (Southern Historical Collection, University of North Carolina at Chapel Hill); Francis Fries Woolen Mill Diary, 1840–1842 (North Carolina Department of Archives and History); *House Executive Document #6*, 29th Congress, 1st Session (1845), 677. Samuel McAlister's Adams County, Mississippi, steam mill employed thirty blacks.

attention, which was tiring, monotonous work. And dangerous, too—cut, split, and broken fingers were common injuries. The crude machinery used in most southern plants and the unusually poor preparation of materials that characterized American manufacturing practices generally in the nineteenth century, made work difficult in another way. Poorly carded cotton often broke in the spinning stage. In factories where the work was well managed, children who tended the spinners might sit for much of the day because well-prepared cotton required little piecing. But in American, and southern, mills the children walked about the whole day piecing the poorly-prepared, broken strands. While a full day's work at a cotton mill was fatiguing enough for an adult, for a child it could be debilitating. Children became so tired they had no time, or inclination, for mischief.[21]

However hard, labor was not continuous. At smaller mills linked to plantations, the work day varied according to the demands of farming. Some mills in regular operation shortened the actual time spent tending machinery to allow slaves and overseers to clean and inspect the machines and the products. Breakdowns of machinery, erratic flows of water, lapses in supervision, and shortages of raw materials also interrupted production with discouraging regularity—or so thought factory owners. (There is no evidence that the operatives complained of such interruptions.) At Bell Factory in Alabama there were frequent stoppages. The mill wheel broke, the head weaver left, the local supply of cotton and wool declined, and in each crisis the slaves stood idle. The mill manager tried to "keep them employed if they but earn their salt," but the work pace slowed considerably.[22]

Holidays also relieved slaves from factory work. Textile manufacturers observed the custom of granting holidays at Christmas and other occasions and they gave time off as rewards for good work or recompense for hard driving. Granting holidays was an effective work incentive, and an expected one.[23]

As a rule, masters and factory managers spared slaves the rigorous, intrusive Christian indoctrination that white operatives underwent in many southern mill villages. Only the Moravians were an exception. They encouraged regular religious instruction among blacks, brought those at the Fries cotton mill in Salem

[21] On the quality of American work, see the perceptive remarks of Anthony F.C. Wallace, *Rockdale: The Growth of an American Village in the Early Industrial Revolution* (New York, 1978), 182–183.

[22] Patton, Donegan & Company to Peebles & Co., November 29, 1847, to Shepherd & Duncan, March 20, 1848, to Fearn, Donegan & Co., September 12, 1848, to James A. Patterson, September 16, 1848, Letterbook, Patton, Donegan and Company Papers (Huntsville Public Library).

[23] See, for example, the time books in the Bell Factory File (Huntsville Public Library), the Graham Cotton Mill Papers (University of Kentucky), and the Woolley cotton and woolen mill accounts, Woolley Papers (University of Kentucky).

under Moravian discipline, and also supported a Methodist revival conducted at the factory. But the Moravian preoccupation with the spiritual welfare was extraordinary; in fact, it reflected the intense religious obligations that they imposed upon themselves. More typical was the experience at the Holt mill in North Carolina. There the owner chose not to interfere in the religious affairs of his bondsmen. He allowed preachers to stage revivals and baptize workers, a few of whom were slaves, but otherwise he showed no inclination to promote religion. The absence of references to religion among bondsmen in the records of other southern textile manufacturers, some of whom wrote feelingly and fully about enlisting evangelical Protestantism to uplift the morals and work habits of white workers, suggests that the masters conceded the religious function to the slaves. At least they did not appear to oppress them with their own brand of Christianity.[24]

The food offered at most textile mills was the standard southern fare of corn and hogback. Although it was coarse and mean, it was still abundant. Masters did not scrimp on rations in order to cut maintenance costs, as some have argued. To be sure, owners watched food prices closely so that they could buy at the lowest price, and those who employed both free and slave labor sometimes reported that the cost of feeding slaves was less than for whites. At the Graham cotton mill in Kentucky, for example, the food expenses for slaves were roughly one-third less than for whites. Such reports, however, did not consider that the large number of women and children working in the mills probably had smaller appetites than the adult male workers with whom they were compared. Visitors to southern mills agreed at least that bondsmen appeared well-fed. The records of the Warrior Factory (later the Tuscaloosa & Northport Manufacturing Company), the Bell Factory in Alabama, and the Roswell factory in Georgia confirm these observations. Slaves added to their diet by purchasing flour, sweets, and coffee with their overwork pay or credits. Some slaves raised their own food at the mill compounds. Nobody went hungry.[25]

Masters devoted special attention to living arrangements, for housing directly affected health and social stability. William Len-

[24] Fries et al., eds., *Records of the Moravians*, IX, 4734–4735, 4886, 4914, 4956; E.M. Holt Diary, entries for August 8, September 13, 1852, April 24, 1853 (Southern Historical Collection, University of North Carolina at Chapel Hill).

[25] Daybook and Inventory, 1837–1841, Graham Cotton Mill Papers; John Ewing Colhoun Commonplace Book (Clemson University); *Hunt's Merchants' Magazine*, 15 (1846), 417; Columbia, S.C., *Carolina Planter*, July 22, 1840. See the daybooks and journals of the Warrior factory and the Tuscaloosa & Northport Manufacturing Company in the Jemison Papers; Patton, Donegan & Co. to Robert Williams, April 1, 18, 1846, to Southwick & Co., August 31, 1846, to Haddock, Hesseltine & Co., December 11, 1847, Letterbook, Patton, Donegan and Company Papers; Bell Factory File; Roswell cotton factory accounts in Barrington King Papers.

oir of Tennessee built tight frame houses with brick chimneys for his workers. The forty female slaves at Arcadia factory in Florida were "comfortably lodged" in cabins arranged by family, although the women who were married lived with their husbands who worked on farms nearby. The slaves at Bell Factory in Alabama lived in thirty-eight cabins, organized by household, inside the factory compound, which was surrounded by a wall. Blacks at Dog River mill and at Scottsville, both in Alabama, inherited the comfortable cottages originally occupied by white workers. Black children hired to David Williams's cotton mill at Society Hill, South Carolina, bunked together in a large house with two bedrooms and a central fireplace. Williams entrusted them to the care of an old negress who stayed with them day and night, while another elderly woman cooked for them and other slaves. The child-bearing women at Williams's mill shared the house with the children. A nurse attended them. As the force of "little homony [sic] eaters" grew, Williams sought another "kind, motherly, and industrious" woman, to assist in washing, mending, cooking, and nursing. The children and pregnant women prospered under such care, enjoying sound health and "good spirits," and Williams counted many births, but no deaths, among his slaves.[26]

The living arrangements at the mills seemingly extended the manufacturer's control over workers. The wall at Bell Factory had a night watch and a patrol that closed the mill to outsiders and staked the boundaries of the slaves' world. At other mills, cabins organized by household provided an easy means of checking the workers' presence. But the living arrangements also adumbrated the limits of the masters' power by marking the family as the basic social unit. Mill owners respected this enough to lodge slaves by household, which also meant that they regarded these people as social beings rather than as anonymous drones harnessed to machines.

For reasons of cost and control, manufacturers often hired slave children and young women. The period of employment was short, and the mills were located near the plantations that supplied the bondsmen. By hiring slaves from local planters, mill owners entered the intricate and extended family network. Aunts, and even mothers, of slave children were likely to be among the women working at the mills or, as at the Williams factory, supervising the children in boarding houses. Older relatives watched over

[26] William B. Lenoir to William Lenoir, December 27, 1834, Lenoir Family Papers; *Hunt's Merchants' Magazine*, 15 (1846), 417; Miller, *Cotton Mill Movement*, 128–129, 205, 209, 109, 207; David R. Williams to James Chestnut, October 26, November 16, 1828, January 18, 1829, David R. Williams Papers (South Caroliniana Library, University of South Carolina).

younger ones. Slave children were not socially isolated in textile factories and so were not wholly pliable subjects for the masters to manipulate.[27]

Manufacturers had to be solicitous of the needs of slaves, for owners would not tolerate abuse, and insisted on good food, clothes, shelter, and safe working conditions. Robert Jemison of Alabama, who hired bondsmen for his many industrial enterprises including cotton mills, complained that such demands under-mined discipline. He compelled slaves in his mills to subscribe to the general rules governing operations and to submit peace-fully to disciplinary action for infractions. Not all complied. When Jemison whipped one unbending individual, the miscreant re-ported the incident to his master, who criticized Jemison's con-duct. The ability of blacks to appeal to their masters over the manufacturers who hired them, and the willingness of some masters to intercede on their behalf, not only circumscribed the coercive power of the manufacturer, but also threatened to inspire other slaves to demand similar "rights." Slavery in the mills, opined Jemison, was "different from views of proper discipline amongst Negroes, tending to spoil the Negroes to whom such privilege is granted and to corrupt others." [28]

Manufacturers eager to hire experienced hands had to accept the terms of the owner who was careful about his property. Robert L. Caruthers of Tennessee suffered "trouble, perplexity, & ex-pense" at his textile mill because he turned away experienced slaves who made too many demands on him, but after he rehired the "old hands," Caruthers reported much improvement in fac-tory production. The bondsmen returned, no doubt, because Caruthers persuaded their owners that he would meet the basic needs of the slaves.[29] The owners' concern for the welfare of their people at hire gave slaves leverage, for masters were not likely to hire them out to persons the bondsmen found obnoxious. To do so invited trouble. A disgruntled slave might run away, thus costing the insensitive master his whole investment and the wages from the period of hire. The scarcity of disciplined, skilled labor in the 1850s of necessity favored the slaves' interest. Man-ufacturers who needed to hire them could not afford to have reputations as hard-driving, cruel employers.

[27] On slave hiring contracts, see the Bell Factory File. On the proximity of mills to plantations, see John W. Fries, "Reminiscences of Confederate Days," February, 1923, Fries Papers (North Carolina Department of Archives and History); Thompson, *From Cotton Field to Cotton Mill*, 251; David R. Williams to James Chestnut, November 16, 1828, Williams Papers.

[28] Robert Jemison to J.S. Clements, March 18, 1852, Misc. Letters, D, 216, and to (?), May 12, 1845, Misc. Letters, B, 112, Jemison Papers.

[29] John Topp to Robert L. Caruthers, January 25, 1839, and Andrew Allisan to Caruthers, January 7, 1842, Robert Looney Caruthers Papers (Southern Historical Collection, University of North Carolina at Chapel Hill).

Manufacturers adopted various stratagems to motivate slaves so that it would not be necessary to discipline them. One simple device was to pay them for overwork—beyond the prescribed time from dawn to dusk. While this system committed bondsmen to complete their required tasks before they could earn cash or credits, it also kept them busy after dark and on weekends—the times when manufacturers and masters exercised the least control. It also eased the pressure on maintenance costs, for bondsmen often purchased food and sundries with their extra "pay." Furthermore, by accepting the payments, they also became what Ronald Lewis has termed "rational economic men" who "fused their interests with those of the masters." Slaves earning cash or credits for overwork had an investment in the mill's progress, and since overpayments were held on account until the end of the year, the practice also checked mischief and resistance. No one wanted to risk losing his or her "earnings." [30]

Nonetheless, the overwork system was not so important in textile manufacturing as it was in coal mining and iron making. The reason was that beyond a general competence to tend certain machines, individual skills were not always important. However widely applied in cotton mills, the overwork system illustrated again the duality of control. The system extended the master's power, but the slave did not have to accept the opportunity to earn overpayments. By trying to convince a person to perform extra work, the master acknowledged the bondsman's right to his own time, and by choosing to accept or to reject overwork, the slave claimed an area of discretion for himself. He became, in a small way, his own man. [31]

In a cotton mill manual dexterity, quickness, and stamina—traditionally the components of a craftsman's skill—were important in improving output, but they were not the means of a worker's advancement. Mill owners promoted people who were knowledgeable about the technical aspects of production and, more important, were able to direct a group of individuals to produce efficiently. Such men possessed the ability to command or persuade as the case warranted, and the ability to mediate between the workers' human needs and the owner's economic ones. In the large plants most manufacturers looked to northern-born supervisors to provide the training and guidance for their workers, but such men commanded handsome salaries, at least

[30] On the master's advantages in using the overwork system see Starobin, *Industrial Slavery*, 104. Lewis, *Coal, Iron, and Slaves*, 112.

[31] Dew, "Disciplining Ironworkers in the Antebellum South," 407, makes this point for the iron industry; it can be applied to the textile industry. For examples of overpayments, see the accounts and ledgers of the Warrior factory and the Tuscaloosa & Northport Manufacturing Company in the Jemison Papers; the accounts of the Roswell cotton factory in the King Papers; and the accounts in the Woolley Mill Papers.

by southern standards, and they did not always establish the good rapport necessary for untrammeled, successful production. Consequently, manufacturers who employed slave labor sometimes elevated talented bondsmen to head up the carding, spinning, and weaving operations.

Francis Fries, for example, entrusted his Salem cotton mill to a black overseer, who directed all operations and business when Fries was away. David Williams also relied on a slave to supervise his factory hands, composed largely of young children, women, and old men. Such supervisors worked well. Williams reported much success in training young children to tend machinery and obey rules. At Bell Factory the slave Branch, "a fine, intelligent fellow," managed forty hands in the spinning room. His charges were "quite expert at their business and gave their overseer little or no trouble." Branch also repaired machinery belts, covered the rollers, and weighed the thread and waste. Each day he entered his people's progress in a journal, which he gave to the factory superintendent each Saturday. Branch was the indispensable man in the spinning room. He was also the middle man, serving as a conduit for the master's commands to the slaves and as a spokesman for them. The third floor of Bell Factory was Branch's domain. As long as his people performed well, a black man stood there to guide and protect them.[32]

Men like Branch presented slaves with tangible evidence of the possibility of mobility and prestige in the factory system, and of the masters' "benevolence." Upward mobility perhaps siphoned off the discontents of talented, ambitious blacks by offering a degree of latitude in their lives, a measure of self-direction, and a degree of power. For the workers below, men like Branch potentially offered insulation of a sort from the owner's intrusions into their world..Such bondsmen could work out accommodations with black overseers who needed their support—their willingness to move with the machines and to stay out of trouble—as they needed the overseers' protection.

Yet control never meant dominion, and accommodation never meant contentment. Slaves resisted attempts to dominate them. Resistance took many forms, although it rarely developed into direct confrontations. The physical confines of the typical textile mill imposed restraints, and in such a closed and highly organized world, sluggishness, incompetence, and truculence did not go unnoticed. Each floor and each operation had its own supervisor.

[32] Stokes, "Black and White Labor," 113; Francis Levin Fries Diary (typescript), *passim* (North Carolina Department of Archives and History); Cook, *David Rogerson Williams*, 140; David Williams to James Chestnut, November 16, 1828, Williams Papers, for the composition of the work force; *New York Herald Tribune*, March 8, 1860.

Working in buildings of roughly 150 to 250 by 50 to 100 feet, factory slaves had small opportunity to steal away for a nap, break a loom, or plot some terrible misdeed with fellow bondsmen. The supervisor knew the minimum daily output of each card, spindle, or loom, and the wise slave did at least that much work.

But masters and overseers could not be everywhere at once, and slaves slipped into the interstices of supervision to gain relief from prying whites. They showed their discontent by stealing, running away, and worse. While runaways could be caught and returned, theft was a common problem for which manufacturers never discovered a solution. Some bondsmen appropriated cuttings and scraps for their own use; others developed an illicit traffic in stolen goods, exchanging raw cotton, wool, yarn, and cloth for food and other items. Malingering also vexed factory owners. More serious than any other problem, however, was arson, which posed a constant threat to manufacturers. Deliberate burning occurred often enough to remind masters that slaves were a troublesome property. In one instance in 1831, a vengeful man, who had been accused of a theft, put the Vaucluse factory in South Carolina to the torch, destroying the whole plant. In 1833 another incendiary razed the Metcalfe mill in Tennessee, and in 1841 a bondsman at Bell Factory set fire to that mill. Although some blazes may have been wrongly attributed to slaves, and carelessness rather than malevolence the real cause, masters were still convinced that slaves were not afraid to wield the torch, and so the threat of arson gave bondsmen a power over their masters, for it touched their vulnerability.[33]

CONCLUSION

Slaves in antebellum southern textile mills were not creatures riveted to an impersonal, mechanistic factory system. By the eve of the Civil War they represented an efficient and self-confident work force that was not brutalized by industrial bondage, but rather found sufficient social space to fend off the total domination of their masters. As slaveowners came to depend on their slaves for industrial prosperity, as they developed subtle forms of accommodation to push production with minimal disruption, they conceded a measure of autonomy to them. The fabric of control in textile mills was like that in other antebellum southern industries—it was loosely woven into a pattern of grays.

[33] On thefts, see Starobin, *Industrial Slavery*, 80; *Pendleton* (S.C.) *Messenger*, August 3, 1831; on malingering and flight, see, for example, Patton, Donegan & Co. to Fearn & Crenshaw, May 10, 1847, Letterbook, Patton, Donegan and Company Papers; on arson, see *Pendleton* (S.C.) *Messenger*, August 3, 1831; *Columbia* (S.C.) *Daily Telegraph*, November 17, 1848; William B. Lenoir to William Lenoir, May 18, 1833, Lenoir Papers; *Huntsville Democrat*, July 3, 1841.

Work and Culture: The Task System and the World of Lowcountry Blacks, 1700 to 1880

Philip D. Morgan

Who built Thebes of the seven Gates?
In the books stand the names of Kings.
Did they then drag up the rock-slabs?
And Babylon so often destroyed,
Who kept rebuilding it?
In which houses did the builders live
In gold-glittering Lima?
Where did the brick-layers go
The evening the Great Wall of China was finished?
. . .

Even in legendary Atlantis
Didn't the drowning shout for their slaves
As the ocean engulfed it?
. . .

So many reports
So many questions.

Bertolt Brecht, 1939

WITHIN the realm of slavery studies there has been a pronounced preoccupation with the external or institutional aspects of the slave system. Despite repeated clarion calls for
investigations of life in the slave quarters, little scholarly attention has
been directed to the domestic economy of the slaves, their work routines,

Mr. Morgan is a member of the Department of History at Virginia Polytechnic Institute and State University and was a Post-Doctoral Fellow at the Institute of Early American History and Culture when this article was written. He wishes to thank members of an Institute colloquium, panel members at a Southern Historical Association meeting, and Stanley Engerman and Edward Steiner for their comments on an earlier version of this paper. He is also grateful to Ira Berlin, Joseph Reidy, and particularly Leslie Rowland for their help in guiding him through the very valuable files of the Freedmen and Southern Society Project at the University of Maryland.

their attitudes toward resource allocation, their attempts to accumulate, and their patterns of consumption.[1] This academic shortsightedness is more easily identified than remedied. Attitudes toward work and patterns of work constitute an area of inquiry that sprawls awkwardly across academic demarcations: the subject is all too easily neglected.[2] In addition, the genre to which this type of history is most akin, namely, labor history, often suffers from its own myopia: studies that begin by aiming to uncover the experience of workers can all too readily focus instead on management priorities.[3] Moreover, what has been said with respect to the English farm laborer applies even more forcefully to the Afro-American slave: "No one has written his signature more plainly across the countryside; but no one has left more scanty records of his achievements."[4]

Mindful of these difficulties and pitfalls, this article accepts the challenge posed by Brecht's questions: it attempts to bring history closer to the central concerns of ordinary people's lives—in this case, the lives of Afro-American slaves in the lowcountry region of South Carolina and Georgia. In this light, perhaps the most distinctive and central feature of lowcountry slave life was the task system. In Lewis Gray's words, "Under the task system the slave was assigned a certain amount of work for the day, and after completing the task he could use his time as he pleased," whereas under the gang system, prevalent in most Anglo-American plantation societies, "slaves were worked in groups under the control of a driver or leader . . . and the laborer was compelled to work the entire day."[5] While previous commentators have drawn attention to the task system, few have explored how this peculiarity arose and how it structured the world of those who labored under it. In order to shed light on the first matter, I shall open three windows onto different phases in the develop-

[1] Comparative studies of slavery have been especially prone to the institutional or external perspective. Even one of the best studies of slave life—Eugene D. Genovese's *Roll, Jordan, Roll: The World the Slaves Made* (New York, 1974)—devotes only a few pages to the domestic economy of the slaves (pp. 535-540), although slave work routines (pp. 285-324) and aspects of consumption patterns (pp. 550-561) are explored sensitively and at length.

[2] Anthropologists, for example, have been criticized for neglecting the subject. See the introduction to Sandra Wallman, ed., *Social Anthropology of Work*, Association of Social Anthropologists, Monograph 19 (London, 1979).

[3] The labor history that is practiced in *History Workshop* and in the volumes published in the *History Workshop* series are the kind to which this article aspires. Also noteworthy is a recent trend in American labor history that treats the reality of work as the focus, or starting point, of investigation. See David Brody, "Labor History in the 1970s: Toward a History of the American Worker," in Michael Kammen, ed., *The Past before Us: Contemporary Historical Writing in the United States* (Ithaca, N.Y., 1980), 268.

[4] Alan Everitt, "Farm Labourers," in Joan Thirsk, ed., *The Agrarian History of England and Wales*, IV (Cambridge, 1967), 396.

[5] Lewis Cecil Gray, *History of Agriculture in the Southern United States to 1860* (Gloucester, Mass., 1958 [orig. publ. Washington, D.C., 1933]), I, 550-551.

ment of this labor arrangement: its origins in the first half of the eighteenth century, its routinization during the Revolutionary era, and its full flowering by the time of the Civil War. I shall also explore the ramifications of the task system for the slaves by analyzing its most distinctive feature so far as they were concerned: the opportunities it provided for working on their own behalf once the stipulated task had been completed.[6] I shall argue, then, that a particular mode of labor organization and a particular domestic economy evolved simultaneously in the colonial and antebellum lowcountry.[7]

This argument can best be secured by broadening our horizons to take in not only colonial and early national developments but also those of the antebellum and even postbellum years. On the one hand, such a strategy will show how colonial developments bore directly on nineteenth- and even twentieth-century realities. To take a minor example, the basic task unit still current in the minds of freedmen in the 1930s will be shown to have had a precise colonial origin. On the other hand, the opportunities that the task system presented slaves can be understood only in the light of mid-nineteenth-century experiences. To take a more significant example, the resemblance between the experiences of some lowcountry slaves and of the protopeasants found among the slaves of certain Caribbean plantation societies emerges most clearly from a glance at the behavior of slaves and freedmen in the years surrounding the Civil War.[8] In other words, to understand the evolution of the task system and its concomitant domestic economy, we shall need a telescope rather than a microscope.

I

If the Negroes are skilful and industrious, they
plant something for themselves after the day's work.
Johann Bolzius, 1751

The earliest, fragmentary descriptions of work practices in the low-country rice economy indicate that a prominent characteristic of the task system—a sharp division between the master's "time" and the slave's

[6] Equally, we could investigate more fully than will be possible here the special role of the black driver, the marketing opportunities, or the occupational structure that a rice tasking system produced.

[7] The word *particular* is important here because I do not intend to suggest that the independent production of goods and the accumulation of property by slaves was necessarily predicated on a task system. From situations as diverse as a sugar plantation in Jamaica to an iron foundry in the United States, slaves were often able to control the accumulation and disposal of sizable earnings and possessions. Rather, in the lowcountry, a particular conjunction arose that probably led—but this would need much greater space for comparative presentation—to a distinctive internal economy among the slaves.

[8] In exploring these resemblances, I have found the work of Sidney W. Mintz to be particularly helpful. See "The Origins of Reconstituted Peasantries," in

"time"—was already in place. In the first decade of the eighteenth century the clergy of South Carolina complained that slaves were planting "for themselves as much as will cloath and subsist them and their famil[ies]." During the investigation of a suspected slave conspiracy in mid-century, a lowcountry planter readily acknowledged that one of his slaves had planted rice "in his own time" and could do with it as he wished.[9] The most acute observer of early work practices, Johann Bolzius, described how slaves, after "their required day's work," were "given as much land as they can handle" on which they planted corn, potatoes, tobacco, peanuts, sugar and water melons, and pumpkins and bottle pumpkins.[10] The opportunity to grow such a wide range of provisions on readily available land owed much to the early establishment and institutionalization of the daily work requirement. By mid-century the basic "task" unit had been set at a quarter of an acre. Moreover, other activities, outside of the rice field, were also tasked: in pounding the rice grain, slaves were "tasked at seven Mortars for one day," and in providing fences lowcountry slaves were expected to split 100 poles of about twelve feet in length (a daily "task" that remained unchanged throughout the slave era, as Table I indicates).[11] These tasks were not, of course, easily accomplished, and occasionally planters exacted even higher daily requirements; but, as Bolzius noted, the advantage to the slaves of having a daily goal was that they could, once it was met, "plant something for themselves."[12]

A tried and tested model of labor organization—the gang system practiced on both tobacco and sugar plantations—was available when lowcountry planters discovered their own plantation staple. In fact, many of the first immigrants were from Barbados, where they must have had direct experience of operating gangs of slaves.[13] Why did they and others decide to adopt a new system? U. B. Phillips claimed that temporary

Caribbean Transformations (Chicago, 1974), 146-156, and "Slavery and the Rise of Peasantries," in Michael Craton, ed., *Roots and Branches: Current Directions in Slave Studies* (Toronto, 1979), 213-242.

[9] The Instructions of the Clergy of South Carolina given to Mr. Johnston, 1712, A8/429, Society of the Propagation of the Gospel, London; testimony of Thomas Akin and Ammon, Feb. 7, 1749, Council Journal, No. 17, Pt. 1, 160, South Carolina Department of Archives and History, Columbia.

[10] "Johann Martin Bolzius Answers a Questionnaire on Carolina and Georgia," trans. and ed. Klaus G. Loewald et al., *William and Mary Quarterly*, 3d Ser., XIV (1957), 259.

[11] Dr. Alexander Garden to the Royal Society, Apr. 20, 1755, Guard Book 1, 36, Royal Society of Arts, London; "Bolzius Answers a Questionnaire," trans. and ed. Loewald et al., *WMQ*, 3d Ser., XIV (1957), 258.

[12] "Bolzius Answers a Questionnaire," trans. and ed. Loewald et al., *WMQ*, 3d Ser., XIV (1957), 256.

[13] Richard S. Dunn, "The English Sugar Islands and the Founding of South Carolina," *South Carolina Historical Magazine*, LXXII (1971), 81-93; Richard Waterhouse, "England, the Caribbean, and the Settlement of Carolina," *Journal of American Studies*, IX (1975), 259-281.

absenteeism was responsible: "The necessity of the master's moving away from his estate in the warm months, to escape the malaria, involved the adoption of some system of routine which would work with more or less automatic regularity without his own inspiring or impelling presence." However, while absenteeism may have contributed to the attractiveness of this system, it seems an insufficiently powerful agent to account for its inception. The example of Caribbean sugar production is pertinent here; if the withdrawal of an inspiring master encouraged the development of tasking, why did not sugar planters in the West Indies, where absenteeism began relatively early, adopt the system?[14]

The absence of masters may be an unconvincing explanation for the development of a task system, but perhaps the presence of particular slaves can serve in its place. Peter H. Wood and Daniel C. Littlefield have pointed out that some black immigrants to early South Carolina were already familiar with the techniques of rice cultivation.[15] These slaves' expertise, it might be argued, accounts for the evolution of a system that would operate more or less automatically. It has even been suggested, in this regard, that a work pattern of alternating bouts of intense labor and idleness tends to occur wherever men are to some degree in control of their own working lives (need one look any further than authors?).[16] By displaying their own understanding of the basic requirements of rice cultivation, lowcountry slaves might have gained a measure of control over their lives, at least to the extent of determining the length of their working days. While this is an attractive argument, it is not without problems. The coastal regions that seem to have supplied a majority of slaves to early South Carolina were not rice-producing areas; lowcountry whites have left no record of valuing the knowledge of rice planting that some slaves might have displayed; and familiarity with rice planting is hardly the same as familiarity with irrigated rice culture, practiced in South Carolina from early days.[17] Slaves undoubtedly contributed a great deal to the development of South Carolina's rice economy; but, on present evidence, it would be rash to attribute the development of a task system to their prowess, especially when that prowess went largely unrecognized and may not have been significant.

[14] Ulrich Bonnell Phillips, "The Slave Labor Problem in the Charleston District," in Elinor Miller and Eugene D. Genovese, eds., *Plantation, Town, and County: Essays on the Local History of American Slave Society* (Urbana, Ill., 1974), 9. For Caribbean absenteeism see Richard S. Dunn, *Sugar and Slaves: The Rise of the Planter Class in the English West Indies, 1624-1713* (Chapel Hill, N.C., 1972), 101-103, 161-163.

[15] Wood, *Black Majority: Negroes in Colonial South Carolina from 1670 through the Stono Rebellion* (New York, 1974), 56-62; Littlefield, *Rice and Slaves: Ethnicity and the Slave Trade in Colonial South Carolina* (Baton Rouge, La., 1981), 74-114.

[16] E. P. Thompson, "Time, Work-Discipline, and Industrial Capitalism," *Past and Present*, No. 38 (1967), 73.

[17] Of those slaves imported into South Carolina before 1740 and for whom an African coastal region of origin is known, I calculate that 15% were from rice-

A consideration of staple-crop requirements provides the most satisfactory, if not complete, answer to the question of the system's origins. The amount of direct supervision demanded by various crops offers at least one clue to the puzzle. Unlike tobacco, which involved scrupulous care in all phases of the production cycle and was therefore best cultivated by small gangs of closely attended laborers, rice was a hardy plant, requiring a few relatively straightforward operations for its successful cultivation.[18] The great expansion of rice culture in seventeenth-century Lombardy, for instance, was predicated not on a stable, sophisticated, and well-supervised labor force but on a pool of transient labor drawn from far afield.[19] Nor did rice production require the strict regimentation and "semi-industrialised" production techniques that attended the cultivation of sugar and necessitated gang labor.[20] However, the Caribbean plantation experience does offer parallels to the lowcountry rice economy: in the British West Indies, crops that required little supervision or regimentation—notably coffee and pimento—were, like rice, grown by a slave labor force organized by tasks rather than into gangs.[21]

---

producing areas. Unfortunately, we know little or nothing about the regional origins of the earliest slave vessels to South Carolina. The first association between an African region and the cultivation of rice that I have found comes late in the day and may have been no more than a mercantile gambit. In 1758 the merchant firm Austin and Laurens described the origins of the slave ship *Betsey* as the "Windward and Rice Coast" (*South-Carolina Gazette* [Charleston], Aug. 11, 1758). Whites in other areas of North America are on record as valuing the familiarity with rice planting that some Africans displayed (see Henry P. Dart, "The First Cargo of African Slaves for Louisiana, 1718," *Louisiana Historical Quarterly*, XIV [1931], 176-177, as referred to in Joe Gray Taylor, *Negro Slavery in Louisiana* [Baton Rouge, La., 1963], 14). For the West Africans' widespread unfamiliarity with irrigation see Littlefield, *Rice and Slaves*, 86, and the issue of *Africa*, LI, No. 2 (1981), devoted to "Rice and Yams in West Africa." A fuller discussion of all these matters will be presented in my "Slave Counterpoint: Black Culture in the Eighteenth-Century Chesapeake and Lowcountry" (unpubl. MS).

[18] In 1830 one Cuban planter, with little historical sense, could even argue that the culture of the tobacco plant "properly belongs to a white population, for there are few plants requiring more attention and tender treatment than this does" (Joseph M. Hernandez, "On the Cultivation of the Cuba Tobacco Plant," *Southern Agriculturalist*, III [1830], 463).

[19] Domenico Sella, *Crisis and Continuity: The Economy of Spanish Lombardy in the Seventeenth Century* (Cambridge, Mass., 1979), 121-122.

[20] Dunn, *Sugar and Slaves*, 189-200. The connection between sugar cultivation and gang labor was not absolutely axiomatic, at least in the postemancipation era. See Douglas Hall, *Free Jamaica, 1838-1865: An Economic History* (New Haven, Conn., 1959), 44-45; Jerome Handler, "Some Aspects of Work Organization on Sugar Plantations in Barbados," *Ethnology*, IV (1965), 16-38; and James McNeill and Chimman Lal, *Report to the Government of India on the Conditions of Indian Immigrants in Four British Colonies and Surinam* in *British Parliamentary Papers*, 1915, Cd. 7744, 7745 (I am indebted to Stanley Engerman for the last reference).

[21] B. W. Higman, *Slave Population and Economy in Jamaica, 1807-1834* (Cambridge, 1976), 23-24, 220. A Jamaican bookkeeper reported that the only work on

In addition to the degree of direct supervision required by a crop, the facility with which the laborers' output could be measured also shaped different forms of labor organization. For example, the productivity of a single coffee and pimento worker could be measured accurately and cheaply, particularly in the harvesting cycle. It was easy to weigh an individual's baskets of coffee or pimento berries, and tasking may have first developed in this stage of the respective crop cycles before being extended to other operations. Conversely, the much larger volumes involved in the cane harvest would have proved far less easy and much more expensive to measure on an individual "task" basis; not surprisingly, gang labor was employed at this and other stages of the sugar cycle.[22] In the case of rice, it was less the harvesting and more the cultivation of the crop that lent itself to inexpensive and efficient measurement. As Phillips pointed out, drainage ditches, which were necessary in lowcountry rice cultivation, provided convenient units by which the performance of tasks could be measured.[23] The ubiquity and long-standing history of the quarter-acre task suggest that the planting and weeding stages of the rice cycle provided the initial rationale for the task system; once tasking became firmly established, it was extended to a whole host of plantation operations.

Thus various staple-crop requirements seem to have served as the most important catalysts for the development of particular modes of labor organization. Undoubtedly other imperatives contributed to the attractiveness of one or the other labor arrangement: absenteeism and the ease with which slaves took to rice cultivation may well have encouraged a more widespread and rapid diffusion of the task system in the lowcountry than might otherwise have been the case. Moreover, once a task system had been tried, tested, and not found wanting, it could be extended to crops that were produced elsewhere by means of gang labor. In other words, once tasking became a way of life, means were found to circumvent the otherwise powerful dictates of the various staple crops.[24]

Whatever the origins of the task system, its consequences soon became apparent. Indeed, the way in which slaves chose to spend their own "time" created unease among ruling South Carolinians. One of the earliest laws relating to slaves, enacted in 1686, prohibited the exchange of goods between slaves or between slaves and freemen without their masters' consent. A decade later, slaves were expressly forbidden from felling and carrying away timber on lands other than their masters'. In 1714 the

---

a coffee plantation *not* carried out by tasks was the drying of the berries, because "this required constant attention" (*ibid.,* 23).

[22] Barry Higman suggested this to me in a personal communication.

[23] Ulrich Bonnell Phillips, *American Negro Slavery: A Survey of the Supply, Employment and Control of Negro Labor As Determined by the Plantation Regime* (Baton Rouge, La., 1966 [orig. publ. New York, 1918]), 247.

[24] See the relevant discussions, below, of how the task system was extended to the cultivation of cotton and even sugar in the late 18th- and early 19th-century lowcountry.

TABLE I

TASKING REQUIREMENTS, C.1750 TO C.1860

Representative Tasks	*1750s*[1]	*1770s*[2]	*1820s*[3]	*1830s*[4]	*1840s*[5]	*1850s–1860s*[6]
Rice						
Turning up land	$\frac{1}{4}$a		$\frac{1}{4}$a	$\frac{1}{4}$a	$\frac{1}{4}$-$\frac{1}{2}$a	$\frac{1}{4}$a
Trenching/Covering	$\frac{1}{2}$a		$\frac{3}{4}$a	$\frac{3}{4}$a	$\frac{3}{4}$a	$\frac{1}{2}$a
First Hoeing	$\frac{1}{4}$a		$\frac{1}{4}$-$\frac{1}{2}$a	$\frac{1}{2}$a	$\frac{1}{2}$a	$\frac{1}{4}$-$\frac{1}{2}$a
Second Hoeing				$\frac{1}{2}$a	$\frac{1}{2}$a	
Third Hoeing	$\frac{1}{2}$a			$\frac{3}{4}$a	20c	
Reaping					$\frac{3}{4}$a	$\frac{3}{4}$a
Threshing			600s	600s	600s	600s
Pounding	7m					
Ditching			600sf	700sf	500sf	600sf
Cotton						
Listing			$\frac{1}{4}$a	$\frac{1}{4}$a	$\frac{1}{2}$a	$\frac{1}{4}$-$\frac{1}{2}$a
Bedding			$\frac{1}{4}$a	$\frac{1}{4}$a	$\frac{3}{8}$a	$\frac{1}{4}$-$\frac{1}{2}$a
Hoeing			$\frac{1}{2}$a	$\frac{1}{2}$a	$\frac{1}{2}$a	$\frac{1}{2}$a
Picking			90-100lbs	70-100lbs		
Assorting			30-50lbs	60lbs		
Ginning			20-30lbs	30lbs		20-30lbs
Moting			30-50lbs	30lbs		

General				
Splitting rails	100	100	100	100-125
Squaring timber		100'	100'	100'	100'

a = acre   s = sheaves   m = mortars
c = compasses   sf = square feet

[1] "Bolzius Answers a Questionnaire," trans. and ed. Loewald *et al.*, *WMQ*, 3d Ser., XIV (1957), 258; Garden to the Royal Society, Apr. 20, 1755, Guard Book 1, 36.

[2] John Gerar William De Brahm, *Report of the General Survey in the Southern District of North America*, ed. Louis De Vorsey, Jr. (Columbia, S.C., 1971), 94.

[3] "Estimate of the Daily Labour of Negroes," *American Farmer*, V (1823-1824), 319-320; [Edwin C. Holland], *A Refutation of the Calumnies Circulated against ... Slavery ...* (New York, 1969 [orig. publ. Charleston, S.C., 1822]), 53; Basil Hall, *Travels in North America in the Years 1827 and 1828*, III (London, 1829), 219-223.

[4] "A Memorandum of Tasks," *Southern Agriculturalist*, VII (1834), 297-299; W. H. Capers, "On the Culture of Sea-Island Cotton," *ibid.*, VIII (1835), 402-411.

[5] Edmund Ruffin, *Report of the Commencement and Progress of the Agricultural Survey of South-Carolina for 1843* (Columbia, S.C., 1843), 118; J. A. Turner, *The Cotton Planter's Manual* (New York, 1865), 285.

[6] Frederick Law Olmsted, *A Journey in the Seabord Slave States ...* (New York, 1968 [orig. publ. 1856]), 434-435; Francis S. Holmes, *Southern Farmer and Market Gardener* (Charleston, S.C., 1852), 234-236; Weehaw Plantation Book, 1855-1861, South Carolina Historical Society, Charleston; "Tasks for Negroes," *Southern Cultivator*, XVIII (1860), 247; Col. A. J. Willard to W. H. Smith, Nov. 13, 1865 (A7011); testimony of Harry McMillan, 1863 (K78) (see below, n. 81 for explanation of these notations); J. A. Turner, *The Cotton Planter's Manual*, 133-135. See also George P. Rawick, ed., *The American Slave: A Composite Autobiography* (Westport, Conn., 1972), II, Pt. ii, 302, III, Pt. iii, 92, Pt. iv, 117.

legislature enacted its stiffest prohibition; slaves were no longer to "plant for themselves any corn, peas or rice."[25] While this stark ban appears definitive, later legislation suggests its ineffectiveness. In 1734, for example, an act for the better regulation of patrols allowed patrollers to confiscate "all fowls and other provisions" found in the possession of "stragling negroes." That slaves produced provisions independently is further implied in a 1738 act for the licensing of hawkers and pedlars, which aimed to stamp out the illicit traffic in rice and provisions between slaves and itinerant traders. By 1751 the legislators bowed to the inevitable. By outlawing the sale of slaves' rice and corn to anybody other than their masters, they were implicitly recognizing the right of slaves to cultivate such crops.[26] The law of 1714 had thus died a natural death.

From the evidence of plantation account books and estate records, the act of 1751 simply brought the law closer into line with social practice. In 1728 Abraham, a Ball family slave, was paid £1 10s. for providing his master with eighteen fowls, while a female slave received £8 for supplying hogs. In 1736 twenty-two Ball family slaves were paid more than £50 for supplying varying amounts of rice to their master.[27] The extent of this trade in provisions was occasionally impressive; over the course of two years, the slaves belonging to James Hartley's estate were paid £124 for supplying 290 bushels of their corn.[28] Henry Ravenel not only purchased his slaves' provision goods, consisting of corn, fowls, hogs, and catfish, but also their canoes, baskets, and myrtle wax.[29]

Masters undoubtedly benefited from these exchanges while displaying their benevolence, but we should not assume that there was no bargaining, however unequal, between the parties. Henry Laurens, for example, advised one of his newly appointed overseers to "purchase of your own Negroes all [the provisions] that you know Lawfully belongs to themselves at the lowest price that they will sell it for."[30] If a master refused to give slaves a fair price for their produce, they could take it elsewhere. One of the most persistent complaints of lowcountry planters and legislators concerned illicit trading across plantation boundaries.[31] A slave who

[25] Thomas Cooper and David J. McCord, eds., *The Statutes at Large of South Carolina* (Columbia, S.C., 1836-1841), II, 22-23, VII, 11, 368.
[26] *Ibid.*, III, 398, 489, VII, 423.
[27] Ball Family Account Book, 174, 32, and unpaginated memorandum, Jan. 21, 1736, South Carolina Historical Society, Charleston.
[28] Administration of James Hartley's estate, Aug. 1758-July 1760, Inventory Book V, 160-175, S.C. Archs., Columbia.
[29] Henry Ravenel's Day Book, particularly for the years 1763-1767, S.C. Hist. Soc., Charleston.
[30] George C. Rogers *et al.*, eds., *The Papers of Henry Laurens*, V (Columbia, S.C., 1976), 41.
[31] Apart from the acts already mentioned, see Cooper and McCord, eds., *Statutes*, VII, 407-409, 434-435. See also Charlestown Grand Jury Presentments, *S.C. Gaz.*, Nov. 5, 1737.

produced rice "in his own time" also traveled more than fifteen miles up the Cooper River to sell a barrel of his crop to his brother, who resided on another plantation.[32] A white boatman, implicated in a slave conspiracy, openly acknowledged that he had exchanged his hog for a slave's deer skin.[33] The records of one lowcountry estate even register payments to a neighboring planter's slaves for their seed rice.[34] In other words, once slaves were allowed to produce provisions, they would always find ways to market them, be it to passing traders, neighboring whites, or fellow slaves.

Lowcountry slaves took the opportunity to raise a wide array of agricultural products, many of which reflected their African background. In the third decade of the eighteenth century Mark Catesby observed two African varieties of corn in the lowcountry but only among the "Planta-tions of *Negroes*." When William Bartram visited the lowcountry in the 1770s he noticed that the tania or tannier (a tuberous root found in the West Indies and tropical Africa) was "much cultivated and esteemed for food, particularly by the Negroes."[35] Bernard Romans claimed that slaves had introduced the groundnut into South Carolina; by the early nine-teenth century, according to David Ramsay's informants on Edisto Island, groundnuts were "planted in small patches chiefly by the negroes, for market."[36] Romans also attributed the introduction of the "sesamen or oily grain" to lowcountry slaves; they used it, he maintained, "as a food either raw, toasted or boiled in their soups and are very fond of it, they call it *Benni*." Over one-and-a-half centuries later, a black sea islander was to be found planting what he called "bene." He used it in the same ways that his ancestors had done. Most significant, when asked where he acquired the seed, he said "his parents always had it and he was told 'Dey brung it fum Africa'."[37] Apparently peppers were also the preserve of slaves. Knowing that his slave old Tom "plants a good deal of pepper," Elias Ball

[32] Testimony of Thomas Akin and Ammon, Feb. 7, 1749, Council Journal, No. 17, Pt. 1, 160.

[33] Testimony of Lawrence Kelly, Jan. 30, 1749, *ibid.*, 85.

[34] Administration of David Caw's estate, Oct. 20, 1761, Inventory Book V, 12-19.

[35] Mark Catesby, *The Natural History of Carolina, Florida and the Bahama Islands* . . . , II (London, 1743), xviii; Francis Harper, ed., *The Travels of William Bartram* (New Haven, Conn., 1958), 297.

[36] Romans, *A Concise Natural History of East and West Florida* . . . , I (New York, 1775), 131; Ramsay, *The History of South Carolina*, II (Charleston, S.C., 1808), 289. The groundnut is a South American cultivated plant which was disseminated so widely and rapidly within Africa that some have postulated an African origin. This is not the case, but Africans apparently introduced the plant into North America (A. Krapovickas, "The Origin, Variability and Spread of the Groundnut," in Peter J. Ucko and G. W. Dimbleby, eds., *The Domestication and Exploitation of Plants and Animals* [London, 1969], 427-441).

[37] Romans, *History of East and West Florida*, I, 130; Orrin Sage Wightman and Margaret Davis Cate, *Early Days of Coastal Georgia* (St. Simons Island, Ga., 1955), 163.

desired him to send "sum Read pepper pounded and corked up in a pint Bottle." In 1742, when Eliza Lucas sent her friend some of the same product, she referred to it, in revealing fashion, as "negroe pepper."[38] The only tobacco grown in early eighteenth-century South Carolina belonged to the slaves.[39] Janet Schaw was so impressed by the way in which Carolina slaves used their "little piece[s] of land" to grow vegetables, "rear hogs and poultry, sow calabashes, etc." that she thought they cultivated them "much better than their Master[s]." Furthermore, she believed that "the Negroes are the only people that seem to pay any attention to the various uses that the wild vegetables may be put to."[40]

The cultivation and subsequent exchange of provisions allowed some slaves to claim more substantial items of property. In 1714 the South Carolina legislature denied the slaves' claim to "any stock of hogs, cattle or horses." This directive apparently fell on deaf ears, for in 1722 it became lawful to seize any hogs, boats, or canoes belonging to slaves. Moreover, this later act referred to the "great inconveniences [that] do arise from negroes and other slaves keeping and breeding of horses"; not only were these horses (and cattle) to be seized, but the proceeds of their sale were to be put to the support of the parish poor. The irony of slave property sustaining white paupers was presumably lost on South Carolina legislators but perhaps not on the slaves. Once again, legislative intentions seem to have been thwarted, for in 1740 more complaints were to be heard about those "several owners of slaves [who] have permitted them to keep canoes, and to breed and raise horses, neat cattle and hogs, and to traffic and barter in several parts of this Province, for the particular and peculiar benefit of such slaves."[41] The most dramatic example of property ownership by a lowcountry slave in the first half of the eighteenth century involved not horses or canoes, but men. According to a deed of manumission, a slave named Sampson "by his Industry and the Assistance of Friends" had purchased and "procured in his owne Right and property and for his owne Use" another Negro slave named Tom. Sampson then

[38] Elias Ball to Elias Ball, Feb. 26, 1786, Ball Family Papers, University of South Carolina, Columbia; Elise Pinckney, ed., *The Letterbook of Eliza Lucas Pinckney, 1739-1762* (Chapel Hill, N.C., 1972), 28.
[39] "Bolzius Answers a Questionnaire," trans. and ed. Loewald *et al.*, *WMQ*, 3d Ser., XIV (1957), 236; John Glen to the Board of Trade, Mar. 1753, C.O. 5/374, 147, Public Record Office; Bernhard A. Uhlendorf, trans. and ed., *The Siege of Charleston: With an Account of the Province of South Carolina* ... (Ann Arbor, Mich., 1938), 353. The cultivation of tobacco spread rapidly through West Africa during the 17th century, so that 18th-century black immigrants to South Carolina might well have been familiar with the crop. See, for example, Jack R. Harlan *et al.*, eds., *Origins of African Plant Domestication* (The Hague, 1976), 296, 302, and Philip D. Curtin, *Economic Change in Precolonial Africa: Senegambia in the Era of the Slave Trade* (Madison, Wis., 1975), 230.
[40] Evangeline Walker Andrews and Charles McLean Andrews, eds., *Journal of a Lady of Quality* ... (New Haven, Conn., 1923), 176-177.
[41] Cooper and McCord, eds., *Statutes*, VII, 368, 382, 409.

exchanged his slave Tom for "fifty years of his [that is, Sampson's] Life time and Servitude (to come)."[42] If the task system had created the opportunities for Sampson's "Industry" to manifest itself in this way, it truly was a potent force.

II

> Once a slave has completed his task, his
> master feels no right to call on him.
> Daniel Turner, 1806

By the late eighteenth century the task system had taken deep root in the lowcountry. Tasks were set for almost all operations—from clearing new ground (one-eighth of an acre) to the weekly task of a pair of sawyers (600 feet of pine or 780 feet of cypress).[43] However, the basic unit, a quarter-acre, was still the yardstick for virtually all rice-planting operations.[44] In recognition of this reality, one Georgia absentee in 1786 sent a chain "for running out the Tasks" to his plantation manager. "It is 105 feet long," he noted, "and will save a great deal of time in Laying out the field, and do it with more exactness." Henry Ferguson, an East Floridian who had spent seventeen years in South Carolina and Georgia, was able to specify precisely how much land his slaves had cleared "from the Tasks which he set to his Negroes having measured the Ground frequently for that purpose." He added that "a Task was a quarter of an Acre to weed p. day."[45] Even opponents of the task system testify to its pervasiveness. William Butler, a keen observer of rice culture, argued in 1786 that slaves "should always be Kept in Gangs or parcels and not scattered over a field in Tasks as is too generally done, for while in gangs they are more immediately under the Superintendants Eyes, [and] of course may be much better and more immediately inspected."[46]

[42] Mr. Isaac Bodett's Release to a Negro for Fifty Years, Nov. 13, 1728, Records of the Secretary of the Province, Book H, 42-43, S.C. Archs., Columbia.

[43] John Gerar William De Brahm, *Report of the General Survey in the Southern District of North America*, ed. Louis De Vorsey, Jr. (Columbia, S.C., 1971), 94.

[44] William Butler, "Observations on the Culture of Rice," 1786, S.C. Hist. Soc., Charleston. One plantation journal recorded completed daily tasks and acres planted. The quarter-acre task was uniformly applied throughout the planting season. See Plantation Journal, 1773, Wragg Papers, S.C. Hist. Soc.

[45] J. Channing to Edward Telfair, Aug. 10, 1786, Telfair Papers, Duke University, Durham, N.C.; Wilbur H. Siebert, ed., *Loyalists in East Florida, 1774 to 1785*, II (DeLand, Fla., 1929), 67.

[46] Butler, "Observations," 1786. There was a parallel debate in England at this time between the advocates of regularly employed wage-labor and the advocates of "taken-work." One of those who censured the recourse to taken-work made a similar point to that of Butler: people only agreed to tasking, this critic alleged, in order "to save themselves the trouble of watching their workmen" (Thompson, "Time, Work-Discipline," *Past and Present*, No. 38 [1967], 78-79).

The extension of the task system to the cultivation of sea island cotton confirms the failure of Butler's advice. Since both the long- and short-staple varieties of cotton required close attention, especially in the tedious hoeing and thinning phases of their cultivation, they were ideal candidates for gang labor. Most upcountry South Carolina planters adopted this arrangement from the first, and sea island planters were encouraged to do the same: one lowcountry planter from Georgia advised his South Carolina colleagues that "there is no possibility of tasking Negroes" in cotton culture. However, his peers proved him wrong. By the early nineteenth century the tasking requirements of all sea island cotton operations were well established. They remained substantially unchanged throughout the nineteenth century (see Table I).[47]

Perhaps the profits being generated under the existing task system discouraged lowcountry planters from adopting gang labor, for they were not likely to restructure an arrangement that was so patently successful. In 1751 James Glen reported that South Carolina planters expected a slave to pay for himself within four to five years. Dr. Alexander Garden calculated that in 1756 planters made between £15 to £30 sterling for every slave they employed in the field, which he noted was "indeed a great deal." At that rate, a slave would pay for himself in two to three years. In 1772 a visitor to South Carolina noted that indigo planters made from £35 to £45 sterling for every able Negro; in this case, a newly purchased slave paid for himself in less than two years.[48] The rate of return of a 200-acre rice plantation, employing forty slaves in the late colonial period, was estimated to be 25 percent, more than double the opportunity cost of capital.[49] And although the Revolutionary war was enormously disruptive of the lowcountry economy, the 1790s were boom years for planters, as they replaced one highly profitable secondary staple (indigo) with another (sea island cotton). So profitable was this second staple that planters on

[47] Letter to printers, *City Gazette* (Charleston), Mar. 14, 1796. The readiness with which sea island planters extended the task system to sea island cotton planting suggests prior familiarity which, in turn, suggests that indigo planting had been subject to tasking. No direct evidence of this connection is available, so far as I am aware. Few upland cotton plantations employed a thoroughgoing task system. One that did—the Silver Bluff plantation belonging to Christopher Fitzsimmons, subsequently owned by James Henry Hammond—was run as an absentee property and was more than likely populated by slaves already inured to tasking when resident on Fitzsimmons's tidewater plantation (Drew Gilpin Faust, personal communication).

[48] James Glen to the Board of Trade, July 15, 1751, C.O. 5/373, 155-157, P.R.O.; Garden to the Royal Society, May 1, 1757, Guard Book III, 86; G. Moulton to [?], Dec. 20, 1772, Add. MSS 22677, 70, British Library.

[49] John Gerar William De Brahm, *History of the Province of Georgia ...* (Wormsloe, Ga., 1849), 51; Ralph Gray and Betty Wood, "The Transition from Indentured to Involuntary Servitude in Colonial Georgia," *Explorations in Economic History*, XIII (1976), 361-364.

Edisto Island in 1808 averaged a return of between $170 and $260 for every field hand.[50]

Crucial to the continuing profitability of rice plantations was the wholesale transfer of production from inland to tidal swamps, a process that was well underway by the late eighteenth century. John Drayton, writing at the turn of the century, identified some of the advantages of this shift in location: "River swamp plantations, from the command of water, which at high tides can be introduced over the fields, have an undoubted preference to inland plantations; as the crop is more certain, and the work of the negroes less toilsome." Surely it was a tidewater rice plantation that a Virginian witnessed in 1780 when he observed that "after the ground is once well cleared little cultivation does the ground [need] being soft by continual moisture."[51] In short, the development of tidewater rice culture reduced the heavy hoeing formerly required of slaves in the summer months. As might be expected, the daily task unit expanded, and squares of 150 feet (approximately a half of an acre) appeared in tidewater rice fields.[52] The other side of this coin was the increase in heavy labor required of slaves in the winter months, for tidewater cultivation demanded an elaborate system of banks, dams, canals, and ditches. By the turn of the century, no doubt, lowcountry laborers were as familiar with the daily ditching requirement (about 600 to 700 square feet or ten compasses) as they had ever been with the quarter-acre task.[53]

Although the precise definition of daily tasks had advantages from the slaves' point of view, the potential conflict that stereotyped tasks and their careless assignment could engender should not be underestimated. Indeed, the evidence of conflict should alert us to a battle that undoubtedly was being waged but that rarely surfaces in the historical record; namely, the constant warring between taskmaster and laborer over what constituted a fair day's work. After one such altercation between a black driver and a group of slaves, the latter took their case to their master in Charleston.

[50] Ramsay, *History of South Carolina*, II, 278-280. High rates of profit continued to characterize the large rice plantations (see Dale Evans Swan, *The Structure and Profitability of the Antebellum Rice Industry, 1859* [New York, 1975]).

[51] John Drayton, *A View of South-Carolina as Respects Her Natural and Civil Concerns* (Spartanburg, S.C., 1972 [orig. publ. Charleston, S.C., 1802]), 116; James Parker's Journal of the Charlestown Expedition, Feb. 5, 1780, Parker Family Papers, 920 PAR I 13/2, Liverpool City Libraries, Liverpool, England.

[52] Timothy Ford speaks of half-acre tasks (Joseph W. Barnwell, ed., "Diary of Timothy Ford, 1785-1786," *S.C. Hist. Mag.*, XIII [1912], 182). However, the first specific reference that I have so far found to the 150-square-feet task is in Edmund Ruffin, *Report of the Commencement and Progress of the Agricultural Survey of South-Carolina for 1843* (Columbia, S.C., 1843), 104.

[53] See Table I. Time and space do not permit an investigation of the effect of developments in machinery on slave work routines. However, to give but one example, the pounding task of the early 18th century was, by the end of the century, redundant. Agricultural manuals in the 19th century do not set daily tasks for pounding.

When he asked them "why they could not do their Tasks as well as the rest," they answered that "their Tasks were harder." The master was sympathetic, knowing that "there is sometimes a great difference in Tasks, and Paul told me he remembered that Jimmy had a bad Task that Day. I was sorry to see poor Caesar amongst them for I knew him to be an honest, inoffensive fellow and tho't if any will do without severity, he will. I inquired his fault, & Paul told me . . . he had been 2 days in a Task."[54] Hoeing was at issue in this dispute; on another plantation, threshing became a source of conflict. Three slaves belonging to George Austin—Liverpool, Moosa, and Dutay—"ran off early in December, for being a little chastis'd on Account of not finishing the Task of Thrashing in due time."[55] By the early nineteenth century, a *modus vivendi* had apparently been reached on most lowcountry plantations. One South Carolina planter reckoned that the "daily task does not vary according to the arbitrary will and caprice of their owners, and although [it] is not fixed by law, it is so well settled by long usage, that upon every plantation it is the *same*. Should any owner increase the work beyond what is customary, he subjects himself to the reproach of his neighbors, and to such discontent amongst his slaves as to make them of but little use to him."[56] The task system's requirements were hammered out just as much in conflicts with the work force as in the supposedly inevitable march of technological progress.

However onerous tasking could become for some slaves, the system at least had the virtue of allowing the slave a certain latitude to apportion his own day, to work intensively in his task and then have the balance of his time. With the institutionalization of the task system, the slave's "time" became sacrosanct. The right not to be called on once the task had been

---

[54] Richard Hutson to Mr. Croll, Aug. 22, 1767, Charles Woodward Hutson Papers, University of North Carolina, Chapel Hill.

[55] Josiah Smith to George Austin, Jan. 31, 1774, Josiah Smith Letterbook, Univ. N.C., Chapel Hill.

[56] [Edwin C. Holland], *A Refutation of the Calumnies Circulated against . . . Slavery . . .* (New York, 1969 [orig. publ. Charleston, S.C., 1822]), 53. In the antebellum era, the role of the laborers continued to be significant in the evolution of the task system. For a particularly good example of the difficulty in modifying a long-established task (in this case, threshing), see James M. Clifton, ed., *Life and Labor on Argyle Island: Letters and Documents of a Savannah River Rice Plantation, 1833-1867* (Savannah, Ga., 1978), 8-9. Frederick Law Olmsted also noted that "in all ordinary work custom has settled the extent of the task, and it is difficult to increase it." If these customs were systematically ignored, Olmsted continued, the planter simply increased the likelihood of "a general stampede to the 'swamp' " (*A Journey in the Seabord Slave States* [New York, 1968 (orig. publ. 1856)], 435-436). James Henry Hammond waged what appears to have been an unsuccessful battle with his laborers when he tried to impose gang labor in place of the task system much preferred by his slaves (Drew Gilpin Faust, "Culture, Conflict, and Community: The Meaning of Power on an Ante-bellum Plantation," *Journal of Social History,* XIV [1980], 86).

completed was duly acknowledged by lowcountry masters.[57] One of the advantages of such a right is neatly illustrated in an incident that befell a Methodist circuit rider, Joseph Pilmore. On March 18, 1773—a Thursday—he arrived at the banks of the Santee River in the Georgetown district of South Carolina. After waiting in vain for the appearance of the regular ferry, he was met by a few Negroes. Presumably they told him that they "had finished their task," for that is how he explained their availability in his journal. He then hired their "time" so that he could be ferried across the river. The actual time was about three o'clock in the afternoon.[58] Slaves could not only complete their work by mid-afternoon; they might then earn money on their own account.

In the same year that Pilmore visited the Georgetown district, another observer of lowcountry society, "Scotus Americanus," testified more fully to the advantages that a fully institutionalized task system presented to slaves:

> Their work is performed by a daily task, allotted by their master or overseer, which they have generally done by one or two o'clock in the afternoon, and have the rest of the day for themselves, which they spend in working in their own private fields, consisting of 5 or 6 acres of ground, allowed them by their masters, for planting of rice, corn, potatoes, tobacco, &c. for their own use and profit, of which the industrious among them make a great deal. In some plantations, they have also the liberty to raise hogs and poultry, which, with the former articles, they are to dispose of to none but their masters (this is done to prevent bad consequences) for which, in exchange, when they do not chuse money, their masters give Osnaburgs, negro cloths, caps, hats, handkerchiefs, pipes, and knives. They do not plant in their fields for subsistence, but for amusement, pleasure, and profit, their masters giving them clothes, and sufficient provisions from their granaries.[59]

---

[57] Daniel Turner to his parents, Aug. 13, 1806, Daniel Turner Papers, Library of Congress (microfilm). Equally sacrosanct, at least to some slaves, was the product of their "time." Thus, in 1781 a set of plantation slaves attempted to kill their overseer because he tried to appropriate the corn that they were apparently planning to market (*South-Carolina and American General Gazette* [Charleston], Jan. 20, 1781).

[58] Frederick E. Maser and Howard T. Maag, eds., *The Journal of Joseph Pilmore, Methodist Itinerant: For the Years August 1, 1769 to January 2, 1774* (Philadelphia, 1969), 188.

[59] ["Scotus Americanus"], *Information Concerning the Province of North Carolina, Addressed to Emigrants from the Highlands and Western Isles of Scotland* (Glasgow, 1773), in William K. Boyd, "Some North Carolina Tracts of the Eighteenth Century," *North Carolina Historical Review*, III (1926), 616. This account almost certainly refers to the Cape Fear region of North Carolina. For slightly less-detailed accounts see François Alexandre Frédéric, duc de La Rochefoucauld-

As we shall see, planting for "amusement, pleasure, and profit" continued to be a prerogative of lowcountry slaves.

Pilmore and Scotus Americanus alert us to the ways in which lowcountry slaves continued to acquire money. It should hardly surprise us, then, that lowcountry bondmen still aspired to the ownership of more substantial items of property. In spite of the acts of 1714, 1722, and 1740, slaves remained singularly reluctant to relinquish their claims to horses. In 1772 the Charleston District Grand Jury was still objecting to "Negroes being allowed to keep horses . . . contrary to Law."[60] In a transaction that bore a remarkable similarity to the one effected by Sampson a half-century earlier, a slave named Will showed even less regard for the law by exchanging his horses for his freedom. A witness to the exchange heard Will's master, Lewis Dutarque, say to

old fellow Will that he had been a faithful servant to him and if he had a mind to purchase his freedom he should obtain the same by paying him three hundred pounds old currency and says he Will you have two Horses which will nearly pay me. I will allow you hundred pounds old currency for a Roan Gelding and forty five currency for your Gray for which the fellow Will readily consented to the proposals and Mr. Dutarque took possession of the Horses and the fellow Will was to pay the Balance as soon as he could make it up. Mr. Dutarque also borrowed of the fellow Will a small Black mare which he lost and he said she was worth six Guineas and would allow him that price for her.[61]

One begins to wonder how many horses Will possessed. Horse trading may even have been possible within the slave community, if a notice placed in a South Carolina newspaper in 1793 is any indication: "On Sunday last was apprehended by the patrol in St. George's parish, a certain negro man who calls himself *Titus* and his son about 10 year who is called *Tom*; he was trading with the negroes in that neighbourhood, and he had in his possession 2 horses . . . one poultry cart, and several articles of merchandise, consisting of stripes, linens, and handkerchiefs."[62] Given these examples, one lowcountry master was perhaps right to be sanguine about an unsuccessful hunt that he had launched for a group of seven

Liancourt, *Travels through the United States of North America . . .*, I (London, 1799), 599; Drayton, *View of South Carolina*, 145; and Edmund Botsford, *Sambo & Tony, a Dialogue in Three Parts* (Georgetown, S.C., 1808), 8, 13, 34.

[60] Charlestown District Grand Jury Presentments, *S.C. Gaz.*, Jan. 25, 1772.

[61] Declaration of John Blake, Apr. 25, 1788, Miscellaneous Record Book VV, 473, S.C. Archs., Columbia.

[62] *State Gazette of South-Carolina* (Charleston), Oct. 26, 1793.

absentees. He was "convinced these runaways would not go far, being connected at home, and having too much property to leave."[63]

III

> Q. You think that they have a love for property?
> A. Yes, Sir; Very strong; they delight in accumulating.
>   Testimony of Rufus Saxton, 1863

By the middle of the nineteenth century the task system dominated agricultural life in the lowcountry. Indeed, the term so pervaded the region's agricultural terminology that its varied meanings have to be disentangled. For example, a lowcountry planter might say that he had planted "seven tasks (within one task of two acres, as a planter well knows)." At this time, a slave was expected to be able to sow two acres of rice a day; this is presumably what this planter had in mind when referring to the single task of two acres. And yet, the early eighteenth-century definition of a task as measuring one-quarter of an acre was still very much current. It was possible, therefore, to speak of seven units, measuring one-quarter of an acre each, within a larger unit measuring two acres.[64] Similarly, a planter might say that he had penned "thirty head of cattle on a task for one week" (the "task" here refers to one-quarter of an acre); or he might mention setting a "task" of three rice barrels a day for his cooper.[65] In other words, in common usage the term "task" not only referred to a unit of labor (a fixed or specified quantity of labor exacted from a person is the dictionary definition) but also to a unit of land measurement (almost invariably one-quarter of an acre or 105 square feet).

Slaves were completely conversant with this terminology, as the recollections of ex-slaves attest. Testifying before Southern Claims Commissioners in 1873, Peter Way knew precisely what constituted a "task" as a unit of land measurement. "Five poles make a task," he noted authoritatively, "and there is twenty-one feet in a pole."[66] Using the term in this

---

[63] William Read to Jacob Read, Mar. 22, 1800, Read Family Papers, S.C. Hist. Soc., Charleston. For another description of property owning by lowcountry slaves in the early 19th century, see Sidney Walter Martin, ed., "A New Englander's Impressions of Georgia in 1817-1818: Extracts from the Diary of Ebenezer Kellogg," *Journal of Southern History*, XII (1946), 259-260.

[64] A Georgian, "Account of the Culture and Produce of the Bearded Rice," *South. Agric.*, III (1830), 292. For the evidence that about two acres was the sowing "task," see "A Memorandum of Tasks," *ibid.*, VII (1834), 297, and Ruffin, *Report*, 118.

[65] A Plain Farmer, "On the Culture of Sweet Potatoes," *South. Agric.*, V (1832), 120; for the cooper's task see the sources cited in the footnotes to Table I.

[66] Testimony of Peter Way, claim of William Roberts, July 4, 1873, Liberty County, Georgia, Case Files, Southern Claims Commission, Records of the 3d Auditor, Record Group 217, Records of the U.S. General Accounting Office,

sense, former slaves might say that "Mr. Mallard's house was about four or five tasks from Mr. Busby's house" (about 420 or 525 feet distant), or that Sherman's troops were "about three tasks off in the woods. I could see [them] from [my] house" (about 315 feet away).[67] When Mason Crum interviewed an old Negro woman (a former slave) in the 1930s, she told him that she owned her land "and that she had in the tract t'ree acres and a tass'," by which she meant three-and-a-quarter acres.[68] When freedmen referred to the crops that they had produced for themselves in "slavery times," they used the units acres and "tasks" interchangeably (tasks here again refer to quarter-acre plots).[69] At the same time, ex-slaves used the term "task" to connote a unit of labor. A freedman, referring to the terms of the contract that he had signed with his employer, spoke of giving "five tasks, that is, I work five tasks for him and plant everything he has a mind to have it planted in for all the land myself and wife can cultivate."[70] The dual meaning of the term is nowhere better illustrated than in the words of one former slave, interviewed in the 1930s, who in one and the same breath recalled "de slave [having] but two taks ob land to cultivate for se'f" (by which he meant half an acre) and "in daytime [having] to do his task" (by which he meant a quantity of labor depending on the operation at hand).[71]

Tasking was so much a way of life in the antebellum lowcountry that virtually all crops and a whole host of plantation operations were subject to its dictates. The cultivation of corn was discussed in terms of the number of hills in a "task-row" and the number of "beds" in a task.[72] Sea

---

National Archives. Hereafter, only the name and date—county and state will be added whenever a claim originates from an area other than Liberty Co., Ga.—will be given, followed by the abbreviation, SCC.

[67] Testimony of Philip Campbell, claim of Windsor Stevens, July 12, 1873, SCC; claimant's deposition, claim of Diana Cummings, June 17, 1873, Chatham County, Ga.; see also testimony of Henry LeCount, claim of Marlborough Jones, July 30, 1873.

[68] Mason Crum, *Gullah: Negro Life in the Carolina Sea Islands* (Durham, N.C., 1940), 51; for a similar use of the term, but by a son of former slave parents, see Wightman and Cate, *Early Days of Coastal Georgia*, 81.

[69] For example, see the claim depositions of James Anderson, William Cassell, Prince Cumings, Hamlet Delegal, and Thomas Irving of Liberty Co., Ga., SCC.

[70] Claimant's deposition, claim of Marlborough Jones, July 30, 1873, SCC; see also claimant's deposition, claim of Somerset Stewart, July 30, 1873.

[71] George P. Rawick, ed., *The American Slave: A Composite Autobiography*, III (Westport, Conn., 1972), Pt. iii, 200-201. A black Edisto Islander, born in 1897, interviewed in 1970, was also conversant with the dual meaning of the term "task" (Nick Lindsay, transc., *An Oral History of Edisto Island: The Life and Times of Bubberson Brown* [Goshen, Ind., 1977], 27, 46-47, 50, 53).

[72] "Memoranda of a Crop of Corn Grown in St. Andrew's Parish," *South. Agric.*, III (1830), 77; "Account of the Mode of Culture Pursued in Cultivating Corn and Peas," *ibid.*, IV (1831), 236. An intensive application of tasking to operations that ranged from the construction of post and rail fences to the digging of groundnuts

island cotton had its own task-acre as distinct from the task-acre utilized in tidewater rice culture.[73] Even when lowcountry planters experimented with sugar cultivation in the 1820s and 1830s, they attempted to retain the notion of a task: a hundred plants, according to one authority, were to be put in a task-row and two hands could then both plant and cut a task a day.[74] On Hopeton plantation, where sugar was grown on a large scale, task work was "resorted to whenever the nature of the work admits of it; and working in gangs as is practiced in the West Indies and the upper country, is avoided. The advantages of this system are encouragement to the labourers, by equalizing the work of each agreeably to strength, and the avoidance of watchful superintendance and incessant driving."[75] Whether this attempt to adapt sugar cultivation to the task system contributed to the failure of lowcountry sugar production is difficult to say; but it is possible that sugar, unlike cotton, just could not be successfully grown without gang labor.

Tasking was ubiquitous in another sense: those slaves not able to benefit from the system's opportunities had to be compensated in other ways. The proposition that drivers, as a group, suffered discrimination is barely credible, but in the lowcountry, at least, such was the case. As one ex-slave recalled, "I suppose the Foreman had advantages in some respects and in others not, for he had no task-work and had no time of his own, while the other slaves had the Evenings to themselves." The son of a Georgia planter remembered that his father's driver was "obliged to oversee all day," whereas the field hands "were allowed to work in any way they chose for themselves after the tasks were done."[76] By way of compensation, lowcountry drivers were entitled to receive a certain amount of help in tending their own crops. Thomas Mallard's driver "had the privilege of having hands to work one acre of corn and one acre of rice" on his behalf; the driver on Raymond Cay's plantation had Cay's field hands plant one

---

can be found in the Plantation Journal of Thomas W. Peyre, 1834-1851, esp. 259, 332, 365, S.C. Hist. Soc., Charleston. (I am grateful to Gene Waddell, Director of the Society, for bringing this to my attention.)

[73] Even Lewis Gray and U. B. Phillips, the two standard authorities on the task system, are confused on this issue. The task-acre in tidewater rice cultivation ideally took the form of a field 300' x 150', divided into two half-acre "tasks" of 150' square. The task-acre on inland rice and sea island cotton plantations was ideally a square of 210', divided into four quarter-acre squares, each side 105' in length. See R.F.W. Allston, "Sea-Coast Crops of the South," De Bow's Review, XVI (1854), 596, 609; cf. Phillips, Negro Slavery, 247, 259, and Gray, History of Agriculture, I, 553.

[74] Jacob Wood, "Account of the Process of Cultivating, Harvesting and Manufacturing the Sugar Cane," South. Agric., III (1830), 226.

[75] The Editor, "Account of an Agricultural Excursion Made into the South of Georgia in the Winter of 1832," ibid., VI (1833), 576.

[76] Testimony of William Winn, claim of David Stevens, July 17, 1873, SCC; testimony of James Frazer, claim of John Bacon, July 7, 1873.

acre of corn and three to five "tasks" in rice on his account.[77] One ex-slave recalled that "drivers had the privilege of planting two or three acres of rice and some corn and having it worked by the slaves"; and, in order to dispel any misimpressions, he emphasized that "these hands worked for [the drivers] in the White people's time."[78] Other occupational groups received different forms of compensation. A former slave plowman recalled that he "didn't work by the task but at the end of the year [his master] gave [him] 6 bushels of corn" by way of redress. A former slave carpenter recollected that "when [he] worked carpentering [his] master allowed [him] every other saturday and when [he] worked farming [his master] gave him tasks."[79] In this man's mind, apparently, these "privileges" were about equal.

The central role of the task system in lowcountry life can best be gauged by investigating its fate immediately after emancipation. Throughout the postwar cotton South freedmen firmly rejected most of the elements of their old system of labor: from the first, gang labor was anathema.[80] At the same time, however, freedmen in the lowcountry were tenaciously striving to retain—and even extend—the fundamentals of their former system. A Freedmen's Bureau official, resident in lowcountry Georgia in 1867, identified a basic response of the former slaves to their new work environment when he observed that they "usually stipulate to work by the task."[81] Lowcountry freedmen even demonstrated their attachment to the task system when they rejected one element of their former slave past by refusing to do the ditching and draining so necessary in rice and sea island cotton cultivation.[82] This work was arduous and disagreeable, of course, and since ditching was more amenable to gang labor than any other operation in lowcountry agriculture, blacks appropriately sought to avoid it at all costs. But in an 1865 petition a group of planters from Georgetown district touched on an even more compelling reason for the freedmen's refusal to perform this familiar task. They pointed out that "it is a work which, as it does not pertain to the present crop, the negroes are

[77] Claimant's deposition, claim of Joseph Bacon, Aug. 12, 1873, SCC; testimony of Peter Way, claim of Silvia Baker, Aug. 9, 1873.

[78] Testimony of Tony Law, claim of Linda Roberts, July 19, 1873, SCC. See also D. E. Huger Smith, A Charlestonian's Recollections, 1846-1913 (Charleston, S.C., 1950), 29.

[79] Claimant's deposition, claim of John Crawford, Mar. 3, 1874, SCC; claimant's deposition, claim of Frank James, Mar. 14, 1874.

[80] See, for example, Leon F. Litwack, Been in the Storm So Long: The Aftermath of Slavery (New York, 1980), 410.

[81] Lt. Douglas G. Risley to Col. C. C. Sibley, June 2, 1867 (A123), Freedman and Southern Society, files of documents in the Natl. Archs., University of Maryland, College Park. (Hereafter reference to documents read at the Society will be given in parentheses.) But cf. Litwack, Been in the Storm, 410.

[82] Bvt. Maj. Gen. Charles Devens to Bvt. Lt. Col. W.L.M. Burger, AAG, Oct. 29, 1865, and Nov. 13, 1865 (C1361, Pt. 1, C4160, Pt. 1); Brig. Gen. W. T. Bennett to Bvt. Lt. Col. W.L.M. Burger, AAG, Oct. 11, 1865 (C1361, Pt. 1).

unwilling to perform." The recipient of this petition, Colonel Willard, was a sympathetic and sensitive observer, and his elaboration of this rationale penetrates to the heart of the issue. The freedmen's real fear, he explained, was that having prepared the ditches for the forthcoming crop, the planters would "insist on having them by the month." This arrangement would be absolutely unacceptable, because the freedmen had "been accustomed to working by the task, which has always given them leisure to cultivate land for themselves, tend their stock, and amuse themselves." If they gave way on this issue, he continued, "their privileges will go and their condition will be less to their taste than it was when they were slaves."[83]

Precisely to avoid such a condition was the overriding imperative governing the actions of lowcountry freedmen. Once this is understood, the multifarious and fluid labor arrangements that characterized the postwar lowcountry become comprehensible. In 1865 and 1866 two basic forms of labor contract (with many individual variations) were employed in the lowlands of South Carolina and Georgia. Either the freedmen worked for a share of the crop (anywhere from one-half to three-quarters, a higher share than found elsewhere in the South), with the freedmen's share being divided among them on the basis of tasks performed, or they hired themselves for the year, with payment being made on the basis of the numbers of tasks completed (usually fifty cents a task, although payment was by no means always made in cash).[84] Whatever the mode of reimbursement, the task was central to most early contracts.

In 1866 a third labor arrangement arose that soon became general throughout the lowcountry. Known as the "two-day" or, less frequently, "three-day" system, it simply extended the concept of task labor, for it drew an even more rigid demarcation between the planters' "time" and the laborers' "time." The Freedmen's Bureau agent for eastern Liberty County, Georgia, observed as early as February 1867 that there were in his district no freedmen working by the month and only a few for wages. Some were working for a share of the crop, but most were employed by the "two-day" system, working a third of the time on the employers' crop

[83] Ben Allston et al., to Col. Willard, Oct. 30, 1865 (C1602, Pt. 2); Lt. Col. A. J. Willard to Capt. G. W. Hooker, AAG, Nov. 7, 1865 (C1614, Pt. 2).

[84] This information was derived from Lt. Col. A. J. Willard to Capt. G. W. Hooker, AAG, Nov. 7, 1865, and Dec. 6, 1865 (C1614, Pt. 2, C1503, Pt. 1); case #104, James Geddes v. William B. Seabrook, Feb. 11, 1867 (C1534, Pt. 1); contract between William H. Gibbons and 120 Freedmen, Chatham Co., Ga., Mar. 1, 1866 (A5798); Maj. Gen. James B. Steedman and Bvt. Brig. Gen. J. S. Fullerton to E. M. Stanton, June 4, 1866 (A5829); Capt. Henry C. Brandt to Lt. Col. A. W. Smith, Jan. 12, 1867 (A5395). See also John David Smith, "More than Slaves, Less than Freedmen: The 'Share Wages' Labor System During Reconstruction," *Civil War History*, XXVI (1980), 256-266, for the example of a contract, *not* the analysis that accompanies it. A detailed analysis of the labor contracts in operation in these years would undoubtedly enrich, and perhaps modify, this section.

and receiving land to work on their own account for the remainder of the time.[85] The agricultural census of 1880 reported that the "two-day" system was ubiquitous on the South Carolina sea islands. For ten months of the year, slaves worked two days in each week for their employers and received in return a house, fuel, and six acres of land for their own use, free of rent. Proprietors were said to dislike the system because their employees only cultivated about two acres in the owners' "time." However, the report continued, "the laborers themselves prefer this system, having four days out of the week for themselves." As a result, "they are more independent and can make any day they choose a holiday."[86]

The reasons for the slaves' (and the freedmen's) attachment to the task system should be readily apparent, but the subject is worth a moment's extra consideration because we are in the privileged and rare position of being able to listen to the participants themselves. The most obvious advantage of the task system was the flexibility it permitted slaves in determining the length of the working day. Working from sunup to sundown was the pervasive reality for most antebellum slaves; but ex-slaves from the lowcountry recall a different reality. Richard Cummings, a former field hand, recalled that "a good active industrious man would finish his task sometimes at 12, sometimes at 1 and 2 oclock and the rest of the time was his own to use as he pleased." Scipio King, another former field hand, reckoned, as he put it, that "I could save for myself sometimes a whole day if I could do 2 tasks in a day then I had the next day to myself. Some kind of work I could do 3 tasks in a day."[87] Exhausting as task labor undoubtedly was, its prime virtue was that it was not unremitting.

A second advantage concerned the relationship between the slaves' provisions and the planters' rations. Whatever slaves produced beyond the task was regarded as surplus to, not a substitute for, basic planter allocations of food and clothing. One former slave recalled that his master continued to dispense rations "no matter how much they [the slaves] made of their own . . . [which] they could sell . . . if they chose." July Roberts, another ex-slave, emphasized that "every week we drew our rations no matter what we raised." When one former slave claimed the loss of corn,

[85] A. M. McIver to Lt. J. M. Hogg (SAC), Feb. 28, 1867 (A5769); see also Lt. W. M. Wallace to Capt. E.W.H. Read, Jan. 8, 1867 (C1619); D. M. Burns to [?], Mar. 17, 1867 (A7188); and Joel Williamson, *After Slavery: The Negro in South Carolina during Reconstruction, 1861-1877* (Chapel Hill, N.C., 1965), 135-136.

[86] Harry Hammond, "Report on the Cotton Production of the State of South Carolina," in U.S. Census Office, *Tenth Census, 1880* (Washington, D.C., 1884), VI, Pt. ii, 60-61.

[87] Testimony of Richard Cummings, claim of Lafayette Delegal, July 11, 1873, SCC; claimant's deposition, claim of Scipio King, July 9, 1873. A number of lowcountry freedmen made similar statements. For the general recollections of ex-slaves see, obviously, George P. Rawick, *From Sundown to Sunup: The Making of the Black Community* (Westport, Conn., 1972), and Paul D. Escott, *Slavery Remembered: A Record of Twentieth-Century Slave Narratives* (Chapel Hill, N.C., 1979), 38.

rice, and clothing taken by Federal troops, an attempt was made to deny him his title because these represented rations and "so belonged to the master." The response of this freedman's attorneys no doubt reflected the prevailing attitude of former slaves: "It is obvious to remark that if these things had not been taken from the claimant by the army, he would have had them after 'freedom came' and were to all intents his property."[88] Not only did slaves plant in their own time for "amusement, pleasure, and profit," they claimed the master's rations as their own to do with as they wished.

In view of these advantages, we might expect the scale and range of property owning by slaves to have assumed significant dimensions by the middle of the nineteenth century. An analysis of the settled claims submitted by former slaves to the Southern Claims Commission for loss of property to Federal troops provides the best test of this hypothesis.[89] Taking the Liberty County, Georgia, claimants as a sample, former field hands outnumber all other occupational groups. While most were mature adults when their property was taken, 30 percent were under the age of thirty-five. In terms of occupation and age these claimants constitute a relatively broad cross section of the slave population. Moreover, whether field hands or artisans, young or old, virtually all of them had apparently been deprived of a number of hogs, and a substantial majority listed corn, rice, and fowls among their losses. In addition, a surprising number apparently possessed horses and cows, while buggies or wagons, beehives, peanuts, fodder, syrup, butter, sugar, and tea were, if these claims are to be believed, in the hands of at least some slaves. The average cash value (in 1864 dollars) claimed by Liberty County former slaves was $357.43, with the highest claim totaling $2,290 and the lowest $49.[90]

Some claims were spectacular. Paris James, a former slave driver, was described by a neighboring white planter as a "substantial man before the war [and] was more like a free man than any slave."[91] James claimed,

[88] Testimony of Peter Stevens, claim of Toney Elliott, Aug. 8, 1873, SCC; testimony of July Roberts, claim of Nedger Frazer, Feb. 27, 1874; report of R. B. Avery and testimony of Gilmore and Co., attorneys for claimant, claim of Jacob Dryer, Nov. 1, 1873.

[89] The settled or allowed claims from ex-slaves for Liberty and Chatham counties, Ga., and Beaufort, Charleston, and Georgetown counties, S.C., were investigated. For a fuller presentation of my findings, see "The Ownership of Property by Slaves in the Mid-Nineteenth-Century Lowcountry," *Jour. So. Hist.* (forthcoming).

[90] The Liberty Co., Ga., claims are the most numerous and most detailed. They contain few urban claimants and form the ideal sample for the purposes of this study. Eighty-nine former slaves from this county submitted claims that were settled: 50 of the 89 were field hands and 25 of 86 were under the age of 35 when their property was taken. For a fuller discussion of the reliability of these claims and an analysis of the claimed property, see my article cited in n. 89.

[91] Testimony of Raymond Cay, Jr., claim of Paris James, June 2, 1874, SCC. Cay also said that he "looked upon [James] as one of the most thrifty slaves in Liberty County." His claim totaled $1,218.

among other things, a horse, eight cows, sixteen sheep, twenty-six hogs, and a wagon. Another slave driver, according to one of his black witnesses, lived "just like a white man except his color. His credit was just as good as a white man's because he had the property to back it." Although the claims commissioners were skeptical about his alleged loss of twenty cows—as they explained, "twenty cows would make a good large dairy for a Northern farmer"—his two white and three black witnesses supported him in his claim.[92] Other blacks were considered to be "more than usually prosperous," "pretty well off," and "hardworking and moneysaving"—unremarkable characterizations, perhaps, but surprising when the individuals were also slaves.[93] Alexander Steele, a carpenter by trade and a former house servant of Chatham County, Georgia, submitted a claim for $2,205 based on the loss of his four horses, mule, silver watch, two cows, wagon, and large quantities of fodder, hay, and corn. He had been able to acquire these possessions by "tradeing" for himself for some thirty years; he had had "much time of [his] own" because his master "always went north" in the summer months. He took "a fancy [to] fine horses," a whim he was able to indulge when he purchased "a blooded mare," from which he raised three colts. He was resourceful enough to hide his livestock on Onslow Island when Sherman's army drew near, but some of the Federal troops secured boats and took off his prize possessions. Three white planters supported Steele in his claim; indeed, one of them recollected making an unsuccessful offer of $300 for one of Steele's colts before the war. Lewis Dutarque's Will, a horse owner of note in the late eighteenth century, had found a worthy successor in Alexander Steele.[94]

The ownership of horses was not, however, confined to a privileged minority of slaves. Among the Liberty County claimants, almost as many ex-field hands as former drivers and skilled slaves claimed horses. This evidence supplies a context for the exchange recorded by Frederick Law Olmsted when he was being shown around the plantation of Richard J. Arnold in Bryan County, Georgia. Olsmsted noticed a horse drawing a wagon of "common fieldhand negroes" and asked his host

"[do you] usually let them have horses to go to
    Church?"
"Oh no; that horse belongs to the old man."
"Belongs to him! Why, do they own horses?"
"Oh yes; William (the House Servant) owns
    two, and Robert, I believe, has three now;

[92] Testimony of W. A. Golding, claim of Linda (and Caesar) Roberts, July 19, 1873, SCC. His claim totaled $1,519.

[93] Report of R. B. Avery, claim of Jacob Quarterman, July 5, 1873, SCC; report of R. B. Avery, claim of Prince Stewart, July 29, 1873; report of the Commissioners of Claims, claim of James Stacy, Aug. 15, 1873.

[94] Claimant's deposition and testimony of John Fish, claim of Alexander Steele, Aug. 17, 1872, Chatham Co., Ga., SCC.

that was one of them he was riding."
"How do they get them?"
"Oh they buy them."[95]

Although a few freedmen recalled that former masters had either prohibited horse ownership or confined the practice to drivers, most placed the
proportion of horse owners on any single plantation at between 15 and 20
percent.[96] A former slave of George Washington Walthour estimated that
"in all my master's plantations there were over 30 horses owned by slaves.
. . . I think come to count up there were as many as 45 that owned
horses—he would let them own any thing they could if they only did his
work."[97] Nedger Frazer, a former slave of the Reverend C. C. Jones,
recalled that on one of his master's plantations (obviously Arcadia, from
Frazer's description) there were forty working hands, of whom five owned
horses; and on another (obviously Montevideo) another ten hands out of
fifty owned horses.[98] This, in turn, supplies a context for an interesting
incident that occurred within the Jones's "family" in 1857. After much
soul-searching, Jones sold one of his slave families, headed by Cassius, a
field hand. A man of integrity, Jones then forwarded Cassius the balance
of his account, which amounted to $85, a sum that included the proceeds
from the sale of Cassius's horse.[99] Perhaps one freedman was not
exaggerating when he observed in 1873 that "there was more stock
property owned by slaves before the war than are owned now by both
white and black people together in this county."[100]

The spectacular claims and the widespread ownership of horses naturally catch the eye, but even the most humdrum claim has a story to tell. Each
claim contains, for instance, a description of how property was accumulated. The narrative of John Bacon can stand as proxy for many such
accounts: "I had a little crop to sell and bought some chickens and then I
bought a fine large sow and gave $10.00 for her. This was about ten years
before the war and then I raised hogs and sold them till I bought a horse.

[95] Charles E. Beveridge et al., eds., The Papers of Frederick Law Olmsted, II
(Baltimore, 1981), 182. Twenty-four field hands, out of a total of 53 slaves,
claimed horses.

[96] Two Liberty Co. freedmen testified to a ban on horse ownership on their
plantations; three recalled that only drivers had horses; and fourteen supply the
proportions mentioned here.

[97] Claimant's deposition, claim of Paris James, June 2, 1874, SCC.

[98] Claimant's deposition, claim of Nedger Frazer, Feb. 27, 1874, SCC. This is
the same Niger, as he was known as a slave, who objected to being hired out in
1864 because he was unable, as he put it, to "make anything for himself," and who
pretended to have yellow fever so that Sherman's troops would not deprive him of
his property (see Robert Manson Myers, ed., The Children of Pride: A True Story of
Georgia and the Civil War [New Haven, Conn., 1972], 1162, 1237).

[99] Myers, ed., Children of Pride, 244, 306.

[100] Testimony of W. A. Golding, claim of Linda (and Caesar) Roberts, July 19,
1873, SCC.

This was about eight years before freedom. This was a breeding mare and from this mare I raised this horse which the Yankees took from me."[101] This was not so much primitive as painstaking accumulation; no wonder one freedman referred to his former property as his "laborment."[102] And yet, occasionally, the mode of procurement assumed a slightly more sophisticated cast: some slaves recall purchasing horses by installment;[103] some hired additional labor to cultivate their crops;[104] two slaves (a mill engineer and a stockminder) went into partnership to raise livestock;[105] and a driver lent out money at interest.[106] Whatever the mode of accumulation, the ultimate source, as identified by virtually all the ex-slaves, was the task system. As Joseph James, a freedman, explained, "They all worked by tasks, and had a plenty of time to work for themselves and in that way all slaves who were industrious could get around them considerable property in a short time."[107]

By the middle of the nineteenth century, in sum, it is possible to speak of a significant internal economy operating within a more conventional lowcountry economy. According to the depositions of the freedmen, this internal economy rested on two major planks. The first concerns the degree to which some slaves engaged in stock raising. One white planter, testifying on behalf of a freedman, recalled that "a good many" slaves owned a number of animals; he then checked himself, perhaps realizing the impression that he was creating, and guardedly stated that "what I mean was they were not allowed to go generally into stock raising."[108] And yet some slaves seem to have been doing just that. One ex-slave spoke of raising "horses to sell"; another claimed to have raised fourteen horses over a twenty-five-to-thirty-year period, most of which he had sold;

[101] Claimant's deposition, claim of John Bacon, July 7, 1873, SCC.
[102] Report of R. B. Avery, claim of Robert Bryant, Oct. 6, 1877, Beaufort Co., S.C., SCC.
[103] Claimant's deposition, claim of William Drayton, Feb. 20, 1874, Beaufort Co., S.C., SCC; testimony of Sterling Jones, claim of Sandy Austin, July 21, 1873.
[104] James Miller, for example, recalled that "many times I would get some one to help me, and get along that way, I would pay them whatever they asked according to the time they worked" (report of R. B. Avery, claim of James Miller, July 29, 1873, SCC). See also claimant's deposition, claim of Pompey Bacon, Aug. 7, 1873.
[105] Claimant's deposition, claim of Edward Moddick and Jacob Hicks, Mar. 17, 1873, Chatham Co., Ga., SCC.
[106] Report of J.P.M. Epping, claim of Pompey Smith, n.d., Beaufort Co., S.C., SCC.
[107] Testimony of Joseph James, claim of Linda and Caesar Jones, Aug. 1, 1873, SCC.
[108] Testimony of T. Fleming before R. B. Avery, claim of Prince Wilson, Jr., July 28, 1873, Chatham Co., Ga., SCC. The widespread ownership of animals is also indicated in the records of one lowcountry plantation. In 1859 almost 40 slaves, over half the adult males on the plantation, owned at least one cow, cow and calf, steer or heifer. Only about 10 of the 40 held skilled or privileged positions (Weehaw Plantation Book, 1855-1861, 87, S.C. Hist. Soc., Charleston).

and one freedwoman named some of the purchasers, all of whom were slaves, of the nine horses that she had raised.[109] The other major foundation of this internal economy was the amount of crop production by slaves. Jeremiah Everts observed that the slaves in Chatham County, Georgia, had "as much land as they can till for their own use."[110] The freedmen's recollections from all over the lowcountry support this statement: a number of ex-slaves reckoned that they had more than ten acres under cultivation, while four or five acres was the norm.[111] The proprietorial attitude encouraged by this independent production is suggested in one freedman's passing comment that he worked in his "own field."[112] Through the raising of stock and the production of provisions (together with the sale of produce from woodworking, basketmaking, hunting, and fishing), slaves were able to attract money into their internal economy. Robert W. Gibbes knew of an individual slave who received $120 for his year's crop of corn and fodder; Richard Arnold owed his slaves $500 in 1853 when Olmsted visited him.[113] Thus, while produce and livestock were constantly being bartered by slaves—"swapping" was rife, according to the freedmen—one observer of the mid-nineteenth-century lowcountry was undoubtedly correct when he noted that "in a

[109] Testimony of Fortune James, claim of Charles Warner, Aug. 6, 1873, SCC; claimant's deposition, claim of Prince Wilson, Jr., July 28, 1873, Chatham Co., Ga.; claimant's deposition, claim of Jane Holmes, July 21, 1873.

[110] Jeremiah Evarts Diary, Apr. 5, 1822, Georgia Historical Society, Savannah, as quoted in Thomas F. Armstrong, "From Task Labor to Free Labor: The Transition along Georgia's Rice Coast, 1820-1880," *Georgia Historical Quarterly*, LXIV (1980), 436.

[111] The Liberty Co. claimants who mention such acreages include Daniel Bryant, William Cassell, Prince Cumings, George Gould, Ned Quarterman, Paris James, and Richard LeCounte. The Chatham Co. claimants include Dennis Smith and Alfred Barnard. The Beaufort Co. claimants include John Morree, Andrew Riley, Pompey Smith, Moses Washington, and Benjamin Platts. When James Miller's brother, Lawrence, a student at Howard University, was asked whether the hundred bushels of rice claimed by his brother was not excessive, he replied, "I should not think so—not in his condition." James's "condition" was only that of a field hand, but he was the "director" of the family, and the family planted five acres (testimony of Lawrence Miller, claim of James Miller, July 29, 1873, SCC).

[112] Claimant's deposition, claim of Adam LeCount, Feb. 26, 1874, SCC.

[113] Gibbes, "Southern Slave Life," *De Bow's Review*, XXIV (1858), 324; Olmsted, *Journey*, 443. Fanny Kemble noted that two carpenters on the Butler estate sold a canoe to a neighboring planter for $60 and that slaves could earn large sums by collecting Spanish moss (Frances Anne Kemble, *Journal of a Residence on a Georgian Plantation in 1838-1839*, ed. John A. Scott [New York, 1961], 62, 364). Unfortunately, there are no estimates of the proportion of money circulating among the slaves. The handling of money certainly gave rise to some discernment: one freedman remembered paying $60 in "good money" for a horse. He continued, "I call silver money good money, I call confederate money wasps' nests" (claimant's deposition, claim of Simon Middleton, June 2, 1873, Chatham Co., Ga., SCC).

349

small way a good deal of money circulated among the negroes, both in the country and in the towns."[114]

The autonomy of this internal economy is further indicated by the development of a highly significant practice. By the middle of the nineteenth century, if not before, slave property was not only being produced and exchanged but also inherited. The father of Joseph Bacon bequeathed him a mare and all his other children $50 each.[115] Samuel Elliot claimed a more substantial legacy, for his father "had 20 head of cattle, about 70 head of hogs—Turkeys Geese Ducks and Chickens a Plenty—he was foreman for his master and had been raising such things for years. When he died the property was divided among his children and we continued to raise things just as he had been raising."[116] The role of less immediate kin was also not negligible. Two freedmen recalled receiving property from their grandfathers; another inherited a sow from his cousin; and William Drayton of Beaufort County, South Carolina, noted that when his father died he "left with his oldest brother, my uncle, the means or property he left for his children," and Drayton bought a mule "by the advice of my uncle who had the means belonging to me."[117] There were rules governing lines of descent. One female claimant emphasized that she had not inherited any of her first husband's property because she had borne him no children; rather, his son by a former marriage received the property.[118] The ability to bequeath wealth and to link patrimony to genealogy serves to indicate the extent to which slaves created a measure of autonomy.

The property rights of slaves were recognized across proprietorial boundaries as well as across generations. Slaves even employed guardians to facilitate the transfer of property from one plantation to another. Thus when Nancy Bacon, belonging to John Baker, inherited cattle from her deceased husband who belonged to Mr. Walthour, she employed her second cousin, Andrew Stacy, a slave on the Walthour plantation, to take charge of the cattle and drive them over to her plantation. According to Stacy, Mr. Walthour "didn't object to my taking them [and] never claimed them."[119] The way in which slave couples took advantage of their divided

[114] Alice R. Huger Smith, *A Carolina Rice Plantation of the Fifties* (New York, 1936), 72.

[115] Claimant's deposition, claim of Joseph Bacon, Aug. 12, 1873, SCC.

[116] Claimant's deposition, claim of Samuel Elliott, July 17, 1873, SCC.

[117] Claimant's deposition, claim of York Stevens, Mar. 2, 1874, SCC; claimant's deposition, claim of Edward Brown, Feb. 20, 1874, Beaufort Co., S.C.; claimant's deposition, claim of William Roberts, July 4, 1873; claimant's deposition, claim of William Drayton, Feb. 20, 1874, Beaufort Co., S.C.

[118] Claimant's deposition, claim of Jane Holmes, July 21, 1873, SCC. Twenty-three Liberty Co. freedmen referred to inheriting property within the same plantation.

[119] Claimant's deposition and testimony of Andrew Stacy, claim of Nancy Bacon, Mar. 14, 1874, SCC; Stacy performed the same service for Clarinda Porter (claimant's deposition, claim of Clarinda Porter, Feb. 18, 1874). Nine Liberty Co. freedmen referred to inheriting property across plantation boundaries.

ownership is suggested by Diana Cummings of Chatham County, Georgia. Her husband's master, she explained, "allowed him to sell but mine didn't," so Diana marketed her crops and stock through her husband and received a part of the proceeds. On her husband's death, she received all his property for, as she put it, her "entitle" (surname) was then the same as her husband's. She had since changed it, through remarriage to Sydney Cummings, but she noted that Cummings had "no interest in [the] property [being claimed]."[120]

By the middle of the nineteenth century the ownership of property by lowcountry slaves had become extensive and had assumed relatively sophisticated dimensions. This, in turn, gives rise to an obvious question. What significance was attached to the practice by the slaves? What was the *mentalité*, the moral economy, of this property-owning group? Certainly some freedmen spoke of "getting ahead" and of "accumulating" under slavery.[121] Jacob Monroe, a freedman, admitted that as a slave under the task system he "could go and come when [he] pleased, work and play after [his] task was done," but he pointedly emphasized that "he chose to work."[122] Competitiveness was also not alien to the slave quarters. One freedman recalled how the young adults on one plantation "were jealous of one another and tried to see which would get their days work done first."[123] William Gilmore referred to the disparities in property ownership that characterized Raymond Cay's slaves; he likened them to the "five wise and five foolish" and disparaged those who "slept and slumbered the time away."[124] Similar impressions are derived from those Northerners who came into contact with sea island blacks in the early 1860s. B. K. Lee observed that "they are very acquisitive indeed"; Henry Judd described their "passion for ownership of horses or some animal"; and Rufus Saxton was impressed to find that "they regard the rights of property among themselves. If a man has a claim upon a horse or sow he maintains his right and his neighbours recognize it."[125]

Acquisitiveness and respect for property had other overtones, as Rufus Saxton's resonant phrase—"they delight in accumulating"—suggests.[126] Display and ostentation, while not on any grand scale, of course, seem an accurate characterization of some slaves' behavior. The ownership of horses undoubtedly had practical purposes—one freedman explained that "some of the slaves had families a good ways off and they used their horses

[120] Claimant's deposition, claim of Diana Cummings, June 17, 1873, Chatham Co., Ga., SCC.

[121] See, for example, claimant's deposition, claim of Silvia Baker, Aug. 9, 1873, SCC; claimant's deposition, claim of Hamlet Delegal, Mar. 7, 1874; and claimant's deposition, claim of William Golding, May 16, 1874.

[122] Claimant's deposition, claim of Jacob Monroe, July 18, 1873, SCC.

[123] Testimony of Joshua Cassell, claim of George Gould, Aug. 11, 1873, SCC.

[124] Testimony of William Gilmore, claim of York Stevens, Mar. 2, 1874, SCC.

[125] Testimony of B. K. Lee, 1863 (K72); testimony of Henry G. Judd, 1863 (K74); testimony of Brig. Gen. Rufus Saxton, 1863 (K70).

[126] Testimony of Saxton, 1863 (K70).

to visit them. The masters said it was for their interest to have us own horses so that we could get back home to work."[127] But the exhibition of status appears also to have been involved. William Golding's ownership of a horse and saddle was proved because "he was given to riding about on Sundays." Frederick Law Olmsted not only witnessed a head house-servant mount his horse after church service but, in true paternalistic fashion, slip a coin to the boy who had been holding its reins.[128] Ex-slaves commonly justified their ownership of a horse and wagon by their need to go to church on Sunday. This was not just a practical matter: Leah Wilson could not disguise the sense of status she derived from being able to drive "right along together with our master going to church."[129] A horse, as Edward Philbrick observed in 1862, was more than a means of transport; it was "a badge of power and caste." Sea island blacks had no respect for people who could not present themselves on a horse. "They will hardly lift their hats to a white man on foot," he noted, and viewed a "walking nigger" with contempt.[130]

Although we find elements of display, of accumulation for its own sake, and of "getting ahead," the *mentalité* of the slaves cannot be reduced to any one of these traits and was indeed much more. We can uncover better the meaning and limits of such behavior by exploring, once again, the slaves' immediate response to freedom. In terms of their attitude toward labor, the freedmen firmly resisted the overtures of northern reformers and proclaimed a resounding attachment to what may be resonantly character-ized as a task-orientation. Employers and Freedmen's Bureau officials alike constantly bemoaned the impossibility of persuading the freedmen to "perform more than their allotted tasks."[131] In 1867 Frances Butler Leigh observed freedmen who begged "to be allowed to go back to the old task system" when the agent of the Freedmen's Bureau attempted to have them work by the day. "One man," she reported, "indignantly asked Major D—— what the use of being free was, if he had to work harder than when he was a slave."[132] Few freedmen would work a full day, a full week, "and very seldom a full month steady," complained one employer.[133] One

[127] Testimony of Lafayette Delegal, claim of Richard Cummings, Feb. 28, 1874, SCC.

[128] Report of R. B. Avery, claim of William Golding, May 16, 1874, SCC; Olmsted, *Journey*, 428.

[129] Testimony of Leah Wilson, claim of Prince Wilson, Jr., July 28, 1873, Chatham Co., Ga., SCC. See also the claim depositions of William Gilmore and Hamlet Delegal, and the testimony of Simon Cassell, Henry Stephens, and Fortune James in the claims of Jacob Monroe, Clarinda Porter, and Charles Warner respectively.

[130] Edward S. Philbrick to Pierce, Mar. 27, 1862 (Q12).

[131] Bvt. Lt. Col. R. F. Smith report in Bvt. Maj. Gen. R. K. Scott to O. O. Howard, July 9, 1866 (C1428, Pt. 1). See also Bvt. Lt. Col. B. F. Smith to O. A. Hart, Apr. 25, 1866 (C1617).

[132] Leigh, *Ten Years on a Georgia Plantation* (London, 1883), 55.

[133] E. T. Wright to Lt. Col. H. B. Clitz, Oct. 6, 1865 (C1361, Pt. 1).

Northerner advocated the confiscation of the freedmen's boats so that instead of continuing in their ways of "precarious living," they might develop "habits of steady industry."[134] The freedmen were said to work "when they please and do just as much as they please"; they then relied on hunting and fishing "to make up for what they lose in the field."[135]

This clash between the proponents of Northeastern business methods and a laboring population wedded to an alternative work ethic reverberated throughout the postwar lowcountry. The conflict is neatly illustrated in an exchange that occurred in 1865 between Colonel Willard, a man generally sympathetic to the freedmen's plight, and two ex-slaves who were sawmill workers. Willard was approached by the harassed owner of the mill, who was unable to impress his workers with the virtues of "steady" work: they claimed, for example, at least two hours of rest during their work day. From the standpoint of a Northern businessman, Willard's argument to the two representatives of the work force was impeccable: "Laborers at the North," he pointed out, "got less wages, and worked from sunrise to sunset, this season of the year, only having an hour at noon." The freedmen's reply was equally forceful: "We want," they emphasized, "to work just as we have always worked." Willard was left to expostulate that these former slaves "have no just sense of the importance of persistent labor."[136]

The freedmen's attitude toward the accumulation of property, much like their attitude toward work, was decisively shaped by their former experience under the task system. The argument that "the more they cultivate, the more they gain" had, as one Northern army officer discovered, no appeal. In 1868 Frances Butler Leigh made a similar discovery when she found that some freedmen refused wages and rations, preferring to "raise a little corn and sweet potatoes, and with their facilities for catching fish and oysters, and shooting wild game, they have as much to eat as they want, and now are quite satisfied with that."[137] In short, lowcountry freedmen apparently wished to avoid an unlimited involvement in the market, favoring production for sale only within the familiar context of an assured production for subsistence. This explains, in large measure, why the freedmen would not forego their hunting and fishing activities for a greater concentration on cash crops, why they aspired to the ownership or rental of land, and why they refused to work for wages.[138] The degree to which subsistence (in this case, hunting) formed the priorities of one freedman is captured in a brief anecdote. A special agent,

[134] J. G. Foster to [?], Sept. 20, 1864 (C1334, Pt. 1).

[135] Joseph D. Pope to Maj. Gen. Q. A. Gilmore, June 29, 1865 (C1472).

[136] Lt. Col. A. J. Willard to W. H. Smith, Nov. 13, 1865 (A7011).

[137] Smith report in Scott to Howard, July 9, 1866 (C1428, Pt. 1); Leigh, *Ten Years on a Georgia Plantation*, 124.

[138] I have been influenced by Eric Foner, *Politics and Ideology in the Age of the Civil War* (New York, 1980), 97-127; Willie Lee Rose, *Rehearsal for Reconstruction: The Port Royal Experiment* (New York, 1976 [orig. publ. Indianapolis, Ind., 1964]), 226, 303, 406; and the works by Mintz cited in n. 8.

who toured the lowcountry in 1878 investigating disputed claims, visited the home of Samuel Maxwell, a former slave. He was not impressed with this particular claimant's adaptation to freedom and advised him to participate more fully in the wider society. For a start, he suggested, why not raise hogs rather than dogs? To which Maxwell replied: "A pig won't help us catch coons and rabbits."[139]

The preferences and ambitions of the freedmen reflected, above all, a desire for autonomy not only from the impersonal marketplace but also from individual whites. As one would-be employer found out in 1866, the freedmen who rejected wages and wanted to supply their own seed were expressing a fundamental desire to "be free from personal constraint."[140] They sought, in other words, to build upon a foundation that the task system had laid, consisting of that part of a day, that plot of land, or those few animals that they, as slaves, had been able to call their own. Thus for many, if not most, lowcountry freedmen, the central priorities of subsistence and autonomy shaped whatever propensity for material accumulation and for "getting ahead" they may have had. And what these goals of subsistence and autonomy signally call to mind, of course, are nothing more than the central priorities of peasants throughout the world.[141]

The freedman's quest for a measure of autonomy from individual whites should not be construed, however, as a desire for total disengagement from whites, particularly in the immediate postemancipation years. The moral universe of lowcountry slaves apparently contained notions of social equity and of reciprocal obligations between blacks and whites that were not jettisoned when freedom came.[142] Henry Ravenel's slaves, for example, voluntarily presented themselves before their master in March 1865 and "said they would be willing to take a certain piece of land which they would cultivate for old Master—that they would not want a driver or overseer, but would work that faithfully for him—and that they would take another piece of land to work for their own use." Another set of plantation blacks dumbfounded their former owner in July 1865 when they told him that they now considered the land as their own; perhaps more striking, however, was their readiness to grant "Master" a portion of the crop as "a free gift from themselves."[143] When the promise of land dimmed, the freedmen could be expected to assume a more hostile posture. While evidence of such hostility exists, some sensitive observers

[139] Report of R. B. Avery, claim of Samuel Maxwell, June 8, 1878, SCC.
[140] J. R. Cheves to A. P. Ketchum, Jan. 21, 1866 (A7058).
[141] Apart from the standard works on peasants by Wolf, Shanin, and Mintz, I found the general implications of James C. Scott, *The Moral Economy of the Peasant: Rebellion and Subsistence in Southeast Asia* (New Haven, Conn., 1976) particularly helpful.
[142] For antebellum slaves, and on a general level, this is the argument of Genovese, *Roll, Jordan, Roll*, esp. 133-149.
[143] Arney Robinson Childs, ed., *The Private Journal of Henry William Ravenel, 1859-1887* (Columbia, S.C., 1947), 216; Capt. H. A. Storey to C. B. Fillebrown, July 9, 1865 (C1468). Ravenel still considered his plantation hands to be slaves in Mar. 1865.

were still aware of a basic and continuing paradox. Thus Joseph Le Conte, writing of Liberty County, Georgia, freedmen in the 1890s, noted their refusal to be tied to whites and their rejection of wage labor based, in his view, on their ability to "live almost without work on fish, crawfish, and oysters." At the same time, however, he referred to "the kindliest feelings" existing "among the blacks . . . toward their former masters." While Le Conte may have been guilty of some self-deception, similar observations from his fellow whites suggest the reality of this paradox.[144] Once again, this aspect of the freedmen's world view is strikingly reminiscent of a central feature of peasant life that, according to one authority, is permeated by the moral principle of reciprocity.[145]

The significance of the particular conjunction that this article set out to explore—the conjunction between a certain mode of labor organization and a particular domestic economy—can now be assessed. From the short-run perspective of masters, this conjunction had a number of benefits. They could escape their plantations in the summer months, they were supplied with additional provisions, and their slaves were *relatively* content, or so they believed. Oliver Bostick, a Beaufort County planter, explained that he "allowed [his] slaves to own and have their property and have little crops of their own for it Encouraged them to do well and be satisfied at home." Rufus King, another lowcountry master, was satisfied that "no Negro with a well-stocked poultry house, a small crop advancing, a canoe partly finished or a few tubs unsold, all of which he calculates soon to enjoy, will ever run away."[146] From the short-run perspective of the slaves, this conjunction increased their autonomy, allowed them to accumulate (and bequeath) wealth, fed individual initiative, sponsored collective discipline and esteem, and otherwise benefited them economically and socially.[147] In other words, on a much reduced scale, there were lowcountry slaves who resembled the protopeasants found among Caribbean slaves. This similarity was derived from very different origins: in the lowcountry, from a particular mode of labor organization; in the Caribbean, from the need for slaves to grow most of their own food and provision the free population. There was, in short, a much wider "peasant breach in the slave mode of production" in the Caribbean than in the lowcountry.[148]

[144] William Dallam Armes, ed., *The Autobiography of Joseph Le Conte* (New York, 1903), 234. Long after emancipation, when he had ceased to be a landowner, Daniel Huger Smith still shared in "the same interchange of small gifts of eggs or a chicken or two on the one side and perhaps an article of clothing on the other" that had characterized master-slave relations many years before (*Recollections*, 127).

[145] Scott, *Moral Economy of the Peasant*, 157-192.

[146] Testimony of Oliver P. Bostick, claim of Andrew Jackson, Mar. 10, 1874, Beaufort Co., S.C., SCC; Rufus King, Jr., to William Washington, Sept. 13, 1828, in *American Farmer*, X (1828), 346.

[147] See Mintz, "Slavery and the Rise of Peasantries," in Craton, ed., *Roots and Branches*, 241.

[148] The phrase was coined by Tadeusz Lepkowski, referred to by Sidney W. Mintz, "Was the Plantation Slave a Proletarian?" *Review*, II (1978), 94. I would also

Still, the parallel is suggestive, for in the same way that protopeasant adaptations had a comparable short-term significance for masters and slaves in both Caribbean and lowcountry, there were comparable long-term results. Wherever there were significant protopeasant activities among the slaves, there emerged after emancipation a class of people who had acquired the requisite skills that helped them escape, at least in part or temporarily, their dependence on the plantation.[149] In the lowcountry, the course of the war, the capital requirements of its major staple crop, and the development of phosphates production go some way toward explaining the particular shape of its postwar labor history.[150] But surely certain elements of this configuration had deeper roots, roots that without exaggeration can be traced all the way back to the early eighteenth century. The imperatives so dear to generations of lowcountry slaves achieved a measure of realization in the more distinctive features of the region's postwar labor arrangements. By 1880 the percentage of farms sharecropped in the coastal districts of South Carolina and Georgia ranked among the lowest in the South; the proportion of rural black landowners was one of the highest in the South; it is possible to speak of a "black yeomanry" in the late nineteenth-century lowcountry; and by 1880 one observer in coastal Georgia could describe how most of the Negroes in his county had "bought a small tract of land, ten acres or more [on which they made] enough rice . . . to be perfectly independent of the white man."[151]

---

suggest that there was a significantly wider peasant breach in the slave mode of production in the lowcountry than elsewhere in North America where "incentives," in the forms of garden plots, opportunities to earn money, etc., were accorded slaves. More comparative work is obviously needed, but evidence from one area of the antebellum South supports my supposition (Roderick A. McDonald, "The Internal Economies of Slaves on Sugar Plantations in Jamaica and Louisiana" [unpubl. paper, Southern Historical Association Meeting, 1981]). In any case, I am reluctant to describe the task system as an incentive system; it was more a way of life.

[149] Mintz, "Slavery and the Rise of Peasantries," in Craton, ed., *Roots and Branches*, esp. 226-233. In the same way that I consider there to have been a wider peasant breach in the slave mode of production in the lowcountry than elsewhere in North America (though it was certainly not absent elsewhere), I also believe—and this is almost a corollary—that the ability to escape the plantation, while not unique to the lowcountry, was more effectively secured here than elsewhere in North America.

[150] As we might expect, lowcountry freedmen, particularly sea islanders, proved an unreliable source of labor for the phosphate mines. Their plots of land took precedence, and their earnings from mining formed only a welcome supplement to the income derived from farming (Tom W. Schick and Don H. Doyle, "Labor, Capital, and Politics in South Carolina: The Low Country Phosphate Industry, 1867-1920" [unpubl. paper], 11).

[151] Roger L. Ransom and Richard Sutch, *One Kind of Freedom: The Economic Consequences of Emancipation* (Cambridge, 1977), 91-93; Williamson, *After Slavery*, 155; W.E.B. DuBois, "The Negro Landholder of Georgia," *Bulletin of the United States Department of Labor*, VI, 35 (1901), 647-677; T. J. Woofter, *Black Yeomanry*

To paraphrase Sidney Mintz, nothing else during the history of low-country slavery was as important as the task system and its concomitant domestic economy in making possible the freed person's adaptation to freedom without the blessings of the former masters.[152]

(New York, 1930); *Morning News* (Savannah), Jan. 30, 1880, quoted in Armstrong, "From Task Labor to Free Labor," *Ga. Hist. Qtly.*, LXIV (1980), 443. This last-mentioned article makes a similar argument to the one here.

[152] Mintz, "Plantation Slave," *Review*, II (1978), 95.

Factory, Church, and Community: Blacks in Antebellum Richmond

By JOHN T. O'BRIEN

IN THE WEEKS FOLLOWING RICHMOND'S CAPITULATION TO UNION troops on April 3, 1865, city blacks availed themselves of freedom by welcoming their liberators, celebrating emancipation, seeking work, and reuniting families. Black groups began at the same time to take complete control of their African churches and in cooperation with northern teachers to establish free schools for over a thousand children. These first collective efforts surprised the teachers but were largely ignored by white Richmonders. The whites could not, however, ignore the black community's public demand for legal equality in June 1865. Responding to the brutal enforcement by the police and army of pass and curfew laws which were designed to expel thousands of blacks from the city, black leaders conducted a court of inquiry into official misconduct. Failing to win redress from local officials, they called a mass meeting for June 10 at the First African Baptist Church. The more than three thousand blacks attending the meeting approved a protest memorial and selected seven representatives to present it to the President of the United States. The delegation, which included a representative from each of the five African churches and was financed by collections in the churches, had an audience with President Andrew Johnson, who promised assistance. By the time the delegates returned and reported back to their constituents the pass and curfew laws had been repealed, the civilian government removed, and the offending army officers replaced.[1]

These collective black activities, which profoundly influenced the subsequent course of Reconstruction in the city, raise questions about the community life and organizational structure of antebellum black Richmond. They pose in particular the question of how

[1] John T. O'Brien, Jr., "From Bondage to Citizenship: The Richmond Black Community, 1865–1867" (unpublished Ph.D. dissertation, University of Rochester, 1975), 73–185.

MR. O'BRIEN is assistant professor of history at Dalhousie University, Halifax, Nova Scotia.

the blacks were able to muster the initiative and cohesiveness necessary to establish schools, take control of churches, and mount a sophisticated mass protest so soon after their liberation.

White observers, in response to these events, offered only superficial characterizations of the newly freed slaves. Northern teachers and missionaries claimed that they were the smartest in Dixie, while military and civilian officials described them as a lazy and ignorant people susceptible to outside troublemakers.[2] The freedmen saw themselves differently. They stated in their memorial that theirs was a law-abiding community with several thousand literate and propertied members, over six thousand regular churchgoers, and a tradition of caring for the sick and the poor through clandestine benevolent societies. Their proved respectability and past loyalty to the Union had earned them humane treatment as free men, they explained, not the abuse and lowly status the army was according them.[3] Their memorial revealed important aspects of their historical development as a community, a past that historians of urban slavery have often slighted by focusing on the disintegrating forces in southern cities that allegedly produced social disorder among slaves.[4]

Recent studies of rural slave societies, of the culture of the quarters, and of the slave family have begun to reconstruct the world of the plantation slaves,[5] but the interior life of urban slave communities still awaits serious study. The collective behavior of Richmond freedmen in 1865 was an expression of their prewar experience and an extension in time and into new conditions of an

---

[2] Henry L. Swint, ed., *Dear Ones at Home: Letters from Contraband Camps* (Nashville, 1966), 159–62; John R. Dennett, *The South as It Is: 1865–1866,* edited by Henry M. Christman (New York, 1965), 27; *Freedmen's Record,* I (June 1865), 98. Richmond *Evening Commercial Bulletin,* June 19, 1865; Marsena R. Patrick, *Inside Lincoln's Army; The Diary of Marsena Rudolph Patrick, Provost Marshal General, Army of the Potomac,* edited by David S. Sparks (New York and London, 1965), 511–12.

[3] New York *Tribune,* June 17, 1865.

[4] The classic work on urban slavery and the one that most clearly argues the theme of social disintegration among urban slaves is Richard C. Wade, *Slavery in the Cities: The South 1820–1860* (New York, 1964), 3, 4, 117–24, 243–81. Wade's thesis that urbanization undermined slavery and the idea put forth by others that hiring created a "twilight zone" between slavery and freedom were disputed in Robert S. Starobin, *Industrial Slavery in the Old South* (New York, 1970). Neither historian paid much attention to the community life of urban slaves, each focusing on what was done to the slaves. Much light on black community life is shed by Ira Berlin, *Slaves Without Masters: The Free Negro in the Antebellum South* (New York, 1974), 250–315, 343–95.

[5] Three of the most impressive works on black life under slavery and in freedom are Eugene D. Genovese, *Roll, Jordan, Roll: The World the Slaves Made* (New York, 1974); Herbert G. Gutman, *The Black Family in Slavery and in Freedom, 1760–1925* (New York, 1976); and Joel Williamson, *After Slavery: The Negro in South Carolina During Reconstruction, 1861–1877* (Chapel Hill, 1965).

order the slaves and free blacks had created earlier. The sources of their behavior were deeply imbedded in the slave past and demonstrated the impact of the two largest institutions of the Richmond black world, the tobacco factories and the African Baptist churches.

Between 1820 and 1860 the population of Richmond more than tripled, reaching 37,910 on the eve of the Civil War and making Richmond the twenty-fifth most populous city in the nation. The number of whites rose from 6,445 in 1820 to 23,635 in 1860, of free blacks from 1,235 to 2,576, and of slaves from 4,387 to 11,699. The average percentage increase per decade over the forty years was 38.5 percent for whites, 28.3 percent for slaves, and 22.1 percent for free blacks.[6] Industrial development sparked the city's growth in population. Richmond contained the South's most important iron-making and machine-building works, the two largest flour mills in the country, and the nation's largest tobacco-manufacturing industry. The output of these three industries and other shops and factories in 1860 made Richmond the thirteenth most productive industrial center in the United States. Its forty-nine factories turned out more chewing tobacco in that year than all other southern factories outside the state.[7] The tobacco industry relied exclusively on black workers. Its rise was intimately linked to the growth of the city's slave population.

Tobacco manufacturing accounted for the unique demographic profile of Richmond's slave population which, unlike most urban slave communities, grew between 1820 and 1860 and consisted of more males than females. In 1820, when the industry was in its infancy, males made up 49.5 percent of the slave population, but by 1860, at the height of industrial prosperity, 56.7 percent of the slaves were males. Tobacco factories in 1860 employed 3,364 men and boys, most of whom were slaves, and in this year the entire male slave population of the city stood at 6,636. More than half of all employees counted in the industrial censuses of 1850 and 1860 worked in these factories. Tobacco factory operatives accounted for 69.8 percent of all workers in 1850 and 50.3 percent of the total ten years later. They worked in larger groups than most other white

[6] Federal census returns for Richmond's population between 1820 and 1860 are printed in Wade, *Slavery in the Cities*, 327–30.

[7] Emory M. Thomas, *The Confederate State of Richmond: A Biography of the Capital* (Austin and London, 1971), 21–22; Joseph C. Robert, *The Tobacco Kingdom: Plantation, Market, and Factory in Virginia and North Carolina, 1800–1860* (Durham, 1938), 187–88. The number of tobacco establishments in Richmond in 1860 is often cited as fifty-two, but only forty-nine were chewing-tobacco factories. See for example Starobin, *Industrial Slavery*, 16; and also Federal Industrial Manuscript Census for Richmond City, 1860 (Virginia State Library, Richmond, Va.).

and black workers. The average number of laborers in tobacco establishments was 84 in 1850 and 69.4 in 1860. Over the decade the number of tobacco factories rose from thirty-one to forty-nine. By contrast, the average number of workers in shops and factories in the city whose output exceeded $500 annually was 20.6 in 1850 and 26.1 in 1860. Tobacco factories were the major employers in Richmond and the chief users of male slave workers.[8]

Most tobacco manufacturers owned some of their factory hands and hired additional workers when market conditions warranted. James Thomas, Jr., for example, owned 88 of the 178 slaves who worked in his factory in 1853.[9] Ownership assured manufacturers of a steady supply of slave workers skilled in preparing tobacco for market and accustomed to the rhythms, disciplines, and conditions of the factories. The main disadvantage was that ownership required large capital outlays that proved increasingly burdensome to entrepreneurs who started or expanded operations in the 1850s, a period of rapidly rising slave prices. Many therefore turned to hiring slaves and free blacks to fill their labor needs, and by 1860 over half the Virginia tobacco workers were hired.[10] As the demand for black hirelings increased the rates of hire soared. James Thomas, Jr., for instance, hired Edmund from William B. Towles for $100 in 1852, for $125 in 1853, and was asked to pay $140 in 1854.[11] Thousands of bondsmen were sent to Richmond during Christmas week each year to be hired out. They came from planters and urban slaveholders with surplus workers, from widows and elderly persons who depended on the hiring out of slaves for their income, and from executors of estates seeking to earn money for the estates' heirs.

Several distinct hiring practices developed over the years. Manufacturers sometimes negotiated directly by letter with slaveowners for the services of their slaves. This method was often employed when employers and owners knew each other personally, when they had enjoyed prior, satisfactory dealings, or when owners

[8] These figures are based on materials from the Federal Industrial Manuscript Census for Richmond City in 1850 and 1860; see also Wade, *Slavery in the Cities*, 325–30; and also Berlin, *Slaves Without Masters*, 220, for the number of skilled and unskilled free, adult, male workers in Richmond in 1860. Berlin counted 4,078 free workers. That the tobacco factories employed nearly 3,400 slaves in the same year suggests the importance of the industry to the slave work force and the entire working population of the city.

[9] Receipt from sheriff of Richmond for personal-property tax paid by James Thomas, Jr., for 1852; list of winter clothing distributed to hands in 1853, James Thomas, Jr., Business Records (Duke University Library, Durham, N. C.).

[10] Robert, *The Tobacco Kingdom*, 197–200; Starobin, *Industrial Slavery*, 129–30.

[11] Towles to Thomas, January 3, December 31, 1852; January 6, 1854, Thomas Business Records.

sought to send young slaves to the city for the first time. In these negotiations the reputations of all parties counted heavily. John Y. Mason, in charge of hiring out three of his father's slaves, left the terms of their hire to James Thomas. "My father," he wrote, "leaves the hire of the boys entirely to you, whatever they are worth he knows you will pay."[12] William B. Wyatt was more demanding in his negotiations. "I understand by letter from my son that you want Anthony for the present year. You can keep him at $150 which I think he must be worth from the prices I have been offered."[13] Even in such direct negotiations the slaves could make their wishes known. Benjamin Fleet told Thomas in 1856 that "Charles is exceedingly anxious to go back to Richmond on account of its being so much more convenient for him to visit his wife from there, than here, and under the circumstances, I feel inclined to indulge him as I can but appreciate the feeling that seems to influence him."[14] Other owners and factory managers, who perhaps had not built up extensive contacts, frequently employed hiring agents located in Richmond to place or find slave hirelings.[15]

Most slave hirelings were placed for the year by their owners in face-to-face negotiations with employers, or they found work by bargaining directly with employers in the streets of the city during the annual Christmas-week hiring period. One newspaper observed at the close of 1853 that Richmond had been "thronged with negroes, hirers, owners and buyers, as is the annual custom. Thousands of dollars changed hands, thousands of negroes changed homes and masters."[16] Main streets were generally so crowded with hirelings that merchants complained that holiday shoppers were frightened away.[17] The heaviest criticism, however, was directed at the practice of permitting hirelings to find employers and bargain for the terms of their own hire.

Just before the 1853 hiring season the Richmond *Daily Dispatch* tartly predicted that "Main street will be converted into one vast unroofed intelligence office, and the owners, masters and hirers, in accordance with the annual custom, will briefly dance attendance upon their black attendants."[18] The *Southern Planter* joined the

[12] Mason to Thomas, January 9, December 28, 1853, *ibid.*; quotation from January 9, 1853.
[13] Wyatt to Thomas, January 1, 1853, *ibid.*
[14] Fleet to Thomas, January 8, 1856, *ibid.*
[15] Frederick L. Olmsted, *A Journey in the Seaboard Slave States, with Remarks on Their Economy* (2 vols., New York and London, 1904), I, 33–34 (hereinafter cited as Olmsted, *Seaboard Slave States*); Starobin, *Industrial Slavery*, 128.
[16] Richmond *Daily Dispatch*, January 3, 1853.
[17] *Ibid.*, January 4, 1854.
[18] *Ibid.*, December 22, 1852.

attack on this growing custom, recalling that in years gone by "the owner himself exercised care in selecting a master for his slave . . . but now the negro is permitted to 'choose his master,' as it is called . . . ." Naturally, the slave "selects a master who he knows will indulge him, will exact but little labor, and grant him many privileges and a good deal of time for himself, or he is bribed by money, or the promise of privileges, to live with some one who, possibly from hope of a certain profit to accrue from a modicum of labor, is willing to take him on such terms . . . ." The indulgent employer, the *Southern Planter* warned, "plants the germ of rebellion in the contract for obedience, and stipulates himself into a certain amount of servitude."[19] Repeated warnings of the social dangers of permitting slave hirelings to find their own employers failed to halt the practice.

The custom of allowing slaves to choose their masters flourished in the 1850s because owners and employers found it convenient and profitable. It freed owners from the chore of traveling to Richmond during the holiday or of paying a 5 percent commission to a hiring agent.[20] Since slaves liked the freedom and bargaining power it gave them, their masters could grant it as a reward for faithful past service or offer it as a lure for continued good behavior. Slaves may have won the privilege either by promising to work harder and thereby making themselves more valuable or by offering their owners a sum higher than the market rate for their yearly hire, paying the extra amount out of their factory earnings. Once owners allowed the slave to "choose his master" employers had little choice but to bargain directly with him. Judge John Taylor Lomax was one of many employers who dealt with slave hirelings in the streets at Christmas. He sought a dining-room servant for a year, found a likely slave, and struck a bargain with him. Before concluding the agreement the slave went off to "inquire into the standing and character of the Judge." A local newspaper, outraged at the slave's impudence, fumed that similar incidents "occur with us every day during the Christmas week."[21] They undoubtedly multiplied when demand for hirelings rose in 1852 as a result of the opening of five new tobacco factories.[22]

For the hired slaves there were two matters of great importance. The first was whether or not they would have the opportunity to

[19] Quoted, *ibid.*
[20] Robert, *The Tobacco Kingdom*, 201.
[21] Quoted in Richmond *Daily Dispatch*, December 29, 1856.
[22] *Ibid.*, September 23, 1852.

earn money for themselves. According to a white Richmonder "All slaves had perquisites of some kind. If called on to do extra work, or to serve at unusual times, or if they showed marked fidelity, they were generally recompensed."[23] Dining-room servants, porters, and coachmen collected tips, while domestic servants and factory slaves often received cash instead of clothing.[24] Slaves at the Tredegar Iron Works regularly earned small sums for lighting and cleaning furnaces after working hours.[25] Nowhere was money payment more thoroughly part of the daily production process than in tobacco factories. All tobacco workers had to fill daily production quotas, and they received piece-rate bonuses for all production above the quota. Surviving factory records do not list bonus payments, but contemporary observers did make rough estimates. The *Daily Dispatch* guessed in 1852 that factory hirelings earned about $120 annually. Five years later the Richmond *Whig* claimed that "Many of the hired negroes in the tobacco factories in Richmond make from $8 to $12 per week, overwork, without any extraordinary labor."[26] The *Whig*'s estimate was certainly too high, but earnings seem to have been considerable. Freed black tobacco workers complained in late 1865 that their total earnings were half of what they had been before the war.[27]

The second significant point was whether or not they would be allowed to make their own arrangements for board and room. The practice of giving board money to slave hirelings and to slaves owned by the manufacturers had been rare in the 1820s but had become widespread in the industry by 1850. Many tobacco manufacturers adopted this practice to attract slaves hirelings, to retain

[23] Robert Ryland, "Origins and History of the First African Baptist Church," in Henry A. Tupper, ed., *The First Century of the First Baptist Church of Richmond, Virginia* (Richmond, 1880), 271-72; hereinafter cited as Ryland, "Origins."
[24] *Ibid.*, 271. Robert Ryland frequently gave his slaves money instead of clothing at their request and supposed that "other families pursued the same course." James Thomas gave twenty of his hands money instead of clothing in 1853; see list of winter clothing distributed to hands in 1853, Thomas Business Records. Ryland noted elsewhere that it was customary to tip slaves for work or services that were especially well done or were beyond the normal call of duty. See Ryland, "Reminiscences of the First African Baptist Church," *American Baptist Memorial*, XIV (November 1855), 322; hereinafter cited as Ryland, "Reminiscences."
[25] Charles B. Dew, *Ironmaker to the Confederacy: Joseph R. Anderson and the Tredegar Iron Works* (New Haven and London, 1966), 26-32.
[26] Richmond *Daily Dispatch*, January 3, 1852; Richmond *Whig*, January 21, 1857. The *Daily Dispatch*, January 16, 1857, also stated that "In some factories servants, after performing their regular tasks, earn from $8 to $12 per week over work, without any extraordinary labor." See also Luther P. Jackson, *Free Negro Labor and Property Holding in Virginia, 1830–1860* (New York and London, 1942), 158–59.
[27] John T. Trowbridge, *A Picture of the Desolated States and the Work of Restoration, 1865–1868* (Hartford, Conn., 1868), 230-31.

their services from year to year, and to cut expenses.[28] Slaves preferred boarding out for the freedom of movement and privacy it afforded them. Manufacturers favored it because it freed them from the expense of building dormitories on factory premises and from the responsibility of policing the slaves after working hours. Moreover, they integrated the boarding-out system into their bonus-incentive plan by paying slaves niggardly board stipends, which in the 1850s usually amounted to less than a dollar a week, thus making the slaves use part of their bonus earnings to pay for their board. By keeping board payments low and bonus scales high manufacturers maximized the force of production incentives.[29]

Critics of the board system, the payment of cash to slave workers, and the lax hiring practices frequently campaigned for reforms. They charged that boarding out shifted the employers' responsibility for controlling their slaves to the police and the public treasury, that bonus payments corrupted slaves by encouraging gambling and drinking among them, and that their bargaining power at hiring time made slaves haughty and impudent.[30] Above all, the critics feared that these practices were actually concessions that employers had made to slaves out of a sense of dependence on them. The *Daily Dispatch*, for example, argued that manufacturers had been "compelled, in order to secure labor, first to purchase the consent of the negroes to live with them, and then to hire them of their owners, and in order to do so, have allowed the servants to dictate their own terms as to the amount of board money to be given, the extent of daily labor to be performed, and the price to be paid for such overwork as they may feel disposed to do."[31] However, the critics overshot the mark. It is true that the manufacturers' reliance on slave labor, particularly when demand was high, had given slave hirelings an opening which they broadened over time, but it had never given them the power to dictate terms. Slave hirelings could bargain and maneuver only within the limited boundaries of the racial etiquette imposed by whites. In this extended bargaining they transformed the role laid down for them by slave law, but they did not reverse it.

Critics called on the City Council to abolish the "evils" that had developed in the factory slave-labor system. Responding to these attacks on the boarding-out system the council proposed an ordinance in 1852 that would have required owners and employers to

[28] Richmond *Daily Dispatch*, October 25, 1852; Robert, *The Tobacco Kingdom*, 203–204.
[29] Richmond *Daily Dispatch*, October 25, 27, 1852.
[30] *Ibid.*, October 21, 25, 1852.
[31] *Ibid.*, December 18, 1856, quoted in Robert, *The Tobacco Kingdom*, 203.

board slaves on their premises. A majority of the tobacco manufacturers counterattacked. They argued that the board system had improved the health and demeanor of their slaves, they claimed that they could not afford to build dormitories for them on factory premises, and they warned that many of them would be forced to evade the law if it were passed. They also asserted that many rural and city slaveowners strongly favored continuing the boarding-out system.[32] Faced by the combined opposition of the influential manufacturers, slaveowners, and boardinghouse keepers, the council backed down, but the controversy persisted.

The financial panic of 1857 weakened the manufacturers' resistance to reforming the board system. Most tobacco factories and other establishments in the city closed by October 1. Newspapers noted that destitution was stalking working-class neighborhoods and that many laborers, particularly free blacks thrown out of work at the tobacco factories, were turning to petty crime to survive. Among working people only slaves seemed untouched by the economic crisis, for they had "masters to supply their wants, however tight the times may be." Manufacturers were sorely pressed by having to provision their own slaves and their slave hirelings. Therefore, they listened intently as Robert A. Mayo, one of Richmond's leading tobacco manufacturers, declared at their December convention "that the practice prevailing in factories of giving light tasks, paying for overwork and furnishing board money, was ruinous to the servants in every respect, unjust to the manufacturers and injurious to owners." The *Daily Dispatch* warmly welcomed Mayo's speech but warned that "No one manufacturer can now say that he will not give board money and over work, and expect to hire a sufficient force to carry on his business; but, by a general understanding, all of them could say so, and the system could be broken up without the slightest inconvenience to themselves."[33] When the City Council passed a new ordinance two weeks later, outlawing the old board system and the practice of permitting slaves to hire themselves out to employers, the manufacturers supported it. The new ordinance did not require owners and hirers to board slaves on their premises, the major stumbling block to earlier reform efforts. It merely directed them to pay board money to those who boarded their slaves instead of to the slaves themselves and required them to inform the mayor where the slaves resided.[34] The victory, however, was more apparent than real.

[32] Richmond *Daily Dispatch*, October 27, 1852.
[33] *Ibid.*, December 3, 7, 1857.
[34] *Ibid.*, December 24, 1857.

Critics of the over-work and bonus system did not win even a cosmetic reform. The *Daily Dispatch* spoke for many white Richmonders in arguing that the over-work system was a "curse" to many valuable factory slaves, for "Money in their hands leads to drinking and gambling, and these, in their turn, to other vices and crimes." Paying slaves for work they ought to perform, when their basic material wants were already provided, was a "mere waste of means" that should be "suppressed," the paper reasoned.[35] A few manufacturers agreed, but most demurred. The majority recognized that the lure of bonuses combined most effectively with the threat of punishment to maintain high production levels. However necessary coercion may have been for slave labor, exclusive reliance on it could backfire. Harsh employers risked injuring valuable slave property, antagonizing owners of hired slaves, and repelling those slaves who found their own employers. Punishments unmixed with rewards provoked work slowdowns, worker demoralization, and such retaliatory acts as physical attack and incendiarism.[36] The promise of bonuses reduced the need for coercion by making it the slaves' interest to labor efficiently and steadily. The promise, moreover, easily became a form of discipline, for employers could dock pay for lateness and unruliness and could cancel the rewards of those who tried to run away. Bonuses were simply too important in the hiring and productive processes to be abolished, despite what editors and elected officials said about their socially subversive consequences.

The range of choice open to slave hirelings narrowed after the hiring period, but their ability to shape their working and living conditions did not end after they entered the factory gates. A highly concentrated labor force averaging about seventy-five men and boys per factory, tobacco hands developed a sense of group interest as slaves and free blacks and as workers with wants and needs different from and occasionally opposed to those of their employers. As working groups have generally done, tobacco workers recognized some of their fellows as leaders and created ways of initiating newcomers into their company and of familiarizing them with the customs of the factory.

White overseers, many in their late teens and early twenties, were set above the workers. Theirs was a ticklish job. It required them to maintain order and high productivity, both of which depended upon cooperation from the workers. The overseers gave

[35] *Ibid.*, December 30, 1853.
[36] For instances of factory burnings see Richmond *Whig*, March 18, 1850; July 4, 19, 1853; see also Richmond *Daily Dispatch*, February 16, March 23, 24, July 1, 1852.

orders to slaves who, in many cases, were older, stronger, and more knowledgeable about making tobacco products than they and who had often seen several overseers come and go, had broken them in, and had learned to exploit their inexperience.[37] The successful overseers learned to balance rewards and punishments, to command respect without provoking hatred, and to win cooperation without surrendering all authority. The unsuccessful frequently relied too heavily on the whip. William Jackson, a nineteen-year-old overseer, was killed by a young slave stemmer he was whipping for slovenly work.[38] Another overseer, a hot-tempered lad with a penchant for whipping slaves while he was enraged, lost his job because, his employer said, "the negroes generally had an antipathy against him . . . ."[39] Manufacturers, however, usually defended their overseers. William Graenor remained steadfastly loyal to his overseer in the face of a threat by some of his slave workers to burn his factory if he failed to discharge the man.[40] Many overseers began taking arms with them into the factories in 1852, which suggests that they wanted more than their employers' moral support.[41]

The slaves' chief resource and defense as workers in the factories was not their capacity to retaliate against employers and overseers by attacking their persons and property, though this served to remind managers that their power was limited. It was, instead, the control slaves had of their own labor and, since no factory before the war had adopted power-driven machinery, of the pace and quality of production. Quotas, bonuses, and coercive measures channeled the slaves' energies into production, but they never fully succeeded in giving managers complete control of the slaves' labor and of the production process. Scattered evidence suggests that slaves might have regulated the work pace and thereby have had a hand in determining quota and bonus levels. It is conceivable, though ultimately unprovable, that they conspired after hours to

[37] Twelve overseers appeared in the 1850 census, six of whom were twenty-five and under. It is unclear whether all twelve worked in tobacco factories. In any case, tobacco factories employed many more than twelve, and they were probably listed under the amorphous title of "tobacconist," which included all who were associated with the industry. Of the 110 tobacconists listed in 1850, 19 were twenty-five or under, and another 37 were between twenty-six and thirty-five years old. See Manuscript Census Returns, Seventh Census of the United States, 1850, City of Richmond, Henrico County, Virginia, Free Schedules, National Archives Microfilm Series, M-432, rolls 1352–53. For an excellent discussion of the role of the plantation overseer see Genovese, *Roll, Jordan, Roll,* 7–25.
[38] Richmond *Daily Dispatch,* February 28, 1852.
[39] *Ibid.,* March 13, 1852.
[40] *Ibid.,* February 1, 2, 1854.
[41] *Ibid.,* May 12, July 28, November 15, 24, 1852.

set the tempo of work. More likely, because it rests on strong but ambiguous evidence, is the possibility that slaves used song to determine the work pace. Their singing constituted a minor tourist attraction in Richmond. James Grant's slaves sang "several beautiful hymns" for Julia Lord Noyes Loveland and her companions from the North.[42] The manager of another factory told William Cullen Bryant that he encouraged his slaves to sing because "the boys work better while singing." But he could not command them to sing. "They must sing wholly of their own accord, it is of no use to bid them do it." The slaves decided when to sing. The same manager remarked "Sometimes they will sing all day long with great spirit; at other times you will not hear a single note."[43] They also decided what to sing and worked in time to their music. Through singing slaves set the pace of work. Some slaves apparently believed they had outsmarted their employers. They bragged to their pastor that "they sometimes received on Saturday night more wages for themselves than they had earned for their masters."[44]

Six days a week the slaves toiled in factories whose conditions they had partly shaped. On the seventh day many joined thousands of other slaves and free blacks in churches over which they exercised far greater influence. On that day the community turned out in its finery. Marianne Finch, an English visitor, observed that the blacks' weekday apparel was dull and ordinary. A black person, she noted, only "appears in full-bloom on Sunday, and then he is a striking object; whether male or female, whether in silks or muslins; or beaver and broadcloth."[45] Another English visitor, finding himself seated with the choir of the First African Baptist Church, noticed that the men "were dressed *en grand toilette*, handsome black coats and trousers, white waistcoats, and white ties; the women in silks and muslins flounced *en dernière mode*, of the gayest colours, with bonnets and mantles to match."[46]

For all the important differences that existed between Sabbath

[42] Journal of Julia Lord Noyes Loveland, April 26, 1855 (typescript, Duke University Library), 18.

[43] Bryant, *Letters of a Traveller; or, Notes of Things Seen in Europe and America* (New York and London, 1850), 73–75 (quotation on p. 75); see also Robert S. Starobin, "Disciplining Industrial Slaves in the Old South," *Journal of Negro History*, LII (April 1968), 112, for a misreading of Bryant. Starobin quoted the manager only as desiring the slaves to sing, and thus he saw singing merely as a managerial technique for extracting additional labor from slaves.

[44] Ryland, "Origins," 271.

[45] Finch, *An Englishwoman's Experience in America* (London, 1853), 295.

[46] Charles R. Weld, *A Vacation Tour in the United States and Canada* (London, 1855) 294–97.

and weekday activities, between the church and the factory, the links connecting them were strong. They were but two connected parts of the life experience shared by thousands of Richmond blacks. The hymns of worship, for example, were frequently the songs of work. One visitor to the factories remarked that the workers "think it is dreadful wicked to sing anything but sacred music."[47] Bryant's informant noted that "their taste is exclusively for sacred music; they will sing nothing else." The majority were regular churchgoers. "Most of them are of the Baptist persuasion; a few are Methodists," he added.[48] The money they made in the factories helped finance their African churches. The group consciousness and modes of organization created in one institution were transferred and adapted to the other, but in the churches they were more clearly articulated and were afforded more room for expression.

The history of the spread of Christianity among Virginia blacks is generally divided into three periods. The first sustained missionary activity among them occurred between 1750 and 1790. The Baptists and Methodists were most successful because they enlisted numerous black preachers and exhorters and mixed antislavery sentiments with the Gospel. This activity flagged after 1790, but regained momentum as a white-directed, proslavery movement after Nat Turner's rebellion in 1831 and the subsequent debate over slavery in the Virginia legislature. Virginia chose to retain slavery and passed laws making it illegal to teach blacks to read and write, suppressing independent black churches, and outlawing black preaching. Virginia's evangelical sects, having lost their black preachers and having committed themselves to defend slavery, redoubled their efforts to attract black converts and to reform the most odious features of slavery. The religious history of Virginia after 1830 formed, according to Eugene D. Genovese, "part of the great thrust to reform slavery as a way of life and to make it bearable for the slaves."[49]

Well before 1830 hundreds of Richmond slaves and free blacks had become Christians and members of Protestant churches in which, consigned to separate areas, they worshiped with their white coreligionists. Most became Baptists, and they easily outnumbered

---

[47] Loveland Journal, 18.
[48] Bryant, Letters, 75; Fredrika Bremer, The Homes of the New World: Impressions of America (3 vols., London, 1853), III, 315–16, heard Richmond tobacco factory slaves "singing at their work in large rooms" and noted that they "were all Baptists, and sung only hymns."
[49] Genovese, Roll, Jordan, Roll, 183–93; quotation on p. 186.

their white brethren. In 1823 ninety-one free black Baptists, complaining that existing churches could not adequately accommodate the nearly seven hundred black Baptists, free and slave, petitioned the legislature for permission to establish an African Baptist church. Although they promised to obey laws passed for the "proper restraint" of black persons and had the support of prominent local whites, their petition was rejected.[50] By 1828 the First Baptist Church counted about 1,000 blacks among its 1,300 members.[51] The Baptists' humble origins, the democratic and mildly antislavery appeals of their early evangels, and their rough, emotional preaching contributed to the success of the church among Virginia blacks. Equally important to that success were the work of its black preachers and exhorters and its form of church government, which permitted members, even slaves, a degree of self-rule.

Baptist churches had regularly licensed black preachers and exhorters prior to the legislative ban on black preaching. This proved a troublesome duty, for several blacks with unorthodox views or without official sanction preached and exhorted. In 1828, for example, a white committee of the First Baptist Church inquired into the extent of the "evil arising from the exercise of public gifts by the coloured brethren not authorized by the church . . ." and recommended that the church formally reexamine all black preachers and exhorters. Only a third of the eighteen men who had preached and exhorted passed the test and received licenses.[52] When the law silenced these men it created a severe shortage of ministers able or willing to conduct funerals and other religious services for blacks.[53] Baptist churches with racially mixed memberships operated on a two-tier plan. White pastors and deacons elected by the white members were in command. Under them were black deacons elected by the entire church. These black deacons scrutinized black members, settled disputes among them, investigated reports of

[50] John H. Russell, *The Free Negro in Virginia, 1619–1865* (Baltimore, 1913), 142–43. For an interesting discussion of white Baptist attitudes toward slaves and slavery see W. Harrison Daniel, "Virginia Baptists and the Negro in the Antebellum Era," *Journal of Negro History,* LVI (January 1971), 1–16.

[51] Minutes of the First Baptist Church of the City of Richmond (1825–1830), (typescript, Virginia Baptist Historical Society, Richmond, Va.), November 3, 1827 (p. 30); October 4, 1828 (p. 40); cited hereinafter as FBC Minutes.

[52] *Ibid.*, March 13, 1828 (p. 35); July 9, 23, 1829 (p. 49); October 3, 1829 (p. 52); October 14, 1830 (p. 62); quotation from March 13, 1828.

[53] Free blacks applied unsuccessfully to the legislature for permission to have black preachers officiate at funerals. For a description of the 1834 petition see Luther P. Jackson, "Religious Development of the Negro in Virginia from 1760 to 1860," *Journal of Negro History,* XVI (April 1931), 206–207. Despite this setback, local authorities permitted blacks to conduct funerals provided a white man attended the services. See Olmsted, *Seaboard Slave States,* I, 26–29; Writers' Program, Virginia, *The Negro in Virginia* (New York, 1940), 77.

misconduct, and presented candidates for admission or readmission to the church. The entire church membership made final decisions after receiving the black deacons' recommendations. The authority of the black deacons was tightly circumscribed, but within a limited area bounded by white supervision the deacons and their black constituents decided with whom they would have "fellowship" and the standard of conduct they would demand.[54]

The Baptist church acted both as a staunch supporter of the slave regime and as a subtle subverter of its underlying rationale. Committed to slavery, the church required that its slave members be obedient servants. Numerous slave members were expelled from the First Baptist Church for disobeying their masters and for attempting to run away, but masters were rarely punished for mistreating slaves. Only once between 1825 and 1830 did the First Baptist Church exclude a master. It expelled William Muse in 1825 for "breach of promise, toward a man formerly owned by him and sent to New Orleans without giving him an opportunity to get a master in this place, and for making misstatements to the church concerning the same."[55] Although the church enforced moral standards that frequently overlapped the state's slave code, it also undercut the central premise of that code. In its view slaves were not mere property. They were, instead, persons whose souls God prized, and who, therefore, ought to be sober, properly married, taught Christian truths, and treated humanely by their temporal masters.[56] For all the obvious weaknesses of exhorting masters to treat slaves in a decent manner as fellow human beings while simultaneously defending slavery and its inhumane racial mores and legal apparatus, the churches provided slaves with more psychological leverage, stronger moral claims, and greater protection in dealing with their masters than did either the law or racial theories. Baptist churches were socially conservative institutions, and blacks occupied subservient positions in them, but the churches did insist on the slaves' humanity and did provide them a small measure of self-government.

Despite legislative rebuffs Richmond's black Baptists continually pressed for churches of their own, and when success was achieved it came as much from the desire of white Baptists to separate from them as by their own efforts. The Baptist message of salvation was

[54] FBC Minutes, April 10, 17, 1827 (pp. 20–21).
[55] Ibid., April 19, 1825 (p. 4).
[56] Ibid., October 25, 1825 (p. 8); April 11, 1826 (p. 10); February 20, 1827 (p. 17); March 20, 1827 (p. 18); June 11, 1829 (p. 48); see also Robert Ryland, The Scripture Catechism for Coloured People (Richmond, 1848), 139–40.

being received by far more blacks than whites. When Jeremiah Bell Jeter assumed the pastorship of the First Baptist Church in 1836 he found only 400 whites among its 2,400 members. Baptist success among blacks became embarrassing, for its churches were susceptible to being stigmatized as black churches and thus becoming unattractive to potential white converts. According to one white minister some fastidious whites "did not like to resort to a church, where so many colored folks congregated, and this was thought to operate against the growth of the white portion of the audience."[57] White Baptists sat uncomfortably beneath galleries packed with poor, mostly illiterate blacks and grew irritated with the blacks' style of worship, their tardiness, and, indeed, their close proximity. Ministers fretted over composing sermons that would engage whites and appeal to blacks. The small white minorities carried much of the responsibility for financing their churches.[58] Many white members became convinced that trusted blacks could best control their black brethren. According to one white minister a large portion of the black congregation, "being slaves, could not be reached and disciplined, except by persons of their own color."[59] The solutions to the problems created by the influx of black converts varied. White members of the Second Baptist Church ruled by 1843 that "no coloured members would be received except under peculiar circumstances."[60] The white congregation of the First Baptist Church decided to build a new church for themselves and sell the old one to the blacks.

Before that decision could be effected the legality of establishing an African church had to be determined. White church officers consulted legal experts, who advised that the law would permit such a church provided a white preacher became its minister. Having settled the legal question, church officers sought to allay public hostility to the project by creating an eighteen-member white superintending committee drawn from three Baptist churches. The majority of committee members came from the First Baptist Church, which acted as the parent church for the proposed First African Baptist Church. Although the old church building was appraised at $13,500, the white congregation demanded far less

[57] Ryland, "Reminiscences," 262; Jeter, The Recollections of a Long Life (Richmond, 1891), 209; FBC Minutes, June 3, 1830 (p. 58).
[58] FBC Minutes, December 11, 1827 (p. 30); January 6, 1830 (p. 54); December 6, 1830 (p. 64).
[59] Ryland, "Origins," 247–48.
[60] Minutes of the Second Baptist Church of the City of Richmond (Virginia Baptist Historical Society), August 3, 1843 (pp. 24–25); hereinafter cited as SBC Minutes.

from the blacks. It received slightly less than $6,500. Nearly $3,000 was raised by James Thomas, Jr., and other fund raisers from white citizens, particularly tobacco manufacturers and merchants. The black congregation contributed $3,500.[61] Shortly after the First African Baptist Church opened in 1841, the First Baptist Church reaped the benefits of separation. In 1842 during a series of revivals that swept Richmond 170 whites joined the church, among whom, Jeter noted with satisfaction, were "heads of families, men of business and influence, who added greatly to its strength and efficiency."[62]

The constitution of the First African Baptist Church, drawn up by Jeter, created a form of government that was "more presbyterial than congregational," in that the black congregation enjoyed less autonomy than was customary among Baptists. It stipulated that the pastor be a white minister nominated by the superintending committee and approved by the elected black deacons. The committee received the power to oversee the African church's affairs, to hear appeals from its decisions, and to rule on changes in the constitution, but it rarely exercised its constitutional authority. Committee members were obliged to take turns attending all African church services, but some, according to the church's pastor, honored the obligation only intermittently. They never had to rule on amendments, and they acted on only three appeals between 1841 and 1865.[63] The constitution did not depart totally from congregational government. It gave the congregation power to elect thirty deacons who, together with the pastor the congregation accepted, constituted the church's "permanent ruling power." The pastor and the deacons ruled the church for twenty-four years relatively unfettered by interference from the superintending committee.

The committee nominated, and the black members accepted, Robert Ryland as pastor. At the time of his nomination and for several years after Ryland also served as president of Richmond College, a Baptist institution of higher learning. Deriving most of his income from the college, Ryland required an annual salary of only $500 from the church. He had impeccable credentials as a safe southern minister, for he defended both slavery and the southern church's concern for slaves against abolitionist attacks. Though he defended the institution, he harbored misgivings about the moral-

[61] Ryland, "Reminiscences," 263; Jeter, *Recollections*, 211, identifies James Thomas, Jr., as the chief fund raiser for the African church among white Richmonders.
[62] Jeter, *Recollections*, 240.
[63] *Ibid.*, 209–12; Ryland, "Origins," 249–51.

ity of destroying slave families merely for the profit of their owners and of obeying state laws against black preaching and literacy, fearing that they retarded missionary work among blacks.

Ryland's defense of slavery, which he shared with Jeter and some other Virginia ministers, rested in part on the assumption that slavery was part of the divine plan to introduce enslaved Africans in America to Christ and to bring Christ to Africa through the agency of repatriated Afro-American missionaries. The laws silencing black preachers placed added obligations on white ministers, and Ryland, who felt keenly this obligation and wanted a city pastorate, eagerly welcomed the call from the First African Baptist Church. The prohibition of black literacy created a dilemma for ministers like Ryland. He and Jeter among others had opposed slavery as young men. During the 1820s and 1830s, however, they followed most white Virginians and embraced the institution. To justify their new commitment they anxiously searched the Bible for evidence supporting slavery and resolved that it was a divinely approved means for spreading the Word. State law threatened to thwart divine purpose. Torn between the conflicting claims of religious mission and secular law, Ryland opted for the former. He admitted on at least one occasion in the 1850s that he was encouraging blacks to read and was distributing Bibles and religious tracts among them.[64]

Unfortunately, more is known about Ryland than about his congregation and the deacons it elected. The church began with 940 members and, also benefiting from separation, grew to 1,600 in a year. It had over 3,000 members by 1856. The status of the founding members is unknown, but slaves far outnumbered free persons among members admitted after 1841. Of 2,388 members added between 1841 and 1857, 1,203 were male slaves; 932, female slaves; 92, male free blacks; and 161, female free blacks.[65] Free blacks, however, held most of the deaconships. The identities of twenty-four of the original thirty deacons have been established and eighteen were free men. Ten of the original thirty had long been active in church affairs, having served as deacons and committeemen in the First Baptist Church between 1825 and 1830. Most of the twenty-nine deacons elected between 1841 and 1859 were also free men, usually tradesmen and property owners.[66] Their domination

[64] Ryland, "Reminiscences," 291–92; Jeter, Recollections, 211–13.

[65] Minutes of the First African Baptist Church of Richmond, Virginia, microfilm (Virginia State Library), 1841–1859 (pp. 1–331); hereinafter cited as FABC Minutes.

[66] These findings are based on correlations between names of deacons and committeemen found in the FBC Minutes and the FABC Minutes with names of free blacks listed in federal census returns for Richmond City in Henrico County and for Chesterfield County and in the personal property and land tax returns for Richmond City for 1857 and 1858, microfilm (Virginia State Library).

of the Board of Deacons did not go completely unchallenged. Three church members complained to the pastor in 1850 about "partiality" shown to "free persons in the administration of church matters." Their complaint touched off a heated debate which so divided the church that the superintending committee made one of its rare interventions. The settlement imposed by the committee did not noticeably diminish the free blacks' influence.[67]

The First African, as the largest and most prestigious black Baptist church in Richmond, served as a model for three others founded before the war. Their constitutions, for example, virtually replicated its constitution.[68] Most of the black congregation of the Second Baptist Church departed in 1845 to form the Second African Baptist Church. The First African built the Ebenezer or Third African Baptist Church in 1858 and sent several hundred of its members to form the new congregation. In 1860 black members of the Leigh Street Baptist Church began meeting as a separate congregation in the basement of their old church. Black Baptists outnumbered whites by a margin of at least two to one by 1860, and their four African churches claimed 4,600 members or about a third of the city's black adults.[69] Only the records of the First and Ebenezer African churches are extant for the antebellum period, but because the First African and its pastor set precedents that the other churches followed and because these two churches claimed three-fourths of Richmond's black Baptists much of the history of the black Baptist community can be reconstructed through their records. The minutes of the First African, which span an eighteen-year period, reveal how the congregation worked with the pastor, deacons, and parent church and how it operated as a semi-autonomous body within the restrictions laid down by secular white society.

The pastor and deacons formed the governing body of the First African, and their decisions were usually final. As governing officers they guided the congregation's affairs and scrutinized the members'

---

[67] FABC Minutes, May 5, 1850, to November 19, 1850 (pp. 169–75); quotation from May 5, 1850.
[68] A copy of the constitution of the First African Baptist Church can be found in FBC Minutes (1841–1844), July 8, 1841 (pp. 4–5). For other constitutions see SBC Minutes, July 27, 1845 (pp. 79–80); Minutes of the Ebenezer African Baptist Church of Richmond (manuscript in the custody of the church), July 18, 1858 (pp. 5–7). For thumbnail sketches of these churches see *The Inventory of Church Archives in Virginia: Negro Baptist Churches in Richmond, Virginia* (Richmond, 1940), 13–18.
[69] Jackson, "Religious Development," 221, 232.

conduct, but they were also responsible to the congregation. Candidates for the pastorship had to win majority support among the congregation. When support evaporated, as it did at the Second African in 1858, the pastor resigned.[70] Deacons owed their positions even more directly to the constituents who elected them. Because they antagonized a large portion of the congregation two deacons of the First African had to retire, although one had strong backing from Pastor Ryland.[71] Nevertheless, deacons exercised great influence. They disciplined members who broke Baptist moral commandments, arbitrated disputes between members, decided whether to admit new members and readmit penitent offenders, and conducted the church's financial affairs. Selected from all areas of the city and suburbs, deacons were the church's listening posts, its disciplinarians, and the guardians of its moral code.

When reports of misconduct reached the church the deacons residing near the parties concerned made investigations and alerted the parties to the church's interest in them. They later reported their findings to the monthly meetings of the pastor and Board of Deacons, who conducted a trial, heard the testimonies of the accused and witnesses, and rendered judgments as to their guilt or innocence. The pastor and deacons also convened special meetings to consider requests for readmission from expelled members. The constitution gave the pastor and deacons greater authority in disciplinary matters than their counterparts in white Baptist churches enjoyed, for the black congregation could not vote in such determinations. It was their exclusive control over membership in the most important institution in the black community that gave the deacons such impressive authority.[72]

The moral code upheld and enforced by the black deacons was essentially the same as that white deacons enforced. It prized harmony and fellowship, love, charity, marital fidelity, sexual continence outside marriage, and sobriety as virtues, and it condemned fighting, fornication, adultery, drunkenness, stealing, gambling, and cheating as vices. For some infractions, such as stealing and adultery, convicted offenders were immediately expelled.[73] For most other offenses the deacons were far more concerned with

[70] SBC Minutes, January 24, 1858.
[71] FABC Minutes, September 11, 1842 (p. 30); October 2, 1842 (p. 35); October 30, 1842 (p. 40); December 4, 1842 (p. 43); May 2 to June 13, 1856 (pp. 200–202).
[72] Ryland, "Reminiscences," 263.
[73] FABC Minutes, September 20, 1857 (p. 298). Between November 1847 and October 1857 a total of 400 persons were expelled from the church, 265 of whom had been convicted of adultery.

reforming offenders and conciliating quarrelsome parties than with expelling them. Only after reform measures and compromise settlements failed and only when the guilty parties failed to show sufficient repentance did the deacons resort to exclusion. Deacons frequently labored for months to save troubled marriages, to reform drunkards and forgive them if they promised to abstain from drinking, to reclaim gamblers who returned their winnings, and to postpone disciplining debtors if they showed even the slightest willingness to repay. Only after it became obvious that their efforts at reform had failed did the deacons exclude the offenders from the church. Later they might readmit those who demonstrated that they had been reformed.[74]

Monthly disciplinary meetings functioned in two important ways for the community. First, they provided a type of judicial apparatus unavailable to slaves and free blacks elsewhere. In municipal court the admissibility of black testimony was severely circumscribed since blacks could not testify against whites. Slaves rarely initiated suits, and then only through white spokesmen. Most slaves and free blacks who appeared in the mayor's court were defendants picked up by the police for some infraction of the law. White men heard their cases and handed down verdicts that usually reflected their interest in maintaining the social order and black subservience. In their churches, however, slaves and free blacks brought their claims and complaints before peers they had elected, whose purpose was to reestablish Christian harmony as well as to uphold the moral code. Church disciplinary hearings were the black community's small-claims courts, offering a service that no other body provided.[75] Second, although black deacons enforced the moral code common to all Baptists, the social effects of their activities were different, as different as the economic, social, and political conditions of blacks were from those of whites. When, for example, deacons upheld slave marriages and punished members who violated norms of marital fidelity they honored a practice that had no legal standing and that was only intermittently recognized by whites. They counterbalanced through community action the disintegrating tendencies inherent in secular slave society. When deacons reconciled quarreling members or creditors and debtors they offered a regular, peaceable alternative to individualistic, possibly

[74] See for example FABC Minutes, July 16 to August 6, 1848 (pp. 131–32); May 5, 1850 (p. 169); September 16, 1855 (p. 258); July 6, 11, 1857 (pp. 294–95); September 6, 1857 (p. 297); and February 7, 1858 (p. 304).

[75] *Ibid.*, February 5, 1843 (p. 45); November 1, 1844, to February 2, 1845 (pp. 71–74); November 19, 1848 (p. 137); and March 3, 1850 (p. 155).

violent, settlements in the streets or to employing white men as arbitrators. The deacons also modified white Baptist practice in at least two ways. They granted divorces and permission to remarry to slaves whose marriages had been broken by forced separation, and they thus adapted their moral code to the harsh realities of slavery. In addition they generally did not expel runaways as the white-dominated churches had done.[76] In black Richmond, because of the relative absence of legal and institutional mechanisms for dealing with mundane personal and social problems, the pronouncements of the African churches, the only bodies over which blacks had considerable influence, resonated with extraordinary power.

The churches' charitable work must be viewed in the same light. The municipal government usually appropriated funds to provide food and fuel for the white and free-black poor over the late winter months and periods of recession. It felt no responsibility, however, for assisting needy slaves, whose upkeep was viewed as the responsibility of their owners. The African churches considered the slave and free-black indigent to be equally deserving of their charities. Each month the congregation of the First African contributed to the "Poor Saints" fund, which was distributed to the needy by a seventeen-member committee staffed by five deacons from each of the city's three wards, a secretary, and a treasurer. Through such church bodies and an unknown number of illegal benevolent societies the black community cared for many of its poor. The Poor Saints Committee of the First African distributed over $2,000 between 1849 and 1858. During eight of those years the smaller, wealthier, white Second Baptist Church raised little more than $700.[77]

Most of the money raised to maintain the church, purchase the church building, and pay the salaries of the pastor and sexton came from the congregation in weekly penny collections. Pews were not rented as they were in white Baptist churches, and, therefore, seating arrangements did not reflect wealth distinctions. Another source of revenue came from renting the church building to political parties, entertainers, and lecturers. A third source of income was the church's popular choir, which gave concerts periodically for the

[76] FBC Minutes, February 20, 1827 (p. 17); June 19, 1828 (p. 37); September 18, 1828 (p. 39); February 5, 1829 (p. 45); April 30, 1829 (p. 47); and August 6, 1829 (p. 50) for expulsions of runaways; see also FABC Minutes, November 14 and December 4, 1841 (pp. 8–9) for the single instance of expelling a runaway from the African Baptist Church; see *ibid.*, March 3, 1850 (p. 166) for an instance of a divorce proceeding.

[77] SBC Minutes, April 18, 1858; FABC Minutes, 1849–1858; *ibid.*, December 4, 1848 (pp. 138–39) for the charter of the Poor Saints Committee.

general public. When the church undertook unusually expensive projects, such as building the Ebenezer African Baptist Church, it had the choir perform, and it appointed its most prominent members to solicit subscriptions in the white and black communities.[78] Money derived from these sources paid salaries, insurance and maintenance costs, and the more than $9,000 owed for the First African and Ebenezer churches. In addition to these routine expenses, the church gave money to a number of Baptist enterprises and secular humanitarian causes. It joined other black churches in buying the slave deacon Thomas Allen and the slave families of two free-black preachers to enable the three to embark on missionary work outside the South.[79] It donated entire collections to struggling black congregations in seven Virginia towns and in Detroit, Philadelphia, the District of Columbia, Savannah, and Buxton, Ontario.[80] It contributed money to aid yellow-fever victims in Norfolk and Portsmouth and to feed the poor of famine-stricken Ireland.[81] The deacons conducted the church's financial affairs with efficiency and skill. Ryland wrote in 1855 that he had never "discovered one instance of an attempt to defraud, or palpable negligence of duty, or a want of competence to the office assumed." Anyone who doubted the blacks' abilities or regarded them "as a set of simpletons," he added, would "very quickly transfer the charge of folly from them to himself."[82]

Relations between the pastor and the church were generally cooperative and cordial because each accommodated to the other's needs, peculiarities, and traditions. Ryland, a college president and defender of slavery, preached submission and obedience, lessons some of his listeners rejected. A cynical free black told James Redpath, an abolitionist writer who visited Richmond, that he had heard Ryland state from the pulpit "that God had given all this continent to the white man, and that it was our duty to submit." He also heard one of his brethren reply: "*He be d---d! God am not sich a fool!*" When Redpath asked whether Ryland always preached to suit slaveholders, his informant answered wearily that Ryland

---

[78] FABC Minutes, July 6, 1856 (p. 275); November 9, 1856 (p. 287); July 6, 1857 (p. 294); August 16, September 20, 1857 (pp. 297–98); November 1, 1857 (p. 300); December 6, 1857 (p. 302); February 7, 1858 (p. 304); April 3, 1859 (p. 322).

[79] *Ibid.*, March 5, 1843 (p. 47); April 6, 1845 (p. 77); January 5, 1851 (p. 177); and November 5, 1854 (p. 248).

[80] *Ibid.*, April 1, 1849 (p. 144); December 1, 1850 (p. 176); May 1, 1853 (pp. 220–21); October 7, 1855 (p. 261); April 5, 1857 (p. 290); and July 6, 1857 (p. 295).

[81] *Ibid.*, March 7, 1847 (p. 114); August 12, 1855 (p. 258).

[82] Ryland, "Reminiscences," 264.

"wouldn't be allowed to preach at all if he didn't."[83] Ryland attempted to inculcate habits of chaste living, sedate and mannered behavior, and punctuality through "didactic" preaching, which he admitted was unexciting and less popular than emotional appeals to his listeners' "passions." He claimed considerable success. He believed that their sexual habits had been elevated and that their religious notions had become more rational. Because of his efforts church members, he announced, "have less superstition, less reliance on dreams and visions, they talk less of the palpable guidings of the Spirit as independent of or opposed to the word of God." They were also learning to "avoid habits of whining, snuffling, grunting, drawling, repeating, hic[c]oughing, and other vulgarities in prayer...."[84] A stickler for punctuality, Ryland never succeeded in communicating its importance. An Englishwoman who visited the church in 1853 observed that it was thinly attended when services began but that afterwards members trickled in without disturbing services, "though they all shook hands with the friends near them, and nodded to the more distant...."[85]

If, as Ryland claimed, his preaching and example modified the behavior of many in his congregation, it is also true that the traditions and needs of his congregation shaped his ministry. Two traditions that some free blacks and more than a few slaves had developed and that the laws of 1831 had suppressed but not destroyed were literacy and preaching. Already troubled about these laws, Ryland easily and with good conscience distributed Bibles and religious tracts among church members and established an informal lending library for them. He also incorporated their preaching into religious services. After the war Ryland recalled that "There were several ministers of respectable gifts in the church, who, at the request of private families and by the connivance of the officers of the law, often attended funerals in the city and the adjacent country." By law they could not preach from the pulpit, "But, as a sort of recompense for this slight, they, and others, were called on to pray, several times, at each religious service." Their prayers, which were actually extemporaneous orations, "exhibited great fervency and power, and afforded the highest degree of comfort, both to those who offered them and to those who heard them."[86] After regular services some blacks preached to those re-

    [83] James Redpath, *The Roving Editor: or, Talks with Slaves in the Southern States* (New York, 1859), 19–20.
    [84] Ryland, "Reminiscences," 265, 289–91.
    [85] Finch, *An Englishwoman's Experience*, 297–99.
    [86] Ryland, "Reminiscences," 289–92; Ryland, "Origins," 258–59 (quotations).

maining, who responded in ways Ryland would have disapproved. A visitor noticed that "there was an amateur performance of singing and exhortation, in which a few old people got very much excited, swinging their bodies about, stamping their feet, and shaking hands frantically with everybody near them, myself among the rest." She noted that the "most active, were those who had slept during the sermon, though, to do them justice, these were few, generally they had been very attentive."[87] Speaking of one of these preachers, Ryland admitted frankly that "he was heard with far more interest than I was."[88]

At the monthly meetings conducted by Ryland and the deacons a majority of deacons usually voted with their pastor, perhaps because his arguments were particularly persuasive. Occasionally, however, his side lost, and his vote counted as only one of thirty-one.[89] He also intervened periodically in matters where the deacons believed he had no business, and they were quick to tell him gently that his advice was unappreciated. At the death of Deacon Joseph Abrams, for example, they purchased a tombstone and pondered what epitaph to inscribe on it. "When I learned that an inscription was to be prepared for his grave," Ryland recalled, "in my simplicity, I offered my services to write it." His friends, however, "thought their own literary taste fully equal to the occasion, and declined my proposal." The funeral attracted eight thousand persons and "one of the largest processions ever seen in Richmond, including more than fifty carriages, followed the remains to the tomb."[90] The congregation's independence sometimes embarrassed Ryland. When a South Carolina judge offended the congregation while delivering a temperance lecture their displeasure "was painfully evident by loud murmurs, and by their leaving the house in large numbers!"[91]

Though compromise characterized the relations between the pastor and the deacons, the superintending committee's interventions allowed the deacons little maneuvering room. Twice the committee imposed settlements on a divided congregation, and it also acted once when the church overstepped the boundaries laid down by the white parent church. The last incident demonstrated the limits of the congregation's autonomy. As long as the deacons

[87] Finch, *An Englishwoman's Experience*, 298–99.
[88] Ryland, "Reminiscences," 354.
[89] FABC Minutes, October 2, 1842 (p. 35); December 4, 1842 (p. 43); January 1, 1843 (p. 45); November 24, 1844 (p. 71).
[90] Ryland, "Reminiscences," 354.
[91] FABC Minutes, June 6, 1852 (p. 201).

operated within the sphere whites believed proper for church government their control was almost complete, but beyond it submission was demanded. The incident arose when the church, having paid its debt for the church building, tried to name three free blacks and two whites as legal trustees of the property. After receiving the deacons' nominations the superintending committee withheld confirmation pending consultation with the Virginia attorney general on the legality of the arrangement. The attorney general ruled that the property would be best secured if all the trustees were white men. Ryland then asked the deacons to revise their choices, but they adamantly refused. The superintending committee broke the stalemate by unilaterally picking five white trustees. The deacons surrendered, but only after announcing that "we do not admit to the propriety of such a restriction." Nor did the matter rest there. At a subsequent meeting, which Ryland characterized as "exciting and somewhat disorderly," representatives of the committee appeared to assure the deacons that the new appointments guaranteed title to the church to the black congregation for its "exclusive and perpetual benefit."[92] At this point the church could do no more than grudgingly accept the committee's terms, for to challenge them again would be to challenge white supremacy openly and perhaps trigger a dangerous white reaction. The church's survival depended on appearing to conform to the whites' rules while subtly broadening its area of autonomy.

The black church's relations with the larger white society were mixed. On the one hand, many whites, especially Baptists, supplied time, money, and public support. White officials, for instance, permitted black preachers to officiate at funerals if they paid or persuaded white men to attend them. On the other hand, many whites remained suspicious and critical of African churches, seeing them as nurseries of rebellion or at least of impertinent behavior, particularly during tense periods. For example, after Jane Williams, a member of the First African, confessed to having murdered two members of her master's family editors and public officials wondered aloud whether the church pacified slaves or created rebels, and they demanded tighter police control over the church.[93] A similar reaction occurred when the police discovered that runaway slaves were using a mailing system, set up in the church by Ryland for sending and receiving conduct references for members, to en-

[92] *Ibid.*, December 4, 1848, to May 6, 1849 (pp. 137–47); quotations from meetings of April 1 and May 6, 1849.

[93] Richmond *Daily Dispatch*, July 20–22, August 6, 10, 13, September 15–16, October 23, 25, 28, 1852.

courage others to run away and to inform them of the best escape routes.[94] The church survived these and other scandals because its white patrons defended it and, more important, because the church never openly criticized slavery or overtly challenged white dominance. Many of its members secretly criticized their bondage, but until slavery was destroyed they could not demonstrate their opposition without incurring murderous reprisals. They emphatically demonstrated their hostility on April 3, 1865.

Thousands of tobacco factory workers and African church members welcomed Federal troops to Richmond. For many the transition to the free-labor system came easily, for they had long been accustomed to finding work, bargaining with employers, and managing finances. They seemed far more eager to recommence working than did the disheartened Confederate veterans.[95] They had already developed modes of self-help and collective action which they activated and redirected after emancipation. Their shadowy secret societies surfaced and proliferated at an astonishing rate, numbering over four hundred by 1873.[96] They seized control of their churches by June 1865, named new pastors, and used church buildings for schools, employment offices, and staging areas for organizing public protests and celebrations. Not without reason did whites come to hate these churches. Incendiaries destroyed the Second African Baptist Church because it housed a freedman's school and because organizers used it to plan a massive celebration of April 3, 1866, the first anniversary of the black liberation and the white defeat.[97]

Long membership in the churches had not won blacks over to their pastors' views on race and slavery nor to the claims that God sanctioned slavery. Cyrus Hughes had joined the First African in 1848 and remained a member and a slave until the soldiers arrived. Three days later he told his former mistress, who asked him to continue working without wages until the harvest, that he would not work for promises, that "there was to be no more Master and Mistress now, all was equal . . . ."[98] For Hughes and thousands of other former slaves and free blacks, emancipation verified Scrip-

[94] Ryland, "Reminiscences," 323–24.

[95] *National Freedman*, I (August 15, 1865), 223; *American Missionary*, 2d Ser., IX (September 1865), 199.

[96] Margaret R. Neary, "Some Aspects of Negro Social Life in Richmond, Virginia, 1865–1880," *Maryland Historian*, I (Fall 1970), 108; O'Brien, "From Bondage to Citizenship," 328–34.

[97] *Freedmen's Record*, II (June 1866), 115–16; *National Freedman*, II (April 1866), 120–21.

[98] Emma Mordecai to Edward, April 5, 1865; Emma Mordecai, Diary, April 13, 1865, Myers Family Papers (Virginia Historical Society).

tural truth and shattered the fetters that had wrongly held them in bondage. Black spokesmen frequently compared emancipation to conversion, the former being the temporal fulfillment of the latter. Conversion, the enslavement of one's soul and will to God, had not legitimatized one man's claim to another as his property. From the same pulpits where Ryland and his white colleagues had delivered countless sermons on servants' duties to their masters came a different message. Whenever freedom was mentioned in the churches, a northern newspaperman observed in April 1865, "emotion kindles over the whole audience, and repeatedly have I heard them quote in prayer the language of God to Moses: 'I have surely seen the affliction of my people which are in Egypt, and have heard their cry because of their taskmasters; for I know their sorrows, and I am come down to deliver them.' "[99] Blacks brought notions about freedom, moral sensibilities, work habits, familial and communal ties, and modes of collective activity to the years of Reconstruction. Into that process of creating something new in a slaveless world they took a culture and organizational structure they had created as slaves and free blacks, as church members and factory workers.

[99] New York *Times*, April 30, 1865.

Historians and the Extent of Slave Ownership in the Southern United States

Otto H. Olsen

IN A RECENT BRIEF AND THOUGHTFUL VOLUME, David Brion Davis has directed attention to what he calls a "paranoid style" affecting the antebellum debate over slavery in the United States.[1] Encouraged by insecurities as well as convictions, this style has remained a lasting as well as distorting force in American thought and its influence upon the posture of the victorious "free" society has had enduring consequences. Then and since, slavery has served as a convenient and perfect enemy. It epitomized evil and became a symbol that has been used to define and justify the social conditions and history of a capitalist, free labor society. A symbol of such convenience obviously would invite distortion; that it has, in fact, done so is suggested by the persistence of certain questionable assumptions about the nature of slave ownership in the antebellum South.

For generations historians have been almost unanimous in emphasizing that black slaves were owned by a surprisingly small minority of whites. Allan Nevins states in his distinguished history of the Civil War era that "from the terms used in the angry discussion of slavery, it might have been supposed that almost the whole Southern population had a direct interest in it. Actually, of the 6,184,477 white folk in the slave States, *only* 347,525 were listed by the census of 1850 as owners, and even this number gave an exaggerated impression of the facts." Adding members of slave owning families and other involved individuals, Nevins increases the figure, but retains the emphasis, concluding that the number of whites directly involved in slavery probably "did not exceed 2,000,000. If so, *not one-third* of the population of the South and border States had any direct interest in slavery as a form of property. This is a fact of great important [*sic*] when we attempt to estimate the effect of slaveholding upon the culture and outlook of the Southern people."[2]

Nevins' conclusion is invariably affirmed by prominent commentators. According to the standard account by James G. Randall and David Donald "the total number of slaveholders in 1850 was *only* 347,525 out of a total white population of about six million in the slaveholding areas." Donald is even more emphatic elsewhere when he complains that "writ-

[1] David Brion Davis, *The Slave Power Conspiracy and the Paranoid Style* (Baton Rouge, 1969).

[2] Allan Nevins, *Ordeal of the Union* (New York, 1947), I, 415-16. Italics added.

387

ers speak of the Southern interest in slavery, even when they perfectly well know that in the 'plantation' South *only* one fourth of the white families owned any slaves at all."[3] Roy F. Nichols and Elbert B. Smith assume the same stance,[4] as do the authors of practically all the outstanding college textbooks on the history of the United States. Typically these textbooks include such statements as "only a minority of the whites owned slaves," "at all times nearly three-fourths of the white families in the South as a whole held no slaves;" "only one family in four held any at all;" "slave ownership in the South was not widespread;" "not more than a quarter of the white heads of families were slaveowners, and even in the cotton states the proportion was less than one-third;" "in 1850, only one in three owned any Negroes; on the eve of the Civil War, the ratio was one in four;" and slave owners "probably made up less than a third of southern whites."[5]

While one seldom can quarrel with the statistics presented by these many writers, serious questions can be raised respecting the significance of this degree of slave distribution in the South. Although the constant conclusion has been that the number of whites owning slaves was remarkably small and that the South was therefore an unusually oligarchical society, the comparative basis for such a judgment has never been firmly established. Instead, that judgment appears to have rested primarly upon a moral repugnance toward slavery and an exceedingly simplistic conception of the meaning of slave ownership. But was the slave South really more oligarchic, especially in an economic sense, than, say, the nineteenth century North or the United States today? And precisely how does one determine this? What should the distribution of slave ownership be compared with in non-slave societies? Without considering such questions it is difficult to see how the extent of slaveholding in the antebellum South can be properly evaluated.

The most apparent origin of the accusation that southern slavery was politically and economically oligarchical was, of course, the antebellum

[3] James G. Randall and David Donald, *The Civil War and Reconstruction* (Boston, 1961), p. 67, italics added; David Donald, *Lincoln Reconsidered: Essays on the Civil War Era* (paperback ed., New York, 1961), p. 214, italics added.

[4] Roy F. Nichols, *The Disruption of American Democracy* (New York, 1948), p. 32: Elbert B. Smith, *The Death of Slavery: The United States, 1837-1865* (Chicago, 1967), pp. 5-6, 21, 26.

[5] T. Harry Williams and others, *A History of the United States to 1877* (3rd. ed., New York, 1969), p. 484; John M. Blum and others, *The National Experience* (New York, 1963), p. 202; John A. Garraty, *The American Nation. A History of the United States* (New York, 1966), p. 331; Harry J. Carman and others, *A History of the American People* (2nd. ed., New York, 1960), I, 587; Henry Bamford Parks, *The United States of America: A History* (3rd. ed., New York, 1968), pp. 211-12; Richard B. Morris and William Greenleaf, *U.S.A. The History of a Nation* (Chicago, 1969), I, 592-93; Richard Hofstadter and others, *The United States: The History of a Republic* (2nd. ed., Englewood Cliffs, 1967), p. 343. The interpretive impact is suggested by the last work, which finds four of five roots of southern loyalty dependent upon racial considerations and the fifth upon "the social ambitions of the small planters." *Ibid.*, p. 352-53.

antislavery movement. Popular northern concepts of a "Slave Power," a "Slave Oligarchy," and a "Slave Conspiracy" reflected that attitude, and Frederick Law Olmsted directly related this purported lack of democracy in the South to the extent of slaveholding among whites. Speaking of Virginia slave owners, Olmsted concluded that "they are not, I suppose, one to a hundred of the people," although they were in fact about one to four of the people. In Georgia, utilizing census figures, he reported far more accurately, but with the same emphasis, that "only twenty-seven in a hundred of the white families . . . are possessed of slaves."[6] Olmsted also correctly pointed to the concentration of most slaves in the hands of a much smaller number of large planters to bolster the oligarchical thesis.

The crucial political endorsement of this view point was provided by the Republican party. "There is not a State in the Union in which the slaveholders number *one-tenth* part of the free white population," stated that party's address to the people of the United States in 1856, neglecting to include in its percentage figure, as it should have, all of the members of slaveholding families. Continuing in a similar distorted fashion the address asserted that non-slaveholders in the South "were reduced to a vassalage little less degrading than that of the slaves themselves, . . . although the white population of the slaveholding States is more than six millions, of whom but 347,525, or less than *one-seventeenth*, are the owners of slaves."[7] The appearance from within the South of Hinton Rowan Helper's *The Impending Crisis of the South* the following year immeasurably strengthened this conception.

In succeeding years convictions of the concentrated nature of slave ownership obviously encouraged northern Republican leaders to discredit and seriously underestimate the popularity of both secession and the Confederacy. During and after the war the same belief can readily be detected in antislavery glorifications of the Union cause, in the opposition to Lincoln's ten per cent plan for Reconstruction, and in the support of plans for confiscation or other forms of federal intervention in the South.

Additional important confirmation of the Republican point of view came from abroad. One lasting voice was added by Karl Marx and Frederick Engels, who repeatedly referred to a narrow "oligarchy of the 300,000 slave lords" arrayed "against the 5,000,000 whites."[8] It would appear that in their eagerness to emphasize the importance of the class struggle Marx and Engels utilized statistics as carelessly as Republicans

[6] Frederick Law Olmsted, *A Journey Into the Seaboard Slave States With Remarks on Their Economy* (New York, 1856), pp. 213-14, 535. Davis, *The Slave Power Conspiracy*, details a variety of the early stereotyped conceptions of the Slave Power.

[7] "Address to the People of the United States," in Robert W. Johannsen (ed.) *The Union in Crisis, 1850-1877* (New York, 1965), pp. 117, 118-19.

[8] *The Civil War in the United States by Karl Marx and Frederick Engels* (paperback ed., New York, 1961), pp. 68, 79, 227.

had. The same attitude also pervaded the full length analysis of slavery by the Irish political economist John Elliott Cairnes that appeared in 1862. After arbitrarily excluding non-slaveholders of substantial condition as not properly a part of slave society, Cairnes depicted the South as composed solely of slaves, a small minority of slave owners, and "an idle and lawless rabble" numbering "about seven-tenths of the whole white population." Elsewhere he used a different figure. "When the whole wealth of a country is monopolized by a thirteenth part of its population," he wrote, apparently referring to slaveholders in general, "the only possible result is that which we find—a despotism, in the last degree unscrupulous and impatient of control, wielded by the wealthy few."[9]

It appears then that the conception of a narrow distribution of slave ownership in the antebellum South, which is sometimes presented as a recent corrective to past distortions, largely originated with the early opponents of slavery. That conception was utilized to promote a negative view of slave society, particularly respecting its oligarchic nature and sometimes respecting the degraded state of the mass of southern whites as well.

For some reason antebellum defenders of slavery displayed little concern with the distribution of slaveholding among whites, although George Fitzhugh and Daniel R. Hundley did reply with some related effectiveness to accusations of general economic injustice within the South.[10] A direct confrontation with the extent of slave ownership in the South was provided, however, by James D. B. De Bow the noted publisher and editor from New Orleans and superintendent of the national census of 1850. De Bow was a racist who deigned even to count blacks as part of the population, but he did establish the number of slaveholders more precisely than others and raised a number of pertinent issues that have escaped appropriate consideration ever since.

Assuming the published returns . . . to be correct, it will appear that one-half of the [white] population of South Carolina, Mississippi, and Louisiana, excluding the cities, are slaveholders, and that one-third of the population of the entire South are similarly circumstanced. . . .

It will thus appear that the slaveholders of the South, so far from constituting numerically an insignificant portion of its people, as has been malignantly alleged, make up an aggregate, greater in relative proportion than the holders of any other species of property whatever, in any part of the world; and that of no other property can it be said, with equal truthfulness, that it is an interest of the whole community. Whilst every other family in the States I have specially referred to, are slaveholders, but one family in every three and a half families in Maine, New Hampshire, Massachusetts and Connecticut, are holders of agricultural land; and, in European States, the proportion is almost indefinitely less. The proportion which the slaveholders of the South, bear to the entire population is greater than that of the owners of land or houses, agricultural stock, State, bank, or other corporation securities anywhere else.

[9] John Elliot Cairnes, *The Slave Power. Its Character, Career, and Probable Designs* . . . . (paperback reprint, New York, 1969), pp. 83, 95-97, 375-76.

[10] George Fitzhugh, *Sociology for the South or the Failure of Free Society* (reprint ed., New York, n.d.), p. 254; Daniel R. Hundley, *Social Relations in Our Southern States* (reprint ed., New York, 1960), pp. 77, 84-85.

No political economist will deny this. Nor is that all. Even in the States which are among the largest slaveholding, South Carolina, Georgia and Tennessee, the land proprietors outnumber nearly two to one, in relative proportion, the owners of the same property in Maine, Massachusetts and Connecticut, and if the average number of slaves held by each family throughout the South be but nine, and if one-half of the whole number of slaveholders own under five slaves, it will be seen how preposterous is the allegation of our enemies, that the slaveholding class is an organized wealthy aristocracy. *The poor men of the South are the holders of one to five slaves, and it would be equally consistent with truth and justice, to say that they represent, in reality, its slaveholding interest.*

The fact being conceded that there is a very large class of persons in the slaveholding States, who have no direct ownership in slaves; it may be well asked, upon what principle a greater antagonism can be presumed between them and their fellow-citizens, than exists among the larger class of non-landholders in the free States and the landed interest there? If a conflict of interest exists in one instance, it does in the other, and if patriotism and public spirit are to be measured upon so low a standard, the social fabric at the North is in far greater danger of dissolution than it is here.[11]

Of course De Bow's concluding prophecy was dramatically disproven soon thereafter and his general arguments discredited and forgotten by an entirely free labor nation. In the future, although the statistical exaggerations of the antislavery enthusiasts were properly modified, the general conclusion remained the one which they had reached—that a remarkably small minority of southern whites had owned slaves or derived any direct benefit from slavery. Even within the South there was a new reluctance to see any supposed advantages to whites in the discredited institution. In a face saving gesture, cultivators of the myth of the Old South recalled slavery only as a selfless burden rather than means of gain; while such prophets of the New South as Henry W. Grady and Daniel A. Tompkins more accurately characterized abolition itself as a blessing that opened up new and exciting economic opportunities for the former slave states.

During the decades following the conclusion of the Civil War, leading historians continued to insist upon the monopolistic nature of slave ownership.[12] Perhaps Woodrow Wilson best revealed how carelessly such conclusions were drawn, when after expanding the proportion of whites involved with slavery to almost 50 per cent, he could still conclude that "less than half the white people of the southern States should be classed among those who determined the tone and methods of southern

---

[11] *The Interest in Slavery of the Southern Non-Slaveholder. . . .* 1860 Association. Tract No. 5 (Charleston, 1860), pp. 3-4. Qualifications must be added to De-Bow's utilization of Tennessee, which did have a large absolute number of slaveholders but did not have one of the larger slave populations or larger percentages of slaveholders, and also to his utilization of nonagricultural northern states.

[12] John W. Draper, *History of the American Civil War* (New York, 1867-1870), I, 538; II, 98-99; James Schouler, *History of the United States of America Under the Constitution* (New York, 1880-1913), V, 225; Woodrow Wilson, *Division and Reunion, 1829-1909* (New York, 1893), pp. 128-29; Hermann E. Von Holst, *The Constitutional and Political History of the United States,* John Lalor and Alfred B. Mason, trs. (Chicago, 1876-1892), I, 342 n. 1, 348.

politics. The ruling class in each State was small, compact, and on the whole homogeneous."[13] The only discovered modification of that attitude came, appropriately enough, from a French nobleman, the Comte de Paris, who suggested that although the slaveholders of the South did form "a real caste," they were "too numerous to constitute an aristocracy."[14]

The most influential historical contribution to the standard view was undoubtedly made by James Ford Rhodes' multivolume history of the Civil War era. According to Rhodes, "the political system of the South was an oligarchy under the republican form. The slave-holders were in a disproportionate minority in every State."[15] Rhodes, a very wealthy stockholder, failed to note that similar comments were being made by some social critics about nineteenth century capitalists. Instead views such as his justified the Civil War to white Americans by identifying the South with oligarchical characteristics that violated a national commitment to political and economic democracy for whites. Nor was that all. Another embarrassment remained—that of reconciling the supposed economic opportunity of the new age of freedom with the manifest poverty of the white as well as black South. Again the heritage of slavery rather than new forms of internal and external exploitation provided a convenient and soothing explanation.

The scholarly profession overwhelmingly continued to endorse the oligarchical thesis expressed by Rhodes. Edward Channing, an historian, and John W. Burgess, a political scientist, soon did so, and in 1896 a journalist and freelance writer, Edward Ingle, focused attention upon the broader consideration that "the greater part of southern wealth was held by a comparative few. . . ."[16] Some years later Albert Bushnell Hart and French Ensor Chadwick added the more original claim that, therefore, the willingness of the southern white population to follow the pro-slavery leadership of the South was "one of the perplexing things in human history."[17] It was not made clear why this should have been more

[13] Wilson, *Division and Reunion*, pp. 128-29.

[14] Comte de Paris, *History of the Civil War in America* (Philadelphia, 1875-1888), I, 87.

[15] James Ford Rhodes, *History of the United States from the Compromise of 1850 to the Final Restoration of Home Rule at the South in 1877* (New York, 1893-1900), I, 345.

[16] Edward Channing, *The United States of America, 1765-1865* (New York, 1897), p. 263; John W. Burgess, *The Civil War and the Constitution, 1859-1869* (New York, 1901), I, 28; Edward Ingle, *Southern Sidelights: A Picture of Social and Economic Life in the South a Generation before the War* (New York, 1896), p. 43. Ingle added an important qualification in viewing the slaveholding and landowning class "as a great middle class, the foundation and wall of conservatism and safety in any land." *Ibid.*, p. 19.

[17] Albert Bushnell Hart, *Slavery and Abolition, 1831-1841* (New York, 1906), p. 76; French Ensor Chadwick, *Causes of the Civil War, 1859-1861* (New York, 1906), pp. 23-24, 34.

perplexing than the habit of most peoples in the past to follow the leadership of privileged minorities.

The attitude of Hart and Chadwick reflected a growing inclination to disassociate the mass of southern whites from the institution of slavery, a development that undoubtedly reflected the spirit of sectional reconciliation marking the close of the nineteenth century. In 1909 a related attitude was expressed by Ulrich B. Phillips and Walter L. Fleming in a collective twelve volume work appropriately entitled *The South in the Building of the Nation*. According to Phillips not only did "scarcely one-fourth of the Southern white population" belong to slave owning families, but slavery was actually profitable only for the few large holders among them, and therefore "the advantages of the slave labor system were confined to the negroes themselves and to a small proportion of the whites."[18] Phillips was thus disassociating an even larger body of whites from any advantageous connection with slavery, although, largely because of his racist beliefs, he remained sympathetic to slavery and absolved the institution itself of being harmful to the enslaved blacks.

Phillips was also perplexed by the willingness of the white South to support an institution which he had decided was economically unprofitable, and in his well known article of 1928, "The Central Theme of Southern History," he offered as his answer to this dilemma the determination of southern whites to maintain white supremacy. This thesis has become increasingly popular, in part because we have become so aware of the pervasiveness and importance of racism in our history. Without denying the historical importance of white racism in both North and South, it must also be noted that minimizing the number of southerners with an economic stake in slavery encourages an overestimation of the independent force of racism itself.

Throughout the early twentieth century the major works dealing with southern history continued to stress, as did Clement Eaton, that the "overwhelming majority" of southern white farmers did not own slaves.[19] Unusually restrained was Avery Craven's comment that antebellum

[18] J.A.C. Chandler and others, *The South in the Building of the Nation* (Richmond, 1909-1910), V, 123-24, 118.

[19] Clement Eaton, *A History of the Old South* (New York, 1949), p. 458; Robert S. Cotterill, *The Old South* (Glendale, Calif., 1937), p. 265; William Garrott Brown, *The Lower South in American History* (New York, 1930), pp. 34, 46; John Bach McMaster, *A History of the People of the United States from the Revolution to the Civil War* (New York, 1883-1913) VIII, 426-27; William E. Dodd, *The Cotton Kingdom: A Chronicle of the Old South* (New Haven, 1919), p. 24; William B. Hesseltine, *The South in American History* (New York, 1936), p. 268; Thomas J. Wertenbaker, *The Old South: The Founding of American Civilization* (New York, 1942), p. 350; Francis B. Simkins, *The South Old and New: A History, 1820-1947* (New York, 1947), p. 53; James Truslow Adams, *America's Tragedy* (New York, 1934), pp. 67-68; Charles M. Beard, *The Rise of American Civilization* (New York, 1930), II, 7; Rollin G. Osterweis, *Romanticism and Nationalism in the Old South* (New Haven, 1949), p. 18; Avery Craven, *The Growth of Southern Nationalism, 1848-1861* (Baton Rouge, 1953), p. 9.

southerners "were a people close to the soil and some among them held slaves." Some time earlier Craven advised that as an economic interest we could "almost ignore [slavery] in our study of the sectional conflict."[20]

A variety of specialized studies followed the same tradition. Lewis Gray's comprehensive study of southern agriculture concluded that "the proportion of the white population connected with slaveholding was comparatively small."[21] A similar emphasis is found in major studies of slavery on the sectional, state, and local level;[22] in economic histories of the United States;[23] in studies of secession and the coming of the Civil War;[24] in studies of southern states;[25] in the works of Marxist historians;[26] and in the works of black historians.[27] On occasion there has been exaggeration beyond that committed by the early Republicans.[28]

With such a long tradition of agreement on this particular question it is surprising to find the following statement made by John Hope Franklin in 1960:

[20] Craven, The Repressible Conflict (Baton Rouge, 1939), p. 76. A few years later Craven considered it "perfectly clear that slavery played a rather minor part in the life of the South and of the Negro." Craven, The Coming of the Civil War (New York, 1942), p. 93. A major dissenting view, which emphasized the economic importance of slavery, was Robert Royal Russel, Economic Aspects of Southern Sectionalism, 1840-1861 (Urbana, 1923), pp. 290-91.

[21] Lewis C. Gray, History of Agriculture in the Southern United States to 1860 (Washington, 1933), I, 481.

[22] Kenneth Stampp, The Peculiar Institution: Slavery in the Antebellum South (New York, 1956), p. 29; Charles S. Sydnor, Slavery in Mississippi (New York, 1933) p. 193; Edward W. Phifer, "Slavery in Microcosm: Burke County, North Carolina," Journal of Southern History, XXVIII (May, 1962), 141. For a contrasting emphasis see Orville W. Taylor, Negro Slavery in Arkansas (Durham, 1958), p. 56.

[23] Harold U. Faulkner, American Economic History (New York, 1949), p. 327; Gilbert C. Fite and Jim E. Reese, An Economic History of the United States (2nd ed., Boston, 1965), p. 171; Edward C. Kirkland, A History of American Economic Life (4th ed., New York, 1969), p. 123.

[24] Arthur C. Cole, The Irrepressible Conflict, 1850-1865 (New York, 1934), p. 34; Gerald W. Johnson, The Secession of the Southern States (New York, 1932), p. 134. Also see above, f.n. 4.

[25] Rosser H. Taylor, Antebellum South Carolina: A Social and Cultural History (Chapel Hill, 1942), p. 8; Guion G. Johnson, Ante-Bellum North Carolina: A Social History (Chapel Hill, 1937), p. 57; Roger W. Shugg, Origins of Class Struggle in Louisiana.... (paperback ed., Baton Rouge, 1968), p. 2.

[26] Herbert Aptheker, Toward Negro Freedom (New York, 1956), p. 59; Algie M. Simons, Social Forces in American History (New York, 1920), p. 224.

[27] Carter G. Woodson, The Negro in Our History (7th ed., Washington, D.C., 1941), p. 355; W. E. Burghardt Du Bois, Black Reconstruction in America. . . . (paperback reprint, Cleveland, 1964), p. 32; John Hope Franklin, From Slavery to Freedom: A History of Negro Americans (3rd ed., New York, 1967), p. 186.

[28] Herbert S. Klein, Slavery in the Americas: A Comparative Study of Virginia and Cuba (Chicago, 1967), p. 186. Klein asserts that in 1860 Virginia slaveholders "represented only 0.5% of the white population." Perhaps he meant to say 5%, but he should have said 25.9%.

Recent studies of the ante-bellum social structure, for example, have made it clear that the vast majority of southern whites owned no slaves and had no hope of owning slaves. This incontrovertible fact has, of course, only slowly made headway in popular thinking against the more attractive, exotic view, sustained in historical fiction, that slavery provided an idyllic existence for all or most southern whites. But as southern whites come to understand slavery as an institution that materially benefitted a very small segment of the southern population, they may be freed from personal involvement in the defense not only of the Old South's defunct "peculiar institution," but also its surviving corollary, the doctrine of white superiority.[29]

The truth is that historians, at least, have long agreed with Franklin's conception of slave ownership and in good part precisely because of the ideological prejudices that he endorses. But the value of such ideological motivations or results in historical interpretation is, to say the least, doubtful. What, after all, are we to do if more than "a very small segment of the southern population" did benefit from slavery?

There have been surprisingly few modifications of the conviction that slaveholding was narrowly distributed among whites. One of the most important of these is associated with studies of the "plain folk of the Old South" by Frank L. Owsley and what has been called the Vanderbilt school. An earlier similar statement, also a product of Tennessee, was G. W. Dyer's study, *Democracy in the South Before the Civil War* (1905), which professed that competitive conditions were good and life relatively prosperous for the average southern white of the 1850's. Dyer appears to have been diverted from stressing the extent of slave ownership, however, by his anxiety to emphasize the morality and industriousness of southern whites.[30]

While a strong interest in the antebellum southern yeomanry was maintained by numerous other authors, particularly William B. Hesseltine and Roger W. Shugg, as well as by the members of the Vanderbilt school, there was seldom any real concern with the spread of slaveholding among these yeomen. This was obviously the case for Blanche Henry Clark's study of Tennessee, which admittedly focused upon that "large group of middle-class and yeomen farmers who did not own any slaves."[31] Owsley, himself, specifically did include small slaveholders among the mass of plain folk in the Old South, although it is a reflection of his reluctance to stress that identification,[32] that a recent discussion of the Vanderbilt school appears under the title "Slavery and the Non-

[29] John Hope Franklin, " 'As For Our History . . . ,' " in Charles G. Sellers, Jr. (ed.), *The Southerner as American* (Chapel Hill, 1960), p. 15.

[30] G. W. Dyer, *Democracy in the South Before the Civil War* (Nashville, 1905), pp. 40-42, 46, 59.

[31] Blanche Henry Clark, *The Tennessee Yeomen: 1840-1860* (Nashville, 1942), p. xvii.

[32] Compare Owsley's failure to mention slaveholders in his introduction with their subsequent inclusion in the text. Frank L. Owsley, *Plain Folk of the Old South* (Baton Rouge, 1949), pp. vii-viii, 8. Fletcher Green's work also stresses the importance of the plain folk and democracy in the South but does not dwell upon the question of slaveholding. E.g. Fletcher Green, "Democracy in the Old South," *Journal of Southern History*, XII (Feb., 1946), 3-23.

slaveholder." David Potter also described the work of this school as "designed to show that plain *nonslaveholding* farmers occupied an important and respected place in the Southern social structure."[33]

The most infrequent but probably most important modification of the traditional concept of slave ownership concerns the matter of perspective. In 1919, William E. Dodd, while agreeing that the concentration of slave ownership in the South revealed "a dangerous tendency," went on to note that "these figures do not show such extreme concentration of wealth in a few hands as the facts of our own day disclose. . . ."[35] Again, in 1935, Frederick Jackson Turner briefly questioned Rhodes' identification of an interest in slavery solely with planters and certain professional classes allied with them: "Logically, this would lead to the conclusion that the institution of private property in the United States rests on the interest of only the most prosperous, who control the larger portion of the property but constitute only a very small percentage of the population. The great slaveholders of the South represented the concentration of wealth in slaves on a scale comparable with the present concentration of holdings of private property, generally, in the United States." Turner also pointed out another neglected fundamental consideration, that "in the regions where slavery flourished, there was a society which depended upon the institution, and this society was dominant throughout the South."[36]

Corresponding closely to the latter point made by Turner is Eugene Genovese's conception of slavery as the fundamental base of the southern social order. Genovese's approach, together with his criticism of other Marxists for glorifying the lower classes and exaggerating the extent of class conflict in the slave South, might well have led him toward reconsidering the extent of slaveholding. Instead, his interest in the southern aristocracy has led Genovese toward a reaffirmation of the conception of concentrated slave ownership. Southern slavery, he states, was "the foundation on which rose a powerful and remarkable social class: a class constituting only a tiny portion of the white population. . . ."[37] In a subsequent severe judgment of Marxist writings on slavery, Genovese nowhere questions Marx's exaggerated conception of a south-

---

[33] Harold D. Woodman (ed.), *Slavery and the Southern Economy. Sources and Readings* (New York, 1966), pp. 127-54; David Potter, *The South and the Sectional Conflict* (Baton Rouge, 1968), p. 123. Italics added.

[34] *Ibid.*, p. 192. An appreciation of the extent of slaveholding could serve to bolster Potter's thesis that self-interest lay at the heart of southern nationality, but he focuses only upon an undefined "vital interest" and the "dangers of a slave insurrection." *Ibid.*, pp. 78-79.

[35] William E. Dodd, *The Cotton Kingdom: A Chronicle of the Old South* (New Haven, 1919), p. 24.

[36] Frederick Jackson Turner, *The United States, 1830-1850* (New York, 1935), p. 153.

[37] Eugene D. Genovese, *The Political Economy of Slavery: Studies in the Economy and Society of the Slave South* (New York, 1965), p. 4.

ern oligarchy, and when he directly criticizes Marx for a "gross under-estimation of the slaveholding class," he is obviously speaking in quali-tative terms.[38]

It is obvious that the long lasting and almost unanimous interpreta-tion of the slave South has been that a remarkably small percentage of the southern white population owned or directly benefited from the enslavement of blacks. This condition has generally been viewed as, in the words of Louis M. Hacker, "a startling situation,"[39] startling in the sense of constituting a departure from the traditions of democracy and opportunity generally associated with the history of the United States. It is the central contention of the remainder of this essay that these tra-ditional conclusions have minimized and misinterpreted the meaning of the extent to which southern whites were economically involved with slavery.

In accordance with the customary emphasis, historians often include all of the slave states in their statistical presentations. If one is interested in the deterministic impact of slavery, however, it would appear more appropriate to consider only the Confederate states, where fully 31 per cent of the white families owned slaves in 1860. Thus, every third white person in those states had a direct commitment to slavery and, barring occasional dissidents, had cause to be a supporter and propagandist for that system. This appears to be an amazingly large, rather than small, base of support for any economic order, and the figures are more impres-sive when we consider the seven states of the lower South in the pre-cise order of their secession from the Union: South Carolina with 48.7 per cent of the white families owning slaves; Mississippi with 48 per cent; Florida with 36 per cent; Alabama with 35.1 per cent; Georgia with 38 per cent; Louisiana with 32.2 per cent; and Texas with 28.5 per cent.

Even more pertinent is the fact that the significance of these per-centages has been distorted because of an eagerness to view slavehold-ing as something that could be equated with, say, voting percentages, or the possession of horses or cows, or the popularity of styles of dress. But while 31 per cent may not appear large as a voting or even isolated ownership statistic, it is enormous if, as suggested by Turner and Geno-vese, slavery is viewed as the economic foundation of an entire social system and the distribution of slaves is compared to analogous factors in a free society.

The problem of determining the appropriate comparisons for such a test is too complex to be thoroughly examined here, but some rough suggestions can be made. First let me emphasize that we are not con-

[38] Genovese, "Marxian Interpretations of the Slave South," Barton J. Bernstein (ed.), *Towards a New Past: Dissenting Essays in American History* (New York, 1967), p. 96.

[39] Louis M. Hacker, *The Triumph of American Capitalism. The Development of Forces in American History to the End of the Nineteenth Century* (New York, 1940), p. 288.

cerned with general economic comparisons but solely with the beliefs that there was something extremely oligarchical about southern slave ownership and that popular white support for such an economic system was surprising. A comparison with the recent past seems particularly appropriate to testing those conceptions, and dates have been selected arbitrarily to coincide with convenient statistical information. Two criteria that seem unusually appropriate for testing are those of investor and employer, with comparisons made between the percentage of slaveholders in 1860 and the percentage of investors and employers in modern free labor society. In the first instance, taking for the year 1949 the very modest estimate of $5,000 as an investment comparable to the investment in one slave in 1860, we discover that in 1949 only 2 per cent of the spending units (families) in the United States held stock worth $5,000 or more.[40] If one is concerned with estimating the extent of a direct personal interest in the profits of a particular labor system it would then seem appropriate to compare this figure of 2 per cent with the 31 per cent of the white families in the Confederacy who owned slaves. We are excluding, of course, the entire southern black population and the entire question of general welfare, but what we are interested in is the comparative extent to which southern whites directly invested in slavery. In this respect the proportion of whites who invested in and profited from slavery far exceeds the proportion of the total population investing in our own free labor system.

When we compare the opportunity afforded white citizens of the slave South to achieve an employer status with the same opportunity afforded citizens in the twentieth century United States the results are similar. Thus, in 1940, the total number of employers in the nation was less

[40] Our comparison probably minimizes the point being made. Thus, $750 has been used as the average investment represented by the ownership of one slave, although Conrad and Meyer set that amount between $1400 and $1450. Since $750 is about 4½ times the average agricultural wage in 1860 for a full twelve months, it would appear appropriate to compare this to an amount 4½ times the annual income of someone in 1949 earning the established minimum wage of 75c, which amounts to about $7020. Again, however, we utilize instead an even lower figure of $5,000 for our comparison in 1949. At that time, according to a federal survey of "owned stock in corporations open to investment by the general public," but not including "a much smaller number of units that owned stock in only privately held corporations," only 2 per cent of the spending units held stock worth $5,000 or more. It is true that this figure would be slightly higher if we could also include those holding stock in privately held corporations, but the comparative result would be about the same. See Alfred H. Conrad and John R. Meyer, *The Economics of Slavery and Other Studies in Econometric History* (Chicago, 1964), p. 53; Stanley Lebergott, "Wage Trends, 1800-1900," Conference on Research in Income and Wealth, National Bureau of Economic Research, *Trends in the American Economy in the Nineteenth Century* (Princeton, 1960), p. 462; "Survey of Consumer Finances," Part VI, *Federal Reserve Bulletin*, Oct. 1949, 1183.

[41] In 1940 there were 54,447,000 gainfully employed workers in the United States. Of these 81.4 per cent were employees and 18.6 per cent were self employed, the latter including 9.6 per cent in farming, 8 per cent in business, and 1 per cent professional. Not all of the self employed were, however, employers. For

than 10 per cent of the number of households. For a proper comparison with slaveholding this figure should be reduced, since it includes duplication as well as *all* business, agricultural, and professional employers. But even the figure of 10 per cent hardly equals the 31 per cent of white families holding slaves in the Confederate South who may be classed as employers. Again, there appears to be less need to wonder at southern white support for slavery than most historians have assumed. While it certainly is true that the moral, historical, and economic limitations of slavery as a social system are overwhelming, nevertheless the enslavement of black people did provide southern whites with a unique opportunity to exploit human labor. Practically every slaveholder sought to tap that opportunity, whatever the actual rate of profit and whatever the special advantages accruing to the planter class; and even if that opportunity was declining in the 1850's it remained remarkably broad. Indeed, considering the white population alone, race slavery in the Americas may have created one of the largest percentage groups of investors in the direct exploitation of labor that the world has ever seen.

White racism was, of course, essential to the existence and preservation of this economic opportunity for whites, and it is important to recognize just how many southern whites had an economic interest in the development, propagation, and acceptance of racism within the South. While it would be a mistake to minimize the independent force of racism or the impact of psychological and other factors in racist development, it is also a mistake not to recognize that white supremacy was fundamental to the material interests of a very large proportion of the southern white population. Furthermore, this connection between white supremacy and economic opportunity extended beyond emancipation. One third of the white population subject to Reconstruction automatically retained a selfish economic interest in perpetuating the suppression of black labor. The advantages of such subordination included a continuation not only of exploitive opportunities but also of all the accompanying privileges and advantages that had accrued to slaveholders,

---

example, one year earlier 45 per cent of all the business firms in the United States had no regular paid employees. If we apply this same percentage to the total number of those self employed in business in 1940 (4,378,000), we approximate the number of business employers at 4.4 per cent of all those gainfully employed. We then add to our number of business employers 15 per cent of all self employed farmers. Since in 1950 only 9.4 per cent of all farms utilized regular hired labor and another 5 per cent utilized seasonal labor, this is a generous percentage and provides an additional 1.44 per cent of those gainfully employed. Then also adding the entire professional group of 1 per cent we approximate the total employer group at 6.44 per cent of all gainfully employed individuals. This in itself is an appropriate comparative figure, but assuming that each employer is the head of a household, employers constitute 9.97 per cent of the number of the households in the nation in 1940. See Joseph D. Phillips, *Small Business in the American Economy,* Illinois Studies in the Social Sciences, Vol. 42 (Urbana, 1958), 4, 26, 29; *U.S. Census of Agriculture: 1950. General Report,* Vol. II, 250; *The Statistical History of the United States from Colonial Times to the Present* (Stamford, 1965), p. 15.

large and small, during the slave era. Such selfish considerations may well have been more central to the intensification of racism during Reconstruction than were the racist convictions of the public at large or competitive clashes between lower class blacks and whites. Probably it has been the erosion of these economic advantages rather than growing convictions of the limited benefits of racism and slavery, that ultimately has made the most significant contribution to combating racism.

A widespread investment in slavery may also have been as responsible for the South's racist *Herrenvolk* democracy as was any calculated effort on the part of a planter elite to win the support of nonslaveholding whites.[42] Certainly this would help explain why the spread of Jacksonian democracy in the South was accompanied by an intensification of the regional commitment to slavery, and why it was that a political party famed for its equalitarian leanings became the nation's major defender of racism and slavery. While such an interpretation of slaveholding obviously parallels many of the conclusions of the Owsley school, it does so by viewing slavery as central to the well being of many of the plain white folk of the old South. While recent study indicates that it was primarily whites of middle rather than lower circumstances who were deriving these economic benefits,[43] one might still conclude that the South's vigorous endorsement of slavery was more a reflection of popular white will and ambition than it was the defensive response of a small white aristocracy.

The significance or influence of the large slaveholding minority of the antebellum South was additionally enhanced by a wide variety of factors that usually and mistakenly have been identified only with the interests of the planter elite. For example, slave owners were, on the whole, the more successful and influential members of the white population, and in addition their interests were championed by many nonslaveholders who were directly or indirectly involved with the benefits of the slave economy. The geographical concentration of slavery also increased its political power in key regions within the various states, while that power was sometimes further strengthened by slave or property representation at the state level. What is being suggested is that while particular advantages did exist for the slaveholding minority within the South, these advantages were being exploited by a remarkably large proportion of the total white population; and the large size of this minority was crucial to the strength of racism, slavery, and the Confederacy.

Meanwhile, antislavery northerners had difficulty believing that a white Christian population could willingly endorse the evil of slavery,

---

[42] Cf. George Frederickson, *The Black Image in the White Mind* (New York, 1971), p. 68.

[43] Gavin Wright, " 'Economic Democracy' and the Concentration of Agricultural Wealth in the Cotton South," in William N. Parker (ed.), *The Structure of the Cotton Economy of the Antebellum South* (Washington, D.C., 1970), p. 85.

and they found some solution to that paradox, as did many Americans thereafter, by equating slavery with oligarchy. Today it appears particularly ironic that they were not equally disturbed by the evil of racism, for the historical process has reversed itself. Having recently been forced to recognize the existence of American racism, we now seem far more prepared to admit our susceptibility as a people to that evil than our susceptibility to such an extreme economic exploitation as enslavement.

The concept of a popular economic endorsement of slavery is also strongly supported by recent denials that the southern slave economy was either unprosperous or unhealthy. Alfred Conrad and John Meyer have concluded that "slavery was profitable to the whole South," while a study by Richard Easterlin concludes that "the income of the white population in the South exceeded the national average" and that per capita income in the South was probably rising substantially in the 1850's. Robert W. Fogel and Stanley L. Engerman have come to the same conclusion.[44] If these analyses are correct, the confidence and economic interest in slavery on the part of southern whites, slaveholders or not, obviously would remain strong, even if the percentage of slaveholders was declining. In some areas this decline did not even occur.[45] Such economic viability does not, by the way, automatically contradict assumptions that there were internal contradictions and important limitations to the slave system, but it does suggest that it was sufficiently viable in the 1850's to encourage mass southern white support.

A recent study by Gavin Wright, on the other hand, concludes that cotton areas of the slave South were characterized by a more unequal distribution of agricultural wealth than was true of the agricultural North. The social impact of this fact appears minimal, however, and Wright agrees that the distribution of wealth among the free population of the cotton South was not more unequal than the wealth distribution of the nineteenth-century urban North or of the present day.[46]

There are then several important challenges to the traditional assumption that the ownership of slaves and the economic benefits of slavery extended to a remarkably small minority of the southern white population. That assumption largely originated in arguments supporting the antislavery moment and the Civil War; and it has also reflected the presumptions and doubts of a free labor society, the eagerness of scholars to discover class conflict within the South, and a misdirected sympathy for white and black southerners. At various times this tradition has served as a simplistic means of discrediting slave society and, less

[44] Conrad and Meyer, *The Economics of Slavery*, p. 82; Richard A. Easterlin, "Regional Income Trends, 1840-1950," in Seymour Harris (ed.), *American Economic History* (New York, 1961), pp. 527, 530; Robert W. Fogel and Stanley L. Engerman, "The Economics of Slavery" (unpublished manuscript, 1967).

[45] Cornelius O. Cathey, *Agricultural Development in North Carolina, 1783-1860* (Chapel Hill, 1956), pp. 53, 62.

[46] Gavin Wright, " 'Economic Democracy' . . . in the Cotton South," 83-85.

directly, as a means of bolstering faith in our present political-economic system by exempting the mass of southern whites from economic or political involvement in the slave South and by blaming slavery for many of the ills of the free South. Most obviously this emphasis upon the supposedly narrow extent of slaveholding has encouraged an exaggerated conception of the oligarchic peculiarities of antebellum slavery, an underestimation of the impact of economic self interest upon a large proportion of the southern white population, and an excessively detached conception of the role of racism in southern life. The fact is that the enslavement of black people did provide extensive economic opportunities for whites, and viewed from its own racist context, slavery appears a good bit less oligarchical in several significant economic respects than twentieth century free labor capitalism. The ownership of slaves was spread among a remarkably broad proportion of the white population, and the extent of this white investment was central to southern white unity before, during, and after the Civil War.

116

THE ECONOMIC COST OF SLAVEHOLDING IN THE COTTON BELT[1]

APART from mere surface politics, the ante-bellum South is largely an unknown country to American historians. The conditions, the life, the spirit of its people were so different from those which prevailed and still prevail in the North that it is difficult for northern investigators to interpret correctly the facts which they are able to find. From the South itself they have received little assistance; for before the war southerners were content, as a rule, to transmit traditions without writing books and since the war they have been too seriously engrossed in adapting themselves to new conditions to feel any strong impulse towards a scientific reconstruction of the former environment. When the South shall have been interpreted to the world by its own writers, it will be highly useful for students of other sections and other countries to criticise and correct, utilize and supplement the southern historical literature.[2] At the present time, however, the great need seems to be that of interpretation of developments in the South by men who have inherited southern traditions. This consideration will perhaps justify the following incomplete study.

Whether negro slavery was an advantage in the early colonies and whether it became a burden in the later period, and, if so, how the change occurred, and why the people did not relieve themselves of the incubus—these are a few of the fundamental problems.to which the student must address himself. The present essay, based on a study of slave prices, deals with the general economic conditions of slaveholding, and shows the great transformation caused by the opening of the cotton belt and the closing of the African slave trade.

[1] The grant of a fund by the Carnegie Institution of Washington has been of material aid in prosecuting the research of which this article is a product.

[2] In the study of the economic history of American slavery the writer has enjoyed the collaboration of Dr. Charles McCarthy, of Wisconsin, a keen thinker with a point of view which supplements that of a southerner.

As regards the labor supply, the conditions at the outset in the new world of America were unlike those of modern Europe, but similar to those of Asia and Europe in primitive times. The ancient labor problem rose afresh in the plantation colonies, for land was plentiful and free, and men would not work as voluntary wage-earners in other men's employ when they might as readily work for themselves in independence. There was a great demand for labor upon the colonial estates, and when it became clear that freemen would not come and work for hire, a demand developed for servile labor. At first recourse was had to white men and women who bound themselves to serve three or four years to pay for their transportation across the sea, and to English criminals who were sent to the colonies and bound to labor for longer terms, frequently for five or seven years. Indian slaves were tried, but proved useless. Finally the negroes were discovered to be cheap and useful laborers for domestic service and plantation work.

For above half a century after the first negroes were brought to Virginia in 1620, this labor was considered a doubtful experiment; and their numbers increased very slowly until after the beginning of the golden age of the colony toward the end of the reign of Charles II. But the planters learned at length that the negroes could be employed to very good advantage in the plantation system; and after about 1680 the import of slaves grew steadily larger.[1]

In the West Indies the system of plantations worked by slaves had been borrowed by the English settlers from the Spaniards; and when the South Carolina coast was colonized, some of the West India planters immigrated and brought this system with them. In view of the climate and the crops on the Carolina coast, negro slave labor was thought to be a *sine qua non* of successful colonizing. The use of the slaves was confined always to the lowlands, until after Whitney invented the cotton gin; but in the early years of the nineteenth century the rapid opening of the great inland cotton belt created a new and very strong demand for labor. The white farming

[1] For statistics of the increase of slaves in Virginia, see J. C. Ballagh, History of Slavery in Virginia, pp. 10 to 25, *et passim*.

population already in the uplands was by far too small to do the work; the lowland planters began to move thither with their slaves; the northern and European laboring classes were not attracted by the prospect of working alongside the negroes; and accordingly the demand for labor in the cotton belt was translated into an unprecedented demand for negro slave labor.

Negro slavery was established in the South, as elsewhere, because the white people were seeking their own welfare and comfort. It was maintained for the same economic reason, and also because it was thought to be essential for safety. As soon as the negroes were on hand in large numbers, the problem was to keep their savage instincts from breaking forth, and to utilize them in civilized industry. The plantation system solved the problem of organization, while the discipline and control obtained through the institution of slavery were considered necessary to preserve the peace and to secure the welfare of both races. Private gain and public safety were secured for the time being; but in the long run, as we shall see, these ends were attained at the expense of private and public wealth and of progress.

This peculiar labor system failed to gain strength in the North, because there was there no work which negro slaves could perform with notable profit to their masters. In certain parts of the South the system flourished because the work required was simple, the returns were large, and the short-comings of negro slave labor were partially offset by the ease with which it could be organized.

Once developed, the system was of course maintained so long as it appeared profitable to any important part of the community. Wherever the immediate profits from slave labor were found to be large, the number of slaves tended to increase, not only through the birth of children, but by importations. Thus the staple-producing areas became "black belts," where most of the labor was done by slaves. With large amounts of capital invested in slaves, the system would be maintained even in times of depression, when the plantations were running at something of a loss; for, just as in a factory, the capital was fixed, and operations could not be stopped without a still greater loss.

When property in slaves had become important, the conservative element in politics became devoted, as a rule, to the preservation of this vested interest. The very force of inertia tended to maintain the established system, and a convulsion or crisis of some sort was necessary for its disestablishment in any region.

As a matter of fact it was only in special industries, and only in times of special prosperity, that negro slave labor was of such decided profit as to escape condemnation for its inherent disadvantages. But at certain periods in Virginia and in the lower South, the conditions were unusual: all labor was profitable; hired labor was not to be had so long as land was free; indentured white servants were in various ways unsatisfactory, and negro slaves were therefore found to be of decided profit to their masters. The price of Africans in colonial times was so low that, when crops and prices were good, the labor of those imported repaid their original cost in a few years, and the planters felt a constant temptation to increase their holdings of land and of slaves in the hope of still greater profits.

Thus in Virginia there was a vicious circle: planters bought fresh lands and more slaves to make more tobacco, and with the profits from tobacco they bought more land and slaves to make more tobacco with which to buy yet more land and slaves. The situation in the lower South was similar to that in Virginia, with rice and indigo, or sugar, or in latter times cotton, substituted for tobacco. In either case the process involved a heavy export of wealth in the acquisition of every new laborer. The Yankee skipper had a corresponding circle of his own: he carried rum to Guinea to exchange for slaves, slaves to the plantation colonies to exchange for molasses, molasses to New England to exchange for more rum, and this rum again to Guinea to exchange for more slaves. The difference was that the Yankee made a genuine profit on every exchange and thriftily laid up his savings, while the southern planter, as a rule, invested all his profits in a fictitious form of wealth and never accumulated a surplus for any other sort of investment.

From an economic point of view the American system of

slavery was a system of firmly controlling the unintelligent negro laborers, and of capitalizing the prospective value of the labor of each workman for the whole of his life. An essential feature of that system was the practice of buying and selling the control over the slave's labor, and one of the indexes to the economic situation at any time may be found in the quotations of slave prices.

The slave trade had no particular local home or "exchange," but it extended throughout all the slaveholding districts of America. Though the number and frequency of slave sales was relatively small, the traffic when once developed had many of the features of modern stock or produce markets. It cannot be forgotten, of course, that the slave trade involved questions of humanity and social organization as well as the mere money problem; but from the financial point of view the slave traffic constituted simply an extensive commodity market, where the article dealt in was life-time labor. As in any other market, the operations in the slave trade were controlled by economic laws or tendencies. There were bull influences and bear influences, and occasional speculative campaigns. And when at times the supply was subjected to monopoly control, the prices tended to go wild and disturb the general system of finance in the whole region.

In the general slave market there was constant competition among those wishing to sell, and among those wishing to buy. The volume of the colonial slave trade and the rate of slave prices tended to fluctuate to some extent with the tides of prosperity in the respective staple-producing areas; but during the colonial period the plantations in the different regions were of such varied interests, producing tobacco, rice, indigo, cotton, sugar and coffee, that depression in one of these industries was usually offset, so far as concerned the slave-trader, by high profits in another. Barbadoes was the information station. The slave ships touched there and gathered news of where their "ebony" was to be sold the highest.[1] The Royal African Company had the best system of intelli-

---

[1] D. McKinnon, Tour Through the British West Indies, p. 8.

gence, and about 1770 and 1780 it sold its cargoes at a fairly uniform price of £18 to £22 per head,[1] while the independent traders appear to have obtained from £15 to £25, according to the chances of the market.   American-born slaves, when sold, brought higher prices than fresh Africans, because their training in plantation labor and domestic service rendered them more valuable.   The prices of the home-raised slaves varied considerably, but so long as the African trade was kept open, the price of field hands of all sorts was kept reasonably near to the price of the savage African imports.

In the very early period the sellers in the slave market were more eager than the buyers, and the prices ranged nearly as low as the cost of purchasing slaves in Africa and transporting them to America; but great prosperity in all the different groups of plantations at the same period soon greatly increased the demand, and the ships in the traffic proving too few, prices rapidly advanced.   After this, however, there came a decline in tobacco profits; then the war of revolt from Great Britain depressed all the staple industries simultaneously, and following that the American production of indigo was ruined by foreign competition.   Thus in 1790–95 slave prices reached the bottom of a twenty years' decline.[2]

---

[1] *Virginia Magazine*, iii, 167.   Calendar of State Papers, Colonial Series, America and West Indies, 1775–76, p. 155 *et passim*.

[2] The depression of industry in the staple districts toward the close of the eighteenth century is illustrated by several contemporary writers.   Samuel DuBose, in his reminiscences of St. Stephen's parish, describes conditions in lowland South Carolina in the period after the close of the American Revolution:

"When peace was restored every planter was in debt. . . . Ruin stared many in the face.   Besides, with the exception of rice, the country had no staple crop; for since the bounty, which as colonists they had enjoyed on the export of indigo and naval stores, had been discontinued, these products ceased to have any value, and negroes fell in price.   Prime gangs were not unfrequently sold for less than two hundred dollars per head. . . . The people however . . . . were sanguine respecting the future. . . . They strove to reduce their expenses to the lowest possible point; they manufactured clothing for themselves and their slaves; raised abundant supplies of poultry and stock of various kinds, and with these contrived to live in plenty. . . . [At length] the Santee Canal was projected and constructed within their neighborhood.   Everyone availed himself to a greater or less extent of this opportunity of hiring their negroes; for men they received thirty and for women twenty pounds sterling per annum, besides their food.   At times a thousand labor-

The developments following Whitney's invention of the cotton gin revolutionized the situation. Slave prices entered upon a steady advance, which was quickened by the prohibition of the African trade in 1808. They were then held stationary by the restrictions upon commerce, and were thrown backward by the outbreak of war in 1812. But with the peace of Ghent the results of the new cotton industry and of the cessation of African imports became strikingly manifest. The inland fields of the lower South proved to be peculiarly adapted for the production of cotton. The simplicity of the work and the even distribution of the tasks through the seasons made negro slave labor peculiarly available. With the increasing demand of the world for cotton, there was built up in the South perhaps the greatest staple monopoly the world had ever seen. The result was an enormous demand for slaves in the cotton belt. American ports, however, were now closed to the foreign slave trade. The number of slaves available in America was now fixed, the rate of increase was limited, and the old "tobacco South" had a monopoly of the only supply which could meet the demand of the new "cotton South."

ers were employed on this work, which was seven years in being completed. The enterprise, which was disastrous to those who had embarked in it, rescued a large number of planters from ruin. It was commenced in 1792, and finished in 1800. Two or three years after it had been commenced, a few planters in the neighborhood tried the cultivation of cotton on a small scale, but the progress of this enterprise was slow and irresolute, in consequence of the difficulty of preparing it for market. With the improvement of the gins, the cotton culture increased and was extended, until 1799, when Capt. James Sinkler planted three hundred acres at his plantation Belvidere, on Eutaw Creek, and reaped from each acre two hundred and sixteen pounds, which he sold for from fifty to seventy-five cents per pound." This pamphlet of DuBose's is reprinted in T. G. Thomas' History of the Huguenots in South Carolina. N. Y., 1887, *vide* pp. 66–68. The accuracy of the statements quoted is borne out by the very interesting manuscript records of the Porcher-Ravenel family, which are now in the possession of members of the family at Pinopolis, St. John's parish, Berkeley, S. C.

Virginia conditions are indicated in a letter of George Washington to Alexander Spotswood, Nov. 23, 1794, which is published in the *New York Public Library Bulletin*, vol. ii, pp. 14, 15. Spotswood had written that he intended moving west, and asked advice as to selling his lands and slaves. Washington replied that he believed that before many years had passed slaves would become a very troublesome sort of property, and that, except for his principles against selling negroes, he himself would not by the end of twelve months be possessed of a single one as a slave.

Till 1815 "colonial" conditions prevailed, and the market for slave labor was relatively quiet and steady. In 1815 began the "ante-bellum" régime, in which the whole economy of the South was governed by the apparently capricious play of the compound monopoly of cotton and slave labor. The price of cotton was governed by the American output and its relation to the European demand. And the price of slaves was governed by the profits in cotton and the relation of the labor demand to the monopolized labor supply.[1]

For an understanding of slaveholding economics, a careful study of the history of slave prices is essential. Prior to the middle of the eighteenth century, the scarcity of data, the changing value of gold, the multiplicity of coinage systems and the use of paper money with irregular depreciations unfortunately present so many obstacles that any effort to determine the fluctuation of slave prices would be of very doubtful success. For the following periods the study is feasible, although under the best of existing circumstances slave prices are hard to collect and hard to compare. The proportion of the slave population on the market at any time was very much smaller than the student of prices could wish for the purpose of his study; and many of the sales which were made are not to be found in the records. The market classification of the slaves was flexible and irregular; and, except in Louisiana, most of the documents in the public archives do not indicate the classification. To make thoroughly accurate comparison of slave prices at different times and places, we should need to know, among other things, the sex, age, strength and nativity of the slaves; the purity or mixture of blood of the negroes, mulattoes, quadroons, mestizoes, *etc.;* and their special training or lack of it. For such statistical purposes, however, the records have many shortcomings. In many cases they state simply that the slave Matt or Congo or Martha, belonging to the estate of William Jones, deceased, was sold on the date given to Thomas Smith, for, say, $300, on twelve months' credit. Such an item indicates the sex and states the price, but gives

---

[1] *Cf.* De Toqueville, Democracy in America, vol. ii, p. 233.

little else.   In other instances the slaves are classed as infants, boys, men (or fellows) and old men; girls, wenches and old women.   Whole families were often sold as a lot, with no individual quotations given.   Women were hardly ever sold separate from their young children.   In the dearth of separate sale quotations, any study of the prices of female slaves would have to be based chiefly upon appraisal values, which of course were much less accurate than actual market prices.

The sales made by the professional slave traders were generally recorded each in a bill of sale; but in most of the localities these were not transcribed into the formal books of record, and the originals have mostly disappeared.   The majority of the sales of which records are to be found were those of the slaves in the estates of deceased persons.   These sales were at auction; and except in abnormal cases, which may often be distinguished, they may be taken as fairly representative of slave prices for the time and place.

There was always a great difference between the values of individual slaves.   When the average price of negroes ranged about $500, prime field hands brought, say, $1,000, and skilled artisans still more.   At that rate, an infant would be valued at about $100, a boy of twelve years and a man of fifty at about $500 each, and a prime wench for field work at $800 or $900.

The most feasible comparison of prices is that of prime field hands, who may be defined as well-grown, able-bodied fellows, with average training and between eighteen and thirty years of age.   To find the current price of prime field hands in lists where no classification is given, we take the average of the highest ordinary prices.   We ignore any scattering extreme quotations, as applying probably to specially valuable artisans, overseers or domestic servants, and not to field hands.   Where ages are given, we take the average of the prices paid for grown fellows too young to have received special training. We leave aside, on the other hand, the exceptionally low quotations as being due to infirmities which exclude the slave from the prime grade.   The professional slave traders in the domestic traffic dealt mostly in " likely young fellows and wenches." In the quotations of the sales by these traders, when no details are recorded, we may assume that the average, except for children, will range just a little below the current rate for prime field hands.

In view of all the hindrances, the production of a perfectly accurate table of prices cannot be hoped for, even from the exercise of the utmost care and discrimination. The table which follows is simply an approximation of averages made in a careful study of several thousand quotations in the state of Georgia.[1]

The parallel quotations of cotton prices[2] afford a basis for the study of slave-labor capitalization. In examining these quotations it will be noticed that during many brief periods the prices of slaves and cotton rose and fell somewhat in harmony; but that in the whole period under review the price of cotton underwent a heavy net decline, while slave prices had an extremely strong upward movement. The change which took place in the relative slave and cotton prices was really astonishing. In 1800 a prime field hand was worth in the market about 1500 pounds of ginned cotton; in 1809, about 3000 pounds; in 1818, about 3500; in 1826, about 5400; in 1837, about 10,000; in 1845, about 12,000; in 1860, 15,000 to 18,000. In his capacity for work, a prime negro in 1800 was worth nearly or quite as much as a similar slave in 1860; and a pound of cotton in 1860 was not essentially different from a pound of cotton in 1800. But our table shows that within that epoch of three-score years there was an advance of some 1000 or 1200 per cent in the price of slaves as measured in cotton.

---

[1] The sources used for this tabulation are the documents in the Georgia state archives and the records of Baldwin, Oglethorpe, Clarke and Troup counties, all lying in the Georgia cotton belt, together with bills of sale in private hands, travelers' accounts, and articles in the newspapers of the period. Instances of sudden rise or fall in slave prices and sales of large and noted estates were often reported in the local press, with comments. There is no printed collection of any large number of slave-price quotations.

[2] The cotton price averages are made from the tables given by E. J. Donnell in his Chronological and Statistical History of Cotton, New York, 1872, with the aid of the summaries published by G. L. Watkins, Production and Price of Cotton for One Hundred Years, U. S. Department of Agriculture, Washington, 1895.

SLAVE AND COTTON PRICES IN GEORGIA

Year	Average Price of Prime Field Hands	Economic Situation and the Chief Determinant Factors	Average N. Y. Price of Upland Cotton	Years
1755.....	£55			
1773......	60			
1776–1783.	....	War and depression in industry and commerce.		
1784......	70	Peace and returning prosperity.		
1792......	$300	Depression due to Great Britain's attitude toward American commerce.		
1793......	....	Cotton gin invented.		
1800 [1]. ...	450	....	30 cents.	1795–1805
1808......	....	African slave trade prohibited.		
1809......	600	Embargo moderates rise in prices.	19 cents.	1805–1810
1813......	450	War with Great Britain	12 cents.	1813
1818......	1000	Inflation	29 cents.	1816–1818
1819......	....	Financial crisis.................	16 cents.	1819
1821......	700	Recovery from panic.............	14 cents.	1821
1826......	800	Moderate prosperity	15 cents.	1824–1827
1827......	....	Depression.		
1828......	700	....	10 cents.	1827–1828
1835......	900	Flush times...................	17½ cents.	1835
1837......	1300	Inflation—crash	13½ cents.	1837
1839......	1000	Cotton crisis	13½ cents.	1839
1840......	700	Cotton crisis; acute distress......	9 cents.	1840
1844......	600	Depression	7½ cents.	1844
1845......	....	Severe depression	5½ cents.	1845
1848......	900	Recovery in cotton prices. Texas demand for slaves	9½ cents.	1847–1848
1851......	1050	Prosperity	12 cents.	1851
1853......	1200	Expansion of cotton industry and simultaneous rise in tobacco prices.[3]	11 cents.	1850–1860
1859......	1650			
1860 [2].....	1800			

[1] The quotations down to this point are lowland quotations. There were very few slaves in the uplands before 1800.

[2] In the later fifties there were numerous local flurries in slave valuations. In central Georgia prime negroes brought $2,000 in 1860, while in western Georgia and central Alabama the prices appear not to have run much above $1,500. For prices in the other parts of the South in that decade, see G. W. Weston, Who are and who may be slaves in the United States, a pamphlet published in 1856. See also Brackett, The Negro in Maryland; Ingle, Southern Sidelights; Hammond, The Cotton Industry, and De Bow's Review, vol. xxvi, p. 647.

[3] The rise in tobacco prices and the revival of prosperity in Virginia in this decade tended to diminish the volume of the slave trade and contributed to raising slave prices. Cf. W. H. Collins, The Domestic Slave Trade in the Southern States, N. Y., 1904, p. 57.

The decline in the price of cotton was due in some measure to a lessening of cost, through improvements in cultivating, ginning and marketing. The advance in slave prices was due in part to the increasing intelligence and ability of the negroes and to improvements in the system of directing their work on the plantations, and also in part to the decline in the value of money. But the ten-fold or twelve-fold multiplication of the price of slaves, when quoted in terms of the product of their labor, was too great to be explained except by reference to the severe competition of the planters in selling cotton and in buying slaves. Their system of capitalized labor was out of place in the modern competitive world, and burdened with that system all the competition of the cotton planters was bound to be of a cut-throat nature. In other words, when capital and labor were combined, as in the American slaveholding system, there was an irresistible tendency to overvalue and overcapitalize slave labor, and to carry it to the point where the financial equilibrium was unsafe, and any crisis threatened complete bankruptcy.

Aside from the expense of food, clothing and shelter, the cost of slave labor for any given period of time was made up of several elements:

(1) Interest upon the capital invested in the slave.

(2) Economic insurance against (a) his death, (b) his illness or accidental injury, and (c) his flight from service.[1] Of course insurance policies were seldom taken out to cover these risks, but the cost of insurance against them must be reckoned in the cost of slave labor for any given period.

(3) The diminishing value of every mature slave by reason of increasing age. Because of the "wear and tear" of his years and his diminishing prospect of life and usefulness, the average slave of fifty-five years of age would be worth only half

---

[1] Physicians' and attorneys' fees should perhaps be included under the head of insurance. It may be noted that doctors' charges were generally the same for slaves as for white persons. To illustrate how expensive this charge often was, we may cite an instance given in the records of Troup county, Georgia, where Dr. Ware collected from Col. Truitt's estate $130.50 for medicine and daily visits to a negro child, from November 29, 1858, to January 5, 1859.

as much as one of twenty-five years, and after fifty-five the valuation decreased still more rapidly. In computing the cost of any group of slaves it will be necessary to set over against this depreciation the value of the children born; but, on the other hand, the cost by groups would be increased by the need of supporting the disabled negroes who were not in the working gangs.

(4) Taxation assessed upon the capitalized value of the slaves. In the slaveholding region as a whole, in the later antebellum period, the total assessed value of slave property was at least as great as that of all the other sorts of property combined.

The rate of slave hire would furnish a good index of the current price of slave labor year by year, if sufficient quotations on a stable basis could be obtained. But on account of the special needs or wishes of the parties to the individual bargains, there were such opportunities for higgling the rate in individual cases that the current rate is very elusive. The following averages, computed from a limited number of quotations for the hire of men slaves in middle Georgia, are illustrative: In 1800, $100 per year; in 1816, $110; in 1818, $140; in 1833, $140; in 1836, $155; in 1841, $140; in 1860, $150. These were in most cases the years of maximum quotations in the respective periods. The local fluctuations in short periods were often very pronounced; but in the long run the rate followed a gradual upward movement.

The relation between the price of slaves and the rate of their hire should theoretically have borne, in quiet periods, a definite relation to the rate of interest upon capital; but the truth is that in the matter of slave prices there was, through the whole period after the closing of the African trade, a tendency to "frenzied finance" in the cotton belt. Slave prices were largely controlled by speculation, while slave hire was regulated more largely by the current rate of wages for labor in general. The whole subject of these relations is one for which authentic data are perhaps too scanty to permit of thorough analysis.

Negro slave labor was expensive, not so much because it

was unwilling as because it was overcapitalized and inelastic. The negro of himself, by reason of his inherited inaptitude, was inefficient as a self-directing laborer in civilized industry. The whole system of civilized life was novel and artificial to him; and to make him play a valuable part in it, strict guidance and supervision were essential. Without the plantation system, the mass of the negroes would have been an unbearable burden in America; and except in slavery they could never have been utilized, in the beginning, for plantation work. The negro had no love of work for work's sake; and he had little appreciation of future goods when set over against present exemption from toil. That is to say, he lacked the economic motive without which voluntary civilized industry is impossible. It is a mistake to apply the general philosophy of slavery to the American situation without very serious modification.[1]   A slave among the Greeks or Romans was generally a relatively civilized person, whose voluntary labor would have been far more productive than his labor under compulsion. But the negro slave was a negro first, last and always, and a slave incidentally. Mr. Cairnes and others make a great mistake when they attribute his inefficiency and expensiveness altogether to the one incident of regulation. Regulation actually remedied in large degree the disadvantages of using negro labor, though it failed to make it as cheap, in most employments, as free white labor would have been. The cotton planter found the negro already a part of the situation. To render him useful, firm regulation was necessary. The forcible control of the negro was in the beginning a necessity, and was not of itself a burden at any time.[2]

[1] Palgrave's Dictionary of Political Economy contains an excellent article upon slavery, in which it is indicated that harshness and compulsion were not always essential in slave labor; that the motive force was often a sort of feudal devotion to the master; and, further, that negro slave labor was practically essential for developing the resources of the hot malarial swamp regions.

[2] The current rate of hire to-day for negro workmen in agriculture in Georgia is from $8 to $12 per month; but for the year 1904, the state of Georgia leased out its able-bodied convicts at an average rate of $225 per year. When under strict discipline, the average negro even to-day, it appears, is worth twice as much as when left to his own devices.

In American slaveholding, however, the capitalization of labor-value and the sale and purchase of labor-control were permanent features; and when the supply was " cornered " it was unavoidable that the price should be bid up to the point of overvaluation.[1] And this brings us to the main economic disadvantage of the system.

In employing free labor, wages are paid from time to time as the work is done, and the employer can count upon receiving from the products of that labor an income which will enable him to continue to pay its wages in the future, while his working capital is left free for other uses. He may invest a portion of his capital in lands and buildings, and use most of the remainder as circulating capital for special purposes, retaining only a small percentage as a reserve fund. But to secure a working force of slaves, the ante-bellum planter had to invest all the capital that he owned or could borrow in the purchase of slaves and lands;[2] for the larger his plantation was, within certain limits, the more economies he could introduce. The temptation was very strong for him to trim down to the lowest possible limit the fund for supplies and reserve. The slaveholding system thus absorbed the planter's earnings; and

[1] In the periods of high slave prices employers found that slave labor was too expensive to be used with profit except in plantation industry under the most favorable circumstances. Striking proof of this is to be seen in the eager employment, wherever they could be had, of Irish and German immigrants for canal and railway building, ditching and any other labor which might prove injurious to a negro's health and strength. Slaves were growing too dear to be used. W. H. Russell (My Diary North and South, Boston, 1863, p. 272) writing of the Louisiana sugar district in 1860, says: " The labor of ditching, trenching, cleaning the waste lands and hewing down the forests, is generally done by Irish laborers, who travel about the country under contractors, or are engaged by resident gangsmen for the task. Mr. Seal lamented the high prices for this work; but then, as he said, ' It was much better to have Irish do it, who cost nothing to the planter, if they died, than to use up good field hands in such severe employment.' " The documentary evidence in regard to the competition and rather extensive substitution of immigrant labor for that of slaves in the times of high slave prices is quite conclusive, in spite of its fugitive character. Further data may be found in *DeBow's Review*, vol. xi, p. 400; *Harper's Magazine*, vol. vii, pp. 752 *et seq.;* Sir Chas. Lyell, Second Visit to the United States, vol. ii, p. 127; Waddell, Annals of Augusta County, Virginia, pp. 272, 273; and the James River and Kanawha Canal Company's fourth annual report, Richmond, 1839.

[2] *Cf.* F. L. Olmsted, A Journey to Texas, pp. 8–10.

for such absorption it had unlimited capacity, for the greater the profits of the planters the more slaves they wanted and the higher the slave prices mounted. Individual profits, as fast as made, went into the purchase of labor, and not into modern implements or land improvements.[1] Circulating capital was at once converted into fixed capital; while for their annual supplies of food, implements and luxuries the planters continued to rely upon their credit with the local merchants, and the local merchants to rely upon their credit with northern merchants and bankers.

Thus there was a never-ending private loss through the continual payment of interest and the enhancement of prices; and, further, there was a continuous public loss by the draining of wealth out of the cotton belt by the slave trade.[2] With the

[1] This was lamented by many planters, especially in times of low staple prices. *Cf. Southern Agriculturist*, published at Charleston, 1828, vol. ii, p. 1 *et passim;* and especially an address by Dr. Manly before the Alabama State Agricultural Society, Dec. 7, 1841, published in the *Tuscaloosa Monitor*, April 13, 1842. (File in the Alabama State Department of Archives and History.)

[2] This injurious effect of the slave traffic is strikingly illustrated in the account by a Charleston bookseller, E. S. Thomas, of the misfortunes which befell his business by the reopening of the South Carolina ports to the foreign slave trade in 1803. Thomas had found the business opportunities in Charleston exceedingly good; and for some years he had been annually doubling his capital. But in November, 1803, he had just opened a new importation of fifty thousand volumes, when news came from Columbia that the legislature had opened the ports to the slave trade. "The news had not been five hours in the city," he writes, "before two large British Guineamen, that had been lying on and off the port for several days expecting it, came up to town; and from that day my business began to decline.......A great change at once took place in everything. Vessels were fitted out in numbers for the coast of Africa, and as fast as they returned their cargoes were bought up with avidity, not only consuming the large funds that had been accumulating but all that could be procured, and finally exhausting credit and mortgaging the slaves for payment.......For myself, I was upwards of five years disposing of my large stock, at a sacrifice of more than a half, in all the principal towns, from Augusta, in Georgia, to Boston." E. S. Thomas, Reminiscences, vol. ii, pp. 35, 36.

The same general phenomena were observed in various other parts of the South, as is shown by the following extract from a letter written August 22, 1774, by one John Brown, a citizen of Virginia, to William Preston: "Some time ago you told me that you intended to enter the servant trade, and desire[d] me to tell if there was any encouragement our way for the sale of them. I think there is none, for these reasons: (1) the scarcity of money; (2) servants are plenty and everyone has as many as they want; besides, the country is sunk in debt by them already. If you

stopping of the African slave trade, the drain of wealth from the lower South was not checked at all, but merely diverted from England and New England to the upper tier of southern states; and there it did little but demoralize industry and postpone to a later generation the agricultural revival.

The capitalization of labor lessened its elasticity and its versatility; it tended to fix labor rigidly in one line of employment. There was little or no floating labor in the plantation districts; and the planter was obliged to plan in detail a whole year's work before the year began. If he should plant a larger acreage than his "force" could cultivate and harvest, a part of the crop would have to be abandoned, unless by chance some free negro or stray Irishman could be found for the odd job. As an illustration of the financial hardships which might befall the slaveholder, it may be noted that in 1839 William Lowndes Yancey happened to lose his whole force of slaves through poisoning in the midst of the working season. The disaster involved his absolute ruin as a planter, and forced him to seek some other opening which did not require the possession of capital.[1]

In the operations of cotton production, where fluctuating and highly uncertain returns demanded the greatest flexibility, the slaveholding system was rigid. When by overproduction the price of cotton was depressed, it could be raised again only by curtailing the output in the American cotton belt, which had the monopoly. But the planter, owning cotton lands and slaves trained in the cotton field alone, found it hard to devote his fields with success to other crops or to sell or lease his negroes to any one else, for no one else wanted them for any other purpose than cotton production. In fact, the proportion of the southern resources devoted to cotton production tended always to increase. To diminish the cotton output required the most heroic efforts. As a rule, the chances of heavy gains

have not as yet engaged, I think it not prudent for you to do it at the present juncture; you have business enough upon hand, but these things you can better think of than I can." Original MS. in Wisconsin Historical Society, Draper Collection, series QQ, vol. iii, no. 81.

G. W. DuBose, Life of Wm. L. Yancey, p. 39.

from cotton planting outweighed those of loss, in the popular estimation; and the strong and constant tendency was to spoil the market by over-supply.

There were uncertain returns in cotton raising, and great risks in slave-owning. The crop might be heavy or light in any year, according to the acreage and the weather, and prices might be away up or away down. A prime slave might be killed by a rattlesnake or crippled in a log-rolling or hanged for murder or spirited away by the underground railroad. All these uncertainties fostered extravagance and speculation.

In the cotton belt inflation and depression followed each other in rapid succession; but the times of prosperity brought less real advantage and periods of depression caused greater hardship in the slaveholding South than in any normally organized community. For by the capitalizing of labor, profits were generally absorbed through the purchasing of additional slaves at higher prices, while in time of need the cotton-planter found it impossible to realize upon his investment because his neighbors were involved in the same difficulties which embarrassed him, and when he would sell they could not buy.

When after the peace in 1815 the system of industry and finance of the ante-bellum South had fully developed itself, the South and its leaders were seized in the grip of social and economic forces which were rendered irresistible by the imperious laws of monopoly. The cotton-planters controlled the South, and for some decades they dominated the policy of the federal government; but the cotton-planters themselves were hurried hither and thither by their two inanimate but arbitrary masters, cotton and slavery.

Cotton and slavery were peculiar to the South, and their requirements were often in conflict with the interests and ideas prevailing in the other parts of the United States. As that conflict of interests and sentiments was accentuated, it became apparent that the South was in a congressional minority, likely to be overridden at any time by a northern majority. Ruin was threatening the vested interests and the social order in the South; and the force of circumstances drove the southern politicians into the policy of resistance. To the leaders in the

South, with their ever-present view of the possibility of negro uprisings, the regulations of slavery seemed essential for safety and prosperity. And when they found themselves about to become powerless to check any legislation hostile to the established order in the South, they adopted the policy of secession, seeking, as they saw it, the lesser of the evils confronting them.

Because they were blinded by the abolition agitation in the North and other historical developments which we cannot here discuss, most of the later generation of ante-bellum planters could not see that slaveholding was essentially burdensome. But that which was partly hidden from their vision is clear to us to-day. In the great system of southern industry and commerce, working with seeming smoothness, the negro laborers were inefficient in spite of discipline, and slavery was an obstacle to all progress. The system may be likened to an engine, with slavery as its great fly-wheel—a fly-wheel indispensable for safe running at first, perhaps, but later rendered less useful by improvements in the machinery, and finally becoming a burden instead of a benefit. Yet it was retained, because it was still considered essential in securing the adjustment and regular working of the complex mechanism. This great rigid wheel of slavery was so awkward and burdensome that it absorbed the momentum and retarded the movement of the whole machine without rendering any service of great value. The capitalization of labor and the export of earnings in exchange for more workmen, always of a low degree of efficiency, together with the extreme lack of versatility, deprived the South of the natural advantage which the cotton monopoly should have given. To be rid of the capitalization of labor as a part of the slaveholding system was a great requisite for the material progress of the South.

ULRICH B. PHILLIPS.

THE UNIVERSITY OF WISCONSIN.

Journal of Historical Geography, 2, 4 (1976) 329–346

Race, residence and ideology: Charleston, South Carolina in the mid-nineteenth century

John P. Radford

By the eve of the Civil War, Charleston, South Carolina had become the centre of a moral order which was articulated by Tidewater planters who transformed the city, not into an industrial metropolis on the Northern pattern, but into a leisure capital. The utilitarian notions of conventional American urban theory have little to contribute to understanding the allocation of residential space, which was facilitated less by competitive processes than by control along class and racial lines. Analysis of manuscript Federal population census schedules, city directories and local census data for 1860 reveals not only the micro-segregated patterns of a slave city, but also the relegation to the urban periphery of the free black population. A comparable analysis for 1880 shows much less change than might be expected in a city so greatly disrupted by military and political events, thereby supporting recent interpretations which emphasize the failure of Reconstruction to impose lasting change on South Carolina society.

Despite some recent theoretical statements, it remains generally true, as two historians have recently charged, that "geographers do not give much weight to the ideological components coincidental with spatial change".[1] Nowhere has this been more evident than in geographical studies of urban phenomena, in which ideology has been played down, and in which culturally relative concepts have frequently been used as if they were universal axioms. Those who seek to redress the balance, and to confront the ideological components of spatial change, are faced with severe problems. The shortage of documentation poses difficulties, especially in historical studies. But the major difficulty lies in establishing the existence of direct causal links between ideology, social process and spatial pattern. It is a chain of events which all the simulation models in the world are unlikely to be able to reconstruct. Yet, however difficult the task, it is an important one, and one which must be attempted. This paper examines some of the spatial concomitants of racial ideology in a mid-nineteenth century city in the American South. Specifically, it focuses on the racial residential patterns of Charleston, South Carolina immediately before the Civil War, and after the end of Reconstruction.

Charleston has been widely regarded as epitomizing the racial residential patterns of the traditional urban South. In the 1920s T. J. Woofter identified old, small, Southern cities, and especially Charleston, as having highly scattered patterns of black residence throughout the city.[2] This pattern was contrasted with not only the concentrated patterns of blacks in Northern cities but also the clustering of blacks in those Southern cities which had no antebellum heritage. Two decades later, E. Franklin Frazier amplified the distinction between two types

[1] Haley P. Bamman and Ian E. Davey, Ideology and space in the Toronto Public School System, 1844–1882. In James T. Lemon (Ed.), *Internal relationships within the nineteenth-century city.* York University, Dept of Geography, Discussion Paper No. 11 (1975) 9
[2] T. J. Woofter, *Negro problems in cities* (Garden City, N.Y. 1928) 37–8

423

of Southern city.[1] In the older cities most blacks were domestic servants and were interspersed with the white population but in newer cities blacks were often industrial labourers and tended to cluster near to sources of employment. Taeuber and Taeuber also commented on this distinction and identified the dispersed pattern with cities that attained a substantial size before the Civil War when a backyard or alley dwelling pattern would have predominated.[2] Schnore and Evenson confirmed this finding and observed that the relationship between the timing of city growth and residential patterns was still valid in 1960.[3] The authors concluded that "despite the passage of a century since the Civil War, we can be reasonably confident that age of the city is a rather potent factor in affecting its current levels of segregation".[4]

The issue of the origins of so-called "segregated residence" in Southern cities is clouded by a tendency to use the term "segregation" rather loosely. If we continue to use the term "residential segregation" at all, a distinction must be made between micro-spatial segregation and macro-spatial segregation. Micro-segregation is separation of residence by lot or block-segment whereas macro-segregation involves the exclusive occupance of whole sections of a city by a particular group. During the middle and late nineteenth century micro-segregation largely gave way to macro-segregated patterns, which became predominant in the early twentieth century. This trend toward macro-spatial segregation was slower in Charleston, South Carolina than in any other major American city. As late as 1940, its racial residential patterns were highly mixed. Taeuber and Taeuber calculated segregation indices for 109 cities using census data for that year, and Charleston had the lowest score, indicating a high degree of residential intermixture of the black and white populations.[5] As the authors pointed out, even this low score revealed an increase in clustering over previous years and recorded a trend initiated before the Civil War.

Late antebellum Charleston, in fact, offers almost a controlled case to those interested in the changing patterns of black residence in nineteenth-century cities. Most of the social and economic processes which were beginning to produce important spatial changes in other major cities of the eastern United States—CBD differentiation and growth, the emergence of the factory system, transportation innovations—were resisted by many of Charleston's major decision makers.[6] The dominant influence upon the residential patterns of the city were not these market processes but rather the enactment of a particular way of life, based upon an increasingly rigid interpretation of the doctrine of white supremacy.

Most urban theory, rooted in utilitarianism, assumes that urban residential patterns in cities are created by competitive market processes. The allocation of residential space in Charleston, like many other aspects of the life of the city, resulted not from competition but from control. The influence of social control in creating distinctive residential patterns was most clearly recorded in the distribution of the slave population. To Wade the control of slaves in Southern cities was

[1] E. Franklin Frazier, *The Negro in the United States* (New York 1957) 237
[2] Karl E. Taeuber and Alma F. Taeuber, *Negroes in cities. Residential segregation and neighborhood change* (New York 1965) 190
[3] Leo F. Schnore and Philip C. Evenson, Segregation in Southern cities *American Journal of Sociology* LXXII (1966) 56–67
[4] *Ibid.* 65
[5] Taeuber and Taeuber, *op. cit.* 37–41
[6] John P. Radford, Culture, economy and urban structure in Charleston, South Carolina, 1860–1880 (unpubl. Ph. D. dissertation, Clark Univ., Massachusetts 1974) 32–6

enhanced by the dispersed patterns of slave residence which were instigated as a deliberate attempt to prevent the formation of a viable black community.[1] On the plantation a rigid set of rules could be established which not only governed all facets of the lives of the slaves but also reinforced their mental and physical dependence upon their masters. This code could be strictly enforced by means of sanctions and constant supervision on plantations where an isolated location ensured virtually complete control over information reaching the slaves from the outside. Slavery in the urban environment involved the problem of maintaining the isolation of slaves without the "comfortable distances of the plantation".[2] The usual solution was to provide slaves with accommodation on the same lot as the main house, either at right angles to it, or parallel to it at the other end of the lot. The first floor of the accommodation would often be used for storage purposes or as stables. The building faced onto the yard at the back of the main house, the remaining sides of the lot being enclosed by a high wall to form a courtyard. The outside world could only be reached through the main house, or perhaps through a side door. The building plan thus formed a compound which was the architectural expression of the captive status of its inhabitants.

In his portrayal of the urban slave compounds as architectural expressions of racial attitudes, Wade provided a rare insight into the relationship at the micro-scale between ideology and urban form. This "urban equivalent of the plantation" was not, however, completely successful.[3] In Wade's view, slavery was incompatible with the urban environment, with its manifold opportunities for contact and interaction. In part, the weakening of the institution was associated with an increasing tendency to permit "living out". Slaves, seeking escape from constant surveillance, gravitated to particular parts of the city, and especially its periphery, where "segregated" residential districts were created.

This kind of social and residential control extended beyond the slave population. White social leaders in antebellum Charleston were obsessed with a fear of a slave revolt, but it was the free Negroes of the city who were regarded as the most likely instigators of slave unrest. The free Negro was viewed as a threat to the tight-knit relationship between master and slave upon which the perpetuation of the institution was thought to rest. Despite the oft recurring references to a few successful and prosperous free Negroes in Charleston, their position in society in the last three antebellum decades undoubtedly declined. The white community viewed the slave conspiracy of 1822, apparently led by a free Negro, Denmark Vesey, as a direct threat to its existence. The immediate repercussions were trials, mass public hangings, meetings of outraged citizens and ensuing legislation, but the conspiracy also marked the beginning of a new and extended era of repression. The city, in Channing's words, "never again relaxed the outward forms of vigilance".[4] To supplement its sizeable police force the city now established a town guard, a force of 100 men. They were uniformed, trained and heavily armed, being issued with muskets and bayonets as well as alarming devices such as rattles. Whites as well as blacks were dealt with at the guardhouse, but the list of offences for which blacks could be held liable was much larger. Slaves and free Negroes were brought to the guardhouse in 1838 for such offenses as: "being out after beating of the tattoo without tickets", "following military companies", "walking on the Battery

[1] Richard C. Wade, *Slavery in the cities: the South, 1820–1860* (New York 1964)
[2] *Ibid.* 56
[3] *Ibid.* 61
[4] Stephen A. Channing, *Crisis of fear: secession in South Carolina* (New York 1970) 45

contrary to law", "bathing horses at prohibited places" and "loitering in retail shops".[1]

Visitors to the city frequently commented on the guard. William Kingsford from Toronto wrote in 1858:

> "What struck me peculiarly in Charleston was the police organization. It is a perfect *gens d'armerie* . . .. Patrols pass through the city at all hours, and there is a development in this respect that I have seen nowhere else. I heard that a great many desperate men, owing to the position of Charleston, occasionally congregate there . . . hence these precautions. But it struck me that the principal cause of anxiety might be, after all, the slave population."[2]

A visitor from England commented: "The city guard were actively patrolling the streets day and night, for the purpose, as one of them told me, of 'keeping down the niggers'."[3] Another noted "abject fear and timidity" and "servile dread" in the expressions of the Negroes in the streets of the city.[4]

It was widely believed in the white community that a slave revolt would involve arson if only to create a diversion and stretch manpower to its limits. The Charleston Fire Guard, a volunteer force, mobilized during fires to protect the city against any Negro uprising that might occur. The city had good reason to be concerned about the problem. A fire on 27th April 1838 destroyed 1,000 houses in the city at a loss of about $3,000,000. Whether or not it was started by black arsonists, the authorities seemed determined to place the blame there. The City Council Proceedings[5] note the "uncommon number of incendiary attempts that immediately succeeded the fire". Eighteen attempts were discovered in less than four weeks, and in each case "combustibles" were discovered before much damage was done. The report continues: "In every one of these cases, all the slaves attached to the premises in which an attempt was made, were promptly arrested, and committed to the workhouse." The owners or occupants were interrogated, and the slaves were "subjected to close and repeated examinations" from which was gained "a decided impression of the guilt of five individuals who were accordingly directed to be prosecuted either for arson, or for an attempt to commit it". In the weeks following the fire, control of the Negro community was intensified and the Mayor's Report noted that "during the continuance of these attempts, and the prevalence of the alarms rising from them, the community was roused to a state of extraordinary and intense excitement".[6] The city guard was increased from 100 to 120 men, military guards were used, a temporary Committee of Vigilance was appointed, consisting of the Mayor and four Aldermen, and citizen patrols were organized.

Although the period following the Great Fire was one of unusual agitation, at no time in the antebellum history of the city did the white community feel able to relax its control. The diary of Jacob Schirmer[7] abounds with reports of fire alarms.

[1] Charleston City Council, *The Mayor's Report of the Proceedings of the City Authorities from September, 1838 to August, 1839* (Charleston 1839) 66
[2] William Kingsford, *Impressions of the West and South during a six week's holiday* (Toronto 1858) 77
[3] Arthur Cunynghame, *A glimpse at the Great Western Republic* (London 1851) 264
[4] J. Benwell, *An Englishman's travels in America: his observations of life and manners in the free and slave states* (London 1953) 190
[5] Charleston City Council *The Mayor's Report of the Proceedings of the City Authorities from the 4th September, 1837 to the 1st August, 1838* (Charleston 1838) 37–44
[6] *Ibid.* 44
[7] Manuscript at the South Carolina Historical Society

It is clear that throughout the antebellum period the diversion of a false alarm was to be feared almost as much as fire itself. It was at night that the strictest precautions were taken in the city. Daybreak was signalled by a reassuring drumbeat at the guardhouse. The ceremony at "retreat" was a little more extensive.[1] A fife was played, and a drum beaten outside the guardhouse "at quarter past ten o'clock in the summer and quarter past nine in the winter". This was preceded by fifteen minutes of "bell ring" from St Michael's Church on the opposite side of the street, after which the town guard marched into position. After the ceremony, any Negro found on the street without a ticket was arrested. Thus, with church bells and military drum, the racial *status quo* of Charleston was reasserted every night of the year.

Racial residential patterns in 1860

By 1860, after three decades of mounting crisis and ensuing response, Charleston had reached the height of its secessionist fervour. During these years the city's reputation was based upon the preservation of a particular way of life in which white supremacy was axiomatic. On the eve of the Civil War, Charleston was a city of some forty thousand people (Table 1), with a built-up area which stretched from the southern tip of the peninsula to Line Street (Fig. 1). Of the eight wards into which the city was divided, the four to the north of Calhoun Street had been annexed to the city in 1850.

TABLE 1
Population by race, 1860 and 1880

	1860	1880
White	23,376	22,699
Non-white	17,146	27,285
Total	40,522	49,984

Source: Eighth and Tenth Censuses of the U.S.

To determine the racial residential patterns of Charleston in 1860, a ten per cent systematic sample of free households taken from the manuscript schedules of the Eighth Census of the U.S., was mapped (Fig. 2A–C). Whereas the white population was quite evenly distributed throughout the city, the free Negro population had a more northerly bias. It has occasionally been observed that the free Negroes were better represented in the city's Upper Wards than below Calhoun Street.[2] Since the federal census manuscripts distinguish between free *mulatto* and free *black* a further observation can be made: the free black was largely confined to the Upper Wards. Whereas only forty per cent of sample white households were north of Calhoun Street, the Upper Wards accounted for three-quarters of the mulattoes and eighty-six per cent of the blacks.

Apparently there is no way in which the distribution of slave households can be plotted using the U.S. census of population. The slave schedules give the number

[1] The ensuing descriptions of "retreat" in Charleston appear in: D. E. Huger Smith, *A Charlestonian's recollections, 1846–1913* (Charleston, S.C. 1950) 63; William W. Freehling, *Prelude to Civil War: The nullification controversy in South Carolina, 1816–1836* (New York 1965) 7
[2] See, for example, Taeuber and Taeuber, *op. cit.* 45–9

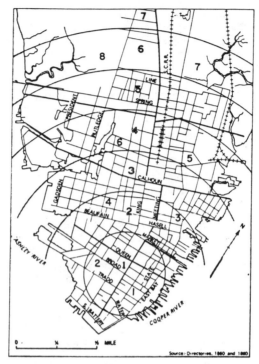

Figure 1. Charleston in 1860—showing streets, the eight wards and seven concentric zones.

and names of slaves owned by each owner, but the addresses are not given, and no other source gives this information. A census of 1861[1] did, however, enumerate slave *houses*, and these are mapped in Fig. 2D. The slave houses were widely dispersed throughout the city and recorded the co-existence on numerous city lots of a streetfront house with slave quarters at the rear. There was, however, some clustering of the slave houses, particularly on the eastern portions of wards four and six. The mill lots of Chisholm's Mill and Bennett's Mill were also points of concentration.[2]

Ideology and residence

Free black residence in Charleston in 1860 was, then, largely confined to the Neck. It is possible that this peripheral location represented a squatter settlement of rural in-migrants, but the growth of the residential areas on the Neck took place at a time when the population of the old city was *decreasing*, and there is strong evidence of a flow from the centre to the edge of the city. The compilers of a census conducted in 1848 observed that the decrease in the population of the city since 1840 could be accounted for by the movement of slaves and free Negroes to the

[1] Frederick A. Ford, *Census of the City of Charleston, South Carolina, for the Year 1861* (Charleston, S.C. 1861)
[2] In the case of mill lots, the Ford census provides numbers of slaves rather than slave houses

428

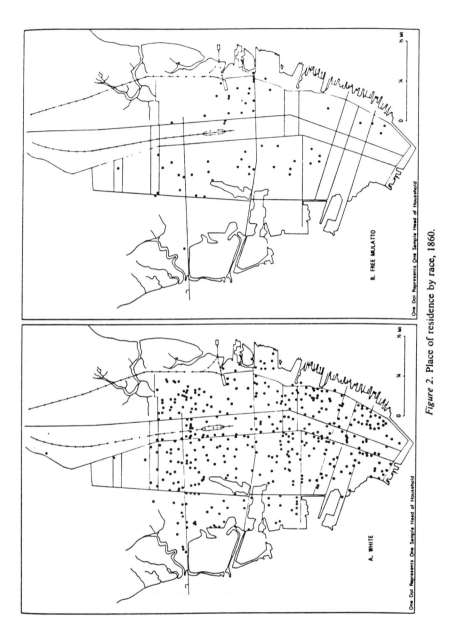

B. FREE MULATTO

One Dot Represents One Sample Head of Household

A. WHITE

One Dot Represents One Sample Head of Household

Figure 2. Place of residence by race, 1860.

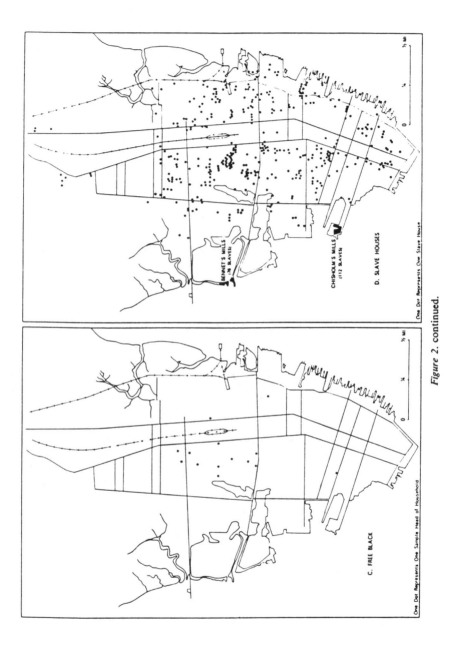

Figure 2. continued.

Neck[1] which had not been annexed at that time. These authors emphasized the "pull" of the area north of Calhoun Street, notably the cheap lots and lower taxes. The Neck held considerable attraction for the slave who had acquired the freedom to "live out". Here he could live in the company of his own choice, beyond the surveillance of his owner.

Although some of the city's inhabitants were attracted to the Neck, others were virtually forced there for the "suburb" on the centre of the Neck contained a large number of city rejects. Evidence exists of a "push" from within the city itself and the settlement of the Neck was in part a consequence of attempts of those in power to make the city a safer and pleasanter place for themselves. The motives for these attempts lie in the value system of a white elite which was both the arbiter of taste and the centre of social power. This elite was dominated by, and to a large extent composed of, Low Country planters. Charleston had long been the focus of antebellum plantation society in Tidewater South Carolina. The increasing prevalence of "country fever" (malaria) in the Low Country during the early decades of the nineteenth century prompted many planters to leave their plantations during the summer months. While many ventured to the North during the "sickly season", others gravitated to the Carolina sea coast. The port of Charleston, the traditional centre of taste and source of information, offered not only salubrious sea breezes but also the promise of an active social life. Here it became increasingly fashionable for "the wealthier and more influential planters to build townhouses" which they normally occupied briefly during the racing season in February, and then from May until after the first frost which usually occurred in October.[2] Others, especially retired planters, lived permanently in Charleston. Their ranks were supplemented by retired lawyers, doctors and wholesale merchants who often laid claim to the prestigious title of "planter".

Wertenbaker observed that, whereas in Virginia, Williamsburg was the centre of planter civilization and Norfolk the centre of the mercantile interests, in South Carolina both rôles were performed by Charleston.[3] In the nineteenth century Charleston became relatively less important as a mercantile centre and more prominent as a focus of the planter interests. When the Tidewater planters came to Charleston they brought with them a set of moral precepts and ideas as to what Charleston should be. Their interests were in health, aesthetics and leisure, and increasingly they regarded the pecuniary activities of the merchant with distaste. Moreover, they possessed the affluence and authority to impose their interests upon the city. As Rogers has written, Charleston's "mental climate" in the 1850s was very different from that which had characterized the city during the Revolution. It was a climate which was "marked by the presence of planters" who were able to "overawe the merchants and factors".[4] The pre-eminence of the planters accounted in large part for both Charleston's precipitous slide down the urban rank size hierarchy in the nineteenth century and the distinctiveness of the city's internal structure.

[1] J. L. Dawson and H. W. DeSaussure, *Census of the City of Charleston, South Carolina, for the Year 1848* (Charleston, 1849)
[2] Lawrence Fay Brewster, *Summer migrations of South Carolina planters* (Durham, N.C. 1947) 11
[3] Thomas Jefferson Wertenbaker, *The Old South: the founding of American Civilization* (New York 1942) 14
[4] George C. Rogers, Jr, *The history of Georgetown County, South Carolina* (Columbia 1970) 323

The tastes of the elite strongly influenced the city's morphology. The main outdoor focus was the Battery at the tip of the peninsula. Here, as one visitor observed, one could during a summer evening see "almost every one of any notability in Charleston".[1] The houses at the edge of the Battery park were highly regarded not only because of the views which they commanded, but also because of their exposure to the salubrious ocean breezes. The limited amount of available space and the opportunity to build new and more luxurious houses encouraged many planters to choose sites further up the peninsula, usually close to the water. Patios and terraces often stretched out on filled land into the Ashley and Cooper rivers. Here, delicately balanced between the "country fever" prevalent as close as the upper part of the Neck, and the strangers' disease (yellow fever) which periodically threatened to emanate from the wharves, the planters entertained in lavish style.

In contrast, the greater part of Charleston Neck long remained a *terra incognita* to the elite.[2] It had a reputation as an unhealthy area, the source, among other things of "bilious, or as it was familiarly termed Neck fever". The dread of this fever "so pervaded the minds of the citizens that to sleep on the Neck between the first of June and frost was considered tantamount to ordering one's coffin".[3] The city dumped much of its garbage on the Neck and much land was reclaimed in this way. One report noted that a large area of the upper city east of King Street had been filled in with rubbish and "scavenger's offal". Half of this area had been built upon by 1870.[4] Reports issued in the 1870s testify to a long-standing neglect of the area. The City Registrar's report of 1870 noted the inadequacy of the drains in the upper part of the city, which resulted in much of the seventh and eighth wards being submerged after heavy rains. The water stayed until it evaporated, causing "malarial fevers during the autumnal months, and catarrhs, pneumonia and other diseases incident to the winter season".[5] The City Inspector's report stated flatly that since there was no drainage system north of Calhoun, it was impossible to maintain wholesome sanitary conditions in that portion of the city.[6] Considerable efforts were made from time to time to improve the health and appearance of the Lower Wards. The records of the Board of Commissioners for Opening and Widening Streets,[7] and the Mayor's Reports, reveal attempts to widen several of the alleyways in the city. The task of "widening" involved the clearing out of the alley inhabitants. The motives were aesthetic and hygienic; but there is an undercurrent of white hostility directed against the free Negroes who inhabited many of these alleys. A committee report of 1854 declared that although the costs would be prohibitive, there was no doubt about the desirability of "opening and widening narrow Lanes and Alleys, as well as dividing into smaller

[1] William Ferguson, *America by river and rail: notes by the way on the New World and its people* (London 1856) 114

[2] It was described thus in a cutting from the Charleston *Courier* pasted in the diary of Jacob Schirmer (Ms. South Carolina Historical Society). See also the *Charleston Mercury*, 22nd June 1860

[3] *Ibid.* A more scientific approach to disease in nineteenth-century Charleston is found in: Joseph Ioor Waring, M.D., *A history of medicine in South Carolina, 1825–1900* (Columbia 1967)

[4] Health District No. 5 Report, *City Registrar's Report for 1867* (Charleston 1867) 80–1

[5] City Registrar's Report, *Annual Reports of the Offices of the City Government to the City Council of Charleston for the Year Ending December 31st, 1870* (Charleston 1871) 40

[6] City Inspector's Report, *Ibid.* 53

[7] Ms. South Carolina Historical Society

blocks the larger squares of the city".[1] The stated motives most frequently appearing in the reports are: the creation of "a continuous and handsome street", increased "security against fire", decreased "nuisance to citizens" and "increased ventilation".

These motives also appear in demands from white citizens that the Battery gardens be further extended. Reaction was particularly strong when in 1860 the City Council decided by a small majority to sell off a few lots on East Bay Street at the edge of White Point gardens and close to some of the best houses in the area. In a petition to the Mayor, 230 citizens protested about the sale of one of the lots. They recalled that the city had originally purchased this lot,

> "to abate without delay the nuisance of a cluster of shops for negro trading, established on the premises", and to facilitate "the future extension of the Battery garden towards Ashley river".[2]

These citizens declared that even in "the ill-managed city of New York, where life and human comfort are so ruthlessly sacrificed to the almighty dollar", pleasure grounds and squares were being opened. They noted that "in this latitude, and with our narrow streets, larger open spaces are of the greatest importance", and that the people of Charleston needed places where they could obtain "pure air and agreeable outdoor exercise".[3] Several letters were published in the local newspapers on the question. One in the *Courier*, signed by MORE TAXPAYERS, was concerned with some lots at the foot of King Street which also impinged on the gardens. It praised the "unobstructed views", and the benefits obtained from the

> "uninterrupted draft from the South and Southwest, which sweeps through King and Meeting-streets in every direction. Our healthiest winds are thus attracted and diffused to an extent that in summer is highly important. Why then, close up this funnel and mar the beauty of the Battery, by making one entire half an Alley-way *along the wall* and the *back-yard* accommodations and *negro houses* of private residences?"[4]

The threat of fire did as much as the elite's conceptions of health and aesthetics to encourage the demolition of inhabited alleyways. The white community lived in constant fear of slave revolt and it was widely assumed that arson would be the major threat.[5] Security against fire was incompatible with the presence of large numbers of free blacks within the city for two main reasons. First, free blacks were seen as the potential instigators of arson and organizers of slave revolts. Secondly, few free blacks could afford housing constructed with other than cheap and highly combustible materials. The city authorities had long tried to limit the construction of wooden buildings, but legislation had proved ineffective, largely because of the high cost of brick and stone in the area. In the aftermath of the fire of 1838, which was widely believed by whites to have been the work of black arsonists, a special committee under the chairmanship of C. G. Memminger recommended a total ban

---

[1] Minutes of the Board of Commissioners for Streets . . ., June 5, 1854
[2] Charleston *Courier*, 1st March 1860
[3] *Ibid.*
[4] Charleston *Courier*, 31st March 1860
[5] The powerfulness of the association between the two threats—arson and revolt—is evident in the tactics which were used during fires. In 1838 the city authorities decreed that, "except for those necessary to carry and guard the caisson, the city guard instead of being required to attend fires should on every alarm repair to the guard house under arms". Mayor's Report for 1837–1838, *op. cit.* 44

23

on the construction of wooden buildings.[1] Despite the objections of a few "self-styled friends of the poor", within two weeks of the fire, the Mayor ratified an ordinance making it illegal to build any wooden or frame building. Since prior to 1850, the city extended only as far north as Calhoun Street, the effect of the ordinance was to confine the construction of cheap houses to the Neck. Many well-maintained wooden buildings which antedated the ordinance survived in the city, but many of the cheaper houses were progressively removed, often as part of alley-clearing "improvements", and were not replaced. As Table 2 shows, there were, on the eve of the Civil War, sharp differences between the Lower and Upper Wards in the numbers and proportions of brick and wooden houses.

TABLE 2

Numbers of brick and wooden houses, by Ward, 1861

Ward	Brick houses	Per cent of total	Wooden houses	Per cent of total	Total
1	498	77·3	146	22·7	644
2	251	40·0	377	60·0	628
3	606	54·1	515	45·9	1,121
4	620	45·2	751	54·8	1,371
5	99	13·2	652	86·8	751
6	79	8·0	907	92·0	986
7	16	3·7	424	96·3	440
8	10	1·3	741	98·7	751
Total	2,179	32·6	4,513	67·4	6,692

Source: Ford (1861).

The free black as outcaste

The use of physical improvement schemes to displace blacks in Charleston was one in a mounting series of pressures against the free Negro in South Carolina. In a society with otherwise clear divisions of class and caste, the free Negro had a loosely defined place, and as white apprehension at attacks upon the caste system mounted sharply in the last three antebellum decades, the distinction between free black and slave grew narrower.[2] Within Charleston, this increasing apprehension was manifested in the residential patterns of the city on the eve of the Civil War. The free Negroes and especially those regarded as free *blacks* were viewed with increasing suspicion. The free black in fact became a virtual outcaste and his position at the edge of the city reflected that status. The existence of cheap accommodation outside the old city boundary, viewed by some writers as a point of attraction, was itself a function of decisions made by an elite which pre-empted the healthiest and most attractive sites and supported legislation which discouraged the persistence of cheap *unallocated* housing in the city proper. The slave, whose housing was usually provided and whose presence was largely desired, remained. The free mulatto was to some extent displaced. The free black was largely pushed out of the old city. Ironically, the intermingling of slaves who were living out on the

[1] Report of Mr Memminger offered to the City Council on 22nd May 1838. *Memorial and Proceedings of the City Council on the Subject of Securing the City from Fires* (Charleston 1838)

[2] Channing, *op. cit. passim*. See also Marina Wikramanayake, *A world in shadow: the free black in antebellum South Carolina* (Columbia 1973)

Neck and the free Negroes who had been forced there produced the very situation which slave-owning whites had carefully avoided in the old city. In the view of these whites, this blurring of the institutional boundaries of slavery posed a grave threat to the safety of the city. Moreover, the intermingling was taking place on the edge of the city, beyond the area patrolled by the city guard and outside the jurisdictional limits of the city court. It was this state of affairs which prompted the annexation of the Neck in 1850. The sole justifications for annexation appearing in the preamble of the enabling legislation are the provision of "a more effectual police" and the avoidance of "a conflict of jurisdiction".[1]

Residential patterns in 1880

Traditional interpretations of the post-war Reconstruction era in the South have emphasized corruption and disruption, and portrayed radical changes in the relative status of white and black.[2] In Charleston, because of the wartime destruction of large parts of the city, the virtual abandonment of the area below Calhoun Street in response to enemy bombardment, the abolition of slavery, the post-war immigration of thousands of recently freed rural blacks and the financial ruin of much of the elite, the persistence of the old residential patterns would appear unlikely. Yet recent interpretations of Reconstruction in South Carolina have noted the failure of that venture to impose lasting social change.[3] This is consistent with those studies of black residential patterns which have stressed the persistence of scattering in old Southern cities well into the twentieth century.[4] Among historians of race relations, meanwhile, opinion is divided on whether "segregation" was imposed as an immediate reaction to the abolition of slavery, or whether it was a phenomenon which appeared only in the 1890s.[5]

The residential patterns of Charleston in 1880, reconstructed on the basis of census data, provide a datum from which changes which occurred during the War and Reconstruction period may be described. A ten per cent systematic sample of households drawn from the census manuscript schedules was mapped, and the racial patterns (Fig. 3A–C) are so scattered that any suggestion of a trend toward a pattern of macro-segregation by 1880 can be dismissed. Although the residential patterns were not drastically altered, some changes did occur between 1860 and 1880. A comparative classification of households according to streetfront or alley location (Table 3) suggests that the antebellum decline in alley populations was reversed. Presumably the city's elite were unable to prevent the re-occupation of

[1] An Act to Extend the Limits of Charleston. Charleston: December 1849. Reprinted in: Mayor Courtenay's Annual Review, *Charleston, S.C. Yearbook, 1881* (Charleston 1882) 351

[2] For a review of traditional and revisionist accounts of Reconstruction, see Kenneth M. Stampp, *The era of Reconstruction* (New York 1969)

[3] For example: Peggy Lamson, *The glorious failure: black Congressman Robert Brown Elliott and the Reconstruction in South Carolina* (New York 1973); Martin Abbott, *The Freedmen's Bureau in South Carolina: 1865–1872* (Chapel Hill, N.C. 1967); Carol K. Rothrock Bleser, *The promised land: the history of the South Carolina Land Commission, 1869–1890* (Columbia, S.C. 1969)

[4] Taeuber and Taeuber, *op. cit.* 190; Schnore and Evenson, *op. cit.*

[5] Compare: Joel Williamson, *After slavery: the Negro in South Carolina during Reconstruction, 1861–1877* (Chapel Hill, N.C. 1965) 274–99; and C. Vann Woodward, *The strange career of Jim Crow* (2nd ed. rev.; New York 1966) 25–6. Tindall itemizes some of the aspects of life in South Carolina in which discrimination practices varied greatly. George Brown Tindall, *South Carolina negroes: 1877–1900* (Columbia, S.C. 1952) 291–302

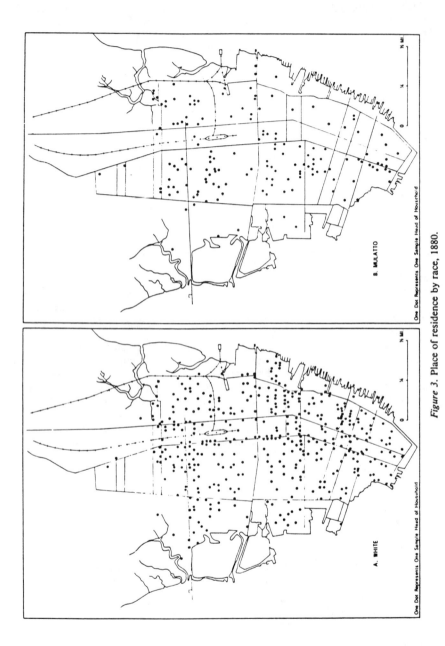

Figure 3. Place of residence by race, 1880.

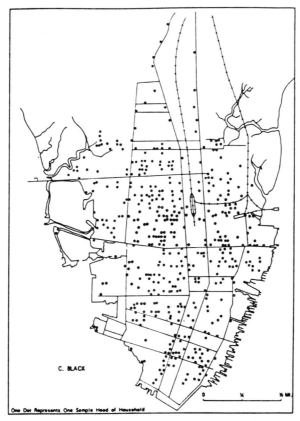

Figure 3. continued.

TABLE 3

*Intra-block distribution of sample heads of household,
by race, 1860 and 1880*

| | 1860 | | | 1880 | | |
	Street	Alley	Other	Street	Alley	Other
White	408	16	2	417	16	2
Mulatto	58	4	0	147	14	2
Black	13	2	1	447	57	11
Total	479	22	3	1,011	87	15

the alleys by blacks at a time when recently freed slaves were crowding into the city. The number of white alley households remained relatively stable and, consequently, there was a southward shift in the centre of gravity of the black population, but only a small lateral movement of whites (Fig. 4).

Direct comparison between the two sets of data is hampered by the extension of full enumeration in 1880 to that segment of the population which in 1860 had

437

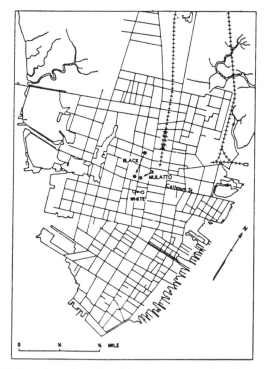

Figure 4. Shifts in centres of gravity of the sample populations by race, 1860–1880.

appeared only in the slave schedules. It is possible to adjust the 1860 data by the addition of estimates of the slave populations derived from the Ford census of 1861 which enumerated slave houses.[1] Tabulations of percentage change by ward and by concentric zones provide a convenient summary of the degree and type of residential change. The distribution of the white population within both sets of spatial units (Tables 4 and 5) was remarkably stable. A somewhat greater change occurred in the distribution of nonwhites, especially in the outer zones and the western and northern wards (except ward 6). Tables of changes in the racial composition of zones and wards by race (Tables 6 and 7) record the increase in the representation of nonwhites in all parts of the city. Every zone except zone four and every ward except ward five experienced an increase in nonwhite population; nonwhites predominated in all seven zones by 1880. The areas of greatest increase were in the north and west of the city. Aggregate patterns of white residence thus remained largely unchanged over the two decades of war and reconstruction. There was some redistribution of the non-white population, but no radical changes. It is possible that more detailed changes would be revealed by analysis of small areas of the city. Nevertheless, the creation of a group of freedmen within Charleston, and the in-migration of large numbers of formerly rural freedmen, scarcely altered the overall residential structure of the city. Visitors in 1880 were just as

[1] Ford, *op. cit.*

struck by the "proximity and confusion so to speak of white and negro houses"[1] as they had been before the War, and their observations are consistent with recent comparative studies of segregation in Southern cities.

This failure of the Civil War and Reconstruction to produce a clear alternative to the carefully contrived residential patterns of the antebellum era lends support to recent studies which have found a high degree of social and ideological continuity in South Carolina between 1860 and 1880.[2] The antebellum attitudes in

TABLE 4

Change in percentage distribution of races over wards, 1860-1880

Colour	1	2	3	4	Ward 5	6	7	8	Mean absolute deviation
White	+1·4	−0·5	+2·7	0	−0·6	−1·2	+0·1	−1·9	1·1
Non-white	0	+4·6	−2·3	+1·7	−7·4	−2·4	+2·5	+3·3	3·0

TABLE 5

Change in percentage distribution of races over zones, 1860–1880

Colour	1	2	3	Zones 4	5	6	7	Mean absolute deviation
White	+0·8	−1·4	+3·1	+1·9	−3·4	−1·3	+0·3	1·7
Non-white	+0·9	+1·0	+1·0	−9·1	+0·7	+2·4	+3·1	2·6

TABLE 6

Change in percentage composition of wards, by race, 1860–1880

Colour	1	2	3	4	Ward 5	6	7	8
White	−3·0	−23·9	+2·6	−8·6	+2·9	−5·8	−19·2	−16·9
Non-white	+3·0	+23·9	−2·6	+8·6	−2·9	+5·8	+19·2	+16·9

TABLE 7

Change in percentage composition of zones by race, 1860–1880

Colour	1	2	3	Zones 4	5	6	7
White	−8·0	−10·2	−3·0	+5·9	−12·9	−14·4	−15·0
Non-white	+8·0	+10·2	+3·0	−5·9	+12·9	+14·4	+15·0

[1] Edward Hogan, South Carolina Today *International Review* **VIII** (1880) 105–19. Quoted in Tindall, *op. cit.* 295

[2] According to Cooper the post-Reconstruction leadership in South Carolina was fully dedicated to antebellum ideals. William J. Cooper, Jr, *The Conservative regime: South Carolina 1877–1890* (Baltimore 1968). Martin Abbott (*op. cit.*) has shown that the impact of the Freedman's Bureau on the status and condition of the black population was slight. Carol Bleser (*op. cit.*) has documented the failure of the South Carolina Land Commission to introduce significant land reforms in the 1870s and 1880s. Peggy Lamson (*op. cit.*) has traced in the life of a black South Carolina congressman the failure of the experiment in racial equality which seemed to promise so much in 1867

Charleston survived Reconstruction, and so too did the antebellum residential patterns. It was not until much more recently that backyard residence and backyard attitudes toward blacks disappeared.

Conclusion

The elite regarded the presence of free blacks within antebellum Charleston as incompatible with the city's continued existence as a safe, clean, healthy and pleasant place in which to live. During the last three or four antebellum decades, the Low Country planters, who formed Charleston's elite, imposed a value system on the city which survived the Civil War and Reconstruction. The Southern planters presided over a society in which prestige was directly related to the ownership of rural land, and in which the normal behaviour pattern of the mass of the population was deferential. Planter ideology, including powerful notions of social control, permeated the whole of Charleston's existence. In particular, a curious amalgam of aesthetic taste, medical ignorance and racial myth affected the evaluation and allocation of residential space within the city. In comparison, those market forces assumed to be dominant in nineteenth-century U.S. cities were insignificant. The main process was residential control, not those competitive mechanisms which are fundamental to the theoretical frameworks within which studies of cities in the United States are frequently cast.

There is no indication that Charleston was a "typical" Southern city; indeed, the evidence suggests that mid-nineteenth century Charleston epitomized rather than typified contemporary Southern society. Whether the cities of the South constitute a distinctive group which may be viewed in contrast to those of the rest of the United States is open to debate. Yet, while re-affirming Warner's observation that U.S. cities, "have grown up within American culture, not apart from it",[1] it is important to stress that American culture has not been homogeneous, and that values apart from the dominant ideology of urban industrial progress have found tangible expression within the nation's cities.

Department of Geography, York University, Toronto

[1] Sam Bass Warner, Jr, *The private city: Philadelphia in three periods of its growth* (Philadelphia 1968) 6

Slave Life Insurance in Virginia and North Carolina

By Todd L. Savitt

In late December 1853 an agent of railroad contractor John Buford stopped at the Southampton County, Virginia, farm of Samuel Drewry and solicited the hire of six healthy male slaves to form part of the crew building the Virginia and Tennessee Railroad. Drewry was aware of the dangers of jobs on public-works construction projects of this sort and of the poor treatment hired slaves sometimes received. He therefore replied that in addition to paying $150 per worker for a ten-month contract (March through December) Buford would have to purchase one thousand dollars of life insurance on each hired hand. After a month's delay, during which Drewry informed Buford that the Great Dismal Swamp Land Company (a wood-and-shingle gathering operation in southeastern Virginia) was paying $160 plus insurance, the two men came to terms—Drewry's terms.[1]

This incident illustrates the interest in slave life insurance that masters were beginning to demonstrate in the late antebellum period. Negroes were frequently employed on dangerous jobs in public-works construction, coal mining, iron manufacturing, and railroad and steamboat operations. A number of industrial concerns that owned slave workers protected their large investments by purchasing life insurance. Similarly, masters who hired out their bondsmen to industry bought life insurance or insisted that the lessee do so; and a few slaveowners took out policies on valuable or favorite servants not hired out.[2] Whatever the reason, during the

[1] Drewry to Buford, January 20, April 14, 1854, John Buford Papers (Manuscript Department, Duke University Library, Durham, N. C.).

[2] See for example C. F. Wills to John McCue, December 7, 1852, McCue Family Papers (Manuscript Department, University of Virginia Library, Charlottesville, Va.); insurance policies of slaves Austin and Mary Jane, June 1, 7, 1860, Haxall Family Papers (items 235 and 236) (Virginia Historical Society, Richmond, Va.).

Mr. Savitt is assistant professor in the Department of Community Health and Family Medicine and the Department of History at the University of Florida. His research was supported in part by a grant from the National Institutes of Health Grant LM 02477 from the National Library of Medicine.

The Journal of Southern History
Vol. XLIII, No. 4, November 1977

late 1840s and 1850s whites were insuring the lives of their slaves in increasing, but never overwhelming, numbers.[3]

Life insurance did not become popular in the United States until the late antebellum period. Prior to 1800 Americans had purchased marine insurance on goods and occasionally a life insurance policy to protect against a pirate's ransom (an important consideration at the time) or the hazards of a long voyage. But people did not buy insurance to cover everyday risks on their lives. Slowly the concept of term insurance gained acceptance as companies began to offer this kind of protection. In 1794 the Insurance Company of North America inaugurated the sale of life insurance policies, followed by the Pennsylvania Company (1809), the Massachusetts Hospital Insurance Company (1818), and the New York Insurance Trust Company (1830). Still, public response was poor until the Girard Life Insurance and Trust Company introduced several years after its founding in Philadelphia in 1836 a new plan whereby management shared some of its profits with policyholders. This idea of distributing profits caught on rapidly and spurred the establishment during the 1840s of other mutual life insurance companies. These firms began actively promoting sales to secure their shareholders' investments and ensure solvency. Given this new impetus, the life insurance business grew rapidly during that and the subsequent decade both in number of companies chartered (at least fifty-nine between 1840 and 1860) and total insurance in force (at least $4,690,000 in 1840 and $204,752,000 in 1860).[4]

The burgeoning life insurance industry did not confine its activities to the northern states, though most business did center in that region. At least sixteen companies were founded in the southern and border states between 1840 and 1860, but, unfortunately, few records exist for these firms. Most firms did not survive for more than a few years, and only one, St. Louis Mutual, was still in existence in 1937, when a major historical survey of life insurance companies was conducted.[5] Those southern companies which did sell life insurance often found sales to white customers scarce. For

---

[3] Virginia legislative petitions, City of Richmond, February 9, 1854 (Virginia State Library, Richmond, Va.); Josiah C. Nott, "Statistics of Southern Slave Population, with Especial Reference to Life Insurance," *De Bow's Review*, IV (November 1847), 275, 286–87; Robert S. Starobin, *Industrial Slavery in the Old South* (New York, 1970), 71–74.

[4] For general histories of the life insurance industry see J. Owen Stalson, *Marketing Life Insurance: Its History in America* (Cambridge, Mass., 1942); Mildred F. Stone, *A Short History of Life Insurance* (Indianapolis, 1947); Terence O'Donnell, comp., *History of Life Insurance in Its Formative Years* (Chicago, 1936). Figures are from Stalson, *Marketing Life Insurance*, 784–86.

[5] Stalson, *Marketing Life Insurance*, 784–86.

example, a group of Virginia agents stated, in a petition requesting lower taxes for out-of-state insurance companies, that "in towns numbering one, two, or three thousand inhabitants there are seldom more than six or eight persons who have their lives insured."[6] Though comparative regional figures are not available, white southerners appear to have been less willing to invest in life insurance protection than northerners. As antebellum southerners' written opinions on the subject of life insurance are rare, it is only a conjecture that residents of the region adopted this innovation as reluctantly and cautiously as they adopted others. Another reason for the difficulty southern firms had in selling policies locally was fierce competition from several large northern firms. Advertisements in most urban newspapers of the South attest to the number of "outside" companies doing business in this relatively small market.

A logical extension of the insuring of white lives was the taking on of slave risks. This form of insurance had existed for some time prior to the 1840s, but mainly as a protection to slave traders transporting blacks from Africa to the New World or from one domestic slave market to another. Few, if any, northern or southern companies insured plantation, industrial, or urban bondsmen on a regular basis until the 1840s, when life insurance began gaining in sales and in the number of new firms.[7] But even after the introduction of slave life insurance owners of bondsmen did not flock to the doors of agents. Had more slaveowners purchased slave life insurance at that time it might have become, as historian Robert S. Starobin asserted, "significant for the future stability of industrial slavery."[8] White southerners wrote little on the subject in diaries, letters, and articles. Historians can thus merely suggest reasons why only about 3 percent of all industrial slaves and a substantially smaller number of plantation bondsmen employed during any year in the 1850s were covered by life insurance.[9] The problem of cost was undoubtedly a major factor. Owners were probably reluctant to lay out an extra five to fifteen dollars annually for every laborer, even if the number insured was limited to prime hands, and small, marginally successful farmers could not afford to buy life insurance

[6] Virginia legislative petitions, City of Richmond, February 9, 1854.

[7] Starobin, *Industrial Slavery*, 71, states that "slave underwriting dated back to at least the turn of the nineteenth century." The proofs he cites, however (p. 254, n. 88), are a series of South Carolina court cases relating to insurance in the international and domestic slave trade. And his example of Jacob, the slave boatman (p. 71), is misleading inasmuch as the insurer was an individual rather than a company.

[8] *Ibid.*, 71.

[9] *Ibid.*, 72. For more on white resistance to slave life insurance see W. P. Burrell, "The Negro in Insurance," *Proceedings of the Hampton Negro Conference*, VIII (1904), 14–15.

for their family slaves.[10] Few white heads of households owned personal policies to protect their surviving spouses and children, much less policies on bondsmen. Though agents advertised frequently in local newspapers, the concept of slave insurance was still so new that many masters must have simply ignored the publicity or put off inquiries for a future time. Then, too, there was the confusion in the Old South between slaves as people and slaves as property. Farmers had been insuring their horses, barns, and even their crops (during transport to markets) for generations. With the introduction of life insurance owners may have had difficulty deciding about the desirability of protecting themselves against the loss of their bondsmen. The situation was more clear-cut when a master hired out his slave or purchased one for dangerous industrial labor. Then the slave was obviously a piece of property, and the investment required financial protection.[11] But on a large plantation, for instance, the bondsman was still treated ambiguously as both person and property.

Some white southerners disapproved the whole concept of slave life insurance. Dr. Josiah Clark Nott of Mobile, Alabama, was probably the best-known and most vocal opponent. He prepared a lengthy article, published in the widely read *De Bow's Review* in 1847, at the very time that slave life insurance was beginning to gain in popularity. Nott feared that bondsmen would be the sufferers in the long run, as masters and mistresses succumbed to temptation and permitted sick or injured slaves to die. Being the working class of the South, Nott argued, blacks "are exposed much to the causes of disease, and are less protected in sickness than the higher classes . . . ." Free men and women have an innate love of life; they and their families naturally do everything possible to save themselves and loved ones from death. However, he continued, "if the slave become unsound and there is little prospect of perfect recovery, the [insurance] underwriters cannot expect fair play—the insurance money is worth more than the slave, and the latter is

---

[10] Eugene D. Genovese, "The Medical and Insurance Costs of Slaveholding in the Cotton Belt," *Journal of Negro History*, XLV (July 1960), 146–47, 155.

[11] It appears that a much higher ratio of bondsmen engaged in certain particularly hazardous pursuits was protected. All five slaves, for example, killed in an 1859 explosion at the Bright Hope Coal Pits in Chesterfield County, Virginia, were insured, as were some forty slaves purchased by the Cape Fear and Deep River Navigation Company (North Carolina) in 1855, and many of the Negroes hired to the Great Dismal Swamp Land Company and to John Buford, the contractor building the Virginia and Tennessee Railroad. Petersburg (Va.) *Daily Express*, April 15, 1859; account books of the Cape Fear and Deep River Navigation Company, XXI, 72; XXV, 10, 14, 34, Henry Adolphus London Papers (Southern Historical Collection, University of North Carolina Library, Chapel Hill, N. C.); Samuel Drewry to John Buford, January 20, April 14, May 18, December 30, 1854, Buford Papers.

regarded rather in the light of a superannuated horse." Nott believed that the typical master treated his Negroes kindly and carefully. But slave life insurance would change his attitude when one of his bondsmen fell seriously ill or became injured: "Any man who will drive a horse cruelly, will drive a negro or operative to death, if he can gain anything by so doing."[12]

Nott's dire predictions did not prevent the formation of companies to insure slaves in Virginia, North Carolina, and other southern states during the late 1840s and the 1850s. The Richmond Fire Association, the North Carolina Mutual Life Insurance Company, the Asheville Mutual Insurance Company, the Lynchburg Hose and Fire Insurance Company, and the Greensborough Mutual Life Insurance and Trust Company all took risks on slaves, but they also heeded Nott's caveats in several ways.[13] They limited the amount for which a slave could be insured, required a medical examination before approving a policy, restricted the term of a slave insurance policy, prohibited the free movement of insured bondsmen from place to place, charged extra premiums for dangerous jobs, and insisted on proof of proper treatment in health and of medical attention in sickness. Each of these means of protecting the company's liability also protected the slave's life.

No insurance company in Virginia or North Carolina insured a slave for full value. The usual maximum was two-thirds or three-quarters of the stated valuation, but not to exceed $800. When John Buford, the railroad contractor, made inquiries regarding the purchase of life insurance on Samuel Drewry's six hired slaves, he learned that the Richmond Fire Association would not take slave risks for $1,000 as Drewry had demanded. The highest the company would go on an eighteen-to-forty-year-old male railroad hand was $600.[14] The North Carolina Mutual Life Insurance Company of Raleigh (not to be confused with the Durham-based, black-owned, postbellum company of the same name) advertised slave coverage at two-thirds of the market value and rejected several applications on slaves written for $1,000. James F. Jordan, Jr., secretary of the

[12] Nott, "Statistics," 286–87.
[13] Virginia Executive Papers (Governor Floyd), June 1851 (Virginia State Library) (Richmond Fire Association policy); Folder 9, London Papers (North Carolina Mutual Life Insurance Company policies); *Woodfin v. Asheville Mutual Insurance Company*, 6 Jones (N. C.) 558 (1859); C. F. Wills to John McCue, December 7, 1852, McCue Family Papers (Lynchburg Hose and Fire Insurance Company); Joseph Adolph Linn Papers, 1855 (Southern Historical Collection) (Greensborough Mutual Life Insurance and Trust Company policy). For examples of other southern companies insuring slave lives see Savannah *Morning News*, December 16, 1851 (Southern Mutual Insurance Company); O'Donnell, *Short History of Life Insurance*, 744–46 (Phenix Insurance Company of St. Louis); *Affleck's Southern Rural Almanac*, 1851, p. 47 (general statement about slave life insurance).
[14] C. F. Wills to Buford, February 25, 1854, Buford Papers.

company, returned one policy in 1855 to an agent in the field, explaining, "In no case at the present time does our company insure for more than $800: unless the slave to be insured is a first rate mechanic and a number 1 risk. The committee have given the limit in this case as Humphrey is only a laborer."[15] Similarly, the Lynchburg Hose and Fire Insurance Company insured slaves "to an amount equal to three fourths of their value provided it does not exceed Eight hundred Dollars the head."[16] By refusing to cover the full worth of a slave, insurance companies were heeding Nott's warning that owners might consider their bondsmen more valuable dead than alive.

Before accepting a slave policy insurance companies required certification that the servant was healthy. Local physicians in major towns acted as regular medical examiners for the firms. In rural areas reputable doctors received a small fee to perform this service when called upon.[17] Some companies routinely required both the family and company physicians to examine slaves. Such was the case with Franklin A. Slaughter, a general insurance broker in Fredericksburg, Virginia. He instructed Dr. Andrew Glasswell Grinnan of Madison Court House to submit with every slave application "a certificate from the slave physician and a personal examination to be made by you as the Medical Examiner."[18] For their efforts physicians received between fifty cents and two dollars per slave examination (the amount was higher for white examinations).[19] Not all doctors were satisfied with the amount of the compensation. Petersburg, Virginia, physicians in 1859 balked at what they considered to be insufficient remuneration for their services. They unanimously adopted a resolution setting the fee for insurance examinations at five dollars for white persons and three for blacks, regardless of any company's established rates.[20]

The quality of doctors' examinations and reports was of the utmost importance to a company. Poorly conducted physical examinations meant approval of poor life insurance risks. Insurance firms

---

[15] Petersburg *Daily Express*, August 13, 1859; North Carolina Mutual Life Insurance Company Minute Book, February 5, 1849 (Archives, State Division of Archives and History, Raleigh, N. C.; hereinafter cited as NC Mutual Minutes); Jordan to J. M. Hirah, January 2, 1855, Orin Datus Davis Papers (Southern Historical Collection). For a similar case see NC Mutual Minutes, August 20, 1851.

[16] C. F. Wills to John McCue, December 7, 1852, McCue Family Papers.

[17] See for example M. W. Davenport to John McCue, July 1, 1852, *ibid.*; Petersburg *Daily Express*, August 13, 1859.

[18] Slaughter to Grinnan, December 15, 1852, Grinnan Family Papers (Manuscript Department, University of Virginia Library).

[19] A. Alexander Little to Andrew G. Grinnan, February 8, 1851, *ibid.*; M. W. Davenport to John McCue, July 1, 1852, McCue Family Papers; NC Mutual Minutes, July 5, 1856.

[20] Petersburg *Daily Express*, February 2, 1859.

insisted that local agents employ regular physicians of good standing in the community, not homeopaths, Thomsonians, hydropaths, or other sectarians.[21] To evaluate medical reports from the field one or more physicians at the home office read each examination statement and brought doubtful cases before the company's directorate or policy committee. The discovery of any chronic disease or serious acute illness automatically disqualified a slave (or white person) from obtaining insurance. For example, the North Carolina Mutual Life Insurance Company rejected a slave suffering from hernia because his occupation was "unfavorable to that disease." Several other male bondsmen were rejected by the firm as "unsound," as were two pregnant slave women.[22] In Virginia three of thirteen black railroad workers scheduled for hire to John Buford failed to receive insurance approval.[23]

This medical check on slave applicants' health sometimes placed owners in awkward positions. When a physician declared Mrs. Clanton's slave Charles "unsound" for life insurance in 1854 Thomas Wrenn, the lady's brother and slave manager, was immediately on the defensive. Had he known that anything had been amiss with Charles, Wrenn explained to his Southampton County, Virginia, neighbor, Samuel Drewry, he would have stated so at the time of application. Yes, Charles had suffered from "a certain disease" last year, but the doctors had cured it, and Charles had been perfectly healthy ever since. Wrenn, therefore, objected strongly to the results of this physical examination.[24] Mr. Drewry himself, having earlier in 1854 driven such a hard bargain with John Buford over the insuring and hiring of his slaves, felt compelled to reaffirm the perfect health of his bondsman Colonel prior to his departure for southwestern Virginia and the railroad. Colonel had died of dropsy and pneumonia a few weeks after his arrival at the work camp, and Drewry apparently feared the insurance company would question the slave's soundness during the months before he began work and decide not to honor his claim. So Drewry disagreed with the doctor's diagnosis of dropsy (usually a chronic condition) and described in detail Colonel's health record for the previous year. "This is the amount of all the sickness I am aware he

---

[21] James F. Jordan, Jr., to W. T. B. Haynesworth, March 21, 1851, James F. Jordan Paper (Archives, North Carolina Division of Archives and History); M. W. Davenport to John McCue, July 1, 1852, McCue Family Papers.

[22] NC Mutual Minutes, February 9, 1858 (hernia); May 12, August 4, 1857 (unsound); October 31, 1849, and November 6, 1857 (pregnancy).

[23] A. C. Mitchell to Buford, April 7, 1854, Buford Papers. For instances from other states of physical examinations for slave life insurance see *Bloodgood* v. *Wilson*, 10 La. Ann. 302 (1855); *Murphy* v. *Mutual Benefit Life and Fire Insurance Company*, 6 La. Ann. 518 (1851); *Durham* v. *Broddus*, 26 Ga. 524 (1855).

[24] Drewry to Buford, April 14, May 18, 1854, Buford Papers.

447

[Colonel] ever had," Drewry concluded in a letter to Buford, "so from these circumstances I think they [the doctor] must be mistaken." He convinced the Richmond Fire Association, for almost a year later Drewry received assurance from the company's agent that his claim would be paid.[25]

Insurance companies also protected themselves and their slave risks by limiting the terms of policies to four or five years. Whites could buy insurance for life at a set annual premium based on age at time of purchase, but slaveowners had to renegotiate policies on their servants every few years and pay higher rates. This gave insurance companies the power to drop from their rolls any bondsmen injured or taken chronically ill during the previous few years. The rule was also designed to protect slaves from "premature" deaths at the hands of mercenary masters. However, during any contracted multiyear term the company had to renew the policy annually as long as the premium was paid, regardless of the slave's health. There was also an upper age limit beyond which slaves could not be insured. Franklin Slaughter of Fredericksburg insured slaves only up to the age of sixty-two, and the North Carolina Mutual Life Insurance Company to age sixty. Superannuated bondsmen thus could not be subjected to maltreatment or neglect for insurance purposes, as companies would not insure them.[26]

Virginia and North Carolina insurance houses limited the movement of insured slaves to certain regions or states. Franklin Slaughter advertised his rates of slave insurance contingent upon a continued residence within the state of Virginia. He was willing to take risks on Negroes "to be conveyed to, or to reside in any slaveholding state in the Union," but at a higher premium.[27] Written into most slave insurance policies were the words: ". . . in case the said slave shall, without the consent of this Company, . . . pass beyond the limits of the State, . . . this Policy shall be null and void."[28] Though designed to protect the company, this rule also helped the slave. "Fevers" were the commonest cause of illness and a frequent cause of death in the antebellum South. Medical opinion held, with some truth, that persons who moved from one place to another, especially in the South, required several years residence to

---

[25] Drewry to Buford, April 14, 1854; Jno. H. Baker to Buford, February 17, 1855, *ibid.*

[26] Richmond *Enquirer,* January 27, 1860; printed circular of Franklin Slaughter, General Broker [1849], Grinnan Family Papers, box 8, folder 20; North Carolina Mutual Life Insurance Company, *Life Insurance: Its Principles, Operations and Benefits* (Raleigh, 1849), 23 (Pamphlet Collection, Duke University Library; hereinafter cited as NC Mutual, *Life Insurance*).

[27] Slaughter circular, Grinnan Family Papers.

[28] See for example slave insurance policies in Linn Papers, 1855; Virginia Executive Papers (Governor Floyd), June 1851; Haxall Family Papers (items 235 and 236).

acclimate to the new disease environment, as different forms of fevers usually prevailed. Residents of the lower South paid, in fact, a higher premium than those of the upper South even when they were acclimated and much more when they were not. For example, a one-year, $1,000 policy on a twenty-two-year-old slave cost $35 in New Orleans in 1854 and only $16 in North Carolina. But even high premiums did not adequately compensate some companies for their slave losses in the Deep South. One Connecticut firm went into bankruptcy under a heavy barrage of claims on bondsmen, and a New York concern ceased issuing slave policies after a two-year trial period.[29] Hence, it was not surprising to read in a slave (or white) policy that the insured could not "go to any locality South of the State, in which he or she now lives" without the company's approval.[30]

Masters did occasionally seek permission to move slaves to other states. In the minutes of the North Carolina Mutual Life Insurance Company's Board of Directors meetings are several instances: Alexander Graham of Fayetteville, North Carolina, was permitted to hire out two insured slaves in South Carolina without additional premium, though William Groves of Wilmington, North Carolina, was allowed to move his insured servants to Florida only if he paid a 1 percent additional premium. The company authorized J. Wells of Hillsboro, North Carolina, to send an insured bondsman to Knoxville, Tennessee, by railroad through South Carolina and Georgia at no extra cost but insisted that W. A. Holeman pay an additional ½ percent premium to send his slave Prince to Alabama.[31] The directors of insurance establishments feared, with justification, that the movement of people through different parts of the South would increase the risk of death.

Slaveowners and hirers paid extra premiums not only for transferring bondsmen but also for putting blacks to work at certain

[29] For more on the diseases and acclimation of slaves in the antebellum South see Todd L. Savitt, "Sound Minds and Sound Bodies: The Diseases and Health Care of Blacks in Ante-Bellum Virginia" (unpublished Ph.D. dissertation, University of Virginia, 1975), 16–48, 518–28, and his forthcoming book, *Medicine and Slavery*. On insurance premiums in the lower South see Genovese, "The Medical Insurance Costs of Slaveholding," 146–47. The insurance premium quoted for New Orleans was taken from a slave policy reproduced in Richard Hooker, *Aetna Life Insurance Company: Its First Hundred Years* (Hartford, Conn., 1956), 14–15. On northern companies' experiences with slave insurance see *ibid.*, 12–13; and James M. Hudnut, *Semi-Centennial History of the New-York Life Insurance Company, 1845–1895* (New York, 1895), 22–23; Shephard B. Clough, *A Century of American Life Insurance: A History of the Mutual Life Insurance Company of New York, 1843–1943* (New York, 1946), 96; Mildred F. Stone, *Since 1845: A History of the Mutual Benefit Life Insurance Company*, ([New Brunswick, N. J.], 1957), 19–20, 41–42.

[30] Insurance policy of slave George, owned by Joseph Myers, April 3, 1858 (Confederate Museum, Richmond, Va.).

[31] NC Mutual Minutes, July 4, November 24, 1851; September 2, 1857; January 12, 1858.

449

occupations. Franklin Slaughter considered that railroad engineers and firemen were at the greatest risk and so added a 2 percent surcharge for slaves so engaged. Miners were charged 1½ percent additional while coal pit, steamboat, and fishing boat laborers, and those involved in coasting were charged 1 percent more. In addition to adding extra premiums for these occupations, the North Carolina Mutual Life Insurance Company also collected more for slaves working in rice fields, "getting oysters," and hauling seines.[32] The Richmond Fire Association refused even to insure slave railroad hands over the age of forty and never for an amount exceeding $600.[33] Most conservative of all was the Lynchburg Hose and Fire Insurance Company. It would take no risks on slaves "employed upon any public improvement, or in any extra hazardous business" and charged an additional 1 percent for carpenters, house joiners, brick or stone masons, and those laboring in "occupation[s] of a like character."[34] Surcharges and severe restrictions on risks protected the insurance firms but did little to deter owners from hiring out their slaves for work at dangerous occupations or from obtaining slave insurance.

A clause commonly found in slave life insurance policies, and designed to protect the servant as well as the company, usually stated that "in case the said slave shall die for want of proper medical or personal attendance . . . this Policy shall be void."[35] Firms required some sort of certificate from physicians and witnesses as to the circumstances surrounding the actual cause of, and the care tendered prior to, death.[36] A typical witness's statement read:

This is to certify that Bill a slave of J. A. Linn, and a Tanner by trade aged about 17 or 18 years- laboured with me in the Tan yard from 1st of August, 1855, to 1st of November, 1856, that said Boy began to complain sometime before the 1st of Nov., 1856, and continued lingering until the 22nd of Feb. 1857 when he expired. I saw him after death and witnessed his burrial, & know him to be the same boy insured in your company in Policy No. 426.[37]

The available evidence does not substantiate Nott's dire predictions of inhumanity to slaves whose lives were insured. The propor-

---

[32] Franklin Slaughter circular, Grinnan Family Papers; NC Mutual, *Life Insurance*. 17.
[33] C. F. Wills to John Buford, February 25, 1854, Buford Papers.
[34] M. W. Davenport to John McCue, July 1, 1852, McCue Family Papers.
[35] See for example slave policies in Linn Papers, 1855.
[36] See for example the forms enclosed in a letter from Jno. H. Bosher to John Buford, February 17, 1855, Buford Papers; insurance policy of slave George, April 3, 1858; NC Mutual Minutes, September 6, 1851.
[37] Draft of a certificate on death of slave Bill, n.d., folder 5, Linn Papers.

tion of deaths among one North Carolina company's white and black clients remained about equal for the years 1857, 1858, and 1860. Companies in Virginia and North Carolina attempted to safeguard their investments by establishing guidelines and rules and in so doing served to protect the lives of black servants.

The North Carolina Mutual Life Insurance Company of Raleigh was probably the major insurer of slaves in the Carolinas. Established in 1849, North Carolina Mutual counted among its directors some of the most prominent business and political figures in the capital city—the mayor of Raleigh (William D. Haywood, vice-president of the company), the cashier and the teller of the Branch Bank of Cape Fear (William H. Jones, treasurer, and F. C. Hill), three respected physicians (Charles E. Johnson, president, William H. McKee, and R. B. Haywood), the principal clerk of the state House of Commons (Perrin Busbee, attorney), the United States attorney for the Raleigh District (H. W. Husted), the editor of the state Democratic organ, the Raleigh *North Carolina Standard* (William Woods Holden), the principal of the Institution for the Deaf and Dumb (William D. Cooke), and an influential local merchant (Charles B. Root).[38] Agents made great use of these prestigious names in assuring prospective clients of North Carolina Mutual's respectability as an insuring and business institution. With sales representatives and policyholders throughout North and South Carolina and in parts of Virginia, Alabama, and Georgia, North Carolina Mutual was by the eve of the Civil War a well-known and trusted firm.[39]

Though established to provide financial security for survivors of white heads of households (motto: "In Distress We Succor"), North Carolina Mutual rapidly became an insurer of slaves. The company approved its first policy on April 1, 1849. In early July it had issued 83 white and 45 slave policies. A year later 610 policies were in force, the majority of which were probably for slaves.[40] By June 1857 (and probably earlier) three times as many slaves as whites were being insured annually (see Table 1).[41] Over the eleven years during which the company grew and prospered (1849–1860) the directors constantly modified and adjusted their handling of slave accounts to keep pace with changing internal and external economic conditions and with the increased volume of slave risks.

[38] James F. Jordan, Jr. to W. T. B. Haynesworth, March 21, 1851, Jordan Paper.
[39] *Ibid.*; NC Mutual Minutes, *passim.*
[40] NC Mutual Minutes, July 7, 1849; July 1, 1850.
[41] North Carolina Mutual Life Insurance Company, *Eighth Annual Report* (Raleigh, 1857), 8. Hereinafter, annual reports of the company will be cited as NC Mutual, *AR,* preceded by the number and followed by the year in parentheses, then the page number. All are located in the North Carolina Room, University of North Carolina Library, Chapel Hill.

Table 1

North Carolina Mutual Life Insurance Company of Raleigh
Data Sheet on Slave and White Policies
1849-1864

For Year Ending	6/20 1850	6/20 1851	6/20 1852	6/20 1853	1854	5/31 1855	5/31 1856	5/31 1857	5/31 1858	5/31 1859	5/31 1860	5/31 1861	5/31 1862	5/31 1863	5/31 1864
Total policies in force	610	1161	1464		2083	2288	2308	2193	2167	2239	2200		1528	1394	1206
White policies in force								500	492		501			425	387
Slave policies in force								1693	1675		1699			969	819
# White losses[1]	1	1	5	6	6	10	10	8	6	5	8	7	7	9	8
# Slave losses[1]	1	10	10	17	25	21	31	17	23	19	25	20	16	13	17
White losses/ 100 white policies								1.60	1.20		1.60			2.12	2.07
Slave losses/ 100 slave policies								1.00	1.37		1.47			1.34	2.08
Money on hand	23,565	46,117	60,911	75,419	91,346	89,754	100,250	114,113	142,180	175,198	191,516		202,027	214,603	209,505
Paid on white losses[1]	1,000	5,000	17,000	22,000	19,000	34,200	25,968	28,283	15,716	14,350	26,000	25,500	19,000	39,000	24,000
Paid on slave losses[1]	400	5,288	5,660	9,132	14,170	13,712	19,116	11,300	14,433	13,200	17,816	14,666	12,533	10,567	14,366
Average paid/ white loss	1,000	5,000	3,400	3,667	3,167	3,420	2,597	3,535	2,619	2,870	3,250	3,643	2,714	4,333	3,000
Average paid/ slave loss	400	529	566	537	567	653	617	665	628	695	713	733	783	813	845

Information was drawn from annual reports and manuscript minutes of the company. Blank spaces indicate that information was not available.

[1] The company paid losses ninety days following claim. Deaths filed later than March 31st of each year (beginning in 1852) were included with figures for the following fiscal year (which began on June 1st).

In their first business prospectus (issued 1849) the directors of North Carolina Mutual included a few remarks on slave life insurance: "The insurance on slaves in this State opens a new field of thought to our Planters, and other slave owners, and proposes to secure them in the possession of that kind of property, which constitutes half of the actual wealth of the State."[42] Despite the fact that insurers of Negroes could not "participate in the profits of the company" as could holders of regular life policies, applications arrived in unexpected numbers, raising several unanticipated problems. According to the rules, for instance, a bondsman could be insured for up to two-thirds of his market value, but the declarations which agents sent to the home office did not include information on the slave's value. Only late in August 1849, almost five months after the start of operations, did the secretary of the company, James F. Jordan, Jr., instruct all agents to rectify this matter. At about this same time J. Hersman, one of the company's traveling agents, presented the directors with the results of his fact-collecting trip to Baltimore on slave insurance.[43] No record of this report or of the directors' reaction to it is available, but the fact that such a mission was even authorized reflects the board's desire to obtain as much information as possible on the subject and to act cautiously until they understood fully the implications of so large a slaveowner response.

During its first fourteen months of operation North Carolina Mutual sold 610 policies and paid only two claims, one slave and one white. This favorable report, the board realized, did not reflect the experiences of other life insurance companies and could not be taken as indicative of future claims.[44] The board's circumspection proved warranted, as the number of deaths increased more than fivefold the following year to eleven, while the number of insured persons only doubled, to 1,161 (see Table 1). This was the one time in the company's sixteen years of full activity that the amount paid in slave losses ($5,288) exceeded that for whites ($5,000). North Carolina Mutual was still financially sound, having $46,117 on hand at the close of the fiscal year (June 1851), but the directors were understandably concerned. Calling these mortality figures to the attention of "those who hold the opinion that the bills of mortality among slaves are not so great as among whites," the board announced in its annual report for 1850/51 a 15 percent increase in slave premiums. It further justified this increase by pointing out that North Carolina Mutual's rates on bondsmen were

[42] NC Mutual, *Life Insurance*, 12.
[43] NC Mutual Minutes, August 29, September 7, 1849.
[44] *Ibid.*, July 1, 1850; December 27, 1849; NC Mutual, *2d AR* (1851), 5.

Table 2

1849 Slave Life Insurance Premiums of
North Carolina Mutual Life Insurance Company
and Franklin Slaughter, Insurance Broker

Age At Next Birthday	Annual Premium per $100 of Insurance			
	for 1 year		for 5 years	
	NC Mutual	Franklin Slaughter	NC Mutual	Franklin Slaughter
10	$1.18	$1.28	$1.30	$1.64
20	1.24	1.36	1.38	1.73
30	1.41	1.57	1.59	1.98
40	1.77	1.95	1.97	2.35
50	2.70	2.98	3.00	3.49
60	5.10	5.65	5.66	6.26

North Carolina Mutual, Life Insurance, 23.

Grinnan Papers (Box 8, Folder 20), Manuscript Department, University of Virginia Library, Charlottesville.

15 to 33 percent lower than those of other companies.[45] A comparison of North Carolina Mutual's premiums in 1849 with those of Franklin Slaughter's for the same year indicates differentials ranging from 7.8 to 20.7 percent lower (see Table 2). The directors made it clear in their annual report that this rate increase was an economic necessity and not a device to discourage slaveowners from insuring their Negroes with North Carolina Mutual: "Its [slave life insurance's] utility has thus far been recognized on all hands; and it is confidently predicted that the day is not far distant when this species of property will be almost universally under insurance."[46]

During the 1851/52 fiscal year the Board of Directors continued to adjust its regulations regarding slave risks. Up to this point neither the bylaws nor the written insurance policies had included any statements refusing payment on claims for death owing to the slaveowner's negligence. Such an oversight could have been very costly to the firm, so on September 6, 1851, the board voted to

[45] NC Mutual, 2d AR (1851), 5–6; NC Mutual Minutes, June 7, July 5, 1851.
[46] NC Mutual, 2d AR (1851), 20.

refuse claims on slaves who had died "from want of proper care during sickness, or from neglect in procuring proper medical attendance." Words to this effect were hereafter included in all policies.[47] A few months later the question arose as to whether the company would insure the lives of free blacks. The board voted unanimously to refuse "this class of risks," no doubt because of the reportedly high mortality rate of members of this usually impoverished and often sickly group.[48]

In June 1852 the directors decided to evaluate the success of their slave insurance program. They found that over the previous three years the company had received $18,206 in premiums and paid out $14,713 in claims on bondsmen. Profits, it was decided, were too small compared with the risks incurred, so another 15 percent rise in premiums was voted.[49] Thus, a master who had paid $7.44 per year in 1849 to insure his twenty-year-old slave for $600 for one year, or $8.28 annually for five years, now, after two rate increases of approximately 15 percent each, had to pay $10.02 for one year, or $11.28 annually for five years (see Table 2). For the remainder of the 1850s premiums on slave insurance remained at the rates established in 1852. The premiums for whites never changed from 1849 to 1860.

Despite the increased cost of insuring slaves, owners and hirers continued to purchase policies in large numbers. In July 1856 the directors acknowledged in their annual report that "insurance on the lives of slaves . . . has become quite an important feature in the transactions of this Company."[50] An analysis of the number of slave and white policies issued was not published until the 1856/57 annual report, but the total policies in force each year between 1854 and 1860 averaged about 2,200, and the racial breakdown remained constant for three of these years at three slave risks for each white risk (see Table 1). During the same period the company paid claims on between two and four times as many bondsmen as whites, a further indication of the large number of slave policies being issued. Mortality rates, as mentioned above, were about equal for both groups. Because North Carolina Mutual took risks only up to two-thirds of a servant's value the total amount paid out for slave losses annually was smaller than the amount for whites. The aver-

[47] NC Mutual Minutes, September 6, 1851.

[48] Ibid., January 3, 1852. For more on the health of free blacks in the antebellum South see Savitt, "Sound Minds and Sound Bodies," 327–49, 453–75, and his forthcoming book, Medicine and Slavery.

[49] NC Mutual Minutes, July 3, 1852; NC Mutual, 3d AR (1852), 4. The figures in Table 1 add up to $11,348, but the directors of the company recorded these losses as $14,713 in the minutes of their meeting on July 3, 1852. Available records do not clarify this discrepancy.

[50] NC Mutual, 7th AR (1856), 5–6.

age coverage for bondsmen (based on claims paid) rose from about $550 in the early 1850s to approximately $800 ten years later, a reflection of the rising purchase price of slaves during the last pre–Civil War decade. Whites usually insured themselves for about four or five times this amount (see Table 1).

During the period of rapid company growth in the mid-1850s, as both white and slave claims began to increase, officials became concerned with the quality of medical examinations provided applicants. In 1854 the board discussed this matter at one of its regular meetings and recommended that insurance examinations "be conducted with the utmost care, and circumspection."[51] Death payments continued, however, to increase during the 1854/55 fiscal year (up over $14,500 from 1853/54) despite company warnings to examining physicians (see Table 1). The directors made their point even more explicit in the next annual report, stating "that the examinations of the applicants for insurance by our Examining Physicians are in many cases insufficient; that they suffer much to escape their attention, which a more thorough and searching investigation would reveal."[52] When white claims dropped some $8,200 during the ensuing year, but slave claims rose, another strong statement from the board appeared and so did a change in policy. Referring to the decline in white claims the directors expressed "their conviction that like benefits and advantages would follow the employment of the same caution and ability in the taking of applications for insurance on the lives of slaves." To encourage such "caution and ability" it was announced that thereafter the company would pay physicians a fee of one dollar for examining slaves. (This had increased to two dollars by 1858). Prior to this North Carolina Mutual had paid two dollars for whites but had refused to reimburse slaveowners or doctors for medical examinations of bondsmen, a practice which had encouraged imperfect if not outrightly dishonest medical reports.[53]

The verbal message and financial incentive may have produced the desired effect, as during the next year (1856/57) claims on slaves dropped from thirty-one to seventeen (see Table 1) and profits on black policies rose from $2,013 to $8,034. Still, the board suspected duplicity on the part of a few agents and examining physicians in the field. Because some deaths "have been the result of chronic constitutional diseases," company officials believed that "sufficient

[51] NC Mutual Minutes, February 4, 1854.
[52] NC Mutual, *6th AR* (1855), 5, 7.
[53] NC Mutual, *7th AR* (1856), 5–6; NC Mutual Minutes, July 5, 1856; NC Mutual, *9th AR* (1858), 11; James F. Jordan, Jr., to W. T. B. Haynesworth, March 21, 1851, Jordan Paper.

care has not been taken . . . to exclude all unsound persons from the benefits of Insurance in this Office."[54] The results of this public exposure must have satisfied the directors, for nothing further on the subject appeared in minutes of board meetings or in annual reports.

Though available records do not contain information on the number of industrial slaves insured by North Carolina Mutual, they do indicate that this group of bondsmen provided the company with a significant amount of business. For instance, included with the table of slave premiums at the end of each annual report was a list of "extra rates of insurance on slaves." With experience, company officials learned that the risk on slaves employed on boats (steam, canal, fishing, pilot) or coasting was greater than for any other kind of work. Consequently, beginning in July 1854 slave insurers paid a 2½ percent surcharge on bondsmen so employed.[55] It was also discovered that slaves engaged in running a railroad incurred more dangers than those who did stationary railroad work such as grading and ditching. By 1855 the insurers of the former were being billed ¼ percent more than the insurers of the latter, and in 1860 slave graders on the railroad from Rocky Mount to Tarboro, North Carolina, were entirely free of any extra premium.[56] Among other industrial slave laborers not subject to surcharge were shingle gatherers and turpentine workers.[57] A number of deaths each year occurred among what appear to be industrial slaves. Causes such as "drowning," "noxious gas in well," "accidents," "falling off embankment," "killed in a well," and "killed on Manchester Railroad" are indicative of the types of employment of some bondsmen.[58] Extant slave insurance policies from several industrial concerns[59] and the appearance of business company names, such as James C. Sproull & Co., Boatwright & Miot, Freeman and Houston, and Dickenson, Grant & Gauze, in the list of claimants for slave losses, further illustrate the importance of industrial slave policies to North Carolina Mutual's business.

During the first eleven years of its existence North Carolina Mutual grew and prospered. By 1860 the company had over $190,000 on hand, compared with less than $90,000 only five years

[54] NC Mutual, *8th AR* (1857), 6–7.

[55] NC Mutual Minutes, July 1, 1854. It is unclear, owing to incomplete records, why the company found it necessary to charge higher premiums for slaves than for whites, since both groups demonstrated approximately equal mortality rates.

[56] NC Mutual, *6th AR* (1855), 31; NC Mutual Minutes, January 7, 1860.

[57] NC Mutual Minutes, January 6, 1855.

[58] NC Mutual, *2d AR* (1851), 7; *3d AR* (1852), 9; *4th AR* (1853), 5; *6th AR* (1855), 10; *7th AR* (1856), 8–9; *8th AR* (1857), 9–10; *9th AR* (1858), 8–9; *11th AR* (1860), 8–9.

[59] See for example slave policies in Linn Papers, 1855, and London Papers, 1855–1856.

earlier (see Table 1). A dividend of 20 percent was declared, with the thought that similar dividends could be declared annually in future.[60] But then civil war and economic chaos disrupted the directors' plans, and within six years, despite several attempts to save it, North Carolina Mutual was forced to cease operations and disband.[61] During its existence the company had insured over 7,200 lives, half to two-thirds of whom were slaves, and had paid to masters more than $176,359 in compensation for the deaths of 265 bondsmen.[62] North Carolina Mutual was, until the outbreak of hostilities, part of a growing network of slave insurance companies which provided a small measure of financial support for the South's "peculiar institution."

[60] NC Mutual. *11th AR* (1860), 3–4.
[61] NC Mutual Minutes, August 6, 1866.
[62] The highest policy number listed in the *15th AR* (1864), 6, was 7,227.

New Orleans Slavery in 1850 as Seen in Advertisements

By Judith Kelleher Schafer

The typical slave in antebellum New Orleans did not, as an old adage has it, get his name in the paper on two occasions, birth and death. Thousands of slaves did make the newspapers, but in the classified section. Slaves were listed for sale and for hire by owners; owners advertised for the return of runaway slaves and described them in detail; and jailers placed notices of captured runaways in the public prints. This article represents a detailed analysis of the several thousand advertisements for bondsmen in the New Orleans newspapers for the year 1850. The resulting picture of labor practices in the Crescent City indicates a booming slave trade in which the equivalent of one in five of the bondsmen in New Orleans were sold annually. Most of the sales were auctions occasioned by a legal procedure, and most sales were of broken lots rather than complete slave families. There were substantial numbers of runaways too. Most slaves ran away to join family members, although most bondsmen chose to run alone. Lighter-skinned slaves tended to be the most likely fugitives, whereas black slaves tended to be more often sold. Women were sold and also became fugitives at an earlier age than men, although there was no seasonal variation for running away among either sex. Rural owners valued their slaves more than did owners in urban areas if the size of the reward can be taken as an indication.

The fragility of the slaves' lives is exemplified over and over by the volume of the slave trade. The fact that a slave could be sold at all was a forceful reminder of his status. The auction block was a compelling symbol of his servitude; it transformed the slave from a person to mere property. As long as any slave sales occurred no normal life was really possible for the bondsman. The chance that an urban black would be sold several times during his life was very great[1] and was dictated by the white family's fluctuating need for

[1] Richard C. Wade, *Slavery in the Cities: The South 1820–1860* (New York, 1964), 197.

Ms. Schafer is a graduate student in history at Tulane University.

The Journal of Southern History
Vol. XLVII, No. 1, February 1981

domestic labor. For example, an urban slave who was a child's nurse might be sold when the white children were grown, whereas a rural field hand would always remain useful.

New Orleans was second only to Charleston in the size of its slave trade in 1850; it was unsurpassed in the lower South. In New Orleans the markets and buyers were numerous, money was plentiful, and the profits large. Seven professional slave dealers placed thirteen different classified advertisements in the New Orleans newspapers in 1850. Most of these dealers advertised for sale slaves from Virginia and Maryland.[2] A typical notice stated that a slave dealer had just received "ONE HUNDRED AND THIRTY Negroes, direct from Baltimore" which included "a choice lot of field hands, waiters, cooks . . . blacksmiths, carpenters and a fine engineer . . . ." To encourage prospective buyers, the vendor stated "I am determined to sell low . . . ."[3]

One slave dealer, Elihu Creswell, specialized in "acclimated SLAVES . . . less subject to diseases of the climate . . . than those recently imported into the State."[4] Carman and Ricardo, who owned a slave depot at 15 Perdido Street (which had accommodations for three hundred slaves), claimed theirs was "one of the most commodious and well-ventilated establishments for the purpose in the United States."[5] Since these advertisements rarely give exact numbers of slaves handled by slave dealers, it is impossible to ascertain how many slaves were sold in this way, but the persistence with which these notices appeared in the New Orleans newspapers indicates a large volume and a high profit for the slave traders. Nevertheless, since numbers for these slave sales are unavailable, individual slave sales as indicated in the newspaper advertisements of New Orleans' nine newspapers in 1850 have been analyzed. All subse-

[2] Vernon A. Wegener, "Negro Slavery in New Orleans" (unpublished M.A. thesis, Tulane University, 1935), 28. Often one advertisement was repeated daily for months. By the late 1840s probably three hundred New Orleans residents were engaged in slave trading. Herman C. Woessner III, "New Orleans, 1840–1860: A Study in Urban Slavery" (unpublished M.A. thesis, Louisiana State University, 1967), 34. One historian thinks that New Orleans was the greatest slave-trading center in the entire South by 1850. Robert C. Reinders, "Slavery in New Orleans in the Decade Before the Civil War," *Mid-America,* XLIV (October 1962), 211.
[3] New Orleans *Bee,* October 29, 1850; the French edition is *L'Abeille.* All citations to New Orleans papers will hereinafter omit the city.
[4] *Daily Picayune,* January 26, 1850.
[5] *Daily Delta,* December 19, 1850. A New Orleans ordinance required slave "traders to keep their merchandise in clean, well ventilated buildings at least two stories high . . . ." Kenneth M. Stampp, *The Peculiar Institution: Slavery in the Ante-Bellum South* (New York, 1956), 252. At least twenty-five slave depots were located within one-half mile of the St. Charles Hotel in 1850. Reinders, "Slavery in New Orleans," 212. Quite a few slave depots had facilities for as many as one hundred slaves. Woessner, "New Orleans, 1840–1860," 34.

TABLE 1

New Orleans Population by Category and Sex in 1850

	Male		Female	
Category	Number	Percent	Number	Percent
White	51,792	57.89	37,667	42.12
Free black	3,999	40.37	5,906	59.63
Slave	6,818	40.08	10,193	59.92

SOURCE: Richard C. Wade, *Slavery in the Cities: The South 1820-1860*, pp. 328-30.

TABLE 2

Slave Ages at the Time of Sale

	Male		Female	
Age	Number	Percent	Number	Percent
0-4	42	9.4	39	7.6
5-9	53	11.9	46	8.9
10-14	49	11.0	46	8.9
15-19	37	8.3	69	13.4
20-24	52	11.7	69	13.4
25-29	69	15.5	59	11.5
30-34	43	9.7	62	12.1
35-39	26	5.8	49	9.5
40-44	29	6.5	32	6.2
45-49	19	4.3	16	3.1
50-54	20	4.5	9	1.8
55-59	4	0.9	6	1.2
60 and over	2	0.4	12	2.3
Total	445	99.9	514	99.9

quent figures are computed on the basis of the published sale notices.[6]

New Orleans newspaper advertisements in 1850 indicate that total slave sales were 3,501, of which at least 523 were male and 604 female (sex was not specified in 2,374). These figures indicate that the equivalent of 20.6 percent of the New Orleans slave population

[6] Of the nine New Orleans newspapers of 1850 (*Commercial Bulletin, Daily Crescent, Daily Delta, Daily Orleanian, Daily Picayune, Daily True Delta, L'Abeille, Le Courrier,* and *Weekly Delta*), seven published daily (except Sunday), and the *Daily Picayune* published twice daily except Sunday and Monday, when it appeared once a day. The *Picayune* classified sections were identical in the morning and evening editions when it published twice a day. As indicated, one paper was a weekly. Nearly complete editions were available for 1850 for eight papers; the *Daily Delta* was available only from October 15 to December 15.

was sold in 1850, or approximately one in five[7] (see Table 1). Of these, there were 919 whose age was specified (56 percent female, 44 percent male). From the figures in Table 2 one can see that peak sale ages for women were between 15 and 24 (26.8 percent) whereas the most frequent ages for male sales were between the ages of 20 and 29 (27.2 percent). Perhaps the younger ages of women sold were swelled by the "fancy girl" market[8] and also by the fact that domestic skills could be learned at an earlier age. Also, girls reached puberty about the age of fifteen and therefore became more valuable as they could bear children. The later peak age of male sales may reflect the fact that slave men were more valuable once they had acquired a skill.

Approximately 21 percent of the male and 17 percent of the female slaves sold were children under ten years of age. Perhaps this sex differential resulted because the slave sellers kept the younger girls at home to perform simple domestic chores, because females of all ages were worth less than males, or because excess males were less useful in domestic employment. Most of these children were sold in a lot with their mothers, as it was against the Louisiana law to sell either the mother of a child under ten away from that child or the child away from its mother.[9] One historian believes that this law was strictly obeyed, but in the classified advertisements of 1850 there appear notices for the sale of twenty-eight children under ten years of age, sixteen males and twelve females. Of these children, three of each sex were orphans, and their sale would not have been a violation of the law.[10] Two of the orphans were brother and sister and

[7] Since some of these slaves were rural, one cannot say that one in five slaves in New Orleans was sold but that the *equivalent* of one in five was sold. Every possible effort was expended to eliminate duplicate advertisements.

[8] There was a great demand in New Orleans for "fancy girls." Eugene D. Genovese, *Roll, Jordan, Roll: The World the Slaves Made* (New York, 1974), 416.

[9] *Acts Passed at the First Session of the Ninth Legislature of the State of Louisiana* (New Orleans, 1829), 48; Bennett H. Wall, "An Epitaph for Slavery," *Louisiana History*, XVI (Summer 1975), 251; Stanley M. Elkins, *Slavery: A Problem in American Institutional and Intellectual Life* (Chicago and London, 1976), 54n. Two young children were listed with their fathers, *Daily Picayune*, February 6, 1850.

[10] Joe G. Taylor, *Negro Slavery in Louisiana* (Baton Rouge, 1963), 41. For example see *L'Abeille*, July 17, 1850; *Le Courrier de la Louisiane* (hereinafter *Le Courrier*), April 29, 1850 (Succession of Mrs. J. B. Colle). Two historians state that many sales of children under ten years of age can be explained by the fact that they were orphans. Robert W. Fogel and Stanley L. Engerman, *Time on the Cross: The Economics of American Negro Slavery* (Boston and Toronto, 1974), 50. Five other historians think that Fogel and Engerman wildly exaggerated the number of orphans in the sales of children under ten. Paul A. David *et al.*, *Reckoning with Slavery: A Critical Study in the Quantitative History of American Negro Slavery* (New York, 1976), 131.

were listed to be sold together,[11] although they may or may not have been separated.

Although older children between the ages of ten and sixteen were sometimes listed to be sold with their mothers, most often they were listed to be sold separately. Approximately 83 percent were listed to be sold away from their mothers; the remainder were listed to be sold together.[12] A typical advertisement stated that Liza, a thirty-five-year-old cook, washer, and ironer, was to be sold with three of her children, ages six years, four years, and fifteen months; her other two children, ages fourteen and sixteen were to be sold separately.[13]

Further fragmentation of the slave family can be seen in the newspaper advertisements of 1850. The very use of the term "family" usually meant a mother and her children, not a husband, wife, and children. This fact can be partially explained by considering that the woman could be a widow, or her husband could belong to a different owner, which would be quite possible in an urban setting. However, another factor to take into account is that full families sold poorly in an urban setting unless they were purchased by a slave dealer to be resold separately. Rural slave families may have remained intact more often, as a family of strong field hands was always in demand.[14]

In the New Orleans newspapers of 1850 there appeared only two classified advertisements which stated that a full family (husband, wife, children) would be sold together; one additional notice stated that the family would be sold either separately or together but that the owner preferred the latter.[15] In another instance, an owner attempted to mitigate the effect of selling a woman and her three children away from her husband and their father. He stated in the advertisement that he would not sell the wife and children to anyone but a resident of New Orleans since her husband remained in his

[11] *Daily Picayune,* June 30, 1850.

[12] For example see *Le Courrier,* April 18, 1850 (Succession of William Carter). The sale of teen-age slaves away from their families cannot be rationalized by saying that at this age many children would choose to leave home. The sale forced an involuntary separation on the young slave and his family. David *et al., Reckoning with Slavery,* 132.

[13] *L'Abeille,* March 28, 1850.

[14] *Ibid.,* October 25, 1850; Wegener, "Negro Slavery in New Orleans," 47.

[15] *L'Abeille,* February 21, 1850; *Commercial Bulletin,* August 8, 1850. In his survey of four New Orleans newspapers between 1850 and 1860, one historian found 120 instances of families being sold together. He defined a family as did the New Orleans newspapers of the time—as a mother and her children. Lawrence D. Reddick, "The Negro in the New Orleans Press, 1850–1860: A Study in Attitudes and Propaganda" (unpublished Ph.D. dissertation, University of Chicago, 1939), 160. *Daily Picayune,* March 9, 1850.

possession.[16] Whether such a limit to the sale was the result of attempting to avoid guilt over splitting the family or to avoid the disapprobation of others, or a combination of both, the sources do not reveal. They do indicate some repugnance to the breaking up of slave families.

In only two other advertisements, however, was there evidence of an effort by an owner to keep family members together. In one auction notice a sister and brother (ages twelve and nine) were required to be sold as a lot,[17] and in one private sale an elderly slave woman (age fifty) was to be sold with her eighteen-year-old daughter. Her son, age twenty-six, was to be sold separately. This last advertisement also stipulated that these three slaves were only to be sold to persons purchasing them for their own use,[18] probably to keep them out of the hands of slave dealers.

Usually when full slave families were listed for sale they were not listed as one lot, nor was it stipulated that they would be sold together. A typical notice of this type was for the sale of slaves in the succession of Phineas Solomon, which listed separately Robert, age fifty, Betsy Streck, "his woman," age fifty-two, and his child, a two-year-old girl.[19]

Of the advertisements of slaves for sale in the New Orleans newspapers, approximately 13 percent of all sales were private (as opposed to auctions). These notices usually were scattered throughout the "For Sale" columns of the publications, often sandwiched in between advertisements for such diverse items as leeches and sardines. Almost all notices for private slave sales stated that the slave or slaves to be sold would be "guarantied against the vices and maladies prescribed by law" or simply "guaranteed."[20] Often the

[16] *Daily Picayune,* January 29, 1850.

[17] *Le Courrier,* December 18, 1850.

[18] *Daily Picayune,* January 16, 1850.

[19] *Le Courrier,* November 21, 1850. Fogel and Engerman claim that 84 percent of all sales of slaves over fourteen years of age were of unmarried individuals, that New Orleans sales records show owners were averse to breaking up slave families, and that only 13 percent of slave sales actually separated families. Fogel and Engerman, *Time on the Cross,* 49–52. Several other historians disagree. They state that families were often split, that 71 percent of the married slave women between the ages of twenty and twenty-four (with children) were separated from their husbands if they were sold. They further assert that of all slave marriages in New Orleans, three of every ten were broken by sale. David *et al., Reckoning with Slavery,* 119–27. My evidence is consistent with Reddick's contention that most slaves were sold in broken lots. Reddick, "The Negro in the New Orleans Press," 160.

[20] *Daily Picayune,* January 10, 1850 (quotation). The guarantee usually meant that the slave had a clear title, was physically sound, and possessed a "good character." Stampp, *The Peculiar Institution,* 252. Occasionally, one may find the statement "not guaranteed except in title," which indicated a serious physical defect. Woessner, "New Orleans, 1840–1860," 38.

prospective vendor would describe the slaves for sale as "splendid" or a "choice lot" or "excellent" and would occasionally make complimentary comments about their character such as "strictly temperate"[21] or "honest, humble"[22] or "a man of good character and habits."[23] One slaveholder praised the female slave he was selling for her "honesty and sobriety and a faithful attendance in sickness."[24] Many private sale advertisements (as well as auction notices) stated that the slave was being "sold for no fault but for want of money"[25] or "sold on account of departure (owner leaving New Orleans)" to assure the prospective purchaser that the seller was not unloading a "bad" slave. The slave's acclimation to the city was also frequently mentioned as a virtue. Many private sale notices stated that the slave for sale had lived "since childhood in the city,"[26] or more simply that he or she was "acclimated."[27] Obviously, a vendor would stress a slave's favorable attributes and be silent about defects such as insolence, laziness, or lack of physical soundness.

Private sale advertisements were usually much more descriptive than auction notices. In these advertisements one can find a nine-year-old girl named Dolly who could speak French and English,[28] a Negro woman of thirty-five who could speak Dutch as well as French and English,[29] and an eighteen-year-old slave who "has commanded the highest wages as a cabin boy on steamboats."[30]

Occasionally, slaveowners who placed private sale advertisements evidenced concern for the future of the slaves being sold. Three masters stated that their slaves would be sold for less than their value if the seller could be assured that they were being purchased by a good master;[31] another owner stated that he would not sell the slave in question "at any price unless I am satisfied that the girl is getting a good home." Two owners were worried about where their slaves would live after the sale. One stated that his slave would not be sold to a city owner, "as it is her wish to live in the country";

[21] *Daily Picayune,* January 4, 1850; October 30, 1850; January 10, 1850.
[22] *Commercial Bulletin,* August 17, 1850.
[23] *L'Abeille,* July 22, 1850.
[24] *Daily Picayune,* April 6, 1850.
[25] For example see *L'Abeille,* November 22, 1850.
[26] *Ibid.,* July 10, 1850 (first quotation); *Daily Picayune,* March 8, 1850; *L'Abeille,* October 11, 1850 (second quotation).
[27] *Daily Orleanian,* December 28, 1850.
[28] *L'Abeille,* March 1, 1850.
[29] *Daily Picayune,* September 13, 1850.
[30] *Commercial Bulletin,* July 25, 1850.
[31] *Bee,* January 19, 1850; *Commercial Bulletin,* October 12, December 24, 1850.

another stated that the slaves he was selling were "mostly raised on the coast and prefer returning to it again."[32]

Although many advertisements of Negroes for hire appeared in the New Orleans newspapers, it is usually impossible to ascertain whether the notices were placed by a slaveowner or by a free black, unless the advertisement is "for sale or for hire." Of these, there are only twenty-four for men and ten for women, only a small fraction of the total sale advertisements for slaves in New Orleans in 1850. In only one advertisement was a hired slave's wages mentioned: a thirty-eight-year-old cook and waiter (male) on a steamboat received wages of thirty dollars per month.[33]

Since only seven advertisements (for ten slaves) in the New Orleans newspapers mentioned the price of slaves, it is impossible to make a generalization about the cost of bondsmen and bondswomen in 1850. The following is a composite of these notices:[34]

Women

Cook, washer and ironer, age 25	$ 700
House servant, child's nurse, bilingual, age 17	$ 600
House servant, washer and ironer, age 25, and her daughter, age 7	$1,000

Men

House servant, carriage driver, bricklayer, age 28	$ 850
Coachman and house servant, age 35	$ 600
Coachman, age 30	$ 600
Cook, dining room servant, carriage driver, age 19	$ 900
Dining room servant, carriage driver (no age given)	$ 750
Barber, age 24 insured for	$1,000

Husband and Wife

Man, house servant, carriage driver and barber, age 25	
Woman, chambermaid, age 22, both for	$1,650

[32] *Daily Picayune,* December 7, March 30, May 18, 1850; quotations appear in order in the cited issues.

[33] *Ibid.,* February 15, 1850.

[34] During the decade 1850–1860 individual slave prices seldom appeared in the New Orleans newspapers. Reddick, "The Negro in the New Orleans Press," 183. Slaves were usually insured for two-thirds or three-fourths of their value; insurance companies thought that if the slaves were insured for their full value, they might be more valuable dead than alive to their masters. Todd L. Savitt, "Slave Life Insurance in Virginia and North Carolina," *Journal of Southern History,* XLIII (November 1977), 587–88. The quoted prices appeared in *Daily Picayune,* January 15, March 8, 14, 1850; *Commercial Bulletin,* August 8, September 20, 30, November 8, 1850.

The overwhelming majority of slaves sold in New Orleans in 1850 were sold at public auction: 3,037 of 3,501 or 86.7 percent. Unlike the private sale, the auction sale implied no mitigating circumstances: the owner could not specify conditions or choose buyers he believed to be kind. Slave auctions were regularly held in New Orleans's two great hotels (the St. Charles and the St. Louis) and in other public places around the city. Slaves sold at public auction were examined by prospective purchasers as though they were livestock—they were poked, prodded, and stripped if the interested party so desired.[35] Auction notices for the sale of slaves in the city's newspapers appeared in a general auction column, along with and often in the same notice as auctions for real estate, furniture, and other items.

Sixty-eight percent of all slave sales reported in the New Orleans newspapers were the result of some legal action, and 78 percent of all auctions were occasioned by some legal procedure. The majority of these judicial auctions were either to settle a succession or an estate or for partition of a succession or an estate. Under Louisiana law no one could be forced to hold property (including slaves) in common with other heirs. If a division of the property could not be agreed upon by the heirs the property was sold at public auction and the proceeds divided among the heirs. Other legally caused auctions were for liquidation of partnership, divorce, settlement of a lawsuit of any type, settlement of debt, or bankruptcy.[36] In many of these auctions, the slave was seized and imprisoned until the date of auction. The high proportion of auction sales for legal reasons shows either that New Orleanians had so much capital invested in slaves that they could not produce the necessary cash to meet their obligations and therefore had to sell some of their slaves or that they chose to sell slaves rather than selling other possessions or parting with their cash. Certainly their slave investments were easily liquidated.

New Orleans was not only a great center for the slave trade; it was a mecca for fugitives. The conditions of slavery in the city both encouraged urban slaves to run away and attracted rural fugitives attempting to lose themselves in the congestion and confusion of the city. Robert Everest, an English visitor to New Orleans in 1853, estimated that 1 percent of all the city's slaves were absent at all

[35] Reddick, "The Negro in the New Orleans Press," 174-75; Wegener, "Negro Slavery in New Orleans," 47-49.

[36] The frequency of estate sales in Louisiana meant that no slave family was secure. Bondsmen could not predict when their owners would die and how the estates would be divided. Herbert G. Gutman, *The Black Family in Slavery and Freedom, 1750-1925* (New York, 1976), 153; Stampp, *The Peculiar Institution*, 199-201. Family ties were generally ignored in judicial sales. *Ibid.*, 200.

times.[37]

It is a rare occurrence to examine any daily New Orleans newspaper on a given date in 1850 and not find at least one runaway advertisement. A total of 475 different notices for fugitive slaves appeared in 1850.[38] These notices were usually scattered throughout the classified advertisements, often near notices for lost dogs or horses. Generally, the notice had a silhouette of either a running man carrying a bundle on a stick over his shoulder or of a woman running and carrying a small bundle in front of her, depending on which was appropriate.

There were two types of advertisements: one was placed by the fugitive's master, and the other by one of the city jailers. The former were generally quite detailed, and the fact that they were placed by the owner shows that the runaway had possibly succeeded in his or her escape. Owners normally did not advertise until the runaway had been gone for several weeks.[39] A fugitive who had been absent for that long a period may be assumed to have had some chance of making good his escape. Sometimes these owner-placed notices appeared daily or weekly for several weeks or even months.

Advertisements placed by the jailer obviously related to an unsuccessful fugitive being detained in one of the city jails until claimed by his or her owner. The law required that detained slaves had to be advertised once a week for three months unless claimed by the master, who had to pay the jailer for keeping the slave. Unclaimed runaways were sold for jail costs after two years. "Detained" notices were usually quite brief, giving only the name, sex, height, color, estimated age of the slave, and the owner's name, which the slave supplied. Seven percent of the incarcerated slaves refused to state the names of their owners, claiming that they were free. In these cases the jailer stated "says he [or she] is free, but supposed to be a slave."[40]

---

[37] Taylor, *Negro Slavery in Louisiana*, 173; Wade, *Slavery in the Cities*, 215; Henry E. Sterkx, *The Free Negro in Ante-Bellum Louisiana* (Rutherford, N. J., and other cities, 1972), 151; Ira Berlin, *Slaves Without Masters: The Free Negro in the Antebellum South* (New York, 1976), 158–59. Everest, quoted in John W. Blassingame, *Black New Orleans, 1860–1880* (Chicago, 1973), 9.

[38] Lawrence Reddick, who used only four New Orleans newspapers, found fewer than six hundred such advertisements between 1850 and 1860. Reddick, "The Negro in the New Orleans Press," 135, 159.

[39] Such notices were detailed, and they were likewise the most objective advertisements concerning slaves. The owner had nothing to sell; he wanted to furnish an accurate description of the fugitive so that he or she could be easily identified and returned. *Ibid.*, 162; Stampp, *The Peculiar Institution*, 110.

[40] Taylor, *Negro Slavery in Louisiana*, 173, 31, 170. It was not unusual for a "detained"

TABLE 3

RUNAWAY SLAVES

Type	Male		Female	
	Number	*Percent*	*Number*	*Percent*
All	324	68.2	151	31.7
Rural	83	25.6	14	9.3
Urban	241	74.4	137	90.7
Possibly successful	160	49.4	84	55.6
Detained	164	50.6	67	44.4
Rural detained	32	19.5	2	3.0
Urban detained	132	80.5	65	97.0

TABLE 4

RUNAWAY SLAVES BY AGE, SEX, NUMBERS, AND PERCENTAGES

Age	Male		Female	
	Number	*Percent*	*Number*	*Percent*
0–4	1	0.3	1	0.7
5–9	2	0.7	4	2.9
10–14	28	9.7	7	5.1
15–19	36	12.5	23	16.9
20–24	53	18.4	29	21.3
25–29	61	21.2	20	14.7
30–34	42	14.6	18	13.2
35–39	23	8.0	16	11.7
40–44	10	3.5	11	8.1
45–49	14	4.9	3	2.2
50–54	11	3.8	2	1.5
55–59	5	1.7	0	0.0
60 and over	2	0.7	2	1.5
Total	288	100.0	136	99.8

NOTE: The totals in this table differ from those in Table 3 because no age was specified in thirty-six advertisements for runaway males and fifteen for runaway females.

The combined totals of possibly successful runaways (owner-placed advertisements) and detained fugitives (jailer-placed notices) are analyzed in Table 3. From these figures one can see that the majority of runaways were urban males but that urban women were possibly more successful in making good their escape than male fugitives.

---

slave to try to pass as a free black. Sterkx, *The Free Negro,* 152. Sometimes a "detained" Negro was a free black without proper identification or a slave without a pass (but not a runaway). Morris K. Hepler, "Negroes and Crime in New Orleans, 1850-1861" (unpublished M.A. thesis, Tulane University, 1939), 88; *Le Courrier,* May 30, 1850 (quotation).

TABLE 5

Monthly Numbers and Percentages of Runaway Slaves

Month	Male Number	Male Percent	Female Number	Female Percent
January	25	7.7	13	8.7
February	19	6.9	12	8.0
March	27	8.4	13	8.7
April	38	11.8	13	8.7
May	25	7.7	14	9.3
June	19	5.9	11	7.3
July	31	9.6	13	8.7
August	33	10.2	15	10.0
September	28	8.7	11	7.3
October	20	6.2	12	8.0
November	28	8.7	17	11.3
December	30	9.2	6	4.0
Total	323	100.0	150	100.0

NOTE: The totals in this table differ from Table 3 because one fugitive advertisement for a man and one for a woman did not specify when they ran away.

Although slaves tried to escape their bondage at every age, certain ages for each sex were the most common. The ages with the highest percentages of runaways correlates roughly with the most common ages of slaves being sold, suggesting that being sold often prompted a slave to run away (see Tables 2 and 4). The figures in Table 4 were not divided into rural and rural detained categories because both types were so evenly distributed among all age groups.

The preponderance of urban slaves among all runaways is reflected in the times of the year during which they chose to leave their owners. As one would expect, there is little seasonal variation; the labor of urban slaves would be rather steady and not affected by planting season or harvest season (see Table 5).

Nearly all owner-placed runaway advertisements promised a reward for the return of the fugitive. Sometimes the owner was content with offering a "liberal" reward, but usually the amount of money was specifically stated. John Bradford, who advertised for his runaway mulatto barber, Shelly Carter, offered the unusual reward of "FIVE CENTS AND AN OLD RAZOR,"[41] but most owners promised a cash reward. Although it is impossible to correlate the skills of the fugitives with the amount of the reward (after all, the amount depended on the financial condition of the master as

[41] *Daily Picayune,* August 10, 1850.

TABLE 6

COMPARATIVE REWARDS FOR RUNAWAY URBAN AND RURAL SLAVES

Reward (in dollars)	Urban		Rural	
	Number	Percent	Number	Percent
5	14	9.8	0	0.0
10	58	40.6	8	17.8
20	22	15.4	4	8.9
25	24	16.8	12	26.7
50	22	15.4	14	31.1
100	3	2.1	7	15.6
Total	143	100.1	45	100.1

well as the value of the slave), rural masters apparently prized their slaves much more highly than did their urban counterparts, probably because rural slaves were a factor of production. The loss of even one would affect the master's crop yield; the owner would also lose the monetary value of the slave.[42] The loss of an urban slave meant losing only the cash value of the slave. Replacement by purchase or hire was not difficult in the city (see Table 6).[43]

Some owners were unable to believe that their slaves would run away voluntarily. Several advertisements of 1850 stated that their slaves were "Missing, supposed to have been stolen . . . ."[44] Another stated that since his slave had "always enjoyed a good [apparently docile] character, it is feared that he has met with some accident."[45] Several owners believed that their slaves were persuaded to run away by persons promising to take them to a free state.[46] One slaveholder was certain that his two slaves had been "enticed" off in this manner. In his notice he stated that he believed his two "boys" had been "decoyed off by a man who ran a trading boat up and down the Coast . . . ." The owner stated that this man "offered to run these Negroes to a free State for $150 each . . . ." Since the fugitives had stolen "a considerable amount of money"

[42] One historian has stated that slaves on sugar plantations died off faster than their offspring could mature, necessitating constant replenishment of the slave labor supply. John S. Kendall, "New Orleans' 'Peculiar Institution'," *Louisiana Historical Quarterly*, XXIII (July 1940), 876. If this statement is true, it is not surprising that slaves should be more valuable to rural owners than to urban.

[43] These figures do not support Reddick's contention that twenty-five dollars and fifty dollars were the most common reward for a runaway. Reddick, "The Negro in the New Orleans Press," 159. Although each of these two amounts were advertised in thirty-six notices, ten dollars was by far the most common, appearing in sixty-six notices.

[44] For example see *Daily Picayune*, July 9, 1850.

[45] *Le Courrier*, January 9, 1850.

[46] *Weekly Delta*, January 14, 1850.

and the trading boat captain had vanished, the slaveowner surmised that the captain had his runaways "in charge."[47] Two owners directed their fury towards the men who "stole" their slaves and described one of the thieves as "a foreigner, stooped shouldered . . . loves brandy, and resembles the ourang-outang."[48] The other owner, bristling with righteous indignation, said in his advertisement that his slave "had been either led astray or kidnapped by one of those rascals that is prowling about the city for the purpose of stealing Southern property."[49]

Some fugitive slaves advertised for by owners and jailers were reported to have run from areas far from New Orleans. One Thornton, a fourteen-year-old house servant, was advertised as the property of Jefferson Davis of Mississippi.[50] Others reportedly came from Memphis, Tennessee; Madison, Georgia; St. Louis, Missouri; Mobile, Alabama; Hinds County, Mississippi; Wilcox County, Alabama; and Sumptner [Sumner] County, Tennessee.[51]

Despite the strain placed on the slave family by bondage, it is clear slaves often ran away to join family members, most often a husband to join his wife. One owner stated that his mulatto "boy" John would probably be in the vicinity of "St. Patrick's Church as he has a wife in that part of the city."[52] Edward H. Pomroy's advertisement for his "intelligent" house servant Henry concluded that he "is probably in the back of the city [Negro district] as he has a wife there."[53] Other fugitive slaves were believed to have traveled longer distances to be united with their families. A slaveholder from St. James Parish said that his "bold look[ing]" slave Etienne ran from the steamboat *Latona* in St. John the Baptist Parish and would probably go to New Orleans "where he has his family."[54] In a similar advertisement, William Dalton's slave Sam ran from Lafayette to be near his wife, whose mistress lived on Bourbon Street.[55] Another slave, Solomon, who was owned by a paint shop operator in Memphis, was believed to have made his way to New Orleans, probably to rejoin family or friends, "as he lived there several

[47] *Daily Picayune*, December 5, 1850.
[48] *Commercial Bulletin*, April 9, 1850.
[49] *Daily True Delta*, May 28, 1850.
[50] *Daily Delta*, October 31, 1850.
[51] *Bee*, April 23, 1850; *Daily Picayune*, May 19, 1850; *Le Courrier*, January 29, March 26, May 13, 31, September 7, 14, 1850.
[52] *Daily Picayune*, April 18, 1850.
[53] *Daily Delta*, November 14, 1850.
[54] *Le Courrier*, June 13, 1850.
[55] *Daily Picayune*, December 12, 1850.

years."[56]

Although most fugitives ran away alone, 6 percent of all runaways reported ran off with one or more other persons. Of these 6 percent, 78 percent were rural. Urban slaves were much more likely to try to escape alone. This fact is not surprising. City slaves were often skilled and acculturated persons accustomed to a great degree of mobility. One historian has found that these bondsmen almost always ran off alone and attempted to pass themselves as free; rural slaves, however, tended to run away in groups and often were merely truants.[57]

Four women were reported as having run away with their children, including one bilingual slave woman named "Indian Fanny," who fled with her five-year-old child.[58] Of all advertisements for fugitive women, none are listed as having run away without their children. Two siblings, Lewis and Elizabeth, ages eight and seven, respectively, were also listed as having fled together.[59] Women with children and children running away together were not very successful. Two of the four women who ran off with their children, and both Lewis and Elizabeth were listed as "detained."

Several male slaves ran off in groups of two or more. Two ingenious slaves, a mulatto named Dennis and a Negro named Cornelius, boarded the steamboat *Shamrock*; once on board Dennis passed for a free man and claimed Cornelius as his slave.[60] Two runaway groups of two men each had been recently purchased from Decatur County, Georgia, and Maryland, respectively, and were believed to be trying to return to their former homes.[61]

In some instances, one slave who ran away seemed to encourage other bondsmen owned by the same slaveholder to follow his example. One New Orleans slaveowner advertised for three male fugitives: Charles, age forty, a mason, who had run away in May 1850; James, age thirty, a seller of beer, who left on June 7, 1850; and Louis, age thirty, also a seller of beer, who ran away on June 14, 1850.[62] The owner of the New Orleans Levee Steam Cotton Press advertised for two of his slaves, Michael Evans and James Williams,

[56] *Daily Delta*, December 3, 1850.
[57] Gerald W. Mullin, *Flight and Rebellion: Slave Resistance in Eighteenth-Century Virginia* (New York, 1972), 36, 56, 106.
[58] *Daily True Delta*, August 29, 1850.
[59] *Daily Orleanian*, November 5, 1850.
[60] *Daily Picayune*, June 16, 1850.
[61] *Ibid.*, December 12, 1850; *Weekly Delta*, February 11, 1850.
[62] *Bee*, June 17, 1850.

who ran away on December 29, 1849, and January 21, 1850, respectively.[63] This same owner placed another notice in April 1850 for his runaway slave Louis Johnson, a mason; he stated that since "two of the best boys belonging to the Company have been enticed away, and got on boats bound for England it is feared that the above named boy, Louis Johnson, is secreted on board of some vessel cleared on Saturday or about leaving port."[64] Before the middle of August 1850 Robert A. Wilkinson placed an advertisement for four slaves who had left his plantation and were believed to be heading for New Orleans; by the end of August he was advertising for one more.[65] According to the advertisements in the New Orleans newspapers a mulatto named Amos ran away from Hewitt and Heran's plantation near Donaldsonville in August 1850; in September he was followed by two slave men from the same plantation, one of whom was Giles, age twenty-two and of "high, copper color." Giles's owner stated that his slave would "perhaps deny his master and change his name."[66] One slave woman, Julia, of "genteel appearance," apparently ran away to join her fugitive husband. Her owner stated that she "will probably try to make her way to Cincinnati, to which place her husband lately escaped."[67]

The survey of 1850 advertisements shows one and possibly two slave husbands and wives ran away together. The more unusual of the two notices stated that two slaves, a "boy," July, and a "small woman," Rhoda, had escaped in a small boat. Their owner, J. A. Kelly of Bayou Sara, declared that they would "pass for man and wife but may change their names, as well as misrepresent who is their owner." If caught in New Orleans, Kelly wanted July and Rhoda to be "put in the chain gang."[68]

One whole slave family ran away, "induced to leave by a hope of escape to a free State where they have been lately preceded by a valuable seamstress Julia, the property of the same gentleman." This family consisted of Kitty, age thirty, a "delicately formed black woman . . . of intelligent, pleasant quiet look and manners"; Papsons, her husband, age thirty-five, of "demure sensible look; a

[63] Daily Picayune, January 27, 1850.
[64] Ibid., April 4, 1850.
[65] Ibid., August 10, 31, 1850.
[66] Ibid., August 7, September 11, 1850.
[67] Ibid., May 18, 1850.
[68] Ibid., June 30, 1850. July and Rhoda may have been husband and wife, mother and son, father and daughter, sister and brother, or merely friends. It is impossible to determine whether the term "boy" should be taken literally; often "boy" was used in newspaper advertisements to describe any black man, even one who was quite elderly.

cook"; their son Henry, age ten, who had a "shrewd, active cunning look"; and Georgiana, their daughter, age six or seven, a "handsome black child, not otherwise remarkable."[69]

Several owners knew or believed that their runaway slaves were "lurking" in New Orleans. (Fugitive slaves were generally not "in" the city, but "lurking" about it.) Thom, a cooper, who ran away from a plantation on Grand Isle, was said by his owner to be "no doubt lurking in the rear of the city, where he has been seen several times."[70] Several newspaper advertisements for slave women stated that bondswomen were "harbored" in New Orleans, one by a free Negro who planned to accompany her to the West, another by a white man who gave the slave woman a forged pass.[71] Eliza, a bilingual fugitive, was "supposed to be harbored by some members of the negro church . . ."; Ellen or Edy, a domestic who spoke French and understood German, was believed by her owner to be "concealed by some black people."[72] Probably the most interesting instance of a "harbored" female is that of Frances, who was bought from E. Creswell, a slave dealer, seven weeks before the runaway advertisement appeared in the newspapers. The new owner believed that a "certain individual" (possibly Creswell himself) was harboring her and would send her up the river or across the lake.[73]

Eight percent of all the fugitive slave advertisements that appeared in the New Orleans newspapers in 1850 show special planning on the part of the runaways. As has already been indicated above, several planned to escape to a free state.[74] One runaway took

[69] *Bee,* August 8, 1850.
[70] Many fugitives had no firm destination in mind when they absented themselves and often never left the city. Hepler, "Negroes and Crime," 71; *Daily Picayune,* April 13, 1850.
[71] Harboring a fugitive or even allowing a slave to sleep in the home of a free person of color was strictly forbidden by law. Donald E. Everett, "Legislation Concerning Free Persons of Color in Orleans Parish" (unpublished M.A. thesis, Tulane University, 1950), 127. Laws against harboring slaves were rarely enforced. Hepler, "Negroes and Crime," 73; *Daily Picayune,* April 7, May 22, 1850. It was not uncommon for free blacks to give aid to runaway slaves. Sterkx, *The Free Negro,* 280; *Daily Picayune,* May 22, 1850. White southerners often aided fugitives by hiding them. Reddick, "The Negro in the New Orleans Press," 138.
[72] *Daily Delta,* November 5, 13, 1850.
[73] *Daily Picayune,* July 7, 1850. This type of fraud was not uncommon in the South. Reddick, "The Negro in the New Orleans Press," 134. Several large slave traders had farms north of New Orleans. If the stock of slaves was not sold by the beginning of the summer, the traders sent the remaining slaves out of the city to avoid the hazards of the summer illnesses common to New Orleans. John S. Kendall, "Shadow over the City," *Louisiana Historical Quarterly,* XXII (January 1939), 153.
[74] For example see *Daily Picayune,* December 5, 1850; *Weekly Delta,* January 15, 1850; *L'Abeille,* August 8, 1850.

with him a fine "bay American horse."[75] Several slaves had false passes with them when they departed.[76] A fugitive named Pierre, who was trilingual and "fond of circus and theater," left with both a false pass and banknotes.[77] A few slave women took clothing with them, the most enterprising of whom was Martha, who left with five "frocks and a Leghorn bonnet, trimmed with red, and blue ostrich feathers."[78] Another fugitive, Mary, took a large quantity of wearing apparel and bedding as well.[79] A few owners thought that their runaway slaves would change their names and that of their masters.[80] Some owners stated that their slaves would attempt to pass themselves as free;[81] and one owner thought his slave would attempt to pass herself for white and free.[82] In a city like New Orleans with a substantial free black population and a white population of varying shades of complexion, such hunches could very well have been true.

A few advertisements for fugitive slaves inadvertently revealed their owners' cruelty. Two men ran away with iron rings or chains on their legs.[83] Another slave ran with a gunshot wound,[84] and several were reported to be "badly marked from [an] old whipping."[85]

Of all of the advertisements for runaway slaves in the New Orleans newspapers in 1850, over 11.5 percent of the fugitives were reported by their owners or jailers as having some type of speech problem. Of these, 32 percent were rural runaways. More than one in four of all country runaways were listed as having some difficulty in oral communication. Nearly all of these were males. The percentage of fugitives with verbal difficulties was probably much higher since "detained" advertisements rarely describe the speech of those

[75] *Daily Picayune,* January 4, 1850.

[76] For example see *Daily Picayune,* May 19, December 5, 1850. Forged passes were a common deception used by fugitive slaves. Sterkx, *The Free Negro,* 153. Slaves were prohibited by law from carrying forged passes but were often not punished if caught. Hepler, "Negroes and Crime," 69.

[77] *Daily Picayune,* May 7, 1850.

[78] *Ibid.,* March 22, 1850.

[79] *Ibid.,* July 2, 1850.

[80] *Weekly Delta,* July 15, 1850; *Bee,* June 1, 1850.

[81] For example see *Daily Picayune,* January 5, April 26, August 3, 1850. Attempting to pass as free was a common ploy of fugitive slaves. Sterkx, *The Free Negro,* 150–51.

[82] *Daily Picayune,* October 22, 1850. Passing for white in New Orleans, with its olive-skinned whites of French and Spanish ancestry, would be easier than in most southern cities. Berlin, *Slaves Without Masters,* 161, 164.

[83] *Bee,* January 14, 1850; *Daily Orleanian,* July 18, 1850.

[84] *Daily Picayune,* August 20, 1850. Louisiana law permitted shooting any runaway slave who refused to stop when ordered to do so. Stampp, *The Peculiar Institution,* 213.

[85] *Daily Delta,* October 15, 1850.

jailed. These findings conflict with those of Gerald Mullin. He found that the slave in eighteenth-century Virginia most likely to have speech difficulties was the acculturated, skilled slave.[86]

The most common problems were that the fugitive was "confused when addressed sharply."[87] This description was often coupled with "has a downcast look" or speaks "in a low tone," or "speaks slow," or "speaks little."[88] Several slaves, all males, were described as stuttering or stammering when spoken to or when excited.[89] Shedrick, who ran from St. James Parish, had such acute anxiety that he was described as "stammering a little" but giving "neither his name not his master's name."[90]

Thirteen percent of all runaway slaves advertised for in the New Orleans newspapers of 1850 were either bilingual or spoke three or four languages (the percentage was probably much higher as "detained" notices were not detailed). These fugitive slaves who spoke more than one language were nearly evenly divided between men and women. For example, a mulatto woman named Suzan spoke English, French, and German;[91] Henry, a "bright mulatto" who had been employed at the New Orleans *Bee,* spoke English, French, and Choctaw.[92]

A few advertisements for runaway slave women were so unique that they defy quantification. Elizabeth, a trilingual slave who formerly belonged to a "free man of color,"[93] was described by her new owner as having a "bad look."[94] Another woman fugitive was described as "ugly" and "pregnant."[95] Aimee, a quadroon, was described by her owner as having "beautiful teeth, fine auburn hair, white eyelids, and has the appearance of a German girl." Her owner offered the exceptionally high reward of two hundred dollars for her.[96] Perhaps the most extraordinary 1850 runaway advertisement

[86] Mullin, *Flight and Rebellion,* 98.
[87] For example see *Daily True Delta,* May 10, 1850; *Daily Picayune,* May 11, 1850.
[88] For example see *Daily Picayune,* September 27 (first quotation), June 6 (fourth quotation), March 7, 1850 (third quotation); *Bee,* August 14, 1850 (second quotation).
[89] *Bee,* May 14, 1850; *Daily Picayune,* January 18, February 15, 1850. Stuttering shows fear, but also anger, resentment, and hostility, emotions one could expect to find in a runaway slave. Genovese, *Roll, Jordan, Roll,* 647.
[90] *Le Courrier,* July 13, 1850.
[91] *Bee,* February 14, 1850.
[92] *Ibid.,* December 9, 1850.
[93] *L'Abeille,* June 7, 1850. Free persons of color who were slaveowners were often cruel. Everett, "Legislation Concerning Free Persons of Color," 129. See also Sterkx, *The Free Negro,* 281.
[94] *Bee,* June 7, 1850.
[95] *Ibid.,* April 22, 1850.
[96] *Ibid.,* May 31, 1850.

for a runaway slave woman was for Marie Amelie, a mulatto with "a prepossessing appearance," "wild looks," "and the scar of a wound inflicted with a whip near the left eye." This slave woman was elegantly dressed in a flowered gown, "a silk shawl with red trimmings, and a small garnet ring mounted with gold."[97] Aimee and Marie Amelie were most probably "fancy girls" or were mistresses of their owners.

Several unusual notices for fugitive men also appeared in the New Orleans newspapers in 1850. One eighteen-year-old slave, whose back was "scarred from flogging," was caught when he secreted himself between the cylinder timbers of a steamboat.[98] Another "intelligent" slave who could read, write, and "understands figures" ran away, his master supposed, to California. This slave showed no signs of physical abuse and his apparently bewildered and uncomprehending owner stated that he ran away "without provocation."[99] Tim, age twenty-eight, was well dressed, had bored ears, and wore "a silver watch and a five dollar gold piece for a breastpin."[100] Another interesting runaway slave named Robert had an "impudent look" and a light complexion, "but he blackens his face to disguise himself."[101] Another owner stated that his fugitive slave Austin Fox had been a stevedore but also played the fiddle and was to be found about cabarets.[102] And finally, at least one owner had a slave who often became a fugitive. This slaveholder stated that his slave's usual occupation as a runaway was that of a chimney sweep.[103]

A survey of both sale and runaway advertisements of the New Orleans newspapers of 1850 shows that the overwhelming majority of all fugitive slaves and slaves for sale had ordinary American or French first names, such as Tom or Etienne, Sally or Marie.[104] A tiny proportion had stereotypical slave names such as Sukey or Sambo; a few had pretentious names such as Cato, Moliere, Voltaire, Othello, and Ophelia; one can find a few ironic names such as

[97] *Ibid.*, February 1, 1850.
[98] *Commercial Bulletin*, March 7, 1850.
[99] *Daily Picayune*, July 7, 1850. This complaint was common in advertisements by slaveowners. Stampp, *The Peculiar Institution*, 111.
[100] *Daily Picayune*, April 14, 1850.
[101] *Le Courrier*, January 4, 1850.
[102] *Daily Picayune*, September 22, 1850.
[103] *Bee*, July 11, 1850.
[104] Classical or whimsical names appeared much less frequently than has been formerly believed. Genovese, *Roll, Jordan, Roll*, 448. By the middle of the nineteenth century nearly all slaves had common Anglo-Saxon names. Gutman, *The Black Family*, 186.

White, Prince, and Queen. A small number were named for months of the year, days of the week, or a feast day, such as Janvier (January), Monday, and Easter, perhaps a conscious (or unconscious) survival of African day names.[105] A few slaves were named for political figures or national heroes such as Henry Clay (a child of five years),[106] and one owner named his slave Profit, a revealing admission.[107] Five percent of all runaways and a few for sale had an alias or alternate first name (mostly men).[108] Seven percent of all runaways and a few slaves for sale were stated to have last names. The most notable of these were Jacques Congo and John American.[109] Probably there were many other slaves who used last names, which either were not mentioned or were not known to their owners. In only one instance was the last name taken by the slave that of his owner.[110]

The color of the slave for sale or the fugitive was often mentioned in the newspaper notices. The figures (in approximate percentages) are analyzed in Tables 7 and 8 (a griff was a term which meant the offspring of a mulatto and a Negro). One can see that those slaves who ran away tended to be lighter in color, and those who were sold tended to be blacker. The lighter colored slaves were probably more skilled and had a better chance to pass as free or white.[111]

Fifteen percent of all fugitive slave notices stated that the runaway possessed a nondomestic skill. The overwhelming majority of these were men. Probably many more were skilled, but the advertisements were often not descriptive enough to mention a skill. The

[105] For example see *Le Courrier*, April 17, October 5, December 18, 1850; *Daily Orleanian*, September 26, 1850. Although Genovese states that slaves were often named for days of the week or months of the year (Genovese, *Roll, Jordan, Roll*, 448), Gutman contends that only a few bondsmen had West African day names. Gutman, *The Black Family*, 186.

[106] *Le Courrier*, January 11, 1850.

[107] *Daily Orleanian*, September 22, 1850.

[108] For example see *Le Courrier*, April 23, 1850 (two instances).

[109] *Ibid.*, March 12, December 28, 1850.

[110] *Ibid.*, July 12, 1850. Sometimes masters gave their slaves surnames, but more often slaves chose their own last names without their owners' permission and often without their knowledge. Genovese, *Roll, Jordan, Roll*, 445.

[111] Sterkx has found that most fugitive slaves were mulattoes or lighter colors. Sterkx, *The Free Negro*, 150-51. However, Stampp finds that most runaways under thirty (in New Orleans the majority of the fugitives) were not of predominantly white ancestry. Stampp, *The Peculiar Institution*, 110. Unfortunately, it is not possible to compare these data with the overall black-mulatto composition of the New Orleans population in 1850, as these categories are not listed in the census of 1850. U. S. Bureau of the Census, *Negro Population, 1790-1915* (Washington, 1918), 211. However, one historian states that in the decade before the Civil War blacks outnumbered mulattoes in the New Orleans slave population, while mulattoes were more prevalent in the free black population. Reinders, "Slavery in New Orleans," 213.

TABLE 7
RUNAWAYS BY COLOR AND SEX

	Male		Female	
Color	*Number*	*Percent*	*Number*	*Percent*
Mulatto	56	20.9	40	30.3
Griff	126	47.0	54	40.9
Black	86	32.1	38	28.8
Total	268	100.0	132	100.0

TABLE 8
SALES OF SLAVES BY COLOR AND SEX

	Male		Female	
Color	*Number*	*Percent*	*Number*	*Percent*
Mulatto	32	19.8	46	17.8
Griff	24	14.8	27	10.4
Black	106	65.4	186	71.8
Total	162	100.0	259	100.0

TABLE 9
SALES OF SLAVES BY SKILL

		Male		Female	
Skill	*Total*	*Number*	*Percent*	*Number*	*Percent*
Domestic	302	66	21.9	236	78.1
Nondomestic	157	149	94.9	8	5.1

existence of a large number of acculturated skilled males concurs with the findings of Gerald Mullin, who concluded that such slaves were most likely to run away.[112] This pattern is striking in the sale advertisements that mention a skill (see Table 9). Skilled slaves were often mechanics, crate layers, pastry cooks, draymen, shoemakers, shirt makers, printing office rollers, carters, blacksmiths, coopers, engineers, masons, clerks (in stores), carpenters, mattress makers, cotton weighers, locksmiths, waiters, cigar makers, railroad laborers, plasterers, barbers, tailors, firemen, boilermakers, house painters, and brass molders as well as those with the usual domestic skills.[113]

[112] This preponderance of skilled males is not surprising. After all, southern cities offered few opportunities for lucrative employment for women of any color. Berlin, *Slaves Without Masters,* 220; Mullin, *Flight and Rebellion,* 36. Another historian states that the most intelligent and accomplished slaves were most likely to attempt to escape. Woessner, "New Orleans, 1840–1860," 47.

[113] For example see *L'Abeille,* November 2, 7, 1850; *Le Courrier,* January 19, May 31, 1850.

Nearly 15 percent of all male runaway notices and 32 percent of all female fugitive advertisements indicate that the slave had a health problem of one type or another.[114] The most common problems for both sexes were missing or decayed teeth, lameness, or some other difficulty in walking, although fugitive health problems included drunkenness, insanity, hernias, and tumors.[115] The physical and mental condition of slaves for sale is much more difficult to assess because vendors naturally tended to stress good features of their slaves, such as intelligence or good disposition, rather than any aspects which would make the slave less salable. Despite this fact, several slaves for sale were advertised as having a variety of diseases and conditions, including drunkenness, mental derangement, fistulas, chlorosis (liver dysfunction), scrofula (tuberculosis of the lymph glands), epilepsy, or asthma, or they are simply described as "sickly."[116]

Slaves for sale were never described as being scarred or burned, but 12 percent of all fugitive men and nearly 14 percent of all fugitive women were described by their owners as bearing these marks. Although occupational accidents were common among slaves, the owners' seeming compulsion to explain away the scars[117] must mean that some of these marks were not accidentally inflicted, or at least a newspaper reader might be expected to believe otherwise because such signs of mistreatment were common. A comment such as "scar on the forehead . . . caused by a kick from a mule . . ."[118] was common.

An examination of the classified notices in New Orleans's nine daily newspapers of 1850 revealed only two evidences of slave emancipation.[119] The first, published under "City Intelligence," listed

[114] One historian claimed that in 1855 only 7 to 8 percent of all slaves were physically impaired or chronically ill according to succession records. William D. Postell, *The Health of Slaves on Southern Plantations* (Baton Rouge, 1951), 160.

[115] For example see *Daily Picayune*, June 6, 7, 1850. Mental and nervous disorders were not uncommon among slaves. Dietary deficiencies often caused diseases such as pellagra, which resulted in lameness. Postell, *The Health of Slaves*, 85, 87. See also Kenneth F. and Virginia H. Kiple, "Black Tongue and Black Men: Pellagra and Slavery in the Antebellum South," *Journal of Southern History*, XLIII (August 1977), 411-28.

[116] For example see *L'Abeille*, November 27, 1850; *Le Courrier*, January 15, February 5, 14, December 18, 1850. Tuberculosis was more common among slaves than has been formerly believed. Postell, *The Health of Slaves*, 79-80.

[117] After abolitionists became outraged by references in southern newspapers to obvious abuses of the slaves allusions to whip marks decreased, and notices referring to scars and burns increased. Stampp, *The Peculiar Institution*, 187; Mullin, *Flight and Rebellion*, 98, 25.

[118] *Daily Picayune*, March 7, 1850.

[119] For a complete discussion of New Orleans emancipation laws and manumission in New Orleans see Donald E. Everett, "Free Persons of Color in New Orleans, 1803-1865" (unpublished Ph.D. dissertation, Tulane University, 1953), 132-66.

thirty owners emancipating thirty-nine slaves. Since many of those freed were by admission children or wives of the slaveholder, it is presumed that these owners were free blacks who had purchased their wives, husbands, or children and then manumitted them.[120] The second instance appeared in an auction notice for the sale of two slave girls, ages fourteen and twelve, and two slave boys, ages fourteen and eight. This auction was held to settle a succession and stipulated that the slaves were to be freed at twenty-one under the terms of the will of the deceased. They were being sold for their service only until they reached that age.[121]

New Orleans newspaper advertisements of 1850 reflect almost every conceivable abuse of the slave and few mitigating circumstances,[122] yet they also confirm that a few remarkable slave men and women managed to have a viable family life, acquire literacy, and plan ingenious escapes. Most of all, this study revealed that while slaves in New Orleans in 1850 might have been declining in numbers, the peculiar institution was nevertheless firmly entrenched in the city's society and economy.

[120] *Le Courrier*, January 14, 1850. Sixty-four slaves were manumitted in New Orleans between January 7, 1850, and August 28, 1851. Hepler, "Negroes and Crime," 104. Of the 1,353 petitions for emancipation submitted to the New Orleans courts between 1827 and 1851, 501 were made by free blacks. Blassingame, *Black New Orleans*, 11.

[121] *Le Courrier*, May 3, 1850 (Succession of Roch Salles). It was illegal to emancipate a slave under the age of thirty. Obviously, this law was at least occasionally ignored. Everett, "Free Persons of Color," 132.

[122] One historian contends that, despite claims in earlier historical writings, "Louisiana's Latin heritage failed to soften slavery, encourage manumission, and foster egalitarian race relations." David C. Rankin, "The Tannenbaum Thesis Reconsidered: Slavery and Race Relations in Antebellum Louisiana," *Southern Studies*, XVIII (Spring 1979), 31.

By Robert S. Starobin
ASSISTANT PROFESSOR OF HISTORY
UNIVERSITY OF WISCONSIN, MADISON

The Economics of Industrial Slavery
In the Old South

❮ *The economics of slavery in the United States has long been a subject of great interest to historians, but the use of bondsmen in southern industries has been little studied. Professor Starobin not only provides new information on industrial slavery, but also offers important conclusions concerning the profitability, efficiency, and viability of this "peculiar institution."*

From the pre-Civil War period until the present day, historians and economists have offered theories and evidence regarding the extent and profitability of southern plantation slavery.[1] After all, if slavery was not economically viable, would not slaveholders have abandoned their "peculiar institution?" Was a bloody civil war necessary if slavery was dying of its own weight? Obviously, the moral question of chattel slavery far transcends economics. But since economic arguments were so prominent in the slavery controversy, then and now, objective analyses of their form, substance, and verity are worthwhile.

Curiously, and despite its political and social significance, scholars have devoted little attention to either the extent to which slave labor was employed in industries in the Old South or to the economic feasibility of such employment. This article is the core of a larger study intended to pose and explore these questions.[2]

THE EXTENT OF INDUSTRIAL SLAVERY

Southern industry's most distinctive aspect was its wide and intensive use of slave labor. In the 1850's, for example, 160,000 to

Business History Review, Vol. XLIV, No. 2 (Summer, 1970). Copyright © The President and Fellows of Harvard College.

[1] H. D. Woodman, "The Profitability of Slavery," *Journal of Southern History*, XXIX (1963), 303–325; S. L. Engerman, "The Effects of Slavery Upon the Southern Economy," *Explorations in Entrepreneurial History*," second series, IV (1967), 71–97.

[2] See *Industrial Slavery in the Old South* (New York, Oxford University Press, 1970), which is based on my doctoral dissertation of the same title, done at the University of California, Berkeley, in 1968. These works contain a full discussion of the use of slaves in southern industries, 1790–1861; working and living conditions; black resistance to bondage and work routines; means of control of slave workers; relations between black and white laborers; and the political relationship of slave-based industrialization to the coming of the Civil War.

200,000 — about 5 per cent of the total slave population — worked in industry. About four-fifths of these industrial slaves were directly owned by industrial entrepreneurs; the rest were rented by employers from their masters by the month or year. Most were men, but many were women and children. They lived in rural, small-town or plantation settings, where most southern industry was located, not in large cities, where only about 20 per cent of the urban slaves were industrially employed.[3]

Many southern textile mills employed either slave labor or combined both bondsmen and free workers in the same mill, contradicting the myth that southern textile manufacturing was the sole domain of native poor whites. The manufacture of iron was also heavily dependent on slave labor, and southern tobacco factories employed slave labor almost exclusively. Slave labor was crucial to hemp manufacturing, and most secondary manufacturing — shoe factories, tanneries, bakeries, paper-makers, printing establishments, and brickmakers — used bondsmen extensively. Sugar refining, rice milling, and grist-milling together employed about 30,000 slaves. At ports and river towns, slaves operated mammoth cotton presses to recompress cotton bales for overseas shipment.

The southern coal and iron mining industry was greatly dependent upon slave labor, gold was mined throughout the Piedmont and Appalachian regions largely with slaves, and lead mining employed many bondsmen. Salt was produced with slave labor; slaves were used to log the pine, cypress, and live-oak in the swamps and forests from Texas to Virginia; and the turpentine extraction and distillation industry was entirely dependent upon slave labor. Southern internal improvements enterprises were so dependent upon slave labor that virtually all southern railroads, except for a few border-state lines, were built either by slave-employing contractors or by company-owned or hired bondsmen. Most southern canals

[3] This figure has been computed from tables on urban slave population in 1850 in Richard Wade, *Slavery in the Cities* (New York, 1964), 30 and appendix; J.D.B. De Bow, *Statistical View of the United States . . . Being a Compendium of the Seventh Census* (Washington, 1850), 94, estimated that about 400,000 slaves lived in southern cities and towns in 1850, while Kenneth Stampp, *The Peculiar Institution* (New York, 1956), 60, estimates that the *total* city, town, and non-agricultural slave population was about 500,000 in 1860. If two-thirds of the *male* population of towns *and* cities was engaged in industrial enterprises and occupations, then the 160,000 to 200,000, or 5 per cent, figure seems approximately correct for the years 1850 to 1860. See tables in my dissertation for some large slaveholdings by deep-South industries. For further estimates, see J. C. Sitterson, *Sugar Country* (Lexington, 1953); J. F. Hopkins, *A History of the Hemp Industry in Kentucky* (Lexington, 1951); J. C. Robert, *Tobacco Kingdom* (Durham, 1938); C. Eaton, *Growth of Southern Civilization* (New York, 1961), 64–65, 134–35, 99–101, and ch. 10; K. Bruce, *Virginia Iron Manufacture in the Slave Era* (New York, 1930); and S. Lebergott, "Labor Force and Employment, 1800–1860," National Bureau of Economic Research, *Output, Employment, and Productivity in the United States After 1800* (New York, 1966), XXX, 117–210.

and navigation improvements were excavated by slave labor, and most other southern transportation facilities — turnpikes, plank roads, ferries, keelboats, and steamboats — were dependent upon slave work forces.

Though little studied, the reliance of municipalities, states, and even the federal government upon slave labor to build public works throughout the South was important. Slaves commonly cleaned and repaired the streets of towns and cities, and some states required the annual service of slaves to build roads and levees and to clear rivers and harbors. Other states purchased or hired slaves to construct state-controlled levees, canals, and railroads. Agencies and departments of the federal government were deeply involved in the industrial use of hundreds of slave hirelings, and only reluctantly disassociated themselves from this practice. Slave stone-quarriers and common laborers helped erect the first national capitol at Washington and participated in its reconstruction after the War of 1812. Slaves manned government dredge boats, and federal fortifications, naval installations, and arsenals also frequently used slaves.[4]

The wide use of industrial slaves by state and federal agencies suggests not only the centrality of industrial slavery to the southern economy, but also the extent of southern control of the national political structure. That private enterprise also relied greatly on slave labor suggests the dependence of the private economic sector upon slavery as well as the determination of Southerners to use that labor system most advantageous to their program of economic development.

THE ECONOMICS OF INDUSTRIAL SLAVERY

To study the economics of industrial slavery requires the consideration of several questions. First, could slave-employing industries expect to earn reasonably profitable rates of return on their capital investments? In this analysis, "profit rate" means either the annual dividend paid on common stock or the annual net income expressed as a percentage of the net worth of the industrial enterprise. A "reasonably profitable investment" means at least a 6 per cent annual return on capital — the average rate of return on other forms of investment.[5]

Second, was industrial slavery *generally* as efficient and as eco-

[4] Starobin, *Industrial Slavery*, ch. 1.
[5] H. O. Stekler, *Profitability and Size of Firm* (Berkeley, 1963), ch. 1 and 2; A. H. Conrad and J. R. Meyer, *The Economics of Slavery* (Chicago, 1964), ch. 3.

nomical as an alternative labor system? Were slaves as efficient as free whites? Was slave labor — directly owned or hired — less expensive to employ than free labor? Did slave labor entail higher capital and maintenance costs than free labor?

Third, were there *specific* competitive advantages to industrial slavery — that is, did the use of slaves enable southerners to compete with the North and with Britain, where industrialization had progressed further? Did the exploitation of slave women and children, the training of slave managers, and the coupling of common slaves with skilled foreign technicians enable southern industries to reduce their costs and to raise their quality in order to become competitive in national market places?

Fourth, what were the sources of capital for slave-based industries? Did southerners have sufficient investment capital to support industries? Did the funding of industries with slave capital have a detrimental effect on financial structures by reducing the flexibility of capital and the mobility of labor? [6]

THE PROFITABILITY OF INDUSTRIAL SLAVERY

Under normal operating conditions, slave-employing industries and transportation projects could expect to earn reasonable profits

[6] U. B. Phillips, "The Economic Cost of Slave-holding in the Cotton Belt," *Political Science Quarterly*, XX (1905), 257–75, U. B. Phillips, *American Negro Slavery* (New York, 1918), especially chs. 18 and 19; C. W. Ramsdell, "The Natural Limits of Slavery Expansion," *Mississippi Valley Historical Review*, XVI (1929), 151–71; E. D. Genovese, "The Significance of the Plantation for Southern Economic Development," *Journal of Southern History*, XXVIII (1962), 422–37; E. D. Genovese, *The Political Economy of Slavery* (New York, 1965); D. North, *The Economic Growth of the United States, 1790–1860* (Englewood Cliffs, 1961), esp. 132. Cf. R. R. Russel, "The General Effects of Slavery Upon Southern Economic Progress," *Journal of Southern History*, IV (1938), 34–54, and "The Effects of Slavery Upon Non-Slaveholders in the Ante-Bellum South," *Agricultural History*, XV (1941), 112–26, and *Economic Aspects of Southern Sectionalism* (Urbana, 1924); D. Dowd, "A Comparative Analysis of Economic Development in the American West and South," *Journal of Economic History*, XVI (1956), 558–74; Wade, *Slavery in the Cities*, esp. chs. 1 and 9, argues that slavery was dying in the largest southern cities and thus tends to lend weight to the old Ramsdell hypothesis.

Certain theoretical and methodological problems also should be noted. While the above questions are obviously interrelated, an affirmative answer to one of them does not necessarily imply an affirmative answer to the others. Much confusion has resulted from a failure to distinguish the differences between the questions. Precise analysis of the economics of industrial slavery is also difficult, since information on the sources of finance, the capital cost and maintenance of labor, and the profits of enterprise is scarce. Available statistics are unsatisfactory because not all businesses kept records and only a few fragmentary accounts have survived. Those that have do not necessarily constitute representative samples of non-agricultural enterprises, since most records pertain to large establishments, and it is not certain whether small industrial operators were as successful as large ones. Moreover, the data on costs of labor and rates of profit is often unclear because of the peculiarities of antebellum accounting and the difficulty of finding long-term statistical series. Company reports tended to underestimate expenses and to exaggerate earnings to promote southern enterprise, while official censuses were haphazardly taken and must be used cautiously. Prices varied, while business cycles caused fluctuating profit rates and frequent bankruptcies. Variables such as location, luck, competition, and caliber of management also make computations of the profitability of industrial slavery difficult for those slave-employing industries whose records survive.

on their capital investments. Some enterprises failed, of course, but most industrial entrepreneurs employing slave labor enjoyed highly satisfactory rates of return on their investments. Most slave-employing enterprises whose records are available matched or exceeded an annual rate of return of about 6 per cent.

The records of southern textile mills employing slave labor indicate that they usually earned annual profits on capital ranging from 10 to 65 per cent and averaging about 16 per cent. The DeKalb, Martin & Weekly, Roswell, and Tuscaloosa textile companies, to give but four examples, annually paid between 10 and 20 per cent. The Woodville mill, which went bankrupt with free labor, annually paid 10 to 15 per cent dividends after switching to slave labor. "The Saluda Manufacturing Company . . . is doing a flourishing business . . . [and] pays large dividends," ran a report of one slave-employing cotton mill (see Table 1).

The available records of southern iron works employing slaves suggest further that substantial profits could be made in this industry. As early as 1813, one slaveowning iron manufacturer reportedly could "afford to work as cheap as others, and always do so but not at an under rate." From 1835 to 1845, a Mobile iron foundry made 25 per cent annually; during the 1850's, a South Carolina iron works earned 7 per cent yearly. The famous Tredegar Iron Company averaged annually better than 20 per cent returns from 1844 to 1861.[7]

Other kinds of manufacturing and processing enterprises employing slave labor evidently earned similar profit rates. One hemp manufacturer testified that he realized more than 42 per cent profits per annum in the 1840's. A tannery reported 10 per cent yearly between 1831 and 1845. A gas works also earned a 10 per cent return in 1854.[8] According to official reports, most Louisiana sugar mills earned better than 7 per cent returns in 1830 and almost 11 per cent in 1845. During the 1850's, a cotton press made 10 per cent; the Haxall Flour Mills of Richmond reportedly "made large fortunes for their owners for over half a century."[9]

Similarly, slave-employing enterprises in the extractive industries

[7] D. Ross to J. Staples, Sept. 16, 1813, Ross Letterbook (Virginia Historical Society, hereafter cited as VHS); De Bow's Review, VI (1848), 295; Charleston Mercury, February 18, 1859; Tredegar Stockholders' Minutebook, reports for 1838–48, and Tredegar Corporate Holdings, 1866, 7–9 (Virginia State Library, hereafter cited as VSL).
[8] Report of Court of Claims, #81, 34 C., 3 s., 1857, 62–64; L. McLane, Documents of Manufactures, House Doc. #308, 22 C., 1 s., 1832, 676–77; New Orleans Picayune, January 2, 1853.
[9] Niles' Register, XXXIX (1830), 271–72; F. L. Olmsted, A Journey in the Seaboard Slave States (New York, 1861), 686–88; Report of the Secretary of the Treasury, House Exec. Doc. #6, 29 C., 1 s., 1845, 708–09, 748; J. G. Taylor, Slavery in Louisiana (Baton Rouge, 1963), 96–101; Sitterson, Sugar Country, 157–66, 178–84, 197, and passim.

generally made handsome profits. Though one turpentine manufacturer "believed sincerely that no money can be made at the business while labour is so extremely high," in the 1850's, turpentine enterprises in North Carolina and Georgia did achieve satisfactory returns. In 1850, *De Bow's Review* proclaimed that "compared to other labor, this [turpentining] has, for the last ten years, been deemed the most profitable of all." The profitability of lumbering is suggested by one Louisiana woodyard that annually earned 12.5 to 25 per cent returns between 1846 and 1850. In addition, the Dismal Swamp Land Company reportedly "realized almost fabulous proceeds from the timber," while a Carolinian maintained that "I have no doubt from all I have heard . . . that more money can be made in this business [West Florida lumbering] than any other when [slave] manual labor is used." Fisheries usually earned at "a level with the ordinary industrial pursuits of the country," though "enormous profits" were "sometimes realized." [10]

Most southern mining enterprises employing bondsmen also earned substantial profits. As early as 1807, the Missouri lead-smelter Frederick Bates declared that "few labors or pursuits in the U. States, yield such *ample*, such *vast* returns — A slave, with a *Pick* and *Shovel* is supposed to do nothing, if the nett proceeds of his labor, do not amount, annually, to the sum of 400 dollars — the price which his master probably paid for him." Later, Bates added: "You will see [in my letter to Albert Gallatin] the vast profits arising from the prosecution of this lucrative business." Official records indicate that between 1834 and 1845, several Key West salt works earned 8 per cent annually. Many southern gold seekers failed, to be sure, but scores of mines were as profitable as, for example, John C. Calhoun's which yielded nearly $1,000,000, and Samuel J. Tilden's which earned $4,000,000. [11]

[10] J. E. Metts to J. R. Grist, December 5, 1858, Grist Papers (Duke University Library, hereafter cited as Duke); letters dated 1854–60, Williams Papers (University of North Carolina Library, hereafter cited as UNC); *De Bow's Review*, VII (1849), 560–62, and XI (1851), 303–05; W. H. Stephenson (ed.), *Isaac Franklin* (Baton Rouge), 1938), 114, 177–80, 213–17; *Harper's Monthly*, XIII (1856), 451, and XIV (1857), 441; J. M. Cheney to E. Bellinger, February 16, 1855, Misc. Mss. (South Carolina Historical Society, hereafter cited as SCHC); C. H. Ambler (ed.), *Correspondence of R.M.T. Hunter*, AHA *Annual Report* (1916), 176–77.

[11] T. M. Marshall (ed.), *Papers of Frederick Bates* (St. Louis, 1926), I, 111–12, 244. For lead mining, see inventory of January 1, 1851, and Will of May 1, 1856, Desloge Papers (Missouri Historical Society, hereafter cited as MoHS); Report on Salt Springs, and Lead and Copper Mines, *House Doc.* #128, 18 C., 1 s., 1824, 20–22, 130–33; Report of Secretary of Treasury, *House Exec. Doc.* #6, 29, C., 1 s., 1845, 660, 664–65; and *Mining Magazine*, 1 (1853), 164–66. For gold mining, see 1828 memo and undated account sheets, Fisher Papers (UNC); High Shoal Gold Mine Records (UNC); letters of 1830–33 and account book, vol. X, 1843, Brown Papers (UNC); Expense Book of S. Burwell and J. Y. Taylor, 1832–39 (UNC); T. G. Clemson to J. C. Calhoun, January 23 and 24, 1843, and T. G. Clemson to P. Calhoun, October 12, 1856, Clemson Papers (Clemson University Library, hereafter cited as Clemson); *Mining Magazine*, XI (1858), 211, and XII (1859–

From the 1790's to 1861, the majority of transportation enterprises employing slaves realized profitable returns. Some southern railroads paid annual dividends as high as 20 per cent, and most other lines averaged about 8 per cent. Some canal companies, such as the Roanoke, did not do as well as most railroads, but others, such as the Louisville & Portland and the Dismal Swamp, paid nearly as well. Plank roads and turnpikes, however, generally did not earn returns greater than 4 per cent on the capital invested (see Tables 2 and 3).

A few unusually complete statistical series for such slave-employing enterprises as sawmilling, steamboating, and gold mining do survive to permit the further computation of the profitability of industrial slavery. As early as 1794, Alexander Telfair's sawmills made him one of Georgia's wealthiest citizens. The Hart Gold Mining Company yielded a similar fortune for another Georgian. The earnings of the *Thomas Jefferson* permitted a Virginia steamboat company to average acceptable dividends between 1833 and 1849.[12]

The surviving records of two rice mills are complete enough so that some idea of the profitability of this industry can be determined. Though it is impossible to separate the profits of rice planting from rice milling, James Hamilton Couper's Georgia rice estate annually averaged 4.1 per cent return on capital between 1833 and 1852, despite his financial losses from natural disasters and from long agricultural experimentation. However, Couper's 4.1 per cent return does not take into account personal expenditures to support his sumptuous living standard and the appreciation of his lands and slaves. Between 1827 and 1841, for example, the plantation appreciated in value as much as 26 per cent; between 1827 and 1845, the slaves multiplied from 380 to about 500 — almost a 20 per cent increase on their original valuation.[13] Couper's average total annual return on capital was therefore greater than 6 per cent. Similarly,

---

60), 365–66; *De Bow's Review*, XII (1852), 542–43; *American Farmer*, series 1, XII (1830), 230; *Hunt's Magazine*, XXXI (1854), 517.

[12] Telfair Account Books, 1794–1861, #s 90, 87, 88, 89, 152, 153, 155, and 156 (Georgia Historical Society, hereafter cited as GHS); Hart Gold Mine Company Accounts, 1855–57, Latimer Plantation Book (University of Georgia Library, hereafter cited as UG); Journal of James River Steamboat Company, 1833–49 (VSL); the Palfrey Account Books, 1842–61 (Louisiana State University Library, hereafter cited as LSU) reveal that Louisiana sugar plantations and mills earned substantial profits.

[13] J. H. Couper Accounts, 1827–52 (University of North Carolina Library, hereafter cited as UNC); the financial statements and reports for Hopeton and Hamilton plantations, 1830's to 1843, 1849, and 1853–65, and J. H. Couper to F. P. Corbin, March 28, 1859, Corbin Papers (New York Public Library, hereafter cited as NYPL) permit the computation of Couper's profits from rice milling beyond the year 1852; T. P. Govan, "Was Plantation Slavery Profitable?" *Journal of Southern History*, VIII (1942), 513–35, demonstrates the profitability of Couper's rice milling enterprise from 1827 to 1852.

the records of the Manigault family's Savannah River rice mills reveal average annual returns of 12 per cent between 1833 and 1839, and 12.2 per cent from 1856 to 1861. The natural increase in the number and value of the Manigaults' bondsmen compensated for losses from three cholera epidemics, the absence of an experienced overseer between 1855 and 1859, a destructive freshet in 1852, and a devastating hurricane in 1854.[14]

The records of those industrial enterprises which hired bondsmen instead of purchasing them outright further reveal that reasonably profitable returns on invested capital could be earned. In such cases, of course, slave hirers computed only the cost of labor against their net income to estimate their profit rate, while slaveowners computed the amount of rent against their investment to estimate their profits for the year. In 1817, Ebenezer Pettigrew noted the expenses and earnings from a hired slave lumberman as follows:

Hire	$80.00
Clothing	17.00
Victuals	27.40
	$124.40

Net proceeds of said fellow geting Juniper
Shingles is found to be $250.00

Moreover, from 1830 to 1860, the annual rates of return from slave hiring ranged, according to one study, from 9.5 to 14.3 per cent in the upper South, and from 10.3 to 18.5 per cent in the lower South.[15] Such earnings suggest that slave hiring was at least as profitable as direct slave ownership for industries.

Finally, it should be recalled that industrial entrepreneurs, like most other slaveowners, profited from slavery's intermediate product — marketable and productive slave offspring. Many industrial establishments owned slave women whose progeny could easily be sold, and both women and children could be employed in light and heavy industries. Slave women and children therefore gave competitive advantages to employers of industrial slaves.[16] It may therefore be

[14] Account Book, vol. IV, 1833–39, 1856–61, Manigault Papers (UNC); Govan, "Was Plantation Slavery Profitable?" 513–35, demonstrates the profitable returns on Manigault's rice milling investment. For the earnings of other rice mills, see J. B. Irving's Windsor and Kensington Plantations Record Books, 1840–52, and T. Pinckney's estate appraisals and account books, 1842–63 and 1827–64 (Charleston Library Society, hereafter cited as CLS).
[15] R. Evans, Jr., "The Economics of American Negro Slavery," *Aspects of Labor Economics* (Princeton, 1962), 217; B. Wall, "Ebenezer Pettigrew" (Ph.D. dissertation, University of North Carolina, 1946), 308.
[16] See below on the use of women, children, and superannuates in southern industries; cf. Conrad and Meyer, *The Economics of Slavery*, ch. 3.

concluded that industrial enterprises, which either owned or hired slave labor, earned profitable returns on their investments.

The General Efficiency of Industrial Slavery

It is possible that industrial slavery was an inefficient or uneconomical labor system, even though it was simultaneously profitable to most industrial enterprises. Slaves were so troublesome and so unwilling, according to some historians, that they were less efficient than free workers. After all, did not slaves have to be coerced, while free workers responded eagerly to wage incentives? Industrial slave labor may also have been so expensive compared to free labor that it was, objectively, an unviable labor system. Given these questions, it is necessary to examine further the general efficiency of industrial slave workers and the costs arising from their ownership.

The available evidence indicates that slave labor was not less efficient than the free labor available in the Old South. To be sure, the slave's indifference to his work and his resistance to bondage tended to diminish his productivity somewhat. But this does not necessarily mean that competent managers could not make industrial slaves work or would have found free labor more efficient to employ. Physical coercion, or the threat of it, was an effective slave incentive, and masters often gave bondsmen material rewards for satisfactory production. In addition, industrial slaveowners could exploit women and children more fully than could employers of free labor. The average industrial bondsman was disciplined more rigorously than the typical free worker. Slaveholders were not troubled by labor organizations and were not obliged to bargain openly with their employees. "These advantages," concludes one authority, "more than compensated for whatever superiority free labor had in efficiency." [17]

In theory, slave labor may be less efficient than free labor over the long run, but for this study the practical comparison is between southern Negro slaves and the alternative free labor — poor whites, yeomen, and immigrants — available to the Old South. If this comparison is made, then it may be seen that the available free labor

[17] Stampp, *Peculiar Institution*, ch. 9, and Starobin, *Industrial Slavery*, chs. 2, 3, and 4, for a discussion of slave resistance and discipline. According to R. W. Fogel and S. Engerman, *The Reinterpretation of American Economic History* (New York, 1968), part 7, the manuscript census schedules reveal that about one-half of the slave population was in the labor force — a figure which is close to, if not at, the maximum possible participation rate. Since 44 per cent of the slaves were children under fourteen years old and 4 per cent were adults over sixty, virtually every able-bodied adult slave and most teen-agers were compelled to work. The slave participation-rate in the labor force was, moreover, 60 per cent greater than that of white workers.

— particularly the poor whites and immigrants — was less efficient than slave labor, since these whites were less tractable than slaves.[18]

Testimony from southern manufacturers who employed free labor supports the conclusion that it was not very efficient. White "hands had to be trained," admitted an associate of Daniel Pratt, the well-known Alabama businessman. "These [whites] were brought up from the piney woods, many of them with no sort of training to any kind of labor; in fact, they had to learn everything, and in learning, many mistakes and blunders were made fatal to success." Southern poor whites were not disciplined to sustained industrial labor, conceded the treasurer of William Gregg's Graniteville, South Carolina, cotton mill — another southern showpiece employing southern white workers.[19] Moreover, such testimony has been confirmed even by those scholars who argue that the level of productivity (that is, output per man) of slave labor was "low." "When white labor was used in Southern factories, it was not always superior to slave labor," admits one historian. ". . . [Southern white] productivity was much lower than in the North. . . . The use of whites did not guarantee a better work force than did the use of Negroes, for the South lacked an adequate pool of disciplined free workers." [20]

The efficiency, or total output, of slave labor compared to free labor can also be estimated by comparing the prices paid for slave hirelings with the wages paid southern free labor. From 1800 to 1861, white wages did not increase substantially; they remained fairly constant at about $300 per annum.[21] On the other hand, between 1800 and 1833, slave rents increased by about 50 per cent. Then, in the 1840's and the 1850's, slave hires again increased by another 50 per cent. At the same time, the value of slaves was increasing proportionately.[22] This suggests that both the productivity of and the demand for slave labor were increasing substantially

[18] For the unreliability of white workers in the South, see Starobin, *Industrial Slavery*, ch. 4.
[19] Genovese, *Political Economy of Slavery*, 226–27; for the politics of industrial slavery, see Starobin, *Industrial Slavery*, ch. 6.
[20] Genovese, *Political Economy of Slavery*, 37 fn. 13.
[21] For evidence on this point, see my dissertation, "Industrial Slavery," ch. 5, fn. 20. The wages of white southern textile workers were somewhat lower.
[22] See appendix on the cost of slave hiring in my dissertation:

Summary of Cost of Slave Hiring at Southern Industries
(in dollars)

Period	Daily	Monthly	Annually
1799–1833	.76	13.14	66.39
1833–52	.77	16.51	100.55
1853–61	1.44	19.68	150.00

during the first half of the nineteenth century. Thus, no matter how inefficient slave labor may have been, it was not less efficient than the free labor available to Southerners at the time.

It is often argued that the use of slaves entailed expenditures that were avoided by the employers of wage labor. The initial investment in blacks, the interest and depreciation on slave capital, the constant risk of financial losses from death, injury, disease, and escape, and the expense of maintaining slaves were all special expenses supposedly peculiar to slave ownership. These extra costs, according to some scholars, made slave labor more expensive and less economical than free labor.

It is clear, however that these special costs did not make slave ownership more expensive than free labor. Many industrialists did not bear the cost of initial slave capitalization, since they had inherited their bondsmen or had shifted them from agriculture to industry. Interest on capital was a current operating expense only if bondsmen were purchased on credit rather than with cash. Depreciation of slave capital was not a cost for most slaveowners, since slaves were appreciating in value and were producing saleable offspring. The prospect of financial disaster from losses of bondsmen was beginning to be alleviated in the 1840's and 1850's as many owners began to insure the lives of their Negroes. Finally, industries that hired slaves rather than purchasing them did not bear directly the cost of initial capitalization.[23]

Yet, when industries did purchase bondsmen, considerable expenditure of capital was involved, which should be compared to the costs of wage labor. The purchase of slaves entailed a different sort of expense than wages of free labor, since it was capitalization of future expenditures on labor and the payment all at once of a portion of what an employer of free labor would pay over a period of years. The cost of Negroes and their maintenance were, as one historian has argued, part of the wages an employer of free labor would expect to pay, and what masters were willing to pay for the right to fully control the time and movements of their workmen.[24] Slavery thus involved long-term capitalization of labor, while free labor involved the current expense of wages.

The surviving evidence also demonstrates that maintaining industrial slave labor cost much less than paying wages to available free

[23] Govan, "Was Plantation Slavery Profitable?" 513–35; Engerman, "The Effects of Slavery," 71–79; Stampp, *Peculiar Institution*, ch. 9; and Starobin; "Industrial Slavery," ch. 3.
[24] Conrad and Meyer, *The Economics of Slavery*, ch. 3; Stampp, *Peculiar Institution*, ch. 9.

labor. For directly-owned industrial slaves the largest annual expenditures were for maintenance and supervision — specifically for food, clothing, shelter, medical care, and management, as well as such incidental expenses as taxes, insurance, and incentive payments (see Table 4). The records of typical slave-employing enterprises reveal that the cost of important maintenance items and of supervision varied considerably. Suits of clothing, for example, ranged in price from $4 to $7, while shoes cost between $1 and $1.50, and boots from $1.50 to $2.50 a pair. Hats and caps sold for 50 or 75 cents, while blankets cost $1 or $2 each. Doctors ordinarily charged from $1 to $3 per visit; treatment of diseases such as syphilis cost from $5 to $15; medicine cost between 50 cents and $1 per illness. Life insurance ranged between $1.66 and $5 per hundred dollar valuation but averaged about $2 per hundred, or 2 per cent of valuation.[25] Depending on self-sufficiency and locale, the annual per capita cost of food varied between $10 and $125; clothing varied from about $3 to $30 annually per capita, housing cost between $5 and $10, and management ranged from about $200 to $3,000 a year.[26]

Despite such wide variations, industrial records indicate that between 1820 and 1860 food annually averaged about $50 per slave and clothing about $15.[27] Medical attention annually averaged about $3 per slave, housing probably cost about $7, and supervision amounted to about $800 per thirty hands, or about $27 per annum per slave. Incidental expenses annually cost little more than $5 per slave.[28] The annual average maintenance cost per industrial slave therefore amounted to about $100. Obviously, this was higher than the maintenance of slaves on plantations, which were much more self-sufficient. But how did these expenses compare with the cost of free labor in the Old South?

In the antebellum South, the daily wages of white common laborers ranged from 75 cents to $2 and averaged about $1 a day, while skilled whites earned daily from $2 to $5 and averaged about $3. The wages of common white workers did not increase appreciably between 1800 and 1861.[29] Thus, for a 310-day working year, and depending on skill, white wages ranged from $225 to $1,500 annually. But the bulk of unskilled white workers who figure in this study averaged only about $310 per year. Like slaves, wage laborers required supervision, but they ordinarily fed, clothed, and

[25] These prices are taken from the records of slave-employing industrial enterprises.
[26] See table 4 on maintenance costs.
[27] Ibid.
[28] Ibid.
[29] For white wages, see Starobin, "Industrial Slavery," ch. 5, fn. 20.

housed themselves, unless their board was furnished for them or they lived in company towns where their maintenance costs were automatically subtracted from their wages. The cost of free labor thus totaled about $335 per annum, including supervision. The annual average maintenance cost per industrial slave was therefore less than one-third the annual cost of wages and supervision of free common laborers.

The surviving reports from those "integrated" companies which used both slave labor and free labor simultaneously (or in succession) in the same workplace also reveal that slave labor was much less expensive than free labor. At the Cape Fear & Deep River Navigation Works, white workers cost 40 cents per day to board, while slaves cost 30 cents. In 1849, the Jackson *Mississippian* reported that whites cost 30 cents per day to board, while slaves cost 20 cents. In the late 1830's and 1840's, the Graham Cotton Mill in Kentucky listed white board at from $65 to $71 per year, while slave board ranged from $35 to $50. The accounts of the Roanoke Valley Railroad for 1852–1853 indicate that slaves were boarded more cheaply than whites, and the records of the Jordan & Davis iron works in Virginia for 1857–1858 demonstrate that whites were boarded for $8 per month, while slaves cost $7.[30]

Similarly, in the 1820's, the proprietors of the Maramec Iron Works in Missouri (another such integrated enterprise) reported that slaves were cheaper than free workers. Whites cost on the average about $15 per month, *excluding* supervision and free housing. Slaves hired for $100 per annum; their supervision and maintenance ran no more than $80 per year. Maramec's proprietors also testified that the cost of labor per cord of wood chopped by slaves compared favorably with the cost when whites performed the task.[31] A Kentucky hemp manufacturer, who converted from free labor to slave labor, claimed that slaves reduced his costs by 33 per cent. In 1854, it was reported that Kanawha River, Virginia, slave miners produced $2 a day more than free miners at Pittsburgh, Pennsylvania, pits. The next year, the Virginia & Tennessee Railroad reported that slave labor cost only about $11 monthly while free labor cost $40 to $50 monthly. The manager of one South Carolina cotton

[30] Boarding bills for October and December 31, 1859, Treasurers' Papers: Internal Improvements: Cape Fear & Deep River Navigation Works (North Carolina Department of Archives and History, hereafter cited as NCA); Jackson *Mississippian*, May 4, 1849; Graham Cotton Mill Daybook and Inventory, 1837–41 (University of Kentucky Library, hereafter cited as UK); vol. XXVI, Hawkins Papers (UNC); account sheet, 1857–58, Jordan and Davis Papers (State Historical Society of Wisconsin, hereafter cited as WSHS). For further information on "integrated" companies, see Starobin, *Industrial Slavery*, ch. 4.
[31] J. Norris, *Frontier Iron* (Madison, 1964), 40–41.

mill estimated that in 1851 slaves cost less than half as much as whites.[32] Therefore, at such integrated industrial enterprises, where the only variable was the nature of the labor force, slave labor was very much less expensive to employ than free labor.

Unusually complete records of several other integrated enterprises provide additional evidence that industrial slave labor was much cheaper than free labor. The labor rolls of the Gosport Navy Yard reveal that in the 1830's slaves produced as much as white workers for two-thirds the cost — that is, the use of industrial slaves was, in this case, almost twice as efficient as the use of whites. This was partly because the daily rent of slave hammerers ranged only from 72 to 83 cents, averaging close to 72 cents. The daily wages of white hammerers ranged from $1.68 to $1.73. Of course, the cost of maintaining the slaves probably amounted to about 30 cents daily, which increased the cost of slave hammerers to about $1 per day. Even so, it was less expensive to employ slaves than whites.[33]

The account sheets for Robert Jemison, Jr.'s Alabama construction projects further indicate that in 1858 bondsmen were 26 per cent cheaper to employ than free laborers. In 1859, slaves were 46 per cent less expensive than whites. The accounts of the Graham textile mill in Kentucky reveal that from 1837 to 1843 unskilled slaves annually cost 26 per cent less than unskilled whites, while skilled slaves cost between 15 and 22 per cent less than skilled whites. As late as 1851, slave carders, weavers, and spinners still cost less than comparable whites. The records of the Woolley textile mill in Kentucky also indicate that, between 1856 and 1861, most skilled slaves annually cost 57 per cent less to employ than skilled whites.[34]

Another integrated industrial enterprise, Richmond's Tredegar Iron Works, offers an interesting example of the cheapness of slave

[32] D. Myerle's testimony in *Report of Court of Claims*, #81, 34 C., 3 s., 1857; memorial of F. G. Hansford, *et al.*, Virginia Board of Public Works Report, 1854, 403; Report of the Virginia and Tennessee Railroad, Virginia *Board of Public Works Report*, 1855; J. S. Buckingham, *The Slave States* (London, 1842), I, 264–65 and II, 112–13; *De Bow's Review*, XI (1851), 319–20; E. M. Lander, "Slave Labor in South Carolina Cotton Mills," *Journal of Negro History*, XXXVIII (1953), 170–71.

[33] Rolls of Labor, 1831–32, and Memorandum of Work, 1831, Baldwin Papers and Selekman Notes (Baker Library, Harvard University Graduate School of Business Administration, hereafter cited as Baker). However, the daily rent of slave *common* laborers averaged about 72 cents, while the daily wages of white common laborers averaged $1.01. Therefore, savings came in the cost of the more skilled hammerers, where slaves were cheaper than whites.

[34] Cost of Hands for 1858, 1859, and undated, loose inserts in Jemison and Sloan Company contract account book, 1856-59, Jemison Papers (University of Alabama Library, hereafter cited as UA); Daybook and Inventory, 1837–41, Ledger and Inventory Book, 1832–45, Factory Time Book, 1847–52, Ledger, 1846–47, and Account Book, 1847–50, Graham Cotton Mill Papers (UK); Wages Ledger, 1856–61, Daybook, 1856–59, and G. Woolley to W. Peck & Sons, June 2, 1861, Lettercopybook, Woolley Papers (UK). However, the Woolley Papers reveal that common slave weavers cost almost as much to hire and to maintain as common white weavers. Again, savings came with skilled labor, where slaves were cheaper than whites.

labor. After commencing to hire slaves in 1848, Tredegar's proprietor, Joseph Reid Anderson, stated that slave labor "enables me, of course, to compete with other manufacturers." Competitiveness was achieved by combining slaves with white iron workers, which reduced the average cost of labor per ton of rolled iron. Between 1844 and 1846, *before* slaves were employed, for example, labor cost more than $12 per ton; from 1850 to 1852, *after* slaves were fully at work, labor averaged $10.59 per ton. The introduction of slaves thus enabled Anderson to reduce his labor costs by 12 per cent.[35]

A confidential report by the chief engineer of the South Carolina Railroad, which employed free labor at its Charleston terminal but used slave labor for its upcountry stations, offers additional evidence on the comparative cost of bondsmen and free workers. "It is a subject well worthy of enquiry whether the labor at the Charleston Depot could not be performed by slaves more economically than by whites," confided the official to the president of the line in 1849. "What cannot fail to strike you in the abstract of Depot expenses for August last is the fact that 1570 days [of] *white* labor at Charleston Depot cost $1,206, or 77 cts per day, while 1033 days [of] *slave* labor cost at the three *upper terminii* only $524 or 51 cts per day," he continued. "This statement also shows that it took 50 per cent more labor to load merchandise and unload cotton [at Charleston by white labor] than to load cotton and unload merchandise [in the upcountry by slave labor], or the cost of the former was two & a third ($2\frac{1}{3}$) times the latter."[36] Similarly, an 1855 report by the State Engineer of Louisiana also reveals that slave labor was much less expensive than free labor.[37]

Whatever the capital costs of slave ownership, these hardly concerned the employers of slave hirelings. Slave hirers bore only the expense of rent, maintenance, and supervision, even though other costs might be hidden in the slave rent. Slave hiring was thus similar to paying wages to free labor. Moreover, industrial slave hirelings, like directly-owned Negroes, were also more economical to employ than the free labor available. This is confirmed by comparing the total cost of hiring slaves with the cost of free labor. Throughout the slave states during the period from 1833 to 1852,

[35] C. Dew, *Ironmaker to the Confederacy* (New Haven, 1966), 18–20, 29–32, tables, and notes for prices of Tredegar iron products; J. R. Anderson to H. Row, January 3, 1848, Tredegar Letterbook (VSL).

[36] J. McRae to J. Gadsden, November 4, 1849, McRae Lettercopybooks (WSHS).

[37] This report is particularly valuable since it was based on detailed accounts and considerable experience with both slave and free labor, *De Bow's Review*, XIX (1855), 193–195.

the average annual rent of slave hirelings was $100; from 1853 to 1861, it was $150. During the same spans, per capita slave maintenance annually averaged about $100. The total cost of employing slave hirelings thus ranged from $200 to $250 per annum from 1833 to 1861. However, between 1800 and 1861, the annual average cost of employing free common laborers remained at about $310, not including supervision. By comparing these figures, it can be seen that slave hirelings remained between 25 and 40 per cent cheaper to employ than wage laborers.[38] Therefore, industrial slaves — whether hired or owned — were apparently more efficient and economical than the free labor available in the Old South.

Specific Competitive Advantages of Industrial Slavery

It is well known that southern industrialization lagged behind that of the North and of Great Britain. At least by the 1830's, northern and British industrialists had longer experience, more efficient management, larger markets, superior technology, and the ability to ship directly to the South. Northern products were of a better quality; Pennsylvania's iron and coal ores, for example, were superior to Virginia's and Kentucky's.[39] The earlier development of internal improvements in the North reduced transportation costs, which in turn reduced the prices of northern products generally. The availability of cheap labor — native and immigrant — in the North lowered prices further; the immigration of skilled Europeans increased the quality of northern products even more. The abundance of commercial capital for industrial investment enabled northern manufacturers to expand production, absorb business losses, withstand depressions, and, most important, to engage in cutthroat competition with southern producers. Thus, whatever the long-range causes and consequences of southern industrial backwardness,[40] the immediate question facing southern businessmen — especially manufacturers — was how best to compete with outside producers.

Southerners attempted to overcome their competitive disadvantages in various ways. They tried to foster direct trade with consumers of cotton, to promote internal improvements, and to recapture western markets.[41] But the most interesting means by which south-

---

[38] For the cost of slave hiring and white wage rates, see my dissertation, "Industrial Slavery," appendices, and ch. 5, fn. 20. In addition, R. Mills, *Statistics of South Carolina* (Charleston, 1826), 427–28, calculated that in Charleston in 1826 black common laborers cost half as much as whites; skilled blacks averaged 82¾ cents per day, while skilled whites averaged $1.37½.
[39] Dew, *Ironmaker to the Confederacy*, 32; North, *Economic Growth, passim.*
[40] See works cited above in fn. 1 and 6.
[41] See *De Bow's Review*, 1846 to 1862, for such programs.

erners attempted to raise the quality and reduce the cost of their products was the use of industrial slave labor in several specific ways. First, southern businessmen extensively exploited slave women and children (and sometimes superannuates). Second, they trained a Negro slave managerial group to complement white overseers. Finally, they "coupled" inexpensive slave workers with highly skilled white technicians — northern and foreign. In short, Southerners attempted to take advantage of the efficiency and inexpensiveness of slave labor to improve their competitive position in national market places.

Slave women and children comprised large proportions of the work forces in most slave-employing textile, hemp, and tobacco factories. They sometimes worked at "heavy" industries such as sugar refining and rice milling, and industries such as transportation and lumbering used slave women and children to a considerable extent. Iron works and mines also employed them to lug trams and to push lumps of ore into crushers and furnaces.[42]

Slaveowners used women and children in industries in several ways in order to increase the competitiveness of southern products. First, slave women and children cost less to capitalize and to maintain than prime males. John Ewing Colhoun, a South Carolina textile manufacturer, estimated that slave children cost two-thirds as much to maintain as adult slave cotton millers. Another Carolinian estimated that the difference in cost between female and male slave labor was even greater than that between slave and free labor.[43] Evidence from businesses using slave women and children supports the conclusion that they could reduce labor costs substantially.[44]

Second, in certain light industries, such as manufacturing, slave women and children could be as productive as prime males, and sometimes they could perform certain industrial tasks even more efficiently. This was especially true in tobacco, hemp, and cotton manufacturing, where efficiency depended more upon sprightliness and nimbleness than upon strength and endurance. The smaller hands and agile fingers of women and children could splice cotton or hempen threads more easily than the clumsy fingers of males. Delicate palms and dexterous digits processed tobacco more carefully. "Indeed it is well known that children are better adapted to some branches of manufacturing labor than a grown person," edi-

[42] See Starobin, *Industrial Slavery*, fn. 42–48.
[43] J. E. Colhoun Commonplace Book (Clemson); J. D. B. De Bow, *Industrial Resources* (New Orleans, 1853), II, 178.
[44] See, for example, Graham Cotton Mill Papers (UK); Woolley Papers (UK); and King Papers (Georgia Department of Archives and History, hereafter cited as GA).

torialized the Jackson *Mississippian*.[45] In addition, some industrialists believed that slave women could do as much work in some heavy occupations as males. "In ditching, particularly in canals . . . a woman can do nearly as much work as a man," concluded a Carolinian.[46]

Third, industrialists used slave women and children in order to utilize surplus slaves fully. "Negro children from ten to fourteen years of age are now a heavy tax upon the rest of the planter's force," editorialized the Jackson *Mississippian*. "Slaves not sufficiently strong to work in the cotton fields can attend to the looms and spindles in the cotton mills," concluded a visitor to a cotton mill where 30 of 128 slaves were children, "and most of the girls in this establishment would not be suited for plantation work." Placing Negroes in cotton mills "render[s] many of our slaves who are generally idle in youth profitable at an early age," observed a textile promoter. "Feeble hands and children can perform this work," concluded a rice miller, "leaving the effective force for improvements or to prepare for another crop." [47]

The intention of industrialists to utilize slave capital fully by employing women and children extensively is confirmed by an analysis of the manuscript census schedules. This study reveals that almost one-half of the slave population was in the labor force — a figure which is close to, if not at, the maximum possible participation rate. Since 44 per cent of the slaves were under fourteen years of age and 4 per cent were adults over sixty, then most slave women, most teen-age slaves, many slave children, as well as most adult males seemed to be at work. Moreover, the slave participation rate in the labor force was 60 per cent greater than the white participation rate.[48] This suggests that slaves of all age groups were forced to labor more extensively than whites.

It has already been seen that one of the greatest costs at southern industries was supervision. Since the cost of management contributed to the price of industrial products, Southerners sought to reduce its expensiveness and to increase its competence. Each of the types of free white management available — personal supervision, native white technicians, and imported directors — had serious

[45] Jackson *Mississippian*, March 19, 1845; cf. *De Bow's Review*, XXV (1858), 114.
[46] *Southern Agriculturist*, VI (1833), 587; *De Bow's Review*, XVIII (1855), 350–51; cf. Northrup, *Narrative*, 155–56; K. W. Skinner to C. Manigault, February 8, 1852, Manigault Papers (Duke).
[47] Jackson *Mississippian*, March 19, 1845; *De Bow's Review*, XI (1851), 319–20, and XXII (1857), 394, 397; Richmond *Enquirer*, October 7, 1827; *Southern Agriculturist*, VII (1834), 582, and IV (1831), 368; New Orleans *Picayune*, October 16, 1858.
[48] Fogel and Engerman, *Reinterpretation*, part 7.

limitations. When more than thirty slaves were employed, personal supervision was difficult, since sales, supplies, and bookkeeping occupied the owner's time. Native white managers were scarce, and they were often technically incompetent. Imported directors — northern and foreign — commanded high salaries for their superior abilities and to compensate for the rigors of the southern climate. No matter what the source, therefore, free white industrial management was expensive, ranging from $200 to $3,000 per annum and averaging about $800.[49] Given these circumstances, industrial enterprises often trained their own Negro slave managers.

Black slave managers were used by many southern industries. Simon Gray and Jim Matthews, slave hirelings of the Andrew Brown Lumber Company of Natchez, were responsible for rafting lumber and sand down the Mississippi River to customers along the way and to a New Orleans depot. Simon Gray directed as many as twenty raftsmen — both free whites and slaves — either owned or hired by the company. He disciplined the crewmen, distributed the wages of the white workers and the overtime payments to the slaves, and he paid the expenses of both. Gray bargained with planters and sawmillers, kept accurate accounts, and collected and disbursed large sums of money. He once delivered $800 to a creditor; on another occasion he escorted a newly purchased bondsman from a slave market to the industrial site — a responsibility ordinarily entrusted only to white men. He had his own pass, and he could charge goods to his personal account at the company store.[50]

Simon Gray had many counterparts in southern industry. As early as the 1790's, Andrew, a slave, rafted lumber down Georgia rivers, directed other slave raftsmen, and responsibly delivered bills of lading as well as valuable lumber for saw-miller Alexander Telfair.[51] Other slave managers handled large sums of money with fidelity. One slave ferryboat operator faithfully collected company tolls, controlled disbursements, and seemed to manage the entire business without difficulty. One railroad company hired Phocian, a slave, who served as a business agent, delivered company correspondence, faithfully handled sums of money ranging up to $200, and received many privileges, including a pass to visit his wife. Harry, a slave, delivered iron and procured supplies for an iron works during the 1830's and 1840's.[52] Other industrial slave managers were

[49] See appendix on the cost of management in my dissertation, "Industrial Slavery."
[50] J. H. Moore, "Simon Gray," *Mississippi Valley Historical Review*, XLIX (1962), 472–84.
[51] Account Books, 1794–1863, Telfair Papers (GHS); Northrup, *Narrative*, 89–99.
[52] G. Rogers, *Memoranda of Travels* (Cincinnati, 1845), 196, 310; D. B. McLaurin to

also trained as business agents. From as early as 1857 until 1862, Nathan, a fifty-seven-year-old bondsman, responsibly transacted much of the affairs of a North Carolina tannery. Without much supervision, Nathan made week-long business trips to sell leather at markets within a fifty-mile radius of the company.[53]

Many slave engineers skillfully operated complicated industrial machinery. Two slave rice millers, Frank the "headman" and Ned the engineer, capably ran the steam engine and the milling machinery at one establishment. Sandy Maybank was the slave head carpenter at another Georgia rice mill. A "full-blooded" black man superintended a Carolina cotton mill; a slave machinist attended the machine shop of a Virginia railroad; and Emanuel, a locomotive engineer owned by a Louisiana line, had an admirable record during ten years' service. One master's coal pits were, according to Edmund Ruffin, "superintended and directed entirely by a confidential slave of his own (whom he afterwards emancipated, and then paid $200 a year wages), and the laborers were also slaves; and they only knew anything of the condition of the coal." [54]

Some slave managers were quite talented. Horace, a slave architect and civil engineer, and Napoleon, his slave assistant, designed and executed Black Belt bridges for Robert Jemison, Jr., a wealthy Alabama planter-industrialist. Horace's most notable achievement for the year 1845 was the erection of a bridge in Columbus, Mississippi, for which he served as "chief architect." This project won Horace his employer's praise as "the most extensive and successful Bridge Builder in the South." Upon the completion of Horace's next project, a bridge in Lowndes County, Mississippi, Jemison wrote: "I am pleased to add another testimony to the style and despatch with which he [Horace] has done his work as well as the manner in which he has conducted himself." [55]

There can be little doubt that industrial slave managers were less expensive to employ than white managers, and that by reducing

---

W. H. Richardson, April 19 and January 27, 1855, and pass dated April 20, 1855, Richardson Papers (Duke); M. Bryan to W. W. Davis, June 30, 1846, Jordan and Davis Papers (WSHS).

[53] Vols. 39, 44, 17, 30, 45, and 46, Hawkins Papers (UNC).

[54] F. Kemble, *Journal* (New York, 1961), 113, 116–17, 168, 176, and 187–88; C. C. Jones to Sandy, August 15, 1853, and C. C. Jones to T. J. Shepard, March 30, 1850, Jones Papers (Tulane University Library, hereafter cited as Tulane); H. T. Cook, *David R. Williams* (New York, 1916), 140; J. B. Mordecai, *A Brief History of the Richmond, Fredericksburg and Potomac Railroad* (Richmond, 1941), 17; Richmond *Times-Dispatch*, January 31, 1943 (VHS); C. Sydnor, *Slavery in Mississippi* (New York, 1933), 7; *Farmers' Register*, V (1837), 315; Duke de la Rochefoucault-Liancourt, *Travels Through the United States* (London, 1799), III, 122–23.

[55] R. Jemison, Jr., Letterbooks, 1844–54 (UA); cf. Olmsted, *Seaboard Slave States*, 553.

the costs of supervision, they increased the competitiveness of southern industries. Simon Gray, the riverman, clearly reduced the management costs for the Andrew Brown Lumber Company. As a head raftsman, Gray at first received twelve dollars monthly; this was about one-fourth the wages of a white head raftsman. Even when Gray's incentive was raised to twenty dollars monthly, the same wages as ordinary white raftsmen, it was still only *half* that of white head raftsmen. A white manager with Gray's skills and responsibilities would have cost the lumber company annually almost as much as Gray's total market value.

Similarly, Nathan, the tannery business agent, cost much less than a comparable white manager. Nathan received for his services only a dollar or two per trip, for about ten trips per year. He incurred in addition only his maintenance, which amounted to several cents per day. A white business agent with Nathan's responsibilities would have cost at least $2.50 daily in wages alone and might have been less trustworthy than the slave. Sandy Maybank, the slave head carpenter at the Georgia rice mill, was as skillful as, yet less expensive than, a comparable white manager. Moreover, his master reaped extra financial benefits from Maybank's ability to hire himself out in the slack season. Horace and Napoleon, the slave bridge builders, cost only five dollars daily plus board; two comparable white managers probably would have cost twice as much. Even at these rates, Jemison considered Horace's services so indispensable and profitable that he continued to engage Horace for many years.[56]

While some industries employed slave managers, others used highly skilled white technicians — imported from the North or Europe — to improve the quality and the competitiveness of industrial products. Of course, imported managers were more expensive than native ones — free or slave; but businessmen discovered that the use of inexpensive slave common laborers made possible the employment of expensive skilled foreign technicians. By "coupling" common slaves with these skilled white managers, industries could raise the quality of products without increasing overall labor and management costs. By engaging the best foreign technicians available, southerners thus attempted to compete with northern and British manufacturers.[57]

Among the many southern industries which coupled cheap slaves

[56] For further information and sources on slave managers in industry, see my dissertation, "Industrial Slavery," ch. 3 and 5, fn. 64.

[57] See earlier discussion on the costs of slave ownership.

with expensive white engineers was textile manufacturing, where competitiveness depended greatly on quality. As early as 1815, cotton millers realized the advantages of skilled management, when one Carolinian who hired three northern superintendents "thought it best so to do — for to depend upon our hands to learn would take a considerable time before we could cleverly get underway." Similarly, a Tennessee textile mill employed a Providence, Rhode Island, foreman; John Ewing Colhoun, whose products were so widely praised, also employed a northern superintendent; and an experienced "Loweller" managed a Mississippi mill.[58]

Combining inexpensive slaves with skilled technicians was also common in extractive industries. Mining companies often hired experienced Welsh, English, Cornish; and other foreign supervisors to direct the blasting, tunneling, seam tracking, and other work performed by common slave miners.[59] Lumbering enterprises often engaged skilled sawyers from Maine or northwest forests to supervise unskilled slave lumbermen. "Those who would engage in a scheme of this kind," advised an early shipbuilding promoter, "would however find it their interest to instruct negroes in the art of working on ships under two or three master-builders." [60]

Experienced foreign civil engineers likewise directed many heavy construction projects, since native southern technicians were scarce. Architect B. H. Latrobe designed the New Orleans Water Works, Loammi Baldwin administered the Gosport Navy Yard, while his brother, James, executed the Brunswick & Altamaha Canal. After 1819, Hamilton Fulton, an Englishman, supervised North Carolina's and then Georgia's river improvement programs. European-trained J. Edgar Thompson planned the Georgia and the Southern Pacific railroads. Charles Crozet, a French engineer, served the Virginia Board of Internal Improvements.[61]

[58] E. M. Lander (ed.), "Two Letters by William Mayrant on His Cotton Factory, 1815," *South Carolina Historical Magazine*, LIV (1953), 3–4; *American Farmer*, series 1, IX (October 12, 1827), 235–314; E. M. Lander, "Development of Textiles in South Carolina Piedmont," *Cotton History Review*, I (1960), 92; Jackson *Mississippian*, December 4, 1844; Charleston *Courier*, February 19, 1845. Another industry which often used white managers was sugar milling.
[59] Report upon . . . the N.C. Gold Mining Co., September 5, 1832, Fisher Papers (UNC); Richmond *Enquirer*, March 23, 1839, and January 9, 1840; B. Broomhead to B. Smith, September 7, 1857, Smith Papers (Duke); Olmsted, *Seaboard Slave States*, 47–48; *Harper's Monthly*, XV (1857), 297; *De Bow's Review*, VII (1849), 546–47, and XXIX (1860), 378; S. Ashmore to C. Thomas, March 26, 1860, Silver Hill Mining Company Papers (NCA).
[60] N. Pendleton, "Short Account, 1796," *Georgia Historical Quarterly*, XLI (1957); J. Baker to S. Plaisted, November 23, 1839, Plaisted Papers (LSU); *Niles' Register*, XLVII (1834), 55; account book, 1812–17, Telfair Papers (GHS); entry for June 6, 1857, D. C. Barrow Diaries (UG); C. L. Benson to M. Grist, October 1, 1855, Grist Papers (Duke).
[61] Latrobe Papers (Tulane); Baldwin Papers (Baker); C. K. Brown, *A State Movement in Railroad Development* (Chapel Hill, 1928), 12; M. S. Heath, *Constructive Liberalism*

The coupling of inexpensive bondsmen with skilled white artisans was also important to the iron industry which attempted to compete with northern and foreign producers. South Carolina's Nesbitt Manufacturing Company imported several New York founders. Four experienced Connecticut Yankees managed the Hecla Iron Works in Virginia. Another iron company employed a "Jersey founder;" William Weaver's hiring agent tried to engage one of Virginia's most famous colliers, while another iron monger sought the services of James Obrian, Weaver's skilled hammerer.[62]

Many southern businessmen clearly understood the competitive advantages of combining skilled white technicians with inexpensive slaves. Textile manufacturers and promoters, such as E. Steadman, who advocated paying cotton mill superintendents well enough to attract the "best talent and skill" to the South, seemed especially aware of these advantages. If the Saluda cotton mill had only hired "a carder, spinner, dresser, weaver, and an active and skillful young man as overseer, taking the best talents that Massachusetts could afford . . . and offered inducements that would have commanded the very best," editorialized the Columbia *South Carolinian* in 1844, the company would have been more successful. "If it is desirable to establish cotton factories in the South," agreed a "practical" English manufacturer who visited South Carolina, "let the proprietors select the proper man to make out the plans, select the machinery, manage the manufacturing details, and let them pay such men sufficient remuneration for their services, and I venture to affirm that there will be no difficulty in building up a manufacturing business, equally as successful, and much more profitable, than the majority of Northern factories.[63]

Other manufacturers were also aware of the advantages of coupling slaves with skilled managers. Manufacturing was less expensive in the South, according to one promoter, mainly because "the manual labor, costing even now as little as northern labor, may be and will be, under a . . . skilful and eminently practical management, made, by the judicious intermingling of slave male and female

(Cambridge, 1954), 241, 261; C. Goodrich, *Government Promotion of American Canals and Railroads* (New York, 1960), 98; *De Bow's Review*, XXVII (1859), 725.

[62] J. M. Taylor to F. H. Elmore, June 25, 1840, and agreements of September 30 and October 5, 1837, Elmore Papers (Library of Congress, hereafter cited as LC); Richmond *Enquirer*, June 3, 1851; Jordan, Davis & Co. to W. Weaver, November 24, 1830, W. Ross to W. Weaver, November 27, 1831, and G. P. Taylor to W. Weaver, October 7, 1831 and May 2, 1832, Weaver Papers (Duke); W. Rex to W. Weaver, January 8, 1859, Weaver Papers (University of Virginia Library, hereafter cited as UV).

[63] E. Steadman, *Brief Treatise on Manufacturing in the South* (Clarksville, Tenn., 1851), 108; Columbia *South Carolinian*, December 18, 1844; *De Bow's Review*, XXVI (1859), 95-96.

labor with that of native whites, and their imported tutors, cheaper than it can possibly be had for in any northern locality. Here then, with all the elements of cost at the lowest rate," he concluded, "the wares of this factory would contend successfully, even for a foreign market, with the keenest Yankee competition." [64]

Transportation companies also comprehended the advantages of skilled management. As early as 1822, the Upper Appomattox Company of Virginia purchased slave laborers and placed them under "as industrious and enterprising an overseer as we could obtain" with excellent results,[65] and during the 1830's and 1840's, other transportation projects also engaged skilled engineers. By the 1850's, as railroad construction forged ahead, the advantages of "coupling" had become widely known.[66] When the directors of the Southern Pacific Railroad pondered the merits of various labor forces, for example, promoter Thomas Jefferson Green proposed to combine common bondsmen with skilled engineers: "It may be safely estimated that the natural increase of negroes upon the healthy line of our road together with the increased value of turning field labour into railroad mechanicks will aqual 15 pr. cent per annum, whilst the interest upon their cost would be 6 pr. cent — leaving a difference of 9 pr. ct. in favor of the company which would go far toward covering Engineering expenses & head mechanics — and other incidental charges." [67] Green thus understood that the use of slaves would save the company enough money to permit the employment of high-salaried civil engineers.

It remained, however, for Joseph Reid Anderson of the Tredegar Iron Works of Richmond, Virginia, consciously to systematize the coupling of common slaves with expensive technicians in order to increase competitiveness. In 1842, Anderson contracted skilled white "puddlers" to train common slave apprentices. Then, in 1847, some of these bondsmen, now more skillful, were promoted to the position of puddler. The next year Anderson explained the theory behind the practice: [68]

---

[64] De Bow's Review, XIV (1853), 622–23.
[65] Report of the Upper Appomattox Company, Virginia Board of Public Works Report, 1822, 33.
[66] Richmond Dispatch, December 9, 1853, for example.
[67] T. J. Green to the Executive Committee of the Southern Pacific R.R. Co., October 14, 1856, Green Papers (UNC).
[68] J. R. Anderson to H. Row, January 3, 1848, Tredegar Letterbook (VSL). However, employing slave labor could not solve Tredegar's problems of competing entirely, since American labor and transportation were costly and Virginia coal and iron were of a low quality. Tredegar's "most glaring weakness" lay not in its use of slave labor, according to Dew, Ironmaker to the Confederacy, 32, but in its "pitifully inadequate raw materials base" and in the southern transportation system.

. . . I am employing in this establishment [Tredegar] as well as at the Armory works, adjoining, of which I am President, almost exclusively slave labor except as to Boss men. This enables me, of course, to compete with other manufacturers and at the same time to put it in the power of my men to do better for themselves.

Throughout the 1850's, Anderson continued these arrangements, and he was soon able to reduce his labor cost per ton of rolled iron by 12 per cent.[69]

The Character of Industrial-Slave Capitalization

It is possible that the capitalization of the slave labor force crippled the finances of industries, even though industrial slavery was both profitable to investors and an efficient labor system. In this respect, industrial slavery may have been unviable in the long run because it reduced the flexibility of capital and the mobility of labor. Slave capital was so frozen, according to some scholars, that it could not easily be converted into cash. To transfer slaves from one place to another or to use them in different kinds of employment was allegedly difficult. "Negro slave labor was expensive," argued one historian, "because it was overcapitalized and inelastic. . . . Circulating capital was at once converted into fixed capital. . . . The capitalization of labor lessened its elasticity and its versatility; it tended to fix labor rigidly in one line of employment" — namely, in agriculture.[70]

Contrary to this view, the available evidence suggests that slave ownership did not seriously lessen the mobility of labor nor did slavery inhibit investment in industrial enterprises. Indeed, the funding of slave-based industries was primarily an internal process, intimately linked to slave-based agriculture.[71] Many industries were actually capitalized by transferring bondsmen from farming or planting to manufacturing, milling, mining, and transportation. And slaveowners themselves, not merchants or bankers, were the chief source of capital for industrial investment.

[69] See earlier discussion on the efficiency of slave labor and Starobin, *Industrial Slavery*, ch. 4 for further information on Tredegar. For sources on the use of white managers at other industrial enterprises, see my dissertation, "Industrial Slavery," ch. 5, fn. 66 and 67.

[70] Phillips, "The Economic Cost of Slaveholding," *Political Science Quarterly*, XX (1905), 257–75; Phillips, *A History of Transportation* (New York, 1908), 388–89; F. Linden, "Repercussions of Manufacturing in the Ante-Bellum South," *North Carolina Historical Review*, XVIII (1940), 328.

[71] As a source of industrial capital, the money derived from mercantile activity — mentioned in L. Atherton, *The Southern Country Store* (Baton Rouge, 1949), ch. 6, 194, 204 — seems less important than agricultural-based accumulation.

Slaveowning planters capitalized many manufacturing enterprises, such as cotton mills and hemp factories, by shifting some less-than-prime field hands or house servants to weaving and spinning. In such cases slave labor itself contributed to capitalization, while profits from planting or slavetrading provided additional funds. "The staples of the lower country require moderate labour, and that at particular seasons of the year," reported a Virginian to Alexander Hamilton, as early as 1791. "The consequence is, that they have much leisure and can apply their hands to Manufacturing so far as to supply, not only the cloathing of the Whites, but of the Blacks also." A visitor to Kentucky calculated: "The surplus [farm] labor is chiefly absorbed by the rope and bagging factories, which employ a vast number of slaves." [72]

To finance larger textile factories, slaveowning planters often pooled their slaves and cash and sold stock to neighboring agriculturists. David Rogerson Williams's South Carolina Union Factory was but one example of a textile mill where close financial relationships developed between investors and the company. James Chesnut, the prominent planter, bought company stock and arranged to rent to Williams's factory several of his surplus slaves. The company credited Chesnut for the amount of the hirelings' rent, against which he drew cotton and woolen goods manufactured at the mill. The factory purchased Chesnut's raw cotton, paying him in cash or credits which he used to buy finished textile goods for his plantation hands. Of course, Chesnut also received a share of the company's earnings. [73] To the company, Chesnut was a welcome source not only of capital, but of labor and raw material at comparatively low prices, while Chesnut's plantation served as a market for its manufactured goods. To Chesnut, the mill absorbed surplus slaves, cash, and cotton, while the company provided comparatively cheap manufactured goods and yielded profitable returns on his investment. Such financial relationships were mutually beneficial to planters and manufacturers alike.

Slaveowning planters also financed many iron works — the Nesbitt Manufacturing Company, a large South Carolina concern, being an

[72] D. Standard and R. Griffin, "Textiles in North Carolina," *North Carolina Historical Review*, XXXIV (1957), 15–16; E. Coulter, "Scull Shoals," *Georgia Historical Quarterly*, XXVIII (1964), 41–43; G. A. Henry to wife, December 3 and November 28, 1846, Henry Papers (UNC); Spinning Book, 1806–7, Taylor Papers (VHS); E. Carrington to A. Hamilton, October 4, 1791, A. H. Cole (ed.), *Correspondence of Alexander Hamilton* (Chicago, 1928), 94, 145; E. G. Abdy, *Journal of a Residence* (London, 1935), II, 349.
[73] Bill, May 9, 1829, account sheet, May 14, 1831, and J. N. Williams to J. Chesnut, May 17, 1831, Chesnut-Miller-Manning Papers (SCHS); same to same, ca. October, 1831, Chesnut Papers (WSHS); account sheets, 1829, 1830, June 19, 1830, and February 14, 1835, Williams Papers (South Caroliniana Library, Columbia, hereafter cited as USC).

interesting case. Like other Nesbitt investors, its president, Franklin Harper Elmore, a leading slaveholding and landowning banker, had strong personal, political, and financial ties in South Carolina and neighboring states. To raise capital, the company's founders agreed to permit investors to purchase stock with an equivalent value of blacks. Financial records reveal that several planters, including Wade Hampton, Pierce Mason Butler, and the Elmore Brothers, each invested thousands of dollars' worth of bondsmen in return for company certificates. The iron works thereby accumulated about 140 Negroes, worth about $75,000. Though two nearby banks loaned cash, a large portion of the company's capital consisted of slave labor.[74]

Similarly, slaveowning planters capitalized many extractive enterprises. As early as 1804, Moses Austin observed Missouri farmers sending or accompanying their slaves to the lead diggings after harvest to supplement their incomes. In the 1840's, John C. Calhoun periodically worked some of his cotton plantation slaves at his Dahlonega, Georgia, gold mines. In 1849, the *American Farmer* reported that Alabama cotton planters were shifting their bondsmen into turpentine extraction and distillation.[75]

Slaveowning planters and farmers also financed the majority of southern railroads, canals, and turnpikes. Some planters bought company stock with cash; others purchased or received shares for the labor of their slaves. "The cleaning, grubbing, grading, and bridging of the road," reported the Mississippi Central Railroad, "have been undertaken by planters residing near the line, who, almost without exception, are shareholders in the company. They execute the work with their own laborers, whose services they can at all times command."[76] Some slave-employing railroad contractors were paid company stock instead of cash, while some planters exchanged their slaves' labor for the privilege of having a railroad pass nearby their plantation.[77] The advantages of such financial relationships were clearly understood by many southern railroad officials, including the president of the Charlotte and South Carolina line, who reported in 1849:[78]

[74] Various financial documents, Elmore Papers (LC and USC); account sheet, ca. 1840, P. M. Butler Papers (USC).
[75] M. Austin, Description of the Lead Mines, 1804, *American State Papers: Public Lands*, I, 207; various letters between T. G. Clemson and J. C. Calhoun, 1842–43, Calhoun and Clemson Papers (USC and Clemson); *American Farmer*, series 4, IV (1849), 252.
[76] *American Railroad Journal*, XXVIII (1855), 577.
[77] For further information on the financing of southern transportation enterprises, see *De Bow's Review, American Railroad Journal, Western Journal and Civilian*, and the reports of boards of internal improvements and public works of the various slave states.
[78] *American Railroad Journal*, XXIII (1850), 9.

The practice of allowing stockholders to pay up their subscriptions in labor, is one of recent origin; is admirably calculated to increase the amount of stock subscribed, to facilitate its payment; and gives to the slave States great advantages over the free in the construction of railroads. . . .

While private investment by slaveowners predominated, public investment in industries and internal improvements by state and local authorities comprised only a small portion of the total capitalization of southern industries. Such public funds went almost entirely into slave-employing transportation projects rather than into other types of industry.[79] Moreover, federal[80] and foreign[81] funding of southern industries was also negligible. This situation contrasted with the process of capitalization in the North and West, where more industrial capital came from commercial surpluses, rather than agricultural, and where state, federal, and foreign funding of industries played an important role.[82] Indeed, the ratio of public to private investment, especially in transportation, seemed lower in the South than in the North. Thus, Southerners derived industrial capital from their own internal, private sources, specifically from the earnings of plantation agriculture. Southerners seemed to be developing industries in their region almost exclusively by their own efforts.

[79] For information on the public capitalization of southern internal improvements and the ratio of public to private investment, see C. Goodrich, "The Virginia System of Mixed Enterprise," Political Science Quarterly, LXIV (1949), 366–69 and tables; Goodrich, Government Promotion of American Canals and Railroads, passim; G. R. Taylor, Transportation Revolution (New York, 1951), passim; Heath, Constructive Liberalism, 287–89; A. G. Smith, Economic Readjustment of an Old Cotton State (Columbia, 1958); 179–83; J. W. Million, State Aid to Railways in Missouri (Chicago, 1896), 232–36; D. Jennings, "The Pacific Railroad Company," Missouri Historical Society Collections, VI (1931), 309; T. W. Allen, "The Turnpike System in Kentucky," Filson Club History Quarterly, XXVIII (1954); 248–58 note; C. B. Boyd, Jr., "Local Aid to Railroads in Central Kentucky," Kentucky Historical Society Register, LXII (1964), 9–16; S. J. Folmsbee, Sectionalism and Internal Improvements in Tennessee (Knoxville, 1939), 28, 122, 135, 265; S. G. Reed, A History of Texas Railroads (Houston, 1941), passim; M. E. Reed, "Government Investment and Economic Growth: Louisiana's Ante-Bellum Railroads," Journal of Southern History, XXVIII (1962), 184, 189; and railroad reports in De Bow's Review, XXVI (1859), 458–60, and XXVIII (1860), 473–77; American Railroad Journal, XXVIII (1855), 771; and the Western Journal and Civilian, XIV (1855), 292. Taylor, Transportation Revolution, 92, estimates that in 1860 about 55 per cent of the investment in railroads in the eleven Confederate states came from state and local authorities. This accounts for neither private investment in internal improvements other than railroads, nor investment generally in such states as Maryland, Kentucky, and Missouri.
[80] For federal funding of southern enterprises, see Goodrich, Government Promotion, 156–62; Taylor, Transportation Revolution, 49–50, 95–96, 67–68; Reed, "Government Investment . . . Louisiana's Railroads," 184, 189.
[81] For foreign funding of southern enterprises, see Kemble, Journal, 104–22; R. Hidy, House of Baring (Cambridge, 1949), 281, 330, 336; B. Ratchford, American State Debts (Durham, 1941), ch. 5; R. McGrane, Foreign Bondholders and State Debts (New York, 1935), 89, and ch. 9–13; Niles' Register, XXIX (1825), 178; XL (1831), 270; and XLII (1832), 91; Governor's Message, Milledgeville Federal Union, November 6, 1849, and December 2, 1845; Barclay, Ducktown, passim; correspondence for 1845–48, and 1855–61, Gorrell Papers (UNC); F. Green, "Gold Mining, Virginia," Virginia Magazine of History and Biography, XLV (1937), 357–65; F. Green, "Gold Mining, Georgia," Georgia Historical Quarterly, XIX (1935), 224–25; American Journal of Science, LVII (1849), 295–99.
[82] Taylor, Transportation Revolution, 97–102, and passim.

Regarding the flexibility of industrial slave capital, the records of several southern enterprises reveal that slave ownership did not cripple industrial finance. It is, of course, possible that larger industrial enterprises and wealthier businessmen were able to manipulate their slave investments more easily than smaller operators and less secure investors. But it is also true that industrial slavery reduced neither the flexibility of capital nor the mobility of labor to the extent that financial problems could not be solved. At the Nesbitt Manufacturing Company, a large South Carolina iron works, for example, finance remained quite flexible. In 1840, a planter-investor proposed to rent twelve blacks to the company rather than to invest them. The annual rate of hire would be $120 for each slave, the duration of hire four years, and the rent paid in company stock at the end of each year. The company accepted this proposal. The same year Pierce Mason Butler decided to withdraw some of his slave capital. Having transferred $12,315 worth of slaves to the company in 1837, Butler now withdrew eight bondsmen worth $4,850, including four whose skill and value had increased. Even when the company terminated operations and settled its obligations, the original stockholders were reimbursed merely by returning their slaves, whose offspring counted as a bonus.[83]

The Nesbitt Company's slave capital was sufficiently flexible so that in the first case the investor obtained shares by renting his slaves, utilized some of his surplus bondsmen, received company earnings, and withdrew his slaves when they had become more skillful and valuable. In the second and third instances, investors suffered little financial embarrassment and they retained appreciated slave capital when the enterprise was terminated. In each case, slave capital seemed sufficiently mobile to meet the company's needs.

Slave labor supposedly was less flexible than wage labor during commodity market fluctuations and business depressions when income dropped and labor costs had to be reduced. However, many slaveowning industries found that during such periods slave labor was as flexible as wage labor, even though whites could be dismissed and slaves could not. "The certainty of a regular and adequate supply of mining labor at reasonable prices is the surest avenue of success in coal mining," privately confided the slaveowning coal miner William Phineas Browne in 1847. "In this respect slave labor owned by the mining proprietors is greatly superior to free labor

[83] Financial documents and letters, Elmore Papers (LC and USC), and P. M. Butler Papers (USC).

even if the latter were as abundant as it is in Europe or in the mining districts of the North." To Browne, the purchase of slave coal miners was less expensive than paying wages to free laborers. To retain large stocks of coal during dull periods the capital required to sustain free-labor mining operations economically would amount to nearly enough to purchase Negroes, he argued. If enterprises owned slaves, on the other hand, sufficient funds could be realized from current sales to maintain full mining operations without financial embarrassments during periods of depressed market conditions. Browne also argued that slave ownership enabled enterprises to capitalize on market fluctuations. Mining companies should therefore depend mainly upon slave labor; free labor should be worked only as a "subordinate adjunct" to the regular slave force. "The employment of slave labor besides being more in harmoney with our institutions," concluded Browne after much experience, "ensures a successful business against all contingencies and will enable proprietors to pass through all disturbing crises without being sensibly affected by them." [84]

Browne's confidence in the flexibility of slave capital was confirmed by the experiences of many southern transportation enterprises. The Upper Appomattox Company of Virginia, which owned its black diggers, was able, in 1816 and again in 1835, to rent out twenty bondsmen to obtain funds to complete the work. The Roanoke Navigation Company of Virginia, which also owned Negroes, was able, in 1823, to obtain capital by either selling or renting out several slaves. During the panic of 1837, this company rented out some bondsmen for five months for $3,167; within a few months the company thereby recouped 23 per cent of its original $14,025 investment in thirty-three slaves. Of course, the company still operated the canal and owned its slaves. In 1839, the company sold half its blacks for $7,044, rented some of the remaining bondsmen to a nearby railroad, and thereafter earned additional income by hiring out slaves each winter and spring, while using them for repairs during summers.[85] Similarly, after 1827, the Slate River Company of Virginia, which owned five Negroes worth $1,900, rented out four of them at $235 per annum each. One Alabama railroad, which owned $9,575 worth of slaves, realized $2,503 annually

[84] W. P. Browne to G. Baker, January 30 and 31, 1857, Browne Papers (Alabama Department of Archives and History, hereafter cited AA).
[85] Reports of Upper Appomattox Company, Virginia *Board of Public Works Reports*, *1816*, ii, and *1835*, 42; Reports of Roanoke Navigation Company, Virginia *Board of Public Works Reports*, *1823*, 69, *1838*, 98, 100, *1839*, 125, and *1854*, 478–88.

(a 26 per cent return) by hiring them out in the 1830's. Upon the completion of the slaveowning Bayou Boeuf Navigation Works in Louisiana, the company totally reimbursed its original investors and continued to pay them dividends.[86]

Confidence in the flexibility of slave capital was also evident in the financial schemes of A. C. Caruthers, a Tennessee turnpike promoter. "We have a Charter for a Road to Trousdale's Ferry," confided Caruthers to a friend in 1838. "We will build our Road — the State takes half. The plan is devised — a few men — 8 or 10 — will take the stock — pay it all in at once — get the State Bonds — & with the fund build the Road." Proposing a clever plan of finance, the promoter concluded: [87]

> With this fund, they can buy say 300 negroes, who will do the work in one year. The interest of the $70,000 borrowed — the tools — support of hands, mechanicks & all cant cost more than $40,000. When the Road is done the $140,000 is theirs — the bond to the Directors is cancelled. The 300 Negroes are theirs — They can sell them for an advance of at least of $100 each = $30,000. The whole sale would be $140,000 original cost & $30,000 profit = in all $170,000. Out of this they must repay the $70,000 borrowed, & the $40,000 expenses in all $110,000 — leaving a clear profit of $60,000 & their road stock, which is $6,000 each partner & $10,000 in road stock. . . .

The experiences of slaveowning industries regarding the flexibility of slave capital have been confirmed by some recent studies. In South Carolina there seemed to be adequate sources of capital for industrial investment, while Texas masters converted slave capital into liquid capital, according to one historian, by selling, mortgaging, or renting out their Negroes. "At the same time that slave labor was being used as an instrument of production, that labor was also creating capital," he concludes. "It is difficult to understand how the notion became current that the slave became a frozen asset and a drain upon the capital resources of a region." [88] Of course, slave hiring was an even more flexible use of capital than slave ownership, and since demand for slaves remained high, slave capital tended to remain liquid.

[86] Report of Slate River Company, Virginia *Board of Public Works Report*, *January 24, 1828*, 23; *American Railroad Journal*, 5 (1836), 817; J. Andreassen, "Internal Improvements in Louisiana," *Louisiana Historical Quarterly*, XXX (1947), 46–47.

[87] A. C. Caruthers to W. B. Campbell, January 28, 1838, Campbell Papers (Duke), for the entire scheme.

[88] Smith, *Economic Readjustment of an Old Cotton State*, 115–34; G. R. Woolfolk, "Planter Capitalism and Slavery: the Labor Thesis," *Journal of Negro History*, XLI (1956), 103–16.

Even if these findings — that slave labor in southern industries was profitable, efficient, and economically viable — are valid, it still should be explained why southern industry did not develop more rapidly. While the reasons for this are, of course, complex, an explanation seems to rest in the limitations of southern markets, the South's difficulty competing with northern and foreign producers, unfavorable balances of southern trade, and, perhaps most important, in the ability of southern agriculture to outbid industry for investment capital.

The slow development of southern industries stemmed partly from various restrictions on consumer demand. Slaveowners usually maintained their slaves at subsistence living standards, and some of the largest plantations were almost entirely self-sufficient. The poor whites lacked purchasing power because they did not produce for regional markets. Isolated from transportation facilities, yeoman farmers produced only for limited markets and had difficulty competing with more efficient planters. Moreover, the South lacked urban markets, since by 1860 only about 10 per cent of its population lived in cities, compared to the Northwest's 14 per cent and the Northeast's 36 per cent. Except for New Orleans and Baltimore, the South had only a handful of cities with populations over 15,000,[89] and many urban dwellers were slaves or free blacks whose purchasing power was minimal. Relatively few foreigners emigrated to the South, where economic opportunity was poorer and the climate sicklier than in the North. In addition, as late as 1861, the southern transportation network still primarily tied plantation districts to ports, rather than providing a well-knit system which might have increased internal consumption. Finally, the distribution of wealth, which helps determine consumption propensities, was less even in the South than in the North,[90] although the rate of growth and the level of southern income compared favorably with other sections.[91]

[89] Genovese, *Political Economy of Slavery*, 20, 24–25, 34, 37, fn. 13, 159–72, 185, 276–77; North, *Economic Growth*, 126, 130, 132, 166, 170, 172–76, 205–06.

[90] Genovese, *Political Economy of Slavery*, passim; North, *Economic Growth*, passim. For further discussion of southern income distribution, see Engerman, "Effects of Slavery," 71–97; F. L. Owsley, *Plain Folk of the Old South* (Baton Rouge, 1949), passim; F. Linden, "Economic Democracy in the Slave South," *Journal of Negro History*, XXXI (1946), 140–89.

[91] However uneven income distribution was *within* the South, recent comparisons of regional and national wealth for 1840 and 1860 suggest that southern income levels and rates of growth compared favorably with those of the free states. See Engerman, "Effects of Slavery," 71–97, especially fn. 35, and R. Easterlin, "Regional Income Trends, 1840–1950," in S. Harris (ed.), *American Economic History* (New York, 1961), 525–47. If one revises upward the maintenance cost of slaves (as Genovese, *Political Economy of*

Southern industries also lagged because southern manufacturers had difficulty competing in national market places. Compared to northern and foreign producers, southerners had less experience, less efficient management, smaller markets, inferior technology, poorer transportation, indirect trade routes, and, perhaps most important, smaller capital resources. Credit arrangements and unfavorable balances of trade drained plantation profits northward and permitted northern merchants increasingly to dominate the commerce in cotton, the leading export both of the South and of the nation. Imports came first through New York, rather than directly to the South, because ships were assured of more cargo on the westward passage from Europe to northern ports than to southern ones.[92] The South would have had to pay for loans and services obtained from the North in any event, but capital accumulated by northern merchants, bankers, and insurance brokers tended to be reinvested in northern industries and transportation enterprises rather than in southern ones.

Southern backwardness was not inevitable; rather, it was the result of human decisions which could have led in a different direction. After all, from the 1780's to about 1815, southern planters had been investing much of their surplus capital in industries and transportation projects. During these years, when the South sustained one-third of the nation's textile mills, southern industrial growth seemed to be paralleling that of the North.[93] After 1815, however, southern industries waned as the rapidly developing textile industry of Britain and New England demanded cotton, the invention of the cotton gin stimulated short-staple cotton cultivation, and fertile southwestern plantations yielded quick profits to investors. Southerners now began to invest more in new lands and in slave labor than in industry and internal improvements. This decision stemmed not only from the agrarian tradition and the prestige of owning real property, but also because the production of staples seemed to promise the easiest financial success. In the competition for capital, agriculture thus outbid industry.[94]

Slavery, 275–80, has done, and as I have also done above), then the size of the southern market and the demand for manufactured goods also increases.

[92] Dew, *Ironmaker to the Confederacy*, 32; North, *Economic Growth*, 122–26; Genovese, *Political Economy of Slavery*, 159–65; W. Miller, "A Note on the Importance of the Interstate Slave Trade of the Ante-Bellum South," *Journal of Political Economy*, LXXIII (1965), 181–87.

[93] Taylor, *Transportation Revolution*, chs. 1 and 10; R. Griffin, "Origins of Southern Cotton Manufacture, 1807–1816," *Cotton History Review*, I (1960), 5–12; R. Griffin, "South Carolina Homespun Company," *Business History Review*, XXXV (1961), 402–14; and Starobin, "Industrial Slavery," ch. 1 and tables.

[94] Taylor, *Transportation Revolution*, chs. 1 and 10; Eaton, *Southern Civilization*, chs. 9 and 10; Stampp, *Peculiar Institution*, 398–99.

As a result of this process, by the 1830's key slave-state industries were already a generation behind those of the free states, and they were having great difficulty competing against outsiders. By 1860, the South had only one-fifth of the nation's manufacturing establishments, and the capitalization of southern factories was well below the national coverage. Thus, as Eugene Genovese has pointed out, southerners could provide a market for goods manufactured by Northerners and foreigners, but that same market was too small to sustain southern industries on a scale large enough to be competitive.[95]

Though these factors helped inhibit southern industries, it is hard to demonstrate that slavery was the *sole* cause of industrial backwardness. Slavery was only partly to blame for the South's difficulty competing with outside manufacturers, for unfavorable patterns of trade, and for restricted consumer demand. Other factors, such as geography, topography, and climate, were at least as important as slavery in retarding southern industry. Can slavery be blamed, for example, for the natural attractiveness of farming in a fertile region? Was slavery responsible for the South's natural waterway system, which delayed railroad development? It therefore seems doubtful that slavery alone decisively retarded the industrialization of the South.[96]

However, it must also be understood that, in the long run, extensive industrialization would have been difficult, if not impossible, under a rigid slave system. To develop according to the British or northern pattern, the rural population of the South would have had to be released from the land to create a supply of factory workers and urban consumers. Greater investment in education for skills and greater steps toward a more flexible wage labor system would have been necessary than were possible in a slaveholding society. Changes in the southern political structure permitting industrialists, mechanics, and free workers greater participation in decision-making processes affecting economic development were prerequisite to any far-reaching program of modernization.

On the other hand, even if slavery is theoretically and practically incompatible in the long run with full industrialization, the point

[95] Genovese, *Political Economy of Slavery*, 165–66.
[96] Stampp, *Peculiar Institution*, 397. Though limited markets restricted southern industrialization, the extent of this phenomenon should not be exaggerated. Plantation self-sufficiency, slow urbanization, and other market factors did not restrict consumption entirely. Recent studies have also shown that plantation and slave consumption were higher than once thought, and that some southern businessmen found substantial markets outside of the slave states. See Genovese, *Political Economy of Slavery*, 25, 159–62, 170, 185, and 276–77; and North, *Economic Growth*, 130.

at which this inconsistency would manifest itself had, apparently, not yet been reached between 1790 and 1861. Tensions were present in southern society, to be sure, but southerners were not yet foundering upon their domestic contradictions. The time when slavery would be absolutely detrimental to southern industries remained quite far off, and the development of slave-based industries was still necessary and desirable, given the imperatives of the proslavery ideology and the political realities of the period leading up to the Civil War.

TABLE 1. EARNINGS OF SLAVE-

Company	Location	Period
a. Woodville	Woodville, Miss.	1850–61
b. Tuscaloosa	Scottsville and Tuscaloosa, Ala.	1841–58
c. Barrett and Marks	Tallapoosa County, Ala.	1845
d. Mississippi	Bankston, Miss.	1849
		1850–60
e. Martin and Weekly	Florence, Ala.	1850–60
		1855
f. Bell	Huntsville, Ala.	1850–60
g. Saluda	Columbia, S.C.	1840–50
		1849
h. Vaucluse	Aiken, S.C.	1849
		1855
i. DeKalb	Camden, S.C.	1838–48
		1849–60
j. Various factories	Augusta, Ga.	1850–60
k. Arcadia	Pensacola, Fla.	1845–60
l. Roswell	Roswell, Ga.	1842
		1843
		1844
		1845
		1846
		1847
		1848
		1849
		1850–53
		1854
		1855
		1856
		1857
		1858
		1859
		1860
		1861

Dividend on Common Stock	Net Profit as a Percentage of Net Worth	Average (%)
10–15		12.5
10–15		12.5
	15	15
"Large dividends"		
	37	37
	10–14	12+
	50	
	"Eminently successful . . . has been for many years [1850's] been paying large profits."	
"Doing a flourishing business . . . pays large dividends."		
5		5
	15.6	15.6
	"Is making money."	
10+		
15		About 13
20–30		25
"The most successful of the cotton factories operating in . . . Florida."		
20		
18		
22		
20		
20		
14		
12		
12		
Dividends not discussed at stockholders' meetings.		
10		
17.5		
10		
10		
10		
15.5		
19		15.2
13		
	GRAND AVERAGE:	16

Sources for Table 1:

a. Vol. I, part 1, p. 46, McGehee Papers (LSU).
b. New Orleans *Picayune*, Oct. 16, 1858; R. Griffin, "Cotton Manufacture in Alabama," *Alabama Historical Quarterly*, XVIII (1956), 294.
c. Report of the Secretary of the Treasury, *House Exec. Doc.* #6, 29 C., 1 s., 1845, p. 649.
d. J. H. Moore, "Mississippi's Antebellum Textile Industry," *Journal of Mississippi History*, XXVI (1954), 86–90; *Niles' Register* LXXV (1849), 344.
e. Charleston *Mercury*, February 26, 1858.
f. *Hunt's Magazine*, XXXVIII (1858), 509.
g. New Orleans *Picayune*, October 23, 1845; Vicksburg *Whig*, November 12, 1849.
h. *De Bow's Review*, VII (1849), 457–58, and XVIII (1855), 787–88.
i. *Ibid.*, VII (1849), 372–73, and XVIII (1855), 787–88.
j. *Ibid.*
k. R. Griffin, "The Cotton Mill Campaign in Florida," *Florida Historical Quarterly*, XL (1962), 269.
l. Roswell Manufacturing Company's stockholders' minutes, 1842–1861 (GA); Charleston *Mercury*, February 26, 1858.

TABLE 2

EARNINGS OF SLAVE-EMPLOYING CANALS AND TURNPIKES, 1805–1861

Company and Location	Period	Dividend (%)	Profit Rate (%)	Average (%)
a. Louisville and Portland Canal, Kentucky	1831–42	8–10		14.7
	1843–55	20		
b. New Orleans Navigation Company, Louisiana	1805–27	6		7.2
	1828	10		
	1829	20		
	1830	19		
	1835	5		
c. Dismal Swamp Canal, Virginia	1850's	6		6
d. James River Canal, Virginia	1808–20	6		14
e. James River and Kanawha Company, Virginia	1835–60	12–16	"Never profitable to the stockholders"	0
f. Roanoke Navigation Company, Virginia	1836	1.5		1.5
g. Barataria and Lafourche Canal, Louisiana	1832	30		
	1833–52		Heavily in debt	
	1853–60		Little debt	
h. Lynchburg and Salem Turnpike, Virginia	1834	4		4

Sources:

a. G. M. Bibb, Report on the Louisville and Portland Canal, *House Doc* #68, 28 C., 2 s. (1845), pp. 7–9, 39; Paul B. Trescott, "The Louisville and Portland Canal Company, 1825–1874," *Mississippi Valley Historical Review*, XVIV (1958), 695, 698, 686, reports that "once completed, the canal made large profits,"

b. Louisiana *Journal of the Senate*, 1827, p. 17; 1829, p. 55; 1830, pp. 47–48; 1831, pp. 38–39, 58; 1836, p. 41.

c. Frederick L. Olmsted, *A Journey through the Seaboard Slave States* (New York, 1861), 151 note.

d,e. Wayland F. Dunaway, *History of the James River and Kanawha Canal Company* (New York, 1922), 34–36, 45, 182–83.

f. Virginia Board of Public Works *Report*, 1836, p. 48.

g. Louisiana *Journal of the House of Representatives*, 1848 session, pp. 148–50; Louisiana *Journal of the Senate*, 1853, p. 28.

h. Virginia Board of Public Works *Report*, 1835, pp. 59–60.

TABLE 3. EARNINGS OF SLAVE-EMPLOYING

Bold figures indicate dividends on common stock; other figures

COMPANY	1835	'36	'37	'38	'39	'40	'41	'42	'43	'44	'45	'46	'47
Montgomery & West Point										**3**	**3**		
Mobile & Ohio													
Georgia			6½	7	8	**8**	4.1	**10**	7.1	6.5	5.5	7.8	4½
Central of Georgia						3.4		2.7	4½	**6**	**6**	**6**	5.7
Macon & Western													
Southwestern													
Western & Atlantic													
Lexington & Frankfort													
Louisville & Frankfort													
Pacific													
Charlotte & South Carolina													
Raleigh & Gaston													
Wilmington & Weldon													
Wilmington & Manchester												6	
Greensville & Roanoke					3.1	3.2	5.7	3.4	2.7	2.3	3.0	3.7	4.2
South Carolina	6	6	6	6	2	4.3	3	5	5.3	**5**	5⅔	5⅓	5.8
Memphis & Charleston													
Nashville & Chattanooga													
Louisa				4½	**6**	4½	0	0	**6**	**6**	**6**	**6**	**6**
Petersburg	10	10		7½	6½	3	7	0	0	3	3½	7	7
Petersburg & Roanoke						(7 to 10 per cent)						7	7
Richmond, Fredericksburg & Potomac				7				7		**6**	**6**		7
Virginia Central													
Richmond & Petersburg												3.6	4.1

Sources:

The American Railroad Journal; De Bow's Review; Hunt's Magazine; The Journal of the Franklin Institute; The Farmer's Register; New Orleans *Picayune;* Virginia *Board of Public Works Reports; Southern Quarterly Review;* Mississippi Central Railroad *Report,* May 1, 1860; Ulrich B. Phillips, *A History of Transportation in the Eastern Cotton Belt to 1860* (New York, 1908); B. H. Meyer and Caroline E. MacGill, *History of Transportation in the United States before 1860* (Washington, 1917); H. D. Dozier, *A History of the Atlantic Coast Line Railroad* (Boston, 1920); Cecil K. Brown, *A State Movement in Railroad Development* (Chapel Hill, 1928); Samuel M. Derrick, *A Centennial History of the South Carolina Railroad* (Columbia, 1930); A. G. Smith, *Economic*

represent net earnings expressed as a percentage of net worth.

'48	'49	'50	'51	'52	'53	'54	'55	'56	'57	'58	'59	'60	'61	'62	AVERAGES	
	8½	9½					8		10	10						7.4
						1.2	2.7	5.4	6.9	10.5	8.0	16.2				7.3
6	6½	7	7	7	7½	8	3½	7½	8	6	7½	8–15			6.3	6.2
8	7–12½	8	8	8	8	14	21.0	19.8	15.4	21	22.6	20.3			10.9	11.1
12.3	17.5	15.2	9.9	12.3	12.1	12.0	14.2	10.4	9.0	11.4	14.5	18.6				13.0
		8	8	8	8		9	8	8	8	8	13				9.2
					7.0	10.4	13.2	15.0	14.3	12.4	13.9	12.8	16.8			12.9
			9.9	11.4	12.3	13.3	8.0									10.9
		6	6				6				6	6			6	
				5	5		5	5	5	5	5	5				5
			5	5	6				13						5.5	9
				6	10½						9					8.5
		6	6							7	8				6.8	
					15				14	8.5						10.9
		7.3			9.2											4.3
2½	4	6	7 ·	7	8	8½	9	10	8	8	8½	7			6.6	3.9
										10	12½	12				11.5
					3.5	5.7				5.6	13.7					7.1
4	4														4.4	
7	7	7	7	7	7	7	0	3	6	6	7½	10	9	12½	6.2	
															7	8.5
		7			7	12						7			6.8	8.3
			7		10	4½	6				7				10	6.1
3.7	2.8	3.9	3.9	4.5	4.2	6.2	6.6	6.0	6.2	7.0	6.5	6.7				5.1
												GRAND AVERAGE:			7.1	8.3

Readjustment in an Old Cotton State: South Carolina, 1820–1860 (Columbia, 1958); Robert Black, *Railroads of the Confederacy* (Chapel Hill, 1962); John B. Mordecai, *A Brief History of the Richmond, Fredericksburg and Potomac Railroad* (Richmond, 1941); Dorothy Jennings, "The Pacific Railroad Company," Missouri Historical Society *Collections*, VI (1931), 288–14; Charles W. Turner, "The Louisa Railroad, 1836–1850," *North Carolina Historical Review*, XXIV (1947), 34–57; Charles G. Woodward, "A Common Carrier of the South Before and During the War," Railway and Locomotive Historical Society *Bulletin*, XLIV (1937), 48–63.
Scattered information is available for a score or more other southern railroads.

TABLE 4

ANNUAL MAINTENANCE COST PER INDUSTRIAL SLAVE, 1820's–1861

(IN DOLLARS)

Location	Year	Food or Board	Clothing	Food Plus Clothing
1. Maramec Iron Works, Missouri	1820's-30's	36.50	29.20	
2. Colhoun's woolen mill, South Carolina	1830	23	5	
3. River snag boats	1829–39			120
4. Various sugar plantations, Louisiana	1830			50
5. Pine Forge, Virginia	1831–33	72		
6. Savannah River Improvement Project, Georgia	1835	54.75		
7. Robert Leslie's tobacco factory, Petersburg, Va.	1835	30		
8. William Clark's hemp factory, Kentucky	1838	72		
9. LaGrange and Memphis R.R., Tennessee	1839	96		
10. Nesbitt Iron Manufacturing Company, S.C.	ca. 1839	73		
11. Cherokee Iron Works, South Carolina	1839–40	10	3	
12. Sugar plantations, Louisiana	1845	10 (pork) 35 low 40 typical 50 high	15	30+
13. Graham cotton mill, Kentucky	1847–50	75	7.50	
14. Louisa R.R., Virginia	1851			33.25–34.25
15. Turpentine distillery, Alabama	1848			30
16. South Carolina R.R., South Carolina	1849	73		
17. A cotton mill, Mississippi	1847		16	
18. Public improvement projects, Virginia	1849	25		
19. Rocks Mill, Virginia	1838–50	120.45		

20. Vicksburg and Jackson R.R., Mississippi	1848–50	28 low, 31.45 average, 33.50 high			
21. Chesterfield R.R., Virginia	1851	52	25		
22. Virginia Central R.R., Virginia	1852	43	14+		
23. James River and Kanawha Canal, Virginia	1854	42			
	1858				
24. Gold Hill Mine, North Carolina	1855	42–48	24.50		
25. Nolensville Turnpike Company, Tennessee	1854	46.40	11.65		
	1855	29	14.30		
	1856	21	6.87		
	1858	15	10.83		
	1859	20.67			
26. Hardinsburg and Cloverport Turnpike Co., Kentucky	1859–60	125			
27. Charleston and Savannah R.R., South Carolina	1855		20		
28. Cape Fear and Deep River Navigation Co., N.C.	1859	109			
29. Blue Ridge R.R., South Carolina	1860	60			
30. Silver Hill Mine, North Carolina	1860	60			
31. Richmond, Fredericksburg and Potomac R.R., Va.	1860				
32. J. H. Couper's rice plantation, Georgia	1859			60	
33. Woodville mines, Virginia	ca. 1850's	23	15	22–25	
34. Evan's estimate		110			
35. Olmsted's estimate of a sugar plantation	1850's	24	15		
36. W. Dearmont, builder, Georgia	1850–61	91.25			
AVERAGES:	1820's–61	51.57	14.50	44.94	

Sources for Table 4:

1. Flyleaf notation, woodchopping book, vol. 10, James Collection (UMo.).
2. J. E. Colhoun Commonplace Book, 1836–1837 (Clemson).
3. H. Shreve, Report on Public Works, *House Doc.* #93, 26 C., 1 s., 1840, pp. 6, 9, 11–12.
4. *Niles' Register*, XXXIX (1830), 271.
5. Account book, vol. 8, 1831–1833, Shenandoah County, Virginia, Collection (UNC).
6. Reports, 1835, Mackay-Stiles Papers, series B (UNC).
7. Bill, December 31, 1835, Leslie Papers (Duke).
8. Accounts, ca. 1838 (Filson).
9. Report, July 17, 1839, *American Railroad Journal*, IX (1839), 80–81.
10. Undated memo, ca. 1839, Elmore Papers (LC).
11. Statement, 1839–1840, Elmore Papers (USC); cf. J. A. Black report, 1840, Elmore Papers (USC).
12. Report of the Secretary of the Treasury, *House Exec. Doc.* #6, 29 C., 1 s., 1845, pp. 708–09, 748.
13. Account Books, 1847–1850, 1851, Graham Papers (UK).
14. Report, November 20, 1848, Virginia *Board of Public Works Report*, 1848, p. 431.
15. *De Bow's Review*, VII (1849), 560–62.
16. Report, 1847, *American Railroad Journal*, XXI (1848), 293–98.
17. Jackson, *Mississippian*, May 4, 1849.
18. *Patent Office Report*, 1849, II, 141.
19. Account book of estate management, pp. 82–84, Muse Papers (Duke).
20. *De Bow's Review*, IX (1850), 456.
21. Cited in R. Evans, Jr., "Some Aspects of the Domestic Slave Trade, 1830–60," *Southern Economic Journal*, XXVII (1961), 336 table.
22. Account, March, 1852, box 201, Brock Collection (Huntington).
23. Report, October 30, 1858, Virginia *Board of Public Works Report*, 1858, p. 277; report of 1854, in *ibid.*, 1854, p. 394.
24. Account book, vol. 3, 1854–1861 (UNC).
25. Nolensville Turnpike Company Minutebook, 1829–1865 (TSL).
26. Hardinsburg and Cloverport Turnpike Accounts, 1859, 1860 (Filson).
27. See footnote 21 above.
28. Bills, October, December 31, 1859, Cape Fear & Deep River Works, Treasurers' Papers (NCA).
29. Statement of costs, July 13, 1860, Hawkins Papers (UNC).
30. Ledger, p. 219 (UNC).
31. C. W. Turner, "The Richmond, Fredericksburg and Potomac," *Civil War History*, VII (1961), 259.
32. J. H. Couper to F. P. Corbin, March 28, 1859, Corbin Papers (NYPL).
33. F. Green, "Gold Mining in Antebellum Virginia," *Virginia Magazine of History and Biography*, XLV (1937), 361–62.
34. See footnote 21 above.
35. F. L. Olmsted, *A Journey in the Seaboard Slave States* (New York, 1861), 686–88.
36. Account book, ca. 1850–1861, Dearmont Papers (Duke).

COMMUNICATIONS

THE PROFITABILITY OF ANTE BELLUM SLAVERY—REVISITED[*]

A recent note in this *Journal* by Edward Saraydar[1] undertakes a criticism of Alfred Conrad and John Meyer's well known article, "The Economics of Slavery in the Ante Bellum South." [2] By reconstructing a typical cotton plantation's production function, Conrad and Meyer had attempted to prove that southern slavery in the latter part of the 1850's was at least as profitable as alternative investment opportunities.

Mr. Saraydar charges that Conrad and Meyer in the course of their calculations confused data from plantations that purchased all food and clothing from outside sources with data from self-sufficient plantations. By using the average yield per slave from the *specialized* plantations and estimates of yearly slave maintenance from *self-sufficient* plantations, one would arrive at too high a profit rate. Saraydar recalculates what he feels to be consistent data and uses them to demonstrate "the general unprofitability of slave operations in cotton." [3]

The relevancy of the rate of profit earned on ante bellum cotton plantations to a number of historical questions has been pointed out by Conrad and Meyer. Primarily, however, interest has been focused on the proposition that the institution of slavery would have destroyed itself without political intervention through its own unprofitability had not the Civil War intervened.[4]

It was primarily to test this hypothesis, and to test it on the historians' ground, that Conrad and Meyer undertook to calculate the rate of return on slave holdings in the last decades before the Civil War. They concluded that:

In sum, it seems doubtful that the South was forced by bad statesmanship into an unnecessary war to protect a system which must soon have disappeared because it was economically unsound. This is a romantic hypothesis which will not stand against the facts.[5]

It is true, if Conrad and Meyer's figures are valid, that the historians' argument "can no longer rest upon allegations of unprofitability." [6] On the other hand, it is important to note that if Conrad and Meyer's calculations are wrong (as Saraydar suggests), this alone would not be sufficient to prove that slavery was about to "topple of its own weight." For what is really of importance to this test is not the profitability of cotton production, which is a short-run phenomenon, but the viability of slavery. If cotton production was unprofitable, it would not mean that slavery was doomed, for presumably alternative uses for slaves existed. If at the existing prices no alternative uses for slave labor were profitable, then the price of slaves, the price of land, or both, would have fallen (had emancipation not taken place) until it was once again profitable to own slaves and to grow cotton. In other words, temporary unprofitability of cotton operations would only mean that land and slaves were overvalued or that resources were misallocated, not that the institution of slavery was economically unsound.

Since slavery is only a peculiar method of providing a labor force, we would expect slavery to be viable as long as it could provide labor at a cost equal to or below that

* I would like to thank Dr. Douglass C. North and Dr. Donald F. Gordon of the University of Washington for their helpful comments on earlier drafts of this paper.

[1] Edward Saraydar, "A Note on the Profitability of Ante Bellum Slavery," *The Southern Economic Journal*, April 1964, pp. 325–32.

[2] Alfred H. Conrad and John R. Meyer, "The Economics of Slavery in the Ante Bellum South," *The Journal of Political Economy*, April 1958, pp. 95–130.

[3] Saraydar, p. 331.

[4] Conrad and Meyer, p. 95.

[5] *Ibid.*, p. 121.

[6] *Ibid.*, p. 122.

of free labor. Since the cost of owning a slave is the cost of his maintenance plus the amortization of his initial price, slavery will always be able to compete with free labor through adjustments in the price of slaves. If free labor posed a threat to slave labor, slave prices would fall and slavery's viability would be maintained. Only if slave prices fell to zero would the institution become economically unviable, and this could happen only if the wages of free labor were at the subsistence level.[7] But this would imply that the free labor force was multiplying at Malthusian rates—a highly unlikely assumption for any period of American history. Thus, it is fairly certain that given reasonably flexible slave prices economic forces could not have brought about an end to slavery directly.

While the profitability figures of both Conrad and Meyer and Saraydar are irrelevant to the question of slavery's viability, they do have a relevance to other questions often connected with ante bellum slavery. For example, a number of historians have argued that low monetary returns to slave owning were counterbalanced by nonpecuniary returns.[8] In other words, the owning of slaves conferred upon the master a higher status in his community, or gave him a feeling of power, or gave him political prestige, or some other nonmonetary return which compensated for low rates of profit.

By calculating the monetary returns, we can test whether such nonpecuniary returns are necessary to explain the patterns of slaveholding. Saraydar's calculations imply that they are necessary, and that Conrad and Meyer were wrong. Despite the fact that there are some problems with Conrad and Meyer's data, it is our contention that

Saraydar has made even more critical mistakes in his calculations, and that they vitiate his conclusion.

There are two sources of error in Saraydar's estimates: (1) he employs an unrealistic assumption about the cotton plantation's production function, and (2) he underestimates the yearly yield of cotton per slave hand. The balance of this note attempts to demonstrate how serious these two factors are to the estimates of profit rate in cotton production.

I

The incorrect specification in Saraydar's production function arises from his implicit assumption that no reproduction of the slave stock takes place. Conrad and Meyer, in their article, employed a concept of a dual production function. One function was used to measure the return from the labor of male field hands, the other the return from the sale of children produced by the female slaves. The two production functions were completely independent of each other.

Saraydar tested only the first of these two production functions; however, he did not retain their independence. Instead, he increased the estimate of the yearly maintenance cost of a male hand used by Conrad and Meyer to include an amount necessary to maintain the females and children.[9] Yet he did not include the returns the females generated by producing salable offspring.

In other words, Saraydar calculates the return to slaveholders by assuming that only the labor in the cotton fields was productive of revenue and that no increase in the stock of slaves took place. In his model, the stream of income provided by an investment in slaves remains constant for thirty years and then stops. In reality, of course, the slave population actually grew throughout the whole period. Thus, an investor in this form of capital would find that as time passed his stock of capital was growing—since under southern law, the children of a

[7] The wages of free labor would not have to fall quite to the subsistence level if a slave were a less productive worker than the free laborer. For even if the free laborer's wage were above subsistence, we would prefer him to a slave for whom we had to provide subsistence, if the free laborer's product were higher.

[8] Ulrich Bonnell Phillips, *American Negro Slavery*, 2d ed. (Gloucester, Mass.: Peter Smith, 1959), p. 394.

[9] Saraydar, pp. 327–28.

female slave belonged to the woman's owner. This growth in the stock of capital would produce a rising stream of income that would continue growing indefinitely.

Thus, if we wish to switch from Conrad and Meyer's dual production function to a single production function (including both male and female slaves as inputs), we must include the appreciation in the slave stock as part of our formulation. Alternatively, if we wished to retain Conrad and Meyer's dual concept, we would not properly include the females and children as inputs to the males' production function, for they are inputs to their own distinct production function. If this is the case, Conrad and Meyer's maintenance costs *are* the appropriate estimates and we cannot charge that they confused "out-of-pocket expenses per *slave* with out-of-pocket expenses per slave *hand* when recording maintenance costs." [10]

To obtain an idea of how critical this error in specification of the production function is, we have recalculated the rate of profit using a single production function concept. This approach has an advantage over the dual production function of Conrad and Meyer in that the rate of appreciation of slave capital can be calculated directly from Census data rather than requiring a large number of assumptions concerning fertility and mortality rates of the slave population.

The single production function model is embodied in the following formula:[11]

[10] Saraydar, p. 327.

[11] The formula is derived in the following way:

$$V_t = R_t \, (1/1 + r)^t$$

is the capital value formula where R_t is the return in the year t, and V_t is the present value of this return. But the return per hand is $pY - c$, and the number of hands in year t is $(1 + a)^t$ times the original number of hands purchased; since we are looking for the present value of a single slave we have:

$$V_t = (pY - c)(1 + a)^t(1/1 + r)^t,$$

since a purchase of slaves will yield an infinite stream of income, the present value of this stream is obtained by summing:

$$r = \frac{1 + a}{1 - \left[\dfrac{pY - c}{K}\right]} - 1,$$

where

r is the internal rate of return,

a is the appreciation rate of the stock of slaves,

p is the price of cotton to the farmer,

Y is the yield per hand in pounds,

c is the yearly out-of-pocket expense per hand, and

K is the initial investment per hand.

Consulting the Census figures, we find that between 1850 and 1860 the slave population increased 23.4 per cent which represents an annual increase of 2.15 per cent.[12] Between 1850 and 1860, slave prices rose 72 per cent or, after adjustment for the increase in the general price level, 68 per cent.[13] Thus the capital value of the slave stock increased 107.6 per cent in ten years—an annual increase of 7.56 per cent.

When we recognize this general appreciation of an investment in slaves, it puts a totally new light on the profitability question. For this 7.6 per cent increase in and of itself is greater than the 6 per cent alterna-

$$K = (pY - c) \sum_{t=0}^{\infty} \left[\frac{1 + a}{1 + r}\right]^t$$

which simplifies to:

$$K = \frac{(pY - c)}{1 - \left[\dfrac{1 + a}{1 + r}\right]}$$

and solving for r gives us our formula.

[12] Census Office, *Population of the United States in 1860*, Eighth Census (Washington, D. C.: U. S. Government Printing Office, 1864), p. ix. The age distribution of the population also shifted between 'fifty and 'sixty, but a calculation of "prime field hand equivalents" showed that they increased only one tenth of 1 per cent more over the ten years than the population as a whole.

[13] Robert Evans, Jr., "The Economics of American Negro Slavery, 1830–1860," *Aspects of Labor Economics*, National Bureau of Economic Research (Princeton, N. J.: Princeton University Press, 1962), p. 224. Evans used a New Orleans price index.

tive rate of return. However, if these capital gains are to be solidly based on rising profitability of slave-operated cotton plantations rather than on short-term speculation effects, we must demonstrate a return to cotton production above 6 per cent *exclusive* of the effects of rising slave prices. For this reason an appreciation rate of 2.15 per cent is used in the following calculations.

To measure how significant the growth of the slave population is to the estimates of profit rate, we recalculated the internal rate of return using Saraydar's own estimates of the yields per hand for each of the regions he examined, and the seven- to eight-cent range in the price of cotton used by Saraydar. However, increases are necessary in both the yearly maintenance cost and the initial investment required to be consistent with the altered assumptions.

For the cost of slave maintenance, Saraydar uses $32 per hand. Since the number of slaves increased at the rate of 2.15 per cent, the stock of land and associated capital must be increased at the same rate to prevent diminishing returns. Using Saraydar's figures of $640 and $793 for the cost of these inputs per hand for the Old South and for the highly fertile alluvial soils respectively means that new investment of $13.76 to $17.05 per hand per year must be added to the $32 maintenance cost.

The nursery costs associated with the birth of slave children must also be included in the yearly maintenance allowance if we are to bring all the costs into the picture. In 1860 there were 113,650 slaves under one year old[14] which would imply 2.87 successful births per year for every one hundred slaves. Conrad and Meyer assumed that the nursery costs were $50 per successful pregnancy[15] which in turn implies a cost of $2.87 per slave hand per year for nursery costs.[16] Thus the total yearly outlay per hand

ranges from $48.70 to $52.00, the numbers we use for c in the formula.

For our calculations, we need to have an estimate of the initial capital investment per hand; this variable should include the cost of the slaves, land, and equipment, and the value of a sinking fund to replace the land as it wears out. Saraydar calculates the value of the land, the equipment, and the sinking fund at $640 for plantations in the Old South and $793 for alluvial soil. The sinking fund was calculated to last only thirty years; however, the necessary increase required to extend this to a perpetual fund is negligible. These data, then, seem reasonable enough as they stand. However, in calculating the necessary investment in slaves we must now include, not just the investment in male field hands, but in women and children as well.

In 1850, 45.4 per cent of the slaves in the United States were under fifteen years of age and 50.87 per cent were between 15 and 60.[17] Conrad and Meyer have reported the average price of a male field hand in prime condition in 1848 as $900 and an adult female as $750 to $800.[18] Assuming that children and slaves over 60 are worth only one half of their adult prices, we can calculate that the average value of a slave was roughly $630 in 1849, the year for which Saraydar measured his yields. Thus, if 50 per cent of the slaves are field hands, the average investment in slaves per hand was $1,260; adding the cost of the other capital as estimated by Saraydar, we come to the final estimate of capital expenditures: $1,900 for the Old South, and $2,053 for alluvium.

Table I compares the returns computed by Saraydar with those from the single production function model. As can be seen, his neglect of the growth of the negro population produced a significant downward bias in his estimates.

---

[14] *Eighth Census of Population*, p. 594.

[15] Conrad and Meyer, p. 108.

[16] Assuming, with Saraydar, that 50 per cent of the slaves are hands.

[17] J. D. B. DeBow, *Statistical View of the United States, Compendium of the Seventh Census* (Washington, D. C.: Beverley Tucker, 1854), p. 103.

[18] Conrad and Meyer, p. 100.

TABLE I

Effect on Estimated Returns of Alternative Models of the Production Function

Region and model	Yield (bales per hand)	Capital cost	Maintenance cost	Return with cotton selling for	
				7¢/lb.	8¢/lb. (percentage)
Older Areas:					
Saraydar's Model	3	$1,640	$32.00	—	1.1
Single Production Function Model	3	1,900	48.70	4.1	4.8
Average for the South:					
Saraydar's Model	3.2	1,690	32.00	—	1.5
Single Production Function Model	3.2	1,950	49.70	4.3	5.0
Average for Alluvium:					
Saraydar's Model	3.6	1,793	32.00	0.9	2.3
Single Production Function Model	3.6	2,053	52.00	4.6	5.4
High for Alluvium:					
Saraydar's Model	6.1	1,793	32.00	6.5	8.2
Single Production Function Model	6.1	2,053	52.00	8.4	9.8

—, less than .025%.
Source for Saraydar's Model: Saraydar, Table I, p. 331.

Saraydar originally calculated a yield for "poor upland pine land"; however, this figure is not reported in Table I since Saraydar's calculations for this region are incorrect by his own method. He chose two counties in northwestern Alabama which he felt had poor soils,[19] and he reported a cotton output per hand of 2.4 bales in one and of 1.7 bales in the other.[20] Yet the correct figures, *using his method*, should be exactly twice this. Apparently he did not divide the slave population in half before calculating his returns.

II

As Table I has shown, the effects of appreciating stocks are fairly significant to

the profitability estimates, but they are not generally sufficient to raise the return above the 6 per cent interest available on alternative investments. This brings us to the second source of error in Saraydar's estimate: his underestimation of the average yield per hand.

Conrad and Meyer's data on the average yield were drawn from three authoritative secondary sources: J. L. Watkins, *The Cost of Cotton Production;* Lewis C. Gray, *History of Agriculture in the Southern United States to 1860;* and Kenneth Stampp, *The Peculiar Institution.*[21] The yields used in Conrad and Meyer's calculations ranged from three bales per hand per year on the worst land to seven bales per hand on the best.[22]

[19] Fayette and Marion Counties, Alabama. There is no evidence that I could find that would indicate that these counties had poor soils. Indeed, E. A. Smith reports the soils are above average in fertility and "quite productive." Eugene A. Smith, "Report on the Cotton Production of the State of Alabama," in Eugene W. Hilgard, Census Office, *Report on Cotton Production in the United States, Part I* (Washington, D. C.: U. S. Government Printing Office, 1884), pp. 120–21.
[20] Saraydar, p. 330.

[21] James L. Watkins, *The Cost of Cotton Production,* U. S. Department of Agriculture, Division of Statistics, Miscellaneous Series, Bulletin No. 16 (Washington, D. C.: U. S. Government Printing Office, 1899); Lewis Cecil Gray, *History of Agriculture in the Southern United States to 1860,* 2d ed. (Gloucester, Mass.: Peter Smith, 1958); Kenneth Stampp, *The Peculiar Institution* (New York: Alfred Knopf, 1956).
[22] Conrad and Meyer, p. 107.

531

TABLE II
YIELDS PER ACRE ON MISSISSIPPI ALLUVIUM IN 1879

County	Pounds of lint per acre	Page reference
Mississippi County, Arkansas	390	p. 587
Tunica County, Mississippi	285	p. 318
Crittenden County, Arkansas	330	p. 587
Coahoma County, Mississippi	380	p. 318
Desha County, Arkansas	430	p. 586
Bolivar County, Mississippi	399	p. 320
Washington County, Mississippi	413	p. 321
Chicot County, Arkansas	470	p. 548
East Carroll Parish, Louisiana	451	p. 145
Issaquena County, Mississippi	418	p. 323
Madison Parish, Louisiana	394	p. 149
Tensas Parish, Louisiana	394	p. 149
Concordia Parish, Louisiana	375	p. 149
Weighted Average	396	

Source: Computed from data in Eugene W. Hilgard, Census Office, *Report on Cotton Production in the United States, Part I*, (Washington, D. C.: U.S. Government Printing Office, 1884). The data were reported in bales and converted to pounds according to the average weight of bales reported on p. 18.

Saraydar charges that these figures are unrealistic in light of present day yields from cotton plantations of the South. He calculates that Conrad and Meyer's average yield of seven to eight bales per hand on alluvial soil (regarded as the best for cotton) implies a yield per acre of 280–320 pounds; yet it was not until 1946–1950 that 280 pounds per acre was achieved as an average for the South, and not until 1951–1955 that it reached 340 pounds.

Saraydar concludes:

> ...this would have the dubious implication that the significant innovations in cotton culture which have served to boost yield per acre since the 30's have been only just sufficient to increase per acre yield to a level commensurate to that achieved on alluvium in 1850....[22]

However, this finding is not as unreasonable as it might first appear. For one thing, Saraydar is comparing the yield from the best lands of the South before the Civil War with the average for all the United States in recent years. It is not immediately obvious that agricultural technology should have improved *average* yields to the extent that they equalled the yields obtainable from the *best* soils before the Civil War.

In fact, if we look at the growth in productivity on alluvial soil we find that it has grown at a reasonable rate. The Census of 1880 provides us with the earliest data on cotton yields per acre by county. We can use these data to compare the 280–320 pounds per acre yield implied by Conrad and Meyer's data, with yields from alluvium in 1879. Table II presents the average yield per acre for the 13 counties in Arkansas, Mississippi, and Louisiana that border the Mississippi River and are characterized by the Census Office as having primarily alluvial soils.

Since these 13 counties produced one half of all the cotton grown on alluvium in that year,[24] the average yield of 396 pounds can probably be taken as an average for a typical Mississippi alluvium operation in 1879. This figure is 24 to 41 per cent higher than the yield implied by Conrad and Meyer's seven to eight bales per hand for Mississippi alluvium.

Saraydar has suggested that the yields reported by Conrad and Meyer were too large, because they came from plantations that bought all their food from the outside rather than growing most of their own.[25] Since the production costs used by Conrad and Meyer are based on the assumption of self-sufficiency, such an error would bias their calculated returns upward.

However, a check of the three sources used by Conrad and Meyer reveals in two of them that the figures given were explicitly stated to be from plantations that *did* produce their own foodstuffs. Conrad and Meyer's figure for the Vicksburg area of Mississippi, for example, is obtained from Watkins:

---

[22] Saraydar, p. 329–30.

[24] Hilgard, Part I, p. 16.
[25] Saraydar, p. 328.

A Vicksburg, Miss., cotton planter [who owned in 1855] ... a plantation of 1,600 acres, 1,000 of which was cleared land, and worked with 75 effective hands worth $600 each and 50 mules worth $130 each, *the corn and meat being produced on the plantation*, states that the yield for an average of ten years would be about 600 bales of 400 pounds each.[26] [Italics mine.]

Simple calculation gives an average yield of eight bales per "effective" hand.

Similarly, the figure from Watkins cited by Conrad and Meyer for DeSoto County, Mississippi (1849), was from a self-sufficient plantation. Here "4 bales of 500 pounds each per hand [was] a fair average." [27] Since Conrad and Meyer based their price on a four-hundred-pound bale, they should have reported five bales a hand from this county—as it is, they *underestimate* the average yield.[28]

Conrad and Meyer cite from Gray a yield of five bales on new land in the Southwest. Gray reports a hand could work eight to ten acres of cotton "besides making provisions." [29] Eight to ten acres with a product of 250 pounds each, yields five to six-and-a-quarter bales, of four hundred pounds each, to the hand.

Thus, it would seem that Saraydar was incorrect in arguing that "as an average for self-sufficient cotton hands working on alluvial land 7–8 bales is very probably high." [30] It can be easily shown that Saraydar's range of 2 to 3.6 bales is an underestimate. In 1859, seven southern states[31] produced 4,824,308 bales (400 pounds each) of cotton

(90 per cent of the U.S. crop). The 1860 slave population of these same states was 2,361,722, but only 1,594,888 were between 10 and 70 years old.[32] If we subtract 10 per cent from this figure for the slaves in the cities,[33] we get an average yield of 3.36 bales per slave, and this completely ignores the fact that a sizable proportion of these slaves were not cotton hands, but worked in tobacco, rice, sugar, or other cash crops, or were domestic servants, or were unable to work for one reason or another.

Because he felt Conrad and Meyer had overvalued the average product of a field hand, Saraydar recalculated yields for several regions of the South. His estimates were arrived at by dividing one half of the slave population of several southern counties into the counties' cotton production, the raw data being taken from the Seventh Census (1850).[34]

The major bias in such a procedure is introduced by using the Seventh Census, which reported the 1849 cotton crop—for this year saw particularly low yields.[35] The total crop of the preceding year (considered a particularly good one) was 25 per cent higher; and not until the outbreak of the War, over a decade later, did the cotton crop fall below the trough reached in 1849.[36] The average annual crop of the 50's was 3,091,843 five-hundred-pound bales, a full 50 per cent above the 2,064,028 bales of the 1849 season.

The short crop sent the price of cotton up to 10.8 cents a pound.[37] If Saraydar had

[26] Watkins, p. 46.
[27] Ibid., p. 45.
[28] Similarly, Conrad and Meyer's 1844 figure of seven bales to a hand was underestimated; as the reference was to 450-pound bales (Watkins, p. 43), the correct figure should be 7.875 bales. And the Cherokee County, Alabama (1855), yield of four bales was for 500-pound bales; the correct figure is therefore five bales. It should also be noted that the yield of 4½ bales per hand for South Carolina coastal plantations cited by Conrad and Meyer actually refers to a plantation in Marengo County, Alabama (Watkins, pp. 44–45).
[29] Gray, p. 912.
[30] Saraydar, p. 330.
[31] Alabama, Arkansas, Georgia, Louisiana, Mississippi, South Carolina, and Texas.

[32] *Eighth Census of Population*, pp. 594–95.
[33] This figure is given by Kenneth Stampp and is cited with approval by Saraydar.
[34] DeBow, pp. 194–337.
[35] Watkins, p. 34.
[36] Gray, Table 40, p. 1026.
[37] Ibid., Table 41, p. 1027. It should be noted that when Conrad and Meyer reproduced these data of Gray in their Table 17, p. 117, they matched average cotton prices with the wrong years' cotton production. If the years are meant to be crop years, then Conrad and Meyer have reported the crop a year late (i.e., the crop of 1849 is reported as that of 1850). If the years are meant to be commercial years, then the prices are reported a year early.

TABLE III
ESTIMATED RETURN FOR 1849

Region	Yield	Internal rate of return	
		9¢/lb.	10¢/lb.
Older areas	3.0	5.5	6.1
Average for South	3.2	5.7	6.4
Average for alluvium	3.6	6.2	6.9
High for alluvium	6.1	11.2	12.8

used a price based on this rate in his calculations, then the error in using the 1849 crop would not be so great; instead, he used a 7- to 8-cent range that was valid for more normal years. Thus, even if Saraydar's yields accurately measured 1849 productivity, his profit rates could not be considered correct.

Between September 1849 and August 1850, the period in which the 1849 crop was sold, cotton prices at New Orleans rose from 9.3 cents a pound in September to 12.2 cents in July 1850. The weighted average price for the year was 10.8 cents.[38] Conrad and Meyer have calculated the cost of marketing the cotton (the cost of freight, insurance, storage, drayage, and commissions) at 0.7 to 0.8 of a cent per pound.[39] Thus, if we use 9–10 cents a pound as the price of cotton, we should not be overstating the farm-gate price relevant to Saraydar's yields.

Table III presents the results of calculating the rate of return using 9- to 10-cent cotton. The model used was the single production function model, with the same capital and maintenance allowances used in Table I.

These calculations show that slavery was profitable for a good many planters in 1849. But still we can hardly expect to find "normal" profits in a year of particularly poor crops. What we would like to do is to recalculate yields for different years than 1849.

If we wish to avoid the cotton crop data from 1849, we are forced to use the data reported in the Census of 1860 for the 1859 crop. But, then we have the opposite problem, for 1859 was one of the best years for cotton production and the yields calculated from these data will overrepresent an average for the decade of the fifties.

However, there are several reasons why it would be interesting to examine the yields of 1859. First, a test for 1859 is more relevant than one for 1849 to the hypothesis of the major proponent of the unprofitability thesis, U. B. Phillips. It was his contention that:

...by the close of the 'fifties it is fairly certain that no slaveholders but those few whose plantations lay in the most advantageous parts of the cotton and sugar districts and whose managerial ability was exceptionally great were earning anything beyond what would cover their maintenance and carrying charges. [Italics mine.][40]

Secondly, there were a number of important changes in the cotton economy between 1849 and 1859. Cotton output more than doubled—largely through expansions into new lands in Louisiana, Arkansas, and Texas (these states' cotton output rose 335 per cent, 462 per cent, and 643 per cent respectively). And, as we have noted, the price of slaves rose 68 per cent during the decade. The price of cotton seemed to be increasing slowly.

Finally, the more detailed data available from the 1860 Census will enable us to devise a more precise method of estimating the yields. Saraydar's method of simply dividing one half the number of slaves into the cotton production of each county introduces several biases into the estimates. We should like to correct for as many of these as possible.

As Saraydar realized, his method assumes all the slaves in the county lived on cotton plantations. Yet an examination of the fourteen alluvial-soil counties of Mississippi, used in part by Saraydar in his calculations, turned up Adams County with 688 slaveowners in 1860 but only 214 farms, and

[38] Ibid.
[39] Conrad and Meyer, p. 105.

[40] Phillips, pp. 391–92.

Warren County with 821 slaveholders and only 396 farms.[41] Of the fourteen alluvial counties examined, all but one had a greater number of slaveowners than of farms in 1860. By including slaves who were obviously not on farms in his calculations, Saraydar's method will bias the yields downward.

A bias in the opposite direction will be present, in so far as free men worked in the fields producing cotton. Data in the *1860 Census of Population* enable us to make at least a partial correction for both of these effects. So that we do not count slaves who lived in cities as farm hands, we have deducted from each county's population the number of slaves reported in each of the towns enumerated by the Census. Since the listing by towns is partial, this will be only an incomplete adjustment. Furthermore, for South Carolina, a number of towns had only the free population reported; for these it was assumed that the same proportion of slaves resided in the city as was found in those towns of South Carolina (excluding Charleston) for which the slave population was reported.

The Census reported in 1860 the occupations of the free population by state. We calculated for each state the percentage of the free population who were reported as farm laborers (see Table IV), and assumed that this ratio held in every county. From this was calculated the estimated number of free field hands, which was added to the slave population. In general, this adjust-

TABLE IV

PERCENTAGE OF THE FREE POPULATION WHO WERE FARM LABORERS, 1860

State	Percentage	State	Percentage
Alabama	2.7	Mississippi	2.2
Arkansas	2.6	South Carolina	2.1
Georgia	3.3	Texas	1.6
Louisiana	1.5		

Source: *Eighth Census of Population*, pp. 662–63, 607.

ment had negligible effects on the productivity.[42]

A minor downward bias is introduced into the calculations because the 1850 Census reports the crops of 1849 but the population of 1850. Since the population grew between 1849 and 1850, too many slaves will be included in the calculations. On the average, this amounts to only about 2 per cent; although in counties that experienced a large in-migration of slaves, this factor might be significant. No adjustment was attempted to correct this bias.

Saraydar's method assumes a labor force participation rate of 50 per cent; although this figure is supported by a number of contemporary sources, it would seem open to doubt. For this rate implies that *all* slaves, male and female, fifteen to sixty years old, would be engaged as full-time hands.[43] Yet, it must be that a number of slaves in this age group were domestic servants or craftsmen, and that many of the women were unable to work in the fields because of advanced pregnancy or child-caring activities. Moreover, very few of the children below fifteen could be expected to be as helpful as a prime field hand (32 per cent of the slave population were under ten).

---

[41] United States Census Office, *Agriculture of the United States in 1860*, Eighth Census (Washington, D. C.: U. S. Government Printing Office, 1864), pp. 206 and 232. According to the Census Office, "It would probably be a safe rule to consider the number of slaveholders to represent the number of families directly interested in the slave population in 1860," p. clxxii. Since there is no reason (such as tax advantage) to believe that there would be more than one slaveholding family per farm, it can be safely assumed that the excess of slaveholders over farmers represents the minimal number of persons who held slaves for nonagricultural purposes.

[42] It might be argued that the white slaveowners should be included in the number of cotton hands along with the slaves and free farm laborers. However, the best evidence is that it was not common for the slaveowner to work alongside his chattel, particularly in the planting regions that we are considering. See Gray, p. 486. Furthermore, a check of the census figures reveals that such inclusion would have little effect on the results.

[43] DeBow, p. 91.

TABLE V
YIELDS OF COTTON—ALLUVIAL REGIONS—1859

Region	Bales per slave (400 lbs.)
Mississippi River Counties, Louisiana[a]	6.27
Alluvial Counties, Southeast Arkansas[b]	4.35
Yazoo Delta, Mississippi[c]	3.88
Upper Red River Counties, Louisiana[d]	3.40
River Counties, Southwest Mississippi[e]	2.69
Tennessee River Valley, Alabama[f]	1.72
28 Alluvial Counties, Miss., La., Ark., and Ala.[g]	3.69

YIELDS OF COTTON—OTHER COTTON REGIONS OF THE NEW SOUTH—1859

East Texas Cotton Counties[h]	3.83
Northwest Alabama[i]	2.74
Black Prairie, Alabama[j]	2.69
Clay Hills Region, Alabama[k]	2.33
Eastern Piedmont, Alabama[l]	2.24

YIELD OF COTTON—COTTON REGIONS OF THE OLD SOUTH—1859

Upper Coastal Plain, Georgia[m]	2.39
Southern Piedmont, Georgia[n]	1.74
Middle and Upper Coastal Plain, South Carolina[o]	1.13
Southern Piedmont, South Carolina[p]	1.17
17 Counties, Georgia[m, n]	2.03
13 Districts, South Carolina[q]	1.25

[a] Carrol, Concordia, Madison, and Tensas Parishes, Louisiana.

[b] Arkansas, Chicot, Deshia, and Jefferson Counties, Arkansas.

[c] Bolivar, Coahoma, Issaquena, Tallahatchie, and Tunica Counties, Mississippi. Part brown-loam uplands.

[d] Bossier and DeSoto Parishes, Louisiana.

[e] Adams, Claiborne, Jefferson, and Wilkinson Counties, Mississippi. Part brown-loam uplands.

[f] Limestone and Madison Counties, Alabama. Rich alluvial river bottoms offset by poorer uplands.

[g] All counties listed in notes a through f, as well as Carrol, Hinds, Madison, Warren, and Yazoo Counties, Mississippi; Rapides Parish, Louisiana; and Crittenden County, Arkansas.

[h] Austin, Fort Bent, Grimes, Walker, and Washington Counties, Texas.

[i] Fayette and Marion Counties, Alabama.

[j] Dallas, Greene, Lowndes, Marengo, and Montgomery Counties, Alabama.

[k] Butler and Pike Counties, Alabama.

[l] Chambers and Coosa Counties, Alabama.

[m] Burke, Clay, Dougherty, Houston, Stewart, Sumter, Thomas, and Washington Counties, Georgia.

[n] Coweta, Hancock, Harris, Meriwether, Monroe, Morgan, Newton, Putnam, and Troup Counties, Georgia.

[o] Barnwell, Clarendon, Richland, and Sumter Districts, South Carolina.

[p] Abbeville, Edgefield, Laurens, and Newberry Districts, South Carolina.

[q] All districts listed in notes o and p as well as: Cheste, Darlington, Marion, Marlborough and Union Districts, South Carolina.

The problem of measuring the labor force participation rate is particularly tricky. One of the important advantages of the single production function is that it allows us to bypass the problem entirely. As can be seen by referring to the formula, the calculation of the internal rate of interest is independent of the proportion of slaves assumed to be field hands. For we can calculate the yield as well as the yearly outlay and capital costs on a per-*slave*, rather than a per-hand, basis. In other words, the proportion of slaves assumed to be hands cancels out of the interest formula. This makes the calculated return for each region dependent on the total cotton output, the total number of slaves on cotton plantations, the price of cotton, and the yearly outlay and capital costs per slave.

Since Saraydar assumes a 50 per cent labor force participation rate, we need only halve the initial capital cost and the yearly maintenance allowance already calculated to return the data to the original per-slave basis.

Table V presents the estimated average yield per slave for several cotton producing regions of the South. The counties included in each region are cited by Gray as the major cotton producing counties of 1859. They follow the groupings which he prepared according to soil and climatic conditions.[44] This method of selecting counties has the advantage of including only those economies known to be primarily based on cotton production, thus preventing the downward bias that would result in counties that produced other staple crops with slave labor. A total of 74 counties was examined; together, they accounted for 38 per cent of the 1859 crop. The average yield from the entire sample was 2.6 bales per slave.

Before we can calculate the returns implied by these yields, we must adjust the data to take account of changes in the price of cotton and of slaves.

The bumper crop of 1859 caused the price

[44] Gray, pp. 531–37.

TABLE VI
The Rate of Return on Cotton Operations in the Ante Bellum South, 1859

	Yield (bales per slave)	Rate of return with:	
		9¢ cotton	10¢ cotton
		(percentage)	
Rich Cotton Lands (K = $2,015, c = $26.00)			
Mississippi River Counties, La.	6.3	11.9	15.1
Alluvial Counties, S. E. Ark.	4.4	8.3	10.4
Yazoo Delta, Mississippi	3.9	7.4	9.2
East Texas Cotton Counties	3.8	7.2	9.0
28 Alluvial Counties, Miss., La., Ark., and Ala.	3.7	7.1	8.7
Upper Red River Counties, La.	3.4	6.5	8.0
Northwest Alabama	2.7	5.3	6.5
River Counties, S. W. Miss.	2.7	5.3	6.5
Black Prairie, Ala.	2.7	5.3	6.5
Tennessee River Valley, Ala.	1.7	3.6	4.3
Older Areas (K = $1,861, c = $24.25)			
Upper Coastal Plain, Georgia	2.4	5.6	6.2
Clay Hills Region, Ala.	2.3	5.5	6.0
Eastern Piedmont, Ala.	2.2	5.3	5.8
17 Counties, Georgia	2.0	4.8	5.3
Southern Piedmont, Ga.	1.7	4.2	4.6
13 Districts, South Carolina	1.3	3.4	3.7
Southern Piedmont, So. Carolina	1.2	3.2	3.5
Middle and Upper Coastal Plain, So. Carolina	1.1	3.0	3.2

of cotton to fall from the previous year's price of 11.5 cents a pound to 10.8 cents. At no time during the selling year did the price fall below 10.5 cents. Thus, a 9- to 10-cent farmgate price is the appropriate one for these yields.

By 1859, the price of slaves had risen substantially. Using the same technique we applied to the 1849 slave prices, we find that the average slave was worth $1,221. This increases the capital costs to $1,861 per *slave* for the Old South and to $2,015 per slave for the alluvial lands.

Table VI presents the returns calculated from the 1859 data, and Table VII digests them into averages, which are compared with Conrad and Meyer's and with Saraydar's estimates.

As the tables show, cotton production was clearly profitable for the alluvial or prairie lands of the New South, when compared with the 6 per cent alternative interest rate.[45] Particularly striking is the close

[45] It should be noted that Conrad and Meyer

parallel between the returns for the South as a whole calculated in 1849 and 1859, and Conrad and Meyer's estimates for a typical cotton plantation, with the 6 per cent return on other forms of capital. This would indicate that we need not rely on the assumption of nonpecuniary returns to slaveholding so often used to explain the willingness of southerners to own slaves.

Another interesting result emerges from the data; it seems that while the return to slave operated plantations remained fairly constant over the decade, returns in the New South were rising while the profits of the older states were declining. This would lead us to expect a more rapid expansion of cotton production in the new areas than in the older states, as capital reallocates itself to

estimated this 6 per cent return by looking at the interest rates on prime commercial paper in New York and Boston. Though this is not the ideal technique the paucity of data makes it about as good as we can do. The 6 per cent rate seems reasonable enough, agrees with contemporary sources, and is accepted by Saraydar.

TABLE VII
THE PROFITABILITY OF ANTE BELLUM SLAVERY

Region	Rate of Return on Slave-Operated Cotton Plantations			
	1849[a]	1859	Conrad and Meyer[b]	Saraydar—1849[c]
Older areas	5.5–6.1	3.6–4.0	2.2–5.4	0–1.1[d]
Average for the South	5.7–6.4	5.8–6.3[e]	4.5–6.5	0–1.5[d]
Average for alluvium	6.2–6.9	7.1–8.7	10.0–13.0	0.9–2.3
High for alluvium	11.2–12.8	11.9–15.1	—[f]	8.4–9.8

[a] From Table III.
[b] Conrad and Meyer, Table 9, p. 107.
[c] Saraydar, Table I, p. 331.
[d] The lower value in the range reported by Saraydar was less than 0.025 per cent.
[e] Calculated from a yield of 2.5 bales per slave, which is the simple average of the 3.7 bales on alluvium and the 1.4 bales of the Older areas.
[f] Conrad and Meyer did not report a high for alluvium.

TABLE VIII
EXPANSION OF COTTON PRODUCTION IN THE NEW AND THE OLD SOUTH—1850 TO 1860

State	Year	Cotton production (400 lb. bales)	Number of slaves	Number of slave holders	Average number of slaves per owner
THE OLD SOUTH:					
Georgia	1850	499,091	381,682	38,456	9.9
	1860	701,840	462,198	41,084	11.2
(Percentage change)		(40.6)	(21.1)	(6.8)	(13.1)
So. Carolina	1850	300,901	384,984	25,596	15.0
	1860	353,412	402,406	26,701	15.0
(Percentage change)		(17.5)	(4.5)	(4.3)	(0)
THE NEW SOUTH:					
Arkansas	1850	65,344	47,100	5,999	7.8
	1860	367,393	111,115	11,481	9.7
(Percentage change)		(462.2)	(135.9)	(91.4)	(24.4)
Louisiana	1850	178,737	244,809	20,670	11.8
	1860	777,738	331,726	22,033	15.0
(Percentage change)		(335.1)	(35.5)	(6.6)	(27.1)
Texas	1850	58,072	58,161	7,747	7.5
	1860	431,463	182,566	21,878	8.3
(Percentage change)		(643.0)	(213.9)	(182.4)	(10.7)
TOTAL for the Old South:	1850	799,992	766,666	64,052	12.0
	1860	1,055,252	864,604	67,785	12.8
(Percentage change)		(31.9)	(12.8)	(5.8)	(6.7)
TOTAL for the New South:	1850	302,153	350,070	34,416	10.2
	1860	1,576,594	625,407	55,392	11.3
(Percentage change)		(421.8)	(78.7)	(60.9)	(10.8)
TOTAL for all Slave States:	1850	2,445,779	3,204,051	347,516	9.2
	1860	5,385,354	3,953,696	395,196	10.0
(Percentage change)		(120.2)	(23.4)	(13.7)	(8.7)

Sources: Cotton production 1850: DeBow, p. 173; 1860: *Eighth Census of Agriculture*, p. 189. Slave population: *Ibid.*, pp. 247–48, 224. Slaveholders: *ibid.*

538

correct the disparities in income. This should be accompanied by transfers of slaves from the Old to the New South.

And this is exactly what was happening. Table VIII demonstrates this by comparing the expansion in cotton production, slaves, slave owners, and the average size of slave holdings for several states of the Old and the New South.

The rather high rates of return calculated for several areas of the New South indicate that the price of land was not high enough to capture its full rent. In long-run equilibrium, we would expect the land rents to adjust so that returns in all parts of the South are equal, save for the differences caused by unequal risk premiums. In the late fifties, it was undoubtedly the case that the free or very cheap (yet highly fertile) lands to the west prevented rents from rising, thus causing disequilibrium.

Several regions of the Old South show normal returns, and if we take into account the capital gains earned in these states when they sold their slaves to buyers in the New South, it is fairly certain that even the poorest areas could show a profit. If this process had been allowed to continue for some time, it might have been the case that the Old South would have run out of slaves before returns were equalized. In this regional sense, therefore, and only in this sense, could slavery have destroyed itself through its own unprofitability.

It is not our intention, however, to exhaust the subject of slave profitability but only to show that Mr. Saraydar was incorrect in challenging Conrad and Meyer's conclusion.

RICHARD SUTCH
University of Washington

THE PROFITABILITY OF ANTE BELLUM SLAVERY—A REPLY

Richard Sutch states that the intent of his paper is "only to show that Mr. Saraydar was incorrect in challenging Conrad and Meyer's conclusion." At the outset, I should like to restate the "conclusion" which I attempted to test, since Sutch himself seems to be somewhat confused as to my purpose.

Conrad and Meyer concluded that, in the period 1830 to 1860, investment in male prime field hands to be utilized in cotton production yielded a rate of return of at least 6% (the relevant interest rate). Although they did not delimit their analysis to the particular thesis that ante bellum investment in field hands was unprofitable (or profitable)—e.g., their article was also concerned with slavery's viability, as well as its implications for Southern economic growth—my paper was clearly concerned with their treatment of this problem alone. Therefore, it is quite appropriate to utilize the capital-value formula which incorpo-

rates returns over the life of this particular investment (indeed, Sutch does not disapprove of this identical production function as employed by Conrad and Meyer; he cites their results with approval, and compares his own rates of return with theirs).

Consequently, I am at a loss to understand the relevance of Sutch's charge that there is an "incorrect specification" in my production function which arises from my "implicit assumption that no reproduction of the slave stock takes place." I do not make this assumption, because it is not required. Reproduction of the slave stock is relevant to Conrad and Meyer's *second* function, the production of the intermediate good, slave labor—i.e., slave breeding.

Sutch argues that I erred in increasing out-of-pocket expenses to include those necessary to maintain females and children as well as male field hands. I am inclined to agree with him; these expenses should properly be charged to the production function for the intermediate good. However, I object to Sutch's use of this rather slim reed to support his allegation that I assumed "that only the labor in the cotton fields was productive of revenue and that no increase in the stock of slaves took place." In fact, the significance of using $21 rather than $32 out-of-pocket costs for the profitability calculation is reflected by, and should be adjudged solely in terms of, the 1.9% rather than .9% rate of return on alluvium which emerges at 7¢ a pound for cotton, and the 3.0% rather than 2.3% rate of return at 8¢ a pound.

The pertinence of Sutch's single production function analysis to the determination of the rate of return to be earned from an investment in slave hands over the period 1830 to 1860 is surely questionable. Conrad and Meyer's (as well as my own) analysis involved an estimate of an *average* price for field hands over the period 1830–50 (since slave prices in the 50's would have introduced an upward bias), *typical* prices for cotton lands over the period 1830–50, an *average* interest rate for the period 1830–60, *typical* out-of-pocket costs in the period 1840–60, and an *average* price for cotton over the period 1830–60. Our major point of dispute centers on the question of whether their estimates or my own (based on 1850 Census data) more accurately reflect slave productivity for the entire period. Neither Conrad and Meyer nor I tried to calculate the rate of return in 1849, 1859, or any other single year.

Why, then, does Sutch insist that a 9¢ to 10¢ range for cotton is more appropriate to my output-per-hand estimates—which are intended to represent an average for the period 1830–60—than the average price for cotton over that same period? Sutch maintains that the higher price is more relevant because my productivity figures are necessarily low, since 1849 was "a year of particularly poor crops." But was 1849 really a year of "particularly low yields"? On the

contrary, it could be argued that 1849 was particularly representative.

The 1849 crop was actually well above (some 10% above) the average for the 40's.[1] Prior to 1849, there were only three cotton crops which were larger: 1844, 1847, and 1848. The 1844 and 1847 crops were not significantly so (1% and 3% respectively), but the 1848 crop stands out; it was almost 39% greater than the average for the 40's. It makes no sense to compare 1849 with the bumper-crop year of 1848, as does Sutch. In an effort to establish that 1849 was not a normal year, Sutch notes that the average crop of the 50's was "a full 50 per cent" above that of 1849. But this proves only that the 50's were especially good years for cotton, not that 1849 was a particularly poor year. The average annual crop of the 50's was also almost 20% larger than the bumper crop of 1848, and "a full" 45% greater than the one-year-earlier 1847 crop (which sold for 7¢ a pound)—and both of these were record years to that time.

Even if we accepted the 9¢ to 10¢ price range, this alone would not be enough to ensure a rate of return greater than 6%. These prices imply rates of return of 4.4%–5.4%, 3.7%–4.8%, and 3.3%–4.3% respectively, on alluvium, as an average for the South, and for older areas.

But these rates of return are calculated without the benefit of Sutch's single production function concept. As noted above, the rate of appreciation is simply not relevant to the production function with which I was concerned. Nevertheless, Sutch recalculates rates of return with his function, to see how "critical" was my "error in specification" in ignoring the growth rate of the negro population.

Sutch devotes a major portion of his paper to a critique of the estimates which I used for slave productivity in my model.

[1] Lewis Gray, *History of Agriculture in the Southern United States to 1860* (Washington, D. C.: The Carnegie Institution of Washington, 1933), Table 40, p. 1026.

First, I should like to acknowledge that he has indeed correctly spotted an arithmetic error in my calculation of output per hand for the two Northwestern Alabama counties of Fayette and Marion. I wanted to choose representative counties characterized by remoteness from market and poor soils; Gray implies that these two counties quite possibly fitted the description.[2] Although cotton producers in both counties faced major transportation problems—even in 1879[3]—which lowered average realized farm price (and thus the rate of return) sufficiently to keep cotton production quite low, cotton acreage was relatively fertile in both counties, and therefore output per hand was relatively high. In fact, of the 52 Alabama counties which produced cotton in 1849, Fayette ranked number four in output per hand at 4.8 bales, and Marion ranked number seventeen at 3.4 bales per hand. More representative counties, for example, were Greene, at 2.3 bales, and Sumter, at 1.9 bales per hand.

In an attempt to confirm Conrad and Meyer's 7 to 8 bale per hand estimate as an average for ante bellum slave productivity on alluvium, Sutch cites a yield per acre figure of 396 pounds as an average for the 13 counties which produced one half of all the cotton grown on alluvium in 1879. He notes that this figure is 24% to 41% higher than the yield implied by Conrad and Meyer's estimate. A weighted average for those alluvial areas which produced 99.8% of all the cotton grown on alluvium generates a figure of 361 pounds per acre on alluvium in 1879.[4] This is some 13% to 29% higher than Conrad and Meyer's implied yield. We may thus conclude that yield per acre on alluvium in 1879 does not in itself invalidate Conrad

and Meyer's estimate for ante bellum slave productivity.

But, surely, neither does it support that estimate. Cotton production in 1879, twenty years after the ante bellum period, exceeded that of any previous year.[5] The 1879–80 season was "propitious" for cotton in all states other than Georgia and Alabama.[6] In fact, contemporary reports by the Department of Agriculture indicate that 1879 was an especially good year for cotton—i.e.:

In the States bordering on the Mississippi River there is considerable increase (in pounds of lint per acre). Louisiana and Mississippi each show the effects of the favorable fall, and make decided gains over last year. Arkansas and Tennessee equal their magnificent yield of 1878.[7]

In reference to this 1879 crop, quoted extracts from correspondence from counties in Louisiana, Mississippi, and Arkansas are replete with statements such as: "unprecedented good weather for gathering," "yields more clear lint to the 100 pounds than previous years," "season very favorable," "as good a yield per acre as ever made in this county," "so far the most favorable fall ever known," "weather finest for years," "better than ever before."[8] I should think, then, that yield per acre figures for alluvium in 1879 are useful only in the sense that they provide some kind of an extreme upper limit for ante bellum yield per acre estimates.

As to the 7 to 8 bale per hand estimates of Conrad and Meyer, I am perfectly willing to concede that *all* of the nine reported yields per field hand listed in Conrad and Meyer's Table 6 might have involved self-sufficient cotton production,[9] whether explicitly reported as such or not. But Conrad

[2] *Ibid.*, Table 13, p. 534, p. 536.
[3] Census Office, *Report on Cotton Production in the United States, Part II* (Washington, D. C.: U. S. Government Printing Office, 1884), pp. 120–21.
[4] *Ibid.*, Part I, p. 16, and summary reports for Louisiana, Mississippi, and Arkansas.

[5] U. S. Bureau of the Census, *Historical Statistics of the United States* (Washington, D. C.: U. S. Government Printing Office, 1960), p. 302.
[6] U. S. Department of Agriculture, *Condition of Crops*, Special Report No. 19 (Washington, D. C.: U. S. Government Printing Office, 1879), p. 15.
[7] *Ibid.*
[8] *Ibid.*, pp. 17, 18.
[9] Alfred Conrad and John Meyer, "The Economics of Slavery in the Ante Bellum South," *The Journal of Political Economy*, April 1958, p. 105.

and Meyer did not make their estimates for slave productivity on the basis of these reports. They merely used them to "illustrate the possible variation in productivity per hand." [10] They do note that this relatively small sample of reported yields agrees (I would say, rather, that it does not disagree) with the "frequent statements in contemporary journals" upon which they base their *own* estimates. I merely suggest that the "frequent statements in contemporary journals" might not have referred to output inclusive of the slave hand's non-cotton (subsistence) product, and this would introduce an upward bias into their estimates.

Sutch avers that "it can easily be shown that Saraydar's range of 2 to 3.6 bales is an underestimate (of ante bellum slave productivity)." He proceeds to do so by dividing total cotton output in 1859 of the seven major cotton states by the total number of slaves (discounted by 10% to account for city-dwellers) between 10 and 70 years old. He gets an average yield of 3.36 bales per slave. The joker in this particular deck is his use of the 1859 cotton crop. The 1859 crop was by no means an "average"; it was 47% greater than the average for the 50's—a pre-Civil War high. In fact, Sutch himself notes that "1859 was one of the best years for cotton production and the yields calculated from these data will over-represent an average for the decade of the fifties." Slave productivity based on this crop would have a strong upward bias. If we utilize the 1850 Census, we find that the seven states cited by Sutch produced 2,150,866 bales in 1849; 1,192,718 slaves in these seven states were between 10 and 70 years old; subtracting 10% to account for those living in cities ("not more" than 10% probably lived in cities and towns), we get an average of 2.0 bales per slave. But, like Sutch's average of 3.36 bales, this neither proves nor disproves that my range of 2 to 3.6 bales is an underestimate.

[10] *Ibid.*, p. 104.

Recognizing that 1859 was a bumper-crop year, and therefore that productivity estimates based on this crop would not be representative of the ante bellum period, Sutch nevertheless feels that "a test for 1859 is more relevant than one for 1849" in spite of U. B. Phillips' contention that by the close of the 50's only a few slaveholders "were earning anything beyond what would cover their maintenance and carrying charges." I would have thought that a test for *neither* year would be, in itself, sufficient to determine the profitability of slave operations in cotton over the period 1830–60. Surely, this is the proper target toward which Sutch should direct his inquiry if, as he says, he wishes to test whether "non-pecuniary returns are necessary to explain the patterns of slaveholding."

Sutch's contention that an analysis of 1859 is superior to one relating to 1849 cotton yields because "the more detailed data available from the 1860 Census will enable us to devise a more precise method of estimating the yields" is frankly puzzling. As far as I can see, the only information he utilizes which is not available in the 1850 Census has little or no effect on productivity estimates arrived at through a simple division of cotton output by slave population.

Sutch dislikes my method of estimating yield per hand, which involves dividing cotton production in particular counties (chosen on the basis of type of soil and zero or relatively negligible production of the non-cotton staples) by one-half of the slave population in each county (on the assumption that plantations typically carried one hand to every two slaves). I claim no great precision for this method; nevertheless, I do maintain that the productivity estimates which emerge *are* more precise than Conrad and Meyers' estimates based on "frequent statements in contemporary journals."

Sutch apparently does not think so. He feels that there must be a significant downward bias, for example, connected with the assumption that "not more" than 10% of the slaves in each county lived in towns or cities. To support his assertion, he points out that "an examination of the fourteen alluvial-soil counties of Mississippi ... turned up Adams County with 688 slave-owners in 1860 but only 214 farms, and Warren County with 821 slaveholders and only 396 farms," and that "all but one (of these counties) had a greater number of slaveowners than of farms in 1860." Apart from the obvious fact that my calculations involved slave residency in 1850 while his figures relate to 1860, it is not clear at all that his results imply that there is a significant downward bias in my method. In fact, for what it's worth, an examination of the 21 alluvial counties which I used for estimating slave productivity on alluvium reveals not one, but *six* counties that had a greater number of farms than slaveowners in 1860.

More importantly, if we subtract the number of farms from the number of slaveholders in the remaining counties, the number of slaves which each of these presumably non-farm slaveholders could have owned, and still not have left more than 10% of the slave population living off farms, ranges from 3 in Adams County, Mississippi, to 66 in Issaquena County, Mississippi; the mean for all 15 counties is 30.

Further, one may judge to some extent the relative importance of farming to slave employment by noting that the median slave holding in each of these counties[11] times the number of farms in each county yields—in every case—a number of slaves which is more than sufficient to account for the total slave population of each county.

Finding that the 1850 Census reports 50.87% of all slaves in the United States as being between the ages of 15 and 60, Sutch is disturbed by my assumption of a 50%

labor force participation rate. He feels that this must imply that all slaves in the 15 to 60 age bracket were employed as hands. According to Sutch, this rate is suspect because "a number" of slaves in this age bracket must have been utilized as craftsmen or servants, and "many" slave women in this group were incapacitated by advanced pregnancy, or cared for children instead of working in the fields. Furthermore, "very few of the children below fifteen could be expected to be as helpful as a prime field hand."

Since the quantities implied by "a number," "many," and "very few" are necessarily vague, I wonder what the proportion of slaves in the 15 to 60 age group would have had to have been in order to satisfy Sutch as permitting a 50% participation rate—52%, 55%, 60%, 100%? It could just as credibly be argued that the proportion of slaves in this age group who were craftsmen or servants, or who were in advanced pregnancy, was insignificant. Moreover, child-caring activities might well have been within the province of older slaves. And, although it is true that not many of those below the age of 15 could be expected to have been as productive as a prime field hand, this is not really the relevant consideration.

Field work age encompassed the years 10 to 54,[12] and, in fact, children were assigned fractional work in the fields at an age as early as six.[13] For the six states that provided the data for my productivity estimates, 52% (in the alluvial counties, 57%) of the slave population was between the ages of 15 and 60 in 1850. But if we (properly) include the 10 to 15 year old group, roughly 65% of the slave population was of field work age. The relevant question, then, is not how many below the age of 15 were as productive as a prime field hand, but rather how many field hands would it have taken to do the field work performed by

---

[11] As estimated by Gray, *op. cit.*, Table 12, p. 531.

[12] Conrad and Meyer, *op. cit.*, p. 116.
[13] Gray, *op. cit.*, p. 549.

those less than 15 years old? My point is that Sutch's observation that 50.87% of all slaves in the United States were between the ages of 15 and 60 does not, in itself, provide sufficient information to cast serious doubt on the 50% labor force participation rate assumption.

The participation rate assumption can in fact be tested. Suppose we make the perfectly reasonable assumption that the highest yield per acre on the best soil in 1879 (470 pounds, Chicot County, Arkansas; see Sutch, Table II) was no less than yield per acre in those areas which Sutch identifies as producing a high for alluvium twenty years earlier in 1859 (the Louisiana Parishes of Carroll, Concordia, Madison, and Tensas). Sutch estimates average yield per *slave* in these areas as 6.27 bales. This in turn would imply a labor force participation rate of *at least* 53% on alluvium in 1859, and (since there is no obvious reason to expect the rate to differ significantly) in 1849 as well. [The participation rate t is derived from the formula $(400b)/(10t) = q$, where: b = bales per slave, q = pounds per acre, at 400 pounds per bale, and 10 acres of cotton land per hand. In 1859, b = 6.27, $q \leq 470$. Therefore, $t \geq (40)(6.27)/470 = 53\%$.]

Sutch feels that he can bypass the problem of estimating the labor force participation rate altogether by using his single production function concept. He estimates yield per slave for a number of counties using 1859 data, and revises upward the price of cotton and of slaves to more accurately reflect the 1859 situation.[14] He

[14] However, he ignores the possibility of rising land prices in the 50's. One might reasonably expect the magnitude of this price increase to be reflected in the movement of the ratio of "cash value of (acres of land in) farms" to "acres of land in farms." Over the census period 1850–60, this ratio increased by 1.7 times for those counties (in Table 5) which Sutch includes in "Cotton Regions of the Old South," by 2.5 times for those counties comprising "Other Cotton Regions of the New South," by 2.6 times for counties which make

then calculates rates of return for the several types of cotton operations, and compares them with those of Conrad and Meyer and myself.

I would like to reiterate two points applicable to Sutch's results. First, whatever the single production function does measure, it does *not* measure the rate of return to be realized from an investment in field hands. Although the participation rate does indeed cancel out of Sutch's formula, the appreciation rate does not—and that rate is just not applicable to a consideration of the returns to be realized from male field hand investment.

His function has implications for profitability which are immediately obvious. For example, Sutch's construction has the property of guaranteeing at least a 2.15% rate of return on an investment in slave hands— *regardless* of the price of slaves, land, or cotton, of slave productivity, or out-of-pocket costs—as long as return per hand is not negative. In other words, if slaves were multiplying at the rate of 6% or more a year, there would be no question of profitability, as long as each slave yielded a net return of, say, as little as 1¢ a year.

Further, his single production function model implies a positive rate of return even if yearly out-of-pocket expense per hand *exceeds* the value of his product. Suppose $c > pY$. As long as $(c - pY)/K < a$, $r > 0$.

According to Sutch, then, it might still be profitable for a planter to purchase a male field hand, even though his yearly net return is negative, if the price of the hand is high enough. In any event, if the hand working in cotton yields a positive net return—no matter how small—it is always profitable to purchase him as long as the negro population is growing at a rate which

up his "Alluvial Regions," and by 3.1 times for those Mississippi River counties which he identifies as yielding a high output per slave on alluvium.

is no less than the rate of interest. Needless to say, the validity of both of these propositions is at least open to doubt.

The final point is that Sutch's estimates in any case are not comparable to those of Conrad and Meyer and myself. Sutch attempts to estimate presumably expected rates of return for the specific years of 1849 and 1859, while we attempted estimates of average rates of return over the period 1830–60. Sutch apparently does not realize this, for he incorrectly labels my estimates in his Table VII as "Saraydar—1849." (He also errs in reporting my estimate of returns from high-yield alluvium; the correct figures are 6.5%–8.2%, not 8.4%–9.8%.)

EDWARD SARAYDAR
University of Rochester, and
*California State College at
Long Beach.*

"ECONOMIC DEMOCRACY" AND THE CONCENTRATION OF AGRICULTURAL WEALTH IN THE COTTON SOUTH, 1850-1860

Economic issues are among the most basic of the many disputed and still largely unsettled questions concerning the antebellum history of the American South. Historians have argued, for example, over whether slavery was a profitable and viable economic institution in 1860 (or whether it might have died out for economic reasons if the Civil War had not occurred); whether southern agriculture was increasingly dominated by wealthy slaveowners with privileged access to capital or whether yeoman farmers formed the real backbone of the economy; and whether slavery (or specialization in cotton, or the plantation system) retarded the economic growth and development of the South as a region. Even such noneconomic topics as the relationship between master and slave contain a fundamental economic question: was plantation slavery an efficient, "capitalist" form of organization or did it more closely resemble a pre-industrial or traditional social institution?

Even so empirical a question as the dominance of large or small landholders and slaveholders has been a point of dispute. In the first section of this article, the most prominent historical treatments are reviewed and judged unsatisfactory. Subsequent sections present new evidence based on manuscript census returns for 1850 and 1860.

PHILLIPS, GRAY, AND OWSLEY

A long tradition of romantic literature, sectional polemics, and colorful history places heavy emphasis on the large plantations of the South. The writings of Olmsted, Helper, and Cairnes tended to divide the white population into two classes: the wealthy slaveholding planter class and the poor whites leading a "semisavage life" on the "outskirts of civilization." While no serious historian has accepted such a stark simplification, Ulrich B. Phillips and those writing in his tradition did base most of their detailed work on large plantations because of the limited availability of letters, diaries, and record books. In addition, Phillips maintained that slavery

GAVIN WRIGHT is Assistant Professor of Economics at Yale University.

63

TABLE 1. DISTRIBUTION OF SLAVES IN CRAWFORD COUNTY, GEORGIA, 1824 AND 1860

1824		1860	
No. slaves	No. owners	No. slaves	No. owners
1	27	1	51
2	18	2	56
3	17	3	30
4	9	4	30
5	7	5	19
6	9	6	19
7	4	7	16
8	1	8	12
9	5	9	16
10	6	10–14	34
11	2	15–19	28
12	1	20–29	20
13	2	30–39	18
15	2	40–49	8
20	1	50–69	7
28	1	70–99	1
31	1	100–199	4
42	1		
Total slaves:	579	Total slaves:	4,270
Total owners:	114	Total owners:	369
Total families:	230	Total families:	630
Average holding:	5.0	Average holding:	11.6

SOURCE: See n. 1.

tended "to concentrate wealth . . . within the hands of a single economic class and within certain geographic areas." [1] As documentation for this assertion, Phillips presented distributions of slaveholdings for a handful of counties from the early 1800s to 1860. His prime example is Crawford County, Georgia, for which the figures are presented for 1824 and 1860 in table 1. Phillips' interpretation of this evidence is: "The most marked feature of the contrast is the growth in number and size of the larger slaveholdings—in a word, the passage of the domination of the community from the men of few or no slaves to the men of the planter class." [2]

But the second half of this sentence is a non sequitur; why, for example, should the four largest slaveholders "dominate the community" any more in 1860 than in 1824? Indeed, they control a smaller fraction of the total slave force in the later year. Furthermore, the figures indicate that the proportion of white families owning slaves rose from 50.4 to 58.5 percent.

[1] Ulrich B. Phillips, "The Origin and Growth of the Southern Black Belts," reprinted version in *Ulrich B. Phillips: The Slave Economy of the Old South*, ed. Eugene Genovese (Baton Rouge: Louisiana State University Press, 1968), 95. (First publication, *American Historical Review* 11 [July 1906].)
[2] Ibid., 98–99.

If Phillips means only that the largest slaveholders of 1860 owned more slaves than the largest holders of 1824, this is obviously true, but this is a statement about the *size* of slaveholdings, not about the *concentration* of holdings. There is no necessary relationship between these two, especially when both free and slave populations are rising. From a social standpoint, surely it is the *relative* status of large and small holders which is important. The same objection holds for Phillips' analysis of other counties in Georgia and Mississippi.

Lewis C. Gray advanced a similar view with respect to the geographical and economic concentration of holdings. He contended that the greatest concentration was in those areas with the best soil and best suited for commercial production. However, in spite of his obviously thorough acquaintance with the available material, Gray never assembled a careful, systematic documentation for his opinion. The following excerpts illustrate his method:

> In general, the concentration varied according to the extent to which production was favored by conditions of soil, topography, climate and accessibility to market. The most extreme concentration existed in the alluvial lands of the Mississippi and its largest tributaries, where conditions of commercial production were especially favorable.... Issaquena County, Mississippi, and Concordia, Louisiana, were characterized by a degree of concentration comparable to that of the rice and sugar regions, with medians of 118 and 117 respectively.... In Claiborne, Jefferson, Adams, and Wilkinson counties, the oldest settled portion of the state, which were located almost entirely in the region of rich upland loams bordering the river, the concentration of slaveholdings was somewhat greater than in the Yazoo Delta as a whole, probably due to the longer period of development....[3]

Gray goes on to describe the entire cotton area in a similar manner, but the glaring flaws in method render the effort to follow him unrewarding. First, Gray's sole measure of "concentration" is median slaveholdings, an index which is deficient not only because it ignores land and farm value and because it is based on *all* slaveholders rather than farms, but primarily because, like Phillips' index of average slaveholdings, it is not a measure of concentration at all. Indeed, a highly skewed distribution might be characterized by a low median and a high average. No evidence is presented, and there is no reason to believe, that the median is sufficient to describe the distribution as a whole.

Moreover, even if one grants that the median slaveholding is a statistic of some interest for a county, Gray's method of testing his hypothesis is so nonrigorous as to make refutation impossible. The elements of transportation cost and length of settlement are introduced in an ad hoc manner to "explain" observations which do not fit the rule with respect to size and soil quality. Thus Gray can dispose of almost any proposed counterexample

[3] Lewis C. Gray, *History of Agriculture in the Southern United States to 1860* (Washington, D.C.: Carnegie Institution, 1933), 533–36.

simply by drawing on one of his three factors, and one is left with no idea whether the correlations are consistent over all of the counties or whether the strength of any of the correlations is sufficient to "explain" the exceptions. Indeed, the phrasing often suggests that Gray's judgment on the adequacy of a county's transportation facilities was deduced from the median slaveholding, rather than vice versa.

Thus the planter-dominance thesis of Phillips and Gray was founded on rather shaky evidence. It was in an effort to correct this historical emphasis that Frank Owsley and his students at Vanderbilt University produced a series of writings[4] emphasizing the "vast middle group of sturdy, self-reliant, law-abiding farmers" who had been "ignored because they were conventional and prosaic." [5] These writers were not interested in writing lengthy prose lyrics about the South. They used quantitative methods, and they drew upon a new set of material—tax records and the manuscript census returns. These studies use virtually identical methodology and make similar assertions, which can be summarized in a few main points:

1) "The farm rather than the plantation was the basic agricultural unit, and yeomen far outnumbered both planters and poor whites." This contention is documented by size distribution figures for counties in all regions of the South, showing that only a small minority of farm operators had extensive holdings of land or slaves. Weaver found, for example, that even in the rich, delta-loess region of Mississippi, "in 1860 only 18.97 percent of the heads of families owned fifty or more slaves and only 22.16 percent owned five hundred or more acres of improved land." [6]

2) "A large majority of the farmers owned land and the total number of landowners was rapidly increasing." [7] This assertion is based on a matching of names from the agricultural and population census returns for 1850 and 1860, and a subsequent development of estimates of the percentage of the agricultural population owning land. Owsley's summary figures indicate that almost all of the slaveholders and perhaps 75 percent of the nonslaveholding farm population did own land.

3) The failure to own slaves did not condemn a man to grinding poverty. "On the whole, the non-slaveowner compared favorably with the slaveholder who cultivated a similar acreage. . . . The majority of slaveless people . . . compared very favorably with the slaveholders owning similar amounts of land." [8] Support for this point involves data on farm value,

[4] The most prominent of these are Blanche Henry Clark, *The Tennessee Yeomen, 1840-1860* (Nashville: Vanderbilt University Press, 1942); Harry L. Coles, "Some Notes on Slaveownership and Landownership in Louisiana, 1850–1860," *Journal of Southern History* 9 (Aug. 1943): 381–94; Frank L. Owsley, *Plain Folk of the Old South* (Baton Rouge: Louisiana State University Press, 1949); Herbert Weaver, *Mississippi Farmers, 1850–1860* (Nashville: Vanderbilt University Press, 1945).

[5] Weaver, *Mississippi Farmers*, 13.

[6] Ibid., 40–41.

[7] Ibid., 63.

[8] Clark, *Tennessee Yeomen*, 8, 45.

wealth, and crop outputs for slaveholders and nonslaveholders of comparable land ownership.

4) The best farm land was not appropriated by large planters from small farmers, or by slaveholders from the slaveless. This argument receives major emphasis in all the studies. "The often repeated statement that the non-slaveholders were pushed off the good lands and even out of the county by the slaveholders is not borne out." [9] "It would be an error to assume, as some writers have done, that the better lands were appropriated by the planters and that the small farmers were pushed back onto the poorer lands." [10] Most emphatically: "The truth of the matter is that the plain farmers settled where they chose and stayed as long as it suited them." [11] The basis for this claim, in all of the studies, is the finding that large and small farmers, slaveholders and nonslaveholders, could all be found in every county "intermingled" on the manuscript census lists. "It is to be supposed that usually the enumerator listed the farmers as he came to them in his rounds. . . . In every county the slaveholders and non-slaveholders are listed one after another on the pages of the Census." [12] Owsley's book includes many maps of counties and precincts in the black belt of Alabama, showing, according to his reading of them, that large and small farms lay close to one another.

One must express admiration and some wonder at the amount of effort and time which went into these studies, all of them completed before the advent of the computer. Further, the studies have been extremely important in pointing to the use of the manuscript census returns. However, it is hard to be so charitable with respect to the methods used or the conclusions drawn. On each of the four major points, the Owsley studies either failed to use the relevant statistical criteria to test their hypotheses, or altered the hypothesis itself into an irrefutable triviality, or, finally, relied on ad hoc explanations to dispense with that portion of their own evidence which pointed in an opposite direction. [13]

1) The size distribution tables in these books are always in terms of the proportion of persons or farms in a given bracket, never in terms of the proportion of acreage or slaves or wealth held by farmers in a given bracket. Thus, the proposition that is demonstrated is only that many small or slaveless farmers existed, not that they were an important part of the social structure. The Owsley studies have shown that the small farm was "typical" or "basic" only in the sense that a random sample of *farms* contained more small farms than large—but a "typical" acre or slave may well have belonged to a large plantation. In the reverse sense, this is the same

[9] Ibid., 67.

[10] Weaver, *Mississippi Farmers*, 45.

[11] Owsley, *Plain Folk*, 52.

[12] Clark, *Tennessee Yeomen*, 67.

[13] Many of these points were first made in Fabian Linden's celebrated article, "Economic Democracy in the Slave South: An Appraisal of Some Recent Views," *Journal of Negro History* 31 (April 1946): 140–89.

criticism made of Phillips' work earlier; the fact that what are essentially the same tables yield opposite conclusions to different people demonstrates that these tables are not the relevant ones for the question at hand.

2) It is uncertain how relevant landownership is as a measure of economic position. Weaver writes: "One of the most important keys to the well-being of farmers or planters was the ownership of land." [14] But in a period when land was cheap and labor dear, surely slaveownership was a better index of economic status, and these percentages were much lower: in the cotton South, less than 50 percent of farm operators held slaves, and this fraction was falling between 1850 and 1860.

Nevertheless, even if one accepts landownership as an index of "economic democracy," in 40 percent of the counties discussed by Owsley this percentage *fell* between 1850 and 1860, most notably in the rich Mississippi and Louisiana black belts. Weaver makes a particular point of asserting that the 1850s were a decade of general prosperity affecting all economic classes. But in his sample counties the percentage of landowners was substantially lower in 1860 than in 1850; since the *absolute* number of landowners increased, he writes that "this decrease was due to the incoming of a large number of immigrants who by 1860 had not gained title to land. This considerable immigration indicates that confidence in the future of agriculture in the state was high." [15] Weaver thus passes over the indication of his own criterion and changes the subject to expectations, which is another matter entirely. Without evidence, he leaves the reader with the impression that these immigrants were going to obtain title to land in the future.

3) It makes little sense to compare slaveholders to nonslaveholders if the comparison is limited to those with no other differences between them. Clark argues that while, obviously, slaveholders were wealthier on the average than nonslaveholders the latter group was in a strong position "compared to the slaveholders of a similar economic status." [16] But if it is already known that they are of "similar economic status," what has been proved? The only question to which such evidence might be relevant is whether the ownership of *one* slave made a crucial economic difference to a farmer. But this is a question of relatively minor interest, compared to the broad issues of economic status and the distribution of wealth under the slave agricultural regime. Clark thus turns the assertion into a near-tautology and ignores the evidence of concentration provided by her own data.

4) It is difficult to take very seriously the results of the alleged "intermingling" of large and small farms based on the order of names in the census. Linden reports finding names in widely different relative positions in the manuscript census returns for 1850 and 1860. Furthermore, no way of measuring this effect is offered, and Owsley's maps may be just as easily read (by this reader, at least) as indicating clusters of similar size farms

[14] Weaver, *Mississippi Farmers*, 163.
[15] Ibid., 63.
[16] Clark, *Tennessee Yeomen*, 45.

rather than as a thoroughly mixed pattern. It is true that Phillips' assertion that a strict "segregation" prevailed between rich and poor, and that planters came into "complete possession" of certain regions, is a serious overstatement, but the destruction of this particular straw man diverts the attention of these studies from the important questions—the distribution of land *value*.

Other studies have considered this set of questions, but for the most part they fall into one of the traps discussed above or are concerned with particular states or counties. This survey, therefore, suggests the following characteristics which would be desirable in a new study of the concentration of agricultural holdings. First, an adequate sample is required, covering the entire region (in our case, the cotton South), but with a subregional breakdown according to geographic and agricultural criteria. Second, the study should have a consistent and relevant index of concentration, preferably not based on arbitrary size classes. Third, the results should be compared with the evidence for other regions of the country; and the rate and direction of change in concentration should be measured by consideration of at least two points in time—in this case, 1850 and 1860. The last two points are designed to make less arbitrary the choice of what is a "high" or "low" degree of concentration. Fourth, the question of the homogeneity of soil quality with respect to farm size should be tested. Finally, statistical tests of alleged differences should be provided as far as possible.

Two additional elements would be needed in a definitive study, both of which will be lacking here. First, we would like to know the wealth distribution for the *entire* free population, rather than for farm operators. Such a study would require an entirely new sample and is outside the range of the present work. However, the evidence available—see, for example, James C. Bonner's study of Hancock County, Georgia[17]—indicates that the full distribution is almost certainly more highly concentrated than the farm-operator distribution. Thus the evidence presented here is conservative with respect to the overall distribution of wealth in the cotton South.

Second, the most ethically objectionable feature of the works surveyed is that slaves are considered only as property, not as members of the population. Unfortunately, this conception of things is largely imposed on us by the available data. However, some estimate can be made of the effect of this characteristic on the overall wealth distribution.

The main source for the tables is the 1860 manuscript census sample for the cotton South, compiled under the direction of William N. Parker and Robert E. Gallman. The 1850 figures are taken from a smaller sample from the 1850 manuscript returns, collected by James Foust.[18] The soil type

[17] James C. Bonner, "Profile of a Late Ante-Bellum Community," *American Historical Review* 49 (July 1944): 663–80.

[18] For a full discussion of both samples, see James Foust, "The Yeoman Farmer and Westward Expansion of United States Cotton Production" (Ph.D. diss., University of North Carolina, 1967). Foust considers several issues related to the questions discussed in this article, and in general his conclusions are consistent with mine.

TABLE 2. SHARES (IN PERCENT) OF SOIL TYPE REGIONS IN COTTON SOUTH, 1850 AND 1860

	Farms		Improved acres		Farm value		Cotton	
	1850	1860	1850	1860	1850	1860	1850	1860
Piedmont	23.3	18.9	27.5	21.4	23.7	12.9	21.7	10.8
Sand hills	2.7	2.8	3.5	2.7	2.8	2.3	2.8	2.0
Valley	5.9	6.0	4.7	4.9	4.7	3.9	4.1	3.0
Western upland	12.6	18.3	7.3	11.5	7.0	10.1	7.0	12.8
Black prairie	6.0	5.0	7.5	9.0	8.2	10.1	12.5	13.4
Brown loam	8.6	6.8	7.2	7.6	10.3	9.2	14.2	10.8
Central plain	18.3	16.4	22.1	20.4	16.7	14.5	20.0	15.2
Coastal plain	4.8	5.1	4.1	4.6	3.7	3.9	2.4	3.5
Alluvial	3.6	4.4	3.9	5.8	8.9	17.4	8.6	17.0

regions used represent a cross-classification of counties based on the divisions of the National Research Program Agricultural Economics Project and the soil classifications of the *Tenth Census of the United States, 1880*, Vol. V. Only the nine largest soil type regions are included in this study, and only seven of these appear in both the 1850 and 1860 samples; a brief description of each region is provided in appendix A. Table 2 shows the distribution of farms, cotton output, improved acreage, and farm value among these regions.

CONCENTRATION OF IMPROVED ACREAGE

The published census for 1860 supplies figures only on the number of farms in a few improved acreage-size classes, by county. Earlier censuses did not provide even this much. The manuscript census sample, therefore, includes a great deal of additional information and allows a true measurement of concentration—the proportion of total holdings in the hands of a given segment of the population. However, the published census is the only source now available for the purpose of comparing the cotton South with other regions of the country, so it is worth going as far as possible with the size-class figures before turning to the manuscript sample.

In table 3 mean and median improved acreage levels are listed for each soil type region in the cotton south and for six northern farm states; also listed are the percentages of farms in five improved acreage size classes. It is clear that the average farm size was larger in the cotton regions than elsewhere, notwithstanding major differences among the soil type regions. However, differences in median farm size are much smaller: the overall median improved acreage for the cotton South was less than that for Illinois, and only slightly higher than that for Ohio. In the size class distributions, all of the cotton regions have higher percentages in the upper two classes than the northern states. However, these percentage differences are not large; even in the alluvial region, for example, only 5.1 percent of the farms are in the largest class. An observer of Owsley's school might conclude that North-South differences in the size structure of agriculture were minor, and that the role of the large plantation has been overemphasized.

TABLE 3. DISTRIBUTION OF FARMS BY IMPROVED ACREAGE, COTTON SOUTH AND OTHER FARM STATES

	Mean im-proved acreage	Median im-proved acreage	Percentage of farms by improved acreage size class				
			0–49	50–99	100–499	500–999	≥1000
Piedmont							
1850	144.8	80.0	26.2	26.2	42.4	4.2	1.2
1860	158.3	75.0	29.4	26.4	37.1	4.6	2.4
Sand hills							
1860	97.0	50.0	44.1	27.3	25.9	0.7	2.1
Valley							
1850	105.4	50.0	50.0	23.6	21.3	2.8	1.4
1860	105.1	55.0	43.5	27.4	24.9	3.8	0.3
Western upland							
1850	72.7	40.0	60.9	21.7	15.8	1.4	0.0
1860	81.9	50.0	49.8	27.3	21.5	1.3	0.2
Black prairie							
1850	209.7	125.0	21.8	16.6	49.7	9.3	2.7
1860	204.8	125.0	28.1	13.9	47.5	8.8	1.8
Brown loam							
1850	167.1	80.0	30.9	21.0	38.3	7.4	2.5
1860	162.7	75.0	30.8	25.1	35.1	6.6	2.4
Central plain							
1850	136.6	50.0	41.6	24.8	28.0	4.8	0.8
1860	161.4	80.0	31.0	24.1	37.8	4.7	2.4
Coastal plain							
1860	87.8	50.0	47.4	26.1	24.9	1.6	0.0
Alluvial							
1850	198.4	110.0	29.8	17.5	40.3	11.4	0.9
1860	209.7	70.0	40.6	15.2	31.4	7.6	5.1
Cotton South							
1850	113.8	75.3	37.7	23.4	33.1	4.8	1.1
1860	135.9	70.6	39.4	24.5	30.8	3.8	1.5
Illinois							
1860	92.1	73.5	32.0	34.5	32.0	0.7	0.1
Iowa							
1860	63.5	47.1	49.3	33.1	17.6	0.1	0.0
Indiana							
1860	65.0	50.9	48.7	33.1	17.8	0.2	0.0
Minnesota							
1860	30.9	26.5	83.3	12.6	3.6	0.0	0.0
Ohio							
1860	72.2	64.8	38.1	38.1	23.5	0.3	0.1
Wisconsin							
1860	54.5	41.8	60.7	25.9	13.2	0.1	0.0

SOURCES: For the cotton South soil type regions, computed from the manuscript census samples; for the other states, from the 1860 published census.

Table 4, however, shows that a small percentage of farms in the upper two classes implies a large percentage of total improved acreage in those two classes. The table shows the percentages for the cotton regions computed directly from the census observations. For the northern states it was necessary to assume that the farms were concentrated at the midpoints of the intervals; an average of 1,200 improved acres was assumed for the largest class. The clustering of farms in the lower ranges suggests that this assumption overstates the average acreage in the largest two classes. But even with this bias the percentages in these classes are much smaller in the North in almost every case. In the alluvial example cited above, the upper 5.1 percent of farms contained 33.5 percent of the total improved acreage.

The degree of concentration implied by these size-class distributions may be summarized in an estimate of the Gini coefficient of concentration: in a Lorenz curve diagram (as in fig. 1), the Gini coefficient is the ratio between the area enclosed by the curve and the diagonal, and the total area under the diagonal. This area was estimated for the approximation to the curve given by the straight-line segments joining the points which represent the five size classes. As the diagram shows, this method underestimates the degree of concentration, and in the case of the cotton regions there is no reason to settle for such a crude estimate. Nevertheless, the calculation was made, in order to have a set of indices roughly comparable for North and South. The index

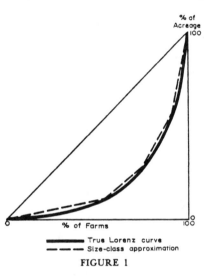

FIGURE 1

ranges from 0 (complete equality) to 100 (complete concentration). The results for 1860 are shown in the last column of table 4.

The figures show that landholding in every cotton region was more highly concentrated than in every northern state. This is true even for those soil types experiencing small-farmer immigration during the 1850s, such as western upland. The aggregate index for the cotton South, which takes into account interregional inequalities as well as intraregional inequalities, is strikingly high. It would be stretching these limited data too far to devise significance tests for these indices, but the test devised for interregional and 1850–1860 comparisons within the South suggests that the order of magnitude of the overall difference is significant.

This evidence, crude as it is, leaves little doubt that holdings of land were more concentrated throughout the cotton South than in the North. It is argued below that this is a conservative test for the comparison of

TABLE 4. DISTRIBUTION OF IMPROVED ACREAGE BY SIZE CLASS, COTTON SOUTH AND OTHER FARM STATES

| | Percentage of total improved acreage by improved acreage size class | | | | | |
	0–49	50–99	100–499	500–999	≥1000	Gini index
Piedmont						
1850	5.2	12.0	54.8	17.5	10.4	
1860	4.1	8.7	36.6	14.5	36.1	62.1
Sand hills						
1860	12.0	17.5	40.5	3.6	26.4	55.0
Valley						
1850	11.7	14.8	41.2	18.4	14.0	
1860	11.1	17.5	44.5	23.9	3.0	51.9
Western upland						
1850	23.4	19.0	45.6	12.0	0.0	
1860	15.5	21.7	49.3	10.2	3.2	48.5
Black prairie						
1850	3.0	5.3	48.4	30.6	12.6	
1860	3.6	4.3	52.5	27.8	11.8	48.5
Brown loam						
1850	4.5	8.2	39.8	32.7	14.8	
1860	5.1	10.1	43.5	23.6	17.8	53.7
Central plain						
1850	7.7	11.5	40.6	24.9	15.2	
1860	5.4	9.7	45.1	17.3	22.5	54.2
Coastal plain						
1860	14.3	19.6	55.1	11.0	0.0	47.0
Alluvial						
1850	3.3	5.7	45.6	36.8	8.6	
1860	4.3	4.7	33.0	24.5	33.5	63.5
Cotton South						
1850	7.5	11.1	47.0	22.9	11.5	
1860	7.3	11.5	43.5	16.9	20.9	57.7
Illinois						
1860	8.1	20.7	65.8	4.2	1.3	43.6
Iowa						
1860	17.8	29.0	52.0	1.0	0.2	44.0
Indiana						
1860	17.0	28.6	51.5	2.0	0.8	45.2
Minnesota						
1860	52.0	24.4	23.4	0.2	0.0	34.2
Ohio						
1860	11.2	28.1	57.8	2.1	0.8	43.8
Wisconsin						
1860	24.6	27.2	46.7	1.2	0.2	45.2

SOURCES: Cotton South soil type region figures computed from MSS census samples; 1850 cotton South totals from MSS census sample total for each soil region (regional weights from published census). Figures for other states estimated from published census by multiplying number of farms in each size class by the interval midpoint (midpoint of 1200 for the largest class.

TABLE 5. CONCENTRATION OF IMPROVED ACREAGE, 1850 AND 1860

	Share of largest 5%		Share of smallest 50%		Index of concentration	
	1850	1860	1850	1860	1850	1860
Piedmont	27.9	32.6	15.7	13.3	52.5	58.1
Sand hills		37.0		15.5		57.1
Valley	38.0	29.0	11.8	14.3	61.7	56.6
Western upland	33.9	27.5	16.6	15.9	52.9	53.7
Black prairie	23.7	23.5	13.9	13.2	53.2	55.6
Brown loam	32.0	28.9	11.0	12.3	61.3	58.9
Central plain	40.2	32.2	10.5	12.0	63.9	59.3
Coastal plain		25.6		16.4		52.8
Alluvial	25.5	33.6	10.2	7.3	57.7	67.2
Cotton South	31.7	29.6	13.4	12.7	57.1	57.5

wealth concentrations, because the distributions of farm value and of other forms of wealth in the South were still more unequal. At this point, however, there is no further reason to rely on size-class tables. From the manuscript census samples, percentile distributions have been calculated for each soil type region in improved acreage, farm value, wealth, slaveholdings, and cotton output. These regional distributions are summarized in tables 5, 6, 7, 8, and 9. Aggregate decile distributions for the cotton South appear in table 10. In what follows, the term "statistical significance" is used without elaboration; the reader should consult appendix B for a description of a fitting of the lognormal distribution to each sample variable, from which the test was derived.

Looking first at the improved acreage distributions, one can see clear differences among the regions.[19] The alluvial region, in which the upper 10 percent of farm operators owned over half the land, had by far the greatest concentration. The difference between the alluvial region and every other region is significant. At the opposite end of the range are the coastal plain, western upland, and sand hills regions, in which the upper 10 percent of farms held slightly more than 40 percent of the acreage. Relatively high-concentration soil types include brown loam, black prairie, and central plain, with piedmont and valley intermediate. Thus, while it is true that the distribution of land was more unequal throughout the cotton South than in the North and West, one should not think of the cotton South as homogeneous in this respect.

To some degree, the overall level of concentration is understated by looking at each soil type separately. Differences in mean improved acreage *between* regions mean that the aggregate distribution is more unequal than

[19] It will be noted that in every case but one the new estimate of the concentration index is higher than the original estimate in table 3. The explanation is given in the text, namely, that calculation of the index by the size-class method yields an underestimate.

an average of the regional concentration indices, weighted only by number of farms. It is even possible that the aggregate index could be greater than any of the regional indices. In fact, however, the aggregate index is 57.5, less than that of four of the regions.

Interregional differences also appear when one considers the change in concentration between 1850 and 1860. In the piedmont and alluvial regions, the share of the largest 20 percent of farms (as well as the concentration index) increased, the corresponding loss in shares being spread over the lower 80 percent. In the valley, western upland, black prairie, brown loam, and central plain regions, the share of the largest 10 percent *fell* during the 1850s; thus some support can be mustered for the view that this decade was a period of general prosperity and equalization of status. However, in all of these regions the major beneficiaries of this loss were the second and third deciles, so that the overall index of concentration changed little. In fact, for the western upland and black prairie regions, *both* the upper 10 percent *and* the lower 40 percent lost ground relatively, in favor of the intermediate farms. In these two regions, if the small farmer was being squeezed out, it was by the medium-sized farmer with less than 500 improved acres, rather than by the 1000-acre planters.

Looking at the South as a whole, however, one can not say that the shifts in the concentration of landholding which took place during the 1850s were important.[20] The aggregate concentration index rose insignificantly from 57.1 to 57.5; the share of the largest 5 percent of farms fell slightly from 31.7 percent to 29.6 percent, but this loss went almost entirely into the hands of the next 15 percent of farms in terms of size.

CONCENTRATION OF FARM VALUE

In many ways the distribution of farm value is more interesting than the distribution of acreage. First, the value of a man's farm is clearly a better measure of his welfare and social position than the number of acres he owns. Second, a comparison of acreage and value distributions enables us to test whether the large planters held higher-quality land than small farmers; this question is one of long-standing controversy. But the use of the farm value figures in this connection requires further discussion.

The census enumerators were required to record for each farm, in addition to acreage, an item called "cash value of farm." Their instructions stated that the meaning of the term was "the actual cash value of the whole number of acres returned by you as improved and unimproved." [21] The figure was *not* to include the value of implements, slaves, livestock, or financial assets, but it did include the value of buildings and improvements. One might argue that the larger, wealthier planters would have spent pro-

[20] The imperfect statistical test in appendix B indicates that none of these changes is statistically significant. See the appendix, however, for qualifications to this statement.

[21] Carroll Wright, *The History and Growth of the United States Census* (Washington: G.P.O., 1900), 52.

TABLE 6. CONCENTRATION OF FARM VALUE, 1850 AND 1860

	Share of richest 5%		Share of poorest 50%		Index of concentration	
	1850	1860	1850	1860	1850	1860
Piedmont	29.3	34.6	12.2	11.0	58.1	61.2
Sand hills		59.3		6.2		76.7
Valley	45.8	39.7	7.1	7.6	70.9	69.5
Western upland	47.7	37.0	7.4	10.9	71.5	64.7
Black prairie	34.4	30.1	8.6	8.4	64.1	64.8
Brown loam	38.2	35.9	9.1	9.0	64.7	65.3
Central plain	51.0	38.0	5.0	8.9	75.0	66.0
Coastal plain		44.7		9.9		66.7
Alluvial	50.9	44.8	4.0	2.9	76.6	78.0
Cotton South	42.4	39.1	7.8	7.8	69.8	67.8

portionately more on the family house, farm buildings, and other improvements, and hence that the value of farm (per acre) would not be a satisfactory measure of soil quality. However, there are several reasons for believing that this upward bias should not have been important.

First, the postwar mythologies about antebellum times have substantially exaggerated the number and grandeur of plantation mansions. Bonner writes: "Travelers ... were frequently astonished at the great number of wealthy men they found living in miserable dwellings. ... The planters' barns, fences, and outhouses were worthy matches for the residence." [22] Furthermore, many planters did not live on their plantations; if they did not live outside of the region, they built their houses in nearby towns: "In general, planters in the Black Belt preferred to reside in small communities rather than on their plantations, which were frequently ... extremely unhealthful in summer." [23] Also, historians are nearly unanimous in finding that "the transitory nature of agriculture in the ante-bellum South gave little encouragement to construction of permanent buildings, roads, or fences." [24] Gray found that "outbuildings were inexpensive in character. Negro houses represented generally an inconsiderable expenditure. ... Barns of large size were unusual on cotton plantations." [25] Finally, it should be borne in mind that the hypothesis of an upward bias requires that these investments increase more than in proportion to acreage. Yet expenditure on external fencing, to cite only one possible example, would increase only in proportion to the square root of acreage. Other fixed capital items, such

[22] James C. Bonner, "Plantation Architecture of the Lower South on the Eve of the Civil War," *Journal of Southern History* 11 (August 1945): 371, 373.

[23] Charles S. Davis, *The Cotton Kingdom in Alabama* (Montgomery: Alabama State Department of Archives and History, 1939), 42.

[24] John H. Moore, *Agriculture in Ante-bellum Mississippi* (New York: Bookman Associates, 1958), 39.

[25] Gray, *History of Agriculture*, 539–40.

as barns or overseers' quarters, would not necessarily have to be increased as acreage grew, and these expenditures would then be proportionately less on large farms. Since the land-labor ratio was more or less constant (certainly not falling) on farms of various sizes, there is no reason to believe that investment in slave quarters increased faster than acreage, and it may have increased more slowly.

Hence there is substantial basis for believing that "cash value of farm," in relation to acreage, is a measure of the value of the soil. There is one remaining problem, however, which is that the census provides no way to allocate the farm value between improved acreage and unimproved acreage; cash value of farm per total acreage is a function of the proportion of the total improved, as well as the quality of the soil. It is widely believed that the big planters held large amounts of unimproved acreage as "insurance against the necessity for moving." [26] A negative correlation between farm size and the proportion of acreage improved would introduce a bias: farm value would be more highly concentrated than improved acreage, not because of soil quality, but because the large farms have proportionately more unimproved acreage to add to the value of their improved acreage. [27]

The evidence from the sample, however, is that the comparison of distributions of farm value and improved acreage is not biased by this phenomenon. It is true that, if farms are ranked by total acreage, there is some negative relationship between size and percentage improved. However, tables 5 and 6 are based on rankings by improved acreage and by farm value. In the first case, the largest farms have a higher proportion of improved acreage; in the second, there is no clear correlation. For the cotton South as a whole, the relevant data are as follows:

Total acres	Percentage improved	Improved acres	Percentage improved	Farm value ($)	Percentage improved
0–49	66	0–49	17	$0–999	27
50–99	45	50–99	23	1,000–1,999	27
100–199	35	100–199	28	2,000–4,999	29
200–299	34	200–299	31	5,000–9,999	50
300–499	30	300–499	34	10,000–19,999	35
500–999	32	500–999	38	20,000–49,999	36
≥1,000	28	≥1,000	50	≥50,000	25

The influence of unimproved acreage on value is small in any case. Regres-

[26] James C. Bonner, A History of Georgia Agriculture, 1732–1860 (Atlanta: Georgia University Press, 1964), 67.

[27] It may be argued that such a phenomenon could only be based on capital-market imperfections and is therefore not entirely different from the alleged appropriation by the wealthy of the richest soil. That is, if both large and small farmers could borrow funds freely at similar rates, then the larger farmers would have had no particular advantage in holding idle land.

sion estimates for the average value of an unimproved acre in 1860 suggest the following figures: piedmont, $3.03; valley, $0.76; western upland, $3.21; black prairie, $0.33; brown loam, $11.65; central plain, $2.91; alluvial, $4.10.[28] For contrast, the estimates of the value of an improved acre range from $12.43 (piedmont) to $107.39 (alluvial). Only in the brown loam region was the value of an unimproved acre substantial, and in that region there was virtually no relationship between farm size and the percentage of acreage improved.

With this discussion as a background, the reader should consult the figures on farm value in table 6. In every soil type region the index of concentration is greater for farm value than for improved acreage. In most cases the difference is large and statistically significant. In the alluvial region, for example, the largest 10 percent of farms contained 50.6 percent of the improved acreage, but the *most valuable* 10 percent of farms controlled 64.1 percent of the total farm value.[29]

The ordering of soil types by concentration of farm value is roughly the same as the ordering by concentration of improved acreage. As in the latter case, the distribution in the alluvial region is significantly more unequal than that of every other region. Piedmont, western upland, and the coastal plain showed the least inequality, with the others in between.

For the cotton South as a whole, the index of concentration of farm value is 67.8, higher than the average of the regions weighted only by number of farms, which is 64.3. The reason for the discrepancy is that, as even Owsley agreed, larger farms were concentrated in the most fertile regions. In other words, the difference in mean farm value among the regions makes for a greater concentration in the aggregate figures. This aggregate index is substantially greater than the index of 57.5 for improved acreage. It thus appears that the North-South contrast is probably understated in the previous section, if we are concerned with the wealth distributions associated with agricultural production.

The same result does hold with respect to changes in the concentration of farm value between 1850 and 1860: essentially there was little overall change. The only statistically significant development was the decline in concentration in the central plain: in that region, the share of the top 5 percent fell dramatically from 51 percent to 38 percent, the gap in shares being spread over the remaining 95 percent of farms. Concentration also fell in the western upland region, and rose somewhat in the piedmont and

---

[28] The estimates were obtained by regressing farm value against improved acreage and unimproved acreage for each soil type. The R^2 values for 1860 range from .500 (western upland) to .756 (brown loam). The coefficients are not necessarily unbiased, but the figures for the cotton South as a whole in the text table suggest that there is, if anything, an upward bias to the coefficient of unimproved acreage.

[29] This does not necessarily imply that the *largest* farms in terms of improved acreage had the *most* valuable land, because the ranking of farms is not the same for the two cases. In fact, it appears that only in the alluvial, sand hills, and valley regions did the largest 5 percent of farms have the most valuable land.

alluvial regions. This contrasting regional pattern, of increasing value-concentration on the large-plantation soils of the piedmont and alluvial counties, and decreasing value-concentration in the small-farm regions, may
account for the conflicting histories of the 1850s which have been written.
One notes, however, that the small farmers on alluvial land were losing
out, not to the very richest planters, but to the "upper-middle-size" planters
in the second decile. For the cotton South as a whole, it cannot be claimed
that the concentration in land value was increasing during the 1850's,
and in fact the aggregate index fell slightly from 69.8 to 67.8.

DISTRIBUTION OF SLAVES, COTTON OUTPUT, AND WEALTH

I have argued that, in an era of cheap land and scarce labor, control over
slaves was probably a better measure of the social and economic standing of
a farmer than control over acreage. Such an assertion is reinforced by the
prestige and political power attached to the institution of slavery. It may
be seen from table 7 that the distribution of slaves was very much more unequal than the land and farm value distributions. With two exceptions
(discussed below), the indices of concentration in slaves are significantly
higher.

Tables 7 and 8 show that the distribution of cotton output is very similar
to the distribution of slaves. Such similarity tends to confirm the observation that the link between cotton production and slave labor was much
stronger than that between cotton and land; one could reasonably own
land and produce only nonmarket crops, but one could hardly invest in
slaves without producing cash crops, and cotton was the only important
cash crop over almost all of the region under study. The two exceptions
mentioned above are instructive. It is probably not coincidence that the
alluvial and black prairie regions, the two soil types for which the distribution of slaves and cotton output are not much different from the dis-

TABLE 7. CONCENTRATION OF AGRICULTURAL SLAVEHOLDINGS, 1850 AND 1860

	Share of largest 5%		Share of smallest 60%		Index of concentration	
	1850	1860	1850	1860	1850	1860
Piedmont	32.6	39.1	9.6	4.3	67.7	75.2
Sand hills		70.9		0.0		83.6
Valley	46.7	43.7	1.2	0.0	80.9	84.5
Western upland	45.0	44.0	1.1	0.0	80.2	82.4
Black prairie	26.1	26.1	14.2	12.6	62.2	64.5
Brown loam	39.5	34.9	6.5	4.5	73.5	73.7
Central plain	48.2	40.8	2.4	3.5	79.2	76.8
Coastal plain		38.8		6.5		77.8
Alluvial	27.7	37.1	17.0	4.8	60.0	74.8
Cotton South	39.0	38.9	7.1	4.3	72.3	74.7

TABLE 8. Concentration of Cotton Output, 1850 and 1860

	Share of largest 5%		Share of smallest 50%		Index of concentration	
	1850	1860	1850	1860	1850	1860
Piedmont	34.6	40.4	9.9	5.5	62.7	71.5
Sand hills		75.3		1.3		83.6
Valley	53.2	46.2	0.3	1.9	84.2	80.5
Western upland	57.7	43.9	1.8	4.5	81.0	75.6
Black prairie	32.8	25.9	7.7	6.9	66.5	64.7
Brown loam	44.9	40.1	5.0	3.7	72.3	73.9
Central plain	50.0	47.2	3.1	3.8	78.2	76.4
Coastal plain		46.0		2.9		76.5
Alluvial	36.1	43.9	4.5	1.4	69.6	78.8
Cotton South	42.5	42.0	5.3	4.0	71.3	73.0

tribution of the value of farms, are also the two regions of most valuable soil. It is often stated loosely that "land was not a constraint" on cotton production, but land was not homogeneous, and high-quality land was very expensive. In these two regions, the purchase of land was as much a commitment to commercial production as the purchase of slaves.

For many purposes the distributions of land value, slaveownership, and cotton output are most interesting: What they tell us, in brief, is the distribution of the stakes in the market economy. It is likely that economic power and status were closely connected with the ownership of cash-value assets (especially slaves) and with the production of cash crops. Furthermore the distribution of *money* income is relevant for such questions as the structure of market demand for various goods, and easily the most important source of money income was cotton sales. The strong suggestion of the evidence is that the impact of the cotton-slavery sector of the economy was to raise the degree of concentration in income and wealth.

Nevertheless, there is really no reason not to try to measure the distribution of wealth directly from the manuscript census. "Wealth" in this measurement is defined as the value of personal property of the farm operator (which includes such things as implements and livestock, though the bulk of the total is the value of slaves) and the value of the farm which he operated.

From tables 5 through 10, one can see that in most cases the concentration index for wealth is greater than that for farm value, and less than that for slaves. With the exceptions of black prairie and alluvial soils, the difference between the concentration of wealth and the concentration of farm value is statistically significant, showing the impact of the still more concentrated distribution of slaves. (The coastal plain is another and a puzzling exception to this generalization.) These exceptional soil types are explainable, not in terms of a less concentrated distribution of slaves, but in terms of more valuable soil and more highly concentrated ownership of it.

With respect to changes between 1850 and 1860 there is a clear contrast between the wealth distribution and the others we have considered. Few significant changes were found in the distributions of land and land value, certainly no marked increase in inequality (with the possible exceptions of the piedmont and alluvial regions). However, in every soil type region major changes occurred in the distribution of wealth during the 1850s. In the piedmont, the share of the top 5 percent rose sharply, while the share of the poorest 50 percent fell by almost 50 percent! This shift appears to reflect the clear pattern of increasing concentration of slaveownership in the piedmont shown in table 7.

Looking only at the columns for the share of the top 5 percent for the remaining regions, one might argue that an opposite trend was present, since in every case the share fell. But this "concentration ratio" alone is highly misleading, because it is also true that in every case the share of the *poorest* half of the population fell, on the average by 25 percent. The same pattern of change is evident in each case: the second, third, and sometimes fourth deciles gain proportionately at the expense of both the richest and poorest members of the population. This common pattern may also help to explain the divergent interpretations of the 1850s: on the one hand there is a trend to equalization among the planters; on the other hand the poor do not share in this redistribution, indeed they lose ground relatively.

Such changes undoubtedly reflect in part the increase in slave prices during the 1850s, but they also have a basis in changes in the distribution of slave ownership. Only in the piedmont and alluvial regions did the share in total slaveholdings of the top 5 percent rise, but in every case there was an increase in the proportion of farm operators owning no slaves. It seems that the small farmer was not so much being squeezed off his land as losing his share of the slaves. These two factors—the rise of slave prices and the shift of slaveownership away from small farmers toward middle-class planters—resulted in an increase in the concentration of wealth for the cotton South as a whole.

URBAN AND RURAL WEALTH DISTRIBUTIONS

Gallman, in another study,[30] contrasts the wealth distribution for the 1860 cotton-county sample with that of three United States cities (Baltimore, New Orleans, St. Louis) and two other farm regions (Louisiana outside New Orleans, and Maryland outside of Baltimore). He found that "the distribution of wealth was much more unequal in large cities than in rural

[30] Robert E. Gallman, "Trends in the Size Distribution of Wealth in the Nineteenth Century: Some Speculations," in *Six Papers on the Size Distribution of Wealth and Income*, ed. Lee Soltow, NBER, Studies in Income and Wealth, vol. 33 (New York: Columbia University Press, 1969).

TABLE 9. CONCENTRATION OF AGRICULTURAL WEALTH, 1850 AND 1860

	Share of richest 5%		Share of poorest 50%		Index of concentration	
	1850	1860	1850	1860	1850	1860
Piedmont	28.7	36.7	12.1	6.4	58.0	68.8
Sand hills		56.3		4.6		78.7
Valley	43.3	37.9	7.6	5.4	70.2	73.6
Western upland	43.8	37.6	7.6	6.9	69.3	69.6
Black prairie	34.0	27.0	9.2	8.0	63.3	63.0
Brown loam	39.6	33.4	8.3	5.8	65.8	68.6
Central plain	44.7	37.9	5.8	5.5	72.0	70.4
Coastal plain		35.1		7.7		66.0
Alluvial	48.0	35.9	4.5	3.3	74.3	72.9
Cotton South	39.5	36.2	8.0	5.9	67.0	68.3

areas," including the cotton South.[31] What implication does this finding have for the results of this paper?

The contrast with which we have been concerned is that between the distribution of agricultural holdings in the cotton South and that of similar holdings in northern farm areas. The North-South agricultural comparison is the relevant one for many historical questions concerned with contrasting social structures and contrasting patterns of economic development. Whether, as Gallman's evidence suggests, there is also a pattern of greater inequality in cities than in rural areas in 1860 is a different question. The state of Maryland, though not part of the cotton South, is definitely not representative of northern agriculture. As Gallman states, we can be sure that Maryland's distribution is "more unequal" than that of "all other" farm regions outside the South. Hence, there is really no argument here, and the evidence presented loses none of its force.

Nevertheless, the contrast between *cities* and the South was a matter of considerable discussion in antebellum times; the North, though still predominantly rural, was urbanizing at a rapid rate in 1860, and it is of interest to look more closely at this comparison as well. With respect to the distribution of wealth among free men, it may be observed that the cotton South distributions derived from the manuscript census samples are understatements of the degree of concentration. They are distributions from a sample of farm operators, not heads of families. This limitation may not be serious for comparing soil type regions within the South, or comparing 1850 with 1860, but for purposes of comparison with the cities, it is probable that the persons who have been excluded—overseers, farm laborers, rural unemployed—are those with little or no wealth.

[31] Ibid. Gallman obtained the following figures for the share of the richest 5 percent: Baltimore, 71.7 percent; New Orleans, 71.6 percent; St. Louis, 67.7 percent; Maryland, 45.4 percent; Louisiana, 57.5 percent; cotton counties, 42.0 percent.

TABLE 10. AGGREGATE COTTON SOUTH DISTRIBUTIONS, 1850 AND 1860

	Percent of total improved acreage		Percent of total farm value		Percent of total wealth		Percent of total slaves		Percent of total cotton produced	
	1850	1860	1850	1860	1850	1860	1850	1860	1850	1860
1st 5%	31.7	29.6	42.4	39.1	39.5	36.2	39.0	38.9	42.5	42.0
1st decile	46.0	46.1	57.1	54.5	54.8	52.8	56.4	56.7	58.9	58.6
2nd decile	16.5	17.3	15.8	17.7	16.6	19.6	18.9	21.0	16.9	18.8
3rd decile	10.6	10.8	9.2	9.9	9.8	10.9	10.6	11.7	9.3	9.9
4th decile	7.7	7.5	6.0	6.0	6.5	6.7	7.1	6.3	5.8	5.5
5th decile	5.8	5.7	4.0	4.1	4.2	4.0	3.7	2.9	3.8	3.4
6th decile	4.6	4.1	3.1	3.0	3.3	2.5	2.1	1.1	2.5	2.1
7th decile	3.4	3.3	2.2	2.2	2.2	1.5	1.0	0.2	1.5	1.3
8th decile	2.6	2.5	1.4	1.5	1.4	1.0	0.2	0.0	0.9	0.5
9th decile	1.9	1.8	0.8	0.8	0.8	0.6	0.0	0.0	0.0	0.0
10th decile	0.9	1.0	0.3	0.3	0.3	0.3	0.0	0.0	0.0	0.0

However, the bias associated with this factor alone—the exclusion of free heads of families other than farm operators—can be assessed by comparison of the cotton South distributions with Gallman's distribution for heads of families in Louisiana outside New Orleans. Agricultural wealth was almost surely more concentrated in Louisiana (which includes the sugar counties) than in the cotton areas, yet the urban distributions are substantially more concentrated than Louisiana.

It appears safe to say, therefore, that the wealth distributions described in this paper are not as unequal as those of urban areas in 1860. It may be observed further that the wealth distribution among free heads of families in the cotton South does not seem to be more unequal than more recent wealth distributions. Robert J. Lampman's figures for the share of the top 1 percent of the population 20 years and over for the period 1922–1956 range from 20.8 percent (1949) to 36.3 percent (1929),[32] shares which are probably greater than corresponding figures for the cotton South. As argued above, use of a 1 percent or 5 percent "wealth concentration ratio" can yield misleading results, but it appears unlikely that the overall 1860 wealth distribution for free persons in the South could be very much more unequal than the wealth distributions of the twentieth century.

[*] Robert J. Lampman, *The Share of Top Wealth-Holders in National Wealth, 1922–1956* (Princeton: Princeton University Press, 1962), 25.

All of this discussion, however, involves the treatment of slaves as property rather than as persons. Such a treatment has practical justification in the nature of the available data, and it may also have analytical justification, as well, in the comparison of northern and southern agriculture. But in terms of the most basic social questions about the distribution of wealth across the population, it may well be argued that slaves should be included as zero-wealthholders. This is especially true for comparison with the urban distributions, which include the poorest industrial laborers, most of whom owned little or no property. Gallman's estimates for the distribution of nonslave wealth, when slaves are included in the population, show that the first decile controlled 79 percent of the wealth (96 percent in Louisiana outside New Orleans), a figure which puts the cotton South in the same general range as the cities. Even here, it may be surprising that the distribution of wealth in the cities was roughly equivalent in concentration to the distribution of nonslave wealth in the South; but the most striking contrast, of course, is between both of these distributions and that of the rural areas.

It should be clear that no one of these comparisons is the "correct" one. Equality is as relative as most economic concepts, and the comparison which is relevant depends upon the purpose or the historical question at hand. One might even make a case that the most pertinent distribution from a social standpoint would include the value of slaves as wealth to the owners and also include slaves as members of the population. The essence of "wealth" is control over productive resources, which is certainly what slaveowning was, but why should this fact necessarily call for the removal of slaves from the population? Such a distribution would of course be much more unequal than any of the distributions yet considered.[33] But perhaps this is merely a way of saying that in the broadest sense the "inequality" inherent in a slave regime cannot be fully captured by a wealth distribution.

CONCLUSIONS

The conclusions of this study may be briefly summarized. First, it was found that the concentration of holdings of improved acreage was substantially greater in all parts of the cotton South than in northern agricultural states. The second finding was that farm value was significantly more concentrated than improved acreage in the cotton South, suggesting that the planters not only held more land, but also more valuable land than their small-farm neighbors. Third, it was found that agricultural wealth

[33] Gallman observes that consistency would require the inclusion of all forms of human capital in the wealth distributions for North and South. Such an inclusion, however, would almost surely accentuate the contrast between free and slave sections, because the zero-wealthholders of the North at least "owned" their own human capital. Some of the wealthier persons in the North might, of course, have possessed substantial human capital as well, but it is difficult to believe that the overall wealth distribution for the free states would not be less unequal than that for nonhuman wealth.

generally was in most areas still more unequally distributed than farm value, apparently because of the high concentration of slaveownership. Both the second and third results suggest that the North-South comparison based on improved acreage alone probably understates the difference in the concentration of agricultural wealth. A fourth conclusion is that there was no general pattern of increasing concentration in land and land value during the 1850s; the contrasts in regional experience may help to account for the contrasting accounts of the decade which have been written. There was, however, a pattern throughout the cotton South of a shift in the wealth distribution in favor of the "upper middle" deciles at the expense (relatively) of both the richest and poorest groups. This shift seems to have had more to do with slaves and slave value than with the ownership of land. In sum, there is little reason to reject the traditional view that the social implication of the slave-cotton regime was a highly unequal distribution of wealth. Such a statement is a relative one, however, and one should be aware of the variety of comparisons which are possible and of the different results which they yield.

It should be emphasized that these conclusions apply only to the cotton South and may not hold for the rest of the slave area. On the one hand, we have excluded some relatively small-farm tobacco and general farming regions in Virginia, North Carolina, Tennessee, and Kentucky, but we have also excluded many of the largest plantations of all in the rice counties of South Carolina and the sugar counties of Louisiana. Even for the cotton South, this study represents only one-half of a complete analysis: the remaining task is to examine the links between the agricultural wealth distributions and the agricultural production characteristics of cotton and slavery.

APPENDIX A

DESCRIPTION OF SOIL TYPE REGIONS

The soil type regions employed in this article are based primarily on the soil types of the *Tenth Census of the United States, 1880,* Vol. V, cross-checked with the regional divisions of the National Research Program Agricultural Economics Project. The distinctions of the 1880 census are somewhat finer than those of the AEP, but the broad groupings of counties are very similar under the two systems. It is obviously somewhat artificial to assume, as we are forced to do, that soil type regions are bounded by county lines. But for the most part, the soil types form broad belts or clusters of counties, with only a few borderline cases. When the two systems classified a county differently, the issue was resolved on the basis of the homogeneity of the size distributions of acreage, farm value, and cotton output. In the case of four counties (Chickasaw and Monroe in Mississippi, Anson and Richmond in North Carolina) the classification was so uncertain that the counties were omitted. Only the nine soil types actually used in the study are described here.

Piedmont: Soil type 1, "granite and metamorphic gray and red lands." Soil type 1 coincides almost precisely with the "Piedmont" AEP region. The piedmont is a broad belt running in a southwest-northeast direction through central North Carolina, South Carolina, and Georgia, reaching into eastern Alabama at its westernmost points. The terrain is rocky, almost mountainous in some places, with irregular soils.

Sand Hills: Soil type 4, "sand hills belt of middle North Carolina, South Carolina, Georgia, and Alabama." Also called "pine barrens," the region is a narrow strip between the piedmont and the central plain.

Valley: Soil type 8, "valley lands of eastern Tennessee, Georgia, and Alabama with narrow cherty ridges." The region consists of a group of counties along the Tennessee River valley, with deep red calcareous soil.

Western Upland: Soil type 16, "oak, hickory, and short-leaf pine uplands." Soil type 16 forms the major part of the "Western Hilly" region under the AEP system. Western upland is a long belt of rolling, hilly land from northwest Alabama through central Mississippi, northern Louisiana, and southern Arkansas, and including a large section of east Texas.

Black Prairie: Soil types 17 and 18, "black and stiff calcareous prairies (Cretaceous)" and "calcareous prairie lands (Tertiary)." These are combined because of the lack of significant differences in size distributions. Named for the dark color of the soil, the black prairie, often referred to as the "black belt" of central Alabama and Mississippi, was second only to the alluvial region in cotton productivity and in the concentration of slave population.

Brown Loam: Soil type 20, "brown loam bluff and table land." This covers a north-south region lying east of the delta in Mississippi and Tennessee, also called "loess." The soil is a brown, siliceous loam, noted for its mellowness.

Central Plain and *Coastal Plain:* The region referred to in the AEP system as the "Coastal Plain" is roughly divided by soil type 23, "central belt oak, hickory and long-leaf pine hills, North Carolina to Louisiana," and soil type 24, "long-leaf pine hills," a belt on the coastal side. Both regions are between the piedmont and the coast in the east, stretching further west across Mississippi into Louisiana. The two soil types are kept separate here because of differences in soil quality and the size distribution of farms.

Alluvial: Soil type 27, "alluvial lands and large upland swamps," generally equivalent to the AEP "river bottom" category. Rich, fertile land along the Mississippi River in Louisiana, Mississippi, and Arkansas, and along the Red River in Louisiana. Includes also three Texas counties at the mouth of the Brazos River.

APPENDIX B

DESCRIPTION OF CURVE-FITTING

Probably the most widely used form for studying skewed distributions, such as the size of firms, income, and wealth, is the lognormal, with the density function:

$$f(x) = \frac{1}{xs\sqrt{(2\pi)}} \exp\left[-\frac{1}{2s^2} (\log x - m)^2 \right]$$

where m is the mean and s is the standard deviation of the distribution of the logarithm of the variable. The frequency curve begins at the origin and may take any of a variety of skewed shapes. More highly skewed distributions are characterized by a higher variance. In fact, it may be shown that the index of concentration described above, the Gini coefficient, is uniquely and monotonically related to the variance for a variable which is lognormally distributed.[*] This fact makes the distribution especially easy to work with.

The test for lognormality is simply a test for normality applied to the logarithm of the variable. Since $f(0) = 0$ for the two-parameter lognormal distribution, the tests were run without zero-valued units. (This restriction is of minor importance for improved acreage, farm value, and wealth.) Three tests were applied:
(1) a test of skewness, using the statistic

$$S = \frac{\frac{1}{n}\sum_1^n |y_i - \bar{y}|}{\left[\frac{1}{n}\sum_1^n (y_i - \bar{y})^2\right]^{1/2}}$$

where $y_i = \log x$;
(2) a test of kurtosis, using the statistic

$$K = \frac{\frac{1}{n}\sum_1^n |y_i - \bar{y}|^3}{\left[\frac{1}{n}\sum_1^n (y_i - \bar{y})^2\right]^{3/2}}$$

(3) a x^2 test based on the deviation of the observed and expected frequencies in the ten deciles for the lognormal distribution.

In tests (1) and (2). the statistics S and K were converted to statistics S^* and K^*, which, in the case of lognormality, will be normally distributed with zero mean and unit variance.

[*] See John Aitchison and J. A. C. Brown, *The Lognormal Distribution* (Cambridge: At the University Press, 1957), esp. chap. 11.

APPENDIX TABLE 1. Tests for Lognormality

		S	K	χ^2 (7)
Improved Acres				
Piedmont	1850	0.293*	0.259*	23.79
	1860	3.314	0.846*	47.78
Sand hills	1860	3.102	2.989	10.26*
Valley	1850	2.373	0.403*	14.00*
	1860	2.019	0.248*	23.74
Western upland	1850	3.145	1.639*	12.59*
	1860	2.793	2.490	80.61
Black prairie	1850	0.186*	−1.935*	7.74*
	1860	−0.087*	−2.607	28.62
Brown loam	1850	−0.375*	0.269*	5.86*
	1860	1.644*	−0.864*	15.89
Central plain	1850	1.770*	1.009*	11.88*
	1860	2.442	1.544*	22.92
Coastal plain	1860	1.888*	−0.173*	11.44*
Alluvial	1850	−0.639*	−1.986*	12.67*
	1860	1.650*	−2.170	23.60
Farm Value				
Piedmont	1850	−1.099*	−0.274*	2.03*
	1860	0.902*	−0.556*	19.41
Sand hills	1860	2.896	2.837	12.13*
Valley	1850	2.481	−0.158*	16.86
	1860	1.318*	−0.656*	23.31
Western upland	1850	2.474	0.249*	26.22
	1860	2.593	3.208	17.62
Black prairie	1850	−0.894	−0.574	1.78*
	1860	0.411*	−2.307	12.37*
Brown loam	1850	0.554*	−1.038*	4.00*
	1860	1.248*	−0.767*	13.04*
Central plain	1850	1.375*	−0.683*	12.52*
	1860	2.760	−1.053*	75.27
Coastal plain	1860	2.839	2.057	16.54
Alluvial	1850	−0.036*	−0.571*	5.33*
	1860	1.319*	−1.826	13.43
Wealth				
Piedmont	1850	−1.358*	0.951*	7.68*
	1860	1.864*	−4.400*	36.57
Sand hills	1850	2.305	0.284*	5.62*
Valley	1850	2.092	−0.038*	10.07*
	1860	3.542	−2.089	39.73
Western upland	1850	1.489*	−0.537*	4.00*
	1860	4.851	−1.872*	57.21

* Cannot reject hypothesis of lognormality at 95% confidence level.

APPENDIX TABLE 1. Tests for Lognormality (cont.)

		S	K	χ^2 (7)
	Wealth (cont.)			
Black prairie	1850	−1.464*	0.353*	14.14*
	1860	−1.825*	−2.960	24.10
Brown loam	1850	0.542*	−0.927*	3.79*
	1860	0.894*	−3.143	14.57
Central plain	1850	0.498*	−0.547*	19.45
	1860	2.111	−4.555	58.85
Coastal plain	1860	1.665*	−1.914*	28.15
Alluvial	1850	0.936*	−0.339*	5.76*
	1860	−0.097*	−2.769	9.80*

The results of these tests are presented for each region in appendix table 1, for the distributions of improved acreage, farm value, and wealth. An asterisk beside the statistic value indicates that the evidence is not sufficient to reject the hypothesis of lognormality at a 95-percent confidence level. Of the total of 144 tests, 52 (or 38 percent) indicate rejection of lognormality. If we look only at tests (1) and (2), lognormality should be rejected in 32 of 96 cases, or exactly one-third of the time.

This evidence cannot be claimed to "confirm" the applicability of the lognormal distribution, since only one-twentieth of the tests should indicate rejection if the sample were truly lognormal. Nevertheless the fit seems to be "close enough" to make significance tests based on this distribution meaningful, especially for comparisons between soil type regions and among the three variables. There appears to be no tendency for greater deviation from lognormality for any one of the three variables; nor, with some exceptions, for deviations to be centered in particular soil type regions. Furthermore, the "failures" with respect to the skewness test are almost all of the same direction and degree: positive skewness, between 2.1 and 3.5 standard deviations from zero. (One should not necessarily associate positive skewness of the logarithmic distribution with especially high levels of concentration, because the lognormal distribution itself allows for high degrees of concentration.)

Under the assumption of lognormality, a test for the significance of a change or difference in concentration is whether the ratio of the two sample variances is significantly different from unity, by the F-test. The tests for regional differences in 1860 show that in all three distributions, the alluvial region was significantly more concentrated than every other region. Comparing alluvial to the second most concentrated region in each case, the hypothesis of equality is rejected with better than 99 percent confidence for improved acreage and farm value, better than 95 percent confidence for wealth. When one ranks the remaining regions in order of concentration, however, in no other case is the difference between *adjacent* regions (in this ranking, not by geography) statistically significant. On the other hand, those regions at the bottom of the list are significantly less concentrated than those near the top. In other words, the test does not tell us precisely where to establish the line separating "high" from "low"-concentration regions, but it is clear that important differences exist. In general, a pattern emerges in which black prairie, central plain, and brown loam regions exhibit "high" concentration of holdings; piedmont, western upland, and coastal plain are "low" concentration regions; the remainder are uncertain.

APPENDIX TABLE 2. LOGARITHMIC VARIANCE RATIOS

		Farm value/ improved acreage	Wealth/ farm value
Piedmont	1850	1.43†	0.89
	1860	1.23*	1.53†
Sand hills	1860	1.86†	2.20†
Valley	1850	1.52*	0.94
	1860	1.78†	1.16
Western upland	1850	2.30†	0.93
	1860	1.51*	1.33*
Black prairie	1850	1.78†	0.90
	1860	1.52*	1.28
Brown loam	1850	1.09	0.98
	1860	1.32*	1.42*
Central plain	1850	1.81†	0.88
	1860	1.36*	1.45*
Coastal plain	1860	1.46*	1.40*
Alluvial	1850	1.72†	0.67
	1860	2.92†	1.02

1860 Value over 1850 Value

	Improved acreage	Farm value	Wealth
Piedmont	1.134	0.980	1.664†
Valley	0.954	1.032	1.376
Western upland	1.257	0.808	1.145
Black prairie	1.069	0.898	1.260*
Brown loam	0.764*	0.929	1.336*
Central plain	0.894	0.673†	1.107
Alluvial	1.110	1.103	1.677†

* Significantly different from 1.0 at 95% confidence.
† Significantly different from 1.0 at 99% confidence.

The test reveals differences between the distributions of the three variables more clearly. In appendix table 2, the logarithmic variance ratios are presented for comparing farm value with improved acreage, and wealth with farm value. In 1860, holdings of farm value were significantly more concentrated than holdings of improved acreage in every region, with at least 95 percent confidence. This significant difference also existed in 1850, in every region but brown loam. Thus the phenomenon of the concentration of the best farm land on large farms came about prior to the 1850s.

The test also shows that in 1860 in all regions but three (valley, black prairie, alluvial) holdings of wealth were significantly more highly concentrated than holdings of farm value. The three exceptions are regions of highest value per acre. This phenomenon was entirely a product of developments in the 1850s: in 1850 there was no case of significant difference between the wealth distribution and the farm-value distribution.

The lognormal test is least satisfactory in measuring changes within regions between 1850 and 1860, because the 1850 distributions fit the lognormal distribution much better than do those for 1860. For what they are worth, the relevant F-ratios are also presented in appendix table 2. The indication is that there was no case of increasing concentration in improved acreage or farm value; but that the concentration of wealth increased significantly in the piedmont, black prairie, brown loam, and alluvial regions.

These results are not different in most cases from one's impressions from perusing the decile distributions. But it is clear that there is not really a one-to-one relationship between the fitted lognormal variance and the index of concentration. Most of the difficulty appears to lie in the changing *form* of the distribution between 1850 and 1860; of the lognormal tests for 1850, only 14 percent indicate rejection; but 57 percent of the 1860 tests call for rejection. In several soil type regions, lognormality fits very well in 1850, but not at all well in 1860. This very result suggests that the changes are "significant"; we have already observed that there occurred in all regions a major loss of share on the part of the top decile and the lower 50 percent. For most purposes, this description is the important one, and it is in a sense arbitrary to insist on reducing "concentration" to a single index.

Nevertheless, in the hope of probing further into the 1850–1860 change, an attempt was made to fit curves of the Pearson family. It developed that, according to the Pearson test criterion, the incomplete-Beta distribution fit the data well for all three variables. This is a very flexible two-parameter distribution described by the density function:

$$f(x) = \frac{1}{B(a+1, g+1)} x^a (1-x)^g,$$

where $B()$ stands for the beta-function; and a and g are the parameters of the distribution. The possible shapes for the incomplete-beta distribution range from single-peaked curves skewed to the left or right to J-shaped or U-shaped distributions. In appendix table 3 are presented the values of the two parameters and the indicated shape of the curve.

An examination of the qualitative behavior of the curves is instructive. The most striking result is that in no case is a curve which begins at the origin appropriate. If both parameters are greater than zero, the curve has one turning point, like the lognormal. But in the present case such a curve does not fit because of the large number of small farms. In over 85 percent of the cases, the fitted curve declines smoothly from a high point at or near the Y-axis.

APPENDIX TABLE 3. Fitted Parameters of Incomplete-Beta Distribution

		α	λ	Description of curve
Improved Acreage				
Piedmont	1850	8.24	−0.80	J-shaped
	1860	2.52	−0.86	J-shaped
Sand hills	1860	−9.001	−0.97	U-shaped
Valley	1850	0.74	−0.91	Twisted J-shape
	1860	1.45	−0.85	J-shape
Western upland	1850	0.60	−0.90	Twisted J-shape
	1860	−0.80*	−434.20*	J-shaped*

* Pearson criteria indicate J-shaped gamma distribution.

APPENDIX TABLE 3. FITTED PARAMETERS OF INCOMPLETE-BETA DISTRIBUTION (*cont.*)

		α	λ	Description of curve
Improved Acreage (*cont.*)				
Black prairie	1850	0.58	−0.77	Twisted J-shape
	1860	14.50	−0.55	J-shape
Brown loam	1850	−0.25	−0.90	U-shaped
	1860	5.53	−0.75	J-shaped
Central plain	1850	3.04	−0.95	J-shaped
	1860	5.16	−0.88	J-shaped
Coastal plain	1860	6.53	−0.70	J-shaped
Alluvial	1850	−0.63*	−149.32*	J-shaped*
	1860	3.91	−0.76	J-shaped
Farm Value				
Piedmont	1850	5.66	−0.77	J-shaped
	1860	−0.88*	−43.91*	J-shaped*
Sand hills	1860	−0.05	−0.99	U-shaped
Valley	1850	−0.03	−0.93	U-shaped
	1860	2.74	−0.91	J-shaped
Western upland	1850	1.17	−0.92	J-shaped
	1860	3.97	−0.95	J-shaped
Black prairie	1850	1.71	−0.83	J-shaped
	1860	2.29	−0.77	J-shaped
Brown loam	1850	3.12	−0.86	J-shaped
	1860	17.66	−0.86	J-shaped
Central plain	1850	1.46	−0.97	J-shaped
	1860	6.17	−0.88	J-shaped
Coastal plain	1860	0.14	−0.99	Twisted J-shape
Alluvial	1850	0.74	−0.97	Twisted J-shape
	1860	0.42	−0.89	Twisted J-shape
Wealth				
Piedmont	1850	9.63	−0.76	J-shaped
	1860	−0.89*	−148.16*	J-shaped*
Sand hills	1860	0.16	−0.97	Twisted J-shape
Valley	1850	0.45	−0.91	Twisted J-shape
	1860	4.66	−0.84	J-shaped
Western upland	1850	0.26	−0.91	Twisted J-shape
	1860	16.22	−0.85	J-shaped
Black prairie	1850	1.83	−0.85	J-shaped
	1860	5.86	−0.62	J-shaped
Brown loam	1850	1.71	−0.89	J-shaped
	1860	−0.74*	−14.30*	J-shaped*
Central plain	1850	2.75	−0.90	J-shaped
	1860	8.14	−0.86	J-shaped
Coastal plain	1860	12.89	−0.83	J-shaped
Alluvial	1850	0.42	−0.98	Twisted J-shape
	1860	2.11	0.78*	J-shape

The fact that the J-shaped curve fits better than a single-peaked curve does not necessarily mean that a test based on the lognormal distribution will yield misleading results, provided the qualitative features of the curve do not change. However, appendix table 3 indicates that this assumption is not always a good one. Of the 21 observations for both 1860 and 1850, in 12 there is a change in the *form* of the fitted curve. These changes in form are helpful in explaining discrepancies between the changes in the calculated Gini index and in the logarithmic variance.

Unfortunately, there is no clear *economic* standpoint for assessing these changes. A change in the entire form of a distribution is "statistically significant" in a rather trivial sense, but in this case we cannot formulate tests of concentration based on the parameters because the "parameters" are not common to the two forms. We are left with the largely negative conclusion that the variance-ratio tests should be understood as being suggestive only: where they confirm the evidence of the calculated Gini index, the result is perhaps strengthened; but if the two conflict, there is still uncertainty. But all of the evidence confirms the observation that major structural changes in the distribution of wealth were taking place during the 1850s, and this is perhaps the most important conclusion.

Acknowledgments

Ira Berlin and Herbert G. Gutman, "Natives and Immigrants, Free Men and Slaves: Urban Workingmen in the Antebellum American South," *American Historical Review* 88 (December, 1983): 1175–1200. Reprinted by permission of the *American Historical Review*.

Alfred H. Conrad, et al., "Slavery as an Obstacle to Economic Growth in the United States: A Panel Discussion," *Journal of Economic History* 27 (1967): 518–60. Reprinted with the permission of Cambridge University Press.

Charles B. Dew, "Disciplining Slave Iron Workers in the Antebellum South," *American Historical Review* 79 (1974): 393–418. Reprinted by permission of the *American Historical Review*.

Charles B. Dew, "Sam Williams, Forgeman: The Life of an Industrial Slave in the Old South," in J. Morgan Kousser and James M. McPherson, eds., *Region, Race, and Reconstruction: Essays in Honor of C. Vann Woodward* (1982) 199–239. Reprinted by permission of Oxford University Press.

Carville V. Earle, "A Staple Interpretation of Slavery and Free Labor," *The Geographical Review* 68 (1978): 51–65. Reprinted by permission of *The Geographical Review*.

Stanley Engerman, "The Effects of Slavery on the Southern Economy," *Explorations in Economic History*, 2nd Ser., 4 (1967): 71–97. Reprinted by permission of *Explorations in Economic History*.

Stefano Fenoaltea, "The Slavery Debate: A Note From the Sidelines," *Explorations in Economic History* 18 (1981): 304–08. Reprinted by permission of *Explorations in Economic History*.

Eugene D. Genovese, "The Low Productivity of Southern Slave Labor: Causes and Effects," *Civil War History* 9 (1963): 365–82. Reprinted by permission of *Civil War History*.

Eugene D. Genovese, "The Significance of the Slave Plantation for Southern Economic Development," *Journal of Southern History* 28 (November, 1962): 422–37. Reprinted by permission of the *Journal of Southern History*.

579

Claudia Goldin, "The Economics of Emancipation," *Journal of Economic History* 33 (1973): 66–85. Reprinted with the permission of Cambridge University Press.

Claudia Goldin, "Urbanization and Slavery: The Issue of Compatibility," Leo Schnore, ed., *The New Urban History* (1975): 231–46. Reprinted by permission of the Princeton University Press.

Sarah S. Hughes, "Slaves For Hire: The Allocation of Black Labor in Elizabeth City County, Virginia, 1782 to 1810," *William and Mary Quarterly*, 3rd Ser., 35 (1978): 260–86. Reprinted by permission of the *William and Mary Quarterly*.

Ronald L. Lewis, "'The Darkest Abode of Man': Black Miners in the First Southern Coal Field, 1780–1865," *Virginia Magazine of History and Biography* 87 (1979): 190–202. Reprinted by permission of the *Virginia Magazine of History and Biography*.

Randall M. Miller, "The Fabric of Control: Slavery in Antebellum Southern Textile Mills," *Business History Review* 55 (1981): 471–90. Reprinted by permission of the *Business History Review*.

Philip D. Morgan, "Work and Culture: The Task System and the World of Lowcountry Blacks, 1700 to 1880," *William and Mary Quarterly*, 3rd Ser., 39, No. 4 (October, 1982): 563–99. Reprinted by permission of the *William and Mary Quarterly*.

John T. O'Brien, "Factory, Church, and Community: Blacks in Antebellum Richmond," *Journal of Southern History* 44 (November, 1978): 509–36. Reprinted by permission of the *Journal of Southern History*.

Otto H. Olsen, "Historians and the Extent of Slave Ownership in the Southern United States," *Civil War History* 18 (1972): 101–16. Reprinted by permission of *Civil War History*.

Ulrich B. Phillips, "The Economic Cost of Slaveholding in the Cotton Belt," *Political Science Quarterly* 20 (June, 1905): 257–75. Reprinted by permission of the *Political Science Quarterly*.

John P. Radford, "Race, Residence, and Ideology: Charleston, South Carolina, in the Mid-Nineteenth Century," *Journal of Historical Geography* 2 (1976): 329–46. Reprinted by permission of the *Journal of Historical Geography*.

Todd L. Savitt, "Slave Life Insurance in Virginia and North Carolina," *Journal of Southern History* 43 (1977): 583–600. Reprinted by permission of the *Journal of Southern History*.

Judith Kelleher Schafer, "New Orleans Slavery in 1850 as Seen in Advertisements," *Journal of Southern History* 47 (1981): 33–56. Reprinted by permission of the *Journal of Southern History*.

Robert S. Starobin, "The Economics of Industrial Slavery in the Old South," *Business History Review* 44 (Summer, 1970): 131–74. Reprinted by permission of the *Business History Review*.

Richard Y. Sutch, "The Profitability of Ante Bellum Slavery-Revisited," and "Reply" by Edward Saradar, *Southern Economic Journal* 31, No. 4 (1965): 365–83. Reprinted by permission of the *Southern Economic Journal*.

Gavin Wright, "'Economic Democracy' and the Concentration of Agricultural Wealth in the Cotton South, 1850–1860," *Agricultural History* 44 (1970): 63-93. Reprinted by permission of the Agricultural History Society.